George Durance
1981

Evaluating Student Progress

6th Edition

Evaluating Student Progress

Principles of Tests and Measurements

J. Stanley Ahmann
Iowa State University

Marvin D. Glock
Cornell University

Allyn and Bacon, Inc.   Boston   London   Sydney   Toronto

To Nancy and Ruth

Previous editions were published under the title, *Evaluating Pupil
Growth: Principles of Tests and Measurements,* Copyright © 1975,
1971, 1967, 1963, 1959 by Allyn and Bacon, Inc.

Library of Congress Cataloging in Publication Data

Ahmann, J Stanley.
  Evaluating student progress.

  Earlier editions published under title: Evalua-
ting pupil growth.
  Includes bibliographies and indexes.
  1. Grading and marking (Students) I. Glock,
Marvin David, joint author. II. Title.
LB3063.A43 1981   371.2'6   80–21715
ISBN 0–205–06561–9

Printed in the United States of America.
10 9 8 7 6 5 4 3 2 1   85 84 83 82 81

Production Editor: *Joanne Dauksewicz*

Contents

Preface

A person who has worked hard for a goal wants to find out to what degree that goal is realized. So it is with students and teachers, regardless of subject matter or grade level. Clearly, evaluation of the degree to which educational goals have been achieved is a basic part of teaching and concerns everyone associated with the school.

It follows, therefore, that teachers, counselors, supervisors, administrators, and other educational specialists need the following:

1. Appreciation of the usefulness of student and program evaluation in education
2. Knowledge of the characteristics of a satisfactory measuring instrument
3. Ability to construct measuring instruments capable of showing to what degree students have attained pertinent educational objectives
4. Knowledge of common achievement and aptitude tests and also personal-social adjustment inventories, which are often included in a schoolwide program of evaluation
5. Ability to select appropriate measuring instruments for use in a continuous evaluation program
6. Ability to interpret properly the data yielded by measuring instruments, to use them in diagnosing and remedying achievement deficiencies, and to report them efficiently and accurately to the students, their parents, and possibly the entire community

The sixth edition of *Evaluating Student Progress* is written for a one-term college course, either at the undergraduate or "fifth-year" graduate level, that is designed on the basis of developing attainments such as these. Each of its five parts contributes directly to one or more of the six goals and indirectly to several others. At the beginning of each of the sixteen chapters is a list of the objectives on which that chapter is based. These are subobjectives of one or more of the foregoing goals.

In Part One, "Evaluation in Education," the role of student evaluation in education is defined, the use of educational objectives as a basis of evaluating is established, and a number of measurement procedures are introduced. Part Two, "Measuring Achievement in the Classroom," contains discussions of teacher-built objective and essay tests, methods by which such tests can be evaluated, and teacher-built instruments recording student performance. Part Three, "Characteristics of a Good Measuring Instrument," is devoted to test validity, reliability, and means of reporting a student's relative test performance. In Part Four, "Standardized Tests, Scales, and Inventories," careful attention is given to commercially available tests and batteries measuring achievement, aptitude, and personal-social adjustment. In the concluding section of the book, Part Five, "Using Evaluation to Improve Learning," the use of measurement data in diagnosis and remediation is explained, methods of grading and reporting student growth are discussed, and the characteristics of a comprehensive schoolwide program of evaluation are listed.

Underlying this book are three significant and, indeed, axiomatic principles. In the first place, the measuring procedures of elementary and secondary school teachers are very similar. Moreover, in those instances in which the procedures differ, secondary school teachers can profit from knowledge of the unique measuring problems and procedures of elementary school teachers, and vice versa. This book is designed to serve both groups. Second, to be competent in educational measurement, teachers must have a speaking knowledge of common statistical techniques, such as the arithmetic mean, the standard deviation, and the correlation coefficient. They do not need to be skilled in the theoretical aspects of statistics, helpful as that would be. To fill the need for a limited command of statistical methods, descriptions of several basic statistical techniques are included in Appendix A. The steps to be followed when computing each of these values are shown. The computations are so planned that no prior training in mathematics beyond fundamental arithmetic is needed in order to follow them with ease. Third, before teachers can successfully build their own measuring instruments or select appropriate commercial instruments for classroom use, they must be thoroughly familiar with the essential principles of measurement and evaluation. For this reason entire chapters are devoted to the topics of item analysis, validity, and reliability. Understand, however, that these chapters, as well as all of the others, are not written for the theorist. The treatment is such that teachers can make practical use of it in their classrooms.

Most of the chapters in this book are interrelated. It is recommended that Part One and Part Two be studied first and in that order. At this point instructors may vary their choices as they wish. If possible, the chapters in Part Three (that is, Chapters 8, 9, and 10), which deal with test scores and norms, reliability, and validity, should be kept together as a group. The same is true of Part Four (that is, Chapters 11, 12, and 13), which deals with standardized tests and inventories.

Scattered within each chapter are discussion questions, usually about eight or nine in number. They are designed to challenge students in that no readily determined answers are available. Often the question requires the students to apply what they are learning. Supporting references to educational and psychological literature are regularly given.

At the end of each chapter is a list of suggested readings that, in the opinion of the authors, provide suitable extensions of the material included in the chapter and are written at an appropriate level. These references will provide a more complete view of many of the important topics. In addition, a list of free and inexpensive materials concerning educational measurement and evaluation is given in Appendix B.

Like all such books, this is the product of the efforts of many people. The authors are indebted to the many students at Iowa State University, Colorado State University, and Cornell University, and to the school personnel in Iowa, Colorado,

New York, and other states who directly or indirectly provided ideas and illustrative material for this book. In addition, the authors wish to express their appreciation to Ruth Glock for her assistance with the last six chapters, and to Nancy Cain Ahmann who thoroughly edited all chapters both for style and for logical consistency. This work was absolutely invaluable.

Finally, many publishers have granted permission to reproduce parts of their publications in this volume. These are acknowledged as they occur.

J. S. A.

M. D. G.

PART ONE

Evaluation in Education

Evaluation is an integral part of our everyday activities. Merchants periodically inventory their stocks to see whether they have realized a profit or loss on transactions and to evaluate the merits of their present merchandising practices. Golfers carefully tabulate the strokes needed to play eighteen holes, check the results against the listed par or perhaps the totals of last Saturday, and then appraise the quality of their games. Surgeons examine their patients for postoperative developments to better assess the success of the operations performed and hence the well-being of those involved. Financiers regularly review their portfolios of stocks and bonds to check values and earnings, and then draw conclusions about the soundness of their present investment programs.

Notice that in each of these illustrations a goal has been identified. Notice also that, to evaluate the effectiveness of each endeavor, information is needed on which a value judgment may be made. After weighing the information with respect to a known goal, the individuals judge the current situation either as successful, with little or no change necessary, or unsuccessful, with recommended changes to be made in the hope of improvement in the future.

Education has a direct parallel. Goals are identified on the basis of students' and society's needs. Educational programs are established so that students can reach these goals and do so in a reasonably efficient manner. Finally, after the program has begun, information such as test scores and observation reports of student behavior is periodically gathered. The success of the student in reaching the goal, and hence the success of the educational program, is evaluated in terms of the objectives. This is the core of educational evaluation.

Part One is a description of the purposes and procedures of educational evaluation. These first two chapters survey the entire field of student evaluation, through identification of its perimeter and principal parts, and present a basic vocabulary for this complex field.

In Chapter 1, "The Role of Evaluation in Education," we discuss the scope of educational evaluation (particularly student evaluation), its purposes, the principal types of testing procedures, the heterogeneous nature of these procedures, and the problems resulting from a lack of accuracy in the information produced by these instruments. In Chapter 2, "Educational Objectives in Student Evaluation," we consider the nature of educational objectives, the taxonomies used to classify them, their degree of specificity, and their role in the development of instruments used in evaluating student progress.

1

The Role of Evaluation in Education

The purpose of this chapter is to enable you to

1. Understand the nature of educational evaluation and its principal uses

2. Differentiate educational evaluation, assessment, and measurement

3. Know the purposes of student evaluation and program evaluation, as well as those of large-scale assessments

4. Identify the major types of education tests and define each

5. Explain the key difference between norm-referenced tests and objective- or criterion-referenced tests

6. Understand the indirect nature of much educational measurement

7. Recognize the various levels of accuracy that commonly exist when measuring student traits

A trip to a crowded beach in the summer is a revealing experience. Anyone but the most indifferent observer is impressed by this fascinating view of more or less undraped humanity. Some try to capture the sight on canvas or film; few forget it. Summer reminds us how unique each human body is.

We can easily identify the most obvious characteristics that contribute to individuality. Differences in height and weight, and the sometimes phenomenal distribution of that weight, are prominent. Hair or lack of it, size of feet and hands, and posture are equally noticeable. So are characteristics of the various parts of the head—ears, eyes, chin, and mouth. Other aspects of the physiological entity called man, which remain unseen mut are nonetheless important, are visual and auditory acuity, breathing patterns, strength of grip, and sense of smell.

Most of the bathers are not acquainted with each other. If they were, an entirely new constellation of individual differences would reveal itself. These differences are psychological in nature. Variations in interests, attitudes, motives, and values certainly exist, and so do differences in aptitude, be they scholastic, mechanical, musical, artistic, or clerical. In terms of achievements, there are literally thousands of additional dimensions that are sources of individuality. Achievement in the common subject matter areas is just one part of the picture. To it must be added achievement in the multitude of additional everyday activities ranging from skill in driving an automobile to the art of making and keeping friends.

The picture is staggering. Small wonder that psychologists have spent lifetimes identifying sources of individuality and developing means of measuring the amount of a given characteristic a person might have at a given moment. These efforts have clearly established the principle that each person possesses a profile of traits, both physiological and psychological, that are the result of the unique heredity (except for identical twins) and environment of each individual.

Teachers are seldom surprised when the factors of individuality are listed. Each succeeding class brings many new students before the teacher; no student is exactly like any other in this class or any in one of the preceding classes. The appearance of new and refreshing changes in the educational "raw material" each year is one of the joys of teaching. It is also the source of one of the most perplexing problems of teaching—learning to know your students so that educational experiences can be planned to capitalize on the individual differences displayed.

In view of this student heterogeneity, how can we succinctly describe the teacher's role in expediting the formal educational process? Actually, this role can be conveniently reduced to four points (Tyler, 1949, p. 1). In the first place, (1) teachers must identify the educational objectives sought. They must know the nature of the student behavior to be displayed when the educational objectives have been achieved. Second, they must determine what educational experiences the (2) students must have in order to achieve the objectives. Third, they must know their students so well that they can design and order the educational experiences to in- (3) corporate varied interests, aptitudes, and prior experiences. Finally, they must evaluate the degree to which the desired changes in student behavior have taken (4)

6

place, that is, the degree to which the educational objectives have been achieved. By means of the last step, the effectiveness of the various educational experiences can be inferred. Within the last two steps lie the purposes of student evaluation.

Uses of Educational Evaluation

Educational evaluation is the systematic process of determining the effectiveness of educational endeavors in the light of evidence. For our purposes, evaluation can be thought of as formative and summative. The former is "midstream" evaluation—evaluation of student progress or program effectiveness at some intermediate point. The latter is evaluation at some logical terminal point, such as at the end of a unit of instruction or an academic term.

The differentiation has been refined still further (Bloom, Hastings, & Madaus, 1971, pp. 91–92) in the realm of student evaluation. Formative evaluations provide feedback to teacher and student about the latter's progress, or lack of it, early enough for any needed changes in the instructional effort to be made. The degree of mastery of a certain learning task is discovered, and those aspects of the task not mastered are identified. In contrast, summative evaluations are determinations of the degree of achievement of major outcomes of a student's course of study. The purpose of these evaluations is often the assignment of final marks or "grades." As we shall see, the types of evaluation instruments typically used change according to the nature of the evaluation.

The uses of educational evaluation are broad and diverse. Four subgroups have been identified:

1. Appraisal of the academic achievement of individual students
2. Diagnosis of the learning difficulties of an individual student or an entire class
3. Appraisal of the educational effectiveness of a curriculum, instructional materials and procedures, and organizational arrangements
4. Assessment of the educational progress of large populations so as to help understand educational problems and develop sound public policy in education

The first two uses constitute student evaluation based on the rationale that all individuals differ from each other. This kind of evaluation examines students as unique individuals. Judgments about their educational growth are based on pertinent data, which then may be compared with similar data about them obtained at an earlier date or with similar data from peer groups obtained concurrently. This is the type of evaluation of greatest concern to us, and it is the major focus of this book. On the other hand, considerable attention is being given to the other two uses of evaluation, namely, program and product evaluation and educational achievement assessment on a large scale. An examination of them, however brief, is also in order (see pages 27–31).

Purposes of Student Evaluation

At this point, our focus on educational evaluation is restricted to student evaluation; it concentrates on the student as an individual and as a member of a classroom unit. Such evaluation has two purposes: (1) to help teachers determine the degree to which educational objectives have been achieved, and (2) to help teachers know their students as individuals. The first purpose is basic, as changes in student behavior are always evaluated in terms of the goals of education. The second purpose is subsidiary to the first; if teachers are thoroughly informed about their students, they will be better able to plan educational experiences for them and determine the degree to which educational objectives have been achieved. It is important to realize this fundamental relationship between the two purposes. In practice, information about the degree of achievement is augmented by earlier knowledge of the student's interests, values, aptitudes, and achievements. Thus the second purpose supports the first.

Determining the Achievement of Educational Objectives

Educational objectives stem from the needs of youth as they are guided and molded by the democratic society in which they live. Suggestions for educational objectives commonly come out of three sources: studies of students, studies of the democratic society in which they live, and analyses by informed educational specialists. Certainly the knowledge and skills students already have, as well as their interests and goals, should influence the educational objectives of the classes they are attending. Hence, objectives should be based on student needs. By the same taken, the democratic society in which the student lives has needs; it must be improved and perpetuated. Finally, the informed specialist in a subject matter area can, after intensive study, identify important trends and interrelations that, when translated into new objectives or allowed to influence old ones, may ultimately improve the breadth and direction of the educational program as a whole.

Stating Educational Objectives.   The modern way of expressing educational objectives is in terms of desired student behavior, that is, in terms of the behavior that students should exhibit if they have achieved certain objectives. Often cited are specific behavioral patterns related to the student's knowledge, understanding, attitudes, appreciation, abilities, and skills in a specified subject matter area. The following shows the type of statement used in expressing specific objectives:

> Curriculum area: Science
> Grade levels: 3–5
>> The student should be able to construct a system of pulleys by means of which approximately 100 grams could lift 300 grams (Fors, 1969, p. 26).

> Curriculum area: Mathematics
> Grade levels: 4–6
>> Given a protractor marked in degrees, and the measure of an angle between 0° and 180°, the student will draw the angle accurately to within five degrees (Michigan Department of Education, 1973, p. 81).

From the point of view of student evaluation, objectives stated in terms of outwardly observable behavior are most suitable. Determining the degree to which objectives have been met means finding out how students are observably different after the educational experiences from the way they were before. Stating the objectives of education in these terms is deceptively difficult.

Identifying Changes in Behavior. There are many ways to discover what changes, if any, have occurred in student behavior as a result of educational experiences. By means of a few liberal interpretations, the multitude of methods can be classified into two groups: testing procedures and nontesting procedures. The testing procedures can be the common paper-and-pencil tests, oral tests, or performance tests. Nontesting procedures include teacher-student interviews, anecdotal records, sociometric techniques, general information questionnaires, and ranking and rating methods that summarize the results of observing samples of student behavior or products of that behavior. Properly or otherwise, the most commonly used is the paper-and-pencil achievement test.

No matter which of the suggested methods is used to identify changes in student behavior, teachers need considerable information in addition to knowledge of technique. That information is a thorough grasp of the typical and atypical behavioral patterns of the students they are teaching. Norm-referenced standardized testing devices attempt to provide these reference points by means of norms, that is, lists of typical scores made by a sample of students thought to be representative of a larger population of students for whom the test is designed. Nontesting procedures customarily require a full knowledge of what students in a given class or age group are like. The more complete this knowledge, the more adequate will be the evaluation of changes in student behavior.

Two notable obstacles prevent a comprehensive evaluation of the degree to which educational objectives have been achieved. First of all, certain educational goals, such as those pertaining to attitudes and interests, are difficult to translate into observable student behavior, and changes can be identified only crudely, if at all. Consequently, it has not been possible to construct evaluation instruments that can adequately measure the degree to which a student has achieved all of the many and varied educational objectives. Second, in some instances the total desired change in student behavior may not be observable until months or years following the educational experience. Of course, teachers will not be on the scene at this auspicious moment. However, they may be able to observe changes in student behavior indicating partial achievement of an educational objective. For example, one of the broad educational objectives often mentioned is that the student will prepare adequately for a suitable vocation. The complete achievement of this objective may not be observable for some time. Yet the classroom teacher may observe partial achievement as the student masters, for example, verbal and mathematical skills.

Helping Teachers Know Their Students

All teachers subscribe to the obvious truth that, to be successful, they must know their students. They can begin by inquiring about names, addresses, previous academic experiences, parents, and parental occupations. By observation, teachers may be able to crudely appraise the socioeconomic level from which a student comes, physical vigor, social training, and even student enthusiasm concerning the anticipated educational experiences.

But what lies beneath the surface? Teachers are more than curious about student aptitudes, the complete story of previous academic achievement, and the degree of personal-social adjustment. These aspects cannot be assessed without relying on some of the many techniques here classified as part of student evaluation. Careful guesses based on informal observations are not sufficient. Appraisals need to be based on objective data and organized in a systematic pattern.

Consider for a moment a given student about whom a teacher is questioned. Let's call him Mike. According to the teacher, Mike is a "fair" student who is "moderately bright" and who seems to be "rather well liked" by most of his classmates. In general, Mike is not very highly motivated, but appears to be content and causes little trouble. You may have often heard such a description. Undeniably it is a helpful thumbnail sketch. Yet it could be infinitely more helpful if it were more specific and less subjective. One might ask how "fair" is "fair" and how "bright" is "moderately bright"? Test scores from achievement tests and a scholastic aptitude test could underpin this description to a sizable degree. Furthermore, according to the teacher's remarks, Mike seems to be an underachiever. Why? Test scores and teacher ratings of earlier academic achievements may shed light on this question, as may various aptitude test scores. Home conditions should not be ignored even though they can only be casually evaluated. Lastly, how "well liked" is "rather well liked"? What kind of trouble is "little trouble"? Sociometric devices and anecdotal records may jointly illuminate these questions.

The list of suggested evaluation techniques could be continued, but the point has been made. The picture of Mike can be brought into focus only by better evaluation techniques. These will never paint a complete profile of a student, but they will reveal enough of that profile to justify the time and money their use demands.

Knowing a child is a prolonged, complex process. Ideally, it combines the skill of the teacher as an impersonal, astute observer, the skill of the test technician who constructs and validates the standardized measuring instruments, and the skill of a clinician who carefully amalgamates all the above information and ferrets out likely causes and effects. Although not confronted by the ideal situation, the average classroom teacher can, through extensive effort, attain useful though typically imperfect results. The rewards for such effort are rich.

PROBLEMS

1. Using for illustrative purposes a class level and subject matter familiar to you, cite the chief arguments for and against the contention that student evaluation is most successful when based on limited, well-defined educational objectives.

2. It is argued that an effective teacher is one who, in a minimum amount of instructional time, can help students reach pertinent educational objectives

commensurate with their abilities. In the light of this statement, to what degree should there be interaction between student evaluation and the evaluation of teacher effectiveness? Why?

Differences Between Measurement and Evaluation

Differentiating between the terms "measurement" and "evaluation" is sometimes difficult. The two terms are related, yet decidedly different. Evaluation is a more inclusive term than measurement. Measurement is only a part of evaluation, although a very substantial one, providing information on which an evaluation can be based.

Characteristics of Measurement

Educational measurement is the process that attempts to obtain a quantified representation of the degree to which a student reflects a trait. The use of a paper-and-pencil test to discover the scholastic aptitude or achievement of a student is an illustration of educational measurement. In the case of scholastic aptitude, for example, one can easily visualize it as a continuum, that is, as a trait that logically varies from much to some to none and that is theoretically capable of being divided into an infinite number of degrees. Each student has a specific position on the continuum. Educational measurement tries to represent that position by means of a numerical value, a scholastic aptitude test score, in as objective a manner as possible.

The measurement process is fundamentally descriptive of the degree to which a trait is possessed by a student and uses numbers rather than words. A teacher can characterize a fourth-grade student as "tall," "gifted," or "underweight." These are word descriptions of traits that are continuous. Measuring instruments can change "tall" to "61.5 inches," "gifted" to "*Wechsler (WISC-R)* IQ of 128," and underweight" to "85 pounds." The advantage of reporting numbers rather than adjectives is obvious. The meaning of any adjective varies from teacher to teacher. Carefully executed measurement data do not change. They are notably less ambiguous than verbal descriptions.

Educational measurement tends to concentrate on a specific, well-defined trait and then strives to determine precisely the degree to which that trait is possessed by an individual student. This is in many ways roughly comparable to the methods of a photographer who, in trying to capture the individuality of a physique, photographs each part separately—first the hand, then the foot, perhaps then the nose, and so forth. Such a photographer would hope that the result of this work would be a series of revealing photographs, each displaying the status of the physique with regard to the particular part. If totally successful, all photographs could be arranged to create a two-dimensional picture of the total physique.

Teachers act like photographers when they examine specific student traits, such as reading comprehension, vocabulary, and scholastic aptitude, with a series of measuring instruments. Each test measures a certain trait, just as each photograph depicts a part of the physique. Unfortunately, the teacher's task is not so simple as the photographer's. Whereas it is possible that some of the photographer's pictures might be blurred because the camera was out of focus, or might have poor color contrast because they are underexposed, such lapses are unlikely. In contrast, the teacher using even the best measurement devices may have nothing but somewhat blurred and underexposed "photographs." Worse than that, some traits of the student cannot be "photographed" at all since no measuring instruments are available. Hence the total picture produced by combining the results of many measurements of various traits is often somewhat unclear, due to the failure of the instruments to yield precise, unequivocal results. It is also invariably incomplete, due to the scarcity of suitable measuring instruments, particularly in the area of personal-social adjustment.

The statement that a measuring instrument fails to yield precise, unequivocal results means that the instrument does not adequately serve the purposes for which it is intended, and that it does not measure with perfect consistency. The failure of an instrument to serve the purposes for which it is intended is known as *lack of validity;* the failure of an instrument to measure consistently is known as *lack of reliability.* The concepts of reliability and validity are described and illustrated in Chapters 9 and 10, respectively.

Characteristics of Evaluation

Student evaluation is a process in which a teacher commonly uses information derived from many sources to arrive at a value judgment. The information might be obtained by using measuring instruments as well as other techniques that do not necessarily yield quantitative results, such as general information questionnaires, direct observation, and teacher-pupil interviews. An evaluation may or may not be based on measurement data, though appropriate measurements are customarily used if they are available. Data from good measuring instruments can provide a sound basis for good evaluation.

The differences between educational measurement and evaluation can be easily illustrated. A common example of the differences between them can be found in the practice of assigning final marks to students at the end of a unit of work. Measurements of the student's achievements and aptitude may have been made before the unit began, and measurements of the changes in behavior follow the termination of the unit. To these pieces of information teachers frequently add their reactions to the student's attitudes, cooperation, motivation, and possibly even punctuality. The final result is generally a single letter or numerical mark that supposedly indicates the relative success of the student in relation to the unit of work. An evaluation process has been completed; a value judgment has been made.

Educational Testing

Educational measurement is usually considered to include educational testing. Whether this is true depends, of course, on the manner in which educational testing is defined. The term "test" is a simple and widely used word but is paradoxically somewhat vague. It can be defined so broadly as to include some evaluation procedures that yield only verbal descriptions of student traits. For instance, it can be defined as any systematic procedure for observing a person's behavior and describing it by means of a numerical scale or a category system (Cronbach, 1970, p. 26). Some of these procedures cannot be included within the definition of educational measurement. On the other hand, educational testing can be defined in a more restricted manner so that, practically speaking, all tests can be called measuring instruments.

It is convenient for the purpose of this book to define the word "test" in the more restricted manner. In the first place, a test is nothing more than a group of questions to be answered or tasks to be performed. The questions might require the student to give the correct meaning of a word, solve an arithmetic problem, or identify missing parts of an animal in a picture. Tasks might require the student to thread beads on a string, assemble a small piece of apparatus, or arrange blocks in a prescribed design. These questions and tasks might be presented to the student orally or in writing; some are even presented by means of pantomime under certain circumstances. The questions and tasks are known as test items. They are intended to be of suitable difficulty and representative of all possible questions and tasks related to the trait measured by the test. A student's responses to the test items are scored in such a way that, ideally, the results indicate the degree to which the specified trait is possessed. The test is a quantitative representation of the trait that it is designed to measure. Certainly educational testing is included within educational measurement when this restricted definition of a test is used.

Types of Tests

Tests can differ from each other in many ways. Some contain items of nearly constant difficulty, whereas others contain items of varying difficulty. Some require that rigid time limits be maintained; others do not. Some demand that the students to whom the test is to be administered have a complete command of the English language; others do not. Some can be administered to large groups of students simultaneously, others to only one student at a time. These and other variations have been used to subdivide tests into a relatively restricted list of eighteen types.*

In the following discussion, two and sometimes three types of tests are grouped together, as in the case of oral, essay, and objective tests. This grouping is made because the types are more or less contrasting. Sometimes the relative merits of each are vigorously debated by both teachers and testing specialists. In any event, it is a useful way of remembering the types and their general characteristics.

Notice also that a test can simultaneously be classified as more than one type. For example, one popular achievement test used in schools today is a group, verbal, objective, standardized, norm-referenced test. Such a multiple classification of a test is actually a highly informative thumbnail description. Mastery of such terminology is a necessary prerequisite to an understanding of this part of educational evaluation.

* Brief descriptions of these and other types of tests can be found in Carter Good, *Dictionary of Education* 3rd ed. (New York: McGraw-Hill, 1973).

Individual and Group Tests

Individual Tests.   Individual tests are tests that can be administered to only one student at a time. The examiners have an opportunity to establish rapport with each student and to gain insight into his or her reaction to the testing situation. They can even ascertain possible reasons for many of the student's answers. Furthermore, the examiners practically always have the responsibility of making a written record of the student's answers. A common illustration of an individual test is the *Wechsler Intelligence Scale for Children (WISC-R)*.

Group Tests.   Group tests can be administered to more than one student at a time. The number of students can range into the hundreds if sufficient test proctors are available. In elementary and secondary school situations, however, students are often tested as a class. Because of its simplicity and low cost, this type of test is far more popular than the individual test.

You have no doubt repeatedly experienced the impersonal atmosphere in which group tests are typically given. As the group of students becomes larger, this problem increases. Certainly, many of the desirable aspects of the individual test are not found in group tests, since they have been sacrificed for the economies of time and money.

Classroom and Standardized Tests

Classroom Tests.   Classroom tests are sometimes called teacher-made tests or "informal" tests. They are tests constructed by classroom teachers for use in particular classes under conditions of their choosing. In practically all instances these tests are group tests and measure student achievement. More of these tests are administered than any other kind. Unfortunately, they often are carelessly constructed and interpreted.

The value of classroom achievement tests stems from one major consideration— the individual nature of every class. This individuality can be traced primarily to the kinds of educational objectives involved in the class and also to the relative emphasis each receives. It also can be traced to the characteristics of the students who compose the class. Teachers certainly know better than anyone else the exact nature of these characteristics. Since the appropriateness of any achievement test is determined by the educational objectives of the class, the teacher is in an excellent position to build test items of suitable difficulty to measure appropriate areas of student achievement. Thus classroom achievement tests, if properly prepared, are tailor-made for a certain class of students taught in a certain manner (see Chapter 2). On the other hand, standardized achievement tests are designed for many classes of a certain type; these tests attempt to cover those achievement areas thought to be common to all classes for which they are designed.

Standardized Tests.   Standardized tests are constructed almost invariably by teams of individuals rather than by a single person. In the case of standardized achievement tests, teachers qualified in the area to be tested work with measurement specialists by helping to identify the scope of an achievement test and its appropriateness. Often they contribute possible test items. In the case of standardized aptitude tests, the role of the teacher is considerably reduced if not nonexistent.

Characteristically, standardized tests are carefully designed. They are pretested in order to determine the level of difficulty of the test items, the amount of testing time required, the sizes of typical scores made by various types of students, and so forth. The manuals accompanying the test contain information concerning the method of developing the test, its purposes, directions for its proper administration, directions for scoring, techniques for interpreting the scores, and reports of research in which the test was involved. In order that any standardized test be used properly, it must be administered only to those students for whom it is designed and strictly in accordance with the manual's directions. Furthermore, the scoring of the instrument and the interpretation of those scores must be performed in the manner prescribed for that test.

Oral, Essay, and Objective Tests

Oral Tests.   Although common in the early history of achievement testing, oral tests are not popular today. Their use as a means of testing the knowledge and understanding of a candidate for an advanced degree is no doubt their principal single function now. Even in this situation they often are not used alone but in conjunction with written tests.

The disadvantages of oral testing are not difficult to identify. First of all, it tends to be somewhat unplanned as a whole. The first questions asked by the teacher can be selected with care; after that, however, the nature of student responses often influences the nature of later questions. Soon the sampling of the student's knowledge and understanding becomes quite narrow. Consciously or unconsciously, the teacher may be grossly unfair to the student. Second, students, like actors, are affected by their audience. The tension created by face-to-face contact with an examiner has caused many students to blurt out the most unusual conglomeration of words, complete with fractured syntax, even though they actually know the correct answer. Third, oral tests generally require too much time for both teacher and student. Fourth, there is no written record of the student's responses.

A principal advantage of oral testing is that it can be diagnostic. Probing questions can reveal the causes of a student's errors. Such information, needless to say, is extremely useful to a teacher. Oral testing has a further advantage in that it reveals how well students can apply knowledge to novel situations, though this can be tested by paper-and-pencil tests as well. To this end, specialists in medicine have designed standardized role-playing situations for the purpose of assessing certain complex skills of gathering data and making judgments, as demonstrated by candidates for certification (Levine & McGuire, 1968). Simulated diagnostic interviews, proposed treatment interviews, and patient-management conferences have been used successfully. In the first two instances, the candidate plays the role of a physician and an examiner plays the role of a patient, while a second examiner uses standard rating scales to record his impressions of the interview. In the third situation, five candidates play physicians and their conference is rated by examiners.

Essay Tests. Since many of the difficulties associated with oral tests disappear when paper-and-pencil tests are used, essay testing has replaced oral testing in part. Instead of asking the students to answer a question orally, they are asked to write their answers. This simple change affects the testing situation drastically. Now many students can be tested simultaneously; each can answer the same questions, except for an optional question or two which some teachers offer. Since only one set of questions is to be used for many students, extensive efforts to obtain a cross-sectional sampling of the subject matter in those questions are certainly justified. Moreover, the students now have a better opportunity to organize their thoughts before they attack each question. Tension is noticeably reduced, but scoring problems are still serious (see chapter 5).

Objective Tests. Objective tests are tests that can be scored in such a manner that subjective judgment is eliminated when determining the correctness of a student's answers. True-false tests, matching tests, and multiple-choice tests are objective tests in the true sense of the definition. Supply tests (e.g., completion tests) are sometimes considered to be objective tests even though the subjective judgment is not entirely eliminated. Occasionally, these are called "semiobjective" test items (see Chapters 3 and 4).

Objective tests are very common; classroom, as well as standardized achievement tests, are constructed as objective tests, and paper-and-pencil aptitude tests are almost invariably of this type. Clearly, objective scoring is in keeping with the whole purpose of using a standardized test. After all, a standardized test tries to be a universal "yardstick" to measure a specified student trait. To prevent the "yardstick" from changing its units, such precautions as uniform testing conditions are required. Uniform scoring procedures are equally vital. The test results obtained should never be affected positively or negatively by the person who happens to score the answer sheets.

Speed, Power, and Mastery Tests

Speed Tests. A speed test is one in which a student must, in a limited amount of time, answer a series of questions or perform a series of tasks of a uniformly low level of difficulty. The near-constant level of difficulty of the questions or tasks is such that, if students had unlimited time, they could easily answer each question or perform each task successfully. The average student does not have sufficient time to attempt all test items. The intent of a speed test is to measure primarily the rapidity with which students can do what is asked, rather than whether they can do it at all.

Excellent illustrations of speed tests can be found in the case of some clerical aptitude tests. One such test requires the student to determine whether two numbers or two names are the same or different. In another, the student must match combinations of two letters, a letter and a number, or two numbers. Rigid time limits that allow too little time for completion of the test are enforced. If this were not the case, any alert person would certainly have a perfect score.

Speed tests, in the ideal sense, are not common in educational measurement. Usually, comfortable (though controlled) time limits are allowed, and the level of test item difficulty is not uniformly low. However, in achievement testing, some instruments tend to be speeded because of poorly chosen time limits. So little time is allowed the students that the number of unattempted test items becomes excessive. On the other hand, tests designed to measure reading speed are closely timed and properly so.

Power Tests.   In contrast to a pure speed test is a power test. The items in a power test are more difficult and, technically, time limits should not exist. In reality, time limits frequently do exist. Little is to be gained by giving a student unrestricted time for writing a test. There seems to be a point in time after which further contemplation of the test items yields practically no profit. Builders of standardized instruments generally agree that a power test should be so timed that a very large percentage of the students for whom it is designed will have ample time to complete all of the questions. Although estimates vary as to the proper size of this percentage, ninety percent seems to be an acceptable minimum. Hence, the test is slightly speeded.

Power tests are widely given, particularly when testing achievement. Teachers and students alike feel that it is desirable to minimize the speed factors in a testing situation. This feeling no doubt stems from the conviction that knowing one's level of maximum achievement as indicated by a power test is more useful than knowing the rapidity with which one can perform simple tasks as indicated by a speed test.

Mastery Tests.   In a mastery test the level of item difficulty is quite low, and the time limits allowed are generous. Its purpose is to measure the knowledge and skill that every student of the class should have acquired. Hence it is expected that virtually all of the students (about eighty-five to ninety percent) will perform perfectly on the test. No attempt is made to discover how much a student may have acquired over and above the minimum everyone should have reached.

Mastery tests are customarily teacher-constructed. A spelling list, a vocabulary list, or a series of arithmetic computations may constitute such a test. Teachers have used them as quizzes with considerable effectiveness. However, when used alone as an end-of-unit or end-of-term achievement test, they are less useful than power tests, particularly at the secondary school level.

Sometimes we underestimate the usefulness of mastery tests. For instance, they can serve as end-of-unit achievement tests when used in conjunction with an appropriately designed classroom power test. By means of the mastery test, the teacher could determine student command of the essentials of the subject matter. Then the power test would be used to sample other material.

Furthermore, emphasis by teachers on learning for mastery means testing accordingly. Here mastery tests are part of a formative evaluation program; in other words, they show the points of difficulty for students who lack mastery and help the teacher to prescribe remedies. Frequent "midstream" use of mastery tests in this context helps ensure that each group of learning tasks is mastered before subsequent tasks are begun. Students are motivated to put forth the necessary effort at the appropriate time.

Also, some large-scale assessments of achievement use various levels of test items, one of which samples the knowledge and skill that practically all examinees have. The same point of view is used with criterion-referenced tests (see page 19) when reporting of test results is "on-off" in nature (for instance, either an eighty-five to ninety percent minimum level of proficiency has or has not been achieved by the student). Finally, mastery tests are used for units of programmed instruction in order to find out whether a student should proceed to new material, repeat the material completed, or study remedial material.

Verbal, Nonverbal, and Performance Tests

Verbal Tests.   A verbal test is one in which the responding student utilizes written or spoken language. This use of language can occur in the directions presented to the student, in the responses to the test items, or in both cases. The widespread use of paper-and-pencil achievement tests in the typical classroom situation clearly illustrates the popularity of verbal tests.

Nonverbal Tests.   Not all persons can be given a verbal test. Illiterates, mentally deficient children, and very young children are incapable of understanding written, and sometimes even oral, directions. Some tests are so constructed that the instructions are given orally and the persons tested respond without use of language. These have been called nonverbal tests, although in the strict sense a nonverbal test does not require the use of language by either the examiner or the person taking the test. Pantomime is used as a means of giving directions. The person may only point to indicate an answer. Geometric drawings and three-dimensional materials have been used in this type of test.

Performance Tests.   In a discussion of performance tests, it is necessary to differentiate between aptitude performance tests and achievement performance tests. In aptitude testing, performance tests are often nothing more than nonverbal tests. They are designed to measure the aptitudes of those persons unfamiliar with the English language. For example, the manipulation of blocks and the tracing of a maze have been used to assess general mental ability. In achievement testing, performance tests are not devoted primarily to the illiterate. Performance tests attempt to appraise the degree to which a skill has been achieved. For example, a typing speed test is a performance test. The student's performance during a specific period of time is scored in terms of the quantity and accuracy of the material typed. Athletic events, musical performances, food preparation, laboratory exercises, and machine operations can serve as performance tests (see chapter 7).

Readiness and Diagnostic Tests

Readiness Tests.   Readiness tests are designed to determine the ability of a student to undertake a certain type of learning. They resemble aptitude tests in that they try to forecast the achievement that would occur if appropriate training were given. They differ from aptitude tests in that they deal with a highly specific kind of achievement, such as reading.

Readiness tests are designed to discover whether a student is sufficiently advanced to profit from formal instruction in a subject area. To accomplish this purpose, reading readiness tests may use tests of visual discrimination, auditory discrimination, vocabulary, and sometimes motor coordination. Tests of student readiness in mathematics and language are also given in secondary school; these are called aptitude or prognostic tests for a given subject matter area.

Diagnostic Tests.   Whereas readiness tests are administered to students before formal instruction is given, diagnostic tests are administered after formal instruction has taken place. The purpose of a diagnostic test is to reveal specific deficiencies in a student's background. This information could also point to specific deficiencies in the instruction given. Alert classroom teachers test in this manner continually, often using mastery tests of their own design.

One outstanding characteristic of diagnostic tests is that any total test scores they might give are of limited value. The desired information comes from subscores based on a few related test items or from an item-by-item analysis of the student's responses. Each individual item or small group of items tests the students with regard to a particular part of the material taught. Thus their answers are studied on that basis.

Norm-Referenced, Criterion-Referenced, and Objective-Referenced Tests

Norm-Referenced Tests.   Test norms are representations of average or common performance based on the results of testing a typical group of students for whom the instrument is designed (see Chapter 8). Thus a student's score can be compared with norm tables, such as those for percentile ranks; relative performance can be determined in terms of rank in a standard group of 100 students, for example, seventy-third from the bottom of the group.

A norm-referenced test, then, finds a student's performance level in relation to levels of others on the same test. This is the usual approach taken in educational testing. Many standardized achievement and aptitude tests are norm-referenced instruments.

Criterion-Referenced Tests.   In contrast, criterion-referenced tests are those used to ascertain a student's status with respect to some criterion, for instance, an established performance standard. We want to know what students can do, rather than how they compare with others. An example of this type of test is the *Red Cross Senior Lifesaving Test* in which an individual must demonstrate certain swimming skills in order to pass. How well others perform is not important. Individual mastery is the primary issue.

On the basis of its appearance, you will not be able to differentiate between a norm-referenced test and a criterion-referenced test in a subject matter area such as mathematics. Yet the test items in a norm-referenced test are selected in order to produce variability among the test scores, whereas those for a criterion-referenced test are designed to be an accurate reflection of a given criterion behavior. Thus these two types of tests differ in terms of purpose.

They also differ in the manner in which they are constructed and the kind of information produced by student responses. Note that test items in a criterion-referenced achievement test must be a representative sample of the tasks identified by the specific educational objectives of the instruction given. This is most easily accomplished if the objectives are stated in terms of the explicit performance to be demonstrated by the student. An analysis of the task structure (e.g., ability to add integers accurately) is necessary so that components of the task and performance criteria are described carefully. The scoring of student responses to test items is such that it provides detailed information about which tasks a student can perform (Glaser & Nitko, 1971). The desired end product is generally a descriptive statement of the student's behavior, for example, "Frank's performance on the test was such that we believe he can accurately add eighty percent of a universe of pairs of positive integers, none of which has more than three digits."

The most difficult and important step in the construction of suitable criterion-referenced tests is to define the limits of the student behaviors that the test items will measure, that is, to establish a set of rules needed to generate the items for the test (Popham, 1978, pp. 89–111, 114–137). In other words, we need to describe a behavior domain that is a *class* of learner behaviors, such as "the ability to add correctly any pair of single-digit numbers," rather than a *single* behavior such as "the ability to add correctly 8 + 9." Unfortunately there are no established procedures for defining satisfactory domains, although some success has been achieved in well-organized learning areas such as mathematics and science (Hively, 1974). Some have labeled this kind of testing *domain-referenced testing,* but for our purposes it will be incorporated within criterion-referenced testing.

A well-designed criterion-referenced test, in short, provides a great deal of information about the behavior repertoires of students. We discover what they can and cannot do, that is, whether or not they achieved some of the immediate outcomes of a learning situation. This type of testing is highly compatible with a teacher emphasis on mastery learning, and can provide information helpful in both student evaluation and program evaluation.

Objective-Referenced Tests.   The primary difference between criterion-referenced tests and objective-referenced tests is the presence of a clearly defined standard of performance. For instance, in some large-scale assessments, achievement test items are constructed to be a direct reflection of a specified objective, but often no performance standard is inherent in the objective. Like criterion-referenced test items, the purpose of these test items is to describe the tasks a student can perform. However, in view of the absence of a clearly stated criterion, they are better called objective-referenced than criterion-referenced.

The difference among norm-, criterion, and objective-referenced tests is not always clear-cut. Sometimes norm-referenced tests are capable of producing criterion-referenced interpretations. Also, the terms "criterion-referenced" and "objective-referenced" are often used interchangeably. The former is the more popular term and is used hereafter in this book to designate objective- as well as criterion-referenced tests. In any event, all types have powerful roles to play in student evaluation and should be thought of as supplemental to each other.

Comparison of Test Types

The major differences and similarities between norm-referenced tests on the one hand and criterion- and objective-referenced tests on the other are delineated in Table 1.1. This table summarizes many of the ideas contained in the foregoing paragraphs. It can be most easily interpreted when one restricts its scope to achievement testing. Even in this context, however, further elaboration is sometimes needed as designated by the page references to sections of other chapters that follow.

PROBLEMS

3. According to the definition of a test used in this chapter, can the following standardized instruments be called tests? (For information about these instruments, see *The Eighth Mental Measurements Yearbook*, edited by O. K. Buros, 1978.)

    a. *Iowa Tests of Basic Skills*
    b. *Strong-Campbell Interest Inventory*
    c. *CIRCUS*
    d. *Mooney Problem Check List*

    For each of the foregoing which you consider to be a test, identify its classification according to the eighteen types of tests described.

4. What are the important differences between criterion-referenced testing for mastery of relatively simple learning outcomes, and testing at the developmental level, where learning outcomes are complex and each student is encouraged to achieve maximum performance (Gronlund, 1973, pp. 22–23)?

Indirect Nature of Measurement Procedures

When carpenters build houses, they engage in direct measurement. When they measure the length of a board or the size of the angles at which it is to be cut, they do not need to infer the characteristic being measured. It is clearly and obviously present and measurable. In contrast, the teacher must frequently engage in indirect rather than direct measurement. For example, a student's general mental ability is inferred by measuring, by means of a test, what are considered to be the *effects* of general mental ability and not by measuring general mental ability as such. Let us examine this situation more closely.

The expression "general mental ability" (or its near synonym "general intelligence") is widely used today. But exactly what does it mean? One writer defines intelligence as a summation of the individual's learning experiences (Wesman,

TABLE 1.1.   Comparison of Norm-Referenced Achievement Tests with Criterion-Referenced Tests

Test characteristic	Norm-referenced achievement tests	Criterion-referenced tests
Planning the test	The test is typically planned on the basis of general descriptions of subject matter topics and process skills.	The test is typically planned in terms of specific, behaviorally stated objectives, each providing the basis for one or several related test items.
Preparing the test items	Test items are constructed to maximize discrimination among students.	Test items are constructed to measure proficiency for a specified task.
Types of test items	All types are used.	All types are used.
Level of difficulty of test items	Test items are of medium difficulty, that is, about thirty to seventy percent of the students answer correctly (see p. 163).	Test items vary widely in difficulty, but regularly are of the mastery type, that is, most students respond correctly after training.
Criterion for mastery	No criterion for mastery is customarily specified.	Objectives for criterion-referenced test items may designate a criterion for mastery or it sometimes can be inferred.
Interpreting the test results	A total score or several sub-scores are computed and a student's relative standing in a group or class is ascertained (see p. 216).	A student's success or failure on a test item or small group of similar test items is determined, and a statement is prepared that describes performance solely with reference to certain performance objectives.
Common uses of the test	1. The relative standing of a student within a normative group is determined (see p. 229).	1. A student's status with respect to established standards of performance is ascertained, thereby determining what he or she knows and can do.
	2. The test is used to assist in selection of individuals for educational programs, employment, etc.	2. Specific student deficiencies in achievement are diagnosed.
	3. The test is used to provide a more-or-less global representation of student achievement in a specified learning area.	3. The success of an instructional program is evaluated.
Availability of standardized tests	Many tests are available covering most of the common curriculum areas.	An increasing number are becoming available, many of which focus on the basic skills.

1975, p. 142). Another says that this term "is commonly used to cover that combination of abilities required for survival and advancement within a particular culture" (Anastasi, 1976, p. 350). Still another believes that, along with the strictly cognitive aspects of general mental ability, one must consider heavily "two additional factors; namely, (1) creativity and (2) resistance to emotional or other forces that distort the process of reasoning" (Stoddard, 1966).

These are but three of the multitude of definitions that have been proposed. The fact that they differ at least slightly among themselves and that other definitions differ to some degree from them does not now concern us. The important factor is their similarity. No matter which definition one may choose as most suitable, general mental ability is clearly a less obvious human trait than others (such as height and weight). In short, it cannot be seen, touched, or handled in a direct manner.

To appreciate the relatively obscure nature of general mental ability, we need only recall how most individuals estimate informally, without the use of instruments, the general mental ability of their acquaintances. Rare are those who have not identified a number of acquaintances as having less mental ability than themselves. Possibly (and with less certainty, perhaps) these same individuals also have classified a few acquaintances as having more mental ability than themselves. How do they arrive at these decisions? Obviously they examine all acquaintances in terms of those aspects and products of their behavior that seemingly reflect the amount of general mental ability present.

Ordinarily, informal estimates of general mental ability are based on such information as one's academic or financial accomplishments, one's facility for quickly and correctly identifying the salient point of a humorous story, or perhaps one's ability to carry on an interesting conversation. Although these pieces of information may not be representative of a person's behavior, nor directly and completely related to variations in general mental ability, judgment is nevertheless rendered.

Formal attempts to measure general mental ability resemble these informal attempts in one respect. They also evaluate general mental ability in terms of its effects. Observable behavior thought to be directly related to general mental ability is identified, and the trait is measured indirectly by evaluating the observable behavior in some way.

A few of the common types of behavior sometimes used in this measurement are the ability to solve arithmetic problems, to identify the meanings of English words, spatial ability,* and the ability to solve number series problems.† If students are "gifted," they should be able to correctly answer difficult questions concerning areas such as those mentioned. If they are "average," they should be able to answer correctly many of the questions but not the very difficult ones. If they are "dull,"

---

* Spatial ability can be evaluated by determining whether a student can visualize how a geometric figure will look after it has been rotated, or how it will look after it has been divided and the parts reassembled in different positions.

† A typical number problem follows:

The numbers in the following series proceed according to some rule. Select the next number from among the five possibilities listed.

Series ·							Next number				
6	7	10	11	14	15	18	17	18	19	20	21

they should be able to answer correctly only the very easy questions, and may even find these troublesome.

Observe that in this approach an important assumption is made. It is assumed that there is a direct and unchanging relationship between general mental ability and the ability to answer questions in the areas mentioned. If this assumption is not true, indirect measurement procedures are worthless. Moreover, if the ability to answer these questions is an effect of only certain aspects of general mental ability, then any measurement of general mental ability based only on the types of questions mentioned is incomplete.

Indirect measurement procedures are common. Temperatures are ordinarily measured indirectly by means of a mercury thermometer and dangerous highway conditions by means of automobile speed limits. Aspects of the personal-social adjustment of students are inferred from written answers to questions. For example, they may be asked to respond with a "Yes," "Uncertain," or "No" to a question such as "Are you frequently afraid of adults?" Attempts have even been made to determine how well students can apply what they have learned by asking them to recite. Presumably, the more information they can recall, the better they can apply it. Changes in a student's attitudes and appreciations have been estimated by rating changes in the student's overt behavior in the classroom or on the playground. Changes there have been interpreted to represent deep-seated, perhaps permanent, changes, which will be manifested in the home or, in later years, in a vocation.

Indirect procedures should be used only when direct procedures cannot be applied. The repeated use of indirect measurement procedures in education stems from the fact that direct ones are often impossible or at least impractical. Measurement of such characteristics as general mental ability, interests, attitudes, and many aspects of achievement is therefore complicated.

PROBLEM

5. Which of the following can be best classified as direct measurement and which as indirect measurement?
    a. Determining the quality of a university library by counting the number of volumes it contains
    b. Determining the adequacy of a student's vision with a letter chart
    c. Determining the teaching effectiveness of an instructor with a paper-and-pencil opinionnaire administered to students
    d. Determining a student's ability to subtract two whole numbers (with a minuend less than ten) by means of a criterion-referenced test

Accuracy of Measurement Procedures

Carpenters building a new house continually vary the accuracy of their measurements according to need and choose their measuring instruments on that basis. For instance, as they assemble rough scaffoldings to assist in the construction, they probably cut the board needed at points found by estimating the desired lengths. When cutting the joists, however, they use a steel rule to measure lengths, and no greater than a one-eighth-of-an-inch error is allowed. Finally, when cutting the interior trim, they use the most precise of steel rules to measure length, allowing no more than a one-sixteenth-of-an-inch error.

Typically, classroom teachers also vary the degrees of accuracy of their measurement procedures as their purposes change. The measurement of general mental ability again offers a convenient illustration. In the first place, teachers do want to know whether their students have a certain minimum amount of capability and can profit from the learning experiences offered. Finding this out requires only rough measurement for most students. Later teachers may want to know whether their students are achieving in proportion to their capacities to learn. Classification of each student as an underachiever, normal achiever, or overachiever requires considerably greater accuracy of general mental ability measurement as well as academic achievement. Determination of the *amount* of overachievement or underachievement demands still greater accuracy.

Finally, certain students may be in competition for a highly specialized and technical training program to be started after completion of secondary school. Assume that the majority of those who are not qualified or interested are initially eliminated and that only a few of the remaining are to be chosen. Under these conditions, selecting those students who, because of their talents and earlier successes, have the greatest chance of success in such a program will demand even more sensitive measurements of general mental ability, prior achievement, and probably other factors.

Teachers are confronted with a relatively low ceiling above which their accuracy of measurement has not yet reached. We simply do not possess instruments that can measure psychological traits with refined accuracy.

Level of Measurement Accuracy

What then, you may ask, is the level of accuracy teachers typically encounter in their measurement attempts? In the first place, the accuracy of measurement procedures varies with the student traits being investigated. Secondly, although the accuracy available to teachers is considerably less than ideal, it is often sufficient to allow the procedure to be highly useful.

Variability of Accuracy. That the level of accuracy should vary with the student trait being investigated is certainly undesirable. Some traits are reasonably well-defined. Perhaps they have been studied more intensively than others, or perhaps they lend themselves more readily to measurement. Accordingly, mental ability is repeatedly mentioned as an area in which the accuracy of measurement procedures is relatively high, though far from perfect. Somewhat the same is said of the procedures used for measuring academic achievement, especially the measuring of a student's ability to recall information. After all, it is not difficult to determine a student's ability to recall the year in which the Battle of Hastings was fought, to properly spell the word "parallel," or to find the product of seven and eight.

The accuracy of the measurement procedures used in such relatively simple instances as those above is superior. Furthermore, well-developed standardized tests permit assessment in quantitative units that are of equal or near-equal size. In other words, a difference of one unit between two amounts is the same or essentially the same as a difference of one unit between any other two amounts, just as a difference of one pound between two given weights is the same as a difference of one pound between any other two given weights. Measuring instruments yielding scores that have equal units are classified as *interval scales*.

In contrast, consider efforts to measure aspects of a student's personal-social adjustment or the degree to which educational objectives pertaining to changes in attitudes and appreciations have been achieved. Now the student traits are subtle, almost nebulous. Such irrelevant factors as "lip service" and the tendency to conform to majority opinion cloud measurement results. Accuracy here is appreciably less than in measurement of general mental ability. To determine the amounts of some personal traits is often impossible. Our measuring procedures may yield information of such a crude nature that a ranking of the students within a group is the most accurate representation of individual differences that is justified. For instance, Sammy's ability to cooperate willingly with his peers in completing various projects of mutual interest may be observably superior to Sandra's; her ability in this respect may be judged to surpass Jimmy's. Hence Sammy is ranked first, Sandra second, and Jimmy third. Unfortunately, we are not at all certain that Sammy surpasses Sandra to the same degree that she surpasses Jimmy. The intervals between successive ranks are not necessarily equal; thus ranking (i.e., the *ordinal scale* of measurement) is clearly a less precise representation of individual differences than determination of amounts.

All too frequently, the crudeness of the information produced by measuring procedures prevents us from even ranking our students. Instead we must be content with a somewhat general verbal description. For example, instead of ranking Sammy first with respect to his ability to cooperate willingly with his peers, our measuring procedures may be so imprecise that the teacher can say only that he "cooperates frequently," or "usually displays little reluctance when the opportunity to cooperate is presented." Verbal descriptions of this type obviously are less precise representations of individual differences than the ranking of members of a group. Classifying students in terms of categories that have no apparent sense of order is known as the *nominal scale* of measurement.

Usefulness of Available Accuracy.   Certainly, lack of absolute accuracy is disturbing. Yet sufficient accuracy may exist to justify the statement that measuring procedures are some of the most useful tools teachers have. At the same time that informed classroom teachers recognize the inaccuracies of the results produced by educational measurement procedures, they also ask a fundamental question: "Can the information yielded by these procedures, inaccurate though it is, tell me more about my students than I can discover by any other means?" Frequently the answer is in the affirmative. Many instruments can reveal consistently more accurate information than the most popular alternative method, namely, informal judgments by teachers. Teacher judgments of students can be exceedingly accurate in a given instance and should be continually made, but they should be used in conjunction with, rather than independently of, evaluation procedures. When you as a teacher search for information about your students, use every means at your disposal, such as standardized tests, interviews, and rating scales, and be keenly aware of the accuracy of the information.

PROBLEMS

6. Classify each of the following in terms of the level of measurement (i.e., nominal, ordinal, or interval) that they represent.
   a. Temperature in terms of the Celsius scale
   b. Scores from a well-developed achievement test
   c. Auto license numbers
   d. Dog show results
   e. Telephone area code numbers

7. There is a fourth level of measurement known as the *ratio level*. In addition to having equal intervals like the interval level, it is characterized by an absolute zero. A zero reading means that zero amount exists of the characteristic being measured. Cite illustrations of this level of measurement within the realm of educational measurement.

Educational Evaluation Today

For our purposes, educational evaluation as it exists today has three outstanding subparts: student evaluation, the evaluation of programs and products, and large-scale assessments of educational achievement. These interlock in important ways, thereby strengthening each other. The testing and nontesting procedures used in student evaluation, for instance, are also very helpful in program evaluation and large-scale achievement assessments. Like student evaluation, the impact on education of the other two subparts is striking.

Evaluation of Programs and Products

Just as there are pronounced individual differences among students, so are there differences of similar magnitudes among curricula, teaching methods, administrative organizations, flexible class scheduling plans, textbooks, school physical plants, teacher's guides, films, and even projectors, tape recorders and encyclopedias. "Over-the-coffee-cup" opinions about these and other aspects of the educational scene are usually easy to obtain. But can a systematic determination of their worth be made? Most certainly yes.

Scriven (1967), Stake (1967, 1975), and Stufflebeam (1971) have described in detail how this can be done. Their models are not concerned with students as individuals. Only group response is needed, and sometimes not even that. They can encompass both formative and summative evaluation of programs and products.

All of the many program evaluation models proposed can be classified into one of four groups without undue difficulty (Popham, 1975, pp. 21–42). These are

1. Goal-attainment models
2. Judgment models emphasizing intrinsic criteria
3. Judgment models emphasizing extrinsic criteria
4. Decision-facilitation models

The first category largely represents the work of Ralph Tyler. According to this classic method, instructional goals for a program are specified, and the program is conducted in terms of these goals. At the conclusion of the program, groups of students are measured in order to determine the degree to which the prespecified goals have been achieved. On the basis of this evidence, value judgments are made as to the worth of the program.

Judgment models emphasizing intrinsic criteria stress the processes of the program rather than its products. The most common example of this category are accreditation evaluations conducted by regional associations of schools and colleges such as the North Central Association. After self-study by the staff of the participating institution, a team of specialists visits the school, reviews the self-study report, and evaluates the program on the basis of previously-established evaluative criteria. The evaluators examine such inputs and processes as the qualifications of the staff, the suitability of the curriculum and teaching methods, and the adequacy of the physical plant.

By contrast there are the judgment models emphasizing extrinsic criteria, that is, emphasizing product criteria involving the impact of the program on students and teachers. A useful example of this is the model designed by Stake (1967).

According to this model, the initial step in the evaluation of an educational program, perhaps a new curriculum, is to establish a rationale. This designates the purpose of the evaluation—the decisions about which you need data. Should the curriculum be adopted permanently or not? Should it be modified in certain respects? Is it an improvement over others designed for largely the same purposes? With questions like these in mind, the evaluator gathers information about the antecedents, transactions, and outcomes of the program being evaluated. They are defined as follows:

1. *Antecedents:* any conditions existing prior to the beginning of the program that may influence the outcomes of the program. These might include the qualifications of the teachers and students as well as the quality of the facilities and equipment.
2. *Transactions:* the countless encounters between students and staff, that is, discussions, individualized instruction, lectures, demonstrations, etc.
3. *Outcomes:* the impact of the program on students, teachers, and others, such as the students' changes in abilities, achievements, and attitudes resulting from the educational experiences.

First, the evaluator describes fully each of the foregoing in terms of what was *intended to occur* in the program, and what was *actually observed.* Then the evaluator must compare the antecedents, transactions, and outcomes separately in terms of standards of accepted and meritorious levels, often arbitrarily established. And finally, the evaluator must judge the degree of importance of any discrepancies found between actual features of the program and the standards listed for them.

The category of decision-facilitation models somewhat overlaps the other three categories described, but there is one central difference. Evaluators using these models try to work hand-in-hand with program staff by repeatedly collecting and presenting data to them to help them make better decisions as the program develops. The final judgments are made by the program leaders rather than by the evaluators. Probably the best known decision-facilitation model is an elaborate one known as CIPP (Stufflebeam, 1971). This acronym is composed of the first letters of the words for four types of evaluation included in the model, namely, context, input, process, and product evaluation.

Note the broad scope of all of these models as well as the sizable degree of subjectivity incorporated within them. Also keep in mind that use of such models leads to systematic evaluation, which in turn enhances efforts to make decisions based on pertinent data. The application of sound principles of program evaluation certainly will improve the meaningfulness of the educational accountability movement as we now know it (Wrightstone, Hogan & Abbott).

Goal-Free Evaluation.   Should we evaluate programs and products only in terms of their effectiveness in meeting their stated goals? Certainly not—to do so would be dangerous. After all, there might be side effects that would be overlooked. On the other hand, should evaluations be conducted without thought of the stated goals? No—this too would be dangerous. Yet some advocates of "goal-free" evaluation (Scriven, 1972) would respond differently. This evaluation strategy emphasizes the evaluation of the actual effects of a program or product, whether or not they are intended. Attention to stated goals, it is argued, might actually be a contaminating step that partly masks the presence of unanticipated effects. For our part, a more balanced position is to assume that goal-free evaluation is a supplement—not an alternative—to goal-based education, whether it be formative or summative in nature.

Large-Scale Assessment of Achievement

Large-scale assessments of achievement are very much a part of the educational scene today. District, state, national, and even international assessments involving thousands of students are being conducted with considerable regularity. Some are thought of as needs assessments to determine areas of strength and weakness in instructional programs, whereas others are test surveys to determine whether minimal competency in basic skills exists, so that a high school diploma can be granted or a grade-to-grade promotion can take place.

The best known large-scale assessment is the National Assessment of Educational Progress (NAEP). Rather than being concerned with the educational achievement of individual students, or even groups of students in a school, school system, or state, NAEP is designed to determine the regional and national educational skills of young Americans at four crucial points in their educational careers: at the end of their elementary school years (age 9); during their intermediate school years (age 13); during their secondary school years (age 17); and following the completion of all degree-seeking efforts (ages 26–35). The major goals of NAEP are—

1. to obtain census-like data on the educational attainment of large portions of our national population, and
2. to measure the growth or decline in educational attainment that takes place over time in key learning areas.

Serious efforts to achieve these goals began in 1963 and continue today. NAEP has identified many learning areas to be assessed; these include reading, mathematics, writing, science, social studies and citizenship, art and music. Review panels of teachers, specialists, and laymen interested in each area assist in the identification of the general and specific objectives for that area. They also determine the suitability of the exercises (i.e., test items) to be used. Each exercise is designed to be a direct reflection of a specified objective. In other words, data regarding group success or failure when responding to an exercise can be used with reasonable safety as a basis for inferring the degree to which the objective in question is being achieved.

The exercises vary considerably. Some are short-answer in nature, others are of the essay type, and still others require interviews, observations of student behavior (e.g., in citizenship), questionnaires, performance tasks (e.g., in music), and appraisal of work products (e.g., in art). NAEP exercises are not grouped to form tests from which total scores are computed. Instead, each exercise is scored separately and the percentages of subgroups of respondents giving correct and incorrect answers are reported.

Literally thousands of pieces of information, many of which are highly specific, have already been obtained regarding the educational attainment of young Americans. In general, NAEP has found sizable regional and community differences in achievement, as well as very large differences among respondents of major ethnic groups. Furthermore, a striking and consistently positive relationship exists between the level of young Americans' educational achievement and the level of their parents' education (Ahmann, 1979a).

Furthermore, important changes in national levels of achievement were detected during the 1970s. Within a three-to-seven year period, declines in reading, writing, mathematics, political knowledge and attitudes, and science achievement occurred for 13-year-olds and 17-year-olds, whereas 9-year-olds improved in both reading and writing, but declined somewhat in political knowledge and attitudes and only slightly in science and mathematics (Ahmann, 1979b).

Supporters of NAEP believe that the information being gathered is descriptive enough to tell us what the younger segment of the population is learning and to provide a partial basis for formulating public policy in education. Others disagree, pointing out the limitations inherent in large-scale assessment of achievement. In any event, NAEP is a unique and most ambitious project. Its true worth can only be determined after it has assessed each of its learning areas at least twice, thereby measuring the degree of change in levels of educational achievement on a national basis.

PROBLEM

8. Much disagreement exists as to the likely reasons why achievement levels have declined in the 1970s, especially among 13- and 17-year-olds (Harnischfeger & Wiley, 1976; Ahmann, 1979b). Do you believe that school variables (e.g., "time on task") are more important than societal variables (e.g., excessive TV viewing) in this regard? Why?

Development of the Evaluation Movement

The principal developments that have contributed to the evaluation movement today have occurred since 1900. This fact more than any other clearly reveals the relative immaturity that characterizes the evaluation movement in psychology and education. Admittedly, modern efforts are less accurate and consistent than we might wish. The physical sciences far outstrip the behavioral sciences in ability to measure the phenomena being studied. Now time can be measured by means of a thallium-beam clock, which is even more accurate than the cesium-beam clock developed only a few years ago. Lasers can make automatic length measurements with an accuracy of 1.8 parts in 10^9. Such refinements as these allow us to make even greater technological advances in the space age. Educational advances are less impressive by far. Yet, instead of being disappointed in the inability of the behavioral sciences to match the physical sciences in measuring, we should be impressed by the fact that evaluation in the behavioral sciences has progressed so far in so short a time.

Educational evaluation is now an important activity of the school and of most teachers who compose its permanent staff. No one knows how many standardized tests are administered each year in the schools of the United States, but the number probably exceeds 200 million per year. The number of teacher-constructed tests given annually cannot even be estimated, but must be many times the foregoing figure. Furthermore, innumerable educational programs are being evaluated in order to determine whether to continue, modify, or terminate them, and numerous large-scale assessments are showing us the many different achievement profiles of American youth and how these change over time.

The merits of educational evaluation are by no means universally acclaimed today. The history of the movement displays the familiar "pendulum" process. The popularity and general acceptance of the movement wax and wane, and the net result is that well-read teachers have come to realize that these tools are but means to an end and are imperfect even though indispensable. Thorough knowledge of the basic principles of evaluation is not only a necessary prerequisite to understanding and capitalizing on today's tools but also a necessary preparation for tomorrow's progress.

SUMMARY

The principal ideas in this chapter can be summarized as follows:

1. Educational evaluation is the systematic process of determining the effectiveness of educational endeavors in the light of evidence. Its four principal uses are (a) to appraise academic achievement of individual students; (b) to diagnose learning difficulties; (c) to appraise the effectiveness of educational programs and products; and (d) to assess the educational progress of a large population. The first two uses constitute student evaluation. The third is known as program evaluation, and the last as large-scale assessment of achievement.

2. The purposes of student evaluation are twofold: first, it helps teachers evaluate the degree to which educational objectives have been achieved; secondly, it helps teachers know their students to such a degree that educational experiences can be planned according to their varied interests, aptitudes, and prior experiences.

3. The procedures used in student evaluation include paper-and-pencil tests, ranking and rating scales, performance tests, anecdotal records, questionnaires, interviewing techniques, autobiographies, sociometric procedures, and unobtrusive measures.

4. Educational measurement and educational evaluation are not synonymous expressions. Measurement is the process that attempts to obtain a quantitative representation of the degree to which a student reflects a trait. Educational evaluation is a process in which a teacher commonly uses information derived from many sources to arrive at a value judgment. The information may be obtained by using measurements and also other techniques that do not necessarily yield quantitative results, such as questionnaires and interviews.

5. Eighteen common types of tests are individual and group tests; classroom and standardized tests; oral, essay, and objective tests; speed, power, and mastery tests; verbal, nonverbal, and performance tests; readiness and diagnostic tests; and norm-referenced, criterion-referenced, and objective-referenced tests. A given test can be simultaneously classified in more than one of these subgroups.

6. Educational measurement methods can be characterized by two features. First, they are primarily indirect rather than direct. Students' traits are appraised in terms of their effects rather than in terms of the traits themselves. Secondly, measurement procedures are not remarkably accurate in terms of any absolute standards, but they are dependable enough to reveal more information about students than other techniques at the teacher's disposal.

7. Models for program evaluation can be classified into four categories, namely, (1) goal-attainment models, (2) judgment models emphasizing intrinsic criteria, (3) judgment models emphasizing extrinsic criteria, and (4) decision-facilitation models.

8. Large-scale assessments to determine levels of achievement for groups of students are being made at the district, state, regional, and national level. Some attempt has been made to determine whether minimum competency in basic skills has been attained.

SUGGESTED READINGS

BLOOM, B. S., HASTINGS, J. T., & MADAUS, G. F. *Handbook on formative and summative evaluation of student learning.* New York: McGraw-Hill, 1971. See chapters 3, 4, and 6.
Chapter 3 is an excellent discussion of mastery learning. Summative evaluation is covered in Chapter 4, formative evaluation in Chapter 6.

DUBOIS, P. H. *The history of psychological testing.* Boston: Allyn and Bacon, 1970.
The development of psychological and educational tests is traced from the civil service tests in ancient China and the oral tests in medieval European universities to the present.

DYER, H. S. Criticisms of testing: How mean is the median? *NCME Measurement in Education,* 1977, 8(3).
The general criticisms of tests are discussed. Suggestions are made with regard to improving the usefulness of testing in schools.

EBEL, R. L. Educational tests: Valid? Biased? Useful? *Phi Delta Kappan,* 1975, *57,* 89–93.
Six current issues related to the use of tests are examined in this article. In a companion article following it, R. L. Green addresses many of the same issues, but from a different point of view. The comparison is enlightening.

GREEN, B. F., JR. In defense of measurement. *American Psychologist,* 1978, *33,* 664–670.
In the author's opinion, the criticism of tests is misplaced and ignores the major advantages of objective measurement. Test data can indicate general tendencies, he believes, even to the point of providing an indication of social problems such as the extent of educational disadvantage of minority groups.

POPHAM, W. J. *Criterion-referenced measurement.* Englewood Cliffs, N.J.: Prentice-Hall, 1978. See chapters 1 and 2.
In Chapter 1, the recent developments in achievement testing are reviewed, with attention to the origins of criterion-referenced assessment. Chapter 2 concerns norm-referenced measurement, its purposes and characteristics.

REFERENCES CITED

AHMANN, J. S. National achievement profiles in ten learning areas. *Educational Studies,* 1979a, 9, 351–364.

AHMANN, J. S. Differential changes in levels of achievement for students in three age groups. *Educational Studies,* 1979b, *10,* 35–51.

ANASTASI, A. *Psychological testing* (4th ed.). New York: Macmillan, 1976.

BLOOM, B. S., HASTINGS, J. T., & MADAUS, G. F. *Handbook on formative and summative evaluation of student learning.* New York: McGraw-Hill, 1971.

BUROS, O. K. (Ed.). *The eighth mental measurements yearbook.* Lincoln, Nebr.: University of Nebraska Press, 1978.

CRONBACH, L. J. *Essentials of psychological testing* (3rd ed.). New York: Harper & Row, 1970.

FORS, G. (Ed.). *Science guide.* Bismarck, N.D.: North Dakota Department of Public Instruction, 1969.

GLASER, R., & NITKO, A. J. Measurement in learning and instruction. In R. L. Thorndike (Ed.), *Educational measurement* (2nd ed.). Washington, D.C.: American Council on Education, 1971.

GRONLUND, N. E. *Preparing criterion-referenced tests for classroom instruction*. New York: Macmillan, 1973.

HARNISCHFEGER, A., & WILEY, D. E. Achievement test scores drop. So what? *Educational Researcher*, 1976, 5, 5–12.

HIVELY, W. Introduction to domain-referenced testing. *Educational Technology*, 1974, 14, 5–10.

LEVINE, H. G., & MCGUIRE, C. Role-playing as an evaluative technique. *Journal of Educational Measurement*, 1968, 5, 1–8.

MICHIGAN DEPARTMENT OF EDUCATION. *Minimal performance objectives in mathematics education in Michigan*. Lansing, Mich.: Author, 1973.

POPHAM, W. J. *Educational evaluation*. Englewoods Cliffs, N.J.: Prentice-Hall, 1975.

POPHAM, W. J. *Criterion-referenced measurement*. Englewood Cliffs, N.J.: Prentice-Hall, 1978.

SCRIVEN, M. The methodology of evaluation. *AERA Monograph Series on Curriculum Evaluation*, 1967, No. 1, 39–83.

SCRIVEN, M. Pros and cons about goal-free education. *Evaluation Comment*, 1972, 3, 1–4.

STAKE, R. E. The countenance of educational evaluation. *Teachers College Record*, 1967, 68, 523–540.

STAKE, R. E. Program evaluation, particularly response evaluation. *Occasional Paper Series, No. 5*. Kalamazoo, Mich.: The Evaluation Center, Western Michigan University, 1975.

STODDARD, G. D. On the meaning of intelligence. *Proceedings of the 1965 Invitational Conference on Testing Problems*. Princeton, N.J.: Educational Testing Service, 1966, 3–11.

STUFFLEBEAM, D. L. (Ed.). *Educational evaluation and decision-making*. Itasca, Ill.: F. E. Peacock, 1971.

TYLER, R. W. *Basic principles of curriculum and evaluation*. Chicago: University of Chicago Press, 1949 (1969 impression).

WESMAN, A. G. *Selected writings of Alexander G. Wesman*. New York: The Psychological Corporation, 1975.

WRIGHTSTONE, J. W., HOGAN, T. P., & ABBOTT, M. M. *Accountability in education and associated measurement problems* (Test Service Notebook 33). New York: Harcourt Brace Jovanovich.

2

Educational Objectives in Student Evaluation

The purpose of this chapter is to help you

1. Understand the basic sources of educational objectives and their hierarchical nature

2. Distinguish general objectives, subobjectives, and specific instructional objectives from each other, and illustrate their interrelationships

3. Explain the classification of educational objectives in each of the three domains—cognitive, affective, and psychomotor

4. State your position regarding the potential loss of accurate interpretation when student behavior is evaluated on the basis of data gathered in somewhat artificial situations, rather than in those that are more natural

5. Outline the steps followed to build a satisfactory norm-referenced paper-and-pencil achievement test as well as a criterion-referenced test, based on the objectives used in the instruction

6. Become aware of the crucial importance of a high degree of content validity in achievement tests and of how to obtain this by developing such tests on the basis of pertinent educational objectives

7. Defend the need for a broadly-based system for measuring and evaluating student achievement, that is, a system that includes not only paper-and-pencil tests of various types, but nontesting data-gathering instruments as well

The sources of our life goals are difficult if not impossible to trace. It is clear, however, that they stem from the needs that each of us experience. The goals are a direct outgrowth of social needs such as recognition, prestige, power, security, and companionship; others develop from physiological needs like hunger and thirst.

The nature of personal goals and their relative importance will vary among individuals, but practically all can be classified into categories such as vocational, recreational, social, educational, and religious. This should not suggest that a goal in one category is independent of goals in any other. For example, an educational goal of acquiring a bachelor's degree from a first-class university may be closely related to a vocational goal of becoming a licensed physician. Again, a recreational goal of raising a bowling average to 175 pins per game may well be a part of a social goal of enlarging one's circle of friends.

At least for the more important goals, we organize programs, formally or informally, that should lead us ever closer to what we want. Some programs may have tentative termination dates; others may not. They may differ in terms of the degree to which they are structured. Programs for educational and vocational goals are, for the most part, based on formal schooling. Those for recreational and social goals may be designed by the individual and be quite casual.

It is only reasonable that, as we follow a specific program, we are concerned about our progress toward the intended goal. We probably search for evidence that will identify our present position. For example, in the case of the educational goal mentioned above, evidence would include the number of college credit hours accumulated and the grade-point average achieved; in the case of the bowling goal, it would be the bowling average for the past several games. With pieces of evidence such as these in mind, we can compare our present position with out initial position and our goal. These two reference points allow us to evaluate the growth we have achieved.

Translation of Needs Into Educational Objectives

At one time the primary purpose of formal education was to teach each new generation all the knowledge that had been accumulated by all previous generations. This conception resulted in a highly rigid school curriculum that made the textbook the strongest single element in the classroom. At the present time this concept of the primary purpose of formal education has been largely superseded by another—to train students in such a way that they are better able to meet their needs as they grow and develop in a democratic society.

The pertinent needs of youth are translated into educational objectives by identifying the new patterns of behavior that students must acquire to meet their needs. These involve development of new knowledge, intellectual abilities and skills, affective patterns, and psychomotor skills. Knowledge includes student behaviors that emphasize remembering, either by recognition or recall, ideas, material, or phenomena. If students can comprehend pieces of information to the point that they can grasp relationships, restate the information in their own words, and take action intelligently on the basis of what they have learned, then they have developed intellectual skills and abilities to an important degree. Affective patterns include changes in interests, attitudes, and values. These pertain to the predisposition of students to react in a particular manner to certain ideas, objects, people, and events. They now have "points of view." They have feelings of attraction or aversion toward aspects of their environments. Finally, psychomotor skills are vital to achievement in physical education, music, art, technical and industrial education, and vocations in these areas.

For purposes of convenience, the entire array of educational objectives is divided into three domains—cognitive, affective, and psychomotor. Taxonomies for classifying objectives have been established for each domain (see page 38), and these greatly assist in reducing communication problems so often associated with objectives.

Classroom teachers and other education specialists have to examine each area of need and decide the nature of the new behavioral patterns that students must develop to be able to meet their needs. Then they must make decisions as to how and when each student will be taught. These decisions should produce a curriculum in which attainable goals, carefully keyed to the maturity levels and various backgrounds of the students in question, have been selected for each area of instruction.

Whether goals should be established for each grade level of each curriculum area is another question, since the grading system can be thought of as little more than a convenient administrative device for grouping students. In any event, within a framework of educational goals, teachers should maintain sufficient flexibility so that they can exploit all the learning possibilities in their fields, and can do so in terms of the individual needs of their students.

The goals of education are student-oriented rather than teacher-oriented. The manner in which they are stated should reflect this fact. In the not-too-distant past, educational objectives were stated in terms of the activities that the teacher was to perform. A certain topic was to be taught at a certain time in a certain manner. The modern way of stating educational objectives reflects the fact that they stem from student needs. To be consistent, therefore, educational objectives must be stated in terms of desired student behavior rather than in any other way.

Types of Objectives

Efforts to translate the needs of youth into educational objectives are typically directed toward producing precise statements that identify the observable changes in student behavior that should take place if the learning experience is successful. Unquestionably, such objectives are excellent starting points for developing the curriculum, planning teaching strategies, and constructing testing and nontesting instruments. Nevertheless, we must recognize that the very preciseness that is so valuable may also be detrimental; it is difficult to identify measurable student behaviors in subject matter areas like the fine arts.

Recognition of this possibility causes some to feel that, in reality, there are two types of objectives, instructional and expressive (Eisner, 1969, pp. 14–17). The former unambiguously specify the particular pupil behavior to be acquired as a result of learning. The latter do not. Expressive objectives describe "educational encounters," situations in which students are to work or problems they are to solve. These encounters are, in essence, tasks that yield student products—a poem, art object, or report.

Unsurprisingly, expressive objectives are most common in curriculum areas such as art, music, drama, dance, creative writing, and speech. Illustrative of this type of objective are the following:

1.   The student will compose a poem depicting a personal impression of a brilliant sunset over the desert.
2.   The student will interpret the meaning of Alexander Pope's "Essay on Man" and prepare a written summary of the interpretation.
3.   The student will build an original mobile having at least five moving parts.

In each instance, the primary means of evaluating student performance would be the evaluation of the merits of the product developed.

Both types of objectives are needed. On the one hand, teachers may find that expressive objectives provide a kind of outreach for their teaching efforts that is exciting to them and their students. On the other hand, instructional objectives are the solid base for both teaching and evaluation. As educational outcomes become prescribable, expressive objectives are not needed and instructional objectives receive their proper emphasis. In this and the following chapters, instructional objectives are given primary attention.

PROBLEMS

1.   Select two school systems that you know well, preferably one in a metropolitan center and one not in such a center, and compare them in terms of the role the schools must play in the process of helping students learn how to satisfy their needs.

2.   In your opinion, are instructional objectives or expressive objectives more important in each of the following teaching situations:
     a.   Elementary school science unit on climate
     b.   Junior high school carpentry shop
     c.   Senior high school English literature class
     d.   Senior high school marriage and family living class

Taxonomy of Educational Objectives

Educational objectives have been classified into three domains, namely, the cognitive, affective, and psychomotor. The cognitive domain includes those educational objectives related to the recall of knowledge and the development of intellectual abilities and skills. The affective domain includes those objectives concerning changes in a student's emotional state or the degree of acceptance or rejection of some entity—it is the domain of personal-social adjustment. The psychomotor domain includes objectives that involve primarily muscular or motor skills, some manipulation of material and objects, or some act that requires a neuromuscular coordination (Krathwohl, Bloom, & Masia, 1964, p. 7).

Cognitive Domain

The taxonomies organized for each domain well represent the hierarchical nature of each. In the case of the cognitive domain, the main organizing principle used is the degree of complexity of the cognitive process involved in the objective. Comparatively simple cognitive behaviors could combine with others of a similar nature and yield more complex student behaviors.

The taxonomy for the cognitive domain contains six subdivisions, and these in turn are subdivided as needed. The subdivisions are as follows (adapted from Bloom, 1956, pp. 201–207):

Knowledge

1.00 *Knowledge*
The recall of specifics and universals, the recall of methods and processes, or the recall of a pattern, structure, or setting. The knowledge objectives emphasize most the psychological processes of remembering.

Intellectual Abilities and Skills

2.00 *Comprehension*
A type of understanding or apprehension such that the individual knows what is being communicated and can make use of the material or idea being communicated without necessarily relating it to other material or seeing its fullest implications.

3.00 *Application*
The use of abstractions in particular and concrete situations. The abstractions may be in the form of general ideas, rules of procedures, or generalized methods.

4.00 *Analysis*
The breakdown of a communication into its constituent elements or parts such that the relative hierarchy of ideas is made clear and/or the relations between the ideas expressed are made explicit. Such analyses are intended to clarify the communication, to indicate how the communication is organized, and the way in which it manages to convey its effects, as well as its basis and arrangements.

5.00 *Synthesis*
The putting together of elements and parts so as to form a whole. This involves the process of working with pieces, parts, elements, etc., and arranging them in such a way as to constitute a pattern or structure not clearly there before.

6.00 *Evaluation*
Judgments about the value of material and methods for given purposes. Quantitative and qualitative judgments about the extent to which material and methods satisfy criteria.

The claim that the six levels represent a hierarchical order, that is, vary from the simple to the complex, has some empirical verification (Seddon, 1978). Evidence supports the ordering of the first four levels more than it does the last two, but a simple hierarchical interpretation is not justified (Miller, Snowman, & O'Hara, 1979).

Affective Domain

The main organizing principle used to develop the affective domain taxonomy is the process of internalization. This is the process whereby ideas, practices, standards, or values successively and pervasively become part of an individual. In the case of the taxonomy, internalization is viewed as a process through which there is at first an incomplete and tentative adoption of only the overt manifestations of the behavior in question and later a more complete adoption. Hence the taxonomy represents a continuum of the behaviors implied by objectives in this domain.

Five chief categories have been identified, each of which has two or three subdivisions as follows:

1.00 *Receiving (Attending)*
       The sensitization of learners to the existence of certain phenomena and stimuli. They are willing to receive or to attend to them. This is the first and crucial step if the learners are to be properly oriented to learn what the teacher intends.

2.00 *Responding*
       Learned responses that go beyond merely attending to the phenomenon. Learners are sufficiently motivated that they are not just willing to attend but to attend actively. This is the category that many teachers find best describes their "interest" objectives.

3.00 *Valuing*
       Recognition that a thing, phenomenon, or behavior has worth. This abstract concept of worth is in part a result of each learner's own valuing or assessment, but it is much more a social product that has been slowly internalized or accepted and has come to be used by the learner as his or her own criterion of worth. This category is appropriate for many objectives using the term "attitude" and, of course, "value."

4.00 *Organization*
       The beginnings of the building of a value system. As learners successively internalize values, they encounter situations for which more than one value is relevant. Thus necessity arises for (a) the organization of the values into a system, (b) the determination of the interrelationships among them, and (c) the establishment of the dominant and pervasive ones.

5.00 *Characterization by a Value or Value Complex*
       Integration of beliefs, ideas, and attitudes into a total philosophy or world view. The values already have a place in the individual's value hierarchy, are organized into some kind of internally consistent system, and have controlled the behavior of the individual for a sufficient time that he or she has adapted to behaving this way.*

* Adapted from *Taxonomy of educational objectives*, Handbook 2: Affective Domain, by David R. Krathwohl et al. Copyright © 1964 by Longman Inc. Previously published by David McKay Company, Inc. Reprinted by permission of Longman Inc.

The utility of the affective taxonomy is influenced by a number of factors. One of these is the lower level of emphasis often placed on these objectives as compared with cognitive ones. This is perplexing since, in keeping with the major objectives of education, we want students not only to have cognitive skills, but also to want to use them. Another factor is the comparatively limited knowledge we have about the affective domain in general. Such terms as *attitude, adjustment, appreciation,* and *interest* are used without being precisely defined. The range of meaning for each is so great that objectives using such terms may be classified in a variety of categories in the taxonomy.

Psychomotor Domain

The difficulty of classifying objectives according to a taxonomic framework is most apparent in the psychomotor domain. Several major efforts have been made to develop a suitable taxonomy. One significant contribution was made by Harrow (1972) in which six major classification levels were arranged along a continuum from the lowest level of observable movement behavior to the highest level, as follows.

1.00 *Reflex Movements*
Those movements which are involuntary in nature. They are functional at birth, developing through maturation.

2.00 *Basic Fundamental Movements*
Those inherent movement patterns that form the basis for specialized complex skilled movements.

3.00 *Perceptual Abilities*
All of the learner's perceptual modalities where stimuli impinge upon him or her to be carried to the higher brain centers for interpretation.

4.00 *Physical Abilities*
Those functional characteristics of organic vigor which, when developed, provide learners with sound, efficiently functioning instruments (their bodies) to be used when making skilled movements a part of their movement repertoire.

5.00 *Skilled Movements*
The result of the acquisition of a degree of efficiency when performing a complex movement task. This classification level includes movements that require learning and are considered reasonably complex. All sports skills, dance skills, recreational skills, and manipulative skills fall into this classification.

6.00 *Nondiscursive Communication*
Behaviors that can be labeled forms of movement communication. These encompass a wide variety of communicative movements ranging from facial expressions, postures, and gestures to sophisticated modern dance choreographies.*

The foregoing taxonomy is not as "clean" as the other two, particularly the cognitive. Cognition can occur with a minimum of motor activity, and perhaps

*Adapted from *A Taxonomy of the Psychomotor Domain,* by A. J. Harrow. Copyright ©
1972 by Longman Inc. Previously published by David McKay Company, Inc.

little feeling. In contrast, psychomotor activity involves both cognitive and affective influences. This seriously complicates work in the third domain.

Value of the Taxonomies

The impact of the taxonomies on educational thinking is indeed powerful. As foreseen, they do assist appreciably in the task of helping teachers and other educational specialists discuss their curricular and evaluation problems with greater precision. We gain a better perspective of the relative importance of our objectives and their interrelationships by using the taxonomies as classification schemes. Also, terminology is standardized to a greater degree than ever before.

The three taxonomies represent the total framework of educational objectives for all types of educational institutions. They also represent, therefore, the total framework within which evaluation procedures are functioning. Hence, after careful study, teachers can classify objectives pertinent to their teaching in appropriate categories, and devise a set of measurement procedures, some of which are tests, to obtain appropriate data on the basis of which broadly-based evaluations can be made. Use of the taxonomies in this way adds meaning to the educational objectives and defines more sharply the limits of the scope of the student evaluation attempted.

Learning Hierarchies

For some purposes, the taxonomies are not sufficiently precise. For instance, the categories of the cognitive taxonomy deal with mental processes and do not recognize other significant aspects of a well-stated instructional objective. Such an objective identifies the specific overt behavior to be performed by the students, the conditions under which they are to perform, and the criteria of acceptable performance. Tools other than the taxonomies are needed if this kind of objective is to be formulated easily.

A categorizing system with a finer mesh has been designed by Gagné (1977). He identifies eight types of learning—eight sets of conditions under which changes in student behavior are brought about. They are ordered as follows:

1. *Signal learning:* Making a general, diffuse response to a signal
2. *Stimulus-response learning:* Acquiring a precise response to a discriminated stimulus
3. *Chaining:* Combining two or more stimulus-response connections
4. *Verbal association:* Learning chains that are verbal
5. *Discrimination learning:* Learning to make *n* different by identifying responses to as many different stimuli as resemble each other
6. *Concept learning:* Acquiring a capacity to make a common response to a class of stimuli that widely differ from each other
7. *Rule learning:* Acquiring a chain of two or more concepts
8. *Problem solving:* Learning that requires thinking; combining two or more previously acquired rules to produce a new capability of a higher order

The hierarchical nature of the breakdown is unmistakable. Achievement in each class depends on learning the preceding one. Thus these varieties of learning can serve as a means of conceptualizing a wide range of educational objectives.

This and other works by Gagné are basic to the preparation of a "learning hierarchy," that is, a set of component tasks that lead to the achievement of a certain educational objective. In other words, the behavioral pattern of a "major" objective of an instruction program is analyzed in terms of the pattern of tasks that must be mastered by the student. The tasks are ordered to form a hierarchy that can then guide teaching and student evaluation. Observe that the hierarchy of component tasks can be considered a hierarchy of specific objectives. We know "what comes first" when the student behaviors identified are ones known to exist among the students when instruction is to begin. Certainly this type of backward analysis is highly useful for student placement and for diagnosis and remediation of learning difficulties. In this regard, criterion-referenced tests are able to play a significant role.

The analysis of learning hierarchies, otherwise known as component task analysis, is highly complex. Its rewards are well illustrated by the results of its application in an elementary school science program (Walbesser, 1968). The author has listed "action verbs" to be used in the formulation of instructional objectives in science. They are:

1. *Identify:* Select the correct object from a set of objects
2. *Name:* Specify what an object, event, or relationship is called
3. *Order:* Arrange three or more objects or events in a sequence based on some stated property
4. *Describe:* State observable properties sufficiently to identify an object, event, or relationship
5. *Distinguish:* Select an object or event from two or more with which it might be confused
6. *Construct:* Make a physical object, drawing, or written or verbal statement
7. *Demonstrate:* Carry out a sequence of operations necessary for a stated task
8. *State a rule:* Provide a relationship or principle that can be used to solve a problem or complete a task
9. *Apply a rule:* Determine the answer to a problem by using a relationship or principle

Use of these nine terms serves to sharpen the thrust of instructional objectives in traditional subject matter areas. It can be argued that only six are needed, namely, *identify, name, describe, construct, order,* and *demonstrate,* provided such highly specific verbs as *add, spell,* and *conjugate* are also used when appropriate (Sullivan, 1969). Be that as it may, the intent of action verbs is to focus attention directly on student behavior. The list should be so heterogeneous that practically every student behavioral pattern with heavy cognitive features could be classified under one of the terms.

PROBLEMS

3. Classify each of the following objectives in terms of the six principal levels of the taxonomy for the cognitive domain:
   a. The student can distinguish between related scientific concepts such as speed and acceleration, kinetic and potential energy, and mass and weight.
   b. The student can list the order of the steps normally followed for a bill to be passed by the U.S. Congress and become law.

4. Classify each of the following objectives in terms of the five principal levels of the taxonomy for the affective domain:
   a. The student finds pleasure in the investigation of natural phenomena such as the activity of an ant colony or tankful of tropical fish.
   b. The student develops awareness of aesthetic aspects of style of dress.

5. Classify each of the following objectives in terms of the six principal levels of the psychomotor domain:
   a. The student can type "smooth-copy" prose at a minimum speed of 40 words per minute (after adjustment for errors) using an electric type-writer.
   b. The student can assume the proper body stance for driving a golf ball.

Levels of Educational Objectives

Even the most casual examination of educational objectives reveals that they vary widely in terms of their degree of specificity. Some are "general" objectives, that is, statements of the main aims or ultimate goals of the educational system. One example is the goal that students become good citizens and function as such throughout their lives. In contrast to the global nature of this, consider the wealth of subobjectives that such a goal can generate. These can be highly specific as in the case of those dealing with a student's ability to distinguish among *to, too,* and *two,* or to add accurately any combination of two integers, neither of which is greater than ten.

At least three main levels of objectives can be established (Krathwohl & Payne, 1971). The first is the most abstract and deals with long-term goals like vocational efficiency or self-realization. The second level, derived from the first, is more concrete and represents objectives to be attained by students successfully completing a course of study. For example, "the student can distinguish among a chemical element, compound, and mixture." Finally, the third level contains highly specific objectives derived from ones at the second level, which state not only the student performance desired, but also the situation that initiates the performance, the criteria of acceptable performance, and, if appropriate, any special conditions related to the performance. Here is an example: "the student distinguishes among *to, too,* and *two* with ninety percent accuracy when provided short written sentences that can be completed by inserting one of the three words at a designated position."

First-Level Objectives: General Objectives

A number of the attempts to formulate first-level objectives have been quite ambitious. Committees as well as individuals have produced impressive lists most often delineating the ultimate goals of the educational system without direct references to traditional subject matter areas. Of greater interest to us are first-level objectives organized along curricular lines.

Primary Objectives for National Assessment.   In the late 1960s and continuing into the 1970s, advisory committees composed of educators, subject matter specialists, and laymen wrote the primary objectives for the National Assessment of Educational Progress in ten curriculum areas. This procedure was used to ensure that every objective should meet three criteria: (1) it should be considered important by scholars; (2) it should be accepted as an educational task by the educational system; and (3) it should be considered desirable by laymen. The following are samples of this work for the second assessment of four learning areas (National Assessment of Educational Progress, 1972a, 1972b, 1972c, 1974):

Science

1. Know the fundamental aspects of science.
2. Understand and apply the fundamental aspects of science in a wide range of problem situations.
3. Appreciate the knowledge and processes of science, the consequences and limitations of science, and the personal and social relevance of science and technology in our society.

Writing

1. Demonstrate ability in writing to reveal personal feelings and ideas.
2. Demonstrate ability to write in response to a wide range of societal demands.
3. Indicate the importance attached to writing skills.

Citizenship

1. Show concern for the well-being and dignity of others.
2. Support just law and rights of all individuals.
3. Know the main structure and functions of government.
4. Participate in democratic civic improvement.
5. Understand important world, national, and local civic problems.
6. Approach civic decisions rationally.
7. Help and respect one's own family.

Reading

1. Demonstrate behavior conducive to reading.
2. Demonstrate word identification skills.
3. Possess skills for reading comprehension.
4. Use a variety of approaches in gathering information.

To be sure, this work is not complete. In some ways, such primary objectives as these are moving targets. Therefore, review and revision occurs every assessment cycle, about every four to eight years.

State Goals for Elementary and Secondary Education.   Increased interest in educational accountability has caused most states to re-examine their major objectives for elementary and secondary education. Existing statements of goals have been carefully reviewed, then revised, and new goals added. Extensive participation by educators and citizens has been common.

A study of the goals of thirty-five states revealed that the learner outcome goals fall into eleven categories as follows (Zimmerman, 1972):

1. Basic skills
2. Cultural appreciation
3. Self-realization
4. Citizenship and political understanding
5. Human relations
6. Economic understanding
7. Physical environment
8. Mental and physical health
9. Creative, constructive, and critical thinking
10. Career education and occupational competence
11. Values and ethics

Within each of these categories are classified a variety of objectives. For instance, within the basic skills area are objectives in reading, writing, speaking, listening, viewing, mathematics, science, art, and humanities. The affective domain is heavily represented in the self-realization, human relations, and values and ethics areas.

Second-Level Objectives: Subobjectives

The first important subdivisions of first-level objectives are often called subobjectives. Illustrations are countless; here are several widely used examples representing both elementary and secondary education.

Elementary Education.   A prominent statement of objectives at the second level for elementary education is the one prepared by the Mid-Century Committee on Outcomes in Elementary Education (Kearney, 1953). Each objective included in the list is thought to be attainable by average children at some time prior to age fifteen or sixteen. No matter how defensible a proposed objective might have been on a purely philosophical basis, it was not included unless it was also deemed attainable during the first fifteen years of the child's life, regardless of whether the school, the home, or some other community agency was instrumental in helping the child reach this goal.

Nine curriculum areas are considered:

1. Physical development, health, and body care
2. Individual social and emotional development
3. Ethical behavior, standards, and values
4. Social relations
5. The social world
6. The physical world
7. Aesthetic development
8. Communication
9. Quantitative relationships

To illustrate the nature of the objectives from two of the curriculum areas, a few of the intermediate-period (end of sixth grade, or an age of about twelve years) objectives are listed below:

Ethical Behavior, Standards, and Values

A. Knowledge and understanding
The student develops an awareness of property rights and of truth and falsehood.
B. Skills and competences
The student is able to like a person in spite of disliking his or her behavior in specific instances.
C. Attitudes and interests
The student is interested in altruistic club activities.

Quantitative Relationships

A. Knowledge and understanding
The student knows how numbers apply to time, weight, and dry and liquid measures.
B. Skills and competences
The student can add, subtract, and multiply decimals.
C. Attitudes and interests
The student respects accuracy and arithmetical orderliness.*

Secondary Education. Similar to the foregoing effort, a study was made of the objectives of the secondary school. Only the objectives for the general education program in the secondary school are included in this report. The basic purposes of this program are to help students realize their fullest potentialities and meet civic responsibility.

The lists of educational objectives are classified under three maturity goals and four areas of behavioral competence. The maturity goals are

* Paraphrased from Part II, pages 68–73 and 113–120, of *Elementary School Objectives: A Report Prepared for The Mid-Century Committee on Outcomes in Elementary Education,* by Nolan C. Kearney. Copyright 1953 by Russell Sage Foundation.

1. Growth toward self-realization
2. Growth toward desirable interpersonal relations in small groups
3. Growth toward effective membership or leadership in large organizations

The four areas of behavioral competence are

1. Attainment of maximum intellectual growth and development
2. Cultural orientation and integration
3. Physical and mental health
4. Economic competence

The educational objectives given below are classified under the maturity goal of self-realization within the area of behavioral competence called attaining maximum intellectual growth and development (adapted from French and Associates, 1957, pp. 92–102). They are considered to be reasonable goals for the most mature high school seniors.

1.111(d) The student uses common sources of printed information efficiency; e.g., dictionary, encyclopedia, Readers' Guide, card catalog in a library.

1.121(a) The student adjusts his or her reading rate and method to the material.

1.123(f) The student demonstrates that he or she can read and understand mathematical reports, charts and graphs, and simple statements of financial accounts.

1.131(e) The student analyzes a problem and can follow the recognized steps involved in scientific thinking.

Subobjectives for National Assessment. For each of the main objectives prepared for the National Assessment of Educational Progress, second-level objectives were also prepared. The following are illustrative of these from the science and citizenship areas (National Assessment of Educational Progress, 1972a, 1972c):

Science

First level
Understand and apply the fundamental aspects of science in a wide range of problem situations.

Second level
1. Understand and apply facts and simple concepts.
2. Understand and apply laws and principles.
3. Understand and apply conceptual schemes.
4. Understand and apply inquiry skills.
5. Understand and apply the scientific enterprise.

Citizenship

First level
Show concern for the well-being and dignity of others.

Second level

1. Treat others with respect.
2. Consider the consequences for others of their own actions.
3. Guard safety and health of others.
4. Offer to help others in need.
5. Support equal opportunity in education, housing, employment, and recreation.
6. Be loyal to country, friends, and other groups whose values are shared.
7. Be ethical and dependable in work, school, and social situations.

Often the subobjectives are further refined for each of four age levels, namely, nine, thirteen, seventeen, and young adult. These refinements are a series of suggestions of the kinds of student behavior that, if present, indicate that the subobjectives and hence the primary objectives are being achieved. Typically the suggested behaviors serve as a fine introduction to third-level objectives.

Third-Level Objectives: Specific Instructional Objectives

The various published statements of educational objectives at the first and second levels are most helpful to the classroom teacher. They point out the kinds of goals that should be achieved by all American youth, regardless of the family of which they are members, the schools in which they are enrolled, or the communities in which the schools are located. In so doing, these statements tend to keep the curriculum of all schools more or less aligned without necessarily specifying the nature of all its parts.

The formal statements of educational objectives cited in the preceding sections have at least two common characteristics not mentioned previously. None of the statements suggests the relative importance of the objectives listed. The order in which they are mentioned is not intended to reflect their order of importance. Nor do any of them suggest the particular objectives that are to guide the instruction by a specific teacher on a stated day with a certain group of students.

As a result, teachers become the most prominent people in the process of identifying instructional objectives for the classroom. They must amalgamate the first-level and second-level objectives with a variety of pertinent local factors to arrive at the proper third-level objectives for the class, and give each one its proper emphasis. Local factors usually considered are the instructional objectives of the courses previously completed by the students, their success in achieving these objectives, the educational philosophy of the school, the facilities of the community, the vocational goals of the students, and the nature of their homes. In other words, difficult as it is, the teacher must become acquainted with the individualized needs of the students. The influence of all local factors should yield a set of realistic and pertinent third-level objectives for classroom use.

Third-level objectives are highly specific. One can imagine literally thousands of them. Certainly for each learning experience the teacher needs a series of very concisely stated objectives that are direct outgrowths of the second-level objectives, which in turn are direct outgrowths of those from the first level. When this occurs, we are truly able to understand and interpret all levels of interrelated objectives.

How do classroom teachers go about preparing third-level objectives? Considerable attention has been given to this question (Mager, 1962; Kibler, Cegala, Miles, & Barker, 1974; Gronlund, 1978). Mager (1962) believes that three basic steps must be taken to prepare the specific objectives:

1. Identify specifically the kind of student behavior that is acceptable as evidence that the objective in question has been achieved. In other words, the objective must state explicitly what the student must be able to do in order to achieve it.

2. Describe the important conditions that influence student behavior. In other words, any support provided the student or any restrictions existing when competence is demonstrated should be mentioned.

3. Specify the criteria of acceptable performance by describing at least the lower limit of such performance. (p. 12)

An illustration of the results of this procedure is the following objective for an elementary mathematics unit:

When provided with accurate drawings of a variety of triangles, each having all needed dimensions shown, the student can compute the area of each correctly to the nearest whole number, at least seventy-five percent of the time.

Note that an attempt has been made to follow each of the three steps. First of all, the student behavior is concisely described, that is, to "compute the area of each correctly to the nearest whole number." Secondly, a condition is introduced; that is, the student is "provided with accurate drawings of a variety of triangles, each having all needed dimensions shown." Finally, the lower limit of performance is established; that is, answers must be correct to the nearest whole number "at least seventy-five percent of the time."

The manner of preparation here described will often produce specific instructional objectives of considerable utility, especially in the cognitive domain. As you fractionate first- and second-level objectives in order to formulate third-level ones, you will gain an excellent insight into the problems of providing good instruction and designing sensitive measuring instruments. (For information about systems for sharing objectives, see page 60).

PROBLEM

6. Using the NAEP second-level science objective "understand and apply facts and simple concepts," formulate a third-level objective for each of three age levels: nine, thirteen, and seventeen years.

Evaluation in Terms of Educational Objectives

Does a fourth level of objectives exist? Yes, in a sense it does. Have you heard of "mini-objectives"? They are statements "representing performances observed when an individual is responding to a particular frame in an instructional test or program" (Smith & Shaw, 1969, p. 137). Often each can be represented by a single test item. In other words, test items and instructional materials can be thought of as the fourth and most specific level of all. They are direct expressions of objectives and, in reality, are operational definitions of them (Krathwohl & Payne, 1971). Thus, using testing and nontesting procedures in the process of evaluating student behavior is a logical extension to the development and use of specific instructional objectives. This is the central core of criterion-referenced testing.

Eliciting Student Behavioral Patterns

Rarely is it a simple matter to determine the degree to which a student's behavior has changed so that it conforms more closely to that defined in an objective. In the first place, students must be given an opportunity to demonstrate that they have or have not reached the goal. Secondly, this demonstration must occur under circumstances that will allow critical evaluation in terms of the appropriate objectives. To accomplish this, a trained observer equipped with suitable measuring tools is needed. This is the only truly meaningful way of evaluating student achievement. All other methods are indirect and, by this very fact, tend to be somewhat inadequate. The practical importance of these inadequacies varies considerably. In some cases they are so serious that the measurement results are practically worthless; in other cases their presence only modestly reduces the effectiveness of the measuring methods.

Behavior in a Natural Situation. The first step requires that goal behavior by a student be elicited within a natural situation. The students involved should feel no compulsion to say the "proper" thing or to behave in the "proper" manner. They should behave as they have learned to, rather than in a feigned manner they might adopt if required to exhibit a pattern of behavior for teacher evaluation. In the natural situation, the true, unvarnished products of their educational experiences are voluntarily displayed.

This description of natural situations actually points out one of the chief difficulties encountered in student evaluation. Since the very essence of natural situations prevents the teacher from controlling them, efforts at evaluation are often hampered. Some natural situations will not occur in the classroom; in fact, some will not occur until after the formal education of the student has been completed. For example, it is reasonable to expect that student behavior related to aspects of educational objectives pertaining to citizenship, home membership, and vocational proficiency is best shown in natural situations, most of which occur outside the classroom. The natural situations that do occur during the student's school career may take place at haphazard times and in sundry places. Needless to say, the teacher should capitalize on them whenever possible, although evaluative efforts in natural situations are at times impractical, if not impossible.

To be sure, direct observation of student behavior in a natural situation can be made of the degree to which students have achieved some of the specific objectives of education. For example, a teacher can observe with relative ease and frequency whether students consistently cover their noses and mouths when sneezing or coughing, whether they can tell time and make change with accuracy, whether they enjoy active games, can read silently with little or no lip movement, or can construct charts and graphs with only minor errors. These and other direct observations of student behavior can be made in lifelike situations outside the classroom or in connection with normal classroom routine. Class projects, teacher-student interviews, field trips, social functions, and other activities may be suitable opportunities for observation even though they are not necessarily designed for this.

Skillful Observance.   Although direct observations may be made if an informal atmosphere, the observation process cannot be as casual if it is to be successful. Skilled observers are intimately familiar with the goals to be reached, the characteristics of student behavior that fall short of these goals to various degrees and in various ways, and the methods of reporting observations. This suggests that they should have a full knowledge of human development, psychology of learning, methods of educational evaluation, and subject matter areas in which instruction is given. Observers must know what they are looking for and must be able to search for it as systematically and objectively as possible. Vague "impressions" are not enough. Ranking and rating procedures, check lists, anecdotal records, and even sociometric devices are tools that can be used.

Artificial Situations and Evaluation Methods.   Evaluative attempts conducted in artificial situations are far more common than those conducted in natural situations. The teacher establishes artificial situations that are as similar to the natural situations as time and convenience will allow. It is hoped that the behavior exhibited by students in artificial situations is closely related to that they would have exhibited in comparable natural situations if given the opportunity. Evaluation devices used in these situations are frequently paper-and-pencil achievement tests, but they could be performance tests, written assignments, or work samples of a multitude of types.

The artificial situations and the evaluative devices used with them vary greatly in the degree to which they elicit student behavior closely related to that found in the corresponding natural situation. Some are quite successful in this respect. For example, paper-and-pencil tests, such as reading and comprehension tests, and performance tests, such as typing and shorthand tests, allow students to demonstrate whether they have acquired the behavioral patterns described as objectives, and to do so in rather realistic settings. The same is true of performance tests given in home economics, industrial art, and distributive education classes. The products of the student's behavior as well as the behavior itself can be evaluated. A typed business letter, a meat roast, or a wooden bookcase could serve this purpose. Note that in these instances teachers do not wait until the student's behavioral patterns occur in the natural courses of events, nor are they certain that the material involved in the evaluation is completely representative of that present in the natural situation.

On the other hand, there are countless other evaluation attempts involving artificial situations that do not elicit student behavior essentially the same as that which the student would display in a natural situation. For example, attitude and interest inventories allow students to indicate how they would (or should) behave in the situations described, but do not actually place them in the situations so that they can overtly display their behavior. Is there a strong relationship between what they say they would do and what they actually do if given the opportunity? Probably not, and so these inventories usually are unsatisfactory.

Additional illustrations of the importance of the foregoing assumption are easily found. For instance, paper-and-pencil tests are sometimes used as a basis for evaluating the student's ability to perform laboratory and shop activities. In a physics class, test items may describe the apparatus and materials necessary for laboratory experiments in electricity and magnetism. After the steps of the experiments have been recounted, the student is required to predict the outcome of each experiment and give reasons why this is the case. In an auto mechanics class, the test items may describe symptoms of an automobile engine that is not functioning properly. The student is required to diagnose the trouble by interpreting the symptoms, select from a list of tools those necessary to repair the engine, and list the steps to be followed when making repairs. In an English class, artificial situations have been used to evaluate a student's writing ability. Rather than ask the student to write a composition, the teacher provides a poorly written passage that must be improved by deleting or adding words, phrases, and punctuation marks.

In each of the three examples mentioned above, the response to the artificial situation is not the same as that which would have been elicited in a natural situation. The test items in physics and in auto mechanics do not allow the students to display skill in the actual manipulation of laboratory apparatus and tools. It is conceivable that they could answer the test items correctly and still not be able to perform the tasks. The same is true of the English composition test. Writing ability involves more than correcting the punctuation and rearranging the words of a passage written by someone else. It also includes selection and arrangement of ideas and style of expression. Elements of originality so important in superior writing ability are scarcely tapped by the test. Nevertheless, in the case of all three examples, the teacher must make the assumption that the abilities of the students measured by the paper-and-pencil test items are related to their abilities to perform the tasks in natural situations.

Planning Norm-Referenced Achievement Tests

No doubt the most common measurement method used in schools today is the norm-referenced, paper-and-pencil achievement test. In several respects its prominence is undeserved. Nevertheless, it shows the way in which measuring methods are designed in terms of a set of selected instructional objectives.

Teachers need take relatively few steps when constructing paper-and-pencil achievement tests. First of all, they must separate from among the objectives those that have verbal and mathematical aspects, thereby excluding many objectives of considerable merit. Secondly, they must determine the relative importance of the verbal and mathematical objectives, a purely subjective process. Teachers with the same objectives differ noticeably with respect to the relative importance they assign to each. As the relative importance varies from teacher to teacher, so does the nature of the instruction. The relative emphasis that an objective receives in the process of instruction is a crude but effective indicator of the emphasis to be given that objective when an achievement test involving it is constructed. Finally, each teacher must build a group of test items, either of the essay or objective type, to constitute a representative sample of all subject matter topics and behavioral patterns included within the objectives. This can be summarized by means of a two-way grid or table of specifications (see the following section). The importance of each cell in the table is roughly equivalent to the number of test items related to it, the difficulty of these test items, the amount of credit allotted to right answers to the test items, or several or all of these simultaneously.

Tables of Specifications.   As an illustration of the foregoing process, consider the case of the secondary school chemistry teacher who is conducting an educational program in terms of a number of second-level objectives, three of which are the following:

1. The student can recall certain facts, definitions, laws, and theories of chemistry.
2. The student can comprehend the scientific method in its relations to the theories and principles of chemistry.
3. The student can apply the principles of chemistry in making predictions, explanations, and inferences.

When teaching a unit devoted to oxygen and some of its common compounds, the teacher stresses the first and third objectives insofar as this subject matter is concerned. From these are derived a large series of third-level objectives, each of which establishes, for the most part, the criterion behavior the students must display if they have achieved the objective, any restrictions placed on them when they demonstrate competence, and the lower limit of acceptable performance. The following three statements, based on the first second-level objective, show the kind of objectives used:

1. When given a list of twenty common compounds containing oxygen, the student can properly classify at least fifteen of them as to whether each, at normal temperature and pressure, is a gas, a liquid, or a solid.
2. Of the ten oxides studied, the student can accurately identify each as an acidic oxide or a basic oxide at least seventy percent of the time.
3. When provided with an incomplete equation showing the ingredients and the conditions needed to synthesize each of twenty common compounds containing oxygen, the student can complete the equation and balance it properly at least sixty percent of the time.

The next step is to group the specific objectives as needed. Notice that the foregoing three deal with recall of chemical information, but each is concerned with a different subject matter topic. Although each deals with common compounds of oxygen, the first speaks of their physical properties, the second of their chemical properties, and the third of their preparation.

A convenient way of gathering and organizing the specific objectives is a table of specifications. In its simplest form, the table of specifications is a two-way table, one dimension of which is a breakdown of behavioral changes, and the other of subject matter topics. The behavioral changes can be classified into many categories, for example, the six principal categories of the taxonomy of educational objectives for the cognitive domain. Less than six are commonly used in teacher-constructed tests. For the chemistry test, three categories were considered significant, namely, the first three principal categories of the cognitive domain taxonomy—knowledge, comprehension, and application.

The subject matter topics are subdivisions of the verbal and mathematical material included in the unit. Normally, many topics are listed. For example, the unit devoted to oxygen and some of its common compounds might be first subdivided into general topics—their physical properties, chemical properties, preparation, and uses. Each could be again subdivided into as many minor topics as the teacher deems necessary.

To build a table of specifications the teacher must decide the relative importance of the behavioral changes and the topics and represent them as percentages. The following decisions may be reached for the oxygen unit:

I. Behavioral changes
    1. Knowledge   35
    2. Comprehension   35
    3. Application   30
        Total   100

II. Subject matter topics
    1. Physical properties of oxygen and its common compounds   20
    2. Chemical properties of oxygen and its common compounds   30
    3. Preparation of oxygen and its common compounds   10
    4. Uses of oxygen and its common compounds   40
        Total   100

The two breakdowns and the assigned percentages are then combined into a simple table, as illustrated in Table 2.1. The entries in the twelve cells of the table are based on the best judgment of the teacher, and are arranged so that the row and column totals are not changed.

The percentages included in the table are rough approximations of the importance of each behavioral change in each topic. Therefore, if an objective test is to be constructed, the percentages could be used as rough approximations of the percentage of test items in the test devoted to the behavior changes of each topic. In actual practice, however, circumstances force the test builder to deviate somewhat from this point of view. For instance, a given test item may refer to more

TABLE 2.1.   Table of Specifications for a Chemistry Unit Devoted to Oxygen and Its Common Compounds.

Subject matter topic	Behavioral changes			Total
	Knowledge	Comprehension	Application	
Physical properties	6%	10%	4%	20%
Chemical properties	10	10	10	30
Preparation	6	4	0	10
Uses	13	11	16	40
Total	35	35	30	100

than one cell in the table. On the other hand, items for some cells might be extremely difficult to construct. Because of the short supply that results, the test may not reflect the designated importance of each cell as accurately as we might hope. Finally, it must be remembered that the percentage weights in the table are, at best, very crude. As the test is being constructed, the builder will sometimes gain better insight into the table of specifications and change it accordingly. The end result is a realistic view of the testing situation. The teacher knows which ideas are measurable and which are not, and thus what the test scores *do and do not* reveal about student behavior. After undergoing this agonizing appraisal, many teachers have *contracted* the scope of their interpretations of classroom test scores!

In spite of the crudeness of a table of specifications and the difficulty of constructing a sufficient number of test items for all of its cells, the use of such a table for building paper-and-pencil achievement tests produces tests vastly superior to those yielded by a casual, unsystematic skimming of lesson plans and textbooks. Furthermore, the effort invested in the development of a table of specifications can pay dividends for a prolonged period of time. With revision as needed, the table may materially assist the construction of paper-and-pencil achievement tests for a number of years.

To use the percentage weights contained in the table of specifications, the teacher must first decide how many essay or objective items the test will contain. This in turn depends on the time available for testing, the type of test item to be used, and the anticipated difficulty of those items. The time factor is frequently determined by the administrative routine of the school. A class period may be the maximum amount of time available. Low student maturity level and the possibility that the test may cause excessive fatigue can be sufficient reasons for the teacher to reduce the time interval even more. In any event, knowing the testing time available, the teacher can estimate on the basis of past experience the number of test items of a given kind and level of difficulty students can answer in the number of minutes allotted.

The techniques for constructing test items of various types are described in detail in the following chapters. Strict adherence to the rules given will yield test items of good technical quality. In spite of this, you will find that objective test items are difficult to build for the analysis, synthesis, and evaluation levels of the cognitive taxonomy. Essay tests, performance tests, and even product and procedure evaluation are used to supplement objective test items.

Content Validity.   Clearly, the central purpose of the procedure just described for building paper-and-pencil achievement tests is to develop a high-quality test, that is, one that will satisfactorily serve the purposes for which it is intended. An achievement test such as the oxygen test has the purpose of determining, at the moment it is administered, how well a student recalls, comprehends, and applies the cross-section of the total amount of subject matter studied. The degree to which the achievement test serves this purpose is its content validity (American Psychological Association, 1974). This is one of three types of test validity (see Chapter 10).

The degree of content validity of a test rises and falls in accordance with (1) the extent to which its table of specifications accurately reflects the relative importance of the various subject matter topics in relation to the various student behavioral changes stemming from verbal and mathematically oriented instructional objectives and (2) the degree to which the test items, built on the basis of the table of specifications, accurately mirror the balance of the cells. A high degree of content validity is customarily attained when carefully contrived tables of specification, or some similar device, are used, and when the many rules of test item construction described in Part Two are conscientiously followed.

Planning Criterion-Referenced Achievement Tests

Increasingly, criterion-referenced tests are being used to measure student achievement. Like the common classroom tests previously described, their most important attribute is a high degree of content validity. Yet this is accomplished without the use of a table of specifications. Instead, third-level objectives, such as those previously mentioned, are used directly as a base for building test items. Each test item needs to be an obvious outgrowth of the objective.

Test Item Preparation.   By way of illustrating the steps for preparing test items, consider the following mathematics objective for middle school students:

> Given (1) a list of articles for sale and their unit prices, and (2) a fixed amount of money to spend, the student can select those he or she can afford to buy, compute the total cost including sales tax, and accurately determine their change at least eighty percent of the time.

No doubt a wide variety of paper-and-pencil test items could be developed for this objective. Catalogs, price lists, and newspaper advertisements could be used as commonly available source materials. The nature of the prices and the sales tax rate to be applied could cause the level of difficulty of possible test items to vary widely. Furthermore, does the learner purchase several items each having the same price (e.g., swimming pool tickets) or a group of dissimilar items (e.g., groceries)? Such decisions about the test item would be largely determined by whether one wishes to test for mastery for a specified group of students. In any event, the source material must be realistic to the students, that is, something within their realm of experience. For instance, consider this sample test item:

The following is the menu at a drive-in restaurant where you wish to eat lunch:

Hot Dogs	$1.00 each
Hamburgers	1.25 each
French Fried Potatoes	.65 per bag
Soft Drinks	.50 per glass
Ice Cream Cones	.65 each
Pie	.80 per slice

List the food you wish to eat, find its total cost, and then add 5% sales tax. If you gave the attendant a $10 bill to pay for your meal, how much change would you receive?

Note how this test item (as well as others that could be constructed) follows directly from the behaviorally-stated objective. Certainly there is a set of potential test situations in which student behavior can be displayed. If desired, one could set up a sampling plan to select a subset of test tasks to be used. Finally—and importantly—the student's performance can be described objectively and meaningfully. A family of similar test items can be designed and administered to determine whether each student has reached the eighty percent level of proficiency.

Specifications for Criterion-Referenced Tests. Very often the typical third-level objective provides a good deal of latitude for teachers when they are preparing a criterion-referenced test composed of a series of similar test items. Since a variety of test items can be generated from a single objective, a somewhat confusing situation may result if the proper procedures are not followed. In an effort to refine this process and therefore to improve both the quality of the test items and our ability to interpret their results, a number of test specifications have been developed (Popham, 1978, pp. 121–137). These identify the basic elements needed for building a family of homogeneous test items based on the same objective. The three critical specifications follow:

1. *General description:* A brief one- or two-sentence statement of the behavior being measured by the test item—for all practical purposes, a statement of the objective under consideration.
2. *Stimulus attributes:* A series of guidelines that delimit the kind of stimulus material used in the test item to which the student responds.
3. *Response attributes:* A series of guidelines that (1) delimit the types of response options from which the student may select a response in the case objective test items or (2) identify the criteria to be used to judge the correctness of a student's response if open-ended responses are required.

Establishing and applying the foregoing specifications will generate strong test items. This is illustrated in the case of the following plan (adapted from

Popham, 1975, p. 147) to build criterion-referenced test items to measure the ability of third- and fourth-grade students to use nouns and verbs properly in simple sentences:

General Description

Given a sentence with a noun or verb omitted, the student will select from two alternatives the word that most specifically or concretely completes the sentence.

Stimulus Attributes

1. The student will be given simple sentences with the noun or verb omitted and will be asked to mark an "X" through the one word of a given pair of alternative words which more specifically or concretely completes the sentence.
2. Each test will omit nouns and verbs in approximately equal numbers.
3. Vocabulary will be familiar to a third- or fourth-grade student.

Response Attributes

1. The student will be given pairs of nouns or pairs of verbs with distinctly varied degrees of descriptive power.
2. In pairs of verbs, one verb will either be a linking verb or an action verb descriptive of general action (e.g., *is, goes*), and one verb will be an action verb descriptive of the manner of movement involved (e.g., *scrambled, skipped*).
3. In pairs of nouns, one noun will be abstract or vague (e.g., *man, thing*), and one noun will be concrete or specific (e.g., *carpenter, computer*).
4. The correct answer will be an "X" marked through the more concrete, specific noun or through the more descriptive action verb in each given pair.

On the basis of the foregoing specifications, a group of homogeneous test items can be generated with comparative ease and uniformity. Note that three stimulus attributes are listed, the first of which clearly defines the stimulus material to be used in the test item (simple sentences with the noun or verb omitted), and the method of response (marking an "X" through the one word of the pair that best completes the sentence). Response attributes determine the nature of the pairs of verbs or nouns to be used and specifically stipulate the essential features of the student's response (an "X" marked through the better choice) that must be present in an acceptable answer. With these attributes established, one of many possible test items that could be used is the following:

Directions: Mark an "X" through one of the words in parentheses that makes the sentence describe a *clearer* picture.

Example: The racer (tumbled, went) down the hill.

In a sense, specifications define "mini-domains" that resemble the larger, more complex domains used in domain-referenced testing. While they do not provide item-writing recipes, they streamline the process significantly. In short, they are a natural extension of third-level objectives and are a practical approach to domain description (Martuza, 1977, pp. 260–263).

Computer-Assisted Test Construction.   Conscientious teachers face a Herculean task: they must design innumerable third-level objectives and prepare at least one evaluation method for each. To help teachers out, systems for sharing objectives have been established by commercial and nonprofit organizations, and occasionally by a group of school districts or a university. Associated with each objective is one or more evaluation techniques, usually a test item.

Such systems have much potential. Literally thousands of specific objectives and their associated test items have been compiled. The Instructional Objectives Exchange (IOX), for example, provides a reservoir of cognitive and affective objectives from which teachers can select appropriate parts for local use. The IOX objectives collections cover many major cognitive subject matter areas and innumerable subareas, and include all grade levels. Each objective is accompanied by one or more illustrative test items. Furthermore, the collections are being continually revised, enlarged and updated.

Computers can assist in an important way in the development of criterion-referenced tests. In one instance (SCORE, Riverside/Houghton-Mifflin), teachers can study catalogs of objectives in mathematics and reading/language arts, then select appropriate parts for test development. Test items associated with these objectives are retrieved by computer and assembled into a machine-scorable test booklet. After administration, the tests are scored and reported, if desired, in a variety of ways. Reports for each student for each objective are available in a relatively short period of time. Thus, the test and the reports it produces are tailored to the needs of the teacher and the class.

Computers can be used in still another way to produce many different tests covering the same subject matter. Instead of storing thousands of test items in a computer and drawing a sample for a test, item programs are stored (Millman and Outlaw, 1977). An item program is nothing more than a computer program that is capable of producing many different versions of test items about a particular knowledge or skill area. Since it is unlikely that any given test item will be repeated when this method is used, every test will be unique.

Item programs are fairly easy to develop for learning areas such as science, mathematics, and writing mechanics, and more difficult in areas that are less well structured. For any set of knowledge or skills, the programs are based on pertinent instructional objectives or on test items already developed. With a bank of such programs, teachers have at their disposal an almost unlimited number of unique test items, thanks to the versatility of the computer.

Determining the Role of Paper-and-Pencil Tests

The acknowledged purposes of elementary and secondary education have expanded greatly since the turn of the century. As they increased, the usefulness of the traditional paper-and-pencil test as a measuring instrument has steadily declined. For a curriculum based on the idea that a school must, above all, serve as a vehicle for transmitting to the new generation all of the knowledge accumulated by previous generations, this kind of test would serve admirably. For a curriculum based upon the idea that a school must help its students learn how to meet their many needs as members of a democratic society, this kind of test still is of major importance, but by no means should it dominate student evaluation to the degree that it now does.

The unjustified popularity of paper-and-pencil tests as measuring instruments can be most disconcerting to students, parents, and teachers alike. After everyone assures everyone else that the objectives of education should reflect the needs of the "whole" child, teachers usually evaluate the behavioral patterns of their students on a highly restricted basis. Both students and parents are understandably confused; the teachers usually feel unduly frustrated. While they no doubt recognize the possibility of injustices when this method is followed, teachers also know that they do not have sufficient data-gathering tools, and that many of those they do have lack the respectability of paper-and-pencil tests.

This dilemma in which teachers repeatedly find themselves has no convenient solution. To use paper-and-pencil instruments to the point where most other techniques are ignored, however, is not the answer to the problem. Instead, consider the following:

> For many objectives of the type suggested, measuring or observational devices concerned with the student's overt behavior while he is yet in school, even though of a rough and opportunistic character, are perhaps much more worthwhile than any written type of tests. The actual behavior of the student in school elections, for example, however fragmentary or limited in sampling, may provide a better clue to his future behavior than anything he professes that he will do in a written test; books actually read by the pupil in his free time may constitute a true indication of his literary tastes than his score on a literary appreciation test; anecdotal records may be more meaningful than scores on personality tests; etc. The problem of deriving comparable measures from such opportunistic observational data now seems to present almost insuperable difficulties, but perhaps no worse than have been resolved before through determined and persistent effort. (Lindquist, 1951, p. 157)

The foregoing remarks were made many years ago, but still are highly appropriate. They should not be interpreted as a general denunciation of written tests or a recommendation that they be abandoned completely. On the contrary, paper-and-pencil tests should be a sizable part of any student evaluation program. These tests should be used in conjunction with, rather than in the absence of, other methods. The very nature of many educational objectives requires that this be so.

PROBLEMS

7. Prepare several third-level objectives of a unit you are teaching or soon will be teaching. On the basis of these objectives, build at least one table of specifications suitable for the construction of a classroom achievement test.

8. Using the third-level objective in mathematics for middle school students (see page 57), develop the stimulus and response attributes needed for constructing a group of criterion-referenced test items based on it. As a result of this experience, do you believe that the use of test specifications noticeably improves the quality of criterion-referenced test items? Why?

9. Attempts have been made to use the cognitive taxonomy to build sets of test items that hold content constant and systematically vary process from simple (that is, knowledge) to complex (that is, evaluation). Evaluate the eight interrelated test items in the physical sciences prepared by Smith (1968) and suggest changes, if any, that you would make.

SUMMARY

The following are the main ideas included in this chapter:

1. The primary purpose of formal education is to teach youths in such a way that they are better able to meet their needs as members of a democratic society. The objectives of elementary and secondary education are developed on this premise.

2. The objectives involve the development of new knowledge, intellectual abilities and skills, affective patterns, and psychomotor skills. Thus the objectives of education are student oriented rather than teacher oriented and are stated in terms of desired behavioral patterns in the student.

3. Taxonomies for objectives in the cognitive, affective, and psychomotor domains are now being used.

4. Three levels of objectives are often used. The first contains statements of major goals. The second is a refinement of the first, whereas the third includes highly specific instructional objectives. A number of formal statements of objectives have been prepared by committees for the first and second levels. Third-level objectives are direct outgrowths of these, and are usually prepared by teachers.

5. Having taught students with the guidance of instructional objectives, of course the teacher must evaluate achievement in terms of them. Ideally this should be done by direct observation of the students' behavior in natural situations. At times this is impractical, if not impossible. Instead, the teacher establishes artificial situations that are as similar to natural situations as time and convenience will allow and evaluates achievement indirectly within these situations by means of a variety of data-gathering devices.

6. The artificial situations and the data-gathering devices used with them vary greatly in the degree to which they elicit student behavior closely related to that found in the corresponding natural situation. Performance tests are quite successful in this respect, as are some paper-and-pencil tests. Others are considerably less successful; obvious illustrations are tests designed to measure student behavior in many areas in the affective and psychomotor domains.

7. Ordinarily, the construction of a norm-referenced paper-and-pencil achievement test involves three steps. First, the educational objectives with verbal

and mathematical aspects must be separated from all others. Secondly, the relative importance of these objectives and their subparts must be identified. Finally, a group of test items must be constructed. These should constitute a representative sample of all subject matter topics and behavioral patterns included within the objectives. The second and third steps can be facilitated by using a table of specifications, and a high degree of content validity can be attained.

8. Criterion-referenced achievement test items are direct outgrowths of third-level objectives. Typically, several of them can be developed for each objective, and a short test created. A recommended procedure for constructing homogeneous test items for a given objective is to establish specifications for stimulus materials to be used in the items and response options offered the student. These also help to describe to test users what the test items (or tests) measure.

9. Above all else, criterion-referenced achievement tests must also have a high degree of content validity.

10. Evaluating student behavior in terms of educational objectives is a complex task. Many methods are used, including paper-and-pencil tests (both classroom and standardized), performance tests, rating scales, inventories, questionnaires, and anecdotal records. Student evaluation ordinarily is centered around paper-and-pencil tests to an unrealistically high degree.

SUGGESTED READINGS

EBEL, R. L. The paradox of educational testing. *NCME Measurement in Education*, 1977, 7(4).
Despite the fact that evaluations of student achievement are greatly demanded by the general public, paper-and-pencil tests are sharply criticized by many. Seven frequently-mentioned criticisms of tests are analyzed.

GRONLUND, N. E. *Stating objectives for classroom instruction* (2nd ed.). New York: Macmillan, 1978.
A succinct presentation concerning the development of instructional objectives for use when teaching and when measuring student achievement.

KIBLER, R. J., CEGALA, D. J., MILES, D. T., & BARKER, L. L. *Objectives for instruction and evaluation.* Boston: Allyn and Bacon, 1974.
A central purpose of this book is to help educators write and use specific objectives. The nature and characteristics of such objectives are described, and various examples are provided.

KRATHWOHL, D. R., & PAYNE, D. A. Defining and assessing educational objectives. In R. L. Thorndike (Ed.), *Educational Measurement* (2nd ed.) Washington, D.C.: American Council on Education, 1971.
A well-written chapter providing significant information regarding levels of objectives, their sources, and their taxonomies. Suggestions are given for utilizing third-level objectives.

POPHAM, W. J. *Criterion-referenced measurement.* Englewood Cliffs, N.J.: Prentice-Hall, 1978. See chapters 5 and 6.
Chapter 5 deals with preparing test specifications for norm-referenced tests; chapter 6 is a companion chapter devoted to the same topic for criterion-referenced tests.

POPHAM, W. J., EISNER, E. W., SULLIVAN, H. J., & TYLER, L. L. Instructional objectives. *AERA Monograph Series on Curriculum Evaluation*, 1969, No. 3. *The four chapters often take quite different views about the sources of objectives and the manner in which they are stated and used. Discussions among the four authors follow each chapter and are well worth reading.*

REFERENCES CITED

AMERICAN PSYCHOLOGICAL ASSOCIATION. *Standards for educational and psychological tests.* Washington, D.C.: Author, 1974.

BLOOM, B. S. (Ed.). *Taxonomy of educational objectives:* Handbook 1: *Cognitive domain.* New York: David McKay, 1956.

EISNER, E. W. Instructional and expressive objectives: Their formulation and use in curriculum. *AERA Monograph Series on Curriculum Evaluation*, 1969, No. 3, 1–31.

FRENCH, W., AND ASSOCIATES. *Behavioral goals of general education in high school.* New York: Russell Sage Foundation, 1957.

GAGNÉ, R. M. *The conditions of learning* (3rd ed.). New York: Holt, Rinehart and Winston, 1977.

GRONLUND, N. E. *Stating objectives for classroom instruction* (2nd ed.). New York: Macmillan, 1978.

HARROW, A. J. *A taxonomy of the psychomotor domain.* New York: David McKay, 1972.

KEARNEY, N. C. *Elementary school objectives.* New York: Russell Sage Foundation, 1953.

KIBLER, R. J., CEGALA, D. J., MILES, D. T., & BARKER, L. L. *Objectives for instruction and evaluation.* Boston: Allyn and Bacon, 1974.

KRATHWOHL, D. R., BLOOM, B. S., & MASIA, B. B. *Taxonomy of educational objectives: Affective domain.* New York: David McKay, 1964.

KRATHWOHL, D. R., & PAYNE, D. A. Defining and assessing educational objectives. In R. L. Thorndike (Ed.), *Educational measurement* (2nd ed.). Washington, D.C.: American Council on Education, 1971.

LINDQUIST, E. F. Preliminary consideration in objective test construction. In E. F. Lindquist (Ed.), *Educational measurement.* Washington, D.C.: American Council on Education, 1951.

MAGER, R. F. *Preparing instructional objectives.* Palo Alto, Calif.: Fearon Publishers, 1962.

MARTUZA, V. R. *Applying norm-referenced and criterion-referenced measurement in education.* Boston: Allyn and Bacon, 1977.

MILLER, W. G., SNOWMAN, J., & O'HARA, T. Application of alternative statistical techniques to examine the hierarchical ordering in Bloom's taxonomy. *American Educational Research Journal*, 1979, *16*, 241–248.

MILLMAN, J., & OUTLAW, W. S. *Testing by computer.* Ithaca, N.Y.: Cornell University, 1977.

NATIONAL ASSESSMENT OF EDUCATIONAL PROGRESS. *Science objectives for the 1972–73 assessment.* Denver: Author, 1972. (a)

NATIONAL ASSESSMENT OF EDUCATIONAL PROGRESS. *Writing objectives for the 1973–74 assessment.* Denver: Author, 1972. (b)

NATIONAL ASSESSMENT OF EDUCATIONAL PROGRESS. *Citizenship objectives for the 1974–75 assessment.* Denver: Author, 1972. (c)

NATIONAL ASSESSMENT OF EDUCATIONAL PROGRESS. *Reading objectives for the second assessment.* Denver: Author, 1974.

POPHAM, W. J. *Educational evaluation.* Englewood Cliffs, N.J.: Prentice-Hall, 1975.

POPHAM, W. J. *Criterion-referenced measurement.* Englewood Cliffs, N.J.: Prentice-Hall, 1978.

SEDDON, G. M. The properties of Bloom's taxonomy of educational objectives for the cognitive domain. *Review of Educational Research,* 1978, *48,* 303–323.

SMITH, R. B. A discussion of an attempt at constructing reproducible item sets. *Journal of Educational Measurement,* 1968, *5,* 55–60.

SMITH, T. A., & SHAW, C. N. Structural analysis as an aid in designing an instructional system. *Journal of Educational Measurement,* 1969, *6,* 137–143.

SULLIVAN, H. J. Objectives, evaluation, and improved learner achievement. *AERA Monograph Series on Curriculum Evaluation,* 1969, No. 3, 65–99.

WALBESSER, H. H., JR. *An evaluation model and its application, a second report.* Washington, D.C.: American Association for the Advancement of Science, 1968. (AAAS Miscellaneous Publication 68–4)

ZIMMERMAN, A. *Education in focus: A collection of state goals for public elementary and secondary education.* Denver: Cooperative Accountability Project, 1972.

PART TWO

Measurement of Classroom Achievement

For the homeowner, the do-it-yourself approach usually dominates such activities as carpentry, painting, and landscaping. The novelty of being your own designer, contractor, and artisan contributes to the popularity of this movement. The self-satisfaction experienced at the completion of a project is virtually matchless.

The do-it-yourself idea is a familiar one to you as a teacher, both within the scope of your professional position and outside of it. Early in your training program you discover that "recipes" for teaching are few, that prefabricated teaching techniques do not exist, and that hiring someone to perform part of your duties is seldom possible. In short, you learn that you must rely on your own skill and ingenuity practically all of the time. The unique characteristics of each teaching situation are too important to permit a standardization of the teaching art.

As one step in the teaching process, student evaluation offers an excellent opportunity for a teacher to display skill and ingenuity. Although outside assistance is available in the form of standardized measuring instruments and measurement specialists who serve as consultants, the lion's share of the evaluation program must be shouldered by the classroom teacher. Frequently you are the one who must design the instrument, administer it, score it, interpret the results, and, finally, appraise the worth of these activities. Your responsibilities here are as clear as those related to the identification of educational objectives and, on the basis of them, the determination of suitable learning experiences for your students.

The teacher's measuring efforts are often centered around the paper-and-pencil achievement test, either objective or essay type. Chapter 3, "Measuring Knowledge Objectively," is devoted to discussions of the construction and use of objective test items to be used in classroom achievement tests, with emphasis on those items that measure recall of information. Chapter 4, "Measuring Complex Achievement Objectively," emphasizes those test items that measure students' ability to use their funds of knowledge. Successful performance means that the student can locate appropriate information and manipulate it to solve new problems. Chapter 5, "Preparing Essay Achievement Tests," identifies the role of essay test items in achievement testing and compares it with that of objective test items. Chapter 6, "Appraising Classroom Achievement Tests," contains descriptions of various methods of evaluating paper-and-pencil tests, particularly those that are norm-referenced.

Not all of the data-gathering instruments built by the classroom teacher are paper-and-pencil tests. Many are ranking and rating scales, check lists, product scales, and the like; and they are also used to evaluate student performance. Chapter 7, "Judging Procedures and Products," describes and illustrates these methods.

Classroom teachers generally cannot build measuring instruments as technically perfect as those produced by teams of testing specialists. However, you have a decided advantage over the specialists because you have far more knowledge about the quality of the students whose achievements are to be measured and the nature of the learning experiences they have had. This in turn means that the classroom instruments you build with care will often compare favorably with the standardized instruments designed to accomplish the same purpose.

The classroom teacher's role as tester is particularly pronounced when he or she prepares criterion-referenced tests. No one is better qualified to select the appropriate, specific objectives to be used as bases for building test items. The number of standardized tests of this type has increased significantly in recent years.

Instead of being discouraged about the likelihood of building useful measuring instruments, you should be optimistic. All you really need is a willingness to make reasonable efforts and to carefully observe a group of simple rules. If you are creative, the task is simpler and the product better.

3

Measuring Knowledge Objectively

After studying this chapter you should be able to

1. List the various types of objective test items and illustrate each

2. Differentiate between objective test items of the supply type and the selection type, and identify the advantages and limitations of each

3. Construct acceptable short-answer, true-false, multiple-choice, and matching test items, adhering in each instance to the many rules that govern construction

4. Appraise and edit objective test items in terms of their (1) relationship to educational objectives, (2) degree of ambiguity, (3) use of irrelevant clues, (4) level of difficulty, and (5) reading level

5. Describe the steps needed to organize a norm-referenced objective test of suitable scope and length for a given purpose

6. Prepare written or oral directions for students who are being administered objective test items to measure academic achievement

7. Recognize the strengths and weaknesses of using computers to score objective tests

8. Apply the formula that corrects for guessing with true-false and multiple-choice tests, and evaluate the impact of its use

As consumers, we repeatedly sample various products on the market and, on the basis of our reactions, draw conclusions about quality. Consider for a moment any of the purchases of food we commonly make. Suppose that we enter a supermarket to buy three items—candy, bakery goods, and breakfast cereal. We first select a pound of gum drops. Within the pound are individual pieces of a variety of colors. A nibble of one of each color may quickly convince us to favor the green gum drops over those of all other colors. For the second purchase, we choose one dozen glazed doughnuts. These we find to be fresh and tasteful, and, as a result, our opinion of the bakery is favorable. Finally, we select a well-known brand of breakfast cereal. If at breakfast the next morning we conclude that, as advertised, the cereal is indeed a "taste treat," we probably will continue to buy the product; if not, we will no doubt refuse to buy another box no matter how persuasive the exhortations of well-known motion picture personalities and professional athletes.

How sound are these judgments? This question is difficult to answer. If our taste sensibilities were reasonably normal at the time we tested the product, and if the sample of the product we consumed was reasonably representative, the judgments are sound. If these two conditions are not met, the soundness of the decision is certainly in doubt. For example, had we been ill shortly before or during the sampling, the first condition would very likely not be satisfied. Had the gum drops, doughnuts, or breakfast cereal been accidentally contaminated in some way, they would hardly be representative of these products when properly handled, and the second condition would not be satisfied.

When acting as consumers of food products, classroom teachers sample and judge them just like anyone else. When evaluating the achievement of students they follow essentially the same procedure; they are actually making the same two basic assumptions. In the first place, teachers believe that the ability and willingness of students to reveal their knowledge and complex intellectual skills are not seriously impaired by any unusual factors. Such factors might be emotional disturbances, greatly reduced teacher-student rapport, physical fatigue, or any of a multitude of minor distractions.

Secondly, teachers conclude that the samples of student behavior they observe are typical of much unobserved current and possibly future student behavior. In the case of achievement testing, the samples of student behavior are elicited by the questions or tasks included in a test. Hence, to obtain a representative sample of all the possible variations of the student behavior in question, the teacher tries to find a representative sample of all the possible questions or tasks that might be presented.

The justification for providing samples for the evaluation of achievement, as well as of food products, is essentially one of practicality. It is not feasible or necessary that a person eat all the gum drops available before deciding that the green ones are the most pleasing. In the same manner, it is not feasible or necessary that a teacher ask students all possible questions or provide opportunities for them to perform all possible tasks to determine the degree to which they have achieved certain educational objectives.

Demanding that a paper-and-pencil achievement test contain a representative group of test items is equivalent to demanding that the test have a high degree of content validity. Notice again that content validity is inherently tied to educational objectives; in the case of paper-and-pencil achievement tests, it is tied to specific objectives with verbal and mathematical aspects. Thus, procedures that are known to improve the degree of content validity of a paper-and-pencil (such as the use of a table of specifications) are important to us here.

PROBLEM

1. Writing test items often helps to clarify the table of specifications. This may cause one to modify table headings and even cell percentages while building test items (Tinkelman, 1971). In your opinion, does the failure of the table to remain fixed tend to reduce or increase the degree of content validity of the resulting norm-referenced achievement test?

Differentiating Types of Objective Test Items

An efficient and convenient way to measure the student's ability to recall the information identified by a table of specifications is to build and administer a series of pertinent objective test items. An objective test item is one that can be scored in such a way that judgment is for all practical purposes eliminated when determining the correctness of a student's answer. To be sure, this is a broad definition. It is not surprising, therefore, to find many different types of test items identified as objective test items while being seemingly quite dissimilar in form.

Objective test items may be usefully designated as the *supply* type of item or the *selection* type of item. When responding to a supply type of item, the student has to provide the words, numbers, or symbols. Possible answers are not listed as part of the item. An illustration of the supply type is the short-answer item, two varieties of which are shown below:

Short-Answer Question

Directions: Within the space provided, write the word or phrase that correctly answers the question.

What is the name of the author of the novel entitled *Pickwick Papers?* (*Charles Dickens*)

Completion Test Item

Directions: Within the space provided, write the word or phrase that correctly completes the statement.

The name of the author of the novel entitled *Pickwick Papers* is (*Charles Dickens*).

The selection type of item allows the student to choose the correct response from the information provided. The well-known true-false test item, multiple-choice test item, matching test item, and countless variations of these typify the selection category.

True-False Test Item

Directions: Determine whether each of the following statements is true or false. If the statement is true, circle the "T" preceding the statement; if the statement is false, circle the "F."

(T)   F   The novel entitled *Pickwick Papers* was written by Charles Dickens.

Multiple-Choice Test Item

Directions: For each of the following questions choose the correct answer from among the four possible answers listed. Write the number of your choice in the blank to the left of the question.

(2)   Who wrote the novel entitled *Pickwick Papers?*
   (1)   William Thackeray
   (2)   Charles Dickens
   (3)   Anthony Trollope
   (4)   George Eliot

Matching Test Item

Directions: Match the title of each novel with its author by writing the letter identifying the author in the blank to the left of the title. It is possible that some authors have written more than one of the novels listed.

		Novels		*Authors*
(F)	1.	*Barchester Towers*	A.	Jane Austen
(B)	2.	*David Copperfield*	B.	Charles Dickens
(B)	3.	*Great Expectations*	C.	Alexandre Dumas
(B)	4.	*Oliver Twist*	D.	George Eliot
(B)	5.	*Pickwick Papers*	E.	William Thackeray
(A)	6.	*Pride and Prejudice*	F.	Anthony Trollope
(D)	7.	*Romola*		
(B)	8.	*Tale of Two Cities*		
(E)	9.	*Vanity Fair*		
(F)	10.	*The Warden*		

There are obvious similarities and differences of form in these types of objective test items. There are important similarities and differences in the ease of construction, applicability, and ease of scoring. These and related topics are discussed and illustrated in the following sections.

PROBLEM

2. Some teachers argue that the differences in the various types of objective test items are seemingly large but actually small. In the case of the three chief variations of the selection type of item, defend their point of view.

Constructing Objective Test Items

When you build norm-referenced achievement tests in terms of tables of specifications, and criterion-referenced tests in terms of specific objectives, you are taking an important step toward assurance that the tests will have high content validity. The value of these procedures, however, is noticeably lessened if the test items are carelessly devised. The test as a whole may lose some content validity if the teacher fails to properly apply a myriad of relatively simple, obvious, and seemingly unimportant rules when building the test items. Many "dos and don'ts" govern the construction of objective test items.

Supply Test Items

The supply test item can be crudely defined as an essay test item demanding a highly abbreviated answer. This answer is often only a single word or number, seldom more than several words or numbers. The student responds to a direct question or incomplete declarative statement by writing the answer in the space provided. Notice that there is little difference between these two. By means of a simple arrangement of words, a short-answer question becomes a completion test item, or a completion test item becomes a short-answer question. They are sometimes haphazardly intermixed in classroom achievement tests; a better practice is to separate them, especially when young students are being tested.

Suggestions for Construction.   Design the supply test item so that it has only one correct answer, which is short and definite. This is unquestionably the most difficult problem a teacher encounters when building supply test items. Although you may have but one short and definite answer in mind for each item, you will be amazed at the students' facility for thinking of synonyms or near-synonyms of the answers, which in many instances must be considered as correct answers. For example, consider the following test item written in two different ways.

> *Poor:*   The novel *Pickwick Papers* was written by (<u>*Charles Dickens*</u>).
>
> *Improved:*   The name of the author who wrote the novel *Pickwick Papers* is (<u>*Charles Dickens*</u>).

The first version of this completion test item could elicit such responses as "a man," "an Englishman," "an adult," "a novelist," or "a genius." All of these are technically correct, but none is the answer expected—"Charles Dickens." If teachers wish to avoid much needless quibbling over answers, they must exercise great care in the development of test items. Some proposed supply test items cannot be conveniently changed to avoid wrong or half-wrong answers—the desired answer might be too obvious and the item practically worthless because the level of difficulty is too low. Changing the item form from a supply to a selection type sometimes helps in these cases.

   Avoid removing statements verbatim from textbooks or other sources and trying to use them as short-answer test items. This practice will, of course, give an advantage to that student who can somehow detect a textbook expression and select answers at least partially on the basis of whether they have a textbook flavor. Moreover, the use of verbatim statements may make the item ambiguous since they are used out of context. For example, the first of the following statements is taken directly from a history textbook and one word is deleted to make it a completion item.

Poor: The power to declare war is vested in *(Congress)*.

Improved: In the United States the power to declare war is vested in *(Congress)*.

Since the test covered aspects of the governments of many other countries, the students were understandably confused by the first version of the test item. Obviously, teachers quickly recognize the trouble when it is called to their attention; they are less likely to anticipate this problem, however, if they continually take statements out of context and use them as short-answer test items. In summary, each test item should be able to stand alone unless deliberately related to other items.

When building completion test items, avoid mutilating the statement until its meaning is all but lost. In an effort to increase the level of difficulty, or test for several pieces of information by means of one item, some teachers greatly increase the number of blanks in a completion item. The temptation to do so is rather strong at times, but seldom is the procedure successful. Using a very small number of well-chosen blanks is more satisfactory. Notice how the following item is improved by reducing the number of omitted words:

Poor: The process by which *(petroleum)* is separated into various component *(parts)* having different *(boiling points)* is known as *(fractional distillation)*.

Improved: The process by which petroleum is separated into various component parts having different boiling points is known as *(fractional distillation)*.

To the student, the second version is a well-defined problem, whereas the first is not. In fact, the first statement would discourage anyone but the person who originally deleted the words.

When building completion test items, try to place the blank or blanks near the end of the statement rather than the beginning, and provide sufficient space for student answers. Often it is a simple matter to place the blanks at either the beginning or end of the test item. Placing the blanks at the end prevents the test item from acquiring a noticeable awkwardness, as well as a degree of artificial difficulty. Less time is needed to arrive at the correct answer, particularly in the case of elementary school tests.

Avoid the use of extraneous hints designed to help the student identify the correct answer. On occasion, teachers try to help the student find the correct answer to a short-answer test item by inserting the first letter of each word of the answer, by drawing a line the length of the answer, or by drawing several lines of appropriate length when the correct answer contains several words. The following short-answer test item in an elementary school geography test is typical of this procedure:

> *Poor:* In which state is the most important seaport on the eastern seaboard located? N*(ew)* Y*(ork)*

> *Improved:* In which state is the most important seaport on the eastern seaboard located? *(New York)*

The first version of the test item encourages guessing more than the improved version. In addition, offering such hints as these is not realistic; if students were required to recall this information outside of the testing situation they undoubtedly would not be offered this assistance. The difference between the testing situation and the natural situation is increased, and therefore the form of the test item is open to criticism.

Also, hints help the students use processes of elimination otherwise unavailable. In attempting to answer the test item, those not knowing the correct answer could quickly eliminate possibilities by remembering that "N————" must mean "New" or "North." Therefore, the correct answer is New Jersey, New Mexico, New York, New Hampshire, North Dakota, or North Carolina. Of these states, only New York has the second word beginning with the letter "Y." This, then, is the answer.

Always indicate the units in which the answer is to be expressed for those supply test items that could have several answers depending upon the units chosen. For computational exercises, this can be an annoying problem for both the students writing the test and the person who must later score it. For instance, the correct answer to the following exercise can be expressed in three different ways.

> *Poor:* A four-foot piece of wire is to be cut into two pieces so that one piece will be six inches longer than twice the length of the second piece. What is the length of the longer piece? *(2 ft., 10 in.)*

> *Improved:* A four-foot piece of wire is to be cut into two pieces so that one piece will be six inches longer than twice the length of the second piece. What is the length of the longer piece? Ans. *(2)* ft. *(10)* in.

The correct answer is 34 inches, 2 5/6 feet, 2 feet and 10 inches, or even 86.4 centimeters! Demanding one type of unit rather than another can change the difficulty level of the exercise as well as the amount of time needed to solve it.

Advantages and Limitations. There are two advantages in using the supply test item rather than other kinds of objective test items. First of all, the supply form reduces the likelihood that students will guess the correct answer. Whereas in the case of the selection form, they need only recognize the correct response from among a relatively small number of given possibilities, in the case of the supply test item, they are confronted with a situation that is not so highly structured. As a result, some argue that this type of item is more difficult.

A second advantage often attributed to supply test items is that they are relatively easy to construct. This is, in a sense, a deceptive statement. Although some teachers find them easier to build than the selection type of item, supply test items are by no means so simple to construct as a casual investigation might indicate. The foregoing suggestions for constructing supply test items offer ample supporting evidence.

Of all of the limitations of using supply test items usually cited, two are outstanding. In the first place, such items are more difficult to score than other kinds of objective test items. Despite the best efforts of the teacher building such a test item, often a variety of answers are totally or partially correct. Assigning total or partial credit can only be done by someone intimately familiar with the test items, the background of the students, and the teaching situation. In other words, it must be done by the teacher, even when it is a difficult and time-consuming task. The scoring of student response is complicated by legibility of handwriting and faulty spelling. The latter may or may not be sufficient cause for reducing the amount of credit a student receives for an otherwise correct response. If one of the purposes of the test is to determine whether a student can spell the correct answer after recalling it, then loss of credit can be justified. If this is not the case, loss of credit for faulty spelling cannot be defended.

The second limitation is the kind of behavioral change involved in the item. Typically these items demand only recall of information rather than more complex aspects, such as the application of principles in new situations. This tendency is traceable in part to the fact that no matter what type of objective test item is to be used, test items requiring only recall of information are usually easier to construct. When building supply test items, the teacher strives to find items with correct answers that are short and clear, and in so doing, often selects test items involving primarily factual details. Vocabulary is heavily emphasized.

On balance, supply test items leave something to be desired. They cannot be considered a versatile, efficient means of measuring a wide variety of student achievements. As a result, they are not commonly used except for teacher-built tests, and even for those their popularity is less than that of selection test items.

PROBLEM

3. In light of the foregoing suggestions for constructing supply test items, improve each of the following:
    a. A hogan is an almost round structure with walls made of (_logs_) and (_mud plaster_).
    b. Selling price equals cost plus (_profit_).
    c. (_Sun_) is the source of most of our heat.
    d. A diameter that is (_perpendicular_) to a chord (_bisects_) the chord.

True-False Test Items

The true-false test item is nothing more than a declarative statement to which the student responds in one of two ways—the statement is true or it is false. Occasionally, the statement is so worded that it is more convenient to ask the student to respond with "Right" or "Wrong" rather than "True" or "False." Moreover, changing the declarative statement to a question need not necessarily increase the number of possible responses. In these instances, the question can be phrased so that a "Yes" or "No" response is requested.

The most common type of true-false test item has already been illustrated. Less common variations are the following:

Correction Variety

Directions: Determine whether each of the following statements is true or false. If the statement is true, circle the "T" following the statement. If it is false, circle the "F" and write in the blank provided the word or words that, when substituted for the word underlined, will make the statement true.

1. The earth is essentially *spherical* in shape. Ⓣ F
2. The sun is a *planet.* T Ⓕ (star)
3. The earth spins on its axis once each *month.* T Ⓕ (day)

Cluster Variety

Directions: The following statements pertain to the location of various European countries. Determine whether each statement about each country is true or false. If it is true, circle the "T" following the statement. If it is false, circle the "F."

Switzerland has a common border with

a. Italy on the south. Ⓣ F
b. France on the west. Ⓣ F
c. Austria on the east. Ⓣ F
d. Czechoslovakia on the north. T Ⓕ

T-F–CT-CF Variety

Directions: Determine (1) whether each of the following statements is true or false and (2) whether the converse of the statement is true or false. If it is true, circle the "T" preceding the statement; if it is false, circle the "F." If the converse of the statement is true, circle "CT"; if the converse is false, circle "CF." Two correct answers must be given for each statement.

Ⓣ F CT ⒸⒻ 1. A square is always a quadrilateral.
Ⓣ F ⒸⓉ CF 2. An equilateral triangle is also an equi-angular triangle.
T Ⓕ CT ⒸⒻ 3. A right triangle is necessarily an isosceles triangle.

T-F–TF Variety

Directions: Determine whether each of the following statements is true, false, or true under some circumstances and false under other circumstances. If the statement is true under all circumstances, circle the "T" preceding the statement; if it is false under all circumstances, circle the "F"; if it is true under some circumstances and false under others, circle the "TF."

T F ⒯Ⓕ 1. If a person is living at a latitude of 40° he is living north of the equator.
Ⓣ F TF 2. The prime meridian is an imaginary line at 0° longitude.

Suggestions for Construction.   When constructing a test item requiring a response of either "True" or "False" and only that, search for statements that are true or false without additional qualifications. All too commonly a true-false test item is *essentially* true or false rather than absolutely true or false. This is perplexing to students. Should they mark statements as true only if they are true under all possible circumstances, and mark all others false even though some might be essentially true? On the other hand, should they mark those statements that are in general true and those false that are in general false, thus ignoring specific and perhaps minor qualifications that might be pertinent? If the method of attack fails to be the one the teacher has in mind, the answer will be wrong even though knowledge of the subject matter is superior.

The following test item illustrates the problem. The intended answer is "True."

> *Poor:*   The water vapor in the air will condense when the air is cooled.
>
> *Improved:*   If the temperature of the air in this room is progressively lowered, a temperature will ultimately be reached at which the water vapor in the air will start to condense.

The first version of the test item may trouble the student because the degree of cooling, the amount of water vapor in the air, and the temperature of the air are not stated. Slight cooling may or may not cause condensation; drastic cooling probably would. Hence, the statement is true under certain circumstances and false under others. Students who know the information normally required to answer the test item correctly may fail to receive credit for their knowledge because they remember too many facts. Incidentally, copying statements verbatim from textbooks or study guides customarily produces true-false items that are not absolutely true or absolutely false.

Avoid the use of specific determiners. Specific determiners are words or expressions that frequently identify a statement containing them as true or false. Words often found in false statements are "only," "never," "all," "every," "always," "none," and "no." Those often found in true statements are "usually," "generally," "sometimes," "customarily," "often," "may," "could," and "frequently." Sophisticated students recognize the situation. If they do not possess the knowledge necessary to answer correctly a true-false test item, they search for a specific determiner. Should they find one and answer accordingly, chances of having identified the correct answer are good. Consequently, the test item may discriminate among students on a basis other than their ability to recall information, and thus its usefulness is impaired.

In an effort to construct true-false test items that are absolutely true or absolutely false, teachers repeatedly resort to the use of specific determiners. The weakening of the test item that customarily occurs is illustrated in the following:

> *Poor:*   None of the people of Switzerland is engaged in farming.
>
> *Improved:*   The mountains of Switzerland prevent the Swiss people from raising grain extensively.

A clever but ill-prepared student would quickly mark the first version of the test item as false. The second version demands a knowledge of the geography of the country as well as the nature of its agriculture. It contains no specific determiners to provide hints as to its correct answer.

The teacher need not always avoid the use of such words as "all," "never," and "usually" because they can serve as specific determiners. On the contrary, they can be deliberately used, and with success, by including them in true-false test items that have correct answers the opposite of those suggested by the words in question. For example:

1. All planets revolve around the sun of our solar system.
2. The sum of the angles of a plane triangle is always 180°.

Try to keep the true-false test items reasonably short, and restrict each to one central idea. True-false test items that are extremely long require undue amounts of response time. The student must search out the truth or falsity of each phrase and dependent clause. Moreover, long true-false test items are more often true than false since the length is sometimes caused by the qualifying remarks needed to make the statement true. Strive to balance the true-false statements in terms of length. If lengthy statements are used, they should be false about as often as they are true.

A serious problem that is sometimes accentuated by lengthy true-false items is that several ideas become involved. If one part of the test item is true, whereas another part is false, students customarily label the test item as false. But this can be confusing not only when the students respond to the test item, but also when they review the test at a later time. Misinformation may result.

An illustration of a true-false test item that is partially true and partially false is shown below:

Poor: Although today the members of the United States House of Representatives are elected by popular vote of the people of the districts they represent, the members of the United States Senate are selected by the state legislatures of the states they represent.

Improved: The members of the Senate of the United States are selected by the state legislatures of the states they represent.

The clause at the beginning of the statement is unnecessary and should be eliminated, as illustrated by the second version of the test item. This deletion serves the additional purpose of reducing the scope of the item to one central idea, which can be judged as true or false.

If true-false tests are used regularly, be certain that the percentage of test items requiring a "True" answer, and hence the percentage of test items requiring a "False" answer, are not relatively constant from test to test. Some students quickly sense any tendency on the part of a teacher to maintain approximately the same percent of true and false statements from test to test. This is true regardless of whether an even balance between the two statements is maintained or an overbalance of one type is used. If a noticeable consistency is detected, the students may use it as a basis for guessing the answers of some of the test items. Moreover, some students quickly discover any pattern that the correct answers may take, such as, F-T-F-T-F-T or T-T-F-F-T-T. Occasionally a teacher arranges the test items so that the correct answers form a systematic plan, thereby simplifying scoring. Such an arrangement also simplifies the task of the alert student who is responding to the test items. An otherwise good true-false test can be seriously damaged by this procedure.

Advantages and Limitations.   The advantages accrued by using true-false test items are outweighed by the limitations. The popularity of these test items is unjustified—a popularity that can be traced primarily to the fact that true-false test items allow the teacher to sample widely a large amount of subject matter without needing a great amount of testing time. Most students can respond quickly to well-constructed items of this type. A second and less obvious advantage sometimes cited in the case of true-false test items is that they are essentially a realistic task for the students. Frequently, in everyday life, they are called upon to judge a statement as true or false in the manner required by the test items. A third advantage of even more doubtful merit is the claim that true-false test items are easy to build. As in the case of the supply test items, the true-false item is by no means so easy to construct as you might suppose.

One of the most serious limitations of the true-false test item is that many are concerned only with small, relatively unimportant pieces of information. Like the supply test item, the true-false item serves best as a means of measuring the students' ability to recall information. Because of the teacher's efforts to find statements that are absolutely true or false, the information needed to answer the items correctly is frequently highly specific. It is difficult to build good true-false test items that involve generalizations, broad principles, and relationships, all of which may be notably more important than the pieces of information involved in the usual true-false test items.

A second serious disadvantage is that true-false test items encourage some students to try to guess the correct response. They argue that, after all, they have a fifty-fifty chance of identifying the right answer without even bothering to read the statement. The use of specific determiners, the tendency of long statements to be true statements, and the practice of arranging the correct responses in a systematic pattern encourage guessing and increase the likelihood of that guessing being successful. Means of correcting for guessing are discussed later in this chapter (see page 105).

Finally, true-false test items can be criticized on the basis that many of them are ambiguous. Careful construction of true-false test items reduces ambiguity, but does not necessarily eliminate it. Words like "several," "many," "some," "frequently," "important," and "principal" can hardly be avoided. But what do they mean? Variations in the meanings of these and similar terms can mean variations in the students' responses to the statements containing them. Hairsplitting distinctions may be necessary, to the distress of teacher and student alike.

PROBLEMS

4. In light of the foregoing suggestions for constructing true-false test items, improve each of the following:
    a. If we feel heat traveling through a steel bar at a certain rate, we can assume that heat will travel through another kind of bar at that rate.
    b. Heat can do work.
    c. The *Reader's Guide* is the best source to use when looking for current material on a subject.
    d. If (+) times (+) equals (+), then (−) times (−) equals (−).

5. In contrast to the statement that the advantages of true-false tests are outweighed by their limitations, Ebel (1975; 1980, pp. 145–164) believes that teachers can measure achievement as reliably with true-false as with multiple-choice items. Evaluate his position.

Multiple-Choice Test Items

A multiple-choice test item is one in which a direct question or incomplete statement is presented and a number of possible responses are given. The student chooses the response that is the correct (or best) answer to the question or that is the correct (or best) expression for completing the statement. The question or incomplete statement introducing the test item is known as the *stem*. Any undesired answer is called a *distracter* or *foil*. Generally four or five responses are listed and all but one is a distracter.

Some multiple-choices test items require a correct answer, others a "best" answer. This difference can be traced to the subject matter. For instance, when selecting the name of the author of a book among four names listed, the student searches for the correct answer; all distracters are completely wrong. However, when selecting the principal reason from among four possible reasons that Ulysses S. Grant was elected to the presidency of the United States, the student searches for the "best" answer. It should be clearly the most outstanding of those listed. As you can easily see, in this illustration the distracters can be actual reasons, but relatively unimportant. Both of these kinds of multiple-choice test items are commonly used.

Introducing a multiple-choice test item by means of an incomplete statement seems to be equally as satisfactory as introducing it by means of a direct question. Often the factor governing the choice of stem is the length of the test item. If the direct question approach yields a short, easily understood test item, it is customarily used; should it not do so, the incomplete statement approach replaces it. For a person inexperienced in building multiple-choice test items, however, the direct question is recommended, since fewer technically weak items result (Wesman, 1971).

There are numerous variations of the multiple-choice test item. The most familiar form is that illustrated earlier in this chapter. Four additional variations are shown on the next page.

Multiple-Response Variety

Directions: For each of the following questions, select the correct answer or answers from among the four listed. Note that for each question there may be as few as one and as many as four correct answers. Write the number(s) of your choice(s) in the blank to the left of the question.

(2, 3) Which of the following compounds are gases when at room temperature and under normal pressure?
- (1) Benzene
- (2) Ammonia
- (3) Carbon dioxide
- (4) Silicon dioxide

Combined-Response Variety

Directions: Each of the following exercises contains a group of objects, people, or events, the members of which are to be arranged in proper order according to the principle stated. Select the correct order for those listed and write the number of your choice in the blank to the left of the exercise.

(1) Arrange the following British statesmen in terms of the dates of their careers, starting with the most recent.
- a.   Robert Walpole
- b.   Stanley Baldwin
- c.   William Pitt, Jr.
- d.   Winston Churchill
- (1)   d, b, c, a
- (2)   b, d, a, c
- (3)   b, a, d, c
- (4)   d, c, b, a

Degree-of-Certainty Variety

Directions: For each of the following questions select the correct response from among the four listed. Write the number of your choice in the blank to the left of the exercise. Then indicate your degree of certainty for your choice by selecting the most descriptive of the three statements shown, and writing its number in the blank provided.

(4) Which of the following cities in the United States is located west of the Mississippi River?
- (1) Chicago
- (2) Detroit
- (3) Washington
- (4) Salt Lake City
- ___   How certain are you of your choice?
- (1)   very certain
- (2)   fairly certain
- (3)   quite uncertain

Suggestions for Construction.   Select the distracters so that all of them are reasonably plausible and appealing to those students who do not possess the knowledge demanded by the item. Your experiences as an examinee are no doubt sufficient to convince you of the importance of this suggestion. When you are confronted with a multiple-choice item to which you do not know the answer, you probably attack by a process of elimination. Any response that appears to be extremely unlikely you eliminate, even though you may have little or no knowledge of it. Often you are able to reduce the number of possibilities to two, sometimes to only one. If some of the distracters are implausible, the possibility of identifying the correct answer is greatly improved.

The following test item shows the ease with which the correct answer to a multiple-choice test item can be found when the distracters are implausible.

Poor: Which of the following men was at one time the Chief Justice of the Supreme Court of the United States?
  (1)   Charles Evans Hughes
  (2)   Nikolai Lenin
  (3)   Chiang Kai-shek
  (4)   John Paul Jones

Improved: Which of the following men was at one time the Chief Justice of the Supreme Court of the United States?
  (1)   Charles Evans Hughes
  (2)   William E. Borah
  (3)   Oliver Wendell Holmes
  (4)   William Jennings Bryan

If a student does not know the answer to the test item as stated in the first instance, a few miscellaneous pieces of information can help to find it. After all, responses 2 and 3 are unlikely possibilities. Names such as these hardly sound "American," so they probably should be eliminated. John Paul Jones will no doubt be remembered as a military hero, perhaps as a Revolutionary War naval hero. Since it seems improbable that a military hero would ever be elevated to the position of Chief Justice of the Supreme Court, this response is eliminated. Response 1 is therefore correctly selected despite the fact that the student knows nothing of Charles Evans Hughes, Nikolai Lenin, and Chiang Kai-shek, and very little about John Paul Jones and the Supreme Court.

The second statement of the test item is greatly improved. All of the persons listed were citizens of the United States and were prominent in public life. They were also contemporaries. All had sufficient qualifications to be considered for such a post as Chief Justice; one of them Oliver Wendell Holmes, was a prominent associate justice of the Supreme Court but never the Chief Justice. This should be a plausible and attractive distracter to the partially informed student. The distracters used in the second version of the test item are more homogeneous than those used in the first version. Increasing the homogeneity of the responses tends to increase the difficulty of the multiple-choice test item.

Plausible distracters are often difficult to find. What is plausible to the teacher may not seem so to the students, yet the teacher must decide which distracters are used. With sufficient planning, however, an alternative technique can be used. By tabulating wrong answers to supply test items, the teacher can amass much helpful information for determining plausible distracters for future testing. Multiple-choice questions can be substituted for supply test items and wrong answers from earlier classes used as distracters.

Vary the number of options included in the multiple-choice test item as needed, anticipating that ordinarily there will be at least three and not more than five. How many options should the typical multiple-choice item have? To answer this question, consider first the test-sophistication of the students. Four-option and even five-option test items are commonly used in achievement tests for students at the junior high school level and above. Certainly this is too many for students in the primary grade levels. Often two-option or three-option test items are used in an effort to avoid reading problems and excessive fatigue.

Another important factor influencing the number of options is the quality of distracters available. Sometimes we slavishly adhere to a fixed number of distracters for all multiple-choice items in a given test. This is unnecessary. The effectiveness of the distracters rather than their number determines the quality of the test item (Wesman, 1971). Instead of having a fixed mold (for example, one correct answer plus three distracters for each item), reduce the number of distracters when few good ones are available. Distracters that are nothing but "fillers" complicate the testing effort without improving our ability to differentiate among students in terms of achievement.

If the number of options varies somewhat from item to item in a test, the students should be told about it at the beginning of the test. Should variation occur frequently, group the test items according to the number of options they have, or even consider changing the item form, for example, to one of the true-false varieties.

Be certain that the length of the responses of a multiple-choice test item is not related to their tendency to be the correct (or best) answer. Because of the need to qualify to make one response the correct (or best) answer, the desired answer would regularly be the longest unless precautions are taken. Notice how obvious this is in the following illustration:

> *Poor:*   Sliced oranges are an excellent source of
> > (1)   protein.
> > (2)   starch.
> > (3)   vitamin A.
> > (4)   vitamin C, if the oranges are freshly sliced.

> *Improved:*   Freshly prepared orange juice is recommended for the diet because
> > it is an excellent source of
> > (1)   protein.
> > (2)   starch.
> > (3)   vitamin A.
> > (4)   vitamin C.

If given the first version of the multiple-choice test item, the ill-prepared student will select response 4 more frequently than any other. Its length probably means that it is the correct answer.

If a multiple-choice test item requires a "best" answer, make certain that one and only one is clearly the best. "Hairsplitting" is a problem in practically all objective test items. This is especially true of "best" answer multiple-choice test items, for a judgment is involved. It is a matter of opinion as to which of many is the *most important* reason why a phenomenon occurred, or which of many is the *chief* result for a given cause. There are many counterparts to such possibilities, and they all too frequently appear in otherwise respectable multiple-choice tests. For example:

Poor: The most serious health problem in the United States today is
    (1) cancer.
    (2) mental illness.
    (3) heart disease.
    (4) the common cold.

Improved: Of the following diseases, which kills the most people at the present time?
    (1) cancer
    (2) mental illness
    (3) poliomyelitis
    (4) tuberculosis

On the basis of the prevalence of the illness, the possibility of its being fatal, or the difficulty of relieving it, any one of the responses to the first version of the test item can be judged the "best." Unanimity or even near unanimity of opinion may be difficult to obtain. However, the test item as revised offers no such problem.

Whenever convenient, design the multiple-choice test item so that the stem includes as much of the item as possible. Multiple-choice test items are usually improved if the stem is relatively long and the responses are relatively short; then the stem more clearly defines the problem on which the test item is based, and less response time is needed by most students. On the other hand, it is sometimes awkward to build each multiple-choice test item with a long stem and short responses. The rule can be ignored to ensure clarity.

Examination of the following two versions of a multiple-choice item from a sixth-grade social studies test shows the advantages of relatively long stems coupled with short responses.

Poor: Yugoslavia
    (1) is larger in area than France.
    (2) borders on the Adriatic Sea.
    (3) is located in western Asia.
    (4) contains the Ural Mountains.

Improved: In which of the following continents is Yugoslavia located?
    (1) Europe
    (2) Asia
    (3) Africa
    (4) South America

The first version is more difficult to understand than the second. With the revised version, based on a single problem explicitly stated in the stem of the item, the student should have no trouble grasping it and can devote time to selection of the correct answer.

Express the responses to a multiple-choice test item so that grammatical consistency is maintained. In other words, if the stem of the multiple-choice is an incomplete sentence, each response must be worded so that it is a grammatically correct completion of the introductory statement. If the stem is a direct question, the responses should be brief statements of parallel construction. Failure to maintain grammatical consistency is often due to carelessness; happily, this defect can be easily corrected in most instances. The following test item illustrates this point:

> *Poor:*   If the north pole of one bar magnet is brought very near the south pole of another bar magnet, the two poles will
> (1)   repel each other.
> (2)   attract each other.
> (3)   no effect.
> (4)   an electric spark will be produced.

> *Improved:*   If the north pole of one bar magnet is brought very near the south pole of another bar magnet, the two poles will
> (1)   repel each other.
> (2)   attract each other.
> (3)   have no effect on each other.
> (4)   produce an electric spark.

The two versions of this test item make it clear that the teacher can avoid grammatical inconsistency by simply checking each response with the stem. If this is done and any appropriate changes in wording are made, the test item is not only more impressive from a grammarian's point of view but it is also less confusing from a student's.

Minimize the use of negative expressions in a multiple-choice test item. Such expressions reduce the clarity of an item and may artificially add to its difficulty. This problem can become serious for less mature students. For instance, consider the following:

> *Poor:*   Which of the following is *not* true of Puerto Rico?
> (1)   It is an island.
> (2)   Its principal language is Spanish.
> (3)   It is *not* a state in the U.S.A.
> (4)   It does *not* have a warm climate.

> *Improved:*   What is the political status of Puerto Rico?
> (1)   It is a state in the U.S.A.
> (2)   It is an independent country like the U.S.A.
> (3)   It is an unincorporated territory of the U.S.A.
> (4)   It is a commonwealth under the U.S. government.

The intended correct answer to both versions is the fourth response. In the case of the first version, notice how awkward—and time consuming—it is to arrive at this conclusion and to confirm it. The second version is much more straight-forward and aims directly at one central point, namely, the political status of Puerto Rico. No negative expressions are needed or desired.

Advantages and Limitations.   The advantages of multiple-choice test items are much more impressive than the limitations. The outstanding feature of the multiple-choice item is its versatility. It can be used to determine how well a student can recall the most specific pieces of information as well as the ability to apply the most important principle in a novel situation.* Moreover, it can do so without introducing the problems of subjective scoring, which weakens the short-answer test items, and without ambiguity, so noticeable when true-false test items are used. Successful guessing by students is reduced but not eliminated. Any teacher with a reasonable amount of patience and ingenuity can build and use multiple-choice items with favorable results. As illustrated by the various items concerning novelists (see page 73–74), you can often convert supply, true-false, and matching test items to multiple-choice form without undue difficulty.

Multiple-choice test items are used at all grade levels with the possible exception of the primary. Even there they can be orally administered if practice test items correctly answered are shown. Multiple-choice test items can also be successfully used in all subject matter areas when verbal and mathematical aspects are being tested. An objection is occasionally raised, however, to the use of these items in testing achievement in mathematics. A student may correctly answer the test item by using the four or five responses given as a basis for solving the problem back-wards. This can be circumvented by using a variation of the standard multiple-choice form, such as the incomplete-response variety.

Multiple-choice test items are not, of course, the panacea for the difficulties of achievement testing. They have distinct limitations, some of which have been mentioned in earlier discussions. They are difficult to build, and suitable distracters are hard to find. Although a teacher's ingenuity can produce many, and others can be found among the wrong answers given to supply test items administered to preceding classes, surpluses are rare. More often than not teachers lack at least one distracter. They may try to fill the void by adding the response "none of the foregoing," "not given," or "can't tell." These cannot be used for "best" answer multiple-choice test items; also, they customarily weaken the correct answer variety if used consistently as a distracter, since they are recognized by the student as more often the wrong answer than the correct one. Such responses need not be avoided but they must be carefully presented. For instance, do not use them as the *answer* to an item when it may include a *large   number of incorrect responses,* as in the case of most questions requiring mathematical computations to arrive at a numerical answer.

Another limitation of multiple-choice test items is the response time they require. For a given amount of testing time, students can complete fewer multiple-choice test items than true-false items. This is particularly noticeable when the multiple-choice test items demand fine discriminations and fundamental understandings.

* The usefulness of objective test items for measuring a student's ability to apply information and principles in a novel situation is discussed in Chapter 4.

PROBLEMS

6. Attempts to improve the quality of "best" answer multiple-choice test items may actually change the test item to the "correct" answer variety. Examine the test item concerning diseases on page 87 and decide whether this has occurred.

7. Evaluate the degree-of-certainty variety of multiple-choice test items as (1) a measurement device and (2) an instructional device (Echternacht, 1972, pp. 217–223).

8. Because some objective test items are considered more important than others, some teachers believe more points (for example, 2 rather than 1) should be given for each correct answer. Does this practice improve the quality of the test (Ebel, 1979, pp. 198–200)?

Matching Test Items

The matching test item in its simplest form consists of two lists of items and a set of instructions for matching each of the items in the first with one in the second. The first is known as a list of *premises,* the second as a list of *responses.* The instructions explain how the students are to match each premise with one or more of the responses. Premises and responses may be statements, names of people or places, titles of works of art, dates, formulas, symbols, or even parts of a picture or drawing. They may vary greatly but will tend to be homogeneous within a given list. Usually the length of each premise or response is (and should be) relatively short, perhaps no longer than a word or two.

In some matching exercises, the number of premises and responses is the same and each response can be used only once; this is a "perfect matching" exercise. In other instances some of the responses do not match any of the premises; this is an "imperfect matching" exercise. An "imperfect matching" exercise can be constructed by making the list of responses longer than the list of premises or, if the lists are of equal length, by including some responses that must be used more than once. Earlier in this chapter an example was given of an "imperfect matching" test item having a shorter list of responses than premises; two responses are used more than once and one is not used at all.

In addition to the types of matching test items mentioned in the foregoing paragraph, there are a number of other variations. Two promising ones are illustrated here.

Compound Matching Variety

Directions: Below is a list of nineteenth century and early twentieth century novelists. For each novelist identify the title of one of his works that is listed in the second column by writing the letter opposite the title in the first of the two blanks to the left of the author's name. Identify his nationality from among those listed in the column below by writing the number opposite it in the second blank.

			Authors		Novels
_(H)_	_(3)_	1.	Alexandre Dumas	A.	The Adventures of Tom Sawyer
_(G)_	_(2)_	2.	George Eliot	B.	Barchester Towers
_(F)_	_(3)_	3.	Victor Hugo	C.	Call of the Wild
_(C)_	_(1)_	4.	Jack London	D.	David Copperfield
_(E)_	_(1)_	5.	Herman Melville	E.	Moby Dick
_(J)_	_(2)_	6.	William Thackeray	F.	Notre Dame of Paris
_(B)_	_(2)_	7.	Anthony Trollope	G.	Romola
_(A)_	_(1)_	8.	Mark Twain	H.	The Three Musketeers
				I.	Uncle Tom's Cabin
			Nationalities	J.	Vanity Fair
		1.	American	K.	War and Peace
		2.	English		
		3.	French		

Classification Variety

Directions: Each of the following statements is a complete sentence. Determine whether the sentence is a simple, complex, compound, or compound-complex sentence. Using the list below, find the letter corresponding to your choice and write it in the blank to the left of the sentence.

    A. simple sentence
    B. complex sentence
    C. compound sentence
    D. compound-complex sentence

_(C)_   1. During the winter the days are short and the nights are long.
_(A)_   2. Jane rode to school on her bicycle.
_(B)_   3. If Mary Lou had been home she could have visited with her grandparents and their friends.

Suggestions for Construction. _Make lists of premises and responses as homogeneous as possible._ Each list should be confined to one type of subject. Then, a title including every member can be placed above the list. In contrast, some poorly constructed matching test items are unnecessarily heterogeneous. Suppose that a certain list of premises contained names of inanimate objects, insects, animals, and people. For many students this simplifies the task of answering the test item correctly. They can eliminate many of the possible responses to a given premise not because they know much about the premise and response, but because there is no conceivable basis for matching some responses to a given premise.

Notice how this process of elimination is possible in the first version of a matching test item intended for use in a junior high school social studies achievement test.

Poor

Directions: Match each description in the first column with one of the names in the second column by writing the letter identifying the name in the blank to the left of the description.

	Descriptions		Names
(C)	1. A river in southeastern Europe	A.	Bucharest
(F)	2. One of the largest countries in the world	B.	Czechoslovakia
		C.	Danube
(G)	3. Mountains in Russia	D.	Poland
(D)	4. A level country	E.	Romania
(A)	5. The capital of a country near Czechoslovakia	F.	Russia
		G.	Ural

Improved

Directions: Match each river with the body of water into which it flows by writing the letter identifying the body of water in the blank to the left of the name of the river. It is possible that several of the rivers flow into the same body of water.

	Rivers		Bodies of Water
(C)	1. Danube	A.	Adriatic Sea
(G)	2. Rhine	B.	Bay of Biscay
(F)	3. Rhone	C.	Black Sea
(E)	4. Seine	D.	Caspian Sea
(G)	5. Thames	E.	English Channel
(F)	6. Tiber	F.	Mediterranean Sea
		G.	North Sea

Both lists of the first test item are quite varied in content. This lack of homogeneity certainly will help the relatively uninformed student find correct answers by a process of elimination.

The revised version of the matching test item is greatly improved. Notice that the titles "rivers" and "bodies of water" are much more accurate and definitive than those used in the first version. Any student, especially one with only sketchy knowledge of the topic, would find it difficult to use the process of elimination in this test item. Additional matching items dealing only with the location of various European cities, mountain ranges, or countries can also be constructed. In other words, several matching test items are needed to lessen the variation of the premises and responses in the first version without excluding any of that information from the test.

Always indicate as clearly as possible the basis on which the matching of premises and responses is to be made. Every effort should be made to clarify the task the student is asked to perform by improving the directions and the titles of the lists. It is not the purpose of a matching test item to find out if the students understand the basis for matching, but rather to see if they can accurately match each premise with a response.

Below is a matching test item intended for an achievement test in elementary school science. Although it is not mentioned in the first version of the test item, the teacher wants the student to match each animal with the kind of food it ordinarily eats.

Poor

Directions: Match each animal with grass, insects, or other animals. Write the number in the box next to the name of the animal.

[1]	cow	1. grass
[1]	sheep	2. insects
[3]	fox	3. other animals
[3]	lion	
[2]	robin	

Improved

Directions: Here is a list of animals. Each of these animals eats many different things each day. However, each animal will most often eat grass, or insects, or other animals. If an animal most often eats grass, write "1" in the box next to the animal's name. If it most often eats insects, write "2" in the box next to the animal's name. If it most often eats other animals, write "3" in the box next to the animal's name.

Animals		*Food*
[1]	cow	1. grass
[1]	sheep	2. insects
[3]	fox	3. other animals
[3]	lion	
[2]	robin	

When confronted with the faulty version of this test item, even the most sophisticated elementary school student will at first be uncertain as to how the matching should be done. Some of the less sophisticated may never understand it and consequently skip the test item; or they may unknowingly establish a false yet semi-plausible basis for matching. For instance, several will choose the response "other animals" each time, arguing that each animal is more like other animals in terms of its activities and structures than it is like insects or grass.

The directions accompanying the improved version of the test item are long and may need to be read to the students. Perhaps an illustration of one animal correctly matched with the food it ordinarily eats should be shown. Either or both of the steps should be taken if the teacher suspects that the students are confused about the mechanics of the test item.

Arrange the premises and responses in a logical order. If the premises or responses are names or titles, they should be arranged alphabetically. If they are dates, they should be in chronological order; if numbers, they should be arranged according to size. Unless there is an excellent reason for doing otherwise, any logical order should be followed. This will noticeably reduce the amount of response time needed for answering matching test items.

In every matching test item always include responses that do not match any of the premises, or responses that match more than one premise, or both. In other words, always construct "imperfect matching" test items rather than "perfect matching" ones. The latter have the serious disadvantage of increasing the likelihood of the uninformed student guessing one of the correct responses. Since in the "perfect matching" test item there are as many responses as premises, and each response can be used only once, the student answering it can determine the last response by a process of elimination.

The following is a "perfect matching" test item; each elementary school student is to identify each word in terms of the part of speech it normally is.

		Words		*Parts of Speech*
(*E*)	1.	with	A.	Noun
(*B*)	2.	am	B.	Verb
(*C*)	3.	red	C.	Adjective
(*A*)	4.	car	D.	Adverb
(*D*)	5.	always	E.	Preposition
(*F*)	6.	and	F.	Conjunction

Should students have trouble matching a response with such a premise as "always" they can pair all other premises and responses, thereby discovering that it matches the fourth response. Of course this is not possible if additional premises are included and hence some responses used more than once.

Keep the list of responses relatively short. When attempting to answer matching test items, the students read a premise and search the list of responses. If this list is long, they may spend considerable time in spite of the fact that they may have a rather clear notion as to what the response should be. Thus, valuable test time is wasted. Incidentally, observe that a lengthy list of premises may likewise increase the amount of time needed to respond to a matching test item. This cannot be called wasted time, however, unless some of the premises cannot be justified.

There is no well-established limit to the list of responses; however, the following is a good rule of thumb: Allow the list to exceed ten only when the maturity of the student and the nature of the subject matter in the test item permit; for younger students restrict the list to about half this number. Should you find the list of responses becoming almost endless, consider the possibility of constructing more than one test item. This will allow you to sample a number of different subject matter topics and will simplify the job of finding lists of homogeneous premises and responses.

Advantages and Limitations.   The primary advantage of using matching items in an achievement test is that a lot of factual information can be included in the test without much testing time being required. Such items are useful for seeing if a student can associate words with their definitions, events with their places and dates, results with their causes, concepts with their designated symbols, authors with their published works, statesmen with their countries and contemporaries, and so forth. Although it is not commonly done, matching test items can be used to measure student's ability to apply the information they have learned. Notice the illustration given on page 91 in which the premises are a list of novel sentences that the student is to classify as simple, complex, compound, or compound-complex sentences. The classification variety can be successfully used to measure products of learning other than simple recall of information.

The main limitation in measuring achievement with matching test items is that good items are difficult to build. Sometimes the subject matter is insufficient in quantity or not well suited for matching test items; in either case, homogeneous premises and responses are extremely hard to find. In others, the subject matter may seem to lend itself to this type of test item, but the teacher has great difficulty in finding plausible but wrong responses as well as correct responses that are not completely obvious because of the terminology used.

PROBLEM

9. Using a teaching situation you know well, construct a matching test item involving two lists in which at least one response matches more than one premise.

Appraising and Editing Objective Test Items

Before any newly constructed objective test items can be incorporated into an achievement test, they should undergo a critical reexamination—essentially an appraising and editing procedure. It consists in verifying the relationship between each test item and the table of specifications or specific objective, rechecking it for any ambiguity or irrelevant clues, and estimating the level of difficulty and reading load. The reexamination of test items in terms of these characteristics may simply reconfirm the worth of many well-constructed items. In some cases, it may reveal grammatical weaknesses; in others, it may uncover glaring faults in test items previously thought to be sound. Regardless of the outcome, the procedure is profitable. When building the test item, the teacher is often preoccupied with details and in the process loses sight of basic features. A later review customarily allows the teacher to see with a new perspective, and any features out of balance can be readjusted.

Appraising and editing objective test items can be done by the person who constructed the test items or, preferably, by someone competent in the subject matter. If the second possibility is not feasible, then the original item builder should make the review, but only some time after the building of the items.

No matter who is involved, a useful technique for appraising and editing is for that person to take the test. The answers given should then be compared to the answers originally listed. Any lack of agreement between any two answers is a certain danger signal. It no doubt means that the test item is ambiguous. Perhaps a qualifying statement is missing, or some of the phraseology should be changed. Disagreement between two answers may be traced to some excessive difficulty of the test item. This flaw may be minor and easily corrected; it could be so serious that the item must be discarded.

On the other hand, the fact that the original answer to a test item and the independent answer later determined are the same is no guarantee that the item is satisfactory. There may be other flaws in it that may not affect the answers arrived at by a reviewer but that could seriously affect the role of the test item in a test and the student's response. The teacher should therefore review each test item by checking it in terms of five questions:

1. Is the test item properly identified with one or more cells of the table of specifications (or, in the case of criterion-referenced test items, with a specific objective)?
2. Is the test item ambiguous in any respect?
3. Does the test item contain any irrelevant clues?
4. Does the test item have an appropriate level of difficulty?
5. Does the test item have a suitable reading level?

After a test item has been so examined and any differences corrected, a smooth copy of the item is made. A highly useful and successful procedure is to type each test item on a 5" x 8" card. Generally there is ample room on the card to add additional pertinent information such as the correct answer to the test item, the name and page of the section of any book or outline on which it is based, and, at a later date, a summary of the responses students made when answering it. As a result, you have all important information neatly summarized in a single place, and your test item file enlarged (see page 173).

Relationship between Test Item and Table of Specifications or Specific Objective

When building test items for norm-referenced tests, teachers use tables of specifications as blueprints to guide their selection of subject matter and behavioral changes to be included in each test item. The relationship between each test item and the part of the table of specifications from which it arose can be recorded by means of a simple coding technique. For example, the cells in the table are numbered, and the numbers of those related to the test item are listed on a card containing a statement of the test item.

The first attempt to establish the relationship between a test item and the cells of a table of specifications is usually successful. Since you began to build the test item with one or more cells in mind, you have little difficulty cross-referring it and the cells. However, practically all test items undergo revisions. Perhaps the technical imperfections are corrected without regard to the manner in which these corrections might affect the relationship between the test items and the table of specifications. Sometimes they do not disturb this relationship. Many times they do. For instance, recall the differences between the two versions of many of the test items shown earlier in this chapter. Repeatedly correcting a technical imperfection may have necessitated a fundamental change in the test item. After revision, the test item may be primarily related to a different cell in the table of specifications. Clearly, if these changes are numerous and go unnoticed, the test loses much content validity.

When building criterion-referenced test items, the same problem exists. The relationship between each test item and a specific objective must be identified, recorded, and rechecked after all known technical imperfections of the test item have been removed. The stimulus and response attributes must be appropriate.

Presence of Ambiguity

Many suggestions for constructing objective test items focus on one central weakness—ambiguity. The dangers of using verbatim quotes from textbooks and the difficulty students encounter when denied some relevant qualifications have already been stressed. Proper phraseology in the test item as well as in the directions to the student is also important.

Individually, these suggestions for avoiding ambiguity can usually be followed with ease. Yet they must be applied in harmony with other suggestions not directly concerned with the problem, which is not always easy to do. In some instances, a teacher building an objective test item will find two suggestions working more or less at cross-purposes. Following one by making a certain revision violates another. Escape from the dilemma may be difficult. No doubt a more common situation is the automatic adoption of the most recently considered suggestion. If the revision happens to violate another suggestion, this is not noticed.

Since ambiguity is one of the chief weaknesses of objective test items, the teacher should make a final check by rereading each test item with one question in mind: Is it possible to word this test item more clearly and directly? In trying to answer this question, teachers may find themselves improving test items previously thought to be as polished as possible.

The importance of avoiding ambiguity in objective test items is primary. The student should never experience difficulty in trying to understand the question. We are trying to find out if students can answer a question they understand, not if they understand the question.

Presence of Irrelevant Clues

The presence of irrelevant clues assists students to varying degrees, thereby giving some an unfair advantage. These are the "testwise" students. A student's ability to capitalize on the characteristics and format of a test or a testing situation to obtain a high score is called testwiseness (Sarnacki, 1979, p. 253). Some aspects of testwiseness are independent of the test builder or the purpose of the test; these include the student's ability to distribute effectively the testing time available among the various test items, to pay attention to directions, and to adopt a good guessing strategy based on the method of scoring. Others are directly dependent on the mistakes of the teacher when building test items, such as the student's ability to identify correct answers on the basis of any consistent idiosyncrasies or specific determiners used by the teacher. The second category emphasizes the potentially influential role of irrelevant clues. This must be reduced at all costs.

The existence of student testwiseness is a simple fact of life with which a teacher must contend. Reasonably similar amounts of this trait within a given group of students can actually simplify test planning, since the teacher can anticipate with some accuracy the kind of test format, terminology, time limits, and so forth, that are appropriate for an achievement test. Of concern are wide differences among students in this regard, which can cause important test score differences not related to student achievement.

Proper Level of Difficulty

An important characteristic of objective test items sometimes overlooked by the teacher is the level of difficulty. Obviously this is not determined exclusively by the idea on which the test item is based, for the manner in which it is stated is also important. A single variation of a word or phrase can change it noticeably. Obtaining the proper level for each item and then the test as a whole is a perplexing problem.

The first consideration for the teacher about level of difficulty is the type of test to be built. In a mastery test the level of difficulty is uniformly low; in a norm-referenced test, it varies somewhat, but concentrates in a zone around the fifty percent level of difficulty after correction for chance. In other words, this is the level at which half of the students have responded correctly to a test item after allowance has been made for successful guessing (see page 163). For a number of reasons, the target zone should be slightly above fifty percent rather than below.

A highly successful way of obtaining estimates of the level of difficulty of test items is to pretest them on a group of students similar to those for whom they are designed. Their answers to the test items can be tabulated and analyzed. On the basis of this analysis, the level of difficulty of each test item is determined. Unfortunately, this procedure is frequently impossible. Without pretesting data, the teacher must depend on subjective judgment.

Subjective judgment yields only a rough approximation, even when the teacher is completely familiar with the situation, the maturity of the students, and many of their past experiences. At best, the teacher can rate the test items on only a five-point scale: "very difficult," "moderately difficult," "average," "moderately easy," and "very easy." Often a three-point scale of "difficulty," "average," and "easy" is all that is appropriate. The principal reference point is the "average" category. Test items so rated are considered suitable for typical students in the class under consideration.

Although crude, subjective judgment is useful. In devising norm-referenced tests, for example, subjective judgment can prevent any test item from being so easy that all students respond correctly or so difficult that no one does. Since the purpose of these tests is to differentiate among students in terms of their achievement, both extremes should be avoided. In contrast, criterion-referenced tests often have quite low levels of difficulty.

Reading Level

Because test items are constructed by adults, they regularly include words and expressions more typical of adults than children. This happens despite the most conscientious efforts of the teacher and can be a severe problem in the case of objective test items designed for elementary school students. After all, to the teacher these words and expressions seem to express the thought behind the test item very clearly. To the students, however, this is probably not true. If they were constructing the test item, they would no doubt choose different words. Often they would use more of them, thereby creating another difficulty. Since there is already much to read, the student needs more response time for each test item. Consequently, fewer can be included, and the breadth of the sampling of the subject matter decreases.

Test items must be carefully reread to eliminate improper vocabulary and cut excessive length. If appropriate adjustments are not made, the students with superior reading ability and vocabulary may have an undue advantage over their less fortunate comrades. Superior reading ability and vocabulary help them to understand more of the questions more quickly and, as a result, they have more time in which to concentrate on obtaining the correct answers. When such items are included in a poorly timed test, they may actually measure the student's reading speed and comprehension more than achievement in a chosen subject matter area such as science or social studies; in other words, the basis on which the test items differentiate students' achievement levels has changed.

PROBLEM

10. Some say that objective test items for measuring achievement are unfair to (1) those who think creatively, (2) those who lack inexperience in taking them, and (3) those who are culturally disadvantaged. Evaluate these criticisms.

Organizing Norm-Referenced Objective Tests

It is often said that a group of test items cannot necessarily be called a norm-referenced test. How true! After each objective test item in the group has been appraised and edited in the manner described in the foregoing sections, that part of the group that appropriately reflects the balance of subject matter topics and the behavioral changes established in the table of specifications is organized into a norm-referenced achievement test. To do this, we must decide the order in which the items are presented to the students and the number to be included. We must also formulate directions and draw up a scoring key. Each of these steps must be taken carefully if the test items are to realize their maximum value.

Arranging Objective Test Items

Objective test items should not be arranged haphazardly in a norm-referenced achievement test. Instead, they should be organized on the basis of one or more of three characteristics: the type of item, the subject matter, and the level of difficulty.

When the items of an objective test are grouped according to type, all supply test items are placed together, as are all true-false, multiple-choice, and matching test items. This simplifies the directions given to the students. Furthermore, they can no doubt complete a test thus arranged more quickly. They acquire a mental set for each type of item and need not change it until all such items have been answered, speeding their progress through the test. Incidentally, it is advisable to restrict the number of different types to as few as conveniently possible.

Arranging the test items according to the subject matter means that the test items are grouped according to a set of subject matter topics, or perhaps according to the cells in a table of specifications. This appeals to the students because they see the test as a miniature of the materials they have learned. It is an integrated, orderly whole rather than a disorganized mosaic of unrelated questions. This arrangement may be attractive to the teacher too, since it may help to reveal any underemphasis in the test.

Objective test items can be grouped according to their levels of difficulty if they happen to vary somewhat—that is, the easy ones first, the more difficult next, and the most difficult last. Such an arrangement has advantages for average and below average students. With this kind of norm-referenced test they use the time allowed more efficiently, and morale is improved. When they later encounter the more difficult test items, they no doubt will have time to attack them. Even if these students fail to answer some, as will very likely happen, the resulting disappointment will be moderated by the knowledge that they already have answered others correctly.

Certainly we cannot expect to use all three ways of arranging test items simultaneously. In reality, teachers can only hope to find the best possible compromise among the three. Sometimes they can escape partially or wholly from the dilemma by eliminating one of the possibilities. For example, suppose that only one type of test item is used. The test can now be designed so that the items are grouped according to major subject matter topic, and within each group they can be arranged more or less in terms of ascending difficulty. As a second example, suppose that the teacher is building a mastery test or, perhaps, a norm-referenced test using test items with levels of difficulties that cluster in a comparatively small zone slightly above the fifty percent level. Now the level of difficulty is unimportant as a basis for arranging test items and should be ignored.

If test items are grouped according to major subject matter topics and, within each group, subdivided according to type of item, the teacher may wish to consider each subject matter group as a subtest. The items in such subtests can be independently numbered and, to ensure that each receives proper emphasis, separate time limits can be imposed.

Determining the Length of Objective Achievement Tests

Ideally, the length of a norm-referenced achievement test should be determined by two key factors: representative sampling and reliability. The test should contain as many items as necessary to sample all the verbal and mathematical aspects of the educational objectives on which the table of specifications is based. The smallest sample of test items (in other words, the shortest test) that can be used without jeopardizing reasonable representation varies with the nature of this table. If the subject matter topics and behavioral changes in the table are hererogeneous, then a larger sample is needed. If they are very much alike, a smaller sample can be used. Remember that too short a test may be unsatisfactory because it is impossible to include items based on some less important cells of the table of specifications. Consequently, the degree of content validity is lessened.

The second key factor is that the length of a norm-referenced test is also related to its reliability, that is, the consistency of its results (see Chapter 9). In general, shortening the test decreases its reliability. If, therefore, the use of the test results demands a high degree of test reliability, the length of the test has to be increased. Test results used to diagnose an individual's strengths and weaknesses in an area must be more reliable than those used only to determine differences between groups of students in terms of their achievement. In the first case, the test may be so long that it is administered in parts and requires several hours. In the second, it may be short that only one class period or less is needed.

In addition to these two factors governing the length of the classroom achievement test, there is another and very practical one: the time available for the administration of the test. Although this factor lacks the theoretical justification of the first two, it is just as important. Indeed, it often influences the length of the test more than factors of content validity or reliability, because the teacher often has so little control over it. Ordinarily, the test must be administered during a regularly scheduled class period which usually lasts forty to sixty minutes.

In this connection, remember the importance of student fatigue. Writing achievement tests can be an exhausting task. For this reason, it is doubtful that time periods longer than one hour should be used for achievement testing even if they were available. Certainly time periods of more than two hours should be discouraged. Any time student fatigue is suspected of being a noticeable influence on test performance, the test should be broken into parts with rest periods permitted between them.

Teachers customarily determine the length of an achievement test in a somewhat backward manner. First, they note the maximum amount of time that administrative routine will allow for giving the test. Then they estimate the number of items to which the students should be able to respond in the time allotted. Finally, they select this number from among those constructed. The teacher selects these in such a way that, as a group, they reflect the established relative importance of the various cells of the table of specifications.

As the restrictions on testing time limit the number of items to be included in the test, so do they also weaken its content validity and reliability. All too frequently, there is no convenient way of overcoming this progression of troubles. Instead, the teacher must recognize the situation for what it is, build the achievement test accordingly, and temper the use and interpretation of the results to compensate for whatever degree of content validity and reliability is lost.

Directions for Students

To perform to the best of their ability, the students must know the purpose of the test and must be thoroughly familiar with its mechanics. The teacher therefore formulates directions that the students read or that are read to them before responding to any of the test items.

The purpose of most classroom achievement tests is quite clear to the students. No doubt the initial announcement of the test is supplemented with remarks concerning the reasons why it is being administered; or, perhaps it is one of a series and the students are well aware of its purposes. In both of these instances, the directions need not include statements concerning the purposes of the test. If, however, the teacher doubts for any reason the completeness of the student's understanding of the purposes of the test, the first part of the directions should be devoted to a brief statement about them. Failure to do so can cause an unnecessary loss of motivation.

The mechanics of the test typically command much more attention in the directions than the purposes. Students need a complete knowledge of the "ground rules" of operation. This means that they must be aware of the time allowed, the manner in which they are to select and record answers, and the scoring system to be used. Also, students should even be instructed in test-room etiquette if circumstances dictate.

Directions for Selecting Answers.   Directions for selecting answers must be carefully written. Notice that the sample instructions of this kind given earlier assume that the student knows nothing about objective test items. This of course is an extreme assumption and, for the most part, an unnecessary one. Yet, stating the directions with too much detail is far less an evil than stating them with too little. This point is particularly important when novel or relatively novel items are being used.

For assurance that these directions are understood, practice test items may be included. They may consist of a typical item correctly answered in terms of the directions, as well as one or more to be answered by the students before beginning the test itself. They are told the correct answers to practice test items so that they can verify their understanding of the directions. Such items can be helpful when testing either elementary or secondary school students. The use of this procedure with the former group is quite common.

Directions for Recording Answers.   How the student is to record the answer is another small detail that cannot be overlooked. When the answer is to be written on the same sheet as the question, this is less of a problem. It is necessary to prepare directions such as those already illustrated, and to design a layout of the test items that allows generous space for circling letters, writing numbers, and filling in blanks. When separate answer sheets are used, the directions are not so simple. The relationship between the test copy and the answer sheet must be explained as well as any features of the answer sheet that would speed or impair the making of responses selected or that would increase or decrease the accuracy of scoring.

If separate answer sheets are used, teachers usually design their own. A typical one is shown in part in Figure 3.1. Notice that it can be used with a test having several types of objective items. These have been grouped according to type and each is numbered independently. The manner in which the student uses the answer sheet is described in the directions provided.

Date _____   Name _____
                                          Last   First
Subject _____   Scores: Part A _____
                                            Part B _____
                                            Part C _____
                                            Part D _____
                                            Total _____

DIRECTIONS: Read with care the general directions at the beginning of the test and the directions preceding each subpart. Then read each test item and decide which answer is correct. Indicate your answer by filling the blank or circling the number or letter provided below. Be certain that the number of the test item corresponds exactly with the number on the answer sheet when you record each answer.

A: SUPPLY		B: TRUE-FALSE		C: MULTIPLE-CHOICE		D: MATCHING	
Item	Answer	Item	Answer	Item	Answer	Item	Answer
1	_____	1	T F	1	1 2 3 4 5	1	_____
2	_____	2	T F	2	1 2 3 4 5	2	_____
3	_____	3	T F	3	1 2 3 4 5	3	_____
4	_____	4	T F	4	1 2 3 4 5	4	_____
5	_____	5	T F	5	1 2 3 4 5	5	_____

FIGURE 3.1.   Section of a Teacher-Designed Answer Sheet.

A wide variety of commercial answer sheets are available. They are designed for machine scoring, probably using a high speed computer, and are quite versatile. In addition to true-false and multiple-choice test items, they can be used for matching test items. The student marks the responses with an ordinary soft or medium lead pencil. The scoring machine reads the marks at an extremely high rate and prints partial or total scores. Various scoring formulas (for example, formulas for correcting for guessing) can be applied by the scoring machine. Also, multiple-response test items can be scored. Finally, it is possible to transfer test score information directly into a computer, which in turn can provide a wide variety of summary data about the test score distribution (for instance, the arithmetic means of the scores).

Norm-referenced tests involving separate test copies and answer sheets can be successfully administered to students as inexperienced as those in the fourth grade. However, if they are used with elementary school students, a training period is necessary prior to testing. Even after this, the students cannot handle the separate answer sheet efficiently. No doubt the time limits should be expanded for them. Secondary school students familiar with separate answer sheets lose very little time using them.

Directions for Scoring Answers.   Students should be informed of the scoring procedure when it is conveniently possible. They are entitled to ask how much credit they will get for each right answer. Usually this can be easily included in the directions because it is constant for each objective item within the subtests or possibly the total test.

Allowing the same number of points for each item is somewhat illogical. After all, they may vary in difficulty and importance, and thus more credit should be allowed for some correct answers than for others. However, attempts to weight the test items in terms of these characteristics tend to be highly subjective. Moreover, research has shown that scores made on an objective achievement test graded with a constant number of points for a right answer correlate very highly with scores obtained on the same test when the right answers are weighted in what is seemingly a more defensible manner. This means that, no matter which scoring procedure is used, the relative position of the students within the class remains unchanged in practically all cases. In view of this, more objective achievement tests are scored by means of the simpler method, which is to allow a constant amount of credit for each correct response to a given type of objective test item.

The directions should also include a statement about correction for guessing. Since the possibility of successfully guessing the correct answers appeals to some students, teachers may choose to discourage such attempts by penalizing the student for any wrong answers. This is known as a correction for guessing. The students have the right to know whether one of these methods is to be used. This information could greatly affect their willingness to omit a test item or try to guess the correct answer with little or no information.

Oral Directions.   Writing clear and explicit directions is of little help if the student refuses to read them or reads them carelessly. Therefore, a number of teachers read the directions aloud as the students read them silently. Any questions the students might have are answered, and then the test begins. This is a wise procedure with elementary school students. With the primary grade levels it must be carried one step further. Copies of the directions for any objective test items are not given to the students. Instead, they are given an answer sheet that is meticulously tailored to the test. After the directions are read and explained, practice exercises are completed. Then the teacher reads the questions one by one, allowing time for a response to each. At the conclusion of the test, some or all are repeated if time allows. Administering tests in this way removes a serious obstacle to the use of objective test items with elementary school students—the reading speed and comprehension problem.

Scoring the Objective Test

To many classroom teachers, the least exciting task of achievement testing is the scoring of the student responses. To handle this task the students are sometimes asked to score either their own or their neighbors' papers. Considering the importance of accurate scoring, the limitations of this procedure are obvious. When scoring the papers the teacher commonly takes a blank copy of the test, fills in the correct responses, and compares this key with the responses on the test copy returned by each student. The number of correct responses by each student is determined and recorded. The total operation may not require much time, but being essentially clerical in nature, it is often viewed with distaste by those who must do it.

Various attempts have been made to reduce the time required for scoring objective tests. These have taken the form of scoring keys designed to assist in hand-scoring individual test copies or separate answer sheets, and machine-scoring procedures using separate answer sheets.

Scoring Keys for Hand-Scoring. Two of the more successful scoring keys for hand-scoring are the fan key and the cut-out key.

The fan key is a sheet of paper on which the correct responses are written in a series of columns. The sheet of paper is the same size as the test copy or the separate answer sheet. Each column corresponds to a page of the test or a column on the answer sheet, and the correct responses are spaced in the column as the student responses are spaced on the page of the test or the column on the appropriate answer sheet. The key is folded along vertical lines separating its columns, thus taking the appearance of a fan. It is superimposed on the appropriate page of the test copy or placed next to the appropriate column on the answer sheet and matched with the corresponding responses.

The cut-out key is also a sheet of paper of the same size as the test copy or answer sheet. However, windows are cut in appropriate positions to reveal the correct response if they are made. The key is superimposed on a page of the test copy or the separate answer sheet and the student's responses are scored.

Machine-Scoring. If the commercial answer sheets are used in conjunction with informal objective tests, teachers can, if they wish, turn over the task of scoring to a scoring machine. Under ideal conditions, the speed and accuracy of scoring can be superior. Furthermore, computers can be programmed to print suggestions for remedial work for students whose patterns of error are typical of identifiable learning difficulties.

The disadvantages of machine-scoring of this type are well-known. First of all, it cannot be used with supply test items under any circumstances. Secondly, the students must be trained in the procedure of marking the answer sheets. The marks in the spaces must be reasonably heavy. Erasures must be complete and stray pencil marks avoided, because they might be recorded by the machine as wrong answers. A third disadvantage is the availability of scoring and computing equipment. Unless a machine is available on relatively short notice, scoring may prove to be more trouble than it is worth as far as classroom achievement tests are concerned. Finally, there typically is no indication on the answer sheet as to whether an answer to a given test item is correct or incorrect. The students cannot identify their strong and weak areas by examining the answer sheet alone.

Correcting for Guessing. The persistent problem encountered with objective achievement tests is the tendency of students to guess when they do not know the correct answer. Sometimes this guess is based on partial knowledge, other times on misinformation, and still other times on no information at all. In the last instance, they may not even have read the test item or, if they did, its answer is a total mystery.

If the score is determined by the number of correct responses, any success the students had when they guessed will raise the score. Obviously, this is not a defensible situation. The test score should reflect achievement only, rather than achievement plus the students' willingness to guess and the amount of success they happened to have in this case. Therefore, some teachers argue that students must be discouraged from wild guessing and be penalized if they do.

The correction for guessing formula for true-false and multiple-choice test items in norm-referenced tests is as follows:

$$S = R - \frac{W}{n-1}$$

where
S = the test score
R = the number of correct responses
W = the number of incorrect responses
n = the number of suggested responses from which one is chosen

R is often called the number of "rights," whereas W is thought of as the number of "wrongs."

For a true-false test, n is two and the formula reduces to

$$S = R - W$$

For a multiple-choice test having four suggested responses, the formula becomes

$$S = R - \frac{W}{3}$$

Notice that to use the formula in any of these cases, the number of omitted test items is ignored.

These formulas assume that all incorrect responses and a chance proportion of the correct ones are the result of wild guessing. This is, of course, not fully justified. The students are often taking "calculated risks" when selecting their responses. Rather than making wild guesses they are making more or less intelligent guesses based on sound but incomplete knowledge. Testwiseness is a definite factor.

Because the foregoing assumption is not completely satisfied, the formulas will overcorrect in some instances and undercorrect in others. Consequently, they are persistently criticized by teachers and students alike.

There is another disadvantage when a correction for guessing formula is applied. Informing the student that such a correction will be made customarily acts as a deterrent, but its effectiveness varies with the student. Some are willing to guess wildly no matter what correction formulas are used. Others are cautious. A correction for guessing will cause them to answer only when they are certain of the correct response, and even intelligent guesses are not ventured. More often than not, the first type of student gains higher test scores than the second. Thus, an extraneous personality factor unduly influences achievement tests designed to measure verbal or mathematical ability.

If sufficient time is allowed for the norm-referenced test so that every student can attempt every item, and if *every* student then answers *every* test item, no correction for guessing is needed for norm-referenced tests. Determining the test score by counting the number of correct responses is perfectly acceptable. Despite the fact that the test scores are different in size when corrected than when not corrected for guessing, the relative position of each student in the class is the same in both cases. The relationship between the uncorrected and corrected test scores under these conditions is perfect. If the purpose of an achievement test is to determine the relative position of each student in the class, the simplest test score may as well be used.

To ensure that all students will answer all test items, they must be instructed to guess when they do not know the answer, even if they must guess wildly. Needless to say, these instructions can hardly be considered good pedagogy. The student may lose respect for objective achievement testing, possibly even for the subject matter or the teacher. The full impact of these instructions is difficult to measure. Admittedly unsavory, they probably have no lasting effect upon most students. (For a review of research relevant to the correction for guessing formula, see Diamond and Evans, 1973).

PROBLEM

11.   Branch-testing or tailored testing is a procedure whereby, with the aid of a computer, the test items to which a student is to respond next are determined by the responses on preceding items (Glaser and Nitko, 1971). Hence he or she is administered a test tailored to a specific pattern of achievement. Study this procedure and react to it in terms of its potential value in conserving testing time, measuring achievement in depth, and improving educational diagnosis.

Organizing Criterion-Referenced Objective Tests

Many of the guidelines to be followed when organizing a criterion-referenced objective test are the same as those for a norm-referenced test of this kind. Certainly this is true for the more conventional aspects of test preparation such as designing directions for students and establishing methods for routinely scoring and reporting the results. On the other hand, important differences exist when one considers the problems of developing a criterion-referenced test that is capable of describing a student's performance with great clarity, and yet does not contain an inordinately large number of test items.

When organizing criterion-referenced tests, we must keep foremost in our minds that they are used to describe a student's status with respect to a well-defined behavioral domain. A behavior domain consists of a set of skills or dispositions that students display when called upon to do so (Popham, 1978, pp. 92–97). For example, a behavior domain in language arts might be the student's ability to use nouns and verbs properly in simple declarative sentences (see page 59). Some domains are more complex than this, whereas others are not. The crucial point is that they be well-defined. A well phrased third-level objective is very helpful in this regard but may need amplification in order to pinpoint exactly what a student's test performance really means.

Since the more complex domains are much more difficult to define specifically than the simpler ones, there is a tendency to organize criterion-referenced tests in terms of student behaviors that can be reasonably well isolated and that perhaps are somewhat limited in scope. Such tests may be of considerable help to teachers trying to diagnose student learning problems, but may be too narrow to provide a great deal of information about student learning in a more general sense. To obtain a broader view of such learning, many tests requiring great amounts of testing time might be necessary. This is often not feasible.

Perhaps a "limited-focus" measurement strategy is useful (Popham, 1978, pp. 117–118). Here a small number of highly important behaviors are identified, these are truly significant, hence not simple, and they probably subsume a number of more elementary behaviors. For those selected, detailed test specifications (that is, stimulus attributes and response attributes) can be designed and adhered to religiously. As a result, the number of tests needed to measure achievement is reasonable, their quality high, and their results useful for students and teachers.

After one is satisfied that the description of the behavior domain is satisfactory, the question of test length must be faced. How many test items must be included to measure adequately the behavior in question? In other words, how many are needed in order to determine with a high degree of certainty whether students are achieving satisfactorily?

This issue has been studied extensively and there is no tidy answer. Certainly tests of one or two items are too short since students are offered very little opportunity to display their degree of achievement. Also, one hundred or more highly homogeneous test items are too many since precious time is needlessly wasted and student morale suffers. As a rule, between five and twenty test items per measured behavior is typically sufficient (Popham, 1978, pp. 179–180). Tests of ten to twenty test items are preferred, especially if the decisions to be made about the student are of considerable significance.

Using carefully drawn stimulus attributes and response attributes based on a well-honed general description of the behavior domain will yield a group of highly similar test items for the test (see page 57). Rechecking these items in terms of the test specifications and one's general knowledge of the teaching-learning situation will permit selecting those to be included in the test. Others will serve as a starting point for building another comparable test at some future date. As in the case of norm-referenced tests, constructing criterion-referenced tests is a difficult, never-ending task.

SUMMARY

The following are the major thoughts included in this chapter:

1. An objective test item is one that can be scored so that subjective judgment is practically eliminated when determining the correctness of a student's answer.

2. There are two types of objective test items, the supply type and the selection type. When responding to the supply type, the student has to provide the words, numbers, or symbols necessary. In contrast, the selection type allows the student to choose the correct response from the information it provides.

3. Illustrations of the supply type are the short-answer question and the completion test item. Those teachers who use supply items in achievement tests do so because the likelihood of a student's guessing the correct answer is minimized and because of their ease of construction over the selection type. However, they also find that student responses to supply test items are more difficult to score, and that often the items measure only the student's knowledge of factual details.

4. True-false, multiple-choice, and matching test items all illustrate the selection type. The true-false item in its simplest form is a declarative statement that the student must judge as true or false. A test of this type can widely sample a large amount of subject matter without requiring much testing time. On the other hand, the true-false test item often involves only trivial pieces of information and, because one of two responses must be correct, students who don't know the right one frequently guess.

5. A multiple-choice test item is one in which a direct question or incomplete statement is presented and a number of responses are given. The student is to choose the correct (or best) answer to a question or the correct expression for completing a statement. This type of objective test is widely used because it is so adaptable. It can be used to measure recall of information or application of a principle in a novel situation in practically any subject matter area with all but the most naive students. The principal disadvantage teachers experience is that the items are relatively difficult to build.

6. The typical matching test item consists of two lists of items and a set of instructions for matching each in the first list with one in the second. It can include large quantities of factual information without requiring a proportionately large amount of testing time. However, some subject matter is not well-suited for matching test items.

7. After a group of objective test items have been constructed, they must be appraised and edited prior to being organized into an achievement test. This process involves (1) rechecking the relationship between each item and the table of specifications or objective on which it is based, (2) removing any ambiguity or any irrelevant clues that still remain, (3) establishing relative level of difficulty, and (4) correcting any feature that seriously increases the amount of time needed by the student to read and understand it.

8. Organizing objective test items into a norm-referenced achievement test requires a number of major steps:

   1. Proportional representation by the test items of the cells in the table of specifications must be ensured.
   2. The length of the test must be established.
   3. The order of the test items within the test must be determined.
   4. Directions to the student must be prepared.
   5. A method of scoring and reporting results must be ready for immediate use.

9. Organizing a criterion-referenced objective test is, in some ways, similar to that for a norm-referenced test. Major issues are defining the behavior domain explicitly and determining the length of the test (typically at least five or ten, and not more than twenty, test items).

SUGGESTED READINGS

EBEL, R. L. *Essentials of educational measurement* (3rd ed.). Englewood Cliffs, N.J.: Prentice-Hall, 1979.
In chapters 3, 4, 5, 7, 8, 9, and 10, the planning of a classroom achievement test, the construction of true-false and multiple-choice test items, and the administration and scoring of achievement tests are discussed. Numerous faulty true-false and muliple-choice test items are shown and criticized.

EDUCATIONAL TESTING SERVICE. *Making the classroom test, a guide for teachers* (3rd ed.). Princeton, N.J.: Author, 1973.
In relatively few pages, the basic rules of test-making for both objective and essay tests are developed and illustrated. Elementary and secondary school examples are given.

GRONLUND, N. E. *Constructing achievement tests* (2nd ed.). Englewood Cliffs, N.J.: Prentice-Hall, 1977.
Attention is given to both norm-referenced and criterion-referenced achievement tests. The planning of achievement tests (chapter 2) and the construction of objective tests of knowledge (chapter 3) are particularly useful.

LIPPEY, G. The computer can support test construction in a variety of ways. *Educational Technology*, 1973, *13*, 10–12.
This article is an overview of twenty-two articles in the same issue of this journal which describe various successful efforts to engage in computer-assisted test construction.

SARNACKI, R. E. An examination of testwiseness in the cognitive test domain. *Review of Educational Research*, 1979, *49*, 252–279.
Testwiseness is defined and methods for minimizing its effects are considered. Available research regarding testwiseness is reviewed.

TINKELMAN, S. N. Planning the objective test. In R. L. Thorndike (Ed.), *Educational measurement* (2nd ed.). Washington, D.C.: American Council on Education, 1971.
In a well-organized manner, the author discusses the steps followed in the development of a table of specifications and the planning for the types of test items, their number, and their level of difficulty. Sound recommendations are given.

WESMAN, A. G. Writing the test item. In R. L. Thorndike (Ed.), *Educational measurement* (2nd ed.). Washington, D.C.: American Council on Education, 1971.

Of all the materials available that are less than book length and deal with objective test items, this is one of the best. This piece contains many illustrations of the various forms of objective test items and numerous suggestions for building them properly.

REFERENCES CITED

DIAMOND, J., & EVANS, W. The correction for guessing. *Review of Educational Research*, 1973, *43*, 181–191.

EBEL, R. L. Can teachers write good true-false test items? *Journal of Educational Measurement*, 1975, *12*, 31–36.

EBEL, R. L. *Essentials of educational measurement* (3rd ed.). Englewood Cliffs, N.J.: Prentice-Hall, 1979.

EBEL, R. L. *Practical problems in educational measurement.* Lexington, Mass.: D. C. Heath, 1980.

ECHTERNACHT, G. J. Use of confidence testing in objective tests. *Review of Educational Research*, 1972, *42*, 217–236.

GLASER, R., & NITKO, A. J. Measurement in learning and instruction. In R. L. Thorndike (Ed.), *Educational Measurement* (2nd ed.). Washington, D.C.: American Council on Education, 1971.

POPHAM, W. J. *Criterion-referenced measurement.* Englewood Cliffs, N.J.: Prentice-Hall, 1978.

SARNACKI, R. E. An examination of test-wiseness in the cognitive test domain. *Review of Educational Research*, 1979, *49*, 252–279.

TINKELMAN, S. N. Planning the objective test. In R. L. Thorndike (Ed.), *Educational measurement* (2nd ed.). Washington, D.C.: American Council on Education, 1971.

WESMAN, A. G. Writing the test item. In R. L. Thorndike (Ed.), *Educational Measurement* (2nd ed.). Washington, D.C.: American Council on Education, 1971.

4

Measuring Complex Achievement Objectively

The content of this chapter will enable you to

1. Appreciate the importance of expanding achievement testing programs to include the measuring of complex student achievements with objective test items

2. Compare paper-and-pencil tests of knowledge with those measuring complex achievement in terms of developing test items, scoring them, and interpreting student responses

3. Outline the steps followed in constructing single-response and multiple response test items measuring complex achievement

4. Devise novel but realistic stimulus material for objective test items along with questions which, to be answered correctly, require students to display complex achievement

5. Delineate the advantages and limitations of measuring complex achievement with objective test items

6. Contrast closed-book and open-book test administration when testing student knowledge and complex achievement

As part of an assessment of literature achievement, children were asked to tell something about various literary characters such as Thor, Achilles, and Paul Bunyan (National Assessment of Educational Progress, 1972–73, p. 3). Some ran into trouble, as illustrated by the following two responses about Moses:

> He opened the sea and when the Russians were coming he closed it—the Jews got through and the rest died.

> He was found in the river bank when he was a baby. He was a Baptist.

Aside from the humor present, these and similar student responses make an important contribution. They reveal the pathetically inadequate grasp that some people have of simple concepts, meanings, and relationships. Words are only partially understood and, as a result, the student commits what might be called "logical errors." In other words, some parts of the student's verbal or mathematical achievements are at best superficial.

There are numerous less extreme illustrations of the same problem. In a science class it is generally possible to find a student who can quickly and properly quote Newton's law of motion but fails to see a connection between any of them and the fact that children of various weights travel varying distances when using the same sled on the same hill. A student in a modern language class can conjugate a French verb perfectly, but fails persistently to use the proper form of this verb when translating an English passage to French. In a social studies class we find a student who can recognize the relationship between latitude and climate north, but not south, of the equator. In a geometry class there are usually several students who have difficulty recognizing two parallel lines unless they are drawn vertically or horizontally, or who have trouble solving problems with right triangles if the right angle is not the lower left-hand angle.

These deficiencies have a far-reaching impact on both norm- and criterion-referenced achievement testing. If a test measures only the student's ability to recall information, some of the students responding to the items may succeed admirably even though they comprehend the subject matter only superficially. Moreover, the teacher may erroneously assume that any student who can recall the information is also capable of using it properly, but the consistency of relationship between these two abilities is not large enough to justify this assumption. To identify more closely the perimeters of the student's verbal and mathematical achievements, the tests must include items that measure complex cognitive achievement as well as knowledge. Both essay and objective test items can be used for this purpose.

Testing for Knowledge and More Complex Achievement

For the purposes of this book, knowledge is composed of pieces of information that students can recall. According to this definition, the students may, but will not necessarily, have some grasp of the meaning, implication, or significance of their knowledge. In other words, all the facts about people, places, events, and things that they acquired by rote and that they can still recall are a part of their knowledge, whether or not they grasp the meanings.

More complex cognitive achievement, on the other hand, is based on the acquisition of meanings. Students gain this when they comprehend the meaning of facts so well that they can restate them in their own words, grasp their inter-relationships, and take action intelligently on that basis. Complex achievement is knowledge with its meaning, implication, and significance attached. Students who have gained this are able to meet the changing situations thrust upon them every day and to intelligently attack the problems they contain. In other words, we are talking about the five levels of the cognitive taxonomy called intellectual abilities and skills: comprehension, application, analysis, synthesis, and evaluation.

Tests for Knowledge

Testing for verbal and mathematical knowledge with objective test items is il-lustrated in the preceding chapter. Most of the test items can be correctly answered by any students willing to memorize. If they fail to gain meaning while memorizing, little is lost as far as these items are concerned.

Since testing for knowledge is comparatively easy, it receives considerable at-tention in the classroom. The teacher experiences little difficulty in constructing test items requiring the student to recall an isolated fact or a series of facts. Con-sequently, classroom achievement tests and many standardized achievement tests are heavily overbalanced in this direction. This in turn has a profound influence on learning and teaching. Students quickly discover the advantages of memorizing the facts on which they are tested. They orient their learning procedures accordingly. Sometimes the teachers are no less susceptible to this pressure, particularly if the students are a part of a citywide or statewide testing program. When the tests stress information recall, they generally teach accordingly, so that the class test results will compare favorably with those of the other classes. In brief, the educational objectives dealing with knowledge become the primary objectives.

The overemphasis on information recall found in achievement tests today should not be replaced with a fault equally as serious: an underemphasis on testing for knowledge. Knowledge is the raw material for developing more complex achievement. Before students can acquire the latter, they must have all pertinent knowledge at their disposal. A severe deemphasis on educational objectives dealing with knowledge could be as damaging as the present overemphasis.

Tests for Complex Achievement

In knowledge testing, the material the student learns is essentially, if not exactly, the same as that included in the test items. Novel material is virtually nonexistent in the test. Novel test items require more of the student than simple recall of information.

It follows that evidence of students' complex cognitive achievements can be obtained by asking them questions about a carefully contrived situation that is new to them. Within this situation they are to apply the appropriate part of their total store of knowledge. To do so successfully, they must know the meaning of the knowledge and be able to reorganize this meaning within a strange but plausible situation. By using a novel situation, the teacher can be confident that the student is doing more than merely parroting memorized material.

An illustration of the use of novelty in testing can be found in the mathematics test item shown in Figure 4.1. The chart shows the number of production workers and the total amount paid in wages to them during one year in each of four geographic regions. The student is to identify the region where the average income per worker was lowest.

Assume that this situation is new to the students but the mathematical procedures involved have been studied. To answer correctly, they must select from their mathematical knowledge the part appropriate to this fictitious but realistic situation and apply it correctly.

What the Test Item Measures

There are instances when we are uncertain as to whether the test item is measuring a student's knowledge or a higher order of learning. This is particularly true when the purpose of the test item is to measure knowledge. The teacher building the test item has no intention of measuring anything except recall of information and, as far as most members of the class are concerned, he or she succeeds. Consider, however, the students who for some reason did not acquire the knowledge in question, yet arrive at the correct answer by a process of deduction based upon related knowledge. For them, more complex achievement is measured.

The multiple-choice test item shown below is an example:

Which one of these countries was first to have a colony in North America?
   (1)   Germany   (3)   Russia
   (2)   Italy   (4)   Spain

If the class studied the colonization of this continent with any care, the test item measures recall of information. Yet a student who does not know the answer might still arrive at it by drawing upon related general knowledge about political, economic, military, and imperialistic aspects of the four countries in the sixteenth century. This correct response represents a higher level of achievement than simply acquiring knowledge.

On the other hand, test items designed to measure complex achievement may measure only recall of information. If the situation on which the test item is based is familiar to a student, the teacher cannot be certain which aspect of the student's achievement is reflected in the answer. For example, it is possible in the case in Figure 4.1 that a student had previously memorized the chart and perhaps the answer itself. Certainly under these conditions it would only be necessary to recall this information to handle the test item successfully.

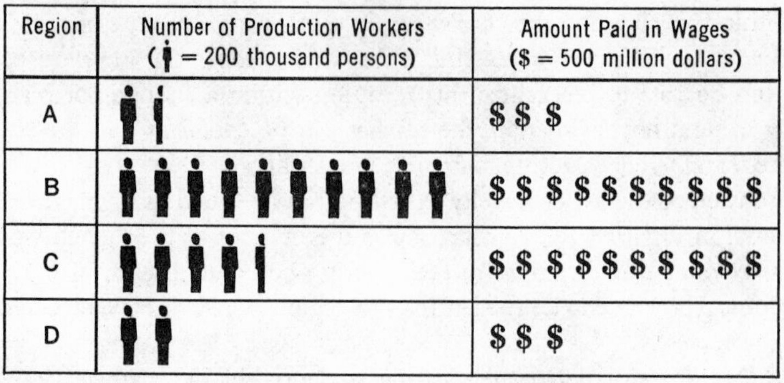

Region	Number of Production Workers (= 200 thousand persons)	Amount Paid in Wages ($ = 500 million dollars)
A	👤👤	$ $ $
B	👤👤👤👤👤👤👤👤👤👤	$ $ $ $ $ $ $ $ $
C	👤👤👤👤👤	$ $ $ $ $ $ $ $ $
D	👤👤	$ $ $

Directions:

By calculating from the chart, find the region in which the average income per worker was lowest. Select the correct answer from among the four listed below.

(1) A
(2) B
(3) C
(4) D

FIGURE 4.1.   Mathematics Test Item Based on Novel Stimulus Material

Adapted from material published by National Assessment of Educational Progress.

Tests of Knowledge and Complex Achievement Compared

The similarities and differences between norm-referenced tests measuring knowledge and those measuring complex achievement have been repeatedly investigated and reported. The studies have tried to answer two questions:

1. Are the gains made by students, as measured in terms of tests of complex achievement, more permanent than those measured in terms of tests of knowledge?
2. Is there a relationship between student performance as measured by tests of complex achievement and as measured by tests of knowledge?

The answer to the first question is an affirmative one. Studies of secondary school and college academic achievement have shown that, as the months pass following instruction, students retain more of the materials included in a test of complex achievement than those in a test of knowledge. In some studies, tests of both types were administered to classes as pretests at the beginning of the school year and as final tests at the end of the period of instruction. The difference between the scores for each student was defined as a gain. Then, without an opportunity to review and relearn the subject matter, the students were retested one, two, and sometimes three years later. The gains in knowledge shrank alarmingly; however, the gains in areas of complex achievement showed no such loss. On the contrary, in some instances they actually increased somewhat.

The relationship between student performance as measured by tests of complex achievement and by tests of knowledge has been found to be positive and somewhat low. Otherwise stated, the student who acquires knowledge in a subject matter area ordinarily acquires more complex learning outcomes too, but this tendency is so imperfect that the second cannot be satisfactorily predicted on the basis of the first. More complex achievement cannot be assessed indirectly by measuring knowledge in a subject matter area; instead, tests specially designed for various levels of the cognitive domain must be used (Solomon, 1965; Smith, 1968).

PROBLEMS

1. Ebel (1980, p. 138) believes that some situational test items may be more an "experience of logic" than a test of student knowledge and understanding. Evaluate his point of view.

2. If a teacher of a class well-known to you built a series of objective test items according to the six principal levels of the cognitive taxonomy, do you think that, working independently, you could properly classify almost every test item according to its intended level? Even if you and the teacher agree as to the classification, have you necessarily identified the cognitive process that each item is intended to measure?

Building and Scoring Test Items Measuring Complex Achievement

Data concerning complex student achievement can be gathered in many different ways. The daily observation of student behavior by the teacher can provide a wealth of evidence. Observation can take place in the classroom, on the playground, or in the student's home, and the information acquired can be organized by anecdotal records or rating scales. Student work products are also useful. An original theme for an English class, a collection or exhibit for a science class, a painting or clay model for a fine arts unit, an apron for a home economics class, or a bookcase for an industrial arts class will quickly reveal some of the student's more complex achievements. Also helpful are teacher-student interviews, diaries of out-of-class activities, and, of course, paper-and-pencil tests.

In addition, the teacher can use the objective test item. Although by no means a universal solution for the problems of measuring complex achievement, it can be extremely effective in science, social studies, mathematics, and the language arts. In such subjects as agriculture, home economics, and industrial arts, objective test items are used less frequently, but still provide much-needed information.

Constructing Test Items

To construct test items that measure more complex student achievement, two basic steps must be taken. First, the teacher must decide which pattern of student behavior is to be measured. Behavioral patterns include the student's ability to apply facts and principles to new situations and the ability to interpret data and recognize cause-and-effect relationships and assumptions underlying conclusions. Another way to think of these is in terms of the last five levels of the cognitive taxonomy, namely, comprehension, application, analysis, synthesis, and evaluation. Of these, comprehension, application, and analysis are usually most important to us.

Secondly, the teacher must devise a novel but realistic situation with questions that, to be answered correctly, require the student to display the pattern of behavior being considered. The situations can be completely original or based on some convenient source such as newspaper or magazine articles or even unfamiliar research reports. If possible, the situations should resemble the familiar, everyday environment. Students are generally impressed with the fairness of a testing approach that requires them to use what they have learned in school to answer questions about situations similar to out-of-school experiences.

Combining an appropriate pattern of student behavior with a suitably novel situation is not simple. Initially, teachers may be hard-pressed to find the situation they want, and then they may experience difficulty in reducing it to an objective test item. Finding the situation is a matter of sensitivity to the relationship between what is taught and the world outside the classroom; reducing it to an objective test item is largely a matter of following many of the suggestions for constructing objective test items described in Chapter 3.

In the search for a novel situation, the teacher starts, of course, with a clear notion of the pattern of student behavior of concern. In a mathematics class, for example, the students have mastered many theorems, one of which is the Pythagorean theorem. To see if they can use this information, the teacher may, in a test item, give them the outer dimensions of a baseball diamond and ask them to compute the distance that the ball must travel when the catcher throws it from home plate to second base. In an elementary school arithmetic unit, the students have studied simple areas. Therefore, the teacher might have them compute the number of square pieces of candy of 2" × 2" size that could be cut out of an 8" × 10" rectangular pan. In a science class the students learned about the law of refraction. Hence, the teacher builds a test item in which they must tell how they would judge the position of a rock at the bottom of a fish pond if they, standing on the bank, were to retrieve it. Finally, the ability of students to read unfamiliar music could be measured by providing each with a sheet of printed music as a recording of it is played; then, as it stops before the end of the music, having them mark the last note heard. Certainly these and many similar illustrations in other subject matter areas are realistic problems to the pupils.

Single-Response Objective Test Items.   Some teachers prefer to ask only one question concerning the novel situation selected. It can be phrased to conform to any of the types of objective test items already described. Condensing the description of the novel situation and the question concerning it into a single test item can sometimes be accomplished without lengthening the test item excessively. For instance, in a secondary school English class teachers may want to check on the students' skill in the proper use of the words *who, whose, whom, which,* and *that.* To do this they could give the students a series of sentences like those below and ask them to select the correct word from the two given, and then write it in the space provided at the right.

1. The man (which, who) is speaking is our president.   1.   *(who)*
2. Do you know the boy (who's, whose) model airplane   2.   *(whose)*
   is broken?

Sometimes not one but several questions can be asked about the novel situation. These questions can be more or less independent of each other—the response to one does not appreciably influence the response to any other. Each correct response may require the students to reveal a different aspect of their ability to use their knowledge.

The following novel situation is one on which a series of test items is constructed. These test items are intended to measure the ability of students in a home economics class to apply certain rules for meal planning. Typical menus are shown and proposed changes are to be accepted or rejected by the students. Since the rules are summarized for the student, these test items demand less recall of information than some of the others included in this chapter.

Directions: Listed below are the menus of meals for two days and certain meal planning rules. Study them carefully.

Breakfast

A. Pear sauce
    Poached egg on milk toast
    Coffee

D. Orange slices
    Soft cooked egg on toast
    Cocoa

Lunch

B. Tomato soup
    Bacon, lettuce, and tomato
    sandwich
    Peaches and cookie
    Milk

E. Chicken soup (broth)
    Cherry jello salad
    Orange
    Tea

Dinner

C. Fried pork chops
    French fried potatoes
    Spinach
    Mince pie
    Coffee

F. Pea soup
    Meat loaf
    Baked beans
    Rolls and butter
    Custard pie
    Coffee

Meal Planning Rules

1. Balance the different types of foodstuffs in each meal.
2. Do not serve the same food twice in the same meal, even in a different form.
3. Do not use many rich or hard-to-digest foods in one meal.

4. Combine bland or soft foods with those of more pronounced flavor or different texture.

5. Plan meals in which the colors harmonize and are appealing.

6. Plan at least one food in each meal that has high satiety value.

Directions: Keeping in mind the above rules, consider the following changes. If the change would not improve the meal, place a zero in the blank. If the change would improve the meal, write the number of the rule supporting your decision in the blank opposite the change. Judge each change independently of all others.

_(4)_   1. Substitute scrambled egg and cinnamon toast for poached egg on milk toast in Menu A.

_(2)_   2. Substitute cream of mushroom soup for tomato soup in Menu B.

_(3)_   3. Substitute broiled steak for the fried pork chops in Menu C.

_(0)_   4. Substitute pecan pie for mince pie in Menu C.

_(0)_   5. Substitute half a grapefruit for orange slices in Menu D.

_(6)_   6. Substitute cream of chicken soup for chicken soup in Menu E.

_(1)_   7. Substitute baked potato for baked beans in Menu F.

Observe that the description of the novel situation is quite long. This is to be expected, since it provides ample material for a series of test items. Also observe that the objective test items following the description can be any one of several types. The true-false and multiple-choice types are commonly used.

Building test items such as the foregoing involves a series of revisions if a high-quality product is to be obtained. The teacher begins by writing a description of the novel situation, then constructs test items on the basis of it. It is soon apparent that revision of the description will strengthen one or more of the proposed items. Minor deletions or additions of material may result in a wealth of new test item possibilities. Thus, the construction of test items suggests changes in the description, and changes in description suggest new or better test items. Persistent efforts along these lines by the teacher will produce a description of the novel situation that is virtually unambiguous and that contains no nonfunctional portions of any consequence; with this description will be a series of test items exploiting practically all the possibilities for measuring complex student achievement in terms of the situation used.

Multiple-Response Objective Test Items. Multiple-response objective test items are also used to measure student understanding. A common instance of this occurs when the teacher wishes to measure the student's ability to apply facts and principles to new situations. In this case the situation is described in some detail. A paragraph or more may be needed. The basic problem within the novel situation is defined and a question asked about it. The students answer the question by selecting the correct response from among several listed. Finally, they select from among many reasons listed those that support the answer. In a sense the students view each reason like a true-false test item. They must decide whether each one is sound or faulty.

An illustration of the above is the following test item intended for use in a secondary school science class. A knowledge of the principles of reproduction, how they operate in plants, and an ability to apply this information in a novel situation are measured by this test item.

A visitor to a rural area noticed that each apple orchard of any size had beehives located in it. This puzzled him, so he asked one of the local farmers why this practice was followed.

Directions: Immediately following are three possible answers to the question asked above. Check the one that best answers the question.

      A.   The bees will be able to get good nectar.

 ✓ B.   The number of apples formed on each tree will increase.

      C.   The apple blossoms will be self-pollinated.

Directions: Following is a list of statements that are suggested as reasons for the above answer. Check the statements that are good reasons for the answer you selected above.

     1.   Yield of apples is increased if bees are present.

 ✓ 2.   Fertilization makes possible the development of mature fruits.

 ✓ 3.   Cross-pollination is necessary for the production of a good apple crop.

     4.   Cross-pollination frequently results in desirable variations.

     5.   Many fruit growers keep bees in their orchards.

     6.   The apple blossoms contain the most desirable type of nectar that can be used in commercial honey.

 ✓ 7.   Flowers from which insects have collected nectar are usually pollinated.

     8.   The only completely satisfactory location for beehives is in the orchard from which they can get nectar.

 ✓ 9.   Even though self-pollination is possible in a flower, it frequently fails to occur.

   10.   Bees pollinate blossoms in order to aid in the production of a good crop.

   11.   All insect-pollinated flowers are cross-pollinated.

   12.   Double fertilization increases the yield.

The construction of test items like the above is, unfortunately, not a simple task. Even after the difficulties of finding a suitable situation and identifying the central problem have been overcome, the teacher must still find two or more plausible answers, each of which is supported by a group of logical reasons. The latter are the most difficult to find. One way of simplifying the task is to submit the situation to groups of students as an essay test item, then screen their answers for attractive but wrong answers and logical reasons for them. These answers can be restated so that an objective test item results.

Two additional features of this kind of objective test item deserve mention. Observe that the students do not know how many of the suggested reasons are good reasons, and that some that are not relevant to the correct answer are nevertheless essentially true statements. An example of this is the fifth reason listed: "Many fruit growers keep bees in their orchards." To avoid confusion these two points are sometimes mentioned in the directions to the students.

Scoring the Multiple-Response Test Item

When a series of more or less independent questions is asked about the same novel situation, the student responses can be weighted and scored in essentially the same manner as any other objective test items of the same type; however, when student responses to one part of the test item are in some way dependent on responses to another part, the weighting and scoring become more complicated. In the scoring of many of these test items, two questions can be asked:

1. How much credit should students receive if they answer one part of the item incorrectly and because of this, respond incorrectly to other parts dependent on the first?

2. When the students are not told how many responses to make, how are their responses scored if they make too few or too many, some of which are correct and some of which are wrong?

Both of these questions can be discussed in terms of the multiple-response objective test item concerning beehives in an apple orchard. Students must select one of three alternatives as the principal advantage of placing bees in an apple orchard, and then they must indicate which of the twelve reasons listed supports the answer. Suppose the students select the wrong alternative and defend their choice well by checking appropriate reasons for it. How much credit should they receive? According to the scoring key, their responses are totally wrong. They argue, however, that only their first response is wrong, since they did check the correct reasons for the wrong alternative. What should the teacher do? Although practices vary, one of the more popular is to allow no credit for any of the reasons checked if the correct alternative is not selected.

The second question deals with the case in which the students check the correct alternative and receive whatever points are allowed for this answer, but do not check the proper reasons. Possibly they check too many reasons, including the correct ones. Or possibly they check too few reasons, yet those selected are correct. In either case, how should their choice of reasons be scored? Again, there is no single, widely accepted answer to this question. Sometimes teachers take the point of view that the students should be penalized if they check any unacceptable reasons. Moreover, students who indiscriminately check *all* reasons should receive no credit.

According to this view, the penalty for any reason erroneously checked will be determined by the total number of reasons listed and the number correct. In the beehives test item, four of twelve reasons are listed on the key as acceptable. Hence, if one point were allowed for each correct reason checked, then one-half of a point would be deducted for every incorrect reason. In this way students who check all reasons will receive four positive points and four negative points, a net of zero. If more than one point is allowed each correct reason checked, the penalty for each incorrect reason is proportionally increased.

PROBLEMS

3. On the basis of each of the following principles in science, describe a novel situation and construct test items that will measure a young student's ability to apply that principle.
    a. Water tends to seek its own level.
    b. An object floating in water will displace water equal to its weight.
    c. The theoretical mechanical advantage of a lever used in conjunction with a fulcrum is related to the position of the fulcrum.

4. Using a table of specifications in a subject matter area of interest to you, design one or more test items that measure comprehension, application, or analysis. Then cross-refer each test item with the table, that is, indicate the cells in the table with which it is primarily related and those with which it is secondarily related (for example, cells concerning knowledge).

Basing Objective Test Items on Pictorial Materials

A picture is said to be worth ten thousand words. This is just as true in achievement testing as in any other aspect of everyday living. Consider for a moment teachers who regularly discover that they need a large number of words to develop a sufficiently unambiguous test item. Many words, they realize, increase the student's reading load and the time required to answer the test item. Hence, they ask the logical question: Could a diagram, map, photograph, picture, or even a table of data be used to construct the test item? When this is done, the number of words needed to make the item specific and understandable is generally reduced, sometimes to less than half that required when no pictorial or tabular material is used. Furthermore, a well-chosen photograph or table serves as an excellent means of describing a novel situation on which the item is based.

Suggestions for Constructing Pictorial Test Items

Use pictorial material only when it makes a unique and sizable contribution to the quality of the test item. The pictorial material must be functional in an important way. It should represent a central idea much better than words can.

Consider the junior high school test item in Figure 4.2, which is designed to measure the students' ability to use knowledge of angles in a new situation. Certainly it would be most difficult to construct test items of this kind without including a diagram. Furthermore, the number of test items based on the diagram can be increased easily, for example, by adding questions about the areas of the lots.

The pictorial material should be no more complicated than needed to accomplish this purpose. Some of the problems experienced in this regard are illustrated in the test items in Figure 4.3, which is designed for primary-level students. Their knowledge of insects is being measured by responding to questions about drawings of insects which they are given. The teacher reads each question at least once and pauses while the students draw a line through the answer each selects.

A real estate agent buys the city block shown in the diagram below and divides it into ten lots as indicated by the dotted lines. The lines CD, EF, GH, and IJ are parallel to the streets AB and KL. Street BL meets street AB at an angle of 72°.

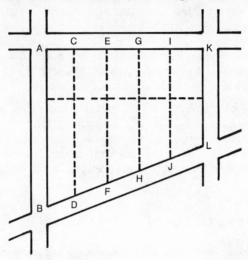

1. What will the agent find to be the size of angle BDC? (<u>108</u>) degrees.
2. What will the agent find to be the size of angle IJL? (<u>72</u>) degrees.
3. Will the lots facing street AK have more, less, or the same frontage as the corresponding lots facing street BL? (<u>less</u>)

FIGURE 4.2.   Mathematics Test Item Based on Pictorial Stimulus Materials

It is difficult to know whether too little or too much detail is included in drawings such as these. The amount used seems to be appropriate, but we cannot be sure of this point without studying student responses and questioning the class members about their incorrect answers.

When necessary, use explanatory statements to clarify the meaning of the pictorial material. Often the pictorial material can stand alone, or virtually so. On the other hand, efforts to avoid complex material can produce ambiguities for some students. Figure 4.4 is an example of how this might happen.

The purpose of the items is to measure the ability of elementary school students to interpret unfamiliar maps. This purpose might not be realized if they fail to understand the symbolism used. Also, they are cautioned not to consider the region shown to be any particular place. Since the drawing vaguely resembles the western end of the Mediterranean Sea, a student who considers it to be that area may believe the cities to be actual localities, thereby adding confusing features to the multiple-choice questions.

Integrate the test items with the pictorial materials so as to reduce the complexity of test items as much as possible. This suggestion is followed in all of the pictorial items shown. Notice that the questions are comparatively short, particularly in Figure 4.4. In addition, the student responds to those items by using the letter of the city selected; numbers for the responses are not provided, thereby streamlining each test item still more.

Teacher: Draw a line through the number that tells you how many legs this insect has.

2
4
6
8
10

Teacher: Draw a line through the number that tells you how many feelers this insect has.

2
4
6
8

Teacher: Draw a line through the number that tells you how many wings this insect has.

0
2
4
6
8

Teacher: Draw a line through the number that tells you how many eyes this insect has.

2
4
6
8

FIGURE 4.3.   Science Test Item Based on Pictorial Stimulus Material

PROBLEM

5. Excellent illustrations of the use of pictorial and tabular materials as a part of test items to measure more than recall of information have been published by the Educational Testing Service (1973). Select one from this publication and analyze it with respect to the student behavioral changes probably involved.

Measuring Complex Achievement with Objective Test Items: Advantages

The advantages gained by measuring complex cognitive achievement with objective test items are in part the same as those obtained by any other means. In other words, their use enlarges the scope of the achievement evaluation program, which in turn increases the attention paid by both students and teachers to the role of educational objectives dealing with a higher order of learning.

DIRECTIONS: Carefully study the map below. Do not consider it to be any particular place. The dots represent cities. Each city is identified by a letter. For each of the questions following the map, choose the correct city from among the four listed. Write the letter of that city in the blank provided.

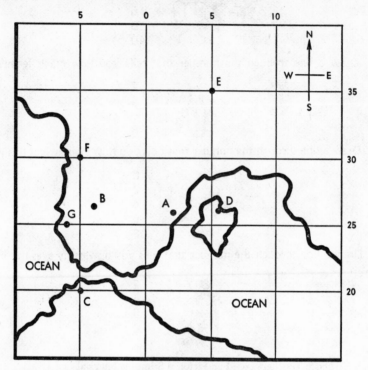

(C)   1. Which city is nearest the equator?
         City C
         City D
         City E
         City G

(D)   2. Which city has the greatest east longitude reading?
         City C
         City D
         City E
         City G

FIGURE 4.4.   Geography Test Item Based on Pictorial Stimulus Material

Moreover, students ordinarily find that objective test items designed to reveal more complex achievement are challenging and practical. Interest can reach the point where more than a few will voluntarily admit that this type of testing is enjoyable and meaningful, a situation particularly probable when pictorial material represents the novel situation. Often we can simulate a natural situation quite well and thereby reduce the degree of artificiality present in the testing situation.

Objective test items measuring complex achievement have several additional advantages. Teachers skilled in objective testing who use it for measuring knowledge find this technique a convenient extension of familiar testing procedures and use it to increase the scope of the achievement evaluations without sacrificing objectivity of scoring. Unlike the evaluation of student work products, for example, the objective test items provide highly structured problems to which the students are to react. Each student is confronted with the same novel situation and responds in terms of the same list of possible answers. This allows comparisons of student performances to be made more easily. Incidentally, the structuring of the problem may also limit the usefulness of objective test items. Complex achievement is reflected in the originality of student performance. Responses to objective test items do not reveal this originality, whereas a creative work product does.

PROBLEM

6. Compare the value of information from objective test items with that gained by examining creative student products when the degree of complex student achievement in the cognitive domain is being evaluated in a subject matter area of interest to you.

Measuring Complex Achievement with Objective Test Items: Limitations

There are three important limitations in the measuring of complex student achievement with objective test items. First, the methods tend to be more difficult to devise and execute than those for measuring knowledge. They demand considerable ingenuity on the part of teachers, especially if they focus their efforts at the upper levels of the cognitive taxonomy. Secondly, the time needed for student response may be excessive. Finally, the results yielded by this procedure cannot be attributed to one—and only one—trait. Instead, they are the products of a combination of student traits; prominent among these are ability to recall information and scholastic aptitude.

Difficulty of Construction

The value of the objective test item in the measuring of complex achievement depends directly on the novel situation selected and the description of pictorial material provided. It is already apparent that the selection of the situation is a painstaking operation. Many possibilities are considered before one is selected.

The description of the situation and any pictorial material used must be prepared with equal care. Since the students cannot add or change any features of the description, it must be complete and, above all, unambiguous. Several rewritings of the description or reconstructions of the pictorial material are ordinarily necessary before this is accomplished.

Another factor that complicates the problem of construction is the relationship between the description of the novel situation and the basic question contained in the test item. These two parts must be clearly interdependent if the test item is to measure complex student achievement. In brief, it must be so designed that it can be answered correctly only if the student recalls appropriate facts and uses them in terms of the information contained in the description. Building this interdependence into the test item sounds like a relatively simple task, but it is not. The following is an illustration.

A janitor saw a strange man walking near the high school on the same night that a door was smashed and $400 stolen. He reported this to the police who promptly arrested the man on a burglary charge. Although the man claimed he was innocent, he was held without bail. A fellow prisoner suggested that he should try to obtain a writ of habeas corpus.

(T) F   1. A writ of habeas corpus is a writ inquiring into the lawfulness of the restraint of a person who is imprisoned.

(T) F   2. When a person who is arrested is held without bail, he is allowed to confer with his lawyer.

Observe that it is possible to answer both true-false test items correctly without reading the introductory material. This item is measuring the student's ability to recall information rather than the ability to recall it and then use it effectively. As appropriate as the description of the stranger's troubles seems to be, it is nothing but window-dressing in the test.

Suppose that the last sentence of the introductory material were deleted and that the following two test items replaced the original pair:

(T) F   1. An effective way to help the stranger would be to obtain a writ of habeas corpus.

T (F)   2. The manner in which the stranger was held (i.e., without bail) is a violation of the Tenth Amendment of the Constitution.

It is difficult if not impossible for the student to answer the above questions correctly without reading the description of the novel situation. These changes make the introductory material functional and greatly improve the degree to which the responses reflect higher levels of the cognitive taxonomy rather than knowledge alone.

Response Time Needed

Class time is a precious commodity. The teacher will be pleased with any measuring procedures that require less time and effort than the techniques already available, and concerned about any that seem less efficient. Objective test items for measuring complex achievement are usually placed in the latter category.

No doubt you are impressed with the length of many of the objective items in this chapter, especially the multiple-response type. The first reading consumes plenty of time, but the several that are usually required dangerously lengthen the response time. Unfortunately, attempts to shorten test items are only partially successful. The description of the novel situation can be abbreviated only so much. Any inappropriate reading load will penalize the poor reader. This reduces the effectiveness of these objective test items, particularly in the elementary school.

Another factor that increases student response time is a lack of confidence in the answer. Unlike the responses to recall-of-information test items, the answers do not carry the conviction of correctness. Hence, the student rechecks. This relative lack of confidence carries over from item to item and tends to slow the pace.

The problem of extended student response time may have acquired exaggerated importance in some quarters. Although it is true that these objective test items often consume unduly large amounts of testing time and at best reflect a small sample of complex student achievement, the teacher can hardly justify not using them on this basis alone, unless there are better means of obtaining as much or more information about these student traits. An increase in testing time is, after all, a small price to pay when the reward is a measurement program broadened to obtain evidence of highly important educational outcomes.

Interpretation of Results

Interpretation of results yielded by test items measuring complex achievement is clouded by a variety of traits contributing to the student's response. Examination of test items in this chapter shows us that behavioral changes at several levels of the cognitive taxonomy are probably intermixed. After all, knowledge is the building material for more complex cognitive achievement. Therefore a correct response means that several correct steps have been taken. Failure to answer a test item correctly means that the students failed to perform one or more steps correctly. Yet the teacher does not know which these are. In a simple case, the teacher might ask whether the students failed to give the right answer because they could not recall the necessary information correctly, or could not use it in terms of the novel situation after they recalled it.

The manner in which the objective test items discussed here are constructed does not provide any appreciable information with which to answer this question. Nor does it allow us to determine the full meaning of a correct response. If students respond correctly, does this mean that they simply followed a correct procedure, or that they followed the most efficient correct procedure? A correct response does not mean that the students have full command of the steps required any more than an incorrect response means that they have no command of them.

Testing techniques have been developed that reveal in greater detail the procedures that examinees follow in attempting to solve a problem. Prominent among these are the tab item technique (Glaser, Damrin, & Gardner, 1960), and written simulation exercises (McGuire & Babbott, 1967; McGuire, Solomon, & Bashook, 1976).

The tab item described is designed to measure the proficiency of technicians in detecting the defective unit in a television set that is not operating properly. They are provided with a description of the malfunction, a diagram of the television set, a list of check procedures that might be employed to determine the cause, and a list of possibly defective units. Opposite each check procedure is a tab, under which is a verbal or diagrammatic description of the results the examinees would have obtained if they had actually performed the procedure. The examinees try to locate the defective unit by making as few check procedures as possible. They begin by selecting one, tearing off the tab, and uncovering the information produced if the procedure is actually followed. They continue to do this until they have diagnosed the difficulty. The pattern of removed tabs reveals all of the steps taken; the sequence of the steps can also be recorded.

Written simulation exercises have been used in medical education for some time. They are designed to test the skill of medical students in gathering data about a patient and making judgments for correcting the ailments described. A brief verbal description or a short color film is provided in which the patient's complaints are recounted. The examinees then choose one of several starting points to be used to alleviate the difficulty, after which they use a special "developer" pen to obtain additional information printed on the answer sheet by a latent-image method. This new information directs the examinees to lists of specific inquiries that are available for each intervention. Usually they can select as many inquiries as they wish, each of which provides additional information of possible use in solving the problem in an efficient manner. On the basis of the new data, they continue the treatment until their efforts result in the patient's recovery, referral to a specialist, or in some cases, death.

Although the construction of simulation exercises is a demanding task, their use in achievement testing is increasing when teachers wish to measure student problem-solving skills in a particular subject matter area. The characteristics of paper-and-pencil exercises designed to simulate the decision-making process are as follows (McGuire, Solomon, & Bashook, 1976, pp. 7–8):

1. The exercise should be initiated in a realistic manner. The problem must be brought to the student's attention in a form resembling that which would be presented in the real world, not as a predigested summary of the salient features of the situation.

2. The exercise should require a series of sequential, interdependent decisions representative of the various stages in the definition, analysis, and resolution of the problem.

3. The exercises must permit the student to make decisions and to obtain realistic information about the results of each inquiry or action as a basis for subsequent decision.

4. Once this information has been obtained, it must be impossible for the student to retract a decision (i.e., "change an answer") even if it is revealed to be ineffectual or harmful.

5. The exercise should be constructed in such a way as to allow each student to approach the task in his or her own way and to follow that approach throughout. Hence, provision should be made for alternate paths through the exercise and for variations in feedback appropriate to the approach each individual student selects.

6. If the simulation is to be lifelike, the problem should evolve and the situation should change in response to the specific actions taken by each student.

7. These changes in conditions must differ among students according to the unique configuration of prior decisions each has made.

Clearly, the simulation exercises differ from tab items in an important way; specifically, the problem is modified by the intervening steps taken by the examinees. For this reason these are called *branched* exercises. Several routes may lead to an acceptable outcome. In the tab technique the same problem is presented to all examinees and it remains the same. This is known as a *linear* exercise. In both cases the path followed by an examinee is well defined and our understanding of the degree of achievement present is enlarged.

Influence of Mental Ability.   A final question that is frequently asked is whether objective tests that measure higher order achievement are appreciably different from tests of mental ability (Madaus, Woods, & Nuttall, 1973). In other words, are these tests achievement tests at all? Certainly the student's mental ability plays an important role; there is evidence, however, that these are not the same as tests of mental ability. The results yielded by the two types of tests are positively related, but not to a perfect degree by any means.

PROBLEM

7. The first four levels of the cognitive domain (that is, knowledge, comprehension, application, and analysis) can be regarded as convergent thinking, whereas synthesis seems to be a type of divergent thinking (Bloom, Hastings, & Madaus, 1971, pp. 193–194). How does this affect the usefulness of objective test items for measuring complex achievement?

Open-Book Testing

Teachers typically administer closed-book tests. The students have no source materials at their disposal that would provide correct answers to any of the test items. They depend exclusively on memory and their ability to manipulate successfully what they remember. Occasionally the teacher modifies the rules slightly; although access to the textbook and many reference books may be forbidden, a restricted number of source materials is allowed. For example, in some mathematics tests the students are permitted to use tables for logarithms, tables of trigonometric functions, or tables of squares, square roots, and reciprocals. During science tests the periodic table of elements is prominently displayed, and various chemical, zoological, and botanical handbooks are available. In social studies tests, the students are sometimes allowed to refer to certain maps and charts. Furthermore, English teachers approve the use of a dictionary during some of their tests. Perhaps these should be called limited closed-book tests.

If the test or test item being administered measures only knowledge, the use of the traditional closed-book approach can be effectively defended. After all, an open-book administration with ample time limits may tell us little more about students' achievement than whether they can use textbooks and other reference materials to find the correct answers to a list of questions. If the test or test item being administered measures primarily complex achievement, however, the use of the traditional closed-book procedure seems to be an unnecessary restriction. An open-book administration is much more realistic. Since a basic purpose of this type of measurement is to discover whether the students can use their knowledge in everyday living, the test situation should simulate the natural situation as much as possible and allow the students the use of the normal tools and aids they would have in the natural situation.

The debate on closed- or open-book testing procedures gets complicated when we try to establish the degree to which the test or test item measures primarily complex achievement. It is clear from inspection of the sample test items included in this chapter that a number of levels of the cognitive taxonomy are involved in each, that the relative amount of each varies from item to item, and that this balance can be controlled by the person building it. Furthermore, no matter what the test item may seem to measure on the surface, the learning experiences of the students answering the test item must also be known before the behavioral patterns it measures can be determined.

The final decision is, of course, in the hands of the classroom teachers. If they believe that tests for knowledge should follow the traditional closed-book procedure and that tests for complex achievement should be open-book, then on the basis of the knowledge of the test items, the students, and the student's experiences, the teachers may separate the test items and administer them accordingly. For those items about which they are in doubt, they must decide which evidence of a student behavioral change is more important and classify the item accordingly.

Building Open-Book Tests

Constructing test items for an open-book test is probably more difficult than constructing those for a closed-book test. Some of the suggestions for constructing objective test items already discussed must be followed with great care. For example, efforts to avoid textbook terminology should be redoubled. Copying verbatim from a textbook, even when designing test items for a closed-book test, is dangerous; for those items to be included in an open-book test, it is very damaging.

Above all, the teacher must construct each test so that the textbook or reference materials will be used in much the same manner as they would be in a similar problem in a natural situation. Although this requirement cannot be fully satisfied, attempts to meet it typically yield good results. For instance, in a mathematics test the textbook may be of little direct help to students as they decide which formula to use to solve the problem, but it does provide an accurate statement of any formula selected. In a social studies test an encyclopedia to which the student can refer may serve a similar function. The students need not trust memory here, any more than they would in a similar everyday situation in which they wanted to use a given formula or historical fact. In other words, the materials to which the student has access in a test should play a supporting role only. The test item should be designed to effect such a condition.

Administering Open-Book Tests

If students are given an open-book test, they should be forewarned. The reference materials they can use should be carefully listed for them. Perhaps there will be no restrictions, or, as some teachers prefer, the list may include only those materials that might be used in a typical out-of-class situation. In any event, the availability of the materials listed will greatly influence the manner in which the students prepare for the test. Quite possibly they will concentrate less on factual details and more on broad principles and relationships. Moreover, they may try to become more familiar with the reference materials' content and organization.

Teachers sometimes argue that if an open-book test is to be used and no restrictions placed on the reference materials, class time need not be used for its administration. Instead, the student can write the test at home. Although the so-called take-home test has some merit, it suffers from two serious disadvantages. First, the teacher has no certainty that the student will work independently. Any assistance destroys the worth of the test results. Secondly, the student writing the test at home does not have an opportunity to ask legitimate questions about the items or procedure. Since tests are rarely so well-constructed that no questions are necessary, the student should not be denied the chance to ask pertinent questions.

PROBLEM

8. Some believe that open-book testing causes students to study less, and that they therefore fail to gain full understanding. Do you agree? Why?

SUMMARY

The primary points raised in this chapter are these:

1. A paper-and-pencil achievement testing program measuring only the student's knowledge is quite inadequate. Where possible, a testing program should be extended to measure their more complex cognitive achievement as well. In other words, it should determine whether the students know the meaning behind the knowledge, grasp the interrelationships among different parts, and can take intelligent action. With enough ingenuity and care, the classroom teacher can construct objective test items capable of eliciting these behavioral patterns from the student.

2. When students acquire higher order achievement, they can use knowledge effectively. Therefore, evidence of this fact can be obtained by asking them questions about a carefully contrived situation that is new. To answer these questions correctly, they must recall the appropriate part of a total store of

knowledge and use it in terms of the novel situation described. If they can do so, they have achieved important, complex educational goals.

3. The novel situations are difficult to develop. First, they must involve one or more of the upper levels of the cognitive taxonomy in which the teacher is interested. Secondly, they must be realistic, relatively commonplace, and plausible. Finally, they should require only a short description and/or comparatively simple pictorial material to be understood.

4. The question or questions concerning the novel situation can be presented as one or more objective test items. Any type of objective item can be used. Integrating the test items with the pictorial material or description of the novel situation requires special care.

5. Objective test items for measuring complex achievement have the principal advantage of offering teachers a convenient extension of familiar testing procedures to increase the scope of their achievement evaluations without sacrificing objectivity of scoring. The principal limitations are that the test items are difficult to build, the students need considerable time in which to respond, and the test results are hard to interpret.

6. The possibility of using an open-book testing procedure should be seriously explored when more than knowledge is being measured, since, in these situations, it is reasonable that the student be allowed to use tools and aids normally available.

SUGGESTED READINGS

BLOOM, B. S., HASTINGS, J. T., & MADAUS, G. F. *Handbook on formative and summative evaluation of student learning*. New York: McGraw-Hill, 1971.
In chapters 8 and 9, objectives and illustrative test items are given for the highest four levels of the cognitive taxonomy, namely, application, analysis, synthesis, and evaluation. Many of the test items are objective, others are essay questions.

EDUCATIONAL TESTING SERVICE. *Multiple-choice questions: A close look*. Princeton, N.J.: Author, 1973.
For the purpose of dispelling the myth that objective test items require no thought or insight by the students who respond, twenty-two test items in a variety of subject matter areas are reproduced in their entirety.

GRONLUND, N. E. *Constructing achievement tests* (2nd ed.). Englewood Cliffs, N.J.: Prentice-Hall, 1977.
In chapter 4, guidelines are given for constructing both simple and complex test items for measuring higher levels of achievement, particularly in the areas of comprehension, application, and analysis.

McGUIRE, C. H., SOLOMON, L. M., & BASHOOK, P. G. *Construction and use of written simulations*. New York: The Psychological Corporation, 1976.
The authors believe that written simulations can be applied in a wide variety of subject matter areas and educational levels. Methods of construction are explained, and several concrete examples are provided. To introduce simulation exercises, an example requiring the reader to assume the role of vacationer and find a distant relative in a foreign city is provided.

SMITH, R. B. A discussion of an attempt at constructing reproducible item sets. *Journal of Educational Measurement*, 1968, 5, 55–60.
Central to this article is a set of eight objective test items based on a novel experiment dealing with the reflection and absorption of light. Each of the six levels of the cognitive taxonomy is represented by at least one item.

WESMAN, A. G. Writing the test item. In R. L. Thorndike (Ed.), *Educational measurement* (2nd ed.). Washington, D.C.: American Council on Education, 1971. See chapter 4.
The last portion of this chapter concerns "context-dependent" objective test items, including items based on pictorial or tabular materials. Suggestions for constructing such items and also illustrations of them are provided.

REFERENCES CITED

BLOOM, B. S., HASTINGS, J. T., & MADAUS, G. F. *Handbook on formative and summative evaluation of student learning.* New York: McGraw-Hill, 1971.

EBEL, R. L. *Practical problems in educational measurement.* Lexington, Mass.: D. C. Heath, 1980.

EDUCATIONAL TESTING SERVICE. *Multiple-choice questions: A close look.* Princeton, N.J.: Author, 1973.

GLASER, R., DAMRIN, D. E., & GARDNER, F. M. The tab item: A technique for the measurement of proficiency in diagnostic problem-solving tasks. In A. A. Lumsdaine & R. Glaser (Eds.), *Teaching machines and programmed learning: A source book.* Washington, D.C.: National Educational Association, 1960, 275–285.

MCGUIRE, C. H., & BABBOTT, D. Simulation techniques in the measurement of problem-solving skills. *Journal of Educational Measurement*, 1967, 4, 1–10.

MCGUIRE, C. H., SOLOMON, L. M., & BASHOOK, P. G. *Construction and use of written simulations.* New York: The Psychological Corporation, 1976.

MADAUS, G. F., WOODS, E. M., & NUTTALL, R. L. A causal model analysis of Bloom's taxonomy. *American Educational Research Journal*, 1973, 10, 253–262.

NATIONAL ASSESSMENT OF EDUCATIONAL PROGRESS. First results for 1970–71 assessment show literary comprehension limited. *NAEP Newsletter*, 1972–73, 6, 1–3.

SMITH, R. B. A discussion of an attempt at constructing reproducible item sets. *Journal of Educational Measurement*, 1968, 5, 55–60.

SOLOMON, R. J. New directions in assessing achievement. *Proceedings of the 1965 Western Regional Conference on Testing Problems.* Princeton, N.J.: Educational Testing Service, 1965, 45–51.

5

Preparing Essay Achievement Tests

The purpose of this chapter is to help you

1. Understand the nature of essay test items and their function in achievement testing

2. Distinguish between extended-response and limited-response essay items, and illustrate their uses when measuring student achievement

3. Construct acceptable essay items for classroom use, adhering in all instances to the guidelines governing their construction

4. Understand the sometimes dangerous degree of unreliability present in the scoring of essay items and prepare adequate safeguards for this process

5. Score student responses to essay test items using either the analytical method or the rating method

6. Differentiate between objective and essay test items in terms of function, construction, scoring, and interpretation of results

7. Develop norm-referenced achievement tests including objective and essay test items to measure both student knowledge and complex achievement

Skilled trial lawyers in action are a pleasure to watch. With great precision and organization, they carefully extract information from witnesses—information that, of course, they hope will be beneficial to the clients. They may do this in such a way as to capitalize on any dramatic effects that are present, and they may later summarize the testimony presented to accentuate whatever casts a favorable light on the case and to deemphasize whatever does not.

It is difficult to imagine the amount of preliminary preparation that lawyers must make before they ever appear in court. Even the framing of the questions to be presented to the witnesses must be carefully planned. The questions need not reveal all the information the witness can recall. Most of this information is irrelevant; some of it may even be damaging to the case. Framing and presenting helpful questions without resorting to leading questions, which the judge might disallow, is a genuine art.

Classroom teachers trying to measure academic achievement with essay tests might tear a page from the lawyer's "how to" book. Teachers are also asking questions of reasonably cooperative subjects; they, too, are interested in soliciting certain kinds of information and no other. Therefore, it seems reasonable to expect that the task faced by the teacher who frames questions for students is essentially the same as that faced by the lawyer who prepares to examine a witness. Each has in mind distinct purposes that the questions are to serve. If the questions are to serve their respective purposes, they must be prepared deliberately.

Unfortunately, the teacher's questions designed to reveal student achievements are usually only partly successful. Consider for a moment oral questioning. Notice how frequently the students attempting to answer a question must ask their own questions to clarify the task. They may want to know the definition of some of the terms, or whether a certain basic assumption should be made when answering, or how much detail is desired. Only after this confusion has been dispelled can the original question be answered. The cost in time and frustration is sometimes considerable.

The essay test items included in a paper-and-pencil achievement test are generally a distinct improvement in this respect. Their preparation is much more systematic. Yet there is still unnecessary student confusion. In spite of the fact that few questions about the test are asked when it is administered, a review of the students' responses customarily reveals considerable uncertainty about one or more questions. Sometimes this review may even lead one to believe that the student would have written a correct answer if he or she had understood the question. In such cases, the questions are clearly not serving the purpose for which they were intended.

When compared with the procedures for constructing objective items, those for constructing essay items seem simple. Nevertheless, you cannot use essay items with consistent success unless the questions are planned. The fact that essay test items are deceptively simple in appearance and hence in construction is the reason why many of their potential values have not been entirely realized.

Characteristics of Essay Test Items

An essay test item is one for which the student supplies, rather than selects, the correct answer. More specifically, an essay item demands a response composed by the student, usually in one or more sentences, of a nature that no single response or pattern of responses can be listed as correct, and the accuracy and quality of which can be judged subjectively only by a person skilled and informed in the subject, customarily the classroom teacher. The important features of this description are the freedom of response allowed the student and the difficulty of scoring the responses. The first is used as a basis for classifying essay items; the second indicates the most perplexing problem associated with essay items, a problem treated in detail later in this chapter.

Freedom of Response

The freedom of response allowed the student may vary appreciably from one essay test item to another. Consider the following items, both of which are designed for use in a secondary school, the first in an American political science achievement test, and the second in a European history achievement test.

> In your opinion is the federal government of the United States more or less democratic today than it was at the end of the eighteenth century? Give reasons for your answer.

> Describe the history of the papacy from its origins to the present, concentrating on its social, political, and religious impact on Europe.

Both of these test items demand extended responses from the students. In fact the typical reaction to each would be ". . . but I could write a book about it." This is justified in both instances. Both items are tapping a higher order of learning than some objective test items; only those students who can recall what they have learned, evaluate it in terms of the question, and then organize it into a suitable answer will succeed.

In contrast, examine the following items, one of which is taken from an elementary school test dealing with a health unit, the second from a junior high school general science test.

> Bill and Tom are students in the sixth grade. They try to take good care of their teeth. Both brush them immediately after their morning and evening meals, but do not brush them after their noon meal or after eating between meals. Both have the dentist inspect their teeth every six months. However, Bill's teeth decay more easily than Tom's. Give possible reasons why this is true.

> An athlete wishes to know the amount of time he needs to run 100 yards. He stations one man at the starting line with a revolver and a second at the finish line with a stop watch. In order to time the athlete accurately, should the man at the finish line start the watch at the moment he sees the flash of the revolver or the moment he hears the sound of the shot? Why?

In terms of freedom of response, these two essay items represent the opposite extremes. The correct responses are now quite specific; notice also that, if the two situations described are novel, more than recall of information is required of the student.

The variations in freedom of response allowed the student offer a crude but useful means of classifying essay test items into types. At least two principal types can be established: the *extended-response* type, as illustrated by the first pair of test items, and the *restricted-response* type, as illustrated by the second pair.

Extended Response. The extended response has much to be said in its favor. It can be extremely challenging to students. To respond correctly, students must display such traits as their ability to organize, evaluate, write clearly, and be creative. Thus, the responses to these test items show how well the students have achieved important educational goals, possibly at the synthesis or evaluation levels of the cognitive taxonomy.

Extended-response essay questions are sometimes more suitably used as term paper topics or "take-home" tests rather than as "in-class" tests. Furthermore, they have value as teaching devices or as stimulus material when measuring writing ability instead of achievement in a subject matter area.

Restricted Response. The restricted-response essay item is of greater concern to us in the measurement of student achievement except as a measure of writing ability. This type of essay item differs from the first in that the perimeter of student response is better defined. A specific problem is presented. It requires the students to recall the proper information, organize it in a suitable manner, arrive at a defensible conclusion, and express it in their own words. In several important respects, it requires students to reveal abilities much like those required by a satisfactory answer to an extended-response essay test item. However, this display must occur within well-defined restrictions. These restrictions simplify the scoring problem, thereby greatly improving the reliability of the scoring.

Observe that the restricted-response essay item is far removed from the supply type of test item described in Chapter 3. In the first place, it differs in the amount of freedom of response allowed. Although the restricted-response essay sets limits in this respect, it does not confine the response to a word or two; on the contrary, a paragraph or more is usually needed if the question is to be answered properly. Secondly, it differs in terms of the behavioral changes reflected. The short-answer test is almost invariably used as a means of measuring student knowledge; the restricted-response essay item can be used for this purpose or designed to measure more complex student achievement. The latter is a very important function of the essay item.

PROBLEMS

1. Construct a supply item for an objective test and a restricted-response item for an essay test. Design the latter so that it overlaps the scope of the objective test item. Compare the two in terms of the cognitive levels of the student behavioral patterns required to respond correctly.

2. Differentiate between essay items designed to measure achievement in a subject matter area and those designed to measure ability to write (Coffman, 1971). Construct a test item of each type.

Constructing Essay Test Items

Essay test items are quite popular in the classroom as a method of measuring educational achievement. Objective items are heavily used in standardized achievement tests, but not to the point of excluding the essay type. Essay questions are an important component of the National Assessment of Educational Progress. They have also been used as a part of the *Sequential Tests of Educational Progress (STEP)* and some of the achievement testing programs conducted by the College Entrance Examination Board (CEEB).

Preparing and scoring writing ability tests have received considerable attention from teachers and testing specialists. To measure writing ability, objective and semi-objective items are being used alone and in conjunction with essay items that often require between twenty to forty minutes of testing time. Combinations of these testing methods seem to be satisfactory means of measuring writing ability (Breland & Gaynor, 1979). Methods of evaluating writing samples are described in Chapter 7.

With the possible exception of those cases in which evidence of writing ability is desired, the extended-response essay item has limited value as a measuring tool. Therefore, the remainder of this chapter is devoted to the restricted-response type.

Teachers usually consider essay items relatively easy to construct since they require less time and technical skill than objective items. The task, however, is not a simple one. Four important considerations confront the teacher in constructing essay items:

1. Relating the essay item to one or more cells of the table of specifications, or a specific objective
2. Sampling the pertinent subject matter adequately
3. Determining the amount of freedom of response to be allowed the student
4. Establishing a suitable time allotment for the student's response

The four categories overlap each other to some degree and are not of equal importance. However, each is sufficiently important that it cannot be ignored in the process of constructing essay items and arranging them as parts of a test. Failure to comply with the suggestions stemming from any one of the categories may cause otherwise well-designed essay items to fail.

Relating Essay Items to Tables of
Specifications or to Specific Objectives

As in the case of the objective test item, the essay test item is a direct outgrowth of one or more cells of the table of specifications or specific objectives. Yet the objective and essay test items do not merely duplicate each other. Like a station wagon and a sports car, they both perform all the necessary functions, but not with equal ease and efficiency.

As you know, objective test items can be used to measure student knowledge with considerable success. Using them, the teacher can sample broadly with a minimum expenditure of time. Measuring complex cognitive achievement with objective test items is an effective approach, but not to the same degree as measuring knowledge. The difficulties of item construction and the length of response time pose problems. The essay item, on the other hand, presents a different picture. It is not as efficient a means of measuring student knowledge as an objective test, particularly because scoring the answers is a demanding task. As a means of measuring complex achievement, however, it offers many encouraging possibilities.

For these reasons, objective items for norm-referenced tests are often developed primarily in terms of the cells of the table involving knowledge, and the essay items in terms of cells involving other levels of the cognitive taxonomy. This means that the achievement test frequently will be composed of both types of items. Such tests offer the student some variety. They also distribute the teacher's work load. The construction of the objective item requires more time before the test, and the scoring of the essay item requires more time after the test.

In addition to differing in the kind of table of specifications cells with which they are associated, the objective and essay items commonly differ in the number with which they are associated. Most often, the objective item is primarily related to one cell and perhaps secondarily to another. The essay item quite frequently is related to several in both cases. It deals with a larger whole than the objective item. The correct response to it has several subparts. These may easily involve one group of cells in the table of specifications in a primary manner and another in a secondary manner.

Care must be exercised if we are to maintain a high degree of content validity in a norm-referenced achievement test containing essay items. For instance, suppose that a teacher using an essay item for measuring complex student achievement finds that it is primarily related to several cells pertaining to knowledge. In addition, it may be secondarily related to still other cells. If this is true, any objective test items included in the same test for measuring knowledge must be readjusted accordingly. Only when the various subparts of the correct response to an essay test item are identified and analyzed can the relationship between that item and the table of specifications be determined. The contribution of the item to the content validity of the test containing it can then be established.

In summary, teachers take the following steps as they build essay test items according to the table of specifications for a norm-referenced test. First, they select the cell or group of cells dealing with complex cognitive achievement (and some dealing with knowledge) to which the item is to be related. With these in mind, they start their search for suitable item content, most likely a novel situation. When the situation is identified, they frame one or more questions. Finally, they compose the correct response, separate it into its subparts, and cross-refer them with the cells in the table of specifications. They may discover that the cells they originally had in mind are not involved in the test item in exactly the manner initially intended. Therefore, they may alter the item to support their first plan, or they may expand or contract in an appropriate manner other essay and objective items to be included.

In the case of criterion-referenced testing, there also may be content validity problems if one is not careful. Objective as well as essay test items should be the direct outgrowth of a specific objective. Ordinarily this relationship is quite obvious. Nevertheless, to be satisfactory, the test item must require that the student clearly display the criterion behavior necessary for mastery of the objective in question. For instance, if the objective requires the student to "list," "contrast," or "state a rule," then the essay item should be designed to require the student to perform accordingly in as direct a manner as possible.

Sampling Subject Matter Adequately

The problems of sampling subject matter for an achievement test are essentially the same as those of a reader selecting a novel in the library. A basic problem in both cases is the size of the sample. How large must the sample be to guarantee that the generalizations based on it will be correct? Both situations have practical restrictions on the size of the sample. The test cannot have more than a certain number of test items because of limited time. The reader thumbing pages at random will not scan endlessly because it requires too much time and may spoil the novel when read in its entirety.

The variety of the population sampled also affects the size of sample needed. For example, sampling a homogeneous mixture, such as a bottle of milk or a bag of well-mixed inorganic fertilizer, is comparatively simple; a relatively small sample will no doubt be sufficiently representative. On the other hand, sampling such heterogeneous "mixtures" as subject matter and complex mental processes is difficult. Inevitably, large samples are needed if one is to have confidence in the breadth of the sample.

In light of this discussion, the inadequate subject matter sampling of the essay test comes into focus. The typical norm-referenced or criterion-referenced essay achievement test contains only a handful of test items; therefore, despite the fact that each item may have a number of subparts, the test is a distressingly small sample when the variety of most subject matter is considered. The possibility that the sample is unrepresentative is increased. Otherwise stated, its content validity is quite possibly less than satisfactory. There is greater likelihood that well-prepared students might have the misfortune to find that one or more test items touch on their weak areas; hence they respond poorly, and the total test results underestimate true achievement.

Restrictions on testing time may cause a classroom achievement test dominated by essay items to seem very narrow in scope when judged in light of the table of specifications or objectives used. Under such restrictions, it is advisable to replace each essay item requiring a long response with several requiring shorter responses. A careful adjustment will cause the degree of content validity and reliability of the test to rise appreciably.

Use of Optional Test Items.   Some teachers try to reduce the sampling limitation of the essay item with optional items. For instance, twelve test items might be listed in a norm-referenced test, and the student allowed to answer any eight of them. Rather than improve the sampling, this procedure weakens it. Since many students will make partially different selections, they are, in effect, confronted with partially different samples. The content validity depends on the particular combination the student chooses, since test content and the meaning of the score varies from student to student. A direct comparison of the various test scores cannot be defended.

A different use of optional test items is that in which a series to be answered by all students is first presented, and a series of paired items follows. The student is to choose one of each pair. The members of each pair are considered to be equivalent test items; they are of the same level of difficulty, require approximately the same response time, are based on the same combination of cells in the table of specifications, and so forth. Thus, ideally, the content validity would be the same for all practical purposes no matter what choices the student made; yet the test is somewhat more flexible.

The last-mentioned use of optional test items is much more defensible than the first described. Nevertheless, it cannot be recommended. It doesn't relieve the basic difficulty, which is that certain cells of the table of specifications are not represented in the test. The pairs are merely independent test items representing the same combinations of cells. Building equivalent test items is, of course, no simple task. Moreover, they increase the scoring labor because the scorer has a great variety of items to score.

Determining the Amount of Freedom of Response

"How much detail should I give?" is a common question asked by students confronted with an essay test item. The answer is particularly important if they are well aware of the fact that the response will be scored in terms of exactly what is written; that is, no credit will be allowed for what they seem to have written or for statements that are essentially correct but not pertinent. Students recognize that they will waste valuable testing time by making a very detailed response if detail is not required, or that they will lose significant amounts of credit for the response if they erroneously assume that the teacher allows no credit for minor but important detail.

The teacher is also penalized by any student uncertainty as to the amount of detailed information that the correct response should contain. If a great deal is expected but this fact is not explicitly known, the students who did not include the details, but could have, will complain when penalized. If the teacher expects only the major elements but does not make this fact explicitly known, some students will include unnecessary information, thus lengthening their responses greatly, and complicating the scoring task.

The essay item must be so framed that all students will easily recognize exactly the task they are to perform. They should all understand the question in the same way. Any confusion or uncertainty that they may experience should be attributed to an inability to answer correctly rather than a failure to understand the purpose of the test item.

To achieve this clarity in an essay test item is often difficult. On the other hand, violations of this principle can be easily identified and corrected, at least partially.

For instance, consider the following essay item, intended for use in a secondary school social studies test:

> Today both major political parties of the United States include members representing practically every shade of political conviction between arch conservatism and extreme liberalism. Suppose that a rearrangement of membership took place so that the Republican Party acquired a truly conservative philosophy and the Democratic Party a truly liberal philosophy. What would happen to the political situation in this country?

Imagine the great variety of responses that this test item would elicit. The impact of such a drastic rearrangement of the political parties could be discussed in terms of the changes in the sizes of the parties, their financial resources, leadership, appeal to the general public, platforms, and control of state legislatures, governorships, the presidency, and Congress. One student could have written successfully about several of these topics, another about several different topics, and yet both could have missed the point of the test item and consequently lost credit. In short, the task to be performed is not clearly defined and, as a result, even the well-informed student will very likely be penalized.

Suppose the question at the end of the test item is replaced by the following:

> Compare the present platforms of the two parties with the platforms that you think the parties would adopt after the rearrangement of membership. Restrict your comparison to the areas of (1) civil rights legislation and (2) energy legislation.

Now the task is better identified. It is only in terms of certain aspects of the platforms that comparisons are to be made between present and hypothetical party composition. A framework for the student's response is established. Incidentally, notice that the test item still requires the student to select information, organize it properly, and present it as an integrated whole. Although the framework restricts the student's freedom of response, it does not do so to the point where the test item elicits only an extremely specific response dealing with superficial knowledge.

Attempts to clearly define the student's task have contributed to the general decline in the use of expressions such as "discuss," "tell about," and "give your opinion of." In their place has come a series of different expressions that, when used individually or in combination, tend to clarify the intent of the test item. Typical of these expressions are the following: "explain," "relate," "interpret," "compare," "discriminate," "select significant ideas," "contrast," and "state the conclusion." The list is suggestive only.

Establishing Suitable Time Limits

Suitable time limits for essay tests are even more difficult to establish than those for objective tests. First, some teachers find it more difficult to estimate the level of difficulty of essay items and overestimate or underestimate the response time needed. Secondly, students vary in terms of the speed at which they can write and, as the test progresses, in their susceptibility to fatigue. Third, a well-designed test item forces the students to marshall the facts and organize them in a suitable manner. To do so they may sketch out the preliminary notes or even a complete outline, and then write the answer on the basis of such notes. The amount of time needed for this is another uncertain variable. Finally, if student responses are to be scored partly in terms of organization, spelling, and grammatical accuracy, they will need more response time.

There is a tendency to allow too little response time for essay tests. The students must rush through at top speed if they hope to finish. The immediate results are, of course, a steady deterioration in the legibility of the handwriting and the organization of the answer, with consequent complications in scoring.

Suitable time limits can be determined by pretesting the items on a similar group of students under normal conditions, and any needed adjustments made on the basis of this trial. Since this can rarely be done, teachers must rely on past experiences with similar test items and students, or they might note the time needed to *write* a complete model answer for each time. Estimating time allotments for each item and listing them on the test copy helps to formulate such judgments. When in doubt, the teacher should allow too much rather than too little time. It is better to have fewer or shorter responses and not have to worry about a speed factor.

PROBLEMS

3. Would the essay item concerning the two political parties (see page 144) be strengthened by stipulating what is meant by a *truly conservative philosophy* and a *truly liberal philosophy?* Why?

4. Criticize and strengthen as you see fit the following essay items which were included in a ninth grade socal studies test administered at the completion of a unit devoted to government organization, functions, and services.
   a. An amendment was proposed in the Congress to have the electoral college vote proportionately, according to actual vote of the people.
      1. How would this change the present system?
      2. Would this proposal strengthen the democratic control of the people and would it lead to a probable increased vote? Give reasons for your answers.
   b. The Supreme Court has nine members. Do you feel this number is too large, too small, or just right to carry the responsibilities of the court? Give reasons.

Administering Essay Test Items

The administration of essay test items involves many of the same principles and procedures described in the two preceding chapters in connection with objective tests. Hence, these need not be repeated here. Two features of test administration that deserve additional comment for essay test items are the directions to the students and the use of open-book testing.

Unlike the directions given in objective tests, those for essay test items are quite simple. Most often the test items are sufficiently self-contained so that few students need any additional information to formulate satisfactory responses. The directions are sometimes omitted, or, if given, are more complicated than the following:

> *Directions:* Answer the following question in as brief a manner as possible. Only a few sentences will be necessary in order to cover the important points needed to answer each.

Special features of the test must be mentioned in the directions. For example, a brief description of the basis for scoring is sometimes included. Classroom teachers can point out if they plan to add or subtract credit for penmanship, style of writing, grammar, or spelling. They should also mention any restrictions on the time allowed or the type of paper to be used, the amount of space on the paper allowed for the response, or the use of pen or pencil.

Using the essay test item primarily as a means of measuring complex achievement suggests an open-book test. If this point of view is accepted, then the question is raised as to whether the students could write the answers at home rather than in the classroom. The open-book, take-home administration of essay test items is somewhat common. The task may now fall under the classification of "homework" rather than a test, but, with the proper design of the questions and the cooperation of the students, it still can serve as a test with generous time limits.

Scoring Essay Test Items

The scoring of student responses to an essay test item is unquestionably the most disagreeable task related to the use of these items. In the first place, teachers are understandably reluctant to allot the great quantities of time that are needed if the job is to be done properly. Also, they are concerned about their ability to recognize the variation of quality in the responses; such judgments may be highly subjective. Perhaps the teacher's state of mind or the name of the student at the top of the page are more powerful factors in determining the quality of the response than the response itself. These and other doubts cause the scoring problem to be an important one.

The problem is also complicated by the testwiseness of the student. This is the same element that reduces the effectiveness of objective achievement tests, but it manifests itself in a different manner here. An imaginative method of faking responses to the essay test item is to practice the art of "precise vagueness." The students take great pains to write at length in a flowing, colorful style. They also take great pains not to commit themselves; they skirt the issue as closely as possible without actually facing it. In short, they want to impress the scorer without revealing their ignorance. An illustration of this technique is the following student response to a test item requiring an evaluation of the causes of Napoleon Bonaparte's fall from power.

There was a day when Napoleon Bonaparte was at the pinnacle of success. People admired him and respected him. He was the outstanding leader in Europe. But this could not last forever. Difficulties arose. These difficulties were political, economical, social, and, of course, military. Moreover, they were not always obvious. Indeed, some were so subtle that even Napoleon himself was not aware of them. Nevertheless, obvious or subtle, these difficulties were sufficiently powerful that, in combination, they toppled him from power.

The relative importance of these difficulties is hard to determine. It would seem that some were clearly more important than others. This is to say that some contributed more directly to Napoleon's fall than did others. . . .

Paragraph after paragraph, perhaps page after page, the student continues to string one vague sentence to the end of another. Each rings of accuracy. Yet the true worth of such an answer is elusive; like a puff of smoke, it seems to disappear as you reach for it. The foregoing response is essentially empty. Yet, in the face of its impressive length and style, it would require a teacher well-schooled in the art of scoring responses to essay test items to recognize this and score accordingly.

Testing specialists have devoted considerable attention to simplifying the task of scoring responses to essay test items and to improving the reliability of the scoring process. Their efforts have been somewhat successful. Well-established general suggestions have been formulated and several methods of scoring have been devised and used.

Improving the Scoring of Essay Items

There are four general suggestions for improving the scoring of essay items.

Score the students' responses anonymously. It has been demonstrated that the "halo effect" can appreciably reduce objectivity of scoring. Because a certain student has written the response, the teacher expects a certain quality of response and has, in effect, prejudged it. The identical response written by a student with a decidedly different reputation will receive a different amount of credit (Chase, 1979).

To conceal the identity of the examinee is not easy. If the teacher is familiar with students' penmanship or writing style, it is virtually impossible. Should this not be the case, the use of numbers, rather than names, to identify the responses, or the practice of having the student's name written on the back of the paper, will provide a simple but effective means of maintaining anonymity.

Score all responses to each test item at one time. Only when this is done, and one item is completely finished, should the responses to any other item in the test be examined. This means that, instead of the responses to all test items by one student being scored at one time, as is most often true of an objective test, the responses to one test item by all of the students are scored at one time.

Two advantages are thereby gained. First, it is easier to maintain a constant or near-constant set of standards on the basis of which each response is to be judged. All details of the completely correct responses can be remembered, and comparisons between and among various responses can be made. Secondly, any "halo effect" that might modify the scoring of all responses by one student in a test tends to be minimized. In other words, the way in which a student answers one test item will not influence the judgment of the teacher when scoring the response to a second test item that is more or less independent of the first.

If the spelling, penmanship, grammar, and writing style of the responses are to be scored, it should be done independently of the subject matter content. In other words, *how* students write should be judged apart from *what* they write. You can easily imagine instances in which one might be of a very different quality from the other. There may also be instances in which the quality of one affects the teacher's judgment of the quality of the other. An all too common occurrence is the case in which accurate spelling, legible handwriting, and pleasant style upgrade the rating of the quality of the content of the response, whereas substandard spelling, handwriting, and style create the opposite effect (Marshall, 1972).

It is frequently asked whether the quality of grammar, spelling, handwriting, and style should be scored at all. The answer is simple. If any or all of these are a part of the educational objectives, they should be scored. If they are not, any deficiencies in these respects can be noted and any superlative achievements can be acknowledged, but no loss or gain of credit can be given. In view of this it is easy to understand why, in tests other than those of the language arts, such aspects as grammar, spelling, and writing style are usually scored on a restricted basis. An example of restricted scoring is the marking of spelling for technical words but not for nontechnical words.

If the results of the test are extremely important, have at least one other person score the responses independently. If this is not possible, score them a second time yourself, doing so without knowledge of your first judgments. The time-proven method of improving the scoring of responses to essay items is to average independent judgments made by competent scorers guided by the same set of standards. The feasibility of this practice is questionable. The next best substitute is the procedure in which two independent judgments are made by the same teacher.

Any radical discrepancies between the scores yielded by independent judgments should be immediately investigated and resolved. Perhaps the services of a third scorer are needed. If the differences cannot be resolved, then the opinion of the person who knows the teaching situation best, the classroom teacher, should be followed.

Methods of Scoring Essay Items

A number of different methods of scoring the responses to essay test items have been developed; only two are discussed here. The first is called the *analytical method;* the second is known as the *rating method.*

Analytical Method.   To use the analytical method of scoring, the teacher must first write out the correct response to each test item. This is analyzed and its component parts identified. The total number of raw-score points allowed for the correct response is distributed among the various subparts. The points may be distributed equally or unequally among the parts, depending on the teacher's feelings about the matter. Finally, each student's response to the test item is read, the various subparts of the correct response that it contains are noted, and the raw score determined accordingly. As far as the scoring is concerned, any extraneous material in the student's response is ignored, whether it is accurately stated or not. Note that this procedure does not prevent the teacher from marking any inaccuracies in the statements containing unnecessary information.

A simple illustration of these procedures can be provided for the test item concerning possible reasons for the differences in incidence of tooth decay of two sixth-grade boys (see page 138). The teacher may decide that the correct response should contain three elements thought to be of approximately equal importance. Therefore, each of the following is allotted one raw-score point.

1. Recognition that the nature of the boys' diets influences incidence of tooth decay

2. Recognition that heredity factors can partly account for the incidence of tooth decay

3. Recognition that all factors causing tooth decay are not known; hence differences between the two boys in terms of unknown factors could account partly for variations in the incidence of tooth decay

With this analysis of the correct response firmly in mind, the teacher should be able to score student responses more quickly and consistently. Moreover, later discussion of the test item, which would include a review of the students' responses and the scoring of items, is greatly facilitated when based on such an analysis. Both teacher and student are much more certain that the scoring is fair, and, in addition, they have isolated any gaps in each student's achievement revealed by the test item.

The analytical method offers several excellent advantages. In the first place, the analysis of the correct response will quite frequently cause teachers to redesign the statement of the test item. They may realize that the item as originally stated will not necessarily elicit the desired response, even when the student is very well informed. Any reframing of the test item and readjustment of the time limits that result from analyzing the correct response are generally distinct improvements. Secondly, the analytical method used by a conscientious grader can yield very reliable scores. This is true when the essay test item is of the restricted rather than the extended-response type.

Attempts have been made to train students to score essay items using the analytical method. The results are so encouraging that it seems reasonable to explore further the possibility of teaching this scoring technique to secondary school students, thereby realizing pedagogical gains as well as conserving teacher time.

Rating Method. The rating method (sometimes called the global or holistic method) also requires that a correct response be written by the teacher for each test item; however, the response is not subdivided. The wholeness of the response is emphasized; the scorer attempts to grasp its complete scope. With this in mind, the student's responses are read. On the basis of the wholeness of each response, the scorer usually classifies it in one of three or one of five categories. The categories represent levels of quality such as, in the first case, good, average, poor, and in the second case, very good, good, average, poor, or very poor. Although the use of five categories is common in classroom testing, as many as nine can be used with good success (Coffman, 1971).

Once the scorer has read and classified all responses, they are read a second time, possibly even a third. The answers in each category are compared with each other. Those that don't fit are shifted to a more suitable category. Homogeneity in each category is desirable, even though the scorer realizes that it depends on the number of categories used. The fewer categories used, the more variability exists within each.

When the scorer is completely satisfied that each response is in its proper category, it is marked accordingly. Total, partial, or no credit is allowed, depending on the category checked. The entire process is then repeated for all other essay items in the test.

The rating method of scoring essay items is a distinct improvement over the single hasty reading in the absence of a clearly understood correct answer. On the other hand, it has not yielded the high scorer reliabilities of the analytical method. A scorer often has difficulty differentiating between the various categories and may even find that the basis for differentiating is changing at times.

The reliability of this method of scoring responses to essay test items can be improved by serious efforts to develop scoring categories representing various levels of quality. Prior to reading all of the answers, teachers analyze a sample of responses to determine mutually exclusive categories (not to exceed nine) based on qualitative differences. After descriptions of the categories are prepared (perhaps with sample responses for each), the teacher can judge the merit of each item response and assign it a numerical value. Then each student answer is read, classified in the appropriate category, and assigned the value associated with it.

An illustration of this procedure is the essay test item shown in Figure 5.1 (Warren, 1977, 1978). This question lists 15 features of the federal government and asks the student to draw on that list to describe a strength and a weakness of our political system. The best responses are those in which the students recall specific information about the government functions listed, recognize how they may be in accord or in conflict with each other, weight the relative importance of each, and formulate a balanced, integrated response.

Five useful response categories can be identified for this item. The following is a description of each category with a possible point value given; each is accompanied by an appropriate student response.

Point Value	Response Category
	Description:
9	The answer makes specific reference to the points of information given in the process of formulating a complete and relevant response.
	Example:
	Power in federal government is divided, so that neither the Executive nor Legislative branch, nor any particular element thereof, can impose its individual will or belief on the

Point Value	Response Category

country. Division of power and authority leads to a disorganized, widely diversified government, where no decisions can be reached nor any continuity and consistency in policy.

Description:

6 The answer asserts a valid generalization about the federal government but fails to associate or integrate it with the points of information provided.

Example:

Strength—people are given a voice in government with many outlets to express opinions. Our government policies are changeable. Weakness—many governing bodies are appointed or controlled by a small group of people.

Description:

4 The answer comments on a single item or specific point of information (sometimes at length) without incorporating it in a general framework.

Example:

Proliferation of the Presidential staff is the greatest weakness. Expanding the staff increases the President's power and creates a bureaucracy. The President appoints specialists who only answer to the President . . .

Description:

2 The answer enumerates various features of the government without explaining how they are strengths or weaknesses.

Example:

Strengths—
Presidential veto
Court restriction of presidential privileges
Congressional power to override a veto

Weaknesses—
Seniority system
Dual system of courts
Nine Supreme Court justices . . .

Description:

0 The answer bears little or no relation to the points of information given; no appropriate synthesis of the variance points is stated.

Example:

It seems to be operating on two opposing principles; one traditional consistent in approach, the other innovative dynamic in approach.

To be sure, it is always possible to develop more response categories. This may prove to be needless, however, if few student responses fall in those categories, or there is no diagnostic need for a more refined classification.

Computer Scoring. Incredible as it sounds, efforts to use a computer to score essay items measuring writing ability have been rather successful (Page, 1966, 1967; Slotnick, 1972). As a point of departure, a distinction was made between intrinsic and proximate variables in an essay. The former are characteristics recognized by the teacher and presumably used in evaluation. Examples are word usage, spelling, and complexity of sentences. Proximate variables are any which, for whatever reason, happen to correlate with expert judgments of writing quality. These vary widely and include such aspects as the number of commas, apostrophes, dashes, relative pronouns, and prepositions present. As many as thirty of these have been used by a computer as it scans essays and assigns scores to each statistically. Believe it or not, these scores based on proximate variables corresponded closely to those for overall quality based on intrinsic variables used by judges.

Furthermore, evidence exists that a computer can detect the presence or absence of a high degree of opinionation, vagueness, or specificity in an essay (Hiller, Marcotte, & Martin, 1969). For instance, in the case of vagueness, it counted the number of times the examinee used any of sixty key words such as *probably, sometimes, usually,* etc. Computer-derived scores on vagueness correlated negatively with

---

STRENGTHS AND WEAKNESSES OF GOVERNMENT

The following features of the major institutions of the American national government, taken together, point to both an obvious strength and an increasingly recognized weakness of our system of government:

Bicameral legislature
Committee system
Seniority system
Presidential veto
Dual system of courts (federal and state)
Courts of primary jurisdiction and appeals courts
Nine Supreme Court justices
New laws possibly circumventing court decisions
Presidents possibly appointing a new crop of judges
Congressional power to override a veto
Court restriction of executive privilege
Proliferation of the presidential staff
Independent regulatory commissions, government corporations,
    and other independent agencies
Presidential power to appoint agency heads
Congressional power to appropriate funds

Without analyzing each of the foregoing items, describe both the strength and the weakness of the federal government that the list suggests.

FIGURE 5.1.   Essay Test Item Concerning the Strengths and Weaknesses of the Federal Government.

essay scores on characteristics such as content, organization, and style as determined by judges. This is the kind of correlation one would expect.

Can computers be used to score restricted-response essay items in a subject matter area? Undoubtedly. While awaiting better research data on which to base their techniques, a few teachers are moving ahead on a tentative basis. Typically they administer essay items requiring only a three- or four-sentence answer. The student prints the answer on a special answer sheet that is converted into a punch card and fed into a computer. Key phrases for each question are specified and assigned various scores so that the computer can compute a total score as it scans each student's response. As a check, the teacher selects a small random sample of the responses and gives these intensive personal study. Usually, these checks verify the scores assigned by the computer.

Unreliability of Scoring

Research shows that seemingly competent scorers frequently cannot agree with themselves, much less with each other, concerning the amount of credit to be allowed a student's response to an essay item (Coffman, 1972). The subjectivity in the scoring process varies according to the nature of the item but is typically large. When the test item approaches the extended-response type, subjectivity increases and reliable scoring becomes an extremely difficult problem. Unfortunately, the student does not always graciously accept any inconsistencies in the teacher's scoring efforts.

The general suggestions for improving scoring that are given in the preceding sections can increase scorer reliability. For this to occur, three conditions must be met. First, the responses must have been elicited by carefully framed test items that present the student with a well-defined task. The problem here resembles that encountered when designing supply items. For instance, consider the plight of the teacher who posed the question: "What is the difference between a king and a president?" One young student responded: "The king has to be the son of his father. The president doesn't."

Second, teachers using the analytical or rating method should master and apply it carefully. Among other things, this may mean practicing the method by scoring student responses several times independently, then analyzing whatever differences have occurred. They may also wish to tackle scoring problems in cooperation with fellow teachers. Such ventures can be profitable. Third, ample time must be allowed. Teachers must be alert, discerning judges at all times, and they cannot be if pressed for time.

PROBLEMS

5. Even though teachers decide to score responses to essay items on the basis of content without consideration of writing style, they may be influenced, consciously or subconsciously, by the quality of writing (Marshall, 1972). To what degree do you think this is true? Does the intensity of this problem depend in part on the subject matter used in the item?

6. After an essay test, some teachers ask their students to record the reasons for their answers on a 3" × 5" card. This information is then used for diagnosing student difficulties and strengthening similar future test items. Identify the advantages and limitations of this procedure.

Comparison of Essay and Objective Tests

At this point, we can identify a number of sizable differences between the essay and objective test as a means of gathering information on which student achievement can be evaluated. Seven general characteristics used as a basis for differentiating between the two types of items follow:

Difficulty of preparing the test item
Adequacy of the subject matter sampling
Relative ease with which knowledge and complex achievement are measured
Study procedures followed by the student in preparing for the test
Originality of the response the student must make to the test item
Relative success of guessing correct responses
Difficulty of scoring the student responses

The differences between essay and objective tests in terms of these seven characteristics are summarized in Table 5.1. This table reveals the fallacy of the

TABLE 5.1.   Comparison of Essay and Objective Tests.

Characteristic	Essay test	Objective test
Preparation of the test item	Items are relatively easy to construct.	Items are relatively difficult to construct.
Sampling of the subject matter	Sampling is often limited.	Sampling is usually extensive.
Measurement of knowledge and complex achievement	Items can measure both; measurement of complex achievement is recommended.	Items can measure both; measurement of knowledge is more common.
Preparation by student	Emphasis is primarily on larger units of material.	Emphasis is often on factual details.
Nature of response by student	Student organizes original response.	Except for supply test items, student selects response.
Guessing of correct response by student	Student is less prone to guess.	Student is more prone to guess.
Scoring of student responses	Scoring is difficult, time-consuming, and somewhat unreliable.	Scoring is simple, rapid, and highly reliable.

argument that one type of test item is unquestionably superior or inferior to the other. Each has peculiar advantages and limitations. There are testing needs for which each is particularly well suited.

No one should needlessly restrict a measurement program by adhering to one type or the other. Recognizing this situation, many classroom teachers build and administer achievement tests containing both types of items. In these cases, students generally prefer to answer the objective items first and the essay items later, thereby making better use of their testing time. This is the order typically followed by national achievement testing programs.

The choice of whether to build an objective or essay test is usually influenced by one additional consideration, namely, the number of students to be tested. If the group is small, less effort may be needed to construct, administer, and score an essay test than an objective one. Sometimes the labor needed to build high-quality objective items can only be justified if the items are incorporated in a test file and used several times (see page 173).

PROBLEMS

7. On the basis of your experience, compare the additional time required to *build* an objective test rather than an essay test with the time required to *score* the essay rather than the objective test.

8. It is said that essay tests encourage the student to learn how to organize his own ideas and express them effectively, whereas objective tests encourage him to build a broad background of knowledge and abilities. Do you agree? Why?

SUMMARY

The following are the main ideas presented in this chapter:

1. An essay test item demands a response composed by the student, usually in the form of one or more sentences. The quality of the student's response can be judged subjectively by an informed scorer, ordinarily the teacher.

2. The freedom of response allowed on an essay item can vary appreciably. In one case, few restrictions are placed on the nature of the student's response; such a test item is an extended-response essay test item. Other test items define quite specifically the task to be performed by the student; these are restricted-response essay test items.

3. Because of the extremely difficult task of scoring answers to extended-response essay test items, their value as a method of measuring subject matter achievement is curtailed. On the other hand, the restricted-response type plays an important role in achievement testing, since its answers can be scored reliably.

4. Four important considerations face teachers when they build essay test items. First, they must relate the item to one or more cells in the table of specifications or to specific objectives involving complex cognitive achievement. Second, they

must sample the subject matter broadly, favoring those essay items that require comparatively short answers and thereby using more items for a given testing period. Third, they must determine the freedom of response to be allowed the student. Finally, they must establish suitable time limits.

5. Scoring responses to an essay item is usually difficult. To help simplify this task and, at the same time, improve the reliability of the scoring process, four general rules should be followed. First, score the students' responses anonymously. Second, score all responses to each test item at one time. Third, if spelling, penmanship, grammar, and so forth are to be graded, score them independently of the subject matter content. Last, if possible, have another person go over them; if this is not possible, score them a second time yourself.

6. Two prominent methods of scoring essay test items are the analytical method and the rating method. In the analytical method, the teacher breaks the correct response into subparts, assigns raw-score points to each, and awards points for a student's answer insofar as each subpart of the correct response is or is not included. In the rating method, the teacher tries to grasp the complete scope of the right answer, and then, on the basis of the wholeness of a student's response, tries to classify it into one of three or five categories representing various levels of quality.

7. It is highly appropriate to use both objective and essay items in the same achievement test. If this is done, the objective items should be administered first, followed by the essay items.

SUGGESTED READINGS

COFFMAN, W. E. Essay examinations. In R. L. Thorndike (Ed.), *Educational measurement* (2nd ed.). Washington, D.C.: American Council on Education, 1971. See chapter 10.
This is a superior discussion of the value of essay test items as a means of measuring student achievement. The limitations of this type of test item, its potential value, suggestions for improving it, and reliable methods of scoring student responses are described.

COFFMAN, W. E. On the reliability of ratings of essay examinations. *NCME Measurement in Education*, 1972, 3, 1–7.
The sources of error in essay examinations are examined and suggestions are made for reducing rating error.

EBEL, R. L. *Practical problems in educational measurement.* Lexington, Mass.: 1980.
The differences and similarities between objective and essay items are recounted in chapter 14, and guidelines for using essay items effectively are included in chapter 15.

GRONLUND, N. E. *Constructing achievement tests* (2nd ed.). Englewood Cliffs, N.J.: Prentice-Hall, 1977.
In chapter 5 there are guidelines given for building and scoring essay test items.

HUCK, S. W., & BOUNDS, W. G. Essay grades: An interaction between graders' handwriting clarity and the neatness of examination papers. *American Education Research Journal*, 1972, 9, 279–283.
Date collected in this study support the hypothesized interaction between the

clarity of graders' handwriting and that of the essays they rated. The authors caution those using essay examinations to be aware of extraneous factors affecting test scores.

REFERENCES CITED

BRELAND, H. M., & GAYNOR, J. L. A comparison of direct and indirect assessments of writing. *Journal of Educational Measurement*, 1979, *16*, 119–128.

CHASE, C. I. The impact of achievement expectations and handwriting quality on scoring essay tests. *Journal of Educational Measurement*, 1979, *16*, 39–42.

COFFMAN, W. E. Essay examinations. In R. L. Thorndike (Ed.), *Educational measurement* (2nd ed.). Washington, D.C.: American Council on Education, 1971.

COFFMAN, W. E. On the reliability of ratings of essay examinations. *NCME Measurement in Education*, 1972, *3*, 1–7.

HILLER, J. H., MARCOTTE, D. R., & MARTIN, T. Opinionation, vagueness, and specificity-distinctions: Essay traits measured by computer. *American Educational Research Journal*, 1969, *6*, 271–286.

MARSHALL, J. C. Writing neatness, composition errors, and essay grades re-examined. *Journal of Educational Research*, 1972, *65*, 213–215.

PAGE, E. B. Imminence of grading essays by computers. *Phi Delta Kappan*, 1966, *47*, 238–243.

PAGE, E. B. Grading essays by computer: Progress report. *Proceedings of the 1966 Invitational Conference on Testing Problems*. Princeton, N.J.: Educational Testing Service, 1967, 87–100.

SLOTNICK, H. Toward a theory of computer essay grading. *Journal of Educational Measurement*, 1972, *9*, 253–263.

WARREN, J. R. *Academic competencies in general education: Selected questions in synthesizing ability.* Princeton, N.J.: Educational Testing Service, 1977.

WARREN, J. R. *The measurement of academic competence.* Berkeley, Calif.: Educational Testing Service, 1978.

6

Appraising Classroom Achievement Tests

The purpose of this chapter is to help you

1. Appreciate the need to reexamine each test item after use in order to evaluate its strengths and weaknesses

2. Recognize that standard item analysis techniques are used primarily with norm-referenced tests, and that special methods are needed for criterion-referenced tests

3. Utilize the formulas for item difficulty level and discriminating power for norm-referenced tests and interpret their results

4. Explain that the appropriate levels of difficulty for test items depend on the purpose of the test, and that different decisions are made for norm-referenced and criterion-referenced items

5. Understand the relationship between item difficulty and discriminating power for norm-referenced tests

6. Demonstrate that study of data from item analysis of a classroom achievement test can yield many inferences about the learning difficulties of individual students and the class as a whole

7. List the most prominent limitations of the application of item analysis to classroom achievement tests

8. Describe the steps to develop a test item file that best capitalizes on item analysis data

The use of measuring instruments in our commercial, scientific, and even recreational pursuits is commonplace. This would be a strange world indeed if desk rulers, bathroom scales, water meters, clocks, thermometers, speedometers, and electrical meters were suddenly removed. These and countless other measuring instruments are constantly feeding us information that we use to make decisions. Without such information, a significant part of our modern civilization would cease to function.

An interesting result of the dominance of measuring instruments is the great confidence we have in their accuracy. True, we may doubt the readings of an ancient wristwatch or an inexpensive outdoor thermometer, but only infrequently do we entertain doubts as to whether the desk ruler is twelve inches long and divided into twelve equal parts, or whether the water and gas meters are measuring volume properly, or whether the speedometer in our automobile is registering as it should. We assume that, for our purposes, their accuracy is sufficient.

Fortunately our confidence in such instruments is well-founded. Extensive efforts are made by the federal government as well as by industrial and scientific organizations to maintain accurate measuring instruments. For example, the United States Bureau of Standards works actively in this field. Among other functions, it maintains the standards against which scientific instruments for measuring distance and weight can be checked. Government officials known as sealers conduct systematic checks of devices, such as the scales used in food stores and the meters used in gasoline stations, thereby protecting the consumer. Also, scientists are constantly recalibrating the thermometers, burets, and weights used in their work to be certain that the accuracy of their measurements is maintained.

The perpetual vigilance in commercial, industrial, and scientific fields should be copied by classroom teachers. They make numerous measurements and, in so doing, use instruments in which they have notably less confidence than in the scales and meters mentioned. This is particularly true when classroom achievement tests are used. Although the product of much time and effort, they no doubt contain numerous unsuspected flaws. After all, many tentative decisions are made as the tests are constructed. Decisions concerning item difficulty, the attractiveness of distracters, or the length of the test, to name just a few, are made on the basis of inadequate evidence and could be at least partially wrong. The teacher will not know the success or failure of these decisions unless the test is carefully reexamined after its administration. Then, and only then, can it be determined how worthwhile it was and how meaningful the scores were.

In addition to determining the worth of a classroom achievement test after it has been given, reexamining test results has other values. For instance, any errors or inadequacies discovered can serve as warnings to teachers when they construct other achievement tests. Although the methods and material used in a class may change from year to year, the important educational objectives are generally stable. Therefore, the classroom achievement testing program changes from year to year, but seldom drastically. In view of this, any past failures and successes can assist the teacher immeasurably in future achievement test construction. Furthermore, a careful inspection of student responses to individual test items or groups of items has diagnostic value. The areas of strength and weakness for each student—or the class as a whole—can be identified.

Item Analysis Methods

Reexamining each test item to discover its strengths and flaws is known as *item analysis*. Item analysis usually concentrates on two vital features: level of difficulty and discriminating power. The former means the percentage of students who answer correctly each test item; the latter is the ability of the test item to differentiate between students who have done well and those who have done poorly.

Indices of discriminating power can be computed for essay or objective items from open-book or closed-book tests. However, this information is most useful to us when the items are a part of a norm-referenced test, rather than a mastery or criterion-referenced test. In other words, the scores are to be used as a basis for ranking student achievement. This means that the scores are spread out from low to high, and standard correlation methods can be used to determine each test item's degree of discriminating power.

In contrast, the purpose of a mastery test is to separate the students into two groups, those who have achieved at least as high as a certain level and those who have not. Consequently, traditional correlation methods used with norm-referenced tests do not work well with criterion-referenced tests (Popham, 1978, pp. 103–111). In view of the special item analysis problems that exist in the latter case, the remainder of this chapter is devoted primarily to the analysis of norm-referenced test items.

Methods of item analysis are essentially mathematical and can take many forms. Various statistical techniques are used, many of them requiring a considerable amount of computing. The methods described in the following sections are, in contrast to many, relatively simple. They are quite satisfactory for classroom teachers. Since teachers do not have the time, facilities, or number of cases often demanded by the more elaborate methods, such methods are of little practical value although they are widely used in the construction of standardized achievement tests.

Item Difficulty

It is easy to determine a test item's level of difficulty. First a tabulation is made of the number of students who successfully answer the item. This figure is then divided by the total number of students attempting the item, and the quotient is multiplied by 100. These steps are summarized in the following formula:

$$P = \frac{N_R}{N_T} (100)$$

where

P = percentage of students who answer the test item correctly
N_R = number of students who answer the test item correctly
N_T = total number of students who attempt to answer the test item

Suppose that an item in a classroom achievement test is answered correctly by eighteen of the twenty-eight students who attempt to answer it. Then the level of difficulty of this test is found as follows:

$$P = \frac{18}{28} \, (100) \, = \, 64$$

In other words, sixty-four percent of the students who attempted the test item answered it correctly.

The formula shown does not alert the teacher to two questions that are often raised about the determination of item difficulty. In the first place, is the number of students who attempt to answer the item the same as the total number who are administered the test? If the time limits are too restrictive, it is conceivable that some students did not have an opportunity to answer test items appearing near the end. Hence, the number who attempt to answer the test item is less than the number to whom the test was administered. Secondly, is the number who know the correct answer the same as the number who answer it correctly? In the case of objective test items, successful guessing may cause the two numbers to be different and thus, to some degree, destroy the value of the computation of item difficulty.

The first question is seldom a problem to the classroom teacher. Sufficient time is allowed for the administration of the test so that each student attempts each item. Therefore the denominator of the formula is the same for each test item.

The second question is the source of widespread debate among measurement specialists. The arguments for and against correcting for guessing are concisely summarized elsewhere (Henrysson, 1971). For our purposes it is not necessary to use formulas for computing item difficulty that incorporate a correction for guessing. In the first place, the added computational burden, though not serious, can be troublesome. Also, the assumptions underlying the formula are not fully satisfied, and the students' reaction to the warning that a correction for guessing is to be made are so varied that extraneous personality factors influence the achievement test scores. Finally, the teacher ordinarily does not need a very accurate measure of item difficulty. Rough approximations are usually sufficient.

Item Discriminating Power

The discriminating power of a test item is its ability to differentiate between students who have achieved well (the upper group) and those who have achieved poorly (the lower group). To determine the discriminating power of a test item we must first specify the characteristics of the upper and lower groups. Here we have considerable latitude. We may wish to use an independent criterion to classify the students. Such a criterion might be the score from a standardized test thought to measure the same aspects of achievement as the classroom test containing the item in question. Or we may wish to use final marks in the same or similar achievement areas, these having been determined without knowledge of the scores yielded by the classroom test. On the other hand, an internal criterion may be used, such as the total scores from the classroom achievement test, the items of which are being studied.

In most cases, the internal criterion is used. This is done not only because independent criteria are customarily unavailable, but also because they are not good measures of the aspects of achievement involved in the classroom test. Achievement tests are, in a sense, "self-defining," that is, the test itself defines what it is to measure. Incidentally, the use of the total test scores as the criterion for classifying students into upper and lower groups, followed by the use of these groups to determine an index reflecting the discriminating power of individual test items, is known as the *internal-consistency* method of computing indices of item-discriminating power.

When the total test scores are used in this manner, a decision must be made as to which part of the distribution of scores is the upper group and which part is the lower group. Some choose the upper and lower halves, others the upper and lower thirds with the middle third discarded, and still others the upper and lower twenty-seven percent with the middle forty-six percent discarded. The last has received a great deal of support by testing specialists, and a number of tables designed to assist item analysis are based on this division. However, for classroom teachers analyzing their own tests, use of the upper and lower thirds is probably a suitable compromise. Fewer cases are lost than when the upper-lower twenty-seven percent method is used, and a more distinct separation between the groups is provided than in the case of the upper-lower halves method.

The rationale behind the scheme for computing an index of item-discriminating power is quite simple. A test item with maximum discriminating power would be one which every student in the upper group would answer correctly and every student in the lower would answer incorrectly; in short, it can discriminate between every student in the upper group and every student in the lower group. Thus, this test item produces a maximum number of correct discriminations. Of course, we cannot expect items to discriminate perfectly. The typical test item will yield some correct discriminations—part of the upper group will respond correctly and part of the lower group incorrectly—and will yield some incorrect discriminations in that the remainder of the upper group will respond incorrectly and the remainder of the lower group correctly.

The discriminating power of a test item is the difference between the number of correct and incorrect discriminations expressed as a percentage of the maximum possible correct discriminations. In simplified form, the formula to compute an index of discriminating power based on this idea is the following

$$D = \frac{U - L}{N}$$

where

D = index of item-discriminating power
U = number of students in upper group who answer the test item correctly
L = number of sudents in the lower group who answer the test item correctly
N = number of students in each of the two groups (Findley, 1956; Ebel, 1980, pp. 219–220).

To use this formula conventionally, one must first find the total raw scores on the test for all students. Then the test papers are ranked according to the raw scores, and the top and bottom thirds of the raw-score distribution are found; the middle third is ignored. For each test item, the number in the upper and lower groups who respond correctly are tabulated. Appropriate substitutions are then made in the formula. For instance, suppose that ten of twelve students in the upper third of the raw-score distribution answer an item correctly, and five of twelve in the lower third answer it correctly. The index of discriminating power for this test item is

$$D = \frac{10 - 5}{12} = +0.42$$

It is evident that the maximum size of the index is $+1.00$ and the minimum size is -1.00. In the first case, maximum discrimination occurs in the desired direction; in the second, in the opposite direction. Any negative value means that the test item discriminates—to some degree—in the wrong direction. Hence, the discriminating power of the test item is unsatisfactory. The larger the positive value, the better. Although it is difficult to establish a suitable minimum positive value below which the discriminating power of a test item is considered faulty, certainly values less than $+0.20$ indicate that the discriminating power of the test item is questionable. A reasonably good achievement test item should have an index of at least $+0.30$.

Difficulty Levels Near Fifty Percent

It has long been known that the discriminating power of an item is influenced by the difficulty of the item. The manner of influence depends on the relative intercorrelation of the items, that is, the degree to which each test item is correlated with every other. In the case of norm-referenced tests containing items that have low intercorrelation, those composed of items with levels of difficulty near fifty percent will display more discriminating power than those composed of items with widely varying levels of difficulty. In the case of tests containing items with high intercorrelations, the reverse is true. The reasons are beyond the scope of this book; further discussion can be found in any of several standard references (Henrysson, 1971).

Since norm-referenced achievement tests rarely are composed of highly intercorrelated items, the recommendation is frequently made that they include only those test items with midrange levels of difficulty, between forty and seventy percent. This recommendation often disturbs teachers who feel that a wide distribution of item difficulty levels is necessary to test very good and very poor students properly. To separate the very good, the good, the average, the poor, and the very poor students from each other, a norm-referenced achievement test with superior discriminating power is needed. To obtain this it is necessary, strange as it may seem, to avoid the use of test items with widely varying levels of difficulty.

Difficulty Levels for Criterion-Referenced Test Items.

In contrast to items used in norm-referenced tests, criterion-referenced items have difficulty levels that may vary considerably, depending on the purpose of the test. For instance, often the primary purpose of a criterion-referenced test is to measure student mastery of specified skills, or to measure the command of knowledge needed for advancement to the next step in a learning program. In these instances, the tests are mastery tests with levels of difficulty at about 85% or higher. In other words, after completing an instructional program, practically all students should select correct answers to virtually all of the test items. By the same token, before completing instruction, we expect that few students will know the correct answers to the same test items. Thus, when used as a pretest, their difficulty levels will be near zero.

In the instances cited, effective items in a criterion-referenced test are those that are very difficult for the student before receiving instruction and quite easy afterwards. Test items like these are exactly the kind that are unsatisfactory for norm-referenced achievement tests, since they tend to be lower in discriminating power.

A common method of selecting effective items for criterion-referenced achievement tests is to determine how sensitive they are to instruction. Highly sensitive items should reveal improved student achievement because of the instruction between pretesting and posttesting. When building standardized criterion-referenced tests, the best items are often selected by trying them out as pretests and posttests for instructional programs with students for whom the test is intended. (For information about the development of a standardized criterion-referenced test, see Chapter 11.)

PROBLEMS

1. By means of a simple experimental study, Ebel (1979, pp. 264–267) demonstrated empirically that an inverse relationship exists between the spread of item difficulty and the spread of test scores. Study the three test score histograms he shows. Are the differences among them striking?

2. Do you think that teachers can study multiple-choice test items and successfully predict the level of difficulty and discriminating power of each? Compare your opinion with the findings of a study in which secondary school mathematics teachers were asked to make such predictions (Ryan, 1968).

Uses of Item Analysis Results

The results of item analysis can serve two main purposes. The first and more obvious one is that the results can give teachers a much better view of the worth of the tests they built and used; they can profit by their mistakes in that they should be able to construct noticeably better tests in the future. The second use can be summarized in a single word: diagnosis. By examining the data from item analysis, the teacher can detect the learning difficulties of individual students or the class as a whole and can plan more suitable remedial programs. Studying the strengths and weaknesses of student achievement will also help the teacher to evaluate more accurately the effectiveness of various parts of the learning situation.

Improving Classroom Achievement Tests

When administering each norm-referenced achievement test, the classroom teacher is usually plagued by countless questions. Will the distracters of the third multiple-choice item be attractive? Is the ninth item so worded that the superior achievers may misunderstand its intent and respond incorrectly? Paradoxically, will the poor achievers not be misled and tend to respond correctly? Is the last item too difficult? The answers to questions such as these can cause a teacher to view the test results with confidence or doubt.

Levels of Item Difficulty.   As a first step in the process of answering questions such as the foregoing, item difficulties can be computed. A quick scanning of these data reveals all items to which 100 and 0 percent respond correctly. Since the purpose of a norm-referenced test is to yield scores that will differentiate among the students, neither type of item is suitable. On the other hand, a possible use of one or two test items to which 100 percent responded correctly would be to place them at the beginning, thereby letting them serve as a gentle introduction to the remainder of the test.

All items of extremely high or low levels of difficulty should be carefully scrutinized. Since any test items with levels of difficulty that are not in the general vicinity of fifty percent (that is, between forty and seventy percent) tend to reduce the discriminating power of norm-referenced test, these can be viewed with suspicion. Their indices of discriminating power should be checked since an item that is extremely easy or difficult cannot possibly have a large D value.

Also, the gross failure of certain test items to approximate the anticipated level of difficulty may be information of great value to the teacher. Is the item poorly designed? Is the effectiveness of the learning experience far different from that expected? If so, why? Is the level of difficulty of this test item affected by the presence of other items in the test? If so, which items? These and other avenues of explanation can be explored.

Indices of Discriminating Power.   The second step that can partly answer some of the questions posed by the teacher is to compute and interpret indices of discriminating power. Any D values about $+0.40$ can be considered very good, any between $+0.40$ and $+0.20$ satisfactory, and any between $+0.20$ and zero poor. It is clear that negative values identify items that differentiate among students in the wrong way. In a well-built classroom achievement test composed of objective test items, probably more than fifty percent of the test items should have D values exceeding $+0.40$, less than forty percent should have values between $+0.40$ and $+0.20$, less than ten percent should have values between $+0.20$ and zero, and none should have negative values. Obviously, these are only guides.

Examination of All Responses to an Item.   An even closer inspection of the effectiveness of test items can be obtained by tabulating and comparing all the responses of the students in the upper and lower groups. For example, in the case of a multiple-choice test item the responses to each of the distracters—as well as the correct response—are counted. Incidentally, this tabulation can be made quickly and accurately by a test-scoring machine or a computer if the proper answer sheets have been used (Warrington, 1972).

To see the kinds of information that can be obtained by scrutinizing all responses, let us examine several multiple-choice items. In each case the discriminating power is represented by a D value, and the difficulty level is estimated by using data from the upper and lower groups only. Such estimates are usually fairly accurate for our purposes. The middle third often divides itself between correct and incorrect answers, much as the other two-thirds combined.

Consider the following test item administered to students developing library skills. (The correct response is designated by an asterisk.)

If you wish to quickly find the page on which a particular topic or subject appears in a reference book, to which of the following would you refer?

   (1)   the appendix
   (2)   the subject index
   (3)   the table of contents
   (4)   the bibliography

The responses of the students in the upper and lower groups are as follows:

Option		Upper third	Lower third
1		0	1
*2		10	8
3		1	2
4		0	0
(Omits)		0	0
	Total	11	11

This test item is too easy, the estimate of P being eighty-two percent. Moreover, its discriminating power is low ($D = +0.18$), although it is almost as high as possible for this easy an item.

Quite possibly, the weakness in the test item is due to the inclusion of the word "subject" in the second option. This may be a clue to the correct response that is so obvious that the students quickly notice it and choose their answer accordingly. The uninformed student will profit more by such a clue than the informed student who didn't need one in the first place. If this word were deleted, it is conceivable that the differential attractiveness of the distracters would increase, thereby improving the item's level of difficulty and its discriminating power.

Another illustration is a test item with a satisfactory level of difficulty but negative discriminating power. It appeared in an elementary school social studies test.

The capital of Switzerland is

   (1)   Bern
   (2)   Zurich

(3)   Lucerne
(4)   Geneva

The responses of the students in the upper and lower groups are as follows:

Option	Upper third	Lower third
*1	5	6
2	2	3
3	1	1
4	5	3
(Omits)	0	0
Total	13	13

The estimated level of difficulty is forty-two percent and the index of discriminating power is −0.08.

We can only speculate as to why more students in the lower group than in the upper group responded correctly and so many in the upper group selected the fourth option. Possibly their familiarity with the League of Nations and the many important international conferences that were held in Geneva caused the students in the upper group to think of Geneva as the most important city in Switzerland and thus the capital of the country. Those in the lower group, on the other hand, may not have known this about Geneva and therefore were not misled by it. Having no preconceived ideas about the importance of these four cities, almost half of them learned that Bern is the capital and responded accordingly. Perhaps the relative importance of the cities of Switzerland and their relationship to each other and the world are not well taught.

These illustrations make it clear that a rich fund of information concerning the test is available to the teacher who takes the trouble to examine all responses to the test items. Although only multiple-choice items are shown, similar information can be obtained from other types of objective test items and even essay test items of the restricted-response type. At the very least, this information should give the teacher a much more realistic view of the value of the test. Ideally, it should also warn of some of the pitfalls encountered in achievement test construction and suggest means of overcoming or circumventing these.

Diagnosing Inadequacies in Achievement

As informative as a student's total raw score can be in many respects, it does not provide very much information about the sources of successes and failures. In other words, the raw score of a student or the arithmetic mean of the raw scores of a class may be interpreted to mean that one or more students are having trouble, but such scores will not tell what the trouble is or where it is located. To locate the nature of the trouble, an item-by-item inspection of the norm-referenced test is necessary.

The first step in diagnosing inadequacies in achievement is to build a chart showing the item-by-item performance by each student. A section of such a chart based on an objective achievement test is shown in Table 6.1. The plus signs indicate correct responses, the negative signs incorrect responses, and the zeros, omitted responses. Incidentally, some teachers have their students participate in the construction of such a chart as this; others use printed reports prepared by computers. In the case of multiple-choice tests, the number of the option chosen by each student can be used in place of the plus and minus signs, thus providing a summary of the popularity of wrong responses for each test item.

The totals listed at the bottom of the table reveal the number of students who responded correctly and incorrectly to each test item. The totals pinpoint the areas of difficulty for the students as a class. Notice that, of the first ten test items, seven students found items, 2, 3, 4, 6, and 8 to be relatively easy, whereas they found 1, 5, and 10 to be moderately difficult, and 9 quite difficult. Now their strengths and weaknesses in achievement can be quickly found by examining the areas of achievement involved in the test items identified and noting the cells of the table of specifications on which they are based. Discussing this information with members of the class immediately following the administration of the test can be most enlightening to them.

Very likely teachers will wish to study the test items that cause difficulty before those that do not. After satisfying themselves that there is nothing technically wrong with such test items and their scoring, they can pose questions as to the reasons why it is difficult. Is little emphasis placed on the point of the test item during the period of instruction? If so, is this lack of emphasis deliberate or accidental? Is there widespread misunderstanding among the students in spite of the fact that careful instruction is given? If so, what is the nature of the misunderstanding? Should the learning experiences related to the areas of difficulty be changed in any way?

There is profit as well in examining test items that the class found to be easy. Again, after a search for technical imperfections fails to reveal any defects, the teacher can raise questions about why the test items are relatively easy: Are the items found to be easy those that primarily measure recall of information rather than more complex cognitive achievement? If so, does this indicate that undue emphasis is being placed on the objectives related to knowledge with a corresponding deemphasis on those involving other levels of the cognitive taxonomy? Can the idea behind one or more of the relatively easy test items be traced to a particular learning experience? If so, is there some feature of that learning experience such as visual aid or supplementary instructional material that is responsible for the students' successes and that should be reused with subsequent classes? Is extreme success with a test item caused by unwarranted hints given before or during the administration of the test? If so, should the test be rescored with this item omitted?

After these questions have been answered satisfactorily, teachers can turn to the responses of each individual student. Just as they attempted to analyze the areas of strength and weakness for the class as a whole, they can now do the same for each student. Following a thorough examination of the item-by-item per-

TABLE 6.1.

Sample Chart for Analyzing Student Responses to Each Item in an Achievement Test

Name of student	Test item number										Total score
	1	2	3	4	5	6	7	8	9	10...60	
1. Steve	$+^a$	$-^b$	+	+	+	−	−	+	−	+ +	39
2. Mary	−	+	+	−	+	−	+	−	−	+ 0^c	21
3. Dick	−	+	+	+	−	+	−	−	+	− −	18
4. Carol	+	−	−	+	+	+	+	+	−	− −	37
5. Becky	+	+	+	−	−	+	−	+	−	+ +	41
6. June	+	+	+	+	−	+	+	+	+	− +	55
7. Sheri	−	+	−	+	+	+	−	+	0	+ −	44
Total No. correct	4	5	5	5	4	5	3	5	2	4...3	
Total No. wrong	3	2	2	2	3	2	4	2	4	3...3	
Omissions	0	0	0	0	0	0	0	0	1	0...1	

[a] Correct response
[b] Incorrect response
[c] Omitted response.

formance of the students, other records of achievement can be consulted, observations of study habits made, and, in many instances, a teacher-student conference held. In this manner, many additional pieces of information come to light as to *why* the student is successful and unsuccessful. These details can be used along with the initial information concerning *what* the areas are as a basis for building a remedial program. Such a program is individually tailored to the needs of the student. If it succeeds, it will not only correct past inadequacies but also provide the means of preventing a number of future difficulties.

Sampling Problem. Analyzing the item-by-item performance of each student has one serious weakness that must be recognized. This is the problem of adequate sampling—the same problem we encounter with other aspects of educational measurement. According to the procedures outlined in the foregoing paragraphs, the teacher may regularly make decisions concerning the achievement on the basis of a response to one or perhaps several test items. Frequently these are very small samples of the achievement areas in question; consequently, the probability that they do not present an accurate picture of the student's accomplishments is uncomfortably large. This means that the information gleaned from the item-by-item analysis must be considered suggestive rather than definitive.

The sampling problem can be corrected in part without destroying all of the diagnostic features of the analysis by modifying Table 6.1 slightly. Instead of listing the test items individually across the top of the table, we can organize them into meaningful groups and list them in place of the individual items. For instance, in an arithmetic test the test items may be grouped in four categories: those requiring addition, subtraction, multiplication, and division. The number of correct and incorrect responses to each group of items by each student can be tabulated.

A recommended scheme for organizing the test items into groups is to use the table of specifications. Items representing the same or similar cells may be combined into one group. The number of groups used, as well as their size, is determined by the teacher and, of course, can vary widely.

Analysis of classroom performance on either an item-by-item basis or with groups of similar items can provide, in effect, criterion-referenced interpretations of norm-referenced test data (Fremer, 1972). This procedure may be less fruitful than anticipated for two major reasons. First, each group of similar items very likely does not represent an explicit domain of tasks, and therefore a criterion-referenced interpretation of the responses is difficult. Second, the item analysis procedures for norm-referenced tests eliminate almost all easy and difficult items from the test—items that would probably be present if criterion-referenced test construction methods had been used originally (Martuza, 1977, pp. 275–276). Because of these problems, any criterion-referenced interpretation of student responses to items in norm-referenced tests should be made with caution.

PROBLEM

3. Study the steps described by Diederich (1973, pp. 1–3) in which an item analysis is completed by the students to whom an achievement test was administered. They performed most of the work involved in the item analysis by raising their hands in response to instructions from the teacher. Demonstrate this procedure with a class you are now teaching or attending. Evaluate the demonstration.

Limitations of Item Analysis

Although item analysis data are useful for evaluating a norm-referenced achievement test and diagnosing weaknesses, several serious limitations exist in application of the techniques. In the first place, while the internal-consistency method is suitable for tests containing items that measure somewhat the same mental functions, achievement tests generally contain test items that are relatively heterogeneous in this respect. Second, the classroom teacher frequently must base an item analysis on a small number of students, forming judgments on limited evidence. Third, analysis of responses to essay test items is less informative than that of responses to objective items. This lessens the utility of the techniques for the teacher using these items. Finally, item analysis results are more relative than some teachers realize. The level of difficulty and discriminating power of a test item are influenced by the test in which the item appears, the conditions under which the test is administered, and the quality of the students.

Uses and Limitations of Internal-Consistency Methods

The internal-consistency method for computing indices of item-discriminating power is appropriate when the student traits measured by the total test scores are homogeneous for all practical purposes. Successful items in a test of this kind are those that are closely related to each other and, of course, that tend to measure whatever the total test scores measure. They will have large positive *D* values. As any test items with low discriminating power are eliminated or changed so that their discriminating power increases, the resulting test will become more and more homogeneous.

The total scores of achievement tests typically represent heterogeneous rather than homogeneous aspects of the students. They contain test items that measure several different kinds of behavior (that is, various levels of the cognitive taxonomy) in unequal amounts. The total score is actually a composite representation of these behaviors. If one trait stands out in the total test scores, well-constructed items that reflect it will have satisfactory indices of discriminating power. On the other hand, test items reflecting less important and somewhat unrelated traits, even though they are well constructed in many technical respects, will tend to have low indices of discriminating power.

This problem can be easily illustrated. Suppose that an achievement test contains forty-five recall-of-information items that are fairly homogeneous and five application-of-principles items that are noticeably unlike the first group. The total score is found by counting the number of correct responses, regardless of which type of test item is being scored. All other factors being equal, we would expect that the items in the larger group would have markedly higher indices of discriminating power than those in the smaller group, if the internal-consistency method of computation is used.

Effect on Content Validity. The true significance of the foregoing statements comes into focus when the problem of content validity is considered. Certainly maintaining high content validity in each achievement test is the primary goal of the teacher who designs and builds it. Yet indices of discriminating power may actually encourage reduction of the degree of content validity of future tests. This would occur if, in the illustration of the fifty-item achievement test, the teacher wishes someday to use it again and either eliminates the items with low indices of discriminating power or modifies them in the hope that the indices will improve. In both cases, large or potentially large changes in content validity could take place. Obviously more is lost than gained.

Of course the problem is largely corrected if it is possible to break down an achievement test in homogeneous subtests with reasonably reliable scores and to use each as the internal criterion for computing indices of discriminating power for items within that subtest. Although this is regularly done with standardized achievement tests, such is not the case with classroom achievement tests because it is often impracticable.

Limits on Numbers of Students

Items analyses for standardized norm-referenced tests are often based on hundreds of cases. Contrast this with the usual class size, which places a limit on the number of cases available to a teacher at one time. This sample is extremely small.

Reexamine for a moment the distributions of the responses made by students in the upper and lower groups to the two test items shown earlier in this chapter. Note how a shift of one response from one option to another can change your opinion of the power of a distractor, or how it might even change the P or D value noticeably. Remembering that some of the reasons why a student selects one option rather than any of the other three can be vague and obscure, you can imagine how easily a shift in choice could have taken place. All of this means that the profile of responses to an item must be considered tentative as long as the number of students is so small.

Difficulties of Analyzing Essay Responses

Item-analysis technique can be applied to the responses to essay items as well as to objective items; it is definitely more difficult, however, and the results are sometimes considered less meaningful. The difficulty is traced to the problems of reliable scoring of essay responses and tabulating the incorrect responses. Both of these activities are time-consuming. The relative lack of meaning of the data is attributed to the fact that the various subparts of the correct are frequently related to each other. The level of difficulty of one subpart may affect the level of difficulty of another; the correctness or incorrectness of a student's response to one part may affect the correctness or incorrectness of his or her response to a subsequent part. These are the principal reasons why responses to essay items are analyzed so infrequently.

The analysis of responses to essay items is most successful if they are of the restricted-response type and are scored by the analytical method. If at all possible, each subpart should be separately considered. This is equivalent to considering each an independent test item with its own level of difficulty and discriminating power. When some or all subparts cannot be logically separated, they should be combined as necessary and the composites treated as separate test items. An analysis based on the internal-consistency method can be used here as it is with responses to objective items.

Relative Nature of Item-Analysis Data

We should like to believe that data from item analysis are completely accurate and meaningful. Clearly this is not justified, both because of the limitations introduced by the use of an internal criterion and a small sample of students and because of the special circumstances surrounding every test item as it is administered.

Some of those special circumstances relate to the students as they respond to the item—their alertness, motivation, and emotional tone. Some relate to the environment in which the test is given—the time of day, the amount of extraneous noise, the temperature of the room and the ventilation. Some relate to the test containing the item in question—its length, the levels of difficulty of the other items, and the order in which they are arranged. Yes, even the attractiveness of a distracter in a multiple-choice item is influenced by the other distracters with which it is used.

It is hard to determine how much these factors influence item analysis data. The influence might be slight, but in a given instance it could be prominent. It must be understood that the P value and the D value are merely representations of the level of difficulty and discriminating power of an item as it appeared in a certain test administered under specific circumstances to one group of students. It is clear that if the test or environment is changed, the values can and do change.

General Considerations

Persistent attempts to follow the suggestions for improving test items should directly and indirectly help produce test items with encouraging item-analysis data. There is no guarantee, however, that this will happen. Very careful construction and even ingenious revision based on item-analysis data may fail to improve the P and D values of a test item satisfactorily. This creates a dilemma: considerations of content validity make it necessary to include the material in the test, yet item analysis suggests that the related items are inferior in some respects. Preference must be given to the content validity. Items based on the material must be included and repeated efforts made to improve their quality. If this fails, then the table of specifications can be changed so that the material can be properly excluded from the test. As a result, the meaning of the total score is changed and evaluation of achievement in the area omitted must be made by other methods, that is, nontesting procedures such as rating methods, product scales, and check lists. These are discussed and illustrated in the following chapter.

PROBLEM

4. For classes of about thirty students or less, item-analysis data are rather un-dependable. Demonstrate the degree to which P values and D values will change by systematically altering the response of one student in the upper third and one in the lower third of the test item concerning Switzerland (see page 167), and recomputing the two values each time.

Test Item Files

The teaching notes maintained by many classroom teachers are voluminous. A syllabus, a variety of outlines, numerous references, several study guides, and a quantity of newspaper clippings and miscellaneous pamphlets are usually a part of this collection. Each assists the teacher in pursuing instructional duties. Some of these are highly prized; they are considered to be proven teaching aids. Although other notes may be of more doubtful value, the practicing teacher would rarely be willing to part with them.

The portion of this mass of teaching notes that often receives the least attention is the evaluation section. Usually it consists of a copy or two of each of the classroom achievement tests administered during the past year or so, and possibly the tables of specifications on which they were based. Nevertheless, more complete materials concerning these techniques could easily simplify the teacher's measurement functions as much as teaching notes simplify instructional functions. A highly successful means of organizing much of the pertinent information on classroom achievement tests, whether norm-referenced or criterion-referenced, is a test item file. Most files are designed for norm-referenced tests, as described in the remainder of this chapter.

Item Data Card.   A test item file is nothing more than a series of cards that record a great deal of the information obtained by item analysis procedures. Usually the file contains as many cards as there are test items, although sometimes the length of the item or the nature of the information about it requires several cards. The cards are customarily 3″ × 5″ or 5″ × 8″ in size and are arranged in any order the teacher desires.

The front of a simple data card is shown in Figure 6.1. Notice that the multiple-choice test item shown is typed so that ample space is allowed for revision. Interlinear notations can be made if the item is to be changed; new options can be written to the right of the original ones if desired. Notice also that the item is cross-referenced with the cells of the table of specifications on which it is based. Each cell is identified by the row (the Arabic number) and the column (the English letter) of the table that intersect to form it. Additional useful information is the page or chapter number of a book or other reference directly related to the subject matter of the item. This allows the teacher to check quickly any detail that might be questioned.

No. 143

If both the President and the Vice President of the United States are unable to serve, which of the following officials will act as President?

(1) Secretary of State
(2) Speaker of the House of Representatives
(3) Secretary of Defense
(4) President pro tempore of the Senate

Cells in table of specifications:			*Reference(s):*
Table No.	*Primary*	*Secondary*	Doe and Colofort
2	4B	—	*American Government Today,* Revised Ed. 1980, pp. 273-274.

FIGURE 6.1.   Front Side of Item Data Card

Test	Unit 2						Comments:
Class	11th grade						4/24 Students are confused about the meaning of the expression "unable to serve." Possibly this should be changed to "die while in office."
Date	4/24						
Item No.	18						
N_T	33						
Type of Adm.	Closed book						
Options	Upper	Lower	Upper	Lower	Upper	Lower	
1	2	4					
2	⑦	②					
3	0	2					
4	2	3					
5	—	—					
Omits	0	0					
P (Est.)	41%						
D	+ 0.45						

FIGURE 6.2.   Reverse Side of Item Data Card

The reverse side of the item data card is shown in Figure 6.2. Space is allowed for summarizing the item analysis data for as many as three separate administrations of the test item or a revision of it and for any appropriate comments made by teacher or students. For each administration, the name of the test, the class to which it was administered, its size, the date of administration, the test item number, and the type of administration are noted. Below these, the responses to all options by the upper and lower third of the class, and the P and D values of the test item are recorded.

Clearly, maintaining item data cards is a serious clerical problem. Fortunately it is not insurmountable. Item data cards such as the one shown can be easily prepared with a duplicating machine. Once an ample supply is available and the necessary item-analysis tabulation is completed, the item data card can be filled out rather rapidly. Regular attention will prevent a backlog of unrecorded data from accumulating and provide a smooth, permanent, and up-to-date record for every test item used.

Some teachers reduce the clerical load by using less elaborate cards. For instance, the data concerning the name of the test, the class to which it was administered, its size, and the type of administration are omitted. If the cards for each test are filed in a separate group, this information need be recorded only once. Others do not fill out cards for all the test items they use. Instead, only very promising test items are filed.

Advantages of a Test Item File

There are significant advantages for maintaining a test item file if you as a teacher intend to reuse test items. On the basis of the item analysis information and the comments made, you can revise the item. A quick check of the table of specifications will reveal whether the relationship between the item and the table of specifications has changed. The fact that the items are on cards facilitates separating and counting them in terms of the cells in the table of specifications. In this way, the degree of content validity of the total test can be estimated. Having the items on cards also simplifies the reproduction of the test. Since the test is built by accumulating a pack of cards, the arrangement of the items in the test can be changed by simply rearranging the cards, and the final copy of the test can be typed directly from them.

Much can be said in favor of using test items again. By constantly reworking test items and adding new ones as needed, the conscientious classroom teacher can develop some excellent achievement tests. In this way, the teacher's investment of time and effort in maintaining a test item file becomes reasonable and profitable. However, test items cannot be used again if there is any chance that students in succeeding classes will be familiar with them before the test is given. To prevent this, some teachers withhold the test copies and answer sheets after the test.

Withholding test materials, however, is neither fair to the students nor good teaching procedure. Students who are aware of their successes and failures can take action to improve their deficiencies and gain a much more realistic view of their achievements. Therefore, the teacher must, if at all possible, return the tests and discuss the results.

Reusing test items, therefore, becomes considerably more difficult. Only after a teacher has developed a large pool of test items over a period of years should any of them be used again. Under these conditions it is unlikely that any students will have any unfair advantage worth mentioning. After all, the vast majority of the previous test copies have been discarded or lost. On the other hand, even if a student had access to all of them, the task of studying them would be more forbidding than preparing for a test in the normal manner. Finally, the test items that are used again are usually revisions of the original items. Even when the revision is minor, it helps prevent a student who may have studied the original item and memorized the answer from gaining a tremendous advantage over others.

Maintaining a test item file also offers advantages to teachers who may not intend to use any of them again. Restudying test items used in the past can provide helpful hints for constructing new ones. The new item may be totally original yet based on the same idea as one in the file, or it might be such a drastic revision of an older test item that its relationship to it is not easily recognized by the students.

In addition, restudying the results of earlier tests can alert the teacher to those cells in the table of specifications that very often are the basis of successful test items and those, if any, that are not. If cells of the latter type are found, efforts at item construction can be focused on them. It is likely that weaknesses of a new test can be detected before it is given.

Limitations of a Test Item File

One of the chief limitations of maintaining a test item file, the great clerical involvement, has already been mentioned. Another limitation is that the method of recording the data is not equally applicable to all types of test items. Although the form shown in Figure 6.1 can be used for many different items, that shown in Figure 6.2 cannot. It is suitable for the common multiple-choice and true-false items but must be modified if short-answer or some of the longer matching items are used. The essay item presents even more problems, since the scoring and analyzing of the responses are so difficult.

Still another possible limitation is that maintaining a test item file will actually have an adverse effect on the teacher's instructional and measurement efforts. The first part of the argument goes this way: if teachers are very familiar with past test items, and if the same or similar test items are used in the future, they may teach toward the test without knowing it. In reality, they may be coaching the students; the instruction may slavishly follow the achievement tests instead of the reverse. The second part is that intimate knowledge of the old test items will tend to dull the teacher's creativity when building new test items. In other words, the teacher falls into a testing rut. The new test items strongly resemble old ones, novel types are typically ignored, and, as a result, the classroom achievement tests become stereotyped.

Certainly these adverse effects are possible. It is difficult to believe, however, that the discerning teacher would tolerate any of them for any length of time. The advantages gained by maintaining a test item file far outweigh these limitations.

PROBLEMS

5. Design a data card for a restricted-response essay test item.

6. Can the data card be used successfully with multiple-response objective test items designed to measure complex achievement, such as the item concerning beehives in an apple orchard shown on page 121? Give reasons for your answer.

SUMMARY

The principal concepts discussed in this chapter can be expressed as follows:

1. Each test item should be reexamined after each use by means of an item analysis in order to study its strengths and weaknesses.

2. Item analysis for norm-referenced tests concentrates on two vital features: level of difficulty and discriminating power. The former means the percentage of students who answer each test item correctly; this is expressed in terms of P values. The latter means the ability of the test item to differentiate between students who achieve well and those who achieve poorly; this is expressed in terms of D values. The students who achieve well and those who achieve

poorly are usually identified by the internal-consistency method. The total scores on the test containing the items to be analyzed serve as the criterion.

3. Appropriate levels of difficulty for test items depend on the purpose of the test. Different decisions are made for norm-referenced items and criterion-referenced ones. In the case of the former, difficulty levels cluster around the middle position (50%).

4. Results of item analysis can serve two significant purposes. In the first place, they provide important information that can help teachers gain a much better idea of the value of the test they have built; teachers should also be able to construct noticeably better tests in the future. The second use is diagnosis. By examining the data from item analysis, teachers can detect learning difficulties of individual students or of the class as a whole.

5. There are four prominent limitations in the application of item analysis. First, the internal-consistency method is suitable for tests containing items that measure somewhat the same mental functions. Achievements typically are not of this type. Second, only a very small sample of students is available for the analysis. Third, it is difficult to analyze responses to essay items. Finally, item analysis data are relative in that they are influenced by the remainder of the test in which the item appears and the particular conditions under which it is administered.

6. A convenient means of organizing much of the pertinent information yielded by item analysis is a test item file. This file is a series of cards on which are typed the item, information about the test administration, and the item-analysis data. Although maintenance creates a difficult clerical problem, a file can greatly assist the teacher who wishes to use some or all of the original test items in later tests. It can also help the teacher who plans to build new test items and, in so doing, wants to capitalize on past experiences.

SUGGESTED READINGS

ANASTASI, A. *Psychological testing* (4th ed.). New York: Macmillan, 1976.
   In chapter 8, item difficulty and discriminating power are treated in a complete fashion. Of special interest are the item characteristic curves showing the relationship between the test item and the criterion—in this case, the total scores on the test containing the item.

DIEDERICH, P. B. *Short-cut statistics for teacher-made tests* (3rd ed.), Princeton, N.J.: Educational Testing Service, 1973.
   In the first three pages, all needed instructions are given for completing an item analysis of an achievement test by students' "show of hands" in the classroom. It is possible to complete an item analysis of a one-period test in ten to twenty minutes.

EBEL, R. L. *Essentials of educational measurement* (3rd ed.). Englewood Cliffs, N.J.: Prentice-Hall, 1979.
   In chapter 13, the value of item analysis data is explained, followed by illustrations of the use of such data for improving faulty multiple-choice items.

HENRYSSON, S. Gathering, analyzing and using data on test items. In R. L. Thorndike (Ed.), *Educational measurement* (2nd ed.). Washington, D.C.: American Council on Education, 1971.

The first part of this chapter is a well-written, nontechnical presentation of the methods and principles of item analysis. In contrast, the second part deals with special problems and methods and has a stronger statistical emphasis.

MEHRENS, W. A. & LEHMANN, I. J. *Measurement and evaluation in education and Psychology.* New York: Holt, Rinehart and Winston, 1978. See pages 323–334. *Item analysis procedures useful in the classroom are discussed and illustrations provided.*

WARRINGTON, W. G. An item analysis service for teachers. *NCME Measurement in Education,* 1972, *3,* (2).
This article describes a computer-based item analysis service for classroom achievement tests. This service produces item response patterns and indices of item difficulty and the discriminating power for each test item, as well as individual student lists and distributions of raw scores for the entire class.

REFERENCES CITED

DIEDERICH, P. B. *Short-cut statistics for teacher-made tests* (3rd ed.). Princeton, N.J.: Educational Testing Service, 1973.

EBEL, R. L. *Essentials of educational measurement* (3rd ed.). Englewood Cliffs, N.J.: Prentice-Hall, 1979.

EBEL, R. L. *Practical problems in educational measurement.* Lexington, Mass.: D. C. Heath, 1980.

FINDLEY, W. G. A rationale for evaluation of item discrimination statistics. *Educational and Psychological Measurement,* 1956, *16,* 175–180.

FREMER, J. *Criterion-referenced interpretations of survey achievement tests.* Test Development Memorandum. Princeton, N.J.: Educational Testing Service, 1972.

HENRYSSON, S. Gathering, analyzing and using data on test items. In R. L. Thorndike (Ed.), *Educational measurement* (2nd ed.). Washington, D.C.: American Council on Education, 1971.

MARTUZA, V. R. *Applying norm-referenced and criterion-referenced measurement in education.* Boston: Allyn and Bacon, 1977.

POPHAM, W. J. *Criterion-referenced measurement.* Englewood Cliffs, N.J.: Prentice-Hall, 1978.

RYAN, J. J. Teacher judgment of test item properties. *Journal of Educational Measurement,* 1968, *5,* 301–306.

WARRINGTON, W. G. An item analysis service for teachers. *NCME Measurement in Education,* 1972, *3,* (2).

7

Judging Procedures
and Products

After completing this chapter you will be able to

1. Recognize the importance of measuring complex student performance
   in a broadly-based achievement evaluation program

2. Differentiate between student procedures and student products and
   identify the measurable characteristics of each

3. Gather evaluative data about student performance by developing
   and using nontesting techniques such as ranking and rating methods,
   check lists, and anecdotal records

4. List the factors which typically create a relatively high degree of
   unreliability when judging student performance

5. Describe the steps followed in developing formal performance tests
   that simulate a criterion situation (such as a job)

6. State your position with respect to the practice of students evaluating
   their own procedures and products as (a) a learning experience or
   (b) part of a total evaluation process to determine the relative quality
   of their performance

The full extent of our achievements cannot always be predicted on the basis of information about part of them. For instance, an investor may reveal widespread knowledge about the economic laws of supply and demand, the histories of prominent industrial companies, and the characteristics of economic cycles in the United States and the world, but still fail to realize anything more than an occasional modest profit when playing the stock market. An avid football fan can no doubt quote at length the rules of the game, recall accurately outstanding contests of past seasons, and even diagnose a quarterback's offensive strategy and plan effective defenses to contain it, yet be unable to play the game himself on a par with his twelve-year-old son. The music critic may command extensive knowledge of the musical score, the instruments played, and perhaps the life of the composer, but not be able to play a single note. Likewise, the mechanical engineer may be completely familiar with the principles of an internal combustion engine, the transmission and the suspension system of a modern automobile, yet not be able to drive or repair it with ease.

There are obvious parallels in formal education. A student studying general science may be able to cite accurately the laws on which an experiment is based and even draw schematically the apparatus needed to conduct the experiment, yet experience great difficulty when trying to set up the apparatus and reproduce the results of the original experiment. In the language arts, a student may quote the rules of English grammar without hesitation, spell a great variety of words, and command a large vocabulary, but be unable to write an acceptable original theme. Students in a home economics class may know many facts and principles about food preparation, yet fail in their attempts to prepare a baked custard that is suitable to serve.

It is clear that attempts to predict the quality of a performance involving physical activity on the basis of verbal and mathematical knowledge are often unsuccessful, not only in everyday experiences but also in the classroom. For information about the student's ability to perform, direct inspection of that performance is called for. This means that the student must be given an opportunity to perform under suitable conditions.

Evaluation of student performance all too often is accorded a secondary place in the evaluation program. A quick study of educational objectives reveals, however, that such an attitude is unjustified. Sprinkled liberally throughout the listings of elementary and secondary school educational objectives are those directed toward development of motor skills, ability to create products of approved quality, ability to perform services efficiently, and so forth. These are largely a part of the psychomotor domain.

Note that some of the objectives of physical and biological science require that the student be able to manipulate apparatus and create products such as drawings of specimens, logs and diaries, and operational mock-ups. In physical education, driver education, art, and music, many of the most important objectives are not verbal or mathematical in nature. The vocational programs, such as business, agriculture, industrial arts, and home economics, also are dominated by educational objectives that stress student performance. Finally, in the language arts, handwriting skill and speaking ability are integral parts of the program.

The importance of these objectives cannot be overestimated. Quite regularly, students' success or lack of success in reaching such goals as these reveals the nature of their higher-order learning. Paper-and-pencil achievement tests are a useful but somewhat limited means of measuring complex achievement. They need to be supplemented. Systematic examination of student performance is often an excellent means of doing this.

No doubt the principal reasons that a relatively small part of the teacher's evaluative effort is directed toward the study of student performance are that (1) the techniques tend to be more subjective and less dependable than paper-and-pencil achievement testing and (2) they are aimed at more complex aspects of behavior, and hence are difficult to administer, score, and interpret. In spite of these two problems, a number of useful instruments have been developed in this area. Some are directed primarily toward the procedure displayed by the student, whereas others are directed toward a product yielded by that procedure. Therefore, as a first step in examining these measurement efforts, it is convenient to divide student performance into two parts—procedures and products.

Procedures and Products

Procedure and product are clearly interdependent, yet in terms of their description they are easily distinguished. Procedures are the sequences of movements executed by the student; products are the results of these procedures. A good illustration can be found in typing. The procedure learned by the student involves assuming a proper posture, placing the fingers on certain keys before beginning, watching the material to be typed rather than the keyboard, and striking only designated keys with each finger, doing so with the proper stroke. The product can be a typed business letter or several paragraphs or pages of prose. Similar illustrations can be found in art, mechanical drawing, handwriting, home economics, agriculture, and industrial arts.

In some educational areas, however, it is difficult to separate the two. Some of the objectives in music, physical education, and speaking are so stated that procedure and product are inextricably intermixed. This is of no great concern to us when evaluating performance.

Measurable Characteristics of Procedures

The complex nature of many procedures prevents teachers from measuring all their subtle aspects. Indeed, teachers often feel fortunate if they can record sufficient data on just the major features. Since the time available is generally short, and a number of the characteristics of many procedures defy measurement for all practical purposes, they are generally faced with a difficult task.

The characteristics that virtually defy measurement may be extremely important. For example, speaking ability should be evaluated in terms of such attributes as rhythm of talking, variety of word usage, and appropriateness of pitch and tone of voice. Shop procedures should display, among other things, an adaptability by the student when unforeseen difficulties arise. Performance in a physical education class should often be characterized by grace, ability, and coordination. Since these are essential features of a student's performance, they must be judged. But how? Clearly, the teacher must, on the basis of training and experience, establish standards for such features as these and then, in a subjective manner, classify the performance by comparing it with the standards.

The characteristics of measurable procedures can usually be classified in one of two categories—those related to the efficiency of the procedure and those related to its accuracy. Efficiency suggests a smoothness of action coupled with rapidity and a general economy of effort. Very often, key data in this category are the speed of performance, as in a typing exercise, or the identification of the sequence of steps followed, as in the use of a microscope. Accuracy means that few errors are committed; moreover, those committed are relatively unimportant. For example, tabulations can be made of the number of words mispronounced and grammatical errors made during a speech. In a singing or instrumental exercise, a similar count could be made of the instances in which the student misjudges the pitch of a note or its duration, or the length of a rest. Clearly it is possible for a given student performance to have some but not all of the characteristics in each category.

Measurable Characteristics of Products

Since the quality of a product is basically a reflection of the quality of the procedure that yielded it, the tendency of a product to be complex varies directly with the complexity of its related procedure. Again, this factor increases the difficulty of the measurement. On the other hand, the time available is an important difference. Seldom does the teacher feel the extreme pressure of time limitation when examining products, as is often the case with procedures. Moreover, some products can, if necessary, be broken down into their component parts and each part analyzed. Many can be subjected to rigorous and varied measurement without such a breakdown—all at a relatively leisurely pace—which simplifies the process.

The study of student products is highly subjective. For instance, the teacher must answer questions such as the following: Is the drawing of the biological specimen sufficiently accurate? How well must a blouse fit before it is a good product? Is the woodworking project in question aesthetically attractive? What must a typing exercise look like before one can say that it is "professional" work? These and a myriad of similar questions can only be answered by the teacher applying certain standards in the same subjective manner as in the case of procedure evaluation.

Measurable characteristics of products are typically numerous. For example, a typing product can be measured in terms of its length and number of errors, a woodworking product in terms of its dimensions and angle sizes. In those cases when the product has been made according to precise specifications (such as blueprint specifications), one can evaluate how closely the product conforms to them.

Notice that these characteristics of products tend to be specific rather than general and that the measurement of them is quite reliable.

Importance of a Natural Situation

Procedures and products are usually studied in a natural situation or one very much like it. This is one of the great strengths of these methods. The elaborate equipment found in the gymnasium, the science laboratories, the industrial and agricultural shops, the art and music studios, the business education rooms, and the home economics kitchens and sewing quarters of the modern school offer realistic settings in which to teach and also to evaluate student growth. Certainly samples of student behavior concerning procedures and products are being observed in a much more natural situation and much more directly when these facilities are used than when paper-and-pencil tests based upon the same specific educational objectives are administered.

The realism of these observation settings is a function of several factors, one of which is the nature and amount of equipment available. For instance, in vocational education or science courses, the equipment may differ greatly from that later used by the students when they leave secondary school for a job or college. Close liaison with business, industry, and colleges plus a flexible budget for purchasing can prevent any serious gap.

Observation Techniques

The instruments used in the observation of procedure and product are primarily of the nontesting type. In other words, they can, but do not necessarily, yield quantitative information. Instead, they commonly include qualitative information coupled with personal impressions or opinions. Many times they function as recording devices. They provide a convenient means of organizing and summarizing teachers' observations of student performances and their reactions to them.

The most widely used techniques for procedure and product observation are ranking, and rating methods, check lists, product scales, and anecdotal records. Of these, teachers often rely on ranking and rating methods more than any of the others.

Ranking. Ranking is one of the lower levels of measurement known as the ordinal scale of measurement. All that is attempted is an ordering of the students according to the merits of the procedures they displayed or the products they made. Under certain circumstances, ranking can be fairly reliable, that is, consistent. This is usually true when a competent judge is ranking a procedure or product on the basis of only one of its characteristics. Thus, members of a driver training class may be reliably ranked according to their ability to brake properly, or students in a mechanical drawing class can be ranked in terms of the thickness uniformity of the straight lines in their drawings. The more clearly defined the characteristic, the more likely the ranking will be reliable.

As the basis for the ranking broadens, its reliability tends to drop. Rankings of the general merit of a procedure or product in which not one but several characteristics are simultaneously considered can be quite unreliable. Certainly the ranking of students' general driving ability (including posture, starting, steering, and stopping) and the general quality of their drawings (including lettering, dimensions, accuracy, and neatness) are no doubt less reliable than the rankings of the single characteristics described. This drop in reliability can be traced to two causes. First, it is difficult to define clearly the meanings of these many characteristics. Second, the relative importance of each characteristic in terms of its contribution to the composite rank is rarely, if ever, completely established. Thus, it is clear that successful ranking normally must be based on a single well-defined characteristic. Moreover, if possible, the ranking should be repeated by either the same observer (without knowledge of the results of the first attempt) or other competent observers.

Rating. Rating scales, which take many forms, are popular devices for summarizing procedure and product information. One of the most common is the continuum form. The basic steps followed in its construction and use are as follows. Characteristics of the performance or product are identified, and a continuum representing degrees of merit is established for each characteristic. The continuum may be divided into as few as two positions or as many as ten or more, each position representing a different degree of merit or quality. The various positions along the continuum are often identified by number and, in the case of the graphic scale, a brief description of the corresponding degree of merit. The observer then rates each characteristic of the procedure or product in question by checking the number or description that corresponds most closely to the degree of merit observed. Illustrations of this type of rating scale are included in the following sections.

Rating based on overall general merit is as difficult a process as ranking on that basis. The failure to clearly define the characteristic to be included, and to definitely establish the relative importance of each, reduces the worth of this type of rating. Again, successful rating, like successful ranking, usually should be based on a single well-defined characteristic and should be repeated.

Using Check Lists. Check lists are highly serviceable instruments for recording student procedures. Usually they list a series of actions, whether desirable or not, that are a part of a typical student's performance. These are arranged in a convenient manner, usually in the order in which you would expect them to occur. For instance, in the case of the check list for the softball batting form shown in a following section, the sequence is: (1) bat grip, (2) preliminary stance, (3) stride, (4) pivot, and (5) swing.

The type of response for each entry in the check list can vary. Very often, it is simply a check mark indicating that the action listed had occurred. In other cases, a yes or no response is required, the yes response meaning that the action had been performed in a satisfactory manner, the no response meaning the opposite. A third type of response is one in which numbers are placed after the actions. The numbers, starting with 1, indicate the sequence in which the actions occurred. In other words, if a teacher is checking the student's skill in using a microscope, the completed check list is a step-by-step summary of the procedure followed.

The development and use of check lists sensitizes teachers to the subparts of each procedure. In this way, they gain a better view of the totality of the procedure and a more reliable technique for reporting information about it.

Using Product Scales.   A product scale is a carefully selected series of products representing various levels of quality. Each product in the scale is usually identified by a number or letter. Each scale is generally composed of five or more products, and an attempt is made to select these so that they are evenly spaced along an "inferior-superior" continuum of quality.

The application of a product scale is quite simple. Each student prepares a product of the kind included in the product scale. This is then compared with those of the scale and as close a match as possible is made. The student's product is then assigned the letter or number of the one in the scale it most closely resembles.

One of the best known product scales is the *Ayres Measuring Scale for Handwriting, Gettysburg Edition,* which is used for determining the quality of young children's handwriting. The children are given two minutes in which to copy the first three sentences of Lincoln's Gettysburg Address. To determine legibility, each student's handwriting specimen is then compared with a scaled series of printed samples. There are eight samples in all. The comparison is made by sliding each specimen along the scale until a printed sample of the same or very similar quality is found. The number for this sample is the value assigned to the specimen.

Teachers can build product scales without great difficulty. For instance, student products, such as drawings involving orthographic projection, sewing samples of hemming, basting, and backstitching, woodworking samples of sawing and nailing, and typing products such as a business letter, can be accumulated over a period of a few years. No doubt their quality will vary widely. Repeated independent attempts to arrange them by quality in equal-appearing intervals will eliminate many products that are near-duplicates or about which there is disagreement. The remainder can serve as a product scale.

Using Anecdotal Records.   Anecdotal records are the most informal of the five techniques mentioned here. The teacher does little more than summarize in writing the major actions of a procedure performed by a student. A definite attempt is made to produce a factual report. A single such record may mean little; however, a series of related anecdotal records can contribute appreciably to the study of student procedures.

Anecdotal records are used most frequently when so little is known about the procedures in question that its characteristics cannot be well defined. Thus, suitable check lists and rating scales cannot be constructed. Anecdotal records are fittingly used in those cases in the fine arts, physical education, social studies, and home economics in which the teacher is interested in expressive educational objectives.

PROBLEMS

1. Identify the measurable aspects of each of the following procedures:
    a. Executing a forehand drive in tennis.
    b. Bending a piece of glass tubing to form a right angle.
    c. Parking an automobile parallel to the curb.
    d. Hemming a dress.

2. Identify the measurable aspects of each of the following products:
    a. A map that is an enlargement of a professionally drawn map.
    b. A short poem
    c. An apron.
    d. A set of wooden whatnot shelves.

3. Five main types of rating scales are descriptive scales, graphic scales, product scales, man-to-man rating scales, and numerical scales. Study each type and determine its merits as a means of gathering data about student achievement.

Observation of Procedures

Techniques most often used in observation of procedures are ranking procedures, rating scales, check lists, and anecdotal records. Among the many variations of these techniques that have been developed are the following: (1) rating scales for evaluating speaking, (2) a check list for evaluating softball batting form, (3) a check list for reporting student behavior when engaged in group work, and (4) a sample anecdotal record concerning achievement in social studies.

Rating Scales for Speaking

The characteristics of speaking have been defined quite clearly. Among those usually listed are enunciation, pronunciation, loudness, word usage, rhythm, pitch, rate, and posture and movements. The skilled observer can separate one from another and, with appropriate rating scales, can record judgments of the quality of a student's performance.

Typical of the graphic rating scales constructed and used by teachers are the pair shown in Figure 7.1, the first pertaining to enunciation and the second to pronunciation. Here only a three-point scale is used. If desired, they could be expanded to five points and appropriate descriptions added as required.

The descriptions beneath each number, though brief, are helpful. They add meaning to the numbers; as a result, the rating scales are improved. The space for comments is often an invaluable addition to the scale. Much useful specific information for evaluation and also remediation can be added. If desired, a tally of the frequency of a flaw in procedure can be added as in the case of the "agin" for "again" error in Scale B.

When a student is to deliver a prepared speech, some teachers prefer rating scales tailored more closely to this activity than a series such as that in Figure 7.1.

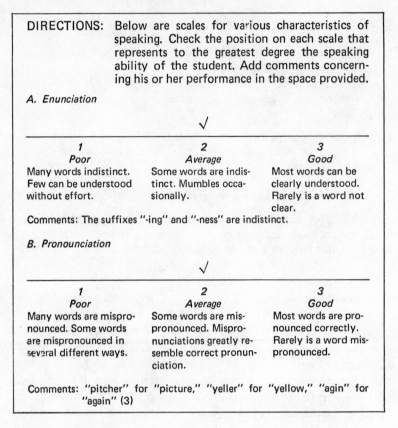

DIRECTIONS: Below are scales for various characteristics of
speaking. Check the position on each scale that
represents to the greatest degree the speaking
ability of the student. Add comments concerning his or her performance in the space provided.

A. Enunciation

✓

1	2	3
Poor	*Average*	*Good*
Many words indistinct. Few can be understood without effort.	Some words are indistinct. Mumbles occasionally.	Most words can be clearly understood. Rarely is a word not clear.

Comments: The suffixes "-ing" and "-ness" are indistinct.

B. Pronounciation

✓

1	2	3
Poor	*Average*	*Good*
Many words are mispronounced. Some words are mispronounced in several different ways.	Some words are mispronounced. Mispronunciations greatly resemble correct pronunciation.	Most words are pronounced correctly. Rarely is a word mispronounced.

Comments: "pitcher" for "picture," "yeller" for "yellow," "agin" for
"again" (3)

FIGURE 7.1.   Sample Rating Scales for Judging Speaking Ability

For example, scales can be constructed for judging the effectiveness of such elements of the speech as the introduction used by the student, the body of the
speech, the transition from topic to topic, and the conclusion. Added to these
might be scales for judging gestures and movements, eye contact, voice, and so
forth.

Batting Check List Form

Check lists and rating scales may not differ as much as descriptions of them
would suggest. The "comments" sections frequently included in rating scales allow
space in which the observer can note specific features of the student's behavior; in
a check list the most common of these features would be listed and, hence, checked
only when appropriate. On the other hand, some check lists include crude representations of continua much like those found in rating scales.

An illustration of a check list that is based in part on a series of rating scales
is that shown in Figure 7.2. This is designed to record observations of batting
form (Scott & French, 1959, pp. 421–423). Each time a student bats, an observer

Date	Rater's initials	Player's name _____
_____	_____	Captain's name _____

Instructions: Rate the player each time at bat. Place a tally mark in the space which precedes the best description of player's form in each of six categories. Indicate your observation of errors in the right-hand half of the page, again with a tally mark. Write in any additional errors and add comments below.

1. Grip
   _____ good
   _____ fair
   _____ poor

2. Preliminary stance
   _____ good
   _____ fair
   _____ poor

3. Stride or footwork
   _____ good
   _____ fair
   _____ poor

4. Pivot or body twist
   _____ good
   _____ fair
   _____ poor

5. Arm movement or swing
   _____ good
   _____ fair
   _____ poor

6. General (Eyes on ball, judgment of pitcher, etc.)
   _____ good
   _____ fair
   _____ poor

Errors
_____ Hands too far apart
_____ Wrong hand on top
_____ Hands too far from end of bat

_____ Stands too near plate
_____ Stands too far away
_____ Rear foot closer to plate than forward foot
_____ Stands too far forward
_____ Stands too far backward
_____ Bat resting on shoulders
_____ Shoulders not horizontal

_____ Fails to step forward
_____ Fails to transfer weight
_____ Lifts back foot from ground

_____ Fails to twist body
_____ Fails to wind up
_____ Has less than 90° of pivot

_____ Arms held too close to body
_____ Rear elbow elevated
_____ Bat not held so that head is higher than wrists
_____ Fails to use enough wrist action
_____ Wrists are not uncocked forcefully

_____ Jerky movements
_____ Tries too hard
_____ Fails to look at exact center of ball
_____ Poor judgment of pitches
_____ Lacks confidence
_____ Poor selection of bat

FIGURE 7.2.   Sample Check List for Softball Batting Form

From Scott and French, 1959; reproduced by permission of M. Gladys Scott.

checks "good," "fair," or "poor" with respect to grip, stance, stride, pivot, and swing. Then the observer checks in the right-hand column the errors that are committed. The list of errors is expanded if necessary. An experienced observer can complete such a check list as this very quickly and with acceptable accuracy.

Check List for Behavior in Group Work

Teachers frequently want to determine whether their students are acquiring and practicing desirable social habits and attitudes. Some of these are revealed when the students are engaged in committee and group work. Of interest in these instances are such student behaviors as willingness to cooperate, volunteering for duties, making worthwhile suggestions, and displaying democratic leadership. To provide a situation in which these behaviors can be displayed, a committee of students is formed to perform certain tasks, such as drawing a map of the playground or planning class observance of a national holiday. The behaviors displayed can be recorded on a check list.

A sample check list of the kind that might be used in these situations is shown in Figure 7.3. Eight kinds of behaviors are listed. Teachers are to check whether each occurred. Should the evidence be insufficient or conflicting, they check the category labeled "Uncertain." Observe that this category is not a middle position between "Yes" and "No." Instead it is a position that indicates that the teacher is unable to make a judgment for any number of reasons. Perhaps the student has no opportunity to display the behavior in question throughout the period that the committee is at work. Perhaps the teacher is unable to observe the student for an appropriate length of time. Perhaps the student behaved inconsistently. The last might be the subject of anecdotal records that would then supplement the check list.

DIRECTIONS: Below are eight kinds of behavior that a pupil might display when participating in committee or group work. Check "Yes" if it occurred; check "No" if it did not. If the evidence available is insufficient or conflicting, check "Uncertain."

BEHAVIOR	YES	NO	UNCERTAIN
1. Starts working promptly			
2. Volunteers for assignments			
3. Displays interest			
4. Cooperates with others			
5. Displays cheerfulness			
6. Makes worthwhile suggestions			
7. Is a follower occasionally			
8. Is a leader occasionally			

FIGURE 7.3.   Sample Check List for Reporting Student Behavior in Group Work

Anecdotal Records in Social Studies

Recording observations of spontaneous procedures is seldom an easy task. Yet much of this spontaneous behavior is very indicative of learning already acquired, and hence it cannot be ignored. The anecdotal record reports the principal details of the procedures observed, and when a series of them is available concerning related procedures, interesting insights into learning can be gained.

The sample anecdotal record shown in Figure 7.4 concerns a comparatively shy junior high school boy who surprised his teacher by insisting that he make his oral report to a social studies class as scheduled, even though he had accidentally left his written notes at home. His level of performance revealed an unusual degree of knowledge and interest in his topic and offered possible clues with regard to ways to involve him to a greater degree in future classroom discussions. Notice the factual nature of the description of the incident as contrasted with the interpretive nature of the comments that follow it.

This case of student behavior differs from those previously considered in this chapter. In speaking and batting skill, the observer is interested in the smoothness and accuracy with which the procedure is executed. These, too, might be the subjects of anecdotal records. Here, however, the observer is primarily concerned with the fact that this behavior happened at all. In other words, a helpful insight into students' achievement in social studies is obtained by noting what they did and how they reacted to it, rather than the quality level of the specific features of their behavior. For example, whether the junior high school boy enunciated clearly or had well-organized material for his oral report is not as important as other factors.

ANECDOTAL RECORD FORM

Date: November 16, 19_____   Pupil's Name: Fred Burke

Observer: R. S. Rover

Description of Incident:

Fred was scheduled to make an oral report to the class concerning cattle branding. Although he forgot his notes, he did not want a postponement. He specifically requested that he report as planned.

He spoke extemporaneously and used the blackboard repeatedly to sketch the various brands he mentioned. Much information was presented, including references to the history of the American West. The class was unusually attentive.

Comment:

This was by far the best report he has given. For the first time he was visibly pleased with his efforts. He evidently knows much about the history of the early West, and enjoys talking about it.

FIGURE 7.4.   Sample Anecdotal Record Pertaining to Achievement in Social Studies

PROBLEMS

4. Would the checklist for reporting student behavior in group work shown in Figure 7.3 be improved if a column entitled "Sometimes" were inserted between the "Yes" and "No" columns and the directions changed appropriately? Why?

5. Using the anecdotal record shown in Figure 7.4 as an example, list the inherent limitations present in this reporting technique.

Judgment of Products

Ranking procedures, rating scales (including score cards), point systems, and product scales are popular means by which student products are studied. As illustrations of some of the many possibilities offered by these techniques, three instruments are described here: (1) rating scales for theme analysis; (2) rating scales for judging student woodworking projects; and (3) a point system for evaluating student drawings representing three-dimensional space on a two-dimensional plane.

Rating Scales for Themes

Many subjects occasionally require that the student submit a largely original written product. English courses are—and should be—especially demanding in this respect. The well-known English theme calls upon the student to select a topic, arrange its subparts in a suitable manner, and develop them in appropriate written form. From a measurement point of view, a theme is both an important and a complex product.

The complex nature of a theme makes its evaluation difficult. To overcome this problem, some teachers divide the characteristics of a theme into two categories: (1) content and (2) matters of form and style. The content categories include the selection of the topic (if topics are not assigned), organization, and the quantity and quality of investigation. The form and style category includes the elements of grammar, punctuation, spelling, capitalization, sentence structure, word usage, and so forth.

The relative importance of the two categories and their respective subparts no doubt varies radically from teacher to teacher, depending on the purpose of the theme and the maturity of the student. For example, themes in a social studies class should be scrutinized more carefully in terms of content than form and style. The reverse may be true for most themes in an English class. In addition, the subparts of a category, such as the quantity and quality of topic investigation and the documentation of the theme, will probably lose importance when one is judging themes from lower grade levels.

Sample rating scales for themes are shown in Figure 7.5. Only two are shown, one from each category. Notice that these are five-point scales although

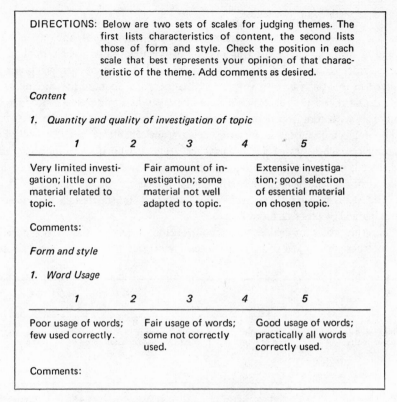

DIRECTIONS: Below are two sets of scales for judging themes. The first lists characteristics of content, the second lists those of form and style. Check the position in each scale that best represents your opinion of that characteristic of the theme. Add comments as desired.

Content

1. *Quantity and quality of investigation of topic*

1	2	3	4	5

Very limited investigation; little or no material related to topic.	Fair amount of investigation; some material not well adapted to topic.	Extensive investigation; good selection of essential material on chosen topic.

Comments:

Form and style

1. *Word Usage*

1	2	3	4	5

Poor usage of words; few used correctly.	Fair usage of words; some not correctly used.	Good usage of words; practically all words correctly used.

Comments:

FIGURE 7.5.   Sample Rating Scales for Judging Themes

only three descriptions are included. An observer vacillating between two of the positions for which descriptions are available may want to select the intermediate position. A series of similar scales can be developed for other characteristics in each category.

Some doubt exists as to the need for such sets of criteria as those mentioned. There is little evidence that they are consistently used by teachers. Moreover, other investigations have established that a fast impressionistic reading of essays by several qualified readers is a reasonably reliable method of measuring student writing ability (Educational Testing Service, 1978, pp. 9–10). This method requires the reader of themes and essays to make global or holistic judgments of each paper rather than analytical judgments. The theme is read quickly for total impressions and given one of three or five ratings; for example, a score of "3" is for a superior paper, "2" is for an average paper, and "1" is for an inferior paper.

Attempts to grade essays by means of a computer are described in connection with procedures for scoring responses to essay test questions (see page 152). This work is useful. If the computer can consistently appraise writing ability as well as, or better than, competent judges can, we have made a significant breakthrough in our ability to evaluate this important work product.

Rating Scales for Shop Products

Many shop products must conform to prescribed dimensions and, as a result, mechanical devices can be used as one means of determining their quality. For instance, rules, combination squares, calipers, and gauges of various kinds are employed in this process. In a very direct manner, one or more measurements are obtained that reveal the success or failure of the student to develop a product of a certain size, with certain proportions, or within certain tolerance limits.

Helpful as mechanical devices are, they are not capable of measuring all of the important characteristics of a shop product. Anyone who has carefully examined wood, metal, or plastic shop products realizes that two such products may have nearly identical dimensions, but still differ noticeably in workmanship. Characteristics such as aesthetic attractiveness, strength, finish, design, and neatness must be judged by other techniques.

Six rating scales for evaluating a woodworking project are shown in Figure 7.6. Many of these scales are related to the characteristics of strength, attractiveness,

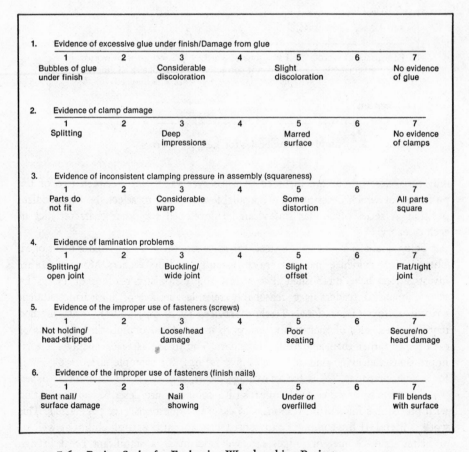

FIGURE 7.6.   Rating Scales for Evaluating Woodworking Projects

From Baldwin, 1971, p. 885; reproduced by permission of McGraw-Hill, Inc.

and neatness mentioned. For example, the presence or absence of clamp damage (#2) and improper use of finish nails (#6) are parts of the attractiveness and neatness category.

Notice that a seven-point scale is given for each factor, with brief descriptions for the first, third, fifth, and seventh position. It is quite possible that teachers find that they are unable to identify this many degrees of quality. If so, the number of points on the scale should be reduced. The number and length of the descriptions can also be varied to satisfy personal preferences.

Point System for Judging Drawings

A widely-used objective in art seeks to determine if students are able to produce drawings that contain various visual components; the objective is specifically concerned with the use of spatial concepts (National Assessment of Educational Progress, 1977, p. 4). One means of determining the degree to which students have achieved this objective is to ask them to complete the following task:

> Pretend that you are standing at one end of a room and at the other end there is a square table with four people sitting at it. Draw the table and the people as you see them from your end of the room. Put one person at each side of the table.

This exercise demands a high level of spatial visualization on the part of the students. Because they have to visualize the drawing schematically before beginning, it is a complex task, and evaluating the product is difficult. One useful method for judging the drawings is to determine the presence of the following twelve characteristics with one point awarded for each:

Use of Converging Lines

1. Table top shown as a foreshortened tilted plane
2. Table legs shown foreshortened
3. Chair legs shown foreshortened

Use of Overlapping Figures and Objects

4. Figures shown overlapping table
5. Table shown overlapping figures
6. Figures shown overlapping figures

Use of Distance

7. Distant figures shown higher
8. Near figures shown lower

Completeness

9. Four figures shown at the table
10. Figures shown seated at the table

11. A figure shown at each side of the table

12. Figures shown complete

Notice that the first eight of the foregoing characteristics are based on three drawing techniques that help to create a sense of space: use of converging lines, overlapping figures and objects, and distance. The students' ability to follow directions is reflected in the last four characteristics.

When responding to the "four people seated at a table" exercise, each student uses an ordinary-size sheet of white paper for the drawing and must complete it in about eight minutes. In Figure 7.7 are three drawings by nine-year-olds. Note that one drawing is awarded 5 points, another 8 points and the last 10 points. Studying the drawings in relation to the point scale shows where each student is having difficulty or is achieving success.

PROBLEMS

6. Seventh-grade students in social studies were required to draw a map showing the principal rivers and lakes in their home state. They were allowed to refer to, but not directly copy, printed maps. The following graphic rating scales were to be used first by the students and then by the teacher to judge the product of their efforts. Revise these scales in any manner that, in your opinion, will strengthen them.

RATING SCALE

5	4	3	2	1
Very neat	Neat	Fairly neat	Somewhat messy	Messy
Words are printed not written	Printed	Some words might not be printed	Written	Written
Has title and key	Both title and key	Might lack correct title or key	Might lack title or key	Lacks both
Has shown rivers and lakes most clearly	Has shown all rivers and lakes	Lacks one or two required items	Lacks several items	Lacks many items

7. Study each of the drawings of four people seated at a table shown in Figure 7.7 and, using the list of twelve characteristics shown, judge each. Are your scores the same as those shown? If discrepancies exist, what do you think caused them?

(8 pts)

(5 pts)

(10 pts)

FIGURE 7.7.   Illustrative Drawings by Nine-Year-Olds of Four People Seated at a Table
From the National Assessment of Educational Progress, 1977, pp. 35–37.

Reliability of Judging Student Performance

Judging student performance is typically less objective and organized than paper-and-pencil testing, and sometimes less satisfying to both teacher and student. Many of these problems are associated directly with a serious weakness of judging performance, that is, a relatively high degree of unreliability. A high degree of unreliability means that the procedures frequently yield inconsistent results.

This can be traced both to the performance evaluated and to the observer. In other words, the reliability of the process is directly related to the degree of successful sampling of student performance and the consistency of the observer in judging that performance.

Sampling Student Performances

Sampling student performances is necessarily limited in scope. How many times is it possible for a student to deliver a prepared speech, build a pair of bookends, or cut out and sew an apron? Teachers may have only one or two opportunities to observe these performances, which may not take place under conditions that they can control as much as they would like. Yet teachers must assume that they are typical representations of achievement.

Some products require considerable quantities of both class and out-of-class time in which to be completed. As a result, unauthorized assistance by a second party is likely. The product then becomes much less useful in terms of judging student achievement.

Ideally, then, the teacher should have at least several opportunities to observe an important student performance. Such samples should truly reflect the student's individual achievement and should take place under suitable conditions.

Improving Observer Reliability

Fatigue, boredom, and indifference can destroy the worth of the observer's attempts to examine student performance. To reduce the impact of these factors, teachers can preplan observations as much as possible, being certain that they spread them out over a reasonable period of time. On the other hand, since these and other factors can never be eliminated fully, multiple observation is desirable. This means that in the case of judging procedures, several competent teachers should observe independently and then reconcile any differences of opinion that exist. In the case of judging products, several persons can participate, or one can judge the product more than once without knowledge of earlier decisions.

Unfortunately, consistent results yielded by efforts to judge a student's performance do not necessarily mean that a proper analysis has been made. After all, the observer or even a team of observers could be consistently wrong. This, of course, is unlikely if the observers are reasonably competent. On the other hand, such factors as the well-known "halo effect," so often present in efforts of this kind, can make the analyses more consistent but less accurate. For improvement of observer reliability, well-defined reference points are needed. In the case of procedures, these may be careful descriptions of the important aspects of various degrees of quality; in the case of products, they may be a variety of specimen products of known quality.

Using Performance Tests to Improve Reliability

Performance tests of considerable complexity are sometimes used for improving the quality of procedures and product evaluation. These are tests in which some criterion (for example, a job) is simulated to a higher degree than is represented by the usual paper-and-pencil test (Fitzpatrick & Morrison, 1971). On the basis of a careful analysis of the education objectives in question, a great effort is made to design a realistic situation for the examinees within which they can demonstrate their skills.

To develop a performance test, it is necessary to specify exactly what the students are to do and the conditions under which they are to do it (Boyd & Shimberg, 1971). One must choose (1) which elements of the task are crucial to success, (2) which of these are to be measured, (3) the necessary equipment and/or materials, (4) the time required, (5) the standard conditions that should exist, and (6) what instructions to give students and observers. Carefully tailored to the foregoing are appropriate rating and check list forms.

With thorough planning, we can design highly useful performance tests in physical education, foreign languages, industrial arts, music, and many areas of vocational education. Such tests typically combine appropriate equipment arranged in a true-to-life environment with a set of explicit instructions to the examinee. These permit a trained observer to use specially designed rating scales or check lists to report on the quality of performance with a comparatively high degree of reliability. The improved reliability is well worth the effort.

The National Assessment of Educational Progress uses test items requiring student performance in a wide variety of subject matter areas such as science (e.g., using a balance), music (e.g., singing a standard piece of music), art (e.g., designing a functional space), and writing (e.g., composing a story about a picture). These items are individually administered on a national basis and present difficult scoring problems. Nevertheless, high degrees of reliability are obtained in many instances. On the basis of this evidence, it is safe to say that classroom teachers can and should do more of this type of testing.

PROBLEM

8. The closer a performance test approaches the real criterion situation it simulates, the more likely the reliability of the measurement of student performance will *decrease* (Fitzpatrick & Morrison, 1971). What causes this?

Judgment by Students

Students as well as teachers can judge performances—their own and also those of their classmates. For example, an audience of students can rate speakers, and they can rate themselves. In a food laboratory, all students including the cook can examine the roast that is prepared and judge its merits by following the same procedures the teacher follows.

Much can be said for this type of multiple evaluation as a learning experience. When both students and teacher use the same instruments to judge the same performance simultaneously and the results are examined in conference, the students gain a much better perspective of the important features of the performance and the teacher's standards concerning them. Particularly informative is the comparison of the self-evaluation by the student with that made independently by the teacher. Certainly a diagnosis of defects and their causes as well as a plan for remediation can be based on such a conference. Most importantly, students are able to gain a realistic view of their achievement.

With regard to sound evaluation principles, there are serious objections to using individual student's judgments or a composite of these judgments in reporting achievement. Certainly we cannot assume that the average student is as competent as the teacher in judging the quality of another's performance or of his or her own. This reduces the value of student observations to a point where they are normally of minor importance. The successful observer has a maturity of judgment and sense of impartiality rarely found in students. They should be regularly allowed to gain experience in observing, but they should not be expected to make sound judgments with great consistency unless carefully trained.

PROBLEM

9. Some teachers believe that as students become skilled in self-evaluation, they actually raise the standards on which evaluations are made. Do you agree? Why?

SUMMARY

The following are the major points included in this chapter:

1. Some educational objectives are such that paper-and-pencil measuring instruments cannot reveal the degree to which students have achieved them. These goals pertain to student performances such as the ability to deliver a speech, write a paragraph, conduct an experiment, or hem a garment. Generally they are quite complex, involving both language and nonlanguage aspects, and are a part of the psychomotor domain.

2. Judgments of student performance can be based on the procedure displayed by the student or the products yielded by the procedure. Both have some characteristics that lend themselves readily to measurement and some that do not. Efficiency and accuracy are the procedure characteristics most often

evaluated. Product characteristics can often be measured more easily; in fact, mechanical devices are available for this purpose for such articles as shop products.

3. The instruments used in judging procedures and products are primarily of the nontesting type. For procedures, ranking and rating methods, checklists, and anecdotal records are frequently applied. For products, ranking and rating methods, point systems, and product scales are used. In all cases, a competent observer is needed.

4. Performance evaluation is not always highly reliable because student performance is not always successfully sampled and the observer is not always consistent. Repeated sampling of student performances and independent observations by one or more qualified teachers increase the reliability of the process a great deal.

5. When students judge their own performances or those of their classmates, they gain excellent experience in this process, although their attempts seldom produce superior evaluative data.

SUGGESTED READINGS

BLOOM, B. S., HASTINGS, J. T., & MADAUS, G. F. *Handbook on formative and summative evaluation of student learning.* New York: McGraw-Hill, 1971.
Chapters 17, 18, 21, and 23 deal with the evaluation of learning in art, science, writing, and industrial education respectively. Evaluation of student performance in these areas is included.

BOYD, J. L., & SHIMBERG, B. *Developing performance tests for classroom evaluation.* Princeton, N.J.: ERIC Clearinghouse for Tests, Measurement, and Evaluation, Educational Testing Service, 1971.
The nature of performance and problems associated with the development of performance tests are discussed.

EDUCATIONAL TESTING SERVICE. *The concern for writing* (Focus 5). Princeton, N.J.: Author, 1978.
The second half of this monograph is devoted to methods of assessing writing ability, describing both objective tests and writing samples scored holistically. Several college-level programs to assess writing ability are discussed.

FITZPATRICK, R., & MORRISON, E. J. Performance and product evaluation. In R. L. Thorndike (Ed.), *Educational measurement* (2nd ed.). Washington, D.C.: American Council on Education, 1971.
Performance tests to measure achievement are described, along with a wide variety of illustrations. Steps for developing and scoring performance tests are presented.

NATIONAL ASSESSMENT OF EDUCATIONAL PROGRESS. *First national assessment of musical performance.* Denver: Author, 1974.
The national music assessment included fifteen performance exercises which required students to sing familiar songs, repeat unfamiliar musical material, improvise, perform from notation, and perform a prepared piece. Sample exercises from each of these categories are discussed and scoring criteria provided.

NATIONAL ASSESSMENT OF EDUCATIONAL PROGRESS. *Design and drawing skills.* Denver: Author, 1977.

One drawing exercise measuring the ability to design functional space, two measuring the ability to use spatial conceptions, and one measuring the ability to show motion are described in detail. For each, a scoring method is explained, along with its application to sample drawings.

REFERENCES CITED

BALDWIN, T. S. Evaluation of learning in industrial education. In B. S. Bloom, T. J. Hasting, & G. F. Madaus, *Handbook on formative and summative evaluation of student learning.* New York: McGraw-Hill, 1971.

BOYD, J. L. & SHIMBERG, B. *Developing performance tests for classroom evaluation.* Princeton, N.J.: ERIC Clearinghouse for Tests, Measurement, and Evaluation, Educational Testing Service, 1971.

EDUCATIONAL TESTING SERVICE. *The concern for writing* (Focus 5). Princeton, N.J.: Author, 1978.

FITZPATRICK, R., & MORRISON, E. J. Performance and product evaluation. In R. L. Thorndike (Ed.), *Educational measurement* (2nd ed.). Washington, D.C.: American Council on Education, 1971.

NATIONAL ASSESSMENT OF EDUCATIONAL PROGRESS. *Design and drawing skills.* Denver: Author, 1977.

SCOTT, M. G., & FRENCH, E. *Measurement and evaluation in physical education.* Dubuque, Iowa: William C. Brown, 1959.

PART THREE

Characteristics of a Good Measuring Instrument

An unknown wit of several generations ago remarked that the only good thing about error was that it created jobs. The truth of this can be demonstrated in many areas, including student evaluation. All of our measuring instruments are somewhat inadequate, a number of them to an appreciable degree. To reduce error, the builders of these instruments are striving constantly to refine their products—which is, in a sense, an endless job. These efforts, in turn, complicate the problems of those who must choose from among many available measuring instruments those that are best suited for a particular need. Each new instrument means that a more careful selection must be made by anyone needing an instrument of that type.

As a classroom teacher, you may find yourself cast in either or both of the following roles: in one case, you may be constructing a paper-and-pencil achievement test to measure the academic achievement of your students; in a second, you may be a member of a teacher committee organized to select a scholastic aptitude or standardized achievement test to be used as part of the school testing program. In either case you need standards. You must be familiar with the characteristics of a good measuring instrument and the methods of determining to what degree a given instrument may possess them.

The characteristics of a good measuring instrument can be classified in many different ways. Here they are grouped under three headings: norms, reliability, and validity. These three headings identify the three chapters that compose Part Three. In Chapter 8, "Using Test Scores and Norms," the need for an instrument to yield easily understood and utilized information is discussed. This need is ordinarily satisfied for criterion-referenced tests by writing statements describing student behavior and for norm-referenced tests by computing norms, that is, by identifying the relative performance of a student in terms of one or more groups of peers. In Chapter 9, "The Reliability of Measurement Methods," the need for an instrument to yield consistent or dependable information is discussed. An instrument that strongly reflects this characteristic will yield virtually the same information each time it is used in an unchanging situation. Chapter 10, "The Validity of Measurement Methods," is devoted to the most important of the three characteristics. A measuring instrument is valid to the degree that it serves the purpose or purposes for which its use is intended.

Chapter 8 concentrates on norm-referenced tests almost exclusively. Chapters 9 and 10 emphasize the reliability and validity of norm-referenced tests, but also treat similar issues for criterion-referenced tests.

Some statistical methodology must be introduced to describe these characteristics and how they are measured. The arithmetic mean, the median, the standard deviation, and the product-moment coefficient of correlation are discussed at appropriate points in Part Three. In Appendix A is an additional explanation of these statistical measures, as well as a step-by-step description of the easiest ways of computing each. Although classroom teachers are seldom required to compute such values, they are often required to interpret them in connection with the validity, reliability, and norm determinations found in test manuals and educational literature.

The purpose of Part Three is to identify the characteristics of a good measuring instrument, to illustrate the most common methods of determining how strongly a specific instrument reflects them, and to provide an adequate background for those statistical techniques commonly used in such determinations. The importance of Part Three can hardly be overemphasized.

8

The Interpretation of
Test Scores and Norms

The purpose of this chapter is to help you to

1. Recognize that a raw score from a norm-referenced test lacks meaning if no additional interpretive reference points are provided

2. Be aware of the prevalence of normally distributed test data and the utility of this kind of distribution when interpreting test results

3. Define and interpret common types of norms, such as percentiles, standard scores, and grade equivalents

4. List the major advantages and limitations of each of the popular norms used in education

5. Defend the use of several norm tables, including those developed locally, when interpreting standardized test scores of a student or class

6. Describe the characteristics of a suitable standardization sample for norming a test for a specified population of students

7. Contrast scores from norm tables with narrative reports from the same test in terms of clarity and completeness of interpretation

Early every morning, practically every radio station in the United States broadcasts a summary of the latest local weather conditions and predicts what they probably will be for the remainder of the day. Here is a typical announcement that might be heard on a mid-April morning:

> The temperature this morning is 50° F (10° C), the barometric pressure 29.8, the wind velocity 10 to 20 miles per hour from the northwest, and the relative humidity 70 percent. Today will be cloudy and mild, with a high temperature of about 60° F (15° C). The probability of measurable precipitation is 5 percent.

To most listeners, this report, brief as it is, is useful. As they prepare for the day's activities informed citizens can readily decide such questions as whether they should wear spring topcoats rather than winter overcoats, make children of preschool age button woolen sweaters before leaving the house, or plan an early season golf or tennis match.

The teacher, who shares a common interest with the public in the weather report, may well ponder two additional features of this example. In the first place, the complexity of the situation being described is almost overwhelming. A one-word description of the weather would be unhappily inadequate. This is also true of a teacher's evaluation of a student. Multiple measurements are involved in a well-designed school testing program just as they are in a weather report. Secondly, it is important to note what both types of measurement reports mean to a relatively uninformed audience. Here the meteorologist has an advantage over the educator. For example, each of us learns at an early age which ranges of temperatures and wind velocities are comfortable. Little more need be said to prepare most individuals for the outdoors. These reference points are understood.

Teachers may understandably envy the meteorologist's ability to present succinct, understandable descriptions of something as intricate as the weather. Although meteorologists have not achieved perfection in their efforts, they can point to notable success. A teacher may well question whether those same individuals who seem to comprehend so much of a brief report on the day's weather would understand comparable amounts of a report on the academic achievement of their child that day in school. It is understandable, therefore, why so much attention is paid to the nature of test scores and their interpretation.

Reporting Raw Scores

The difficulty of meaningfully presenting the results yielded by educational measurement has many illustrations. Assume, for example, that a battery of norm-referenced standardized achievement tests is administered to the students in all of the tenth grades of a city school system. One is a vocabulary test composed of 100 words, the meanings of which have to be identified by each student. The success of each student is then expressed in terms of the number of words correctly identified. Therefore, for each of the 360 students who took the vocabulary test, a numerical representation of effort is available; and it can be no smaller than zero nor larger than 100.

Let us consider for a moment the position of a teacher whose students are involved in the testing program. One of the students, Tom, correctly identified the meaning of 58 of the 100 words. Hence the teacher records a score of a 58. This he properly calls a *raw score*, that is, the quantitative report that is the immediate end product of scoring the test. In the case of this test and many others like it, each student is credited with one point for every correct answer and zero points for any wrong or omitted answer. To be sure, the amount of credit could have varied for each right answer, increasing to two points or more as the words became more difficult. Furthermore, correction for guessing on the part of the student could have been made by subtracting points for wrong answers. Had either or both of these procedures been used, the result of the scoring process would still be called a raw score.

Simply labeling the "58" as one of many raw scores does not answer other questions concerning this representation of degree of success. For example, the teacher may wonder whether 58 indicates that Tom's vocabulary of words is twice as great as that of a student whose score on the same test is only 29. Certainly, it is tempting to assume that this is true. Yet the whole idea, in reality, is absurd. Such a comparison of the raw scores cannot, unfortunately, be made unless the units of measurement possess certain characteristics, that is, the characteristics of a ratio scale. Principal among these is the requirement that a raw score of zero represent a total absence of knowledge of word meanings. Of course, such total absence could not be true in this case.

Absolute Zero

The failure of the raw score of size zero to indicate zero knowledge of vocabulary is equivalent to saying that it is not an absolute zero. In other words, unlike the customary measurement of height and weight, the units of measurement of the vocabulary test are relative. Relativity is a common characteristic of test scores.

Like many achievement tests, the vocabulary test is deliberately constructed in such a way that a score of zero is not an absolute zero. If for no reason other than economy of time and energy, such simple words as *dog, house,* and *bicycle* are not included in the test since they do not differentiate among students of a typical tenth-grade class. On the other hand, words like *immaculate, predicament,* and *conscientious* may very likely be of acceptable difficulty for the class and hence are included in the test. Norm-referenced instruments such as the vocabulary test are generally designed to have a relatively small difficulty spread around the fifty percent level, so that all students to be measured will be represented on the scale rather than somewhere below or above it.

This idea can be translated into a diagram. See Figure 8.1. Although this figure is but an approximate representation of the relationship between the raw scores of the vocabulary achievement test and its level of difficulty, it nevertheless

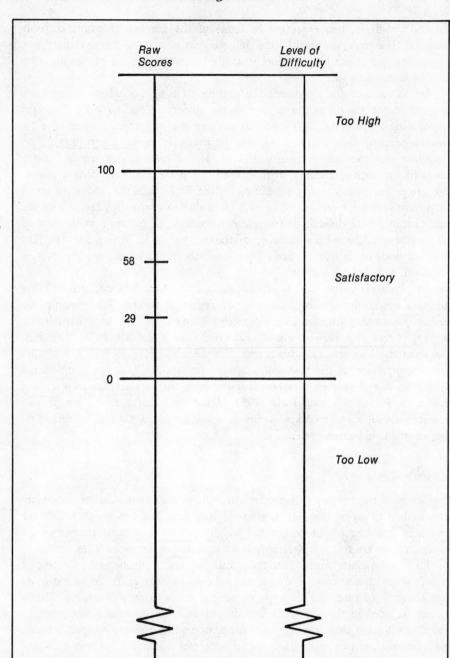

FIGURE 8.1.   Raw Scores and Level of Difficulty of an English Vocabulary Test for
Tenth-Grade Students

illustrates two noteworthy points. First of all, it is evident that a raw score of zero differs from absolute zero by some large and unknown distance. Obviously, the distance between a raw score of 58 and absolute zero is not twice the distance between a raw score of 29 and absolute zero. The second point concerns the level of difficulty of the instrument. Of course, the satisfactory level of difficulty for this achievement test varies with the group of students for whom it is designed. It would move up the scale for twelfth-grade students and down for eighth-grade students. If the test is carefully constructed, its raw-score spread will fall directly opposite the satisfactory level of difficulty as illustrated.

The failure of educational measuring instruments to have an absolute zero is not as serious as it may first seem. The continued successful use of the Fahrenheit and Celsius scales to measure temperature is ample evidence that scales without absolute units still have superior utility.

Differences Between Raw Scores

As teachers examine the raw scores reported for their classes, they may find themselves grappling with other uncertainties. For example, Tom's teacher notices that another student received a raw score of 59 in contrast to Tom's 58. Does this student in fact surpass Tom in terms of the vocabulary test? When answering this question remember that this test, like all tests, is somewhat unreliable. In other words, it does not yield completely consistent results. Test unreliability forces us to interpret each score as an interval rather than a point. These intervals, sometimes called confidence intervals or bands, are found by using the standard error of measurement (see pages 247–248). Study of such intervals shows that small differences between test scores are no doubt due to chance and hence are uninterpretable.

Unequal Units. Further examination of the vocabulary raw scores may reveal a situation such as the following:

Student	Raw score
Sheri	88
Carol	68
Arthur	37
Donald	17

Since the raw-score difference between the two members of each pair is twenty in both instances, can it be said that Sheri surpasses Carol in terms of the vocabulary test by the same amount that Arthur surpasses Donald? If the raw-score units are equal, the question can be answered affirmatively. In all likelihood, however, the difference of twenty raw-score units between the two girls is not exactly the same as the difference of twenty raw-score units between the two boys. It is all too true that educational measurement habitually yields somewhat unequal units. A specified difference, such as twenty raw-score units, cannot be identified at any position along the range, as five inches can be isolated in any position on an accurate yardstick. Hence the requirements of an interval scale are imperfectly met.

In all probability, increasing a raw score in a vocabulary test from 68 to 88 represents greater accomplishment than increasing a raw score from 17 to 37. Hence, Sheri surpasses Carol to a greater degree than Arthur surpasses Donald. It is typical of achievement tests to find "rubber units."

Interpretation of Raw Scores

The individual most vitally concerned about the 58 his teacher wrote in the record book is Tom. When informed of his achievement, he is understandably puzzled. Obviously he lacks reference points against which to compare his information. He needs a raw-score counterpart of "70° F" to help him interpret "58" the way "70° F" helps him interpret temperature reports.

His first reaction might be to convert the number of correct responses to a percent. However, this is not particularly helpful. If the test were composed of simple words, 58 percent might indicate inferior achievement. If the test were composed of difficult words, on the other hand, 58 percent might indicate superior achievement for a tenth-grade student.

No doubt Tom will request information concerning the number of words correctly identified by the other class members. For instance, if the average number of words correctly identified by his classmates is reported, then he can describe his position as "above average" or as "below average" in terms of the vocabulary test.

Three helpful reference points are now available to Tom. They are the maximum number of words correctly identified by any classmate, the minimum number of words correctly identified by any classmate, and the average number of words correctly identified by the entire class. Meager as this information is, it nevertheless provides Tom with the opportunity to interpret his 58 in much the same manner as he would a reported temperature.

Frequency Distribution. To provide Tom with information that will help him interpret his raw score, the teacher must follow several steps. Initially the teacher explains that, in view of the similarity of curriculum and educational environment in general, it is reasonable to compare the raw score of 58 not only with those of other members of Tom's class at his school, but also with those of all (360) students in tenth-grade classes in the city. Then the teacher shows Tom the scores of all other students tested. Needless to say, the columns upon columns of un-arranged raw scores (often called the ungrouped data) are hardly informative. On the other hand, the raw scores can be grouped into intervals and a frequency distribution constructed. To do so, the total spread of the scores from 15 (the lowest raw score) to 94 (the highest raw score) is arbitrarily subdivided into sixteen intervals of a constant size of five raw-score units. This procedure forms

TABLE 8.1.   Frequency Distribution of 360 Raw Scores

Raw-score intervals	Frequency	Percent	Cumulative frequency	Cumulative percent
90–94	4	1.1	360	100.0
85–89	6	1.7	356	98.9
80–84	12	3.3	350	97.2
75–79	20	5.6	338	93.9
70–74	28	7.8	318	88.3
65–69	36	10.0	290	80.6
60–64	40	11.1	254	70.6
55–59	46	12.8	214	59.4
50–54	43	11.9	168	46.7
45–49	39	10.8	125	34.7
40–44	32	8.9	86	23.9
35–39	24	6.7	54	15.0
30–34	13	3.6	30	8.3
25–29	9	2.5	17	4.7
20–24	5	1.4	8	2.2
15–19	3	0.8	3	0.8
Total	360	100.0		

the first column of Table 8.1, which is called the raw-score intervals column. Then each raw score is tallied in the proper interval. Counting the tallies yields the frequencies, that is, the second column in Table 8.1.

The interpretation of the values of the frequency column is by no means difficult. It is clear that three of the students have raw scores somewhere between 15 and 19 inclusive, whereas forty-six have raw scores between 55 and 59 inclusive; one of these is Tom.

To help Tom understand even more clearly his relative position in the group of 360 students, two columns of percentages are added, one based on cumulative frequencies. Approximately thirteen percent of the tenth-graders fall within the same interval as Tom, and forty-seven percent fall within the intervals below his. Thus about forty percent of the students fall within intervals above the one containing his raw score.

Graph Construction.   A further step the teacher may take is to convert the frequency distribution to graphic form. It is common practice to plot the data included in Table 8.1 by spacing the raw-score intervals along a horizontal axis and the frequencies along a vertical axis. In this manner, Figure 8.2 is constructed. The frequency of each interval is plotted directly above the midpoint of that interval.

The curve in Figure 8.2 is fairly characteristic of those resulting from similar plotting of the scores yielded by many different kinds of measuring instruments used in education and elsewhere. Had the students involved been infinite in number and unselected with respect to vocabulary, it is expected that the curve would be smooth and symmetrical rather than erratic. The group of 360 students some-what approximates these conditions, and thus the line resulting approximates a smooth symmetrical curve. Measurements made on smaller groups such as the typical class often yield a very erratic curve.

Normal Curve Distribution.   The curve in Figure 8.2 is shaped, for all practical purposes, like a *normal curve*. The normal curve is distinctively bell-shaped, with the peak of the curve above a point on the horizontal axis corresponding to the average score of the distribution. From the peak, the curve drops rapidly on either side, yielding a symmetrical tapering as it approaches either end of the raw-score distribution.

The fact that the raw scores from the vocabulary test tend to be normally distributed assists considerably in their description. It is immediately possible to say that few students have high raw scores, few students have low scores, whereas many have scores clustering around the average raw score. This statement can be appreciably strengthened by wording it in terms of the standard deviation and the arithmetic mean of raw scores. If the standard deviation is added to and subtracted from the arithmetic mean, points along the horizontal axis are found between which fall a fixed percentage of the scores.

Mean and Standard Deviation.   The arithmetic mean is often called the "average." It is a measure of central tendency or central location, that is, a point at or near which the test scores are clustering. With ungrouped data, it is computed by add-ing all the scores and dividing by the number of scores. However, this procedure cannot be followed when they are arranged in a frequency distribution since, in

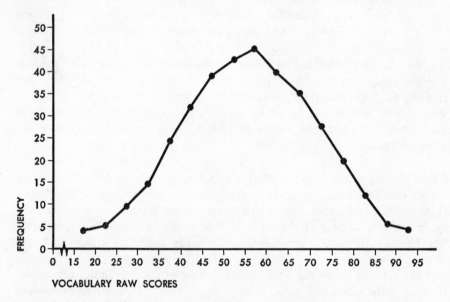

FIGURE 8.2.   Distribution of 360 Vocabulary Raw Scores as Presented in Graphic Form

these instances, the exact test score for a particular student is unknown. A modified formula for computing the arithmetic mean of scores in a frequency distribution is shown in Appendix A. When this formula is applied to the 360 vocabulary raw scores, an arithmetic mean of 55.7 is found.

Like the range, the standard deviation is a measure of the variability or dispersion present in a distribution of test scores. It is a distance expressed in test-score units rather than a point such as the arithmetic mean. Relatively small standard deviations are obtained when the test scores of a distribution are clustered in the vicinity of the arithmetic mean. As the test scores of a distribution spread widely above and below the arithmetic mean, the size of the standard deviation increases.

As in the case of the arithmetic mean, the standard deviation can be computed for test scores that are ungrouped or for test scores arranged in a frequency distribution. Appropriate formulas are shown in Appendix A. For the 360 vocabulary test scores shown in Table 8.1, a standard deviation of 15.3 was computed.

We can add and subtract the standard deviation (σ) from the arithmetic mean (M) in the following manner:

$$M + \sigma = 55.7 + 15.3 = 71.0$$
$$M - \sigma = 55.7 - 15.3 = 40.4$$

and

$$M + 2\sigma = 55.7 + (2)(15.3) = 86.3$$
$$M - 2\sigma = 55.7 - (2)(15.3) = 25.1$$

Because the distribution is approximately normal, about sixty-eight percent of raw scores are higher than 40.4 but no larger than 71.0. Of the 360 students, we should estimate that roughly 245 have scores between 41 and 71 inclusive. On the other hand, about ninety-five percent of the raw scores are larger than 25.1 and smaller than 86.3. Consequently, we should estimate that approximately 342 students have scores between 26 and 86 inclusive. Only when a normal distribution exists can the foregoing estimates be made.

Because finite groups of raw scores never conform to a perfect normal distribution, it is common to speak of the sixty-eight percent of the scores falling between $M + \sigma$ and $M - \sigma$ as the "middle two-thirds" of the distribution. Thus the two remaining tails of the distribution are identified as the "upper one-sixth" and the "lower one-sixth" respectively. Rough as this subdivision is, it is quite useful. For example, the teacher confronted with these almost normally distributed vocabulary raw scores can quickly add the standard deviation to the arithmetic mean, then subtract the standard deviation from the arithmetic mean, and visualize an ideal diagram such as the one in Figure 8.3. He can accordingly classify any raw score above 71 as in the upper one-sixth of the distribution, any raw score larger than 40 but no larger than 71 as in the middle two-thirds of the distribution, and, finally, any raw score of 40 and below as in the lower one-sixth of the distribution. For example, Tom's score of 58 is clearly within the middle two-thirds of the distribution.

Interpretation of Scores from Teacher-Built Tests. In the case of classroom achievement tests, the teacher typically deals with twenty-five to thirty-five raw

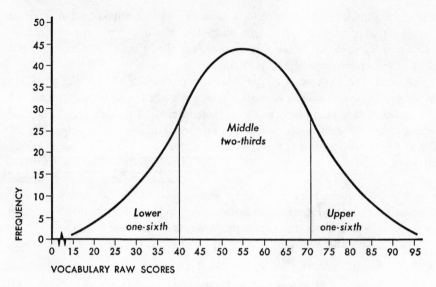

FIGURE 8.3.   Theoretical Normal Distribution of Vocabulary Raw Scores

scores rather than groups as large as the 360 used here. This means that we cannot safely expect a close approximation to the normal curve to exist, and thus interpretation of the test scores in terms of the normal curve is largely lost. Depending on the situation, we may wish instead to interpret these scores primarily in terms of their frequency distribution, mean, range, and highest and lowest values. Furthermore, for such small groups of scores, it is not reasonable to convert them routinely to norms like percentile ranks or standard scores.

PROBLEMS

1. On the basis of data shown on page 211, the statement is made that Sheri surpasses Carol in terms of the vocabulary test to a greater degree than Arthur surpasses Donald. Suppose Carol needed two weeks of study to raise her score twenty points to 88, whereas Donald needed only one week to raise his score twenty points to 37. Ignoring possible measurement errors, can we now say that the difference in vocabulary achievement between the two boys is about half of that between the two girls, even though the raw-score difference is twenty in both cases? (For further elaboration regarding this line of reasoning, see Angoff, 1971).

2. In addition to the arithmetic mean, what other measures of central tendency are commonly computed for raw-score distributions?

Identifying Relative Performance

Attempts to identify the relative performance of a student in terms of a norm-referenced test have been numerous. Furthermore, these attempts have yielded procedures that are vastly less cumbersome and casual than the manipulations of the raw-score distribution described above. The gist of the problem of simplifying the identification of relative performance is to convert the raw scores yielded by a test to some kind of *norms* that have, by their very nature, considerably greater interpretability.

Test norms are representations of typical or common performance based on the results of testing a group of students thought to be representative of those for whom the test is designed. The test is of course administered under the conditions specified by its manual.

Test norms are sometimes confused with test standards. The two expressions are not synonymous. Test norms represent *actual* performance of certain groups of students. In contrast, test standards represent *desired* performance in terms of a specific test. In the case of the vocabulary test, for example, the average number of words correctly identified is 55.7, or slightly more than one-half of the total number of items. This value is an indication of average or common performance on the part of the tenth-grade students and hence falls within the notion of test norms. However, it is possible that the teachers feel that any raw score below 40 is unsatisfactory. If this position is taken, the teachers have obviously established a standard. Presumably, standards are based on the considered judgment of teachers and supervisors who are intimately familiar with the teaching environment related to the characteristic measured by the test and with the talent of the group of students tested.

The most common types of norms can be classified into four groups:

Quartiles, deciles, and percentiles
Standard scores
Grade equivalents
Age equivalents

The very length of this list suggests that none seems to be completely satisfactory. It is common to find test authors and consumers reporting several kinds of norms for the same test. Thus, each type of norm deserves a separate, though brief, description.

Quartiles, Deciles, and Percentiles

Quartiles, deciles, and percentiles are points in a distribution of test scores below which specified percentages of the scores fall. The quartiles are three points dividing the distribution into four equal parts in terms of the number of test scores; deciles are nine points dividing the distribution into ten equal parts; percentiles are ninety-nine points dividing the distribution into one hundred equal parts.

The interpretation of a quartile, decile, or percentile is quite uniform. The first quartile, often identified as Q_1, is the point below which twenty-five percent of the scores fall. The first decile, D_1, is the point below which ten percent of the scores fall. The first percentile, P_1, is the point below which one percent of the scores fall. In a similar manner, the remaining quartiles, deciles, and percentiles are identified symbolically and interpreted.

By definition, equalities have been established between certain quartiles, deciles, and percentiles. For example:

$$Q_1 = P_{25}$$
$$Q_3 = P_{75}$$
$$D_1 = P_{10}$$

The most notable equality is

$$Q_2 = D_5 = P_{50}$$

Interestingly enough, the point in question, namely, the point below which fifty percent of the scores fall, is not known as Q_2, D_5, or P_{50}, but as the median. The median also plays a role in other types of norms described in this chapter.

The computation of any quartile, decile, or percentile can be based on a frequency distribution of raw scores such as the distribution of vocabulary scores shown in Table 8.1. The formula necessary for the determination of any of these values is shown in Appendix A. Repeated application of this formula yields the raw-score equivalents of all of the quartiles, deciles, and percentiles; these values for the first twenty-five percentiles are listed in the fourth column of Table 8.2.

The fact that quartiles, deciles, and percentiles are points and nothing more is reemphasized by examination of the raw-score equivalents. Consider D_1 for a moment. Its raw-score equivalent is 35.8. This value, like the others, is arbitrarily rounded back to one decimal since additional decimal places are of little value. Furthermore, like a great majority of its fellow values, it is not an integer. Hence we can say that a raw score of 35 is slightly below D_1, whereas a raw score of 36 is slightly above. Note that it is not correct to say that any raw score of less than 36 is *in* the first decile. Quartiles, deciles, and percentiles are points, not parts. Raw scores can be above, below, and occasionally at (for example, $P_{65} = 62.0$) a given point, but never in it. Nevertheless, it is common to refer carelessly to Q_1 as the lowest quarter and to D_1 as the lowest tenth of the distribution.

The raw-score equivalents of the quartiles, deciles, and percentiles as presented in Table 8.2 lack utility to some degree. We might ask, for example, what statement can be made about the raw score of 43. Can it be reported that it fell somewhere between P_{21} and P_{22}? Certainly this is true, but it is an awkward way to identify relative performance. Simplification of the wording is not possible if it is necessary to speak of percentiles. However, if *percentile ranks* are to be used, the statement reduces itself appreciably.

Percentile Ranks. Quartile ranks, decile ranks, and percentile ranks are not points, but ranges of raw scores. In the case of percentile ranks, these ranges are customarily quite small. By definition, any raw score of the same size as P_1 or less is given a percentile rank of one. Symbolically, this is PR_1. Any raw score larger than P_1 but no larger than P_2 is given a percentile rank of two, that is, PR_2. The process continues until PR_{100} is reached. Thus the distribution is divided into one hundred percentile ranks.

The last two columns of Table 8.2 list the percentile ranks and the corresponding raw scores. The latter are found simply by inspecting the size of the raw-score equivalents of the percentiles and applying the definition of percentile ranks. A less laborious means of determining percentile ranks is by reading them from an accurately plotted ogive curve, that is, the curve resulting when cumulative percentages are plotted against the raw scores (Cronbach, 1970, pp. 90–91).

Percentile ranks are more commonly reported and used than percentiles. Tables converting raw scores to percentile ranks are standard equipment in many test manuals. Although the last two columns of Table 8.2 perform the conversion function, they are probably not shown in that fashion. Rather, the two columns are rearranged so that the raw-score column is first and the percentile-rank column is second, as in Table 8.3.

TABLE 8.2.   Percentiles and Percentile Ranks for the Bottom Fourth of a Distribution of Vocabulary Scores

Percentile	Decile	Quartile	Raw-score equivalent	Percentile rank	Raw scores
25		1	45.0	25	45
24			44.6	24	
23			44.0	23	44
22			43.4	22	43
21			42.9	21	
20	2		42.3	20	42
19			41.8	19	
18			41.2	18	41
17			40.6	17	
16			40.1	16	40
15			39.5	15	39
14			38.8	14	
13			38.0	13	38
12			37.3	12	37
11			36.5	11	36
10	1		35.8	10	
9			35.0	9	35
8			34.0	8	33, 34
7			32.7	7	32
6			31.3	6	30, 31
5			29.9	5	29
4			28.1	4	27, 28
3			26.1	3	24, 25, 26
2			23.7	2	21, 22, 23
1			20.1	1	20 and below

TABLE 8.3.   Percentile Rank Equivalents of Vocabulary Raw Scores

Raw score	Percentile rank	Raw score	Percentile rank	Raw score	Percentile rank
95	100	68	78	41	18
94	100	67	76	40	16
93	100	66	74	39	15
92	100	65	72	38	13
91	100	64	70	37	12
90	99	63	68	36	11
89	99	62	65	35	9
88	99	61	63	34	8
87	99	60	61	33	8
86	98	59	59	32	7
85	98	58	56	31	6
84	97	57	53	30	6
83	97	56	51	29	5
82	96	55	48	28	4
81	95	54	46	27	4
80	95	53	43	26	3
79	94	52	41	25	3
78	93	51	39	24	3
77	92	50	36	23	2
76	90	49	34	22	2
75	89	48	32	21	2
74	88	47	30	20	1
73	86	46	28	19	1
72	85	45	25	18	1
71	83	44	23	17	1
70	82	43	22	16	1
69	80	42	20	15	1

Table 8.3 shows the percentile rank equivalent for each raw score. As you can see, a raw score of 58 is equivalent to a percentile rank of 56. This means that Tom, with a score of 58 on this vocabulary test ranks fifty-sixth from the bottom in a standard group of one hundred tenth-grade students.

Utility of Percentile Norms. The use of percentiles and percentile ranks to represent relative performance is extremely popular. Authors of norm-referenced standardized tests seldom fail to include these norms in their test manuals. Now that teachers, students, and even parents have been educated to a point that the term "percentile" has become almost a household word, test authors capitalize on the situation and view percentile norms as a convenient way of communicating with a large, heterogeneous audience.

There is a second reason for the continued use of percentile norms: the tables of norms can always be interpreted exactly no matter what the nature of the distribution of raw scores from which they are derived. This distribution may or may not be normal without changing the interpretation of the percentile norms.

The disadvantages of using percentile norms for representing relative performance of students are, however, somewhat damaging. First, and most important of all, the size of percentile units and ranks is not constant. Differences between percentiles are not equivalent to differences between raw scores.

Inspection of Table 8.3 reveals this situation in a typical case. Certainly the percentile ranks are hiding large differences between raw scores when they occur at either the high or low extremity of the raw-score distribution, and also are enlarging small differences between raw scores when they occur near the center of the distribution. A student with a raw score of 15 is no different in terms of percentile rank from a student with one of 20. Both are at the first percentile rank. On the other hand, the raw score of 58 yields a percentile rank of 56. With the present system of scoring the vocabulary test, it is not possible for a student to have a percentile rank of 54 or 55.

Percentile norms have "rubber units"—units of varying sizes. The extent to which the units have been "rubberized" depends on the nature of the distribution of the raw scores. If that distribution is normal or nearly normal, the amount of distortion is large. In Table 8.3 notice that a student at PR_{96} is much farther away from a student at PR_{86} in terms of raw-score units than a student at PR_{56} is from a student at PR_{46}. The difference in raw-score units is nine in the first instance and four in the second. In short, percentile norms are ordinal scales, not interval scales.

The second objection is less serious than the first and sometimes is of little concern to teachers. Simply phrased, it states that percentiles and percentile ranks as such cannot be treated arithmetically and a meaningful end product obtained. One cannot legitimately compute an arithmetic mean of these values or correlate them with other measurements by means of a product-moment coefficient of correlation. Percentiles and percentile ranks are, in effect, terminal values. Test norms such as standard scores do not have this limitation.

Standard Scores

Another popular system for representing relative performance on a norm-referenced test is the standard score. The intent of the standard score is to transform the raw score distribution to a new distribution having a desired arithmetic mean and standard deviation. If the arithmetic mean and standard deviation are known, and if the new distribution is normal, identification of the relative performance of individual students is a simple matter. The same approach is used here that is described in connection with Figure 8.3 when normally distributed raw scores were involved.

Z-Scores. There are many types of standard scores, each with its own arithmetic mean and standard deviation. The "parent" of the group is the well-known *z* score. From this base have sprung the others, three of which are commonly encountered and are described below.

The z scores are computed from the formula

$$z = \frac{X - M}{\sigma}$$

where

z = standard score
X = any raw score of a given distribution
M = arithmetic mean of the raw-score distribution
σ = standard deviation of the raw-score distribution

Examination of the formula reveals that any raw score smaller than the arithmetic mean of the raw scores yields a z score with a negative sign, whereas any larger than the arithmetic mean yields a z score that is positive. When a raw-score distribution is transformed into z scores, the arithmetic mean of the resulting z scores is zero, and their standard deviation is unity.

To change a raw score to a z score, a table of norms similar to that used for percentile ranks is consulted. Such a table is Table 8.4, the second column of which is constructed by successively solving the z score equation for all obtained raw scores ($M = 55.7$, $\sigma = 15.3$) resulting from the administration of the vocabulary test. Any raw score can be readily converted to a z score merely by glancing at the table. For example, a z score of +0.15 corresponds to the raw score of 58. Note that the practical limits of the z score distribution do not exceed +3.00 and −3.00.

Other Multiple-Digit Standard Scores.   Because z scores have negative signs and decimal points, their usefulness decreases. Clerical errors too easily and too often create havoc when test results are reported. To avoid these difficulties, linear transformations of the original z scores are made and an entire family of standard scores is automatically born. One such transformation is

Standard score = 10 (z) + 50

This equation produces a distribution of standard scores with an arithmetic mean of 50 and a standard deviation of 10. In Table 8.4 these standard scores are listed opposite the corresponding z score and vocabulary test raw score. It should be noted that this type of standard score is often called a *T* score, although the original *T* score as proposed years ago is somewhat different.

Another transformation is

Standard score = 20 (z) + 100

Now the arithmetic mean of the standard scores is 100 and the standard deviation is 20. This type of standard score is used with the *Army General Classification Test* and hence is sometimes called the *AGCT* score.

TABLE 8.4.   Standard Scores of Raw Scores Based upon 360 Tenth-Grade Students

Raw score	z	Standard score (M = 50, σ = 10)	Raw score	z	Standard score (M = 50, σ = 10)
94	2.50	75	54	−0.11	49
93	2.44	74	53	−0.18	48
92	2.37	74	52	−0.24	48
91	2.31	73	51	−0.31	47
90	2.24	72	50	−0.37	46
89	2.18	72	49	−0.44	46
88	2.11	71	48	−0.50	45
87	2.05	71	47	−0.57	44
86	1.98	70	46	−0.63	44
85	1.92	69	45	−0.70	43
84	1.85	69	44	−0.76	42
83	1.78	68	43	−0.83	42
82	1.72	67	42	−0.90	41
81	1.65	67	41	−0.96	40
80	1.59	66	40	−1.03	40
79	1.52	65	39	−1.09	39
78	1.46	65	38	−1.16	38
77	1.39	64	37	−1.22	38
76	1.33	63	36	−1.29	37
75	1.26	63	35	−1.35	36
74	1.20	62	34	−1.42	36
73	1.13	61	33	−1.48	35
72	1.07	61	32	−1.55	34
71	1.00	60	31	−1.61	34
70	0.93	59	30	−1.68	33
69	0.87	59	29	−1.75	32
68	0.80	58	28	−1.81	32
67	0.74	57	27	−1.88	31
66	0.67	57	26	−1.94	31
65	0.61	56	25	−2.01	30
64	0.54	55	24	−2.07	29
63	0.48	55	23	−2.14	29
62	0.41	54	22	−2.20	28
61	0.35	54	21	−2.27	27
60	0.28	53	20	−2.33	27
59	0.22	52	19	−2.40	26
58	0.15	52	18	−2.46	25
57	0.08	51	17	−2.53	25
56	0.02	50	16	−2.60	24
55	−0.05	49	15	−2.66	23

Also, the equation can read

$$\text{Standard score} = 100 \ (z) \ + \ 500$$

The arithmetic mean of these standard scores is 500, whereas the standard deviation is 100. Standard scores of this type are used in connection with the *College Entrance Examination Board Tests,* and are often called *CEEB* scores.

Interpretation of Standard Scores. If the distribution of standard scores is normal, their interpretation is not difficult; if it not normal, the interpretation is uncertain. To assume that standard scores are always normally distributed simply because they are standard scores is a common mistake. If the raw scores are normally distributed, then the standard scores computed from them are automatically normally distributed. The standard-score distribution is the same as the distribution of raw scores on which it is based. Since quite a few raw-score distributions are for all practical purposes normally distributed, the interpretation of many standard scores is based on the normal curve.

When interpreting standard scores based on normally distributed raw scores, it is helpful to think of a diagram such as the one in Figure 8.3. For T scores, the middle two-thirds of the distribution falls between 40 and 60; the upper one-sixth is composed of T scores that exceed 60, and the lower one-sixth contains T scores that fail to reach 40. The practical limits for this type of standard score are from 20 to 80, that is, the points that are three standard-deviation units above the arithmetic mean and three below it. These reference points, as well as those for *AGCT* and *CEEB* scores, are listed in Table 8.5.

Unlike the percentile rank procedure, no attempt is made here to interpret more exactly the relative performance of each student. Occasionally, percentile ranks are criticized for leaving a largely artificial impression of exactness. In any event, the normal curve can be broken into more segments than the three mentioned. Should this be desirable for whatever reason, a table of areas under the normal curve can be consulted. Such a table, along with a description of its functions, can be found in most of the available textbooks devoted to statistical methodology (for example, see Twaite & Monroe, 1979, pp. 510–519).

Stanines. The outstanding single-digit standard score used today is the stanine (pronounced *stay-nine*). This word was originally derived from the expression "*sta*ndard *nine*-point scale," which is the system of standard scores developed during World War II. At that time, a simple and workable type of norm was sought. The stanine scale was found to be satisfactory since it employs a single digit to represent relative performance and yet is precise enough for many practical testing problems. It is used for both standardized and teacher-constructed tests.

TABLE 8.5.   Reference Points for Various Standard Scores

Type	Characteristics		Middle two-thirds	Upper one-sixth	Lower one-sixth	Practical limits	
	M	σ	Between	Greater than	Less than	High	Low
T score	50	10	40 and 60	60	40	80	20
AGCT score	100	20	80 and 120	120	80	160	40
CEEB score	500	100	400 and 600	600	400	800	200

When stanine norms are used, raw scores are converted to one of nine stanine scores, which vary from a low of one to a high of nine. The mean of the stanine distribution is five and its standard deviation two. On the other hand, when large numbers of students are involved, some measurement specialists will subdivide the two extreme positions on the scale, thereby creating an eleven-point scale with a low of zero and a high of ten.

The determination of stanine scores is simple. For example, when working with raw scores from smaller groups of students, a teacher can arrange the raw scores from high to low, then determine the median of the distribution, and, with this as a starting point, apply the theoretical percentages of the stanine subgroups. These percentages are as follows:

Stanine	1	2	3	4	5	6	7	8	9
Percentage of Students	4	7	12	17	20	17	12	7	4

The median is theoretically in the center of the middle twenty percent of the distribution. This subgroup is given a stanine of five. By working upward and downward from this subgroup, the remaining subgroups are found and the stanines assigned. Certain minor adjustments of the subgroups are usually necessary to bring actual percentages into closest possible agreement with theoretical percentages. This is necessitated by the principle that every student having the same raw score will, of course, have the same stanine score.

One word of caution: Remember that the percentages used are derived from the normal curve. Therefore, if the stanine scale is to be used, one must be willing to assume that the trait measured follows this curve reasonably well for the students tested.

why use stand. Sc. ✳

Utility of Standard-Score Norms. After comparing the interpretation of the vocabulary raw scores with that of the standard scores based on them, you may wonder about the advantages of establishing standard scores as opposed to raw scores. One is the fact that standard scores have a specified arithmetic mean and *1.* standard deviation. Raw-score distributions usually produce arithmetic means and standard deviations that have somewhat odd sizes and are seldom integers. On the other hand, standard-score distributions have arithmetic means that are easily remembered—for instance, 50, 100, or 500—and a standard deviation that can be speedily added to or subtracted from that mean.

The two disadvantages of percentile norms cannot be attributed to standard-score norms. Because multiple-digit standard scores are simply a linear transformation of raw scores, they are a direct reflection of them, both in terms of unit size and distribution shape. No "rubber units" are generated as in the case of *2.* percentile ranks. Furthermore, standard scores can be treated arithmetically. Find- *3.* ing the arithmetic mean or standard deviation of standard scores is just as legitimate as finding those values for raw scores.

Another advantage of standard scores is the ease of determining a composite *4.* score for a student who has been administered several norm-referenced tests as a part of a test battery. If a composite score representing overall achievement is desired, the standard scores of the subtests can be averaged. Finding the arithmetic mean weights each test score equally. If desired, various weights can be assigned the scores before the arithmetic mean is computed.

Percentiles and all types of standard scores are interrelated if the raw-score distribution from which they are computed is normal. The normal distribution restriction is highly important. In Figure 8.4 these relationships are shown in part. Before the relationships shown in this figure can be considered useful, there must be statistical evidence that the distribution of raw scores is essentially a normal one.

The main disadvantage of standard scores is that they are difficult to interpret when they are not normally distributed. This fact, plus the general public's lack of familiarity with them, somewhat restricts their use.

Grade Equivalents

Representing the relative performance of students with grade equivalents is still another popular method. A grade equivalent of a particular raw score is the grade level of those students whose median (or arithmetic mean) is the same as the raw score in question. In other words, if the median raw score happened to be 63 for a test administered to sixth-grade students just beginning that grade level, all raw scores of 63 have a grade equivalent of 6.0.

The generally accepted way of reporting grade equivalents is in terms of two numbers. The first of the two numbers is designed as the year and second as the month. For example, a grade equivalent of 5.4 is the median raw score of students tested at the fourth month of the fifth grade. Note that the calendar year is divided into ten parts, nine representing the academic year and one representing summer vacation months.

Utility of Grade Equivalents. Despite the limitations of grade equivalents, these scores are amazingly well received, especially in the elementary grade levels. Grade equivalents are easily understood. Contrast these derived scores with standard scores or even percentile ranks. Comparing students' actual grade level with their grade equivalents yielded by tests in various subject matter areas is definitely more comprehensible to many teachers, administrators, and parents than standard scores and percentile ranks. Moreover, grade equivalents offer convenient units for plotting profiles of student achievement. Such profiles are graphic representations of a student's test scores and emphasize areas of overachievement and underachievement.

Several basic restrictions of grade equivalents must be remembered if they are to be properly used and interpreted. The most important of these is that a grade equivalent cannot always be taken at face value. Suppose, for example, that as she begins the fifth grade, Shelly is given a fifth-grade arithmetic test and receives a grade equivalent of 8.0. This does not necessarily indicate that she has mastered all of the arithmetic subject matter in the fifth, sixth, and seventh grades. Although she is displaying superior arithmetic achievement when compared to the

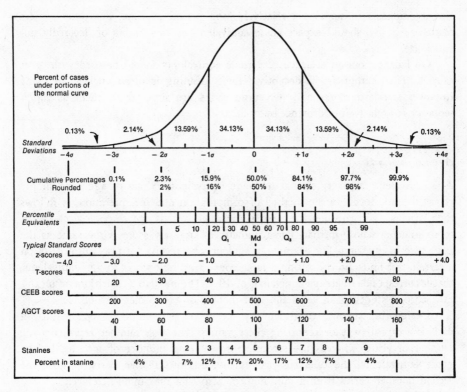

FIGURE 8.4.   Relations among Normally Distributed Raw Scores, Percentiles, and Certain Standard Scores

(From Seashore, 1955)

typical fifth-grade student, in all probability she is not sufficiently well trained at that moment to compete successfully in arithmetic with students beginning the eighth grade. In other words, had Shelly been tested by an eighth-grade arithmetic test, she very likely would have fallen well below the grade equivalent of 8.0.

A second restriction limits the highest grade level to which equivalents may extend. Grade equivalents should not extend beyond the ninth grade since, with the possible exception of English, there is no continuous and systematic instruction beyond the ninth grade for those subject matter areas taught in elementary school. Since this does not occur, grade equivalents like 10.3 and 11.0 are meaningless. Standard scores or percentile ranks should be used to represent relative performance of secondary school students.

Finally, grade equivalents lose accuracy due to "rubber units." There is no assurance that a given difference between two grade equivalents is comparable to the same difference between two other grade equivalents, even though the same test is involved. However, the seriousness of this difficulty varies with the subject matter area being tested. Within the elementary school levels, grade equivalents yielded by tests in areas such as reading, arithmetic, and spelling tend to have equal units. This is true because the subject matter areas are given a consistent emphasis throughout a relatively long period of time. For other subject matter areas, we should expect grade equivalents to have units of decidedly unequal size.

On balance, one must argue that grade equivalents should be used with great caution. Their simplicity is deceptive; their meaning is often unclear. In many instances standard scores and percentile ranks are superior to them as representations of relative performance by students.

Age Equivalents

Age equivalents are very similar to grade equivalents. Years of age have simply replaced grade levels in the method of computation and interpretation. It follows then that an age equivalent of a particular raw score is the chronological age of those students whose median (or arithmetic mean) raw score is the same as the raw score in question. For example, a student who received a raw score of 48 on a certain test finds, on consulting a table converting raw scores to age equivalents, that it corresponds to an age equivalent of 10-4. The median (or arithmetic mean) raw score of students ten years and four months of age is therefore 48.

Designating an age equivalent by means of two numbers separated by a dash is a typical way of reporting these values. The first number represents the number of years, whereas the second represents the number of months. Unlike grade equivalents, the calendar year is divided into twelve parts, so that the second number varies from a minimum of zero to a maximum of eleven.

The utility of age equivalents is as severely limited as that of grade equivalents. They are helpful only when used with students in certain age ranges where the trait measured is known to increase noticeably year by year. In other instances, they are inferior to standard scores and percentile ranks.

PROBLEMS

3. Teachers will often administer the same test before and after a period of instruction, hoping that the difference between the two scores will measure student progress or improvement. Identify the principal measurement problems present in this process (Angoff, 1971). How accurately can the various types of norms reflect student progress?

4. When using grade equivalents, a teacher will sometimes confuse norms and standards by saying that students are progressing satisfactorily if they are performing "up to the norm." What is meant by this statement? What questions would arise if you were to challenge it?

5. As a means of reporting test results from a criterion-referenced test, the percent of students in a given class who successfully complete each test item can be compared with the percent of those who do so in the entire district. Is this an illustration of a norm-referenced interpretation of criterion-referenced test results? Explain.

Using Standardization Group Scores

Throughout the discussion of test norms, repeated mention is made of the standardization or norm group, that is, the group of students whose raw scores are used to identify the raw-score equivalents of the norms computed. The standardization group consists of students for whom the test is designed and who are given the test under conditions recommended by its author. For our illustration, this group comprises more than one tenth-grade class; it comprises the 360 tenth-grade students within the city school system. The appropriateness of interpreting achievement in light of the results of this larger group must be established before taking the trouble to compute any test norms.

A regularly observed principle is that the expression of a student's relative standing in terms of test norms is more meaningful when the standardization group used to determine them resembles that student in terms of any of a variety of salient characteristics. It follows, therefore, that a comparison of Tom's vocabulary skill to that of the 360 students is suitable since, within a single city school system, there is appreciable similarity in the amount and quality of instruction in this subject matter area within the various component schools. There is possibly similarity in the students' backgrounds and abilities as well.

It is only rarely appropriate to compare a student's vocabulary achievement to that of a seemingly very different group. Hence, to support using the 360 students as a standardization group, they should be described in terms of the amount of their previous formal schooling in the area tested, age distribution, scholastic aptitude distribution, socioeconomic ratings, and so forth. Since the averages of these measures do not differ greatly from Tom's position, the comparison of his achievement with theirs would seem to make sense. Should the 360 students as a group be vastly unlike him, the interpretation of his performance relative to those of this group is less useful, barring unusual reasons.

Sampling

The problem so often faced by teachers who wish to use test norms is that their students are not a part of the standardization group. Teachers must know with some certainty if their students can be considered a part of the population which is reflected by the standardization group. Unless they can be considered a part of such a population, norm tables should not be used.

In the past, the sampling problem with test norms has been vastly underestimated in some instances. Tables of norms that are labeled "national" or "regional," without specifying the manner in which the nation or region was sampled, are contributing by omission to the misguided notion that the worth of a sample is determined only incidentally by the method in which it was obtained. More often than not, the size of the sample is impressive and is noted with pride, despite the fact that it is only incidental to the method used for selecting its members.

The task of satisfactorily sampling a group of students is admittedly difficult and quite expensive. For instance, in order to represent the nation, a standardization group should be a national probability sample including appropriate proportions of boys and girls; members of various ethnic groups; those with high, middle, and average income levels; those living in major cities, suburban areas, and rural areas; and those attending large, average, and small schools, both public and private. Even this list is not complete. Any factor that could conceivably affect the test results to an appreciable degree should be considered in the selection of the sample. Test authors have redoubled their efforts to draw suitable national and regional samples, and the representativeness of their standardization groups has correspondingly increased a great deal.

A number of test authors strengthen the utility of their tables of norms by publishing not one but several such tables, each designed for a relatively homogeneous population. In some instances, separate tables are shown for rural schools and urban schools, for schools in different geographical regions, for various levels of scholastic aptitude within a grade level, and for students specializing in various types of secondary school curricula. For each group of students so used, the author then reports data concerning age, educational status, and the like. Every pertinent piece of information characterizing the standardization group helps teachers decide whether their students logically belong in the population sampled by the standardization group.

Local Norms. Even though a variety of tables of norms is available, consideration should be given to the possibiilty of constructing local norms. These are usually expressed in terms of percentile ranks or standard scores. If several hundred or more scores from a certain norm-referenced test are available, and if future use is to be made of that test, local norms should be figured and then revised from time to time as additional raw scores become available. After all, a particular raw score on a test may be equivalent to a standard score of 60 in terms of national norms, 57 in terms of regional norms, 58 in terms of local norms based on one city, or 52 in terms of local norms based on one school.

All these indications of relative performance may be helpful, depending on the purpose of the testing and thus the educational decisions to be made about the student. For instance, local norms are most helpful when we are looking back at what an individual or class has done, but are less likely to be helpful when we look ahead to what they may be expected to do in the future. Further, they are often less useful for counseling purposes (Ricks, 1971).

On balance, local norms are valuable. They supplement national norms, and for some purposes they are more appropriate since they are sensitive to atypical conditions (for example, curriculum practices) in the local schools.

PROBLEMS

6. A senior girl whose percentile rank on a scholastic aptitude test was 85 had a percentile rank of 60 on an achievement test in advanced mathematics. Her mathematics teacher concluded that she was underachieving. What information

must you know about the standardization groups used before you can evaluate the teacher's conclusion on that basis?

7. Study the description of procedures used to select a standardization group and the description of the standardization group finally used for the *Metropolitan Achievement Tests*, 1978 edition. Compare this with similar information provided by any other achievement test battery for the elementary school.

8. In addition to norms for student scores, manuals accompanying the *Iowa Tests of Educational Development* provide information concerning norms for school averages. Evaluate the worth of the school norms.

Using Narrative Format Testing Reports

Are there more understandable ways to report test results to unsophisticated audiences than by using norms? Yes—thanks to computers. Upon scoring a standardized achievement or aptitude test, computers can be programmed to print out an appropriate narrative which provides an interpretation of a student or total class performance (Baker, 1971, pp. 228–229).

Such reports have been prepared for students, teachers, and parents following the administration of the *Iowa Tests of Basic Skills* (Mathews, 1973). These are typically several paragraphs in length. In addition to describing each student's overall performance and achievement on the subtests, various proficiencies and deficiencies are listed. Suggestions for improving performance are included. Progress statements based on a student's change of score from the previous year's test administration can also be formulated by use of a computer.

Increasingly, standardized tests are designed to provide narrative test reports in addition to standard scores and percentiles. For instance, one can obtain a computer-produced counseling report based on students' *Differential Aptitude Tests* scores and their responses to a career-planning questionnaire. Their occupational preferences are compared with the level and pattern of their aptitude test scores, school subjects, and educational plans. The report may confirm their occupational choices or may suggest alternative occupational areas to explore.

Narrative reports about total class performance can also be produced for some standardized achievement tests, for example, the *Stanford Achievement Test*. As a part of a criterion-referenced interpretation for this battery, an interpretive computer report to the teacher provides an analysis of class achievement on small groups of homogeneous test items. Suggestions are made for placing individual students in groups for instructional purposes.

Narrative test reports seem to be less precise than test norms, but they offer highly understandable information to students, parents, and teachers. They are a superior supplement to norms, even when limited to simple designations of student mastery or nonmastery. An example is the individual test record of the *California Achievement Tests* which, in addition to reporting raw scores, grade equivalents, percentiles, and stanines for all subtests, lists each student's mastery or nonmastery of various categories of objectives. For instance, in the case of the mathematics computation subtest there are four categories, namely, addition, subtraction, multiplication, and division. As you see, this is an effort to produce criterion-referenced descriptions of the results from norm-referenced achievement tests. Such descriptions usually should not be interpreted too literally (see page 170).

Reports of Criterion-Referenced Test Results

Results from criterion-referenced achievement tests can be produced in narrative form by computers rather easily. For each student the narrative report can identify the areas of achievement where mastery did or did not occur by describing the objectives of concern. Sometimes these descriptions are rather brief as in the case of the report to the parents of Ricky Cain about his mathematics achievement in third grade, one part of which is shown in Figure 8.5. Note that the heavy use of statements of objectives in an area such as mathematics might introduce terminology that is difficult for parents to understand.

The criterion-referenced mathematics test administered to Ricky is composed of 147 test items based on 20 objectives. Four of the objectives deal with operations, their properties, and number theory. On the average the test includes about eight test items per objective.

For each objective a large majority of the test items associated with it must be answered correctly in order to demonstrate mastery. Ricky performed well in most instances, but, as you can see in Figure 8.5, he did not do well on three of the four objectives in operations, their properties, and number theory. The help he needs is not described in the report to the parents, but suggestions are listed

---

TO THE PARENTS OF RICKY CAIN:

With regard to operations, their properties, and number theory, your child did the following well:

- Multiplying two one-digit numbers and a two-digit number by a one-digit number; dividing by a one-digit number; and relating multiplication to division

He needs help with the following:

- Adding or subtracting with and without renaming, and recognizing the relation between addition and subtraction
- Recognizing properties of zero and one in computation; recognizing and using the commutative and associative properties under addition and multiplication; and recognizing the distributive property of multiplication over addition
- Solving or selecting the operation for addition, subtraction, multiplication, or division in word problems

---

FIGURE 8.5. Narrative Report to Parents Regarding Third-Grade Mathematics Achievement on a Criterion-Referenced Test

in the computer-produced narrative report for his teacher. Among other suggestions, the teacher report mentions that Ricky needs "hand-on" work with physical models of addition and subtraction.

The foregoing reports provide a starting point for teacher-parent conferences and subsequent individual remedial work. Moreover, if nonmastery of certain objectives is fairly common in the class, remedial work in groups may result, followed by retesting. The entire sequence may offer useful insights into the teaching-learning process in this instance.

SUMMARY

The following points have been highlighted in this chapter:

1. The results yielded by measuring instruments frequently lack meaning. For instance, raw scores, which are the immediate quantitative end product of scoring a norm-referenced test, defy interpretation until suitable reference points are known. Three such reference points are the arithmetic mean of a group of raw scores, the value of the highest raw score, and the value of the lowest raw score.

2. Other reference points can be readily located if the distribution of norm-referenced raw scores is normal or practically normal. When this is true, the standard deviation of the raw scores can be successively added to and subtracted from the arithmetic mean to identify distribution points including fixed percentages of raw scores.

3. Raw-score distributions are habitually characterized by two inadequacies. In the first place, a raw score of zero does not correspond to absolute zero. This is not a serious deficiency in terms of lessening interpretability. Secondly, raw-score distributions tend to have "rubber units," that is, unequal units. This deficiency is considerably more serious but hardly disastrous in well-constructed instruments.

4. There have been many efforts to improve the meaningfulness of norm-referenced raw scores. Raw scores are converted into test norms that more readily show the relative performance of a student in terms of the test. Norms are obtained by giving a test to a target group of students under conditions recommended by the manual. Then, with a distribution of raw scores available, norms are computed by applying the necessary formulas or by plotting graphs. The target group is called a standardization group.

5. The most common norms in educational measurement are quartiles, deciles, and percentiles; standard scores; grade equivalents; and age equivalents. Quartiles, deciles, and percentiles are points in a distribution below which specified percentages of raw scores will fall. Standard scores are scores with known arithmetic means and standard deviations. Grade equivalents represent the average test performance of students of various grade levels, whereas age equivalents represent the average test performance of students of various chronological ages.

6. The standardization group used to compute tables of norms must be carefully chosen. It is a sample of a population of students and, ideally, should be selected in accordance with the sampling procedures designed by a competent statistician.

7. Many test manuals contain several tables of norms representing various populations, since, for most purposes, norms become more meaningful as the standardization group used to determine them more closely resembles the students in question. The need for similarity contributes heavily to the importance of local norms.

8. In the case of standardized tests, computer-produced, narrative-format testing reports should be used whenever possible to supplement test norms. Some are criterion-referenced descriptions of student achievement based on norm-referenced test results. In the case of criterion-referenced tests, the narrative reports usually contain descriptions of the objectives on which the tests are based.

SUGGESTED READINGS

ANASTASI, A. *Psychological testing* (4th ed.). New York: Macmillan, 1976.
Chapter 4 includes sections dealing with grade equivalents, percentiles, and standard scores. It concludes with discussions of normative samples and criterion-referenced tests.

ANGOFF, W. H. Scales, norms, and equivalent scores. In R. L. Thorndike (Ed.), *Educational measurement* (2nd ed.). Washington, D.C.: American Council on Education, 1971.
In chapter 15, each of the principal types of norms is reviewed in terms of its purposes, computation, and utility. Considerable attention is given to the problem of selecting suitable standardization groups.

FINK, A., & KOSECOFF, J. How to make sense out of test scores. *How To Evaluate Educational Programs*, 1979, 3 (6).
Attention is given to the interpretation of both criterion-referenced and norm-referenced test scores. The characteristics of various score interpretation systems are shown succinctly in chart form.

JOSELYN, E. G. & MERWIN, J. C. Using your achievement test score reports. *NCME Measurement in Education*, 1971, 3 (1).
All major types of norms are described. Illustrations of standardized achievement test profiles and summary statistics are presented.

RICKS, J. H., JR. *Local norms—When and why*. Test Service Bulletin, No. 58. New York: Psychological Corporation, 1971.
The case for and against local norms is prepared. Scores from the Differential Aptitude Tests *are used as illustrations.*

THORNDIKE, R. L., & HAGEN, E. P. *Measurement and evaluation in psychology and education* (4th ed.). New York: John Wiley & Sons, 1977.
In chapter 4, grade equivalents, percentiles, and various standard scores are described in detail. Also included in this chapter is a section dealing with test score profiles.

REFERENCES CITED

ANGOFF, W. H. Scales, norms, and equivalent scores. In R. L. Thorndike (Ed.), *Educational measurement* (2nd ed.). Washington, D.C.: American Council on Education, 1971.

BAKER, F. B. Automation of test scoring, reporting, and analysis. In R. L. Thorndike (Ed.), *Educational measurement* (2nd ed.). Washington, D.C.: American Council on Education, 1971.

CRONBACH, L. J. *Essentials of psychological testing* (3rd ed.). New York: Harper & Row, 1970.

MATHEWS, W. M. Narrative-format testing approach. *NCME Measurement News,* 1973, *16,* 7–8.

RICKS, J. H., JR. *Local norms—When and why.* Test Service Bulletin, No. 58. New York: Psychological Corporation, 1971.

SEASHORE, H. G. *Methods of expressing test scores.* Test Service Bulletin, No. 48. New York: Psychological Corporation, 1955.

TWAITE, J. A., & MONROE, J. A. *Introductory statistics.* Glenview, Ill.: Scott, Foresman, 1979.

9

The Reliability of Measurement Methods

After completing this chapter, you will be able to

1. Define test reliability and understand its relationship to test validity

2. Describe chance errors that affect test reliability, and differentiate between student-centered and instrument-centered errors

3. List the steps to be followed to determine the degree of reliability of norm-referenced tests when using the stability, equivalence, stability and equivalence, and internal consistency methods

4. Interpret coefficients of reliability and standard errors of measurement for norm-referenced tests.

5. Contrast coefficients of reliability derived from various reliability methods used with norm-referenced tests in terms of the chance errors they reflect

6. Explain that the methods and computations used to determine the degrees of reliability of criterion-referenced tests often differ from those used for norm-referenced tests even though the underlying principles are virtually the same

Prodded by his teenage son, the proud owner of a relatively new automobile decided to determine the number of miles that it traveled for each gallon of gasoline consumed. During a week in early May he carefully tabulated the gasoline consumption and the miles traveled, and computed the gasoline mileage to be 32.1 miles per gallon. Later that same month the owner selected another week, determined the gasoline consumed and miles traveled, and found that the gasoline mileage was 30.4 miles per gallon. The procedure was repeated during the first week of June, and a gasoline mileage of 31.0 miles per gallon was the result.

It is not surprising that the gasoline mileages varied by only small amounts. Because the three one-week periods were separated by relatively short periods of time, and because such factors as weather and traffic conditions were rather uniform during all three trials, it seems reasonable that the results should be consistent if these measurements of gasoline mileage were at all accurate. No doubt the owner ignored the minor differences among the three values and concluded that the gasoline mileage produced by his automobile under the existing traffic and weather conditions was fairly well identified. He might have even averaged the three measurements, and then used this value as the final product of his investigation.

Had he known that the true gasoline mileage had remained unchanged during the three trial periods and was really 31.3 miles per gallon, he would not have been dismayed. On the contrary, he might have been quite pleased with the accuracy of his estimates. Furthermore, if he had been pressed for an explanation as to why his three estimates varied while the true value did not vary, he might have shrugged his shoulders and attributed the small fluctuations to "chance" errors.

The chance errors that he had in mind are many. First of all, the measurement of the gasoline delivered by the pump might have been in slight error. Thus, exactly ten gallons of gasoline drawn from the pump might not necessarily have registered on the meter as exactly ten gallons. Second, the attendant might have filled the gasoline tank to varying degrees of "fullness" each time the owner began and completed the measurement of the gasoline mileage. Third, the odometer might not have registered the miles traveled with perfect accuracy, and the reading of it also might have involved a small amount of estimation. Lastly, the driving conditions probably varied at least slightly from one trial period to another.

Despite these possibilities of error, the gasoline mileages were fairly consistent. Such consistency of measurement is equally desirable in education. A good measuring instrument must yield dependable information; in other words, if it is possible to use it repeatedly in the same unchanging situation, the information yielded by each administration of the instrument should be similar to that yielded by any other administration. For instance, the typing teacher who gives a speed test to students on Friday would hope that the typing rates determined would be the same, for all practical purposes, as those obtained from such an exercise administered on Monday, if the students did not study or practice during the weekend. Likewise, the scholastic aptitude scores yielded by a norm-referenced test given to students at 10:30 a.m. on September 18 are assumed to be essentially the same as those that would be obtained were the test administered at 9:30 a.m. on September 19.

Should there be no assurance that tests such as these do yield reasonably consistent results, their value would be severely limited. Before any measuring instrument should be used, therefore, the question might be asked: If repeated attempts are made to obtain information about an unchanging student attribute with this instrument, will the results tend to duplicate each other? The question can be stated much more simply: Is the measuring instrument highly reliable?

Determining Reliability

Reliability means consistency of results. Unfortunately, all instruments are unreliable to some degree, that is, they are subject to *chance errors*.

Chance Errors

Chance errors, or compensating errors as they are sometimes called, have one vital characteristic: they have a tendency to cancel each other when the instrument is used many times. There are a number of possibilities of chance error in the gasoline mileage determinations, one of which can be traced to the meter on the gasoline pump. Although a given withdrawal of precisely ten gallons from the pump may be recorded on the meter as slightly more than ten gallons, a second withdrawal of ten gallons might be recorded as slightly less. Were the process to be repeated an infinite number of times and the tendency to overestimate and underestimate found to be equal, then the error is a chance error and affects the reliability of the measurement.

There still remains, of course, the possibility that the meter consistently overestimates or consistently underestimates; no canceling takes place no matter how many measurements are made. This is obviously an error in measuring, but not a chance error. It does not lessen the reliability of the measurement, but it does lessen the validity. Thus, the degree of validity of the gasoline mileage measurement is reduced if the readings on the gasoline meter were always, say, one percent less than the actual amount of gasoline delivered by the pump. In the case of the typing speed test and the scholastic aptitude test, similar errors are possible. Either one could have yielded erroneous measurements to the extent that, say, every typing rate is seven percent too low or every scholastic aptitude score is four percent too large. These errors are classified in the second group of errors called *biased errors*, or *constant errors*, and affect only the relative validity of these instruments.

Student-Centered and Instrument-Centered Factors.   Many factors affect the reliability of measuring instruments. Some are associated with the students themselves, whereas other factors arise from the instrument itself. Student factors ordinarily mentioned are state of health, fatigue, motivation, emotional strain, and the like. Two factors associated with the instrument itself are prominent in the paper-and-pencil test. First of all, the test is only a sample of an immense number of possible test items; secondly, the scoring of the test, particularly those with essay test items, may not be consistent, a factor known as lack of scorer reliability. Many additional factors related both to the students and to the instrument and its administration have been listed elsewhere (Stanley, 1971, pp. 363–369).

Certainly the importance of these factors as they affect the information yielded by a measuring instrument is not uniform from student to student or instrument to instrument. The student-centered factors may easily fluctuate from day to day, perhaps from forenoon to afternoon, and, for many students, play only a small role in terms of influencing an instrument's results. Instrument-centered factors tend to be less damaging when, for example, a paper-and-pencil test is lengthened by adding suitable items and when the scoring becomes more objective. Trivial as some of the sources of trouble may seem to be, they can drastically reduce the value of a measuring instrument.

Perhaps it is disconcerting to find such factors as those listed classified as the originators of chance errors. Admittedly, they may not fit as neatly into the scheme as the gasoline meter and its errors do. Yet we can argue that the errors from the sources listed would cancel out if it were possible to measure an unchanging student attribute many times over with each of the many tests for this attribute, with the tests scored independently by many judges.

PROBLEMS

1. On the basis of your experience, order the following in terms of the degree of reliability that probably exists:
   a. Using a common yardstick to measure the height of basketball players
   b. Using a quart bottle to measure volume of bath water
   c. Using a bathroom scale to measure the weight of loaded suitcases

2. Suppose that you were confronted with the problem of estimating the degree of reliability with which a small group of English literature teachers could score student answers to a certain limited-response essay test item. Describe the steps you would take to meet the problem.

Differentiating Between Validity and Reliability

The terms "validity" and "reliability" have too often been used as though they were synonymous or nearly so. Though the concepts are somewhat related, they are by no means identical. The validity of a measuring instrument is the degree to which it actually serves the purposes for which its use is intended; the reliability of an instrument is its capacity to yield consistent information regardless of whether it serves the purposes in question. Thus a highly reliable instrument is not necessarily an equally valid instrument. For example, the heights of male college seniors majoring in education can be measured with considerable reliability. Yet this fact would in no way support the statement that the tall male college senior will be a better classroom teacher in future years than a short one. Educational tests may likewise have superior reliability and still be woefully lacking in validity. A norm-referenced arithmetic achievement test used to measure qualities of leadership is one of many extreme examples.

It is important to emphasize that high validity is the most important characteristic of an instrument. The role of reliability is a vital but secondary one when a measuring instrument is being appraised. Nevertheless, unless a test is reliable it cannot be valid. The importance of both characteristics can be summarized in the statement that the ideal instrument must serve the purpose or purposes for which it is intended and, in doing so, must produce consistent information.

Determining the Reliability of Norm-Referenced Tests

Testing specialists concerned with methods for estimating the validity of a measuring instrument often search for external evidence and try to appraise the instrument's validity in terms of such evidence. Reliability determination, on the other hand, is not based on evidence of this kind. Instead, the instrument is compared with itself or some equivalent form. These procedures can be illustrated readily in the case of norm-referenced tests.

The determination of norm-referenced test reliability is based on one central method. The instrument to be investigated is used (perhaps in conjunction with an equivalent form) to obtain one or more attribute measurements of each member of a group of students. Each measurement identifies the position of each student in terms of the attribute measured. The consistency with which the student maintains his or her position within the group from measurement to measurement is a reflection of the reliability of the test. This consistency can be translated into a *product-moment coefficient of correlation,* called a *coefficient of reliability*. Moreover, a coefficient of reliability can often be interpreted more easily by converting it to a *standard error of measurement.* This is an attempt to estimate the size of the errors of measurement caused by the unreliability of the test.

Coefficients of reliability can result from four separate processes known as the stability method, the equivalence method, the stability and equivalence method, and the internal-consistency method. The first three are classical methods in that they call for correlating two sets of scores.

The Stability Method

We can easily determine the reliability with which we can assess such dimensions as the length or weight of a block of wood. Repeated measurements of the object are made and compared. A similar procedure is sometimes applied when the reliability of educational measuring instruments is under study. Suppose that Mr. Miller, a history teacher, constructs a 100-item norm-referenced test designed to measure eleventh-grade students' knowledge of American history, and that this test has satisfactory content validity. To determine the reliability of his instrument, Mr. Miller may give the test to a sample of eleventh-grade students, tabulate the results, allow an interval of time to pass, and finally readminister the instrument to the same students under the same conditions as before. Unless there is evidence to the contrary, it is assumed that the group has not changed with respect to their knowledge of American history during the time interval. Ideally then, each student would receive the same test score the second time as the first. In reality, the most Mr. Miller can hope for is that students who received high scores on the first test administration will receive high scores on the second test administration and that those who received low scores the first time will receive low scores the second time.

Plotting the results of the two test administrations is most profitable. In Figure 9.1, the horizontal line represents degrees of achievement for the first administration of the test, and the vertical line the degrees of achievement for the second administration. The position of each point is found by locating on the horizontal axis each student's test score for the first administration, and moving upward, parallel to the vertical axis, until the score for that student for the second administration is located. The data for the fifty students have been plotted in Figure 9.1.

Observe that in this figure the points arrange themselves in an elongated manner so as to approximate a straight line. This strongly suggests that the rela-

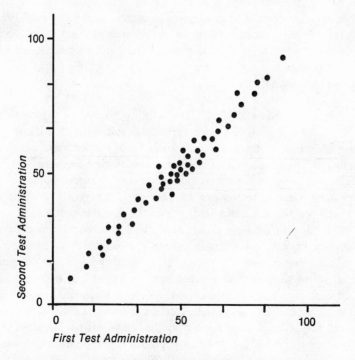

FIGURE 9.1.   Scatter Diagram of Achievement Test Scores Resulting from Two Test Administrations

tive position of each student was the same or nearly so both times the test was administered. In other words, the test is highly reliable in this situation. If the test were very unreliable, the points would scatter considerably, even to the extent that no straight line could satisfactorily represent the total number of points. To identify the degree more precisely, another step is needed, namely, the computation of a coefficient of correlation (r).

The Correlation Coefficient. The correlation coefficient is a number representing the straight-line relationship between the values of two variables, such as the values of the two sets of test scores resulting from double measurement of students in the case of the stability method. If points are plotted, as in Figure 9.1, and all of them fall in a straight line, the value of r will be 1.00. As the points deviate from a straight line, the value of r decreases to zero. In addition, when high values of one variable are associated with high values of the second variable, and low values of one variable are associated with low values of the other (as in the data plotted), the relationship is called positive and the r value carries a positive sign. If high values of one variable are associated with low values of the other, and low values of the first are associated with high values of the second, the relationship is called negative and the r value carries a negative sign. Thus, r values vary from −1.00 to +1.00. The number is indicative of the degree to which the points form a straight line, and the sign reveals the direction of the relationship. It should be noted that positive r values are much more common than negative values in educational evaluation, especially in the determination of test reliability.

Computation of correlation coefficients is somewhat lengthy but simple. The scores of the two test administrations are substituted in the appropriate formula (see Appendix A) for the coefficient of correlation, and a coefficient of reliability is computed. In this instance it is sometimes called a coefficient of stability. An r-value of 0.93 was found.

Usefulness of the Stability Method. The stability method is not considered the most defensible for establishing norm-referenced test reliability. Three apparent defects are the practice effect that may result from the first test administration, the difficulty of establishing a suitable interval of time between test administrations, and the failure to have identical testing conditions both times.

The scores from the second test administration are generally slightly higher because of the practice effect that results from the first test administration. Unlike a block of wood, which can be measured endlessly without any noticeable effect on the block, a student will probably change as a result of the measurement. In the case of achievement tests, the change is customarily slight but discernible.

The length of time allowed between test administrations is critical and must be selected with care. If it is too short, students will remember the answers given at the first test when they answer the questions the second time; if it is too long, the students may change with respect to the characteristic measured. In many cases, a week or two is judged to be an appropriate compromise. Obviously there is no single, widely accepted time interval suitable for all types of tests with all varieties of students.

The most serious weakness in the eyes of some, however, is the fact that the coefficient of reliability reflects student-centered chance errors but not one of the most vital instrument-centered chance errors, namely, the fact that tests are samples of an immense number of possible items. Repetition of a test at different times will reveal inconsistent student behavior; but, since the same test is used twice, the sampling of the items is held constant. Consequently, an important instrument-centered chance error is ignored and the coefficients of reliability tend to be unduly *high.* Some writers recommend that these coefficients not be computed for achievement tests.

The Equivalence Method

Rather than involve administration of the same norm-referenced test twice to a group of students, as in the case of the stability method, the equivalence method utilizes the scores from each of a pair of equivalent tests. The two equivalent tests are given to a suitable group of students with little or no time between the two administrations. Two scores are available for each student, one from each form of the test. When the scores are correlated, a coefficient of reliability results. If the two forms of the test were administered with an intervening time interval as in the test-retest method, then the stability and equivalence method is being followed. In many such cases, the time interval is at least a day and no longer than a week.

The requirement that a norm-referenced measuring instrument be available in two equivalent forms is, of course, a severe limitation. Equivalent forms of classroom tests are seldom found. Teachers usually do not construct them except in the case of "make-up" tests, which are supposed to be equivalent to the tests they replace. Standardized tests, on the other hand, are often published with two equivalent forms, sometimes more. Suppose that Mr. Miller, who developed the 100-item norm-referenced achievement test in American history, wants to construct an equivalent form. The problem he faces is not incidental. One danger to be avoided is the designing of the equivalent form to be so "equivalent" to the original that it is essentially identical. Then he still has but one test in spite of his efforts. The second danger is to design the equivalent form to be so "unequivalent" that it is measuring something quite different from the original. A satisfactory equivalent form is somewhere in between.

The problem of building an equivalent form of the American history achievement test can be attacked systematically. First of all, as emphasized in the discussion of the content validity of achievement tests, Mr. Miller must identify certain educational objectives and from these develop one or more tables of specifications. On the basis of these tables he has to compose a vast number of test items. Pretesting the items at various times with appropriate students helps screen them. In all likelihood, only part of the surviving items are included in the original form of the test. The balance are available for an equivalent form. From this supply Mr. Miller can compile a second cross-sectional sample of test items that represent the same level of difficulty and relative importance with regard to the table of specifications cells as the set of test items composing the original form.

Evidence concerning the equivalence of the two forms can be obtained by methods beyond the scope of this book.

Assume that Mr. Miller completes an equivalent form of the American history test and labels it Form B. The original test becomes Form A. Forms A and B can be administered consecutively to the group of eleventh-grade students for whom the test is designed. The result is a pair of scores for each student, which in turn can be plotted and will yield a scatter of points very much like that in Figure 9.1. A coefficient of correlation computed from the data is a coefficient of reliability (sometimes known as a coefficient of equivalence) and will, of course, fall somewhere between 0.00 and 1.00. An r value of 0.91 is found in the case of the history test.

This coefficient of reliability is clearly not the same representation of test reliability as the coefficient yielded by the stability method. The chance errors involved in the two methods are different. In the equivalence method, the student-centered chance errors are not reflected in the coefficient of reliability. This is because the time interval between the two test administrations is virtually non-existent. On the other hand, the instrument-centered chance error, associated with the fact that the test is necessarily a sample, is manifest in this method. Each form of the test is assumed to be a cross-sectional sample of the same group of items. The opposite is true in the case of the stability method: the student-centered chance errors are operative, whereas the instrument-centered chance error is not.

Mr. Miller may choose to give the two forms consecutively to an appropriate group of students, or he may choose to allow a time interval between the two tests. By the latter process, many student-centered as well as instrument-centered chance errors will influence the reliability estimate. Therefore, since reliability is defined as the relative absence of chance errors in the measurement results, the most logical procedure for estimating test reliability is the stability and equivalence method. Remember that its coefficient of reliability, sometimes known as the coefficient of stability and equivalence, represents stability of performance by the student over a short period of time. This is essential information, since we often want assurance that the student would have obtained a similar test score had he or she been tested on a different day or with an equivalent instrument.

The Internal-Consistency Method

The practical difficulties in the test-retest and equivalent-forms methods of determining reliability emphasize the desirability of estimating test reliability with a single administration of one form of the norm-referenced test in question. The savings in time and labor are obvious. In this undertaking, however, new formulas are necessary and new assumptions must be made.

There are two basic procedures for analyzing the results of a single test administration to assess the reliability of the instrument. The first, sometimes known as the split-half procedure, arbitrarily divides the total test into two halves, scores them separately (thereby yielding two scores per student), and correlates the pairs of scores. The resulting coefficient of correlation is a coefficient of reliability of one-half of the test rather than the total test, and is adjusted to be applicable to the total test. The second procedure, sometimes known as an analysis-of-variance procedure, involves examination of the responses to each test item in terms of the number of students who successfully answered the item and the number who failed it.

Usually the first controversy concerning the application of the split-half procedure is centered around the selection of the two halves. Imagine the number of possible halves that could be obtained by splitting the 100-item achievement test in American history previously mentioned. The most satisfactory set of all possible halves would be that pair composed of the two most equivalent members. In other words, the test items' level of difficulty and the manner in which they reflect the relative importance of the involved cells of the table of specifications should be the same in both halves. Dividing a test haphazardly into halves without thought of equivalence reduces the split-half process of reliability determination to busy work of dubious value.

If two equivalent halves of a test are to be found in the same way as two equivalent forms of a test are constructed, little has been gained in terms of conserving time and labor when the split-half method is used. Therefore, some compromises generally are made. Again the achievement test in American history can illustrate a typical situation. Let us assume that this achievement test, like many norm-referenced achievement tests, follows two general principles of construction. In the first place, the test items' levels of difficulty cluster closely around the fifty percent level. Secondly, the test items are crudely grouped according to content; items relating to each cell in the table of specifications are clustered in a systematic fashion. Under these conditions, a convenient way of selecting two halves that would tend to be equivalent is to separate the odd-numbered items from the even-numbered items. The level of difficulty of the items in the odd half will approximate the level of difficulty of those in the even half. So also will the content of the test items in the odd half approximate that of the items in the even half. Note that had Mr. Miller decided to divide his test so that the items numbered from 1 to 50 composed one half, whereas the items numbered from 51 to 100 composed the second half, the second would sample different material. The lack of equivalence would be striking.

The odd-even division is a popular method of separating a test into two halves of approximate equivalence. If Mr. Miller chooses to use this method, the remainder of the reliability determination is simple. First he gives the complete test (with odd and even test items in their proper order) to a representative group of eleventh-grade students for whom the test is designed. Then he separately scores the odd- and even-numbered items. A correlation coefficient can be computed by substituting the odd-half and even-half scores into the appropriate formula. The correlation coefficient between their scores is 0.73. This is the coefficient of reliability for one-half of the test rather than for the total test. To estimate the expected coefficient of reliability of the total test, an adjustment formula known as the Spearman-Brown "Prophecy Formula" is used.

In modified form the formula is

$$r_{xx} = \frac{2r_{oe}}{1 + r_{oe}}$$

where

r_{xx} = coefficient of reliability of the total test
r_{oe} = coefficient of correlation between the odd-half scores
and the even-half scores

In the American history achievement test the coefficient of reliability is

$$r_{xx} = \frac{(2) \ (0.73)}{1 + 0.73} = 0.84$$

Observe here the increase in the size of the coefficient of reliability as the length of the test is doubled. The main assumption underlying the applicability of the Spearman-Brown formula is that the two halves are indeed equivalent. As they fail to be ideally equivalent, so the coefficient of reliability of the total test is an underestimate. Since the equivalence of the two halves is probably somewhat inadequate, the coefficients of the Spearman-Brown formula are conservative estimates of test reliability.

Computation of a coefficient of reliability by an analysis-of-variance method most often utilizes one of the Kuder-Richardson formulas. This formula, identified as K-R #20, is relatively easy to apply, although its derivation is intricate. An important category of information necessary for solution of the formula is the proportion of students passing and failing each test item. This procedure estimates test reliability on the basis of the consistency of student performance from item to item within the test. In the case of achievement tests, the r values computed are usually smaller than expected because the item content of this type of test is not homogeneous.

The Kuder-Richardson and Spearman-Brown formulas are appropriate only for tests which are administered so that practically all students have an opportunity to attempt every test item. The r values that will result from use of these formulas with a single administration of a pure speed test will be inflated, perhaps substantially. The amount of overestimation is difficult to establish, but tends to decrease as the number of unattempted test items becomes smaller. The preferred procedure for determining the reliability of a speeded test is the stability and equivalence method.

Internal consistency methods of the analysis-of-variance type are becoming increasingly more popular. A number of variations are now being used; the alpha coefficient is one example (Cronbach, 1970, pp. 160–161). This kind of evidence of internal consistency is found in the technical manuals of many unspeeded norm-referenced tests.

PROBLEMS

3. To what degree would one expect the problem of the "practice effect" to reduce the value of a coefficient of reliability from the stability method as a representation of the reliability of a test? Is "practice effect" also a problem when the equivalence method is used? Explain your answer.

4. Serious objections have been raised with respect to the usefulness of the test-retest correlations as representations of degrees of reliability (Cureton, 1969, p. 795). Do these objections justify the position that this type of reliability determination should be avoided?

Determination of the Standard Error of Measurement

Since every test is somewhat unreliable, each score obtained for a student must be considered as an estimate of his or her "true score," which would have been found had the test been totally reliable. Although the coefficients of reliability are useful when test reliability is being appraised, they do not directly offer an estimate of the actual magnitude of scoring error because of test unreliability. The standard error of measurement, on the other hand, is expressed in test score units. The smaller it is for a given type of score distribution, the more reliable the test.

Computing Standard Errors of Measurement. The computation of the standard error of measurement is not difficult. Its formula is

$$S.E._m = \sigma\sqrt{1 - r_{xx}}$$

where

$S.E._m$ = standard error of measurement
σ = standard deviation of total test scores
r_{xx} = coefficient of reliability

The standard error of measurement of the achievement test in American history is 3.2. To obtain this value, we use the coefficient of equivalence of 0.91 along with the standard deviation, which is computed in accordance with a formula shown in Appendix A. The standard deviation value of 10.5 and the coefficient of equivalence are substituted in the standard error of measurement formula as follows

$$S.E._m = \sigma\sqrt{1 - r_{xx}} = (10.5)\sqrt{1 - 0.91} = 3.2$$

Interpreting Standard Errors of Measurement. It is *not* appropriate to say that, in the case of the American history achievement test, a student's "true score" differs from his obtained score by no more than 3.2 raw-score points. Rather, it can be said that the "true scores" will not differ from their respective obtained scores by more than 3.2 raw-score points in approximately two-thirds of the measurements we might make with this test. Or, the standard error of measurement can be doubled and the statement made that the "true scores" will not differ from their respective obtained scores by more than 6.4 raw-score points in approximately ninety-five percent of the measurements we might make. Finally, we could triple the standard error of measurement and say that the "true scores" will not differ from their respective obtained scores by more than 9.6 raw-score points in approximately ninety-nine percent of the measurements.

Although the foregoing interpretations still do not offer a direct, unequivocal statement of the error caused by test unreliabiilty in a given student's obtained score, teachers still consider the standard error of measurement to be a highly meaningful measure of test reliability. The fact that it is expressed in the same units as the test scores contributes greatly to its popularity. Teachers repeatedly argue that it offers a good basis for judging how satisfactory the reported test reliability is for a given testing function.

Because of test unreliability, scores must be interpreted as regions rather than as points. Such regions, often known as "bands," are determined by the standard error of measurement of the test. Since a student's "true score" does not differ from his obtained score by more than the standard error in approximately two-thirds of the measurements we make, it is customary to find the limits of the "band" by adding the standard error of measurement to the obtained score to determine the upper limit of the band and subtracting it from the score to determine the lower limit. Suppose that a student obtained a test score of 70 on a test with a standard error of measurement of 3. The "band" often used would have a lower limit of 67 and an upper limit of 73. A student with a score of 75 would have a 72–78 "band." By the way, because the two "bands" overlap, we can say that there is probably no difference between the two students in terms of this test. Should the two "bands" fail to overlap, there probably is a genuine difference between the students in question. This use of the standard error of measurement, crude as it is, serves to inject caution into the interpretation of small differences between raw scores.

PROBLEM

5. Describe a practical classroom situation in which knowledge of the standard error of measurement would be useful to you. Using layman's terms, how would you explain to a student that a test score should be interpreted as a region (or band) rather than as a point?

Appraising Estimates of Norm-Referenced Test Reliability

The test manuals accompanying commercial tests and sources such as *The Mental Measurements Yearbooks* (see Chapter 10) are extremely valuable sources of information in a study of reliability determinations, just as they are in a study of validity. One or both sources often provide sufficient information to allow the teacher to make at least tentative judgments. Particular attention needs to be given those aspects of the determination that may negatively influence the inter- pretation of the reliability coefficient or standard error of measurement reported.

Coefficients of Reliability

Evaluation of the coefficients of reliability reported for a standardized test should include a discriminating look at (1) the test itself (2) the characteristics of the group of students involved in the reliability determination and (3) the testing conditions.

Characteristics of the Test. Examination of the norm-referenced test itself to find helpful evidence for appraising a coefficient of reliability requires attention to at least three characteristics. These are the tendency of the test to be speeded, the homogeneity or heterogeneity of its content, and the length. The role of strict time limits, as they affect the size of coefficients yielded by the internal-consistency method, and the role of test content homogeneity, when the Kuder-Richardson formula is applied, have already been mentioned. The importance of test length in determining the size of coefficients of reliability is dramatically illustrated by the Spearman-Brown formula. If the number of items in a test is increased by adding items equal in quality to the original ones, the reliability of the test will improve noticeably. With the use of the Spearman-Brown formula, it is necessary to assume the items added are indeed as equal in quality as the originals. Unfortunately this assumption is not always remembered; and an over-generalized statement results, namely, the longer the test, the more reliable it is. Although it is true that longer tests tend to be more reliable in repeated in-stances, lengthening a test does not automatically assure us of greatly improved reliability.

Test items in a norm-referenced test that is comparatively homogeneous usually have higher indices of discrimination (D values) than those from tests of a heterogeneous nature. Furthermore, there is a close relationship between the indices of a test's discrimination and its reliability coefficient. To improve the reliability of a test of a given length, the teacher should use test items with relatively high indices of discrimination.

Characteristics of the Student Group. The group of students cooperating in the reliability determination is a second source of information. As in the case of the determination of tables of norms for a test, the test manual should characterize this group as to any attribute conceivably related to the dimension being measured. For example, the eleventh-grade students taking the experimental American his-tory achievement test should be identified as to grade level, average scholastic aptitude score on some well-known instrument, previous training in history, and geographic location. These and other pieces of information will help the teacher immeasurably in reaching a decision as to whether these eleventh-grade students are comparable to the class for whom the test is being selected. If the class and the experimental group of eleventh-grade students seem to be the same, the teacher can assume that the reliability estimates listed closely reflect the reliability of the measurements to be made.

The variability of the sample of eleventh-grade students with regard to the attribute being measured by the achievement test must never be ignored. A key value in describing the variability of the group in terms of this test is the standard deviation, in this instance 10.5. As the variability in American history achievement increases, so will the standard deviation. Moreover, as the variability increases, so will the coefficient of reliability. An extreme illustration involving the achievement test under consideration can readily illuminate the problem. Suppose that the sample of students had been drawn in about equal numbers from tenth, eleventh, and twelfth grades, in spite of the fact that the test is designed for eleventh-grade students who are completing a course in American history. The tenth-grade students may know relatively little about the material covered in the test; the eleventh-grade students know more; and the twelfth-grade students, having completed American history and probably other history courses, supposedly command even more knowledge. If this is true, the new group of students is extremely variable in terms of American history achievement, and the standard deviation will exceed 10.5. Hence the coefficient of reliability will be larger. Obviously the robust size of a coefficient of reliability based on a highly variable group of students does not indicate the reliability of measurements made on a more uniform group. Therefore, to interpret a coefficient of reliability, one should study the standard deviation of the test scores. Coefficients of reliability become more and more interpretable as the standard deviation of the standardization group approaches that of the teacher's class.

Standardization of Testing Conditions. The uniformity or lack of uniformity of the testing conditions is another point of concern when reports of reliability determination are appraised. Certainly the testing conditions at the time the standardization group is measured must be essentially the same as those recommended by the test manual. This prerequisite is generally attained without difficulty. A persistent problem, however, is student motivation. An appropriately oriented student who is to be given the test only once may be highly motivated throughout the measurement process. By contrast, a student who is the unwilling victim of double measurement, be it by test-retest or equivalent forms, and who is measured at some inopportune time for no apparent reason is undoubtedly less motivated. These differences introduce error. They will, for example, tend to lower the coefficients of stability that might be computed.

Minimum Coefficients of Reliability. Thoughtful consideration of the norm-referenced test itself, the characteristics of the standardization group used, and the testing conditions all inevitably lead to a more intimate grasp of the meaning of the coefficient of reliability. The question is often posed, however, as to what minimum a coefficient of reliability must attain before the test can be used under any condition. The answer is not straightforward. For instance, tests whose reliability coefficients are near 0.50 are used. Either the teacher applied an instrument of limited reliability or did not measure at all, since, as happens periodically in the measurement of personality traits, no other more satisfactory instruments exist. Needless to say, the interpretation of scores obtained from instruments with such low reliability coefficients must be made with extreme caution.

There is no single minimum size a coefficient of reliability must reach since the minimum alters with the purpose for which the test scores are to be used. The minimum size is comparatively low when the level of *group* accomplishment is being measured. It rises for the measurement of the level of *individual* accomplishment. In any event, coefficients of reliability of about 0.85 and higher are regularly found for many norm-referenced achievement and aptitude tests distributed by well-known publishing companies. Values for personality inventories vary considerably but frequently are lower.

Reliability of the Difference between Two Measurements. An important sidelight of the problem of appraising coefficients of reliability is revealed when the purpose of the measurement is to identify differences between two norm-referenced measurements rather than to interpret each measurement as such. Determining the difference between two measurements is relatively common. A teacher may wish to know how much progress her students made as a result of a particular learning experience. She could measure the class before the learning experience, then again after it, and interpret the difference between the two scores. In another case, a test battery composed of three, four, or more achievement and aptitude tests may have been given to a class. Then a test profile for each student was found. Among others, the question might be raised as to whether a student or a class is more competent in English than in general science. Differences between the scores of the two appropriate tests would be most helpful.

Although the coefficient of reliability indicates the reliability of individual measurements, it does not directly show the reliability of the difference between two measurements. This, however, can be computed when we know the coefficients of reliability of the two tests involved in the determination of the differences in question, and the intercorrelation between these tests.

It is unfortunately true that, if there is any important correlation between the two tests yielding scores from which difference scores are obtained, the reliability of these difference scores is substantially lower than the average reliability of the two tests in question. All users of tests should be keenly aware of this fact. In Table 9.1 notice the striking drop in the reliability of the difference scores as the correlation increases between the two tests used.

Standard Errors of Measurement

The foregoing discussion of the coefficients of reliability is appropriate in part to the standard error of measurement. Appraising the significance of standard errors of measurement involves a searching examination of the test itself, the characteristics of the standardization group of students, and the testing conditions. However, fluctuations in the variability of the group with respect to the characteristic being measured are considerably less important when standard errors of

TABLE 9.1.   Reliability of Difference Scores for Tests Having Various Degrees of Reliability

Coefficient of reliability		Correlation between Test A and Test B	Reliability of difference scores
Test A	Test B		
0.90	0.90	0.60	0.75
		0.40	0.83
		0.00	0.90
0.80	0.80	0.60	0.50
		0.40	0.67
		0.00	0.80
0.70	0.70	0.60	0.25
		0.40	0.50
		0.00	0.70

measurement are being considered instead of coefficients of reliability. Whereas differences in variability of the characteristic measured cause considerable fluctuations in the coefficients of reliability, the standard errors of measurement are, for all practical purposes, independent of fluctuations in the variability of the test scores. Hence, the standard error of measurement is a desirable way of comparing the reliability of a particular test administered to two different groups of students. This is precisely what happens when a teacher compares the reliability of a test given to a standardization group with its reliability when it is given to a class.

There are no readily applied suggestions as to how big a standard error should or should not be to ensure that the test is useful for a given purpose. Since it is expressed in the same units as the test scores, and since these units typically vary from test to test, a standard error of measurement of a specific size may be considered small in the case of one test and large in the case of another. Evaluation of standard errors of measurement is largely centralized in the teacher's concept of the importance of score difference in terms of the purposes for which the test has been administered. If a test author reports more than one standard error of measurement and identifies them as being applicable to certain different score levels, the foregoing principle still holds.

PROBLEM

6. Study the procedure for scoring and interpreting the *Differential Aptitude Tests* (see Chapter 12). Compare the interpretation of student profiles plotted on the individual report form to the foregoing discussion of the unreliability of difference scores.

Determining the Reliability of Criterion-Referenced Tests

Like norm-referenced tests, criterion-referenced tests must have a high degree of reliability to be useful. To determine the degree of reliability for these tests, we can again use the principles underlying the stability, equivalence, and stability and equivalence methods. We would be less likely to use the internal-consistency methods that served so well with norm-referenced measures. Often, however, we must use somewhat different procedures and computations (Popham, 1978, pp. 142–155; Millman, 1979, pp. 75–92).

One example of the variations necessary is traced to the fact that the product-moment coefficient of correlation is not always a satisfactory representation of the degree of reliability of criterion-referenced tests. When testing students with two equivalent forms to determine stability and equivalence reliability, for instance, there is normally so little variability among the scores obtained in each administration that standard correlational methods are not meaningful. Instead, one might simply compare each student's *score* from the first test administration with its counterpart from the second and see how much they differ. One could show the degree of unreliability of the test by reporting the percent of students whose two scores differ by very little (0–5 percent), slightly more (6–10 percent), and so forth. A highly reliable test is one yielding pairs of scores which differed very little or not at all.

Another way of studying the degree of reliability of a criterion-referenced test is to investigate the degree to which consistent *decisions* about students are made in terms of its scores. This method could be used for criterion-referenced achievement tests measuring mastery. Assume, for instance, that students are judged to have mastered the domain of behaviors on which the test is based if they can answer 85% of the items correctly. Administering the test once would classify each student in either the "mastery" or the "nonmastery" group. Readministering the test after an interval of time (say, one week) would permit us to classify each student again. We can describe the degree of consistency of our decisions by reporting the percent of identical classifications (i.e., the proportion of students classified in the mastery group both times plus those in the nonmastery group both times).

As you can see, many of the reliability determinations for criterion-referenced tests are somewhat unconventional. This does not necessarily change their worth. It does mean that we must be more flexible in our methods and the interpretations of their results. The importance of the reliability of criterion-referenced tests justifies trying new approaches, especially if they focus on the consistency with which decisions are made about students on the basis of test results.

SUMMARY

The primary ideas in this chapter can be summarized as follows:

1. Reliability is defined as the tendency of a measuring instrument to yield consistent information. It is secondary to validity as a desirable test characteristic, but a test cannot be valid if it fails to possess reliability.

2. A test is reliable to the degree that chance errors do not influence the infor-mation produced when it is given. Common chance errors in educational measuring methods are (1) student-centered errors, such as fluctuations in level of health, emotional strain, and motivation, and (2) instrument-centered errors, which arise from the fact that, for example, a paper-and-pencil test is actually a sample of an immense number of possible items, and it may not be scored consistently.

3. Reliability for norm-referenced tests is practically always expressed in quanti-tative terms, either as a coefficient of reliability or as a standard error of measurement. The coefficient of reliability, as discussed in this chapter, is a product-moment coefficient of correlation that can be determined in one of several ways. These are the stability method, the equivalence method, the stability and equivalence method, and the internal-consistency method.

4. According to the stability method, the coefficient of reliability is computed when a test is administered twice (with an intervening period of time) to a group of students, and the pairs of scores correlated. This representation of reliability has serious limitations.

5. For the equivalence method, the coefficient of reliability is found by admin-istering (with no intervening period of time) two equivalent forms of a test to a group of students, and then correlating the pairs of scores. When a time interval is allowed, the stability and equivalence method is being applied.

6. For the internal-consistency method, two procedures may be followed: the split-half method or the analysis-of-variance method. The split-half method may utilize the Spearman-Brown "Prophecy Formula." One common analysis-of-variance method is the Kuder-Richardson Formula #20.

7. The standard error of measurement is considered a useful indicator of test reliability because it is expressed in the same units as the test score and it is relatively independent of fluctuations in group variability in terms of the characteristics measured.

8. The principles underlying the stability, equivalence, and stability and equiv-alence methods are also useful when determining the degree of reliability of criterion-referenced tests. However, somewhat different procedures and com-putations are usually needed.

SUGGESTED READINGS

AMERICAN PSYCHOLOGICAL ASSOCIATION. *Standards for educational and psychological tests.* Washington, D.C.: Author, 1974.
    One section of this set of standards lists essential and desirable information needed for evaluating the reliability of a test.

ANASTASI, A. *Psychological testing* (4th ed.). New York: Macmillan, 1976.
    Chapter 5 contains sections dealing with the types of test reliability, the re-liability of speed tests, the dependence of test reliability upon the sample used, the interpretation of the standard error measurement, and the reliability of criterion-referenced tests.

CRONBACH, L. J. *Essentials of psychological testing* (3rd ed.). New York: Harper & Row, 1970. See chapter 6.
Strictly speaking, only part of this chapter is devoted to reliability (which the author prefers to call "generalizability"). Analysis of variance methods are stressed.

DIEDERICH, P. B. *Short-cut statistics for teacher-made tests* (3rd ed.) Princeton, N.J.: Educational Testing Service, 1973.
In pages 3–12 the three chief topics considered are the standard error of a test score, reliability, and correlation. Simple methods of computing needed statistical values are demonstrated.

MARTUZA, V. R. *Applying norm-referenced and criterion-referenced measurement in education.* Boston: Allyn and Bacon, 1977. See chapter 17.
Both the reliability and validity of domain-referenced tests are included in this chapter. Various reliability procedures suitable for these tests are described.

POPHAM, W. J. *Criterion-referenced measurement.* Englewood Cliffs, N.J.: Prentice-Hall, 1978. See pages 142–155.
Consideration is given the application of stability, equivalence, stability and equivalence, and internal consistency methods to determine the degree of reliability of criterion-referenced tests. Illustrations are given of the first three methods.

THORNDIKE, R. L., & HAGEN, E. P. *Measurement and evaluation in psychology and education* (4th ed.). New York: John Wiley & Sons, 1977.
In pages 73–101 procedures for determining the degrees of reliability of norm-referenced tests are illustrated. One section deals with the relationship between reliability and validity.

REFERENCES CITED

CRONBACH, L. J. *Essentials of psychological testing* (3rd ed.). New York: Harper & Row, 1970.

CURETON, E. E. Measurement theory. In R. L. Ebel (Ed.), *Encyclopedia of educational research* (4th ed.). New York: Macmillan, 1969, 785–804.

MILLMAN, J. Reliability and validity of criterion-referenced test scores. In R. Traub (Ed.), *Methodological developments: New directions for testing and measurement.* San Francisco: Jossey-Bass, 1979, 75–92.

POPHAM, W. J. *Criterion-referenced measurement.* Englewood Cliffs, N.J.: Prentice-Hall, 1978.

STANLEY, J. C. Reliability. In R. L. Thorndike (Ed.), *Educational measurement.* Washington, D.C.: American Council on Education, 1971.

10

The Validity of Measurement Methods

The purpose of this chapter is to help you to

1. Appreciate the central importance of validity in determining the worth of all measurement methods

2. Define validity and differentiate among its types; namely, content, criterion-related, and construct validity for norm-referenced measurement, and descriptive, functional, and domain-selection validity for criterion-referenced measurement

3. Illustrate the common methods used to determine the degree to which tests possess the various types of validity for norm-referenced and criterion-referenced tests

4. Explain correlation coefficients and expectancy tables, and evaluate their usefulness as estimates of the degree of validity of a test

5. Utilize the *Mental Measurements Yearbooks* and companion volumes when collecting information about the validity and reliability of commercial tests

Some years ago, so it is reported, an anthropologist studying the culture of a primitive community wanted to determine the number of children of each age living there. Since birth records were available for only a few children and parental reports were quite undependable, the anthropologist decided to measure the heights of the children to obtain an estimate of their ages. She did this by first measuring the heights of those few children whose ages were known. Then, by comparing the heights of children of unknown age with the heights of children whose ages were available, she estimated the unknown ages on the basis of height. This maneuver by the anthropologist was probably received sympathetically by her colleagues. It is possible that, had she not estimated ages from heights, she would have departed with no information about ages.

The anthropologist's action is not unlike that of high school seniors who search for a university; they may assess the quality of a university's academic offerings on the basis of (1) the size of its undergraduate student body, (2) the number of games won by its football team, or (3) both criteria at once. In somewhat the same category is the political pundit who evaluates the popularity of the party's agricultural program in terms of the number of unsolicited favorable letters received from the public at large. The economic soothsayer, who describes the economic health of the nation solely in terms of the rise and fall of the stock market, can also be similarly categorized.

Each of the foregoing illustrations may be cynically interpreted by discerning observers who might ask: Do differences in heights of children always indicate differences in age? Is the quality of a university's academic program necessarily a function of its size? Do unsolicited letters received at a political party's headquarters represent a cross-section of voter opinion? Is the stock market completely sensitive to all of the subtle changes in the economic structure? These and similar questions would undoubtedly be embarrassing and difficult to answer.

The individuals using the foregoing measurement methods in such potentially dangerous fashions are possibly somewhat innocent. The very accessibility of such data as height, enrollment, number of letters, and stock market reports tempts most investigators. Furthermore, the accuracy of these data is generally considered good. For instance, height can easily be measured to the nearest one-fourth of an inch. The difficulty then is not centered in the accuracy of the data involved, but rather in the interpretation. To argue that unwarranted interpretations have been made is to argue that validity, to some degree, is absent.

Definition of Validity

In educational measurement, validity is often defined as the degree to which a measuring instrument actually serves the purposes for which it is intended. A scholastic aptitude test is a valid measurement of scholastic aptitude if it truly measures scholastic aptitude. An achievement test in spelling is valid to the extent that it assuredly measures achievement in spelling. In the illustration just cited, it is obvious that the measurement of height by means of an accurate tape measure applied under controlled conditions is unquestionably valid, but it is a doubtful measure of age. Likewise, scores yielded by a scholastic aptitude test may well be quite valid indicators of degrees of aptitude but be inadequate representations of emotional stability.

Validity is clearly the most important characteristic of a measuring instrument. No matter what other characteristics an instrument may possess, if it does not adequately serve the purpose for which its use is intended, it is of no value whatsoever.

PROBLEM

1. The claim is made that some definitions of validity are virtually synonymous with those of test goodness (Ebel, 1979, pp. 301–303). If this is true, then ease of administration, adequacy of norms, reliability, etc., become aspects of validity. Should the definition of validity be this broad? Give reasons for your answer.

Types of Validity

The definition of validity already stated is useful, but still inadequate. To say that a measuring instrument is "valid" in the sense that validity has been defined is not enough. The statement is too vague. An instrument is valid in terms of its purpose or purposes. Examples already have been presented that vividly illustrate the fact that results yielded by a measuring instrument may be highly valid for one purpose and not at all for another. Since the relative validity of an instrument indicates the degree to which its purposes or aims are being achieved, and since the aims of tests vary, somewhat different types of validity are under consideration in various measuring instruments. The types of validity differ with the aims.

The aims of measurement methods are divided into three categories (American Psychological Association, 1974):

1. *To determine how well a student performs today in a certain type of situation or subject matter, a cross-sectional sample of which is present in the measuring instrument.* For example, a teacher might administer a spelling test to a class to determine how much they know at that moment about spelling. In all likelihood, the test would include only a sample of all the words for which the students are responsible.

2. *To predict students' future behavior or to estimate their present standing with respect to some characteristic not directly measured by the instrument.* For example, in the case of future behavior, a scholastic aptitude test could be given to students in a middle school to predict their academic success in senior high school. In the case of a student's present standing, a teacher can administer a paper-and-pencil arithmetic test composed of addition and subtraction problems involving representations of pennies,

nickels, dimes, quarters, half dollars, and dollar bills. The test score is intended to show the accuracy with which each student can actually make change when purchasing articles from retail stores.

3. *To infer the strength of a student trait or quality as reflected in the results yielded by the measuring instrument.* For example, a teacher might give a memory test to a class to make inferences about each student's scholastic aptitude.

The three types of validity are commonly identified as *content* validity, *criterion-related* validity, and *construct* validity. Each can be defined as the degree to which a measuring instrument accomplishes the aim associated with the type of test given.

Of course, an instrument may be designed to meet more than one of the three aims, and hence the person who develops and uses it must investigate more than one type of validity. Also, some types of validity tend to be more vital in certain kinds of tests. For example, content validity plays a key role in achievement testing and criterion-related validity in aptitude testing. To examine these and other ramifications resulting from the classification of validity types, separate consideration of each type is necessary. The emphasis of each of the following discussions reflects the fact that the original classification is based primarily on norm-referenced tests rather than criterion-referenced ones.

Content Validity

Finding the content validity of measuring instruments is equivalent to showing how well they sample certain types of situations or subject matter. An instrument claiming high content validity clearly attempts to include a cross-sectional sample of a great variety of items representing the area in which the student's performance is being measured.

Remember that the primary purpose of achievement measurement is to discover how well students have achieved educational objectives. For example, a teacher may wish to know how well students can add whole numbers or how well they can read. Another may want to determine how much information the class retains from prolonged discussions and readings about the political, economic, and social causes of World War II. These illustrations typify rather well-defined areas of subject matter and behavioral changes in terms of which classroom and standardized achievement tests are constructed. The validity of such tests is determined by the representatives of their contents. Since all possible questions cannot be included, the test is necessarily a sample. To the degree that the sample is not representative, the test lacks content validity.

Content validity is also a useful characteristic of scholastic aptitude tests and personal-social adjustment inventories. In each of these types of instruments, it is generally true that content validity is secondary to another kind. In scholastic aptitude tests, criterion-related validity is paramount, yet content validity is involved in the identification of the great variety of possible test items from which those used are selected.

Criterion-Related Validity

Criterion-related validity can be divided into two parts, namely, the validity of instruments designed to predict future performance, and that of instruments designed to estimate present status with respect to a characteristic not directly measured by the test. The former is known as predictive validity and the latter as concurrent validity. The principal difference between these two classifications is the time at which the student displays the behavior in question. In the first case we wish to predict the future. In the second, we want to gain information about present performance by using information obtained indirectly.

Instruments Predicting Future Performance. The fact that aptitude tests are designed to predict what a student can accomplish with training is another way of saying that aptitude tests, by definition, are fundamentally dependent on the establishment of a high degree of predictive validity. The uses of scholastic aptitude scores for sectioning classes, anticipating success in reading, estimating the likelihood of graduating from secondary school, or guiding a student toward a career in law, amply illustrate the use of a test score or scores to infer tomorrow's successes and failures. This type of validity depends on the accuracy of the predictions of future student behavior.

In spite of the fact that achievement tests are constructed for the primary purpose of determining how much students know or how well they can perform as of that moment, another and less common use is forecasting subsequent achievement. For instance, norm-referenced reading tests are used to section classes in various subject matter areas and to predict academic success in secondary school and college. Criterion-referenced tests covering crucial aspects of a secretarial training program might be used to predict future job performance for graduates. In these cases, high predictive validity is unquestionably necessary.

Instruments Estimating Present Standing. Some measuring instruments try to determine a student's present standing indirectly. The student behavior elicited by this type of instrument is thought to correspond closely to a certain external behavior. If it does, the instrument has acceptable criterion-related validity of the concurrent type.

Like content validity, this type is usually a necessary attribute of achievement-measuring instruments. Consider, for example, the measurement of reading and arithmetic achievement. A reading comprehension test score might be interpreted as being indicative of the student's reading comprehension level when she reads for pleasure. The results of an arithmetic test may be interpreted as related to the accuracy with which a student can compute his hourly wages when he shovels snow after school. A teacher may wish to interpret scores on a language usage test as closely correlated with a tabulation of the student's actual verbal usage at the time.

Concurrent validity is also important when considering the validity of instruments in personal-social adjustment, particularly so when they are used to classify students in groups. For example, an interest inventory may reflect one or more differences between students who have hobbies involving manual skills and those who do not. Also, students in need of immediate counseling may be detected by personal-social adjustment inventory scores and other evidence.

Construct Validity

To describe construct validity, it is first necessary to establish the meaning of the term "construct." A construct is a characteristic assumed to exist to account for some aspect of human behavior. In psychology, many constructs are used, such as cautiousness, tendency to conform, rigidity, insecurity, dominance, and ability to apply principles. These terms serve the useful purpose of providing a convenient means of identifying the psychological concepts they represent. By themselves, however, they do not explain the concept or any theory underlying it.

Whenever a measuring instrument is believed to reflect a particular construct, its construct validity must be investigated. This amounts to determining how well certain constructs account for student performance as measured by the instrument. To make a suitable investigation possible, the construct should be sufficiently well-defined so that verifiable inferences can be drawn from it. Testing the accuracy of the inferences with a measuring instrument is a way of confirming or denying the claim that a certain construct accounts for variations in the performance elicited by the instrument. If the instrument has a high degree of construct validity, its findings will vary from one kind of individual to another, or from one situation to another, as the theory underlying the construct would predict. In many ways, establishing construct validity is the same as validating the theory that defines the construct.

Examples of the importance of construct validity can be found in the measurement of achievement, aptitude, and personal-social adjustment. In the case of achievement measurement, construct validity is a pertinent characteristic of those tests claiming to measure study skills and ability to reason. Is there any proof that the tests actually measure study skills or reasoning ability as defined by the authors of the tests? Aptitude tests can be challenged by questioning whether evidence is available that can describe the complete meaning of the aptitude measured. A teacher using a general mental ability test may demand of its author an explanation of his concept of general mental ability and how the students' activities as they write the test correspond to that concept. Finally, when a personal-social adjustment inventory is thought to reveal the composition of a student's personality, the inventory must have a high construct validity.

PROBLEMS

2. Which of the following activities are illustrations of the need for useful degrees of concurrent validity or predictive validity?
    a. Using the fifth birthday as the minimum age for children to enter kindergarten
    b. Using high school grade-point averages as a basis for selecting the freshmen class at an academically oriented college
    c. Establishing the minimum voting age at 18 years

    d. Studying a quarterly earnings report of a corporation in order to anticipate whether the value of a share of its stock will change

3. Cronbach (1970a, p. 125) believes that the central question asked when the construct validity of a test is being determined is the following: "How can scores on this test be explained psychologically?" What is meant by this question? Illustrate.

Degrees of Validity

A given instrument may have more than one purpose and, thus, should be characterized by more than one type of validity. The demonstration of high validity, then, is commonly a multiple approach rather than a single attempt. The author is obliged to examine carefully the aims of the instrument and, for each aim, to present evidence that the instrument can validly perform that function. This information can be of immeasurable help to those who wish to use the test for a particular purpose and, most important of all, interpret its scores in the most precise manner possible.

Content Validity

Because content validity is oriented toward achievement testing, which is such a formidable part of student evaluation, this section is restricted to achievement testing. Paper-and-pencil achievement tests are developed on the basis of educational objectives with verbal or mathematical aspects and are designed to show how well students have achieved those objectives. Therefore, to construct a test with high content validity, the teacher must begin with the same educational objectives that guided classroom instruction. On the basis of the objectives chosen, test items are developed for criterion-referenced tests; for norm-referenced tests, tables of specifications are built, which in turn guide the development and selection of test items.

    When skilled teachers devise an achievement test for their own classes, the probability increases that the level of content validity will be acceptable. Who knows better than they which of the many proposed test items are probably "trick" or "unfair" items? When thus labeled after careful consideration by either teacher or student, these vernacular expressions mean that the test items (and hence the test as a whole) lack content validity to some degree. The teacher's knowledge of the class and its educational objectives are the most important factors accounting for the superior content validity of carefully constructed classroom tests.

Norm-Referenced Standardized Achievement Tests. To some teachers, norm-referenced standardized achievement tests are unknown quantities. Yet these instruments typically resemble classroom tests, although they are more highly refined and cover a broader area of content. They usually represent the thinking of teachers, supervisors, subject matter specialists and others, and have withstood a rigorous statistical assault by professional testing specialists.

The educational objectives of a course of study and their tables of specifications, which are so important in the identification of the content validity of teacher-built achievement tests, are equally important in the identification of the content validity of norm-referenced standardized achievement tests. Hence, for such a test to have high content validity when measuring student achievement resulting from a given teaching effort, it must be constructed in terms of the table of specifications evolving from the learning experience guided by that teacher in that instance. Beyond question, this rarely happens.

Since a test is to be used by not one teacher but hundreds, and since all teachers have their own peculiar sets of educational objectives and tables of specifications, despite much common ground in many subject matter areas, the author of a test can hope only to orient an instrument toward those educational objectives that appear to be most prevalent. Teachers who propose to use a norm-referenced standardized achievement test are automatically obliged to find convincing evidence that the educational objectives and tables of specifications involved closely correspond to their own.

To aim a standardized achievement test at popularly held educational objectives, the test builders do considerable investigation. A year or more may be spent in the laborious process of scanning lesson plans, state study guides, and widely used textbooks covering the subject matter in question and also in interviewing teachers and supervisors directly involved in the selected field. The process finally yields a core of reference materials thought to be most representative, and possibly a panel of subject matter specialists thought to be well-informed. On the basis of these sources of information, test items are constructed.

If the reference materials are identical with or closely related to those used by a teacher, the possibility of the standardized achievement test having high content validity for that teacher's use is considerably improved. Obviously, the textbooks and courses of study composing the reference materials should be identified for the potential test user. Some, but by no means all, manuals accompanying standardized achievement tests include complete titles and dates of publication of each of the reference materials. If a panel of subject matter specialists in the field is used, either independently of or in conjunction with the reference materials, they should be identified by name and pertinent facts about their professional qualifications should be listed.

Unfortunately, detailed information about the reference materials and any panel of specialists is not given in some test manuals. The inquiring teacher finds only glib statements about the "careful selection" of the test items and the "popular modern textbooks" that were consulted. This is meager fare indeed for any astute reviewer.

Regardless of the limited data of this kind that might be offered in the test manual, at least two other avenues relative to content validity should be explored. In the first place, manuals usually supply ample statements about the purposes of the test and its limitations in terms of subject matter covered. These statements bear careful perusal for evident reasons. Secondly, the test items themselves should be carefully scrutinized. It is highly recommended that a teacher play the role of student and write the answers under similar conditions. Then there should be an additional item-by-item examination. For each item the question must be asked: In view of my educational objectives, the tables of specifications derived from them, and the method of teaching I followed, is this test item appropriate for my students this term? Answers will be regularly affirmative if there is acceptable content validity.

The item-by-item examination should not be a casual operation. On the contrary, it should be tied directly to the teacher's educational objectives and tables of specifications. A tabulation should be made by copying each item number opposite the cell of the table of specifications with which it is associated. If a test item is related to more than one cell, it should be tabulated accordingly. If it is primarily related to one cell of the table and secondarily related to another, a simple coding scheme can identify these differences. Although this process is lengthy, it is necessary if the content validity of a standardized achievement test is to be assessed.

Some norm-referenced standardized achievement tests assist the content validity review by providing the table of specification on which the test was developed and, for each cell, reporting the number of test items primarily related to it. This is illustrated in Table 10.1 in which test items are classified for a survey test measuring the social studies achievement of students finishing elementary school. Six social studies areas are included in the test. Note the comparatively heavy emphasis on geography and history and the light emphasis on economics and anthropology. Also, of the 60 test items, three-fourths (45) require knowledge or comprehension, and one-fourth (15) entail application of facts and principles.

The balance among the cells in Table 10.1 may or may not be suitable for a given testing situation. Even if it is, it may not be acceptable a year or two later. The relative emphasis that teachers place on various combinations of topics and behavioral changes is a moving target. It shifts with time. Ideally, a standardized achievement test must keep pace, step by step. Content validity can be fleeting.

Criterion-Referenced Achievement Tests. The primary mission of criterion-referenced achievement tests is to describe a learner's status with respect to a be-

TABLE 10.1.   Classification of Test Items in a Survey Test in Social Studies

Subject matter topic	Behavioral changes		Total
	Knowledge/ comprehension	Application	
Geography	11	4	15
History	12	4	16
Economics	4	1	5
Political Science	6	3	9
Anthropology	6	0	6
Sociology	6	3	9
Total	45	15	60

havior domain, that is, a class of behaviors such as the ability to add correctly any pair of two-digit whole numbers. The domain must be well defined so that functional test items can be generated. This means that the simple use of instructional objectives for developing test items may not sufficiently delimit the class of behaviors; consequently, independent judges will not consistently agree on whether particular test items actually measure the learner behaviors under consideration. To reduce ambiguity and help improve the quality of criterion-referenced test items, tight test specifications are used. In other words, the test items for a behavior domain are developed in terms of carefully drawn stimulus and response attributes, and therefore tend to be quite homogeneous (see page 58).

The most basic type of validity for criterion-referenced achievement tests is content validity, perhaps better termed *descriptive* validity (Popham, 1978, pp. 155–159). These tests are valid to the degree that they measure the class of learner behaviors included in the domain description. Hence the degree of content validity can be estimated by judges who identify the proportion of test items that is consistent with the domain description. If the domain description is well written and stimulus and response attributes are used successfully, this review by judges can be rigorous—indeed more rigorous than is possible for norm-referenced achievement tests based on tables of specifications.

Criterion-Related Validity

Determining the degree of criterion-related validity for various types of tests can be conveniently illustrated by examining the degree of predictive validity of norm-referenced aptitude tests. The practical value of tests designed to measure mechanical aptitude, clerical aptitude, scholastic aptitude, and similar areas is centered in the accuracy with which a teacher can make predictions on the basis of their scores. It is logical, then, to take a longitudinal approach to the problem of determining predictive validity. A scholastic aptitude test can be administered to a group of students today and predictions of future academic achievement can be made for one or more subjects. Actual academic success can be measured at that future time by achievement tests or, possibly, final marks. Finally, predicted achievement can be compared with actual achievement; and the predictive validity of the scholastic aptitude test as applied in these prediction situations can be evaluated.

Predictions of future academic achievement can also be made in terms of the same units as those of achievement measurement, but they are not always determined in this manner. With the application of appropriate statistical techniques, a teacher may be able to say, for example, that a student whose scholastic aptitude test score is 117 should be expected to score in the vicinity of 80 to 86 on a particular English test. However, the predictions made are usually informal, thus making it awkward to compare predicted and actual achievement. They are often equivalent to saying that students who do well on the scholastic aptitude test will probably achieve well in school, whereas those who do badly will probably achieve poorly. In view of this, comparison of the scholastic aptitude scores and the measures of academic success would yield information concerning criterion-related validity.

TABLE 10.2.   Scholastic Aptitude Test Scores and Achievement Test Scores of Eighth-Grade Social Studies Students

Name	Scholastic Aptitude Test Fall term, seventh grade		Social Studies Test Fall term, eighth grade		Difference in rank
	Score	Rank	Score	Rank	
Leo	135	1	66	9	8
Margaret	130	2	90	1	1
Brian	120	3	68	8	5
Carrie	117	4	85	3	1
Brett	116	5	81	4	1
Louise	114	6	47	17	11
Ralph	113	7	69	7	0
Joyce	112	8	77	5	3
Quinton	111	9	65	10	1
Sandra	109	10	56	15	5
Larry	107	11	89	2	9
Norma	106	12	49	16	4
Frank	101	13	57	14	1
Milton	100	14	58	13	1
Dave	97	15	71	6	9
Joe	95	16	60	11	5
Bill	94	17	38	19	2
Sally	90	18	31	20	2
Mary	88	19	40	18	1
Sue	87	20	59	12	8

Some of the basic steps in establishing the validity of an aptitude test can be examined most directly with an illustration. Suppose that Mrs. Wilson, an eighth-grade social studies teacher, wishes to know how satisfactorily achievement in her class can be predicted from scholastic aptitude test scores received one year earlier. For the sake of simplicity, she is willing to define achievement in social studies in terms of the scores of a comprehensive norm-referenced achievement test given at the end of the term. The result is a double measurement of each student, the data from which may be compiled as shown in Table 10.2.

The twenty students are arranged according to their scores on the scholastic aptitude test. Their achievement scores are listed opposite the scholastic aptitude scores. To facilitate interpretation, both sets of scores are ranked from one to twenty according to the position of each student in the class with respect to each test. If the scholastic aptitude test possesses high validity, the rank of any student on the scholastic aptitude test should be approximately the same as his or her rank on the achievement test. Table 10.2 shows that the aptitude and achievement ranks of some students do not differ by more than one. These cases support the contention that the scholastic aptitude test can predict achievement in eighth-grade social studies. Since other students, however, have differences of eight or more, these cases tend to refute the contention concerning the validity of this test.

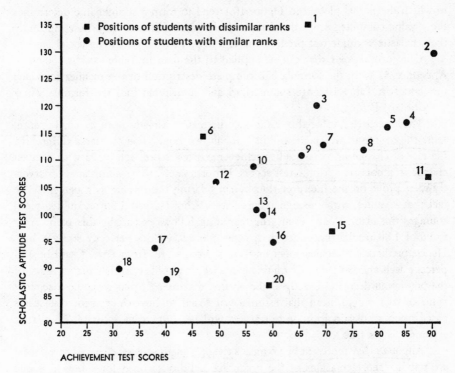

FIGURE 10.1.   Scatter Diagram of Scholastic Aptitude Test Scores and
Achievement Test Scores

The foregoing analysis is casual, if not crude. A precise statement of the
validity of the test is still lacking. Figure 10.1 gives a more comprehensive picture
of the entire class. In this figure are plotted twenty points, one for each student.
The position of a point is found by locating on the vertical axis the scholastic
aptitude test score of that student, and moving to the right, parallel to the horizontal
axis, until his or her achievement in social studies is located. The points are numbered in terms of the ranks of the students on the scholastic aptitude test.

A moment of thought will show that, if the scholastic aptitude test has high
criterion-related validity in this example, the points should arrange themselves in
a straight line. Thus, the greater the tendency of the points to approximate a
straight line, then the greater the predictive validity. All points in Figure 10.1
obviously do not fall in a straight line, yet the eye can detect a definite elongated
pattern that certainly suggests linearity. It is interesting now to observe the positions of points representing the five students whose ranks differ so greatly. The
points are numbered 1, 6, 11, 15, and 20, and are represented by squares rather
than circles. It is not surprising that they are all found along the perimeter of the
pattern, and that their deletion would strengthen the impression that the points
tend to form a straight line.

The computation of correlation coefficient provides a succinct representation
of the predictive validity of the scholastic aptitude test in this instance. The extent

to which the points plotted in Figure 10.1 tend to form a straight line determines the r value computed from the data, and also shows Mrs. Wilson how efficiently the scholastic aptitude test predicts the eighth-grade achievement in social studies.

One formula of r that can be applied to the data in Table 10.2 is shown in Appendix A. With the formula is a complete description of the manner in which the values in Table 10.2 are summarized and substituted into the formula. An r value of 0.61 is found.

The interpretation of this value has, in reality, already been given. It represents the degree to which the points fall into a straight line or, stated differently, the rate of change in social studies achievement test scores compared with a given change in scholastic aptitude test scores. Unfortunately, some uninitiated observers try to improve on the interpretation by considering the r value as a percent. The fact that r values, with the sign ignored, vary from 0.00 to 1.00 undoubtedly encourages this error. In any event, the reasoning follows essentially this path: An r value of 1.00 results from data that, when plotted, yield a perfectly straight line. Hence, prediction of achievement on Test Y from scores from Text X will be 100 percent accurate. On the basis of this evidence, it would seem that the accuracy of the prediction decreases exactly as the r value decreases. If that were the case, an r value of 0.61 would mean that estimates of social studies achievement test scores based upon scholastic aptitude test scores will be 61 percent accurate. This latter argument is not true.

Although they represent by no means the only method, coefficients of correlation are popular representations of the predictive validity claimed for a test. The one described is a *product-moment* coefficient of correlation. Other types of coefficients of correlation, discussions of which can be found in many textbooks of statistical methodology, are also used, but in a minority of instances. The computation of some of these is quite simple and rapid. One is the *rank-difference* correlation coefficient, otherwise known as the Spearman rho. It uses the differences between two sets of ranks such as those in Table 10.2 as a basis for its computation (see Appendix A). In the case of the data in Table 10.2, the rho value is 0.60, a close approximation of the r value. We cannot always expect such a high degree of agreement.

It is clear, certainly, that an adequate grasp of the demonstration of criterion-related validity is highly dependent on an adequate grasp of the meaning of the correlation coefficient. Although teachers such as Mrs. Wilson generally do not find themselves confronted with computations of an r value, they are regularly obliged to interpret them.

Expectancy Tables.   Rather than trying to make "pinpoint" predictions of future student achievement, Mrs. Wilson may wish to predict only in terms of broad categories: that is, whether a student will achieve "above average," "average," or "below average" in her class. If this is the intended use of the scholastic aptitude test, the predictive validity of the instrument can be much more realistically appraised by expectancy tables (Wesman, 1975, pp. 28–35).

An expectancy table is merely a condensed version of plotted data similar to that in Figure 10.1. In the figures, each gradation of the scores of each test is

TABLE 10.3.   Expectancy Table for Scholastic Aptitude and Social Studies Achievement
Test Scores

Scholastic Aptitude Test scores	Social Studies Achievement Test scores			
	Below average (Below 55)	Average (55–75)	Above average (Over 75)	Total
Above average (Over 115)	0	2	3	5
Average (95–115)	2	7	2	11
Below average (Below 95)	3	1	0	4
Total	5	10	5	20

shown; in an expectancy table, the scores are grouped into a convenient number
of intervals. Table 10.3 is an expectancy table based on the data in Table 10.2 in
which each set of test scores is grouped into three intervals. The number within
each cell of the table represents the number of students who have scholastic aptitude and social studies achievement scores within the limits indicated.

The interpretation of Table 10.3 is straightforward. For instance, Mrs. Wilson
can say that none of her students whose aptitude score is "below average" (less
than 95) has an achievement score that is "above average" (greater than 75).
Moreover, none of her students with "above average" aptitude scores (greater
than 115) receives a "below average" achievement score (less than 55). More
inclusive statements could be made in a slightly different manner. Students with
aptitude scores of 95 or greater rarely (2 out of 16) receive achievement scores of
less than 55.

Generally the interpretation of the expectancy table is simplified if percents
are used. This requires a larger number of cases than twenty but can be illustrated
by using the data from Table 10.3. By computing percents for each row separately,
as in Table 10.4, we can estimate the probability of different levels of success in
social studies for students having a given level of scholastic aptitude. For example,
if a student has "average" scholastic aptitude, the probability of having "below
average" achievement in social studies is 18 in 100. The probability of having
"average" achievement is 64 in 100; for "above average" achievement, it is 18 in 100.

Degrees of Predictive Validity.   It is certainly clear at this point that the scholastic
aptitude test in question does not have the greatest possible predictive validity. On
the other hand, although the *r* value is no larger than 0.61 and the expectancy table
shows some students classified in cells other than the ones desired, Mrs. Wilson
cannot automatically say that the validity of the instrument is unsatisfactory. On
the contrary, the instrument may be judged as useful for prediction purposes if,
in spite of its inaccuracies, it can predict future achievement of these students
better than other means.

TABLE 10.4.   Expectancy Table Based on Percents

Scholastic Aptitude		Number of cases	Social Studies Achievement Test scores		
Category	Test score		Below average	Average	Above average
Above average	Over 115	5	0	40	60
Average	95–115	11	18	64	18
Below average	Below 95	4	75	25	0

Actually the *r* value of 0.61 is comparatively large in this case. When attempting to predict future academic achievement we often must work with scholastic aptitude tests with lower *r* values. This does not mean that they are extremely poor. On the contrary, tests yielding *r* values as low as 0.30 can be useful for screening groups of candidates for an educational program or a job.

Predictions of future achievement based on aptitude test data must be viewed in much the same manner as the predictions of life expectancy made by insurance companies. Life insurance companies can predict with striking accuracy the percentage of thirty-year-old men who will be living twenty-five or fifty years from now; yet they cannot predict with similar accuracy which *members* of the group will be alive or dead at these future dates. This is also true of achievement predicted from aptitude-test data. If predictions are made for a group, the accuracy is customarily quite good; a prediction made for an individual member of that group may be distressingly inaccurate.

Criterion-Referenced Tests.   Although descriptive validity is basic to criterion-referenced tests, there are instances where the purpose of the test extends beyond merely describing a student's performance accurately, important as that is. These are decision-oriented functions such as using criterion-referenced test results to anticipate future academic success or job performance. Clearly the need to determine the degree to which such tests can be used successfully for these predictions raises the same questions examined in terms of criterion-related validity for norm-referenced tests. Instead of criterion-related validity, however, this is called *functional* validity in the case of criterion-referenced tests (Popham, 1978, pp. 159–161).

The degree of functional validity of criterion-referenced tests is usually of less concern than their degree of descriptive validity. Keep in mind that, without a high degree of descriptive validity, these tests no doubt have little functional utility in any event.

Test Manual as a Source of Information.   The primary source of information for most teachers as they investigate the validity of commercial tests and inventories is the test manual. Although this compilation is usually highly abbreviated, it regularly provides sizable amounts of data about the authors' attempts to establish acceptable validity and perhaps lists references to reseach conducted by other interested investigators. Examination of the test manual by the potential test purchaser is always sound practice.

Test authors who wish to present the most comprehensible discussion of their tests' validity are certain to find it an exacting task. Among other things, they must carefully describe the criteria with which their tests are correlated and the nature of the students who cooperated in the validation attempt. Both of these descriptions emphasize the fact that the determination of validity as it is outlined is relative to the criteria used and the students measured To the degree that a criterion is weak or the standardization group inadequate in any way, the determination of validity becomes less meaningful.

In theory, there are as many predictive or functional validity determinations as there are suitable criteria. Even if it were possible to gather and report all of this validity information, many potential test users would find much of it of modest value. Some criteria would be so far removed from their needs that they would be uninteresting. Others would be such crude measurements of pertinent variables (e.g., job performance) that they would not provide a basis for a solid estimate of the degree of predictive validity. In short, evidence of predictive validity must be evaluated most carefully before a decision about a test is made.

PROBLEMS

4. What is cross-validation (Anastasi, 1976, pp. 219–221)? Of what significance is it in the determination of the relative validity of a scholastic aptitude test? Give an illustration to support your answer.

5. When homogeneous groups of students are used, the predictive validity of aptitude tests is low. In other words, the r values are small compared with those for the same test used with heterogeneous groups. Explain why this is so (see Kaufman, 1972).

Construct Validity

Many of the methods used to determine the relative validity of the first two types are also suitable when construct validity is being investigated. An analysis of construct validity is supported by total available knowledge of the validity of the instrument in question. In other words, demonstrating what constructs account for variations in performance is a difficult task.

The basis on which the investigation of construct validity proceeds is provided by the theory underlying the construct supposedly involved in the measuring instrument. On the basis of the theory, predictions are made: one group of individuals will differ from another in terms of the data yielded by an instrument involving the construct, or individuals will or will not change after they have experienced certain environmental conditions. The measuring instrument is then used to test the predictions. If the predictions and the data produced by the instrument concur, evidence in support of the construct validity has been found. If they do not, a state of uncertainty exists. Either the instrument does not involve the construct, or the theory is not sound. In any event, the degree of construct validity is in doubt.

Comparisons with Other Instruments.   One method of determining construct validity is to correlate the data from the instrument under study with a second instrument thought to measure the same construct. This is sometimes done with the type of group tests of general mental ability regularly used in elementary and secondary schools. For example, an experimental group test of general mental ability and the *Wechsler Intelligence Scale for Children (Revised)* are administered to a sample of students. The scores from the experimental test and the *Wechsler* test are then correlated. If the *Wechsler* test is an acceptable measure of general mental ability, and its scores are closely correlated with those of the experimental test, the experimental test is said to have high construct validity.

Since complete agreement is seldom obtained as to the quality of the test serving as a standard, the correlation process is often repeated with several tests. When a group test of general mental ability is being studied, the standards are usually individual tests or well-known group tests of this trait. In areas other than general mental ability testing, there is a similar tendency, rightly or wrongly, to use popular tests reputed to measure the same construct as the test under investigation.

Comparisons with Judges' Ratings.   The use of judges is another means of assessing construct validity and has been used in connection with a variety of tests. For example, suppose that a paper-and-pencil inventory has been constructed to measure the social adaptability of middle school students. Each of the 100 items included in the inventory requires them to select one of the four alternatives that best approximates their behavior should they be confronted with the social situation described. The author defines social adaptability as the ability of people, when participating in a social situation, to adjust their behavior in accordance with the nature of the situation and to do so easily.

To discover whether this inventory actually measures social adaptability, the author may employ a group of judges who are to observe independently—and somewhat surreptitiously—the social behavior of a group of students. The judges are, of course, ignorant of the students' scores determined by the paper-and-pencil inventory. They may use rating scales and check lists to record each student's behavior at such events as a playground game, a class party, or a basketball game. If the scores correlate well with the ratings, then the paper-and-pencil inventory has acceptable construct validity.

Serious questions can be raised about the use of ratings of individuals as criteria against which to validate test scores. For ratings to be useful in a validity determination, it is necessary for the raters to know precisely what they are measuring. Unfortunately, ratings regularly reflect different traits from those intended.

Criterion-Referenced Tests. The counterpart of construct validity for norm-referenced tests is *domain-selection* validity for criterion-referenced tests. There are many similarities even though domain-selection validity typically does not involve demonstrating which constructs account for variations in student performance on a test. Instead, we are interested in the degree to which the domain selected will reflect learner status with respect to other related domains (Popham, 1978, pp. 161–164). In other words, can mastery of a specified domain be generalized? Does the fact that students master the domain on which the test was developed mean that they can master other domains as well, perhaps even a more general goal?

Answers to this type of question are badly needed. To obtain them we must have, at a minimum, a careful defense of the procedures followed in the original domain selection. A much more elaborate way of demonstrating the degree of domain-selection validity of a test would be to first prepare test specifications, and subsequently test items, for several domains related to a dimension of general interest. Then it should be empirically determined, through controlled experimentation, whether learner mastery in terms of our test very likely means mastery in terms of the others and, hence, the general goal. The ability to generalize is of great practical importance if we are to measure student performance efficiently.

PROBLEM

6. When two testing instruments are compared to estimate the construct validity of one of them, and the second is considered a standard, is the investigator engaging in a "circular" argument?

General Considerations

Determining the relative strength of any one of the many types of validity in a measuring instrument is sometimes frustrating. If the instrument is commercially distributed, the teacher may faithfully scan the test manual and doggedly sift the references to articles in professional journals in which the instrument is mentioned. Yet it often happens that even this effort leaves the investigator unsatisfied. The information gleaned from the process is often too vague and too limited.

Vague Terms. The complaint of vagueness is traceable in part to the widespread use of a handful of terms that are not as meaningful as often supposed. Expressions such as "face validity," "statistical validity," and "curricular validity" fall into this category. Even the expression "validity coefficient" is applied too generally to contribute much to a discussion of validity.

A paper-and-pencil test has "face validity" when it seems to be valid to someone reading it. In other words, if a person unsophisticated in achievement measurement is handed an English vocabulary test for high school seniors and, after reading it, agrees that it appears to be a "valid" vocabulary test for that group, "face validity" is claimed. Admittedly, this is important to the students writing a test. Certainly they will tend to cooperate more readily if they sense that the nature of the items logically corresponds to the overall purpose of the test. Nevertheless, a flat claim for "face validity" of an instrument does not release its author from the responsibility of establishing the relative strength of one or more of the various types of validity.

"Statistical validity" is not a meaningful expression. As the title suggests, validity determinations in which correlation coefficients of some kind are computed are labeled determinations of "statistical validity." Within this loose framework are many determinations of validity, particularly criterion-related and construct validity. The expression is, therefore, unnecessary.

The expression "curricular validity" suggests the same type of validity as content or descriptive validity. In achievement measurement both are acceptable. In aptitude and personal-social adjustment measurement, however, "curricular validity" becomes an awkward identification because the term "curricular" suggests only that an academic curriculum is implicated in some fashion. To speak of content or descriptive validity does not inject any such restrictions. Therefore, the expression "curricular validity" is not so flexible and thus less useful.

The Mental Measurements Yearbooks.   Fortunately, there is a yet unmentioned source of information about standardized instruments of all kinds. This helps fill the voids one typically finds when searching for definitive evidence about the degrees of validity and reliability present. This source is known as *The Mental Measurements Yearbook,* the first volume of which was published in 1938. Additional volumes are published at fairly regular intervals.

The largest section of each *Yearbook* is entitled *Tests and Reviews* and contains, among other items, materials related to validity and reliability. This section assists in the appraisal of measuring instruments by providing frank, critical reviews of them and comprehensive bibliographies of references concerning each. For a given instrument, it is common to find such information as its complete title, age or grade levels of the individuals for whom it is designed, date of publication, cost, time limits, and the names of the author and the publishing company. In addition, one or more reviews is usually included, and the author identified. Pertinent references are listed without comment and may be numerous, in a few instances as many as one hundred. These contain information on the construction, validity, reliability, use, and limitations of the instrument.

The magnitude of the *Yearbooks* is somewhat startling. For instance, *The Eighth Mental Measurements Yearbook* (Buros, 1978) contains information on well over a thousand tests, along with countless references on the construction, use, and validity of specific tests. When it is remembered that this yearbook supplements rather than supplants the preceding seven volumes, it is eminently clear that these volumes form a colossal body of material.

Several significant companion volumes to the *Yearbooks* have been published. One is *Tests in Print II* (Buros, 1974) which contains information about currently available tests and is cross-referred with the *Yearbooks.* For those test users who are interested in obtaining information about tests in only one or two areas, nine monographs are available. Each contains all of the material relevant to tests in a designated area that is available in previous *Yearbooks*. The monographs are

Personality Tests and Reviews II
Reading Tests and Reviews II
Intelligence Tests and Reviews
Vocational Tests and Reviews
English Tests and Reviews
Foreign Language Tests and Reviews
Mathematics Tests and Reviews
Science Tests and Reviews
Social Studies Tests and Reviews

Counselors, supervisors, and research workers, as well as classroom teachers, find the *Yearbooks* and their companion volumes of inestimable value in their instrument appraisals. As a readily accessible compilation of facts about, and considered criticisms of, measuring instruments, they are unmatched. Certainly no validity or reliability appraisal other than that of a teacher-constructed instrument is complete without including whatever information the *Yearbooks* and test reviews in various measurement journals can provide. (For additional information about noncommercial or unpublished tests, see Johnson and Bommarito, 1971, and Johnson, 1976.)

PROBLEMS

7. Study the reviews in *The Mental Measurements Yearbooks* of two tests or test batteries of interest to you in the area of (a) academic achievement, (b) scholastic aptitude, or (c) interest patterns. On the basis of the evidence presented, compare each pair of tests or test batteries in terms of their various kinds of validity and reliability.

8. Cronbach (1970b) asserts that, in the last analysis, the responsibility for valid use of a test rests on the individual who interprets it. Do you agree? If so, what are the responsibilities for authors of standardized tests?

SUMMARY

Seven basic ideas have been presented in this chapter:

1. Validity, the most vital attribute of any measuring instrument, is commonly defined as the degree to which that instrument actually serves the purposes for which it is intended. Since the purposes of measurement are divided into three categories, validity is classified into three types: (1) content validity, (2) criterion-related validity, and (3) construct validity. In criterion-

referenced measurement, the counterparts to these are descriptive, functional, and domain-selection validity, respectively.

2. Content validity is defined as the degree to which an instrument can be used to measure the present performance of a student in a certain type of situation or in a cross-sectional test sample in a subject matter area.

3. Criterion-related validity exists (1) to the extent that a test can be used to predict a student's future performance (predictive validity) and (2) to the degree that the behavior elicited by a measuring instrument corresponds to external but concurrent student behavior (concurrent validity).

4. An instrument has construct validity if a specified construct accounts for the variations in the student performance it elicits.

5. The demonstration of a measuring instrument's degree of validity is almost invariably a lengthy and laborious task. It may be necessary, for example, to ascertain whether a given instrument is characterized by more than one of the types of validity, perhaps as many as three. Furthermore, suitable criteria and student samples must be found before the validity determination can be completed. This is particularly true of criterion-related validity investigations.

6. The end product of a validity determination may or may not be quantitative in nature. Studies of content validity typically do not yield quantitative evidence, whereas studies of criterion-related and sometimes construct validity do yield quantitative evidence, such as a coefficient of correlation.

7. Before teachers use any measuring instrument, they are obliged to conduct a thorough investigation of its validity. This appraisal commonly is based on the material presented in the instrument's manual, the information provided by *The Mental Measurement Yearbooks* and their companion volumes, and the considered judgment of the teacher.

SUGGESTED READINGS

AMERICAN PSYCHOLOGICAL ASSOCIATION. *Standards for educational and psychological tests.* Washington, D.C.: Author, 1974.
   This bulletin is the result of the third important attempt by the American Psychological Association and other organizations to develop an authoritative statement concerning test standards. Content, criterion-related, and construct validity are defined carefully and illustrations are provided.

ANASTASI, A. *Psychological testing* (4th ed.). New York: Macmillan, 1976.
   Chapter 6 includes descriptions of various types of validity and is nonquantitative in nature. In contrast, Chapter 7 emphasizes quantitative representations of validity and their interpretation. One section deals with expectancy tables, another with test bias.

BACKER, T. E. *A directory of information on tests.* Princeton, N.J.: ERIC Clearinghouse on Tests, Measurement, and Evaluation, Educational Testing Service, 1977.
   This booklet is a directory of books, other printed materials, and information systems useful in the search for test-related information. Also included are strategies for initiating an information search. Annotations are provided for all references.

GAGNÉ, R. M. Observing the effects of learning. *American Psychologist*, 1975, *11*, 144–157.
The proposition that both content and construct validity are important in achievement measurement is explored. A rationale for determining the content validity of criterion-referenced tests is presented.

HOEPFNER, R., et al. *CSE test evaluation series: Preschool/kindergarten*, 1971; *Tests of higher-order cognitive, affective, and interpersonal skills*, 1972; *Secondary school*, 1974; *Elementary school*, 1976. Los Angeles: UCLA Center for the Study of Evaluation.
Commercial tests have been evaluated on the basis of a wide variety of criteria and concise summary ratings are given for each major evaluation factor, one of which is validity. The evaluations systems used are described.

POPHAM, W. J. *Criterion-referenced measurement*. Englewood Cliffs, N.J.: Prentice-Hall, 1978. See pages 155–164.
Descriptive, functional, and domain-selection validity of criterion-referenced tests are explained and methods of determining the degree to which they are present are provided.

WESMAN, A. G. *Selected writings of Alexander G. Wesman*. New York: The Psychological Corporation, 1975.
In pages 28–35, expectancy tables are described as a way of interpreting the relative validity of a norm-referenced test. Examples from several aptitude tests are shown.

REFERENCES CITED

AMERICAN PSYCHOLOGICAL ASSOCIATION. *Standards for educational and psychological tests*. Washington, D.C.: Author, 1974.

ANASTASI, A. *Psychological testing* (4th ed.). New York: Macmillan, 1976.

BUROS, O. K. (Ed.). *The eighth mental measurements yearbook*. Lincoln, Nebr. University of Nebraska Press, 1978.

BUROS, O. K. (Ed.). *Tests in print II*. Lincoln, Nebr.: University of Nebraska Press, 1974.

CRONBACH, L. J. *Essentials of psychological testing* (3rd ed). New York: Harper & Row, 1970a.

CRONBACH, L. J. Validation of educational measures. *Proceedings of the 1969 Invitational Conference on Testing Problems*. Princeton, N.J.: Educational Testing Service, 1970b.

EBEL, R. L. *Essentials of educational measurement* (3rd ed). Englewood Cliffs, N.J.: Prentice-Hall, 1979.

JOHNSON, O. G. *Tests and measurements in child development: Handbook II* (Vols. 1 and 2). San Francisco: Jossey-Bass, 1976.

JOHNSON, O. G., & BOMMARITO, J. W. *Tests and measurements in child development: Handbook I*. San Francisco: Jossey-Bass, 1971.

KAUFMAN, A. S. *Restriction of range: Questions and answers*. Test Service Bulletin, No. 59. New York: Psychological Corporation, 1972.

POPHAM, W. J. *Criterion-referenced measurement*. Englewood Cliffs, N.J.: Prentice-Hall, 1978.

WESMAN, A. G. *Selected writings of Alexander G. Wesman*. New York: The Psychological Corporation, 1975.

PART FOUR

Standardized Tests, Scales, and Inventories

The purpose of Part Four is to acquaint the reader with the nature and availability of various instruments designed to measure achievement, aptitude, and aspects of personal-social adjustment. Considerable attention is given to standardized measuring instruments. Chapter 11, "Standardized Achievement Tests," discusses the construction of such tests in order to give the reader an understanding of their general nature. Selected achievement tests and batteries are used to illustrate their contribution to the evaluation program.

Chapter 12, "Measuring Student Aptitudes," is devoted to an explanation of the various kinds of aptitude instruments. It discusses selected tests to clarify the different purposes for which each should be used, and outlines procedures for their effective use in the classroom and with individual students. A large part of the chapter is concerned with a discussion of scholastic aptitude and its testing both by individual and group instruments. The concepts of mental age and intelligence quotient are developed, and precautionary measures for their use discussed. Differential testing is also explored and its advantages are delineated.

Chapter 13, "Evaluating Affective Behavior," is devoted to the third general area of evaluation. Emphasis is placed upon the strengths and weaknesses of the personal-social adjustment inventories and tests, and suggestions are given for their use in conjunction with less formal methods of evaluation, including observation with use of anecdotal records, rating scales, check lists, and interviews. Measurement of attitudes and interests is also treated as an important aspect of understanding student growth.

11

Standardized Achievement Tests

The purpose of this chapter is to prepare you to

1. Differentiate between achievement and scholastic aptitude tests
2. Explain important differences between standardized and teacher-made achievement tests and discuss the implications of these differences
3. List the various uses of both norm- and criterion-referenced standardized achievement tests and apply each use to an individual, class, or school problem
4. Delineate the concerns in constructing norm-referenced and criterion-referenced achievement tests and indicate how these concerns relate to the use of each
5. Depict the differences between survey and diagnostic achievement tests, and indicate the implications for their use
6. Explain how achievement test batteries are useful for instruction

A golfer "breaking seventy-five" for eighteen holes is considered an outstanding performer. The athlete who runs a mile in four minutes has finished a superlative race. The major league baseball player with a batting average of over .300 will be surpassed by relatively few. On the other hand, the golfer who requires more than 100 strokes to complete eighteen holes is considered a duffer, and the miler who is clocked over 4' 30" would not be likely to make a good college track team. Certainly a baseball player whose batting average is below .225 isn't considered a good hitter.

These performances are evaluated in terms of norms generally accepted as representing various degrees of competence. It makes no difference whether the game is played or the mile run in Kansas City or Seattle. The performances are regulated by specific rules so that the degree of excellence is affected by the ability of the performer. Even though athletes may be considered outstanding when compared with limited competition, their performances may be mediocre on a national scale.

A similar situation exists when norm-referenced standardized tests are administered. There are prescribed conditions for testing. Norms are established. It follows, then, that the performances of students can be evaluated by comparing them with those of a large number of others from many schools.

No such comparisons are made in the case of criterion-referenced tests because they are used for other purposes. Rather than showing how students' performances compare with others, the good criterion-referenced test indicates what they can and cannot do.

If you have studied the foregoing chapters carefully, you already know a great deal about standardized achievement tests. To understand the concepts of validity, reliability, item analysis, test scores and norms, the place of educational objectives in testing, descriptive schemes, and the building and appraisal of classroom tests, means that you already know about the framework on which standardized achievement tests are constructed.

Achievement vs. Aptitude Tests

Both achievement and aptitude tests measure the effects of learning. Therefore, one finds considerable similarities between them. One difference lies in the degree to which the relevant experiences prior to taking the tests are uniform. Aptitude tests measure the effects of learning under relatively uncontrolled and unknown conditions, whereas achievement tests measure the effects of learning under partially known and controlled conditions (Anastasi, 1976, p. 398). Achievement tests are designed to inform the teacher about what a student knows and can do now, whereas aptitude tests are designed to predict future performance. But one must exercise care in making absolute classifications. For example, achievement tests are very useful in predicting subsequent performance. If a student does well on an arithmetic achievement test, the score is a good predictor of performance in algebra or geometry.

There are four important differences between scholastic aptitude and achievement tests:

1. Scholastic aptitude tests sample more broadly.
2. Scholastic aptitude tests sample outside learning as well as school subjects. Achievement tests focus on a particular academic curriculum.
3. Achievement tests sample more recent learning.
4. Scholastic aptitude tests predict future performance, while the achievement tests seek to measure academic progress (Cleary et al., 1975, p. 21).

Actually, achievement tests and scholastic aptitude tests form a kind of continuum in terms of the degree of specificity of experiential background that they presuppose, as shown in Table 11.1. Course-oriented achievement tests, including teacher-made tests, are very specific; in contrast, nonlanguage aptitude tests emphasize the general aspects of learning.

Other continua have been developed, such as a spectrum for comparing tests of scholastic aptitude (Cronbach, 1970, p. 282). Here again, aptitude tests at one end of the continuum are very similar to achievement tests because they measure knowledge and skills that require direct training. As you can see, there is no simple way of differentiating between the many types of achievement tests on the one hand and all of the various kinds of aptitude tests on the other. It is well to remember that aptitude and achievement tests tend to be very highly related whether we compare items or total test scores.

Standardized vs. Teacher-Constructed Tests

The term *standardized* actually refers to specific instructions for administration and scoring, and both criterion- and norm-referenced tests fulfill this requirement. In the case of norm-referenced tests, norms are prepared that represent performance for similar groups. These give teachers an independent yardstick for checking student achievement. While their own tests can measure only the relative performance of the students in their classes, norms provide the opportunity to compare achievement with that of students in other schools. College-bound youth particularly need

TABLE 11.1.   A Continuum of Tests of Developed Abilities

Specificity . . . . *Generality*				
Course-oriented achievement tests	Broadly oriented achievement tests	Verbal-type intelligence and aptitude tests	Non-language tests	Culture-fair tests

Adapted from Anastasi, *Psychology Testing*, 4th ed. New York: Macmillan Publishing Co., Inc., 1976. Used by permission of the publishers.

to know how well they are doing in comparison with future competitors. Teachers, too, can use norms to help judge the effectiveness of their teaching.

Some wonder why we suggest that criterion-referenced tests can be standardized, since there are no norms. Payne (1974, p. 296) gives three reasons why they should be included within this category:

1. The care given the development of objectives
2. The uniformity of administration with regard to directions and scoring
3. The care given to refining the instrument through item and reliability analysis

In constructing criterion-referenced tests we are not concerned with how a student performs in relation to other students. We want the test scores to inform us about students' performance relative to a preestablished standard. Can they perform the tasks? Are they able to add 2 plus 2 correctly? Can they determine the main idea of a paragraph at a given level of reading difficulty?

Some of the factors that distinguish standardized tests from classroom achievement tests relate to their preparation. Planning and construction are probably more careful and thorough for standardized achievement tests, which are handled by specialists, than for teacher-constructed tests. There is also a much more critical analysis of the objectives on which the measurement is based. Exacting procedures are followed in the construction and appraisal of individual test items for standardized tests; in norm-referenced tests, extensive statistical analyses are applied to determine the test items' levels of difficulty and discriminating power. Often there are comparable forms of the instrument so the test can be administered periodically within the school program to measure growth.

In building a classroom test, teachers can take advantage of the individuality of the students and the local community; students can be encouraged to study that which best relates to their experiences. Appreciation of literature can be taught with different literary selections, and the scientific method can be taught through different subjects. Obviously, individual variations in study materials cannot be considered on a test designed for wide use in many schools. It often becomes necessary to include the material on which questions are based. This results in many short selections with a definite limitation on achievement measurement; it is impossible to ask examinees to criticize complete literary works or determine their recall on wide reading. At the classroom level, however, teachers must be better trained in test construction so that they will avoid using assigned materials to measure memorization of content for its own sake. They should instead use these materials as a vehicle for evaluating the lasting results of instruction.

PROBLEMS

1. What arguments might you, as a teacher, offer your school principal to justify using a standardized achievement test as a final examination in your course?

2. Standardized tests are generally recognized as superior in planning and construction to tests prepared by classroom teachers. What techniques used by standardized-test builders could be easily and profitably used by the classroom teacher?

Uses of Standardized Achievement Tests

Although norm-referenced and criterion-referenced achievement tests are designed for largely different purposes, some are the same for all practical purposes. This becomes clear as one compares the uses of standardized norm-referenced tests with those for criterion-referenced tests.

Norm-Referenced Tests

Five uses of norm-referenced tests are of interest to teachers. First they provide teachers with a reference point for checking their own emphasis in teaching. Of course, the use of norms implies that comparisons made between and among students or classes are restricted by the content of the test. If a class has a high mean score on an American history test, it has not necessarily achieved more in this subject matter area than another class with a lower score. Emphasis in one class may have been on facts and details, while the other stressed critical thinking and broad relationships. Test content must be analyzed before final judgment is made. However, when a test proves to include important and generally accepted areas of knowledge and skills, teachers ought to make a critical evaluation of their own educational objectives and instruction if a class does poorly in relation to individual student ability.

A second use of norm-referenced tests is to determine student progress. Generally there are comparable forms of the test available; this allows the teacher to administer one test at the beginning of the year and another at the end. Although cautious interpretation should be made on the basis of individual test scores, group scores representing progress or the lack of it may reliably emphasize particular strengths or weaknesses.

It must also be remembered that a student's mental ability is positively correlated with achievement. Effective teaching cannot always be inferred just because the class average is at the median. A class average below the median may actually represent excellent progress in one case; in another, achievement above the median may still be far below the potential of the group.

A third function of these tests is to provide a comparison of achievement between various subject matter areas and specific phases of a particular area. It is often desirable to determine how student's arithmetic skill compares with their reading ability or to compare achievement in vocabulary, comprehension, and rate of reading. Obviously these comparisons can be made on an individual or group basis. If the group has a particular weakness, then an evaluation of class learning experiences is in order. When problems seem to relate to individual students, the teacher must provide individual attention.

A fourth use of norm-referenced tests is for diagnosis of difficulties in achievement. Often the source of student difficulty may be determined through one or a number of very effective standardized instruments. Because test items have been constructed on the basis of studies that have determined frequent sources of difficulty, it is possible to analyze the adequacy of performance in crucial areas. In diagnosing reading disabilities, for example, one can discover whether the students know the initial consonant sounds, whether they can break words into syllables, and whether they make use of punctuation for improved comprehension. Naturally, teachers will also use their own tests in diagnosis, but norm-referenced tests are helpful in providing a systematic approach. Criterion-referenced tests are also particularly helpful in this regard.

Finally, a fifth use is for purposes of selection and classification. Achievement tests can serve as aptitude tests predicting performance in a given subject area. Not only are achievement-test results helpful in grouping for instruction, but scores are useful in determining whether students can be expected to do well or poorly in given courses.

Criterion-Referenced Tests

Criterion-referenced tests also have a wide variety of uses. They are particularly well suited for the following (Popham, 1978, pp. 218–235):

1. They can contribute to curriculum development. Because criterion-referenced tests describe competencies that are to be attained, they alert educators to the appropriateness of stated objectives. Furthermore, they provide a focus for assessing goals to determine their validity and possibility of attainment.

2. They can contribute to the improvement of instruction, especially that emphasizing mastery learning and individualized instruction. When teachers study carefully the specifications of a test, they should have an understanding of the performance goals and a clear perception of how to help students reach them. If desired competencies are complex, the test provides for task analysis, enabling teachers to identify the necessary subskills. Obviously, the learner must specifically practice this hierarchy of subskills to attain competency. Since these skills are identified, students, as well as teachers, know what must be practiced. Therefore, learning difficulties can be diagnosed, students can be assigned to specific levels of instruction, and the instruction can be evaluated.

3. They reflect effective instruction and provide considerable feedback to both teachers and students. Such positive reinforcement contributes to effective teaching and learning.

4. They are well adapted to the evaluation of educational programs. Well-defined programs based on the competencies measured by good achievement tests are very likely reproducible. They are not pseudoprograms consisting of poorly integrated experiences. The quality of their evaluation can be appreciably improved if criterion-referenced tests tailored to pertinent competencies are used.

PROBLEM

3. One use of standardized tests is grouping students for instruction. Do you consider norm-referenced or criterion-referenced achievement results more appropriate for this purpose? Explain your choice.

Standardized Achievement Test Construction

Norm-Referenced Tests

The expense and effort of building a norm-referenced standardized achievement test demand a very careful appraisal of the need for this particular kind of instrument. First, it should be determined whether there is a group of individuals who will provide a potential test market. Ideally, there should be a substantial need for an instrument and no satisfactory test available. Unfortunately, the motivation for the construction of a new test is sometimes financial gain more than need; often several good instruments that can serve the same purpose are already available.

Nevertheless, once it has been decided that a new instrument will be constructed, representatives from the population of test consumers are consulted to formulate specifications for the instrument. The purpose of the test must be spelled out clearly. Is it to be a survey or a diagnostic test? Is it to be primarily for individual or group guidance? Will there be subscores or just a total score? For what population of students is the test to be designed? Is it for a group of homogeneous ages or for many grade levels? Does it require a high level of reading ability? What will be its general contents? All of these questions and more must be answered before actual test construction begins.

Pretest Construction and Administration. In the discussion of paper-and-pencil achievement tests in chapter 2, three steps were outlined for construction: (1) identifying educational objectives with verbal and mathematical aspects; (2) developing tables of specifications reflecting the relative importance of the objectives; and (3) building the test items on the basis of the tables of specifications. A similar approach is used in developing standardized achievement tests, though test items are generally constructed by several subject matter specialists and examined by test specialists for technical considerations. Practical considerations, such as the typical length of school class periods, help determine test length. Although at times improving the reliability and validity of a test by increasing its length would be desirable, it is not always possible because test administration must be fitted into existing school schedules.

In the development of the better tests, more items are initially constructed than will be used in the final form of the test. These items are assembled into a form called a *pretest.* Before the pretest is administered, the individual items are carefully scrutinized by other subject matter specialists and test experts for inaccuracies and technical flaws.

Directions and accessory materials must be prepared and provision made for recording answers on either separate sheets or the test booklet itself. When the test has been cast into its final form, these accessory materials, including scoring stencils, must be revised to fit it.

Analysis of Pretest Data.   When the pretest form is ready, it is administered to a group of students comparable to those for whom the test is being designed. The results of the pretest administration are studied to determine which items should be kept. If the test is to discriminate among students, the items should be neither so difficult that some will answer them all incorrectly, nor so easy that some can make a perfect score. In either case it is impossible to obtain a true measure of individual achievement. It is absurd to conclude that some students achieved nothing; it is equally erroneous to assume that others achieved the ultimate. Therefore, the difficulty levels of the test items retained should be such that both zero and perfect scores will rarely, if ever, occur.

Items should also be chosen on the basis of their power to discriminate between good and poor students. Therefore, those items are retained that are answered correctly by more good students than poor. By the same token, the distracters or foils should be chosen more often by the poor students.

The total number of items selected for the final form of the test depends on how many can be answered by the students in a given amount of time. One rule of thumb is that about ninety percent of an average class should have an opportunity to attempt all the items in the time allowed. If careful attention has been given to the level of difficulty of these items, an average student should answer somewhat more than fifty percent of them correctly.

Development of Norms.   On the basis of the criteria discussed above and the tables of specifications, items are selected for the final form of the test. It is then given to groups of students typical of those for whom the test is designed but who have not taken the pretest. Their scores provide the basis for setting up the norms of the test by which a teacher or school administrator can compare students' performances. These norms usually are standard scores, percentile ranks, or grade equivalents. Often several different kinds of norms are reported.

Equivalent, Parallel, and Comparable Test Forms.   It is often helpful to have two or more forms of a test so that a student may be tested more than once—perhaps at the beginning and end of a term of instruction. A second test may be helpful at times when there is reason to doubt the validity of a student's first test score—because of illness, for example.

Parallel forms of a test may be developed simultaneously. This is sometimes done by constructing pairs of items that measure the outcome of specific objectives and are of approximately the same level of difficulty. Obviously, the administration procedures and format of both tests should be alike. Parallel forms administered to a large population of students and yielding scores with identical distributions are *equivalent* forms.

When raw scores of two tests can be converted to the same derived-score scale, the tests are said to be *comparable*. Some achievement tests are constructed so that there is a series of difficulty levels. Students' progress can be compared from year to year by means of a scale. The *Differential Aptitude Tests* represent a different kind of comparability. Various subtest scores can be compared because they are based on the same norm group (see p. 331).

Accessory Materials.   In addition to the test booklet, there may be special scoring stencils and, with all of the better tests, a manual. A set of test standards (American Psychological Association, 1974) recommends that certain kinds of information be placed in the manual. Procedures in administration and scoring should be stated so that it is possible to duplicate the conditions under which the test was standardized. The directions should be clearly phrased so the examinees will understand how the author intended them to perform. Although most standardized tests can be scored objectively, whenever there is an element of subjectivity, scoring variations leading to error should be discussed.

Because the name of a test does not always clarify its purpose and sometimes may even misrepresent what the test actually measures, the manual should state the objectives to be measured and assist in the correct interpretation of test results. Competencies required in administration, scoring, or interpretations beyond the typical classroom teacher should be indicated.

Detailed information on reliability and validity should include evidence that can be used in judging whether it is pertinent to the teacher's and the examinee's problems. The method of determining the reliability coefficient should also be reported. Discussion of validity should be specific in terms of whether it is content, criterion-related, or construct validity (see Chapter 10). The nature of any validating criteria and their desirability for a specific test purpose should be reported fully. Statistical data for determining any validity coefficients should be so adequate that the test user may judge their worth.

The manual should contain a discussion of the development of the test norms. Norm groups must be defined, the method of population sampling reported, and the time and conditions under which norm data were secured should be included. It is imperative that measures of central tendency and variability be reported.

Criterion-Referenced Tests

In the construction of criterion-referenced tests we aren't trying to obtain a large spread of scores. In fact, it would be desirable if all students made low scores before instruction and high scores after they had been taught. Unlike norm-referenced tests, criterion-referenced tests are expected to elicit a high degree of uniformity in performance.

Although one would be hard pressed to differentiate between many criterion-referenced and norm-referenced tests by inspection, there are differences that can be traced to the manner in which they are constructed. For instance, some test items in a norm-referenced achievement test may require the more sophisticated kind of knowledge that high achievers have, though many lower achievers do not. These are generally not included in criterion-referenced tests since this depth of knowledge may not be necessary to meet the acceptable standards for mastery of a specific objective.

Another feature to be noted when constructing criterion-referenced tests is the type of item commonly used. Many norm-referenced test items are of the multiple-choice type. In mastery learning, however, objectives are generally not stated in terms of students being able to select correct choices. Intsead they are expected to perform an act such as "balance an equation" or "trace the route of the west-bound caravans." The most straightforward way of measuring the criterion behavior for such objectives may not be with one of the standard objective test items of the selection type, but rather with an open-ended, essay-type item (Hills, 1976, pp. 78–86).

Obviously, improvement of criterion-referenced items cannot be based on statistical procedures used with norm-referenced tests. Item analysis and reliability estimates depend on score variability. On a well-constructed, criterion-referenced test administered after effective learning, the standard deviation of the scores should be zero or nearly so. Teachers would like all students to make a perfect score.

Construction of Criterion-Referenced Tests.   Anastasi (1976, p. 422) lists the problems encountered in the construction of criterion-referenced instruments:

1. Assessing a long list of narrowly defined objectives with enough test items to measure each objective reliably, yet keeping the whole process within manageable length
2. Setting an acceptable performance level as a standard of mastery of each objective
3. Estimating the degree of reliability and validity of such instruments

A description of the procedures used in the construction of the 1976 *Prescriptive Reading Inventory (PRI)* will help you better understand the principles involved in criterion-referenced test construction. The following nine steps were followed:

1. Reading materials used most widely in grades 1–6 were selected.
2. Instructional objectives of these materials were determined.
3. These objectives were consolidated into categories: recognition of sounds and symbols, visual discrimination, phonic analysis, structural analysis, translation, literal comprehension, interpretive comprehension, and study skills.
4. Objectives to be included in the test were specified. Objectives that were not related to the reading process, that required an oral response, that were not appropriate to a group testing situation, or that were implicit in other objectives, were eliminated.
5. Vocabulary and reading difficulty levels for items and passages in the various test levels were determined.

6. Test items were written according to the above specifications.

7. Items for each test level were organized into several tryout booklets to lessen the testing time for each student.

8. A double-testing item tryout, with tests spaced eight to ten weeks apart, was used. There was a pretest and a posttest with normal classroom instruction between administrations. The goal was to determine the sensitivity of each item to instruction. Highly sensitive test items are those that reflect improved performance because of the instruction given between pretesting and posttesting. In selecting test items the first consideration was the sensitivity of the item to instruction.

9. The number of test items needed to measure each objective was determined. Generally this was three or four items per objective. Also, a cutting score was chosen to indicate mastery for a given number of items. To determine cutting scores for nonmastery, review, and mastery of objectives, a generally subjective approach was used after studying the distributions of performance with pools of items. Usually for a three-item test, mastery was equivalent to two correct answers, while one correct answer signified a need for review.

In developing a criterion-referenced test, compromises must be made. In the case of the *PRI* the decision was made to utilize a large number of specific objectives using few items, rather than a lesser number of general objectives measured by numerous items. Statistical reliability was therefore sacrificed to some degree. On the other hand, the position was taken that the more specific the objective, the fewer the test items needed to measure it reliably. Furthermore, the more specific the objective, the greater the potential for uncovering specific deficiencies in achievement. In short, the authors concluded that when teachers study the overall response patterns of students administered the *PRI,* the information about their achievement will be basically correct.

PROBLEM

4. You have an appointment with your principal to present a request to purchase and use a certain standardized achievement test. What specific information about this test should you have prior to the conference? What will be your chief selling point? Present your argument using both a norm-referenced and a criterion-referenced test.

Illustrative Standardized Tests

There are many standardized achievement tests available to the classroom teacher. They attempt to measure a wide variety of areas, including such skills as critical thinking, reading, and listening. There are also tests in subject areas such as arithmetic, physics, and history. A discussion of a few selected tests and batteries is included here. The survey test, test battery, and diagnostic test are highlighted.

Norm-Referenced Survey Tests

Whether a test can be called a survey test depends partly on the purposes for which it is used and also on the number of its subscores. Although a test yielding only one score is not generally thought of as being inherently diagnostic, it could well be used for diagnostic purposes if one were to analyze the performance of the examinee on individual questions. As the number of subtests is increased, the instrument begins to assume a diagnostic flavor.

Tests generally thought of as survey instruments are often used along with scholastic aptitude tests to determine whether students are underachieving. For example, underachieving readers are those who do not read as well as they should for their ability. They may be reading above their grade level; but if they are bright children, they still may be underachievers. On the other hand, children who read below their grade level are not necessarily underachieving; their performance may be adequate for their mental capacity. The reading survey test actually provides a measure of the level of difficulty at which students can read. In general it contains at least two measures, one of vocabulary and the other of comprehension. A measure of reading rate is often included. A useful illustration of a reading survey test is the *Gates-MacGinitie Reading Tests.*

Gates-MacGinitie Reading Tests.   The plan of the second edition of the *Gates-MacGinitie Reading Tests* (1978) is as follows:

Basic R—Grade 1—Adapted to the wide range of reading skills of first grade children, from prereading to beyond the level of first graders

Level A—Grade 1—Vocabulary and comprehension

Level B—Grade 2—Vocabulary and comprehension

Level C—Grade 3—Vocabulary and comprehension

Level D—Grades 4, 5, 6—Vocabulary and comprehension

Level E—Grades 7, 8, 9—Vocabulary and comprehension

Level F—Grades 10, 11, 12—Vocabulary and comprehension

The vocabulary test in *Level A* is primarily a measure of decoding skills. *Level B* also tests decoding ability. *Levels C, D, E,* and *F* are tests of word knowledge.

Comprehension tests in *Levels A* and *B* focus on understanding the relationships of words and ideas within a passage. At *Levels C, D, E,* and *F* students are required to read complete prose passages with understanding. The subtests for *Basic R* include letter recognition and letter sounds in addition to vocabulary and comprehension. All test items are of the multiple-choice, best-answer type.

Additional information about the tests is available in a technical manual provided with each level. They include discussions of test norms, validity, and reliability. Content validity was stressed in the selection of vocabulary words and reading passages. Words found in popular reading series have been used in the construction of vocabulary tests at all levels. Natural science, social science, and humanities materials were sampled for the comprehension tests. All passages are written in standard English, and both literal and inferential questions are included to test the understanding of these passages.

PROBLEM

5. What kinds of information should the subtests of a good reading survey test yield? Which of these do you consider most significant?

Norm-Referenced Test Batteries

In any survey of student strengths and weaknesses, information is needed concerning relative achievement in the basic skills and the various subject areas. Do students excel in reading but do poorly in arithmetic? Are they high achievers in the physical and biological sciences but lacking in information and skill for dealing with problems in social studies? Standardized tests can provide information for evaluating a student's relative status. However, scores from single tests standardized on different populations are not necessarily comparable. For example, the standardization group for one test may have higher achievement or aptitudes than for another, resulting in more exacting norms for the first test. The representativeness of the normative sample may vary in terms of school size, location (urban or rural), geographical area, and so forth. Norms may also vary according to the time of year when the test was administered. The recentness of norms can also affect a student's standing. Over time, there are discernible upward and downward national trends in achievement (Ahmann, 1979).

This limitation inherent in the use of separate tests is overcome through the use of test batteries standardized on the same population. By comparing subtest scores, it is possible to determine whether a student has any real differences in his or her achievement pattern.

Profiles. We have seen that the raw scores students earn on a test can be converted to test norms such as percentile ranks, standard scores, and grade equivalents. If a battery of tests is given, students' raw scores cannot be compared, but their norm scores can if all are based on the same standardization group. A student may, for example, have a percentile rank of 80 in vocabulary and a percentile rank of 90 in spelling. It appears that achievement in spelling is greater than that in vocabulary. But this is not necessarily so. Neither test has perfect reliability, and the reliability of the difference between two scores is less than the reliability of either test. In the better standardized tests, information is included in the manual that will help the test user determine when real differences exist.

After the students' raw scores are converted to standard scores, percentiles, and the like, there are various ways of reporting them. Computers can easily produce tabular reports of district, school, and class averages. Furthermore, teachers routinely receive class record sheets on which all students are listed by name and their scores for all subtests are printed. Such a report for a fifth-grade class is shown in Table 14.1 (see page 400).

In addition to class record sheets, a profile can be plotted in graphic form for each student. Figure 11.1 is an illustrative profile chart of Brian Allison. His percentile ranks for five achievement subtests are reported at the top of the figure. These tell only part of the story. They are more easily understood if a graph is

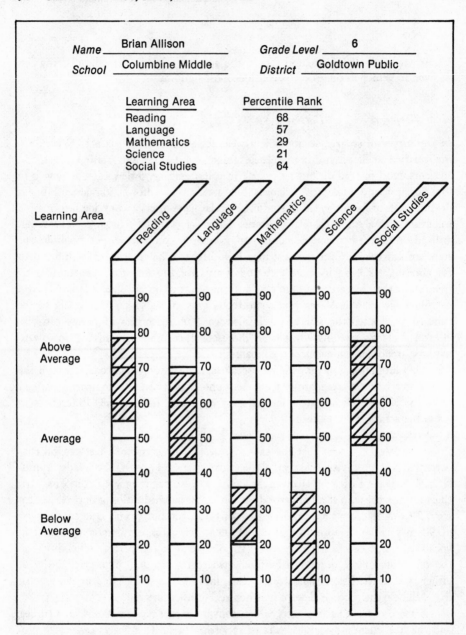

FIGURE 11.1.   Illustrative Student Profile Chart for an Achievement Test Battery

prepared showing Brian's relative position on each of the subtests as a region or band (rather than as a point). In this way each subtest's degree of unreliability, as represented by its standard error of measurement, would be reflected in the interpretation of his profile.

Brian's profile of percentile bands is shown in the lower half of Figure 11.1, and can be interpreted in terms of whether or not the various bands overlap. Can we say, for example, that Brian's score in reading (PR=68) is probably higher than his score in social studies (PR=64) and language (PR=57)? No, because the three bands overlap. On the other hand, it is reasonable to infer that his reading, social studies, and language scores are probably higher than his mathematics (PR=29) and science (PR=21) scores since the first three bands do not overlap the mathematics and science bands. As you can see, the profiles for each student vividly display the achievement pattern which exists, and the use of bands inserts caution in our interpretations.

Elementary School Test Batteries. There are a number of achievement test batteries available for elementary school use. Those batteries listed in Table 11.2 are widely used. The table presents a rough classification of the emphasis in the different areas of achievement for the intermediate grades. In some cases, this includes grades four, five, and six, and in others, only grades five and six. Time limits allotted to the various subtests are used in determining the percentage listed. Because the total time of test administration varies, caution should be exercised in comparing percentages between tests. They can best be used in noting the degree of emphasis.

Note that only two of the batteries listed, the *Metropolitan Achievement Tests (Survey)* and the *Stanford Achievement Test,* include subtests in social studies and science. The *Iowa Tests of Basic Skills* does not include these two areas as a standard part of the battery, but optional subtests are available. In contrast, the *California Achievement Tests* are confined to basic skills.

Note also that content of test batteries is based on what is considered important on a national scale. Certain local objectives may be deemphasized or even omitted. For example, some schools may teach a good deal about math sets, but this may not be adequately represented in the mathematics subtests of a given test

TABLE 11.2. Elementary School Test Batteries and Percentages of Total Testing Time Allotted to the Various Areas

Learning areas	California Achievement Test	Iowa Tests of Basic Skills	Metropolitan Achievement Tests (Survey)	Stanford Achievement Test
Reading comprehension	20.8%	17.2%	21.0%	10.9%
Vocabulary	6.0	6.1	0.0	7.8
Language	18.4	16.4	21.0	17.1
Spelling	4.2	4.9	0.0	6.2
Fundamentals of arithmetic	14.9	18.4	21.0	17.1
Arithmetic reasoning	20.8	10.2	0.0	10.9
Reference/study skills	14.9	26.6	0.0	0.0
Listening comprehension	0.0	0.0	0.0	10.9
Social studies	0.0	0.0*	18.4	9.3
Science	0.0	0.0*	18.4	9.3
Total Working Time (Minutes)	168	244	190	320

* Optional subtests are available.

TABLE 11.3.   Levels of the Iowa Tests of Basic Skills, 1978 Edition

Battery	Level number	Grade level
Primary	5	K.1–1.5
	6	K.8–1.9
	7	1.7–2.6
	8	2.7–3.5
Multilevel	9	3
	10	4
	11	5
	12	6
	13	7
	14	8–9

battery. In such instances, a careful item-by-item review of the mathematics sub-tests of various test batteries is needed in order to find the most appropriate one.

Iowa Tests of Basic Skills.   Representative of the many well-developed achievement test batteries for elementary school students are the *Iowa Tests of Basic Skills.* They have two major parts, the multilevel battery and the primary battery. The multilevel battery is designed for students in grades three through eight, and is composed of six levels as shown in Table 11.3. To it has been added the primary battery for students in kindergarten through the middle of the third grade. This battery has four levels. Each level in both batteries is numbered to correspond roughly to the chronological age of the students to whom it would most likely be administered. The levels overlap, thereby reflecting the continuous nature of the development of basic skills.

Eleven subtests are included in the multilevel battery. As shown in Table 11.4, these were developed in terms of 208 skills objectives grouped into 61 major categories. This classification varies in terms of degree of specificity. In reading comprehension, for example, sixteen skills objectives have been grouped in three categories: facts, inferences, and generalizations. On the other hand, in capitalization and punctuation, specific skills are relatively discrete and a more elaborate categorization is used. For instance, one of the five categories used in punctuation for its 34 skill objectives is the use of terminal punctuation, which in turn has three skills objectives: use of the period, use of the question mark, and use of the exclamation mark.

The foregoing shows the careful planning required to build an achievement test battery. It creates the base for a high level of content validity. To obtain such a goal, a distribution of the test items across the various categories and skills objectives is needed. This distribution should reflect the proper emphasis of each category and objective for every level of the battery.

The number of test items representing each skills objective varies considerably across all levels. In total there are 1,141 multiple-choice test items in the battery, an average of 18.7 items per skills category and 5.5 items per skills objective.

TABLE 11.4. Classification of Skills Objectives According to the Subtests of the Iowa Tests of Basic Skills

Subtest	Major Categories	Skills Objectives
Vocabulary	3	3
Reading comprehension	3	16
Language skills		
Spelling	10	10
Capitalization	7	27
Punctuation	5	34
Usage	5	17
Work-study skills		
Visual materials	8	25
Reference materials	8	21
Mathematics skills		
Concepts	6	34
Problem solving	3	9
Computation	3	12
Total	61	208

The meticulous steps taken to produce the *Iowa Tests of Basic Skills* permit a variety of uses to be made of the test results. As one would expect, grade equivalents and standard scores are available. These are converted to percentile ranks in grade and stanines. Furthermore, item analysis data are used for criterion-referenced or norm-referenced interpretations. The percent of the students who correctly answer each test item can be compared to a subjective standard (teacher's judgment) or to an objective standard (national item data). The differences between these percents offer starting points for identifying achievement deficiencies with regard to skills objectives and planning remediation. To assist in this process, narrative reports of student achievement can be obtained. The teacher's guides also contain specific classroom suggestions for teaching basic skills when weaknesses are found.

Secondary School Test Batteries. Although achievement test batteries have been constructed for secondary school students, meaningful norms for the content subjects are difficult to develop. This is so because the populations are different for each subject area and, often, students included in the norm group have not studied the subject in question. Students enrolled in physics have not necessarily completed a course in world history. When the same students constitute the norm group for all subject areas whether or not they have received instruction in them, the norms are meaningless; the test is invalid for those who have not received instruction.

One popular test battery is the *Sequential Tests of Educational Progress (STEP III)*. This series of achievement tests is designed to measure critical skills in learning application in the fields of reading, mathematics, writing skills, listening, science, and social studies. A serious attempt is made to measure the ability of students to use what they have learned in the classroom rather than merely to recall it.

All subtests of *STEP III* are included in each of the six levels covering grade levels 3.5 through 12.9. Furthermore, *STEP III* is integrated with *CIRCUS,* thereby providing continuous assessment measures from kindergarten through twelfth grade. *CIRCUS* also includes measures of problem solving, productive language, phonics, listening, and school interests and preferences (see page 335).

Various types of norms are provided, including percentile bands and standard scores for individual student interpretation as well as norms for school averages. Furthermore, there are special group norms for high and low socioeconomic groups and for large city schools. It should also be noted that grade equivalents are not provided. Instead, students take a short "locator test" to determine whether the achievement test should be taken at their grade level or one level above or below. These test results identify grade level for the purposes of selecting a test level. The students are then administered the proper test and appropriate norm tables are used.

STEP III is a high-quality achievement test battery. There is ample evidence that its reliability is adequate, and considerable attention has been given to the development of suitable content validity. For instance, each test item in each test level has been classified according to the knowledge and skill it is designed to measure. In summary, it is evident that careful attention has been given to the many steps that must be followed in norm-referenced achievement test construction.

PROBLEMS

6. What, in your opinion, are the outstanding advantages of using the *Sequential Test of Educational Progress* or the *Iowa Tests of Basic Skills* for the purpose of measuring student achievement in the elementary school?

7. Two persistent criticisms of norm-referenced standarized achievement tests are that they (1) determine the school curriculum and (2) force us to teach according to a national standard (Rudman, 1977). Do you agree? Why?

Criterion-Referenced Tests for Diagnosis

Norm-referenced survey tests, whether individual or battery, help the teacher screen out those students who have serious learning disabilities. They provide some diagnostic information. The teacher, however, needs many more data on the specific difficulties of a student to be able to provide adequate remediation. Diagnostic tests serve this purpose.

Such tests must, therefore, be considerably longer than the typical survey test to make the necessary subtests sufficiently reliable. Instead of the three scores typical of reading survey tests—vocabulary, comprehension, and rate—they may provide numerous scores. A reading diagnostic test may give scores in syllabication, knowledge of consonant sounds, blending, reversals, wrong beginnings, and endings. Whereas an arithmetic survey test may provide two scores, computational and reasoning, a diagnostic arithmetic test may provide information on the difficulties encountered by a student in each of the fundamental processes as well as in fractions and decimals. Some students, for example, may have difficulty in long division because they make mistakes in subtraction. Others make errors in multiplication that give them an incorrect answer. Some children have difficulty in their placement of zeros in the quotient. A good diagnostic test will reveal to the teacher the source of each student's difficulty.

The more detailed diagnostic tests are individually administered and require greater administrative skill than survey tests. Interpretation is also more complex. Furthermore, because diagnostic tests often tend to be subdivided into numerous subtests, sampling is frequently limited, and doubt is thereby cast on their reliability. Such scores should be supported by further data if the test's potential usefulness is to be realized.

Criterion-referenced tests are both diagnostic and prescriptive and the scores are keyed to instructional materials, generally on an individually placed basis. Although some diagnostic tests prescribe instructional procedures on the basis of test scores, one should not expect a complete package of tests and instructional materials to be available.

There are somewhat fewer criterion-referenced than norm-referenced standardized achievement tests commercially available. Most of these focus on the basic skills, such as the *Diagnostic Mathematics Inventory* and the *Prescriptive Reading Inventory,* and are aimed primarily at the elementary grade levels. Their worth must be evaluated differently since it is difficult to produce counterparts of such standard indicators as the reliability coefficients used with norm-referenced tests.

Furthermore, a test design issue must be squarely faced. Given that the total testing time is fixed and that one wishes to measure student competencies associated with a large number of specific objectives, we have the choice of measuring a small number of competencies well or a large number less precisely (Hambleton et al., 1978). Choosing the second alternative is somewhat common, resulting in the use of a very small sample of test items for a given objective. Attention to this point is crucial when examining and interpreting criterion-referenced tests.

Prescriptive Reading Inventory. Using criterion-referenced testing techniques, systems of diagnosis and prescriptions for individualizing instruction have been developed. One of these is the *Prescriptive Reading Inventory (PRI),* which provides for individual student diagnosis to be followed by a planned instructional program for remediation. There are six levels designed for students in kindergarten to sixth grade as shown in Table 11.5.

The *PRI* was developed on the basis of 102 objectives, some of which are tested at more than one level. The objectives are classified in seven process groups. In the case of *Levels I* and *II* they are

1. Auditory discrimination
2. Visual discrimination
3. Alphabet knowledge
4. Language experience

TABLE 11.5.   Levels of the Prescriptive Reading Inventory

Level	Grades	Number of objectives
I	K.0–1.0	10
II	K.5–2.0	10
A (Red)	1.5–2.5	34
B (Green)	2.0–3.5	41
C (Blue)	3.0–4.5	42
D (Orange)	4.0–6.5	38

5. Comprehension
6. Attention skills
7. Initial reading

For *Levels A* through *D* the seven groups are

1. Recognition of sound and symbol
2. Phonic analysis
3. Structural analysis
4. Translation
5. Literal comprehension
6. Interpretive comprehension
7. Critical comprehension

There is an average of six test items per objective in *Levels I* and *II* and three to four per objective for *Levels A* through *D*.

Test results for each student are reported in the form of a "diagnostic map," as shown in Figure 11.2. The sample map contains information about all of the reading objectives that appear in a student's particular test level. A plus sign (+) signifies mastery of an objective; a minus sign (−) is recorded for nonmastery. If review is needed (incomplete mastery), an *R* appears next to the specified objective. A blank by an objective indicates that the student made no attempt to respond to items related to that objective.

The diagnostic map provides a means to plan each student's reading growth. Learning activities are individually prescribed in terms of a student's areas of reading need by means of the *Individual Study Guide*. This is based on the existing pattern of objectives mastered and not mastered. In addition, *Program Reference Guides* are available for each reading instruction program keyed to the *PRI*. They list the pages in textbooks, teacher editions, and workbooks where each objective measured by the *PRI* is taught.

The *PRI* also provides a *Class Diagnostic Map* to aid in planning instruction for the class as a whole or for subgroups within the class. This map gives the

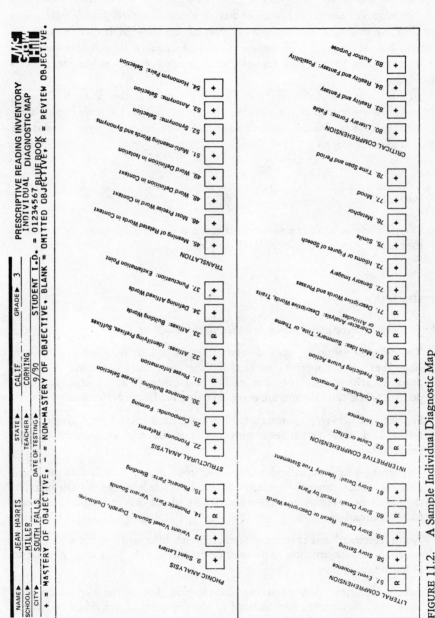

FIGURE 11.2. A Sample Individual Diagnostic Map
Reproduced by permission of the publisher, CTB/McGraw-Hill, Monterey, CA. 93940. Copyright © 1972 by McGraw-Hill, Inc. All Rights Reserved. Printed in the U.S.A.

303

teacher a picture of the total class pattern; it summarizes results for each objective for the class and records the percentage of students who demonstrate mastery of each objective. For *Levels A* through *D* there is also a *Class Grouping Report* which identifies any reading needs common to part of the class. When students fail to show mastery of 60 percent of the objectives in a category, their names are listed. Those listed can be grouped for special instruction aimed at the deficiencies identified.

In short, a great quantity of information is given the teacher about the reading proficiency of every student. In addition to offering a base for individualized instruction, these data also are highly useful for interviews with parents about the child's academic progress.

PROBLEM

8. Do you believe that criterion-referenced achievement tests are as useful at the secondary as at the primary level? Explain.

SUMMARY

The following are the major points included in this chapter:

1. The different names for aptitude and achievement tests have led to confusion, since they often appear to be similar. The most basic difference is one of purpose: achievement tests are meant to measure level of academic competence, while aptitude tests are designed to predict future performance.

2. Standardized achievement tests are, in general, more carefully constructed than teacher-built achievement tests, with greater attention given to technical considerations.

3. The strength of standardized achievement tests lies in their use as an added criterion of measurement against which teachers may judge the adequacy of their content selection and the effectiveness of the leading experiences they have organized.

4. Norm-referenced and criterion-referenced tests differ in their use and in construction. All construction steps must be followed with great care in order to produce quality tests.

5. Achievement test batteries at the secondary as well as the elementary level are used as survey tests, administered to identify areas of individual and group weakness.

6. A distinct advantage of the achievement battery is the availability of a profile providing a more adequate interpretation of a student's educational strengths and weaknesses.

7. Diagnostic tests can be administered to further analyze areas of weakness initially identified by the survey achievement test.

8. The frontier in standardized achievement testing lies in the development of instruments measuring cognitive and affective behaviors rather than specific information taught.

9. Criterion-referenced standardized tests are becoming increasingly available and are serving an important function in mastery learning and individualized instruction.

SUGGESTED READINGS

ANASTASI, A. *Psychological testing* (4th ed.). New York: Macmillan, 1976.
In chapter 14 the uses and limitations of achievement tests and batteries and problems in construction are emphasized. A number of achievement tests in special areas are described, and some of the items are illustrated. Criterion-referenced tests are discussed.

BERK, R. A. (Ed.) *Criterion-referenced measurement: The state of the art.* Baltimore, Md.: The Johns Hopkins University Press, 1980.
This is an excellent source for information on criterion-referenced measurements. Part One deals with content domain specification/item generation. Part Two discusses item and test validity. Part Three deals with the topic of reliability.

EBEL, R. L. The case for norm-referenced measurements. *Educational Researcher*, 1978, 7, 3–5.
Strong arguments are presented for the continued use of norm-referenced tests.

KATZ, M. *Selecting an achievement test: Principles and procedures* (3rd ed.). Princeton, N.J.: Educational Testing Service, 1973.
This monograph is designed to help laymen make a more intelligent choice among the many available tests. The basis for test selection consists of certain universal elements, namely, student population, school objectives, purposes in testing, and use of the test scores.

LEVINE, M. The academic achievement test: Its historical context and social functions. *American Psychologist*, 1976, 31, 228–238.
The author follows the development of achievement tests to give us a better understanding of their present status and use.

MEHRENS, W. A., & LEHMANN, I. J. Standardized test in education (3rd ed.). New York: Holt, Rinehart and Winston, 1980.
This volume contains information on how to select, administer, and use standardized tests correctly.

POPHAM, W. J. The case for criterion-referenced measurements. *Educational Researcher*, 1978, 7, 6–10.
The author maintains that norm-referenced tests are essentially worthless for instructional purposes.

SHOEMAKER, D. M. Toward a framework for achievement testing. *Review of Educational Research*, 1975, 45, 127–147.
The author tells us that the approach to achievement testing, with few exceptions, is identical to that used fifty or sixty years ago. He maintains that the approach is not adequate for today and that we need new ways and means for assessing student achievement in an instructional program.

TALMADGE, H. *Statistics as a tool for educational practitioners.* Berkeley, California: McCutchan, 1976.
Help in the use of statistics for the evaluation of standardized tests is provided in chapter 10. This volume presents case studies with responses for you to evaluate your answers.

REFERENCES CITED

AHMANN, J. S. Differential changes in levels of achievement for students in three age groups. *Educational Studies,* 1979, *10,* 35–51.

AMERICAN PSYCHOLOGICAL ASSOCIATION. *Standards for educational and psychological tests.* Washington, D.C.: Author, 1974.

ANASTASI, A. *Psychological testing* (4th ed.). New York: Macmillan, 1976.

CLEARY, T. A., HUMPHREYS, L. G., KENDRICK, S. A., & WESMAN, A. Educational uses of tests with disadvantaged students. *American Psychologist,* 1975, *30,* 15–41.

CRONBACH, L. J. *Essentials of psychological testing* (3rd ed.). New York: Harper & Row, 1970.

HAMBLETON, R. E., et al. Criterion-referenced testing and measurement: A review of technical issues and developments. *Review of Educational Research,* 1978, *48,* 1–47.

HILLS, J. R. *Measurement and evaluation in the classroom.* Columbia, Ohio: Charles E. Merrill, 1976.

PAYNE, D. A. *The assessment of learning: Cognitive and affective.* Lexington, Mass.: D. C. Heath, 1974.

POPHAM, W. J. *Criterion-referenced measurement.* Englewood Cliffs, N.J.: Prentice-Hall, Inc., 1978.

RUDMAN, H. C. The standardized test flap. *Phi Delta Kappan,* 1977, *59,* 179–185.

Technical report, Prescriptive Reading Inventory. Monterey, Calif.: CTB/McGraw-Hill, 1976.

12

Measuring Student Aptitudes

The discussion in this chapter should enable you to

1. Name the various aptitude tests and explain what they measure
2. Utilize the strengths and weaknesses of individual and group aptitude tests for specific purposes
3. Defend a position on the relationship of environment and heredity to scholastic aptitude test scores
4. Delineate the major legal issues related to grouping on the basis of testing
5. Utilize the differences among verbal, performance, and nonlanguage ability tests for several specific purposes
6. Explain what is meant by a culture-fair test, determine the implications for its use, and summarize the arguments concerning bias in aptitude tests
7. Define terms such as mental age, ratio intelligence quotient, and deviation IQ, and specify precautions for their use
8. Explain the issues associated with the stability of the intelligence quotient throughout a lifetime
9. Explain how differential aptitude tests are constructed and used
10. Defend a position on the implications of the issues related to estimating overachievement and underachievement
11. Describe the probable causes for the decline in college scholastic aptitude test scores

Visit any classroom with a democratic social climate and you will observe as many kinds of behavior as there are students. Within a fifth-grade class you find some students working arithmetic problems while another group turns, fascinated, to the production of a play they have written. One boy is building a model to illustrate the operation of a machine studied in a science unit; one of the girls is writing a poem. Other children are reading and seem to be totally absorbed in a story. Several students are staring out the window; occasionally they will try to work at an assignment, but they seem to give up easily. Another child is buzzing around the room, enjoying a series of social calls, and is soon called back to work.

You also notice that performance varies considerably. Some children seem adept at manipulating scissors or blocks. Others paint very well, though the art work of their peers seems immature. Certain students offer many ideas as they work with others; some tend to follow and do as they are told.

The many individual differences you observe reflect interests, attitudes, experience backgrounds, and innate ability. All these factors form the basis for the students' ability to learn. Ability to learn is called aptitude; achievement refers to what has been learned. As we shall see, tests that measure aptitude and achievement differ not so much in their content but in the functions they perform.

Certain inherited traits are basic to specific aptitudes. Early studies of individual differences revealed that some people react to stimuli more quickly than others. Take, for example, the case of a certain astronomer engaged in recording the instant at which he saw the images of stars as they crossed the field of his telescope. When a consistent time-lag appeared in his reports, his employers discharged him promptly, thinking him simply careless. This occurred before scientists discovered that individuals react to stimuli with varying rapidity. Those who react quickly have an advantage in some kinds of work. Certain manual skills require long fingers and a deftness of manipulation. In those areas, individuals who are more awkward using their fingers will find themselves at a definite disadvantage.

In most instances, aptitude represents more than innate ability. Two individuals with identical inherited capacities, like identical twins, may have quite different aptitudes because their experiences have been different. One may learn or perform a task with ease; she has a high aptitude for that work. The other may find the task difficult; she is inept at improving this skill, having little aptitude for the work. Theoretically, each twin could develop this special genetically based aptitude to the same degree, but this may not happen because of the important part achievement plays in aptitude potential (see Cleary et al., 1975).

The concert pianist has not only high musical aptitude, but high general ability as well. High general ability is necessary for the development of superior specific aptitudes. An individual with superior native endowment is also more likely to have a wider range of aptitudes than one who is less intellectually mature. Such a student may be talented in the graphic arts, exhibit physical prowess, and show high scholastic achievement as well.

Knowledge of students' aptitudes is of value in counseling them on vocational plans and in preparing them for jobs in which they are likely to succeed. It is also helpful in organizing learning experiences for the individual. For example, low achievement may be the result of lack of effort or ability; we want and need to know how much a student can achieve. Of course, reliability of prediction is dependent on the stability of the aptitude. If an aptitude is unstable, it cannot be measured reliably and will have low correlation with achievement. The findings of research dealing with the constancy of aptitudes indicate some disagreement among psychologists. However, in general, aptitudes seem to be fairly stable. Many aptitudes seem to become crystallized in childhood and develop in a predictable, relatively constant way.

In developing instruments for evaluating aptitudes, some investigators have emphasized that we proceed from general to "purer" aptitudes. Any list of aptitudes we choose will be arbitrary, depending on the extent to which we find measuring discrete aptitudes helpful as opposed to lumping them together for practical purposes. For instance, it is often useful to know students' mechanical aptitudes in addition to having a measure of their general mental abilities. Yet mechanical aptitude is a composite of spatial visualization, perceptual speed and acuity, and mechanical information. At the present time, however, it is probably more useful to take a global approach to aptitude measurement rather than an "atomistic" one, which in this case would make a separate analysis of mechanical aptitude.

The discussion that follows focuses on those aptitude tests of particular importance to school personnel. Hence, special attention is given to individual and group scholastic aptitude tests and to differential aptitude test batteries that include other skills, such as clerical aptitudes and mechanical reasoning.

Scholastic Aptitude Tests

Some scholars have concluded that intelligence is what intelligence tests measure. Since the correlations between the scores of intelligence tests are not perfect, we seemingly have about as many definitions of intelligence as there are tests. Furthermore, most formal definitions do little more to clarify the concept and, though many have been offered, they all fail in some sense.

In measuring achievement, we sample different areas of learning; and if our test and testing situation are adequate, we can arrive at some fairly defensible conclusions about student skills. However, in measuring intelligence, we must consider unequal educational opportunities. Since we cannot measure directly, we establish problem situations that represent important intellectual functions. Though we try to exclude problems whose solutions have been taught in school, the tools the students use are learned. If they are to answer questions on a group intelligence test, they probably will have to know how to read. Some items will demand arithmetic; others, the development of specific concepts (such as *liter, quarter, capital, civil war,* and so forth). Because a student's ability to do well on these tests is so closely related to success in school, the commonly used measures of general intelligence are known as scholastic aptitude tests or tests of developed abilities. These tests, like achievement tests, measure the effects of learning (see Figure 11.1, p. 296 and Cronbach, 1970, p. 282).

Scholastic aptitude tests are designed to predict achievement in situations where instruction is relatively nonadaptive (Glaser and Nitko, 1971). This kind of instruction is directed at the total group that one finds in the average classroom; it is not generally adjusted for maximum effectiveness on an individual basis. Nonadaptive instruction assumes that all students can develop a certain degree of proficiency in a given task. However, adaptive instruction demands a different approach to prediction. In essence, it involves determining a specific instructional methodology for each learner and predicting success on the basis of each learner's characteristics.

Individual Tests

The individual scholastic test, as the name implies, is designed for face-to-face administration to the individual student. Commonly used instruments in this category are the *Stanford-Binet Scale (Form L-M), Wechsler Preschool and Primary Scale of Intelligence (WPPSI), Wechsler Intelligence Scale for Children (WISC-R),* and *Wechsler Adult Intelligence Scale (WAIS).* Of these, the *Stanford-Binet Scale* and the *WISC-R* deserve the most attention.

Stanford-Binet Intelligence Scale, Form L-M. The first Binet scales appeared at the turn of the century in France. Terman and his co-workers prepared American revisions, the most recent of which is *Form L-M* published in 1960. The scale was not restandardized until 1972 (Terman and Merrill, 1973a, Part 4). Test content was not revised, but nationally representative norms, including minority group norms, were developed.

The test is grouped into twenty age levels, each composed of a group of tests, usually six. Beginning at Year II the levels are placed at six-month intervals up to Year VI. This grouping allows for the assessment of the rapid growth of preschool children. Each level has six tests; one month of credit toward the mental-age score is allowed for each test. From Year VI to Year XIV, twelve-month intervals are used. Since there are also six tests in each of these levels, each receives two months of credit. Topping the scale are four increasingly difficult levels, the Average Adult, the Superior Adult Level I, Superior Adult Level II, and the Superior Adult Level III. *Form L-M* reflects the conclusions of longitudinal studies that improvement in performance on the test continues after sixteen years of age. It recognizes improvement to age eighteen.

The tests demand both verbal and nonverbal performance. In some cases, simple memory is sufficient; in others, reasoning is necessary. The student must rely on past experiences as well as his or her talent to solve problems in new situations. Test materials consist of toy objects, printed cards, a test booklet for recording responses, and the test manual.

Below are samples of some of the tests from various age levels:*

---

* Sample items from the *Stanford-Binet Intelligence Scale, Form L-M: Manual.* Copyright © 1973 and 1960 by Houghton Mifflin Co. Reproduced by permission.

Year II—*Identifying Objects by Name (Alternate)*

Material: Card with dog, ball, engine, bed, doll, and scissors attached.

Procedure: Show the card with the six small objects attached and say, "See all these things? Show me the dog." "Put your finger on the dog." "Where is the dog?"

Year IV—*Mutilated Pictures*

Material: Card with mutilated pictures.

Procedure: Show subject the card with mutilated pictures and pointing to each in turn, ask, "What is gone in this picture?" or "What part is gone?"

Year XIV—*Orientation: Direction I*

Procedure: Read the following directions distinctly, emphasizing the critical words:

(a)   "Which direction would you have to face so that your left hand would be toward the east?"

The authors emphasize three requirements for a valid test administration (Terman and Merrill, 1973b):

1.   The standard procedures must be followed.
2.   The student's best efforts must be enlisted by the establishment and maintenance of adequate rapport.
3.   The responses must be correctly scored.

Examiners must have special training in test administration and scoring before they can meet these criteria. They must also have background information in testing and a considerable amount of practice with the instrument to administer it well. Any variation of the standardized procedure invalidates the test to some degree. Too much attention to detail excludes continuing rapport with the student and may result in a less-than-adequate performance. Test administration is further complicated by the fact that scoring is simultaneous with administration. Cues for the next step in the procedure are dependent of the student's success or failure.

No student takes all the tests. Tests taken are determined by the lower and upper limits of ability. Provision is made for the spoiling of tests by making an alternative test available at each of the age levels. About one hour is usually needed for test administration; the time required may vary from as little as thirty to forty minutes for younger children to an hour and one-half or more for older children.

The test manual specifies the desired performance on each test for credit at a particular level. For example, in *Identifying Objects by Name* for Year II, the child must correctly identify at least five of the six objects to pass. Scoring is on an all-or-none basis. The child who identifies three objects correctly receives no more credit than one who identifies two. Both children fail.

Some tests are used at more than one age level and require higher standards of performance for success at the higher age levels. If a test is administered at a lower level, it is not given again at the higher level, but is scored and credited for the proper age level at that time. For example, consider one of the test items from the *Opposite Analogies I* test of Year IV: *

Brother is a boy; sister is a ———.

For Year IV, the child needs to have only two of such items correct; however, if three or more are right, he is given credit for the same test in Year IV-6.

The mental age of a child is determined by scoring the successful responses to the various tests. Traditionally, the intelligence quotient (IQ) had been found by dividing mental age (MA) by chronological age (CA) and multiplying by 100. However, this method prevents IQs having the same meaning at different age levels. At one CA an IQ of 120 may be the highest score of eighty-five percent of the age group while, for another age group, an IQ of 115 may be the top figure for the same percentage of that population. To overcome this problem, in *Form L-M* of the *Stanford-Binet,* a deviation or standard score IQ (sometimes known as DIQ) is found by entering a table with the proper MA and CA values for the student in question. In essence, DIQs for the *Stanford-Binet* are standard scores with an arithmetic mean of 100 and a standard deviation of 16 (see page 327).

Like any other aptitude test, the *Stanford-Binet* does not measure pure native capacity, but innate ability and learning. Only if we could assume that the test is completely valid and reliable and that influencing environments are identical could we infer that the students tested have the same native capacity. At that, it would be sounder to infer only that they had the same ability to learn. But no psychological test has perfect reliability or validity; rapport and effective tapping of students' maximum potential are always problems. They may know the answer to a question and refuse to respond; they may give an incorrect answer for many reasons. Students with academic disabilities may have a particularly strong dislike or even a fear of the kinds of items included in the *Stanford-Binet.*

The improbability that children will experience the same environments extends even to siblings. The older children may be asked to assume more responsibility, for example, to supervise younger brothers or sisters. Perhaps more sharing is demanded of them. Because older children serve as models of behavior, younger members of the family are likely to participate in certain activities at an earlier age that their older siblings.

Differences also exist among family environments. One home may provide a great deal of social interaction, another almost none. Reading may be a central interest of all members of one student's family; a classmate's family may lack even a daily newspaper. Bilingual homes present a special problem for children. Because the *Stanford-Binet* is highly verbal, students from bilingual homes are likely to be severely affected by problems of verbal stimulation. Although they may have other types of ability, they may not be effectively sampled by this test.

* Sample item from the *Stanford-Binet Intelligence Scale, Form L-M: Manual.* Copyright © 1973 and 1960 by Houghton Mifflin Co. Reproduced by permission.

It should also be noted that the *Stanford-Binet* is not designed to differentiate among the various aspects of intelligence. There are no separate scores, only a composite.

Despite these limitations, the *Stanford-Binet* has proved over the years to be a valuable instrument. Although superior performance on the test is generally dependent on success in school, the test may also be the instrument for predicting such success; verbal ability is an important factor in school and this highly verbal test enables an examiner to assess the student's verbal facility. It also helps spot deficiencies in arithmetic, problem solving, and the fund of information.

During the administration of the *Stanford-Binet*, one can observe children's reactions. Although the quality of their performances should be interpreted cautiously by an experienced examiner, problem-solving ability, work habits, and reactions to success and failure can be examined. When the students fail, the examiner seeks to determine whether they are disturbed, irritable, argumentative, or depressed. When they are successful, their reactions are also observed. Reaction time should be noted; it can be indicative of certain personality characteristics. Is it delayed, blocked, or irregular? Is there any indication of negativism, or are the responses given quickly and impulsively? On the basis of this and other evidence, the examiner can gain insights to the student's personality.

The Wechsler Scales. Form I of the original *Wechsler Intelligence Scale* was published in 1939 and was called the *Wechsler-Bellevue Intelligence Scale. Form II* was adapted from a scale developed during World War II. Scales of both forms were designed for adults rather than children. The tasks in existing instruments, such as the *Stanford-Binet,* do not hold enough interest to motivate many adults. In addition, the speed factor present in many tests is particularly detrimental in assessing adult intelligence when a test is standardized on children.

The items in these scales reflect Wechsler's specific objective, namely, to construct an instrument that would enable examiners to better understand adult patients at New York's Bellevue Hospital. A test was lacking to determine patients' intelligence and personality aberrations; therefore, an instrument with diagnostic properties in addition to those measuring "global" intelligence was needed.

From this work were developed three scales, namely, the *Wechsler Intelligence Scale for Children (WISC)* for ages six through sixteen (introduced in 1949 and revised in 1974 as the *WISC-R*); the *Wechsler Adult Intelligence Scale (WAIS)* for older subjects (introduced in 1955); and the *Wechsler Preschool and Primary Scale of Intelligence (WPPSI)* for ages four to six-and-a-half (introduced in 1967). The pattern of subtests in each of the three scales is quite similar. As displayed in Table 12.1, the scales are organized into subtests, five or six composing a verbal score and another five designed to yield a performance score. Note that in addition to subtests used regularly (indicated by check), there are alternate tests to be used if, for instance, the administration of one of the regular subtests was faulty.

Unlike the age scales used in the *Stanford-Binet,* the *Wechsler* tests are a series of point scales. In other words, each test item is assigned points for a correct response. Points for each test represent raw scores that are changed to scaled scores

TABLE 12.1.   Subtests for Three Wechsler Scales

Subtest	WPPSI (Ages 4 to 6½)	WISC-R (Ages 6 to 16)	WAIS (Adult)
Verbal			
Information	√	√	√
Comprehension	√	√	√
Arithmetic	√	√	√
Similarities	√	√	√
Vocabulary	√	√	√
Digit span		Alternate	√
Sentences	Alternate		
Performance			
Picture completion	√	√	√
Block design	√	√	√
Picture arrangement		√	√
Object assembly		√	√
Mazes	√	Alternate	√
Digit symbol			√
Animal house	√		
Geometric design	√		
Coding		√	

by means of a table. The respective subtests in the *Verbal Scale* and the *Performance Scale* are added to secure the verbal and performance scores. By the use of tables, the intelligence quotients may be determined.

Student IQs are determined, therefore, by a comparison of the score representing their test performance with those scores earned by the individuals in the standardization sample of a single age group. If the standard deviation of IQs is held constant and the total mean score for each age group equated, the IQ is made comparable for students of different ages. Individuals are assigned an IQ on the basis of the amount that they deviate from the average performance of those in their age group.

It should be noted that the *Wechsler* IQs are deviation IQs as in the *Stanford-Binet*. One difference exists, however. The *Wechsler* scores have a standard deviation of fifteen in contrast to the sixteen used for *Stanford-Binet* scores. Therefore, for comparably bright students, the DIQ on the *Stanford-Binet* will be slightly higher than on the *WISC-R*. With comparably dull children, the DIQ on the *Stanford-Binet* will be a little lower.

The *Wechsler* manuals emphasize that the test examiner must be well-trained and have access to a quiet testing room and proper materials. The directions for test administration must be followed specifically. Rather than change the wording of the questions, the teacher should read the instructions from the manual. The conditions under which the child performs certain tasks have been carefully standardized; norms of performance have been prepared under the conditions of the instructions. As in the administration of the *Stanford-Binet*, the examiner has an opportunity to note any unusual behavior that bears on the child's personality.

The examiner must always be concerned with securing optimum performance, and very skillful questioning is required. Often the child's response needs clarification, which can be accomplished by nonevaluative querying. For example, the examinee may be asked "Please explain further," or "Tell more about it." Also, in maintaining rapport it is sometimes necessary to encourage with supporting statements, such as, "This is a little difficult; you will find it easier when you are older." One should not build up an expectancy for approval because the children may come to interpret no comment as disapproval. On balance, the *Wechsler* scales are more easily administered than the *Stanford-Binet*.

Unlike the *Stanford-Binet,* which provides only one IQ score, the *Wechsler* scales have separate verbal and nonverbal IQs. This feature is often valuable in diagnosing students' educational problems. As you might expect, many studies have compared performance on the *Wechsler* scales with that of the *Stanford-Binet.* Coefficients of correlations usually found vary between 0.60 and 0.80. Correlations based on the *Performance scale* alone tend to be somewhat lower than those based on the *Verbal scale* alone.

PROBLEMS

1. Teachers usually look only for the actual IQ score when an individual psychological test has been administered. Few bother to read the detailed report prepared by the examiner. What dangers are inherent in this practice? What information should you as a teacher look for and expect to find in a psychological report? In what respects might a psychological report of a *Stanford-Binet* test differ from one on the *WISC-R* in terms of the kinds of information given?

2. How might one account for the low correlations between scores on ability tests for very young children and later measures of intelligence?

Group Tests

In most school situations, neither time nor trained personnel is available for the administration of the individual tests described. Group tests, therefore, are much more extensively used, since they may be administered to a large group of students by an examiner with minimum training. In general, they are verbal, and if they do not require reading, the examinee must at least be able to understand the verbal instructions of the examiner. Therefore great care must be taken in interpreting test scores, for a low score may indicate a lack of verbal facility rather than intellectual immaturity.

Although many good group intelligence tests are available for school use, all of them cannot be discussed here. We take the logical alternative of mentioning briefly several tests that represent somewhat different approaches to the measurement of mental ability. In addition, a summary of the important college aptitude tests is included (see p. 341).

Otis-Lennon School Ability Test. In 1918, publication of the *Otis Group Intelligence Scale* marked the development of the first group test of mental ability for school use. During the intervening years various forms and editions have been published, including the *Otis-Lennon School Ability Test (OLSAT)*. It is basically a revision of the *Otis-Lennon Mental Ability Test,* retaining the same rationale and using similar types of test items.

The primary purpose of the *OLSAT* is to measure abstract thinking and reasoning ability in order to predict student success in cognitive achievement areas. The test taps a broad range of cognitive abilities measured by the spiral omnibus form. This means that, instead of using subtests of homogeneous items, the test introduces all easy items first, whatever their nature, and proceeds in the same way through the more difficult ones.

The *OLSAT* is designed for students in grades one through twelve and has five levels (see Table 12.2). Each level yields a single score which has the same statistical properties as a DIQ but called a school ability index (SAI). In addition to the SAI, test results can be reported as percentiles and stanines.

The *Otis-Lennon School Ability test* was standardized concurrently with the 1978 edition of the *Metropolitan Achievement Tests.* Comparative achievement and ability information is thus provided for students from first grade through secondary school. This makes it possible to use a student's SAI to predict future achievement in terms of grade equivalents for the subtests of the *Metropolitan.* These predictions are ranges of grade equivalents within which the student could be expected to score in each of the five achievement areas of the achievement test battery.

Other Group Scholastic Aptitude Tests. Unlike the *Otis-Lennon School Ability Test,* some group scholastic aptitude tests yield more than one score. Examples of these are the *Short Form Test of Academic Aptitude (SFTAA)* and the *Cognitive Abilities Test (CAT).*

The *SFTAA* provides an index of general academic aptitude for students in grade levels 1.5 through 12. It has four subtests, namely, *Vocabulary, Analogies, Sequences,* and *Memory.* These scores can be combined to yield separate measures of language and nonlanguage aptitude as well as a single measure of academic aptitude.

TABLE 12.2.   Grade Level, Number of Items, and Time Limits of Each *OLSAT* Level

Test level	Grade level	No. of items	Time limit
Primary I	1	60	80*
Primary II	2–3	75	80*
Elementary	4–5	70	45
Intermediate	6–8	80	45
Advanced	9–12	80	40

* Approximate number of minutes of testing time.

TABLE 12.3.   Subtests of the *Cognitive Abilities Test* Arranged in Three Batteries

Verbal (V)	Quantitative (Q)	Nonverbal (NV)
Vocabulary	Quantitative relations	Figure classification
Sentence completion	Number series	Figure analogies
Verbal classification	Equation building	Figure synthesis
Verbal analogies		

In addition, the *SFTAA* is used in conjunction with the *California Achievement Tests* to determine anticipated achievement scores. Achievement scores are based on grade equivalents or scale scores from the *California* that were obtained by other students with similar age and grade characteristics who performed similarly on the *STFAA*. It is suggested that the difference between an anticipated grade equivalent based on a student's performance on the *STFAA* and the actual grade equivalent on the achievement test is an estimate of the amount of overachievement or underachievement present. Caution: Only large differences are significant, and even these may be unstable.

The *Cognitive Abilities Test (CAT)* provides verbal, quantitative, and nonverbal measures of ability for a wide age range, basically kindergarten through secondary school. It has ten subtests divided into three batteries as shown in Table 12.3.

Each battery uses a different type of symbol, namely, words, numbers, and figures. In turn, each subtest of each battery requires students to work with the symbol of that battery in different ways. Their success at these tasks for each battery is represented by "standard age scores" (a normalized standard score with a mean of 100 and a standard deviation of 16 for each age group), percentile ranks by age or grade, and stanines by age or grade. No total score representing a combination of the three batteries is reported.

The *CAT* was standardized concurrently with the *Iowa Tests of Basic Skills*, for the elementary and middle school grades, and the *Tests of Achievement and Proficiency*, for the high school grades. As a result, it is possible to use a student's performance on the *CAT* to determine predicted levels of achievement on these achievement batteries.

PROBLEM

3. Compare the *Short Form Test of Academic Aptitude* to the *Otis-Lennon School Ability Test* in terms of validity evidence, standardization groups, and interpretability of scores.

Individual vs. Group Tests

The individual intelligence test can be administered to only one person at a time. The only numerical limitation on a group intelligence test is the number of facilities and proctors available. Administering group tests is not difficult in most instances, although certain problems arise when young children are being tested. Two of the most common problems encountered with young children are a short attention span and difficulty in following instructions. The examiner can be trained rather quickly, however, to administer group tests successfully.

The same is not true for the individual test; special training is necessary if the examiner is to capitalize on the testing situation to learn something of the individual's work habits and personality. One of the most important factors in any test administration is motivating the examinee to optimum performance. It is much easier to obtain good motivation when the examiner's attention can be concentrated on one person. In group testing, lack of interest, along with lapses of attention and effort, are more difficult to determine.

Scoring of responses on individual tests tends to be more subjective than on group tests. Although scoring guides are furnished, the examiner must interpret the correctness of the response. For example, in the *Stanford-Binet Vocabulary* the examinee is asked, "What is an orange?" The response "tree" is listed as a correct answer but "lemon" is not. The *Memory for Designs* test at years nine and eleven requires the examinees to reproduce two designs after looking at them for ten seconds. In scoring, they are allowed full credit for the *A* designs but only one-half credit for the *B* designs shown in Figure 12.1. On the other hand, a group test is generally scored in terms of the number of items right and, in most instances, no such fine interpretation need be made. Ordinary clerical or machine scoring can be employed.

Each type of test has advantages and disadvantages. The group test is used more in the schools because it does not require highly trained personnel for administration and is more economical in time and cost to administer. An individual

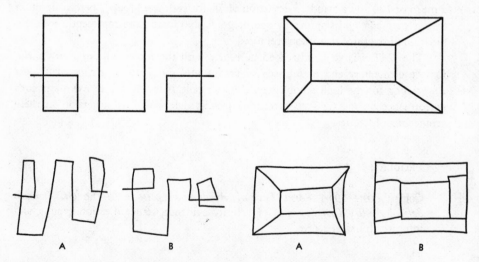

FIGURE 12.1.   Memory for Designs—Stanford-Binet Scale Years IX and XI

Sample item from the *Stanford-Binet Intelligence Scale, Form L-M, Manual.* Copyright © 1973 and 1960 by Houghton Mifflin Co. Reproduced by permission.

intelligence test should be administered when one suspects that group-test results are invalid. They are also required in certain cases because of a student's emotional, physical, or perceptual characteristics. Because the group test emphasizes reading ability more than the individual test, considerable caution should be exercised lest a low score be interpreted as lack of native ability rather than as low reading achievement.

PROBLEM

4. Bill received an SAI of 107 on the *Otis-Lennon* and an IQ of 107 on the *Stanford-Binet*. What justification can you see for the additional time and expense involved in the use of the individual test?

Verbal vs. Performance and Nonlanguage Tests

Performance tests generally require the subject to manipulate some object, put parts of a figure or picture together, set up a color design, and so forth. Generally they call for individual administration. They are often designed for those individuals with some physical anomaly and are exemplified by speech and hearing tests for illiterates or those who cannot speak English. Scoring procedures vary. In some instances, only the time to complete the test is recorded. In other tests, the examiner scores the number of moves in addition to keeping a time record, and sometimes tabulates false movements.

Nonlanguage tests are paper-and-pencil tests designed for group administration. No knowledge of written or spoken language is necessary, and although some test instructions are given orally, they are very simple and can be translated into another language without affecting test validity. Pantomime is often used to clarify instructions. Test items may require a subject to complete paper-and-pencil mazes, determine the number of cubes in a pile, complete a series in which X's and O's have different patterns of arrangement, mark identical pairs of numbers, draw in missing parts of pictures, and solve a spatial relations test.

One test requires the examinee to determine which geometric figure cuts another into parts of a certain shape; find missing parts on reversed geometric figures; determine the resulting design of a pattern synthesis, in which two geometric figures are superimposed; determine the next position of a sequence of geometric figures in a movement sequence; determine spatial relations in a manikin test, in which the position of the manikin is changed and the correct figure in terms of hand placement must be determined; and identify, in paper folding, how the paper would look after it had been folded, cut, and opened again.

It should be understood that both the performance and nonlanguage tests measure different aspects of intelligence from those measured by verbal tests. It is doubtful if they tap higher order abilities, since the verbal tests demand the manipulation of verbal symbols through thinking. Performance and nonlanguage tests rely on spatial and perceptual abilities.

The tests are useful in supplementing data obtained from verbal tests on certain occasions. Children who have failed in school may not be motivated to do items on a verbal test so similar to school work. On the contrary, they may find the tasks in performance and nonverbal tests novel and exciting. Some clinicians assert that performance tests are helpful in the observation of a child's behavior, but their use requires training beyond that of the average teacher. Despite certain limitations, the verbal test is a better instrument for prediction of academic success.

PROBLEM

5. What place would you allocate to performance and nonlanguage tests in a public school testing program? Defend your answer.

Test Bias

In a sense, tests are culturally biased since they inevitably reflect our culture. This does not mean that they are always unfair. For instance, unfairness may be traced to faulty test construction or improper use. To illustrate, a criterion-referenced achievement test is certainly culture-bound, but can be extremely fair if its content is representative of a well-defined domain of tasks and it is appropriately administered and interpreted.

The most common sources of test bias are the content of the test itself; the atmosphere in which, and the procedures by which, the test is administered; and the use to which the test results are put. The last is of great significance, especially in the case of aptitude tests. A test is not biased or unbiased in the abstract; rather, it is biased or unbiased in terms of a particular use (Flaugher, 1978).

As a case in point, scholastic aptitude tests of a verbal nature are designed to predict future academic achievement in verbal learning areas and can do so in a reasonably unbiased manner. On the other hand, if scores from such a test were used as a basis for deciding who would succeed as a plumber, then the test use is quite biased. Obvious as this seems, the issues involved in determining degrees of test bias are very complex and deserve careful study.

Laosa (1977, pp. 10–11) has summarized the criticisms of testing practices associated with test data that opponents believe to be biased.

1. Standardized tests do not reflect the experiences or the cognitive, linguistic, and cultural styles and values of minorities.
2. Data used from these tests to form homogeneous classroom groups have severely limited educational, vocational, economic, and various other societal opportunities.
3. Test administration is often inferior because the test administrator fails to elicit optimum performance from those taking the test. Often this results from a lack of understanding about the culture and language of minorities.
4. Testing practices may foster low-level achievement through the self-fulfilling prophecy.
5. Educational change is restricted by those measurements that promote rigid school curricula.

6. Norm-referenced tests typically used are not helpful for instructional purposes.

7. Only a part of the important educational changes in children are appraised by these tests.

8. Standardized measurements suggest to some that only innate and fixed abilities and characteristics are measured.

Laosa (1977, pp. 11–17) also reviewed the assessment practice trends emerging today that attempt to cope with these criticisms. These trends fall into three categories. There is increasing recognition and acceptance that our society is varied with respect to the patterns of culture and linguistics. New views are evolving concerning educational practices and philosophies. Educators are responding to the pressures of organized groups attempting to modify existing practices.

Culture-Fair Tests

To respond to needs created by varied cultural and linguistic patterns, culture-fair tests have been constructed. This type of test is sometimes spoken of as a *culture free* test, which, of course, is not an accurate description. Every individual's development bears the imprint of some culture. The concern is that the typical scholastic aptitude test is unfair to those reared in a much different environment. We often question whether our commonly used tests give a valid indication of students' intelligence when they come from such an educational environment.

Various kinds of items have been utilized in an attempt to avoid penalizing this kind of student. Mazes, symbol copying, classification of pictures, explaining the essence of a picture, and identification of similar drawings have been employed. Because speed is a cultural factor, it has been deemphasized. Tests placing a premium on quick recall have not been used.

Despite an attempt to eliminate cultural bias, studies in general show that lower-class children do not perform any better on this type of test than on other tests of mental ability. Consider the following:

> ... We may find that the problem is really too big for the test author. It may turn out that the kinds of cultural impact associated with social class differences affect the course of mental development of children as well as their performance on intelligence tests.
>
> Social class differences are real differences, substantial psychological phenomena with which schools and society must deal. It may be that we cannot build valid intelligence tests which will not at the same time discriminate among the social classes. Or, if we start the other way round by designing tests which will not discriminate among social classes, we may find that the tests are poor predictors of academic achievement (Stroud, 1957, p. 85).

Passage of time has not altered the validity of this conclusion. But there is another aspect to the use of scores from our typically culturally biased aptitude tests. A number of children coming from "disadvantaged" environments and having values and classroom behavior at variance with that of their teachers, do well on the tests, in contrast to their daily academic performance. Without objective test results, some of these noncomforming children would be categorized adversely by the typically middle-class professional staff.

To be sure, we should continue to look for a variety of different meanings in the mental ability scores of minority children. Rather than considering these scores as evidence of fixed potential, we should plan activities to help children overcome their academic handicaps. Interpreting their scores sometimes is complicated by the influence of certain nonintellective factors on test performance such as student motivation, testwiseness, and emotional state.

Other Approaches to Reduce Test Bias

A wide variety of approaches are being taken to reduce the influence of cultural bias in student evaluation. They include the following:

1. Existing tests have been translated for non-English-speaking children. Care must be taken, however, if an appropriately equivalent test is to result. More than mere translation and superficial adaptation is required (Laosa, 1973).

2. Regional and ethnic norms have been established. Unfortunately, they can be the basis for negative comparisons between various ethnic and racial groups. Poor scores are assumed to be indicative of lower potential.

3. Attempts have been made to develop tests designed specifically for each of the major subcultural groups in American society. One such instrument is the *Black Intelligence Test of Cultural Homogeneity (BITCH-100)* (Cronbach, 1978). It is a 100 multiple-choice item vocabulary test dealing exclusively with the black experience. A serious problem with this type of instrument is its low predictive validity for academic success.

4. Pluralistic assessment procedures (Mercer and Ysseldyke, 1977) are now being tried. The sociocultural characteristics of the individual are considered when evaluating the scores on tests of intellectual aptitude. A pluralistic evaluation method is applied whereby multiple normative frameworks for various sociocultural, socioeconomic, racial, ethnic, and geographic groups are developed. Children are then evaluated as normal, subnormal, or superior depending on where their scores fall in a distribution of scores predicted for other children from similar sociocultural settings.

    Mercer and Lewis developed the *System for Multi-Pluralistic Assessment (SOMPA)* containing both parent interviews and student assessment materials. The former includes sociocultural scales, an adaptive behavior inventory for children, and a health history inventory. The latter includes physical dexterity tasks, the *Bender Visual Motor Gestalt Test*, and the *WISC-R*. The system provides an opportunity to study children from a biological, cultural, and educational perspective, and thereby estimate "learning potential" in a manner less influenced by cultural bias (Nuttall, 1979).

5. A Piagetian alternative is available; it is quite different from the use of ordinary aptitude tests. Six of the Piagetian-based concepts used by De Avila and Pulos (1978) are types of conservation (area, distance, length, horizontality, substance, number, and weight); the problems are presented

in a cartoon format. They point out that recent studies have found that Piagetian tasks "assess some traits not measured by traditional tests of intelligence and . . . these traits significantly improve the prediction of academic performance" (p. 506).

6. Attempts have been made to familiarize students to a greater degree with the testing situation. Test administrators are engaged who possess special language skills and have a cultural awareness so as to elicit optimum performance from students.

7. The use of lay boards to monitor the use of test results for assigning students to special education classes for the mentally retarded is recommended by the U. S. Office of Civil Rights (Gerry, 1973). The members of such boards would be parents of children in the schools and representative of the ethnic composition of the student body. The primary function of the board is to make certain that consideration is given to cultural factors unique to the particular race and national origin of the student being evaluated. This may affect the test results and any subsequent decision to assign that student to special classes.

It should be obvious that these replacement procedures themselves may have serious limitations. Each should be evaluated carefully and systematically to determine the best solutions to the problem on bias in testing. (For a thorough discussion of test bias in selection for admission to educational programs and employment, see Jaeger, 1976).

Increasing Mental Ability

Because of government programs such as Head Start, designed to improve the learning aptitude of culturally disadvantaged children, there has been considerable discussion about the possibility of increasing mental ability and scholastic achievement. Jensen (1969a, 1969b) argues forcibly that compensatory education efforts have failed to make permanent gains on children's IQ and achievement. He questions the rationale on which these programs have been based—that variance of the environment and the cultural bias of scholastic aptitude tests are the main causes of IQ differences. Finally, he concludes that genetic factors are of greater importance in producing these differences than is environmental influence.

The Jensen position has generated vigorous debate. Some seriously question his conclusions (Sanday, 1972), whereas others believe they are valid at least in part and suggest further research (Shockley, 1972). Unsurprisingly, many questions have been raised. For instance, if variations in environment are gradually reduced, will the effect of heritability on mental ability correspondingly increase?*

How much then we can boost mental ability and scholastic achievement? Garber and Heber (1978) tried to answer this question by studying the infants

* Further questions have been raised about Jensen's findings since he used in part Sir Cyril Burt's data on identical twins, and some of these data are considered faulty (Hearnshaw, 1979). However, Jensen has continued and enlarged his study of bias in mental testing and believes that (1) the most widely used standardized mental ability tests yield unbiased measures for all native-born English-speaking minority groups and (2) nonverbal mental ability tests give unbiased results even for those whose first language is not English (Jensen, 1980).

of a small group of inner city families who were considered high risks for having mentally retarded children. One half of the families participated in an intensive enrichment program for 72 months. The program emphasized the educational and vocational rehabilitation of the mothers and provided an equally personalized educational program for the infants. The program for the children focused on language and problem-solving skills. The other half of the families served as a control group.

By 18 months the development of the children in the control group had fallen behind that of children in families receiving the enrichment program. As they grew older, the differential was maintained. For example, when administered the *Wechsler* tests in the elementary school, the control group children averaged 20 or more IQ-points lower than the children in the enrichment program. In view of this consistent pattern, the investigators believe that the intervention program during infancy and early childhood was effective. However, whether children in such programs can continue to maintain and develop their cognitive skills in a difficult environment still must be determined.

Further answers to critics who attack the effectiveness of the Head Start Program and other early educational interventions are given in a summary of the findings of fourteen longitudinal studies of low-income children (Lazar and Darlington, 1978). These children had participated in experimental infant and preschool programs over a fifteen-year period.

The authors of this report conclude that effective early education programs improve the ability of low-income children to cope with school tasks. They found that these children did significantly better on the *Stanford-Binet* tests for a three-year period after attending the preschool programs. The authors emphasize that these are precisely the years when the basic skills are taught. However, when the *Wechsler* tests were administered ten to fifteen years after preschool, no differences were found between the experimental and control groups of children aged thirteen or older. Only in those projects with younger children nine and twelve years old were the scores significantly greater for the experimental group.

In many ways the foregoing results are encouraging. Nevertheless, there is insufficient evidence to support the claim that early interventions such as those studied raise mental ability levels on a prolonged basis.

PROBLEM

6. What are the major common fallacies about heredity, environment, and human behavior existing today (Anastasi, 1973)? Identify possible reasons for each.

Mental Age and Intelligence Quotients

Mental Age

When buying clothing for school-age children, we do not ask for something to fit a ten-year-old; we ask for a definite size because children of the same age vary.

Intelligence testing is the same; students of the same age do not have the same amount of intelligence. The outstanding feature of the *Stanford-Binet Scale* is that the tests are grouped according to the age at which a majority passed. For example, children passing the items at the ten-year level and failing those at the eleven-year level have a mental age of ten. If their chronological age (CA) is less than ten, they are bright; if their chronological age is greater than ten, they are either duller than average or some factor has interfered with test performance. In actual testing practice, however, a child may receive a mental age of ten and yet miss some items in the scale below the ten-year level and pass some above this level.

Mental age (MA) may be determined in other tests from the raw score, such as the total number of items correct. The mean raw score earned by a particular age group in the standardization sample would represent the mental age for that group. If the group were seven-year-olds, the mental age would be seven. A child who makes a raw score equal to the average of seven-year-olds would, therefore, have a mental age of seven. It should be emphasized that more than mental age is necessary to determine the brightness of a child. Mental age refers only to the level of mental development.

Other characteristics inherent in the concept of mental age make interpretation difficult. Unlike the measurement of height or weight, no absolute zero point exists, and it would be difficult to define the point of no intelligence in a human being. Moreover, mental age units are unequal. As the individual grows older, the mental age units represent decreasing development. Since the increase in mental age units compared to the increase in the CA is quite small, the concept of MA becomes meaningless for students in their late teens. Actually, the growth pattern is not unlike that for height. Between two and four years of age, there is a much greater increase than between the years of sixteen and eighteen. It is for this reason that percentile ranks and standard scores, rather than IQs, are used for older students.

Another problem is in the interpretation of identical mental age of two students who have different chronological ages. If mental age is assumed to represent a student's level of mental capacity, then an MA of eight represents the same degree of intellectual maturity no matter if one child has a CA of six and another a CA of ten. However, these two students are quite different intellectually. Further difficulties in the interpretation of the MA must be dealt with when extrapolating to determine an IQ value for the superior student. How does one interpret a mental age of twenty-two obtained from the norm table when the mean adult age on the test is fifteen years?

We should not conclude from this discussion or from the use of the deviation IQ (DIQ, which does not use the MA/CA rates) that the MA has no value. When the teacher recognizes the limitations, the concept of mental age can be of help in suiting a learning task to the student's ability. We know that understanding concepts of number, time, and distance requires a certain degree of mental maturity. Much research about teaching children to read has established that general intelligence is the most important factor in reading readiness; mental age is closely related to the student's success or failure. Harris and Sipay summarize the evidence as follows:

1. There is a substantial relationship between mental age and ease of learning to read; most children who fail in reading in the first grade have mental ages below 6 years. The more mature children not only learn more easily but also retain what they learn better than the less mature children.

2. Most 6-year-old children who have IQs within or above the normal value and are free from special handicaps can be successfully taught to read in the first grade.

3. It is not possible to set a definite minimum mental age for learning to read because too many other factors are involved. Children with mental ages as low as 5 years can be taught to read first-grade materials provided they are ready in other respects.

4. A systematic readiness training program which precedes the beginning of reading instruction enables some children to make better progress when they do start, but is not needed by all. Many are ready to read before the first day of school. A delayed start without specific efforts to improve readiness is not recommended. (1975, p. 23)

Intelligence Quotients

Information concerning a child's rate of mental development is also useful to teachers. They need to know when some children are maturing more or less rapidly than the average child. If their mental age scores are valid and are greater than their chronological ages, they are brighter and will eventually be more mentally mature than their duller peers. If all other things are equal, they will be more rapid learners.

Levels of intelligence have been classified in relation to IQ intervals, as listed in Table 12.4. These descriptive levels are helpful in communicating about individuals with different degrees of intelligence and in roughly predicting academic success. It is well to remember that these classifications are useful guides, not rigid divisions.

TABLE 12.4.   Distribution of Deviation IQs for the Stanford-Binet Scale

IQ	Percent	Classification
Above 148	0.1	Near genius
124–148	6.5	Very superior
112–123	16.0	Superior
88–111	54.7	Normal
76–87	16.0	Dull
64–75	5.5	Borderline defective
Below 64	1.2	Mentally defective

Adapted from Pinneau, 1961, p. 70; reproduced by permission of Houghton Mifflin Company.

The Deviation IQ. In order to determine how bright a student was in comparison to his or her peers, the IQ was initially determined by the ratio of mental age to chronological age multiplied by 100 (IQ = MA/CA × 100). When MA and CA were equal, an IQ of 100 resulted, indicating an average intelligence. When MA was greater than CA the IQ was more than 100, indicating above average intelligence. On the other hand, when MA was less than CA an IQ value of less than 100 resulted. These persons had below average intelligence.

There was a problem with this procedure, however. Scores have differing variabilities at different ages. In other words, the standard deviation varies with age. As a result, it is possible that an IQ of 110 for a nine-year-old and an IQ of 120 for an eleven-year-old are both one standard deviation above the mean. Although their IQs are different, both students have the same relative position among their peers in terms of mental ability.

Because of this problem, ratio IQs have largely been abandoned and replaced by the deviation IQ (DIQ), a type of standardized score with a mean of 100 and a predetermined standard deviation. If we use a standard deviation of 16 and a mean of 100 in reporting scores for any age group and for any intelligence test, the sizes of the IQ values for that test will be comparable to those of the *Stanford-Binet*. This is most helpful because test users have become accustomed to the "meanings" of IQs of 60, 80, 120, and so forth. It should be emphasized, however, that not all tests use a standard deviation figure of 16 and, therefore, it is important to check closely the standard deviation of the scores of a test before making any interpretations.

Constancy of the IQ. How stable is the IQ of an individual? Does it effectively predict an individual's ability over a long period of time? This question is of great importance in educational and vocational planning. Test intelligence demands achievement as a means for sampling innate ability; inherited capacity cannot be measured directly. If heredity is highly significant, and if we could measure it accurately, it might yield a more stable score. If environment were more important, its influence could vary from time to time and change the size of intelligence quotients. We have reason to believe that both heredity and environment influence effective intelligence. Someone has said that "heredity sets the limit, while environment determines how closely an individual approaches this limit." In other words, individuals probably do not fully develop their innate capacities.

What are some of the other reasons why the IQ seems less stable than is really warranted? Unreliability of measuring instruments is one prime reason; IQs can vary five to ten points because of the unreliability of the tests used. Also, few instruments are effective for measuring the entire range of abilities found in the typical classroom. Less able students will be crowding the "floor," while the "ceiling" will be too low for the able. Such factors as motivation in test taking, language deficiencies, and emotional characteristics may also influence scores. Other possible causes could be transitory psychological or physical conditions, such as illness or poor rapport between the examiner and the subject. On the other hand, the irregularities might reflect real changes in intellectual maturity.

It should be noted that the relative positions of students in a group tend to change in relation to the amount of time between tests.

Less shifting of relative positions occurs with increasing age. Also, verbal IQ scores tend to be more stable than nonverbal IQ scores; by grade four, verbal scores appear to be completely stable. After grade seven there is little difference in the stability of the scores of individual and group tests, while in the early grades the individual tests tend to be more stable. Girls' scores are slightly more stable than those of boys through the school years (Hopkins and Bracht, 1975). Therefore, two important considerations in determining IQ constancy are the student's age at the time of testing and the type of test used.

There are two other factors that may affect the stability of the measured IQ score. One is the variability of scores for different age groups taking a given test. Second, for certain students, test scores from different scholastic aptitude tests may vary greatly. Hence, the report of these scores should always include identity of the test from which they were derived (e.g., SAI (*Otis-Lennon School Ability Test, Intermediate Level*): 93).

There are considerable data supporting IQ constancy from the elementary grades through college for the general population of students (McCall et al., 1973). One explanation for this is that future learning depends on present achievement. The students with inadequate academic skills will have difficulty with their future intellectual development. On the other hand, the able student has mastered the necessary tools for continued growth. In contrast to the total group of students, individual boys and girls may experience IQ fluctuations. These shifts may be caused by critical changes in their lives.

Conclusions. We may conclude that the IQ is quite stable throughout a typical individual's life if we consider it to be a rough classification. Certainly, the child with high mental ability will tend to remain an individual with considerable intellectual prowess. A student who has an IQ well below 100 will probably become an adult who functions on a lower intellectual level, unless the score is the result of poor academic progress. We are assuming also that the IQ is not based on an infant test since such tests are quite unreliable. Because of the numerous factors that may influence test scores, a teacher should never rely on the results of a single test. In addition to other test scores, data obtained through observation and other means should be used to evaluate mental maturity.

PROBLEMS

7. An elementary school is grouping students in the intermediate grade levels according to the total scores from a well-developed, group scholastic aptitude test. Is this defensible? Explain.

8. There is controversy about the implications involved in making school records, including the reporting of actual IQ-scores, available to parents of minor children. What is your reaction to this legal requirement?

Differential Aptitude Tests

The basis of multiple measurement is rooted in trait and factor psychology. A trait is an enduring pattern of behavior that is exhibited by everyone in varying degrees. We should use the multiple-trait approach in studying individual differences. After all, we are attempting to change behavior along several dimensions (for example, verbal as well as quantitative). Furthermore, the affective domain as well as the cognitive must be considered in predicting a student's performance. Motivation, to mention one such trait, is obviously a factor in achievement.

Useful insights into a student's strengths and weaknesses may be found through a battery of tests standardized on the same population. A profile of aptitude scores can be determined and comparisons made among an individual's cognitive, perceptual, and sensorimotor aptitudes. Recently, batteries of tests standardized on the same population have made a comparison of scores more meaningful. Representative of this kind of test battery are the *Academic Promise Tests* (*APT*) designed for grades six through nine, the *Differential Aptitude Test* (*DAT*) for use in the secondary school, and the *General Aptitude Test Battery* (*GATB*) for ages sixteen and over.

Structure of the Intellect

In an effort to provide a theoretical basis for the construction of multiple aptitude batteries, complicated statistical techniques have been used to systematically identify different abilities that can be considered as subparts of "intelligence." Once the various abilities have been identified, it is argued, the construction of aptitude tests could proceed. The end product would be differential aptitude test batteries that would reveal an individual's aptitude profile in detail.

One of the most interesting theoretical models classifying the factors of the intellect was proposed by Guilford (1959). His model shown in Figure 12.2 contains 120 cells, each corresponding to at least one factor or ability. His threefold model includes the process of operation performed (cognition, memory, convergent thinking, divergent thinking, and evaluating); products (units, classes, relations, system, transformations, and implications); and contents (figural, symbolic, semantic, and behavioral). Although some cells have as yet not been fully identified, the model proves most helpful in aiding the formulation of hypotheses for further research designed to explore the nature of the intellect.

Theoretically, it may some day be possible to predict any cognitive behavior from Guilford's model, whether it be performance in algebra or architecture. At the present time, however, the validity of available aptitude tests enables us to predict criterion behavior only within certain limits. In some of the widely used instruments, the verbal and quantitative scores are still the best predictors of academic success.

Creativity. Each of the 120 cells is described in terms of its three dimensions, namely, operation, content, and product. For instance, verbal comprehension is

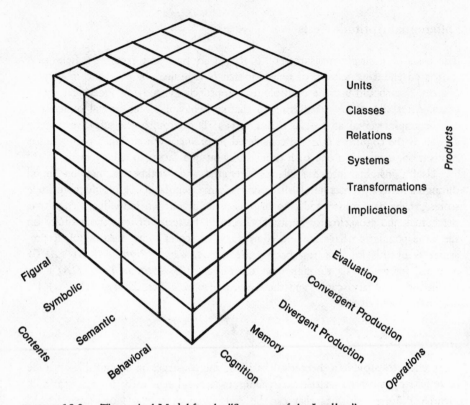

FIGURE 12.2.   Theoretical Model for the "Structure of the Intellect"

From Guilford, 1959; redrawn by permission of the author and the American Psychological Association.

identified as cognition of semantic units and can be measured by vocabulary tests. Also, the cells labeled "divergent production" are prominent in creative activity. Measurements for these typically require the student to make multiple responses to a stated task such as "How many uses can you think of for a brick?" Responses are scored for originality (infrequent responses compared to those generally given); flexibility (variety of categories used); and fluency (the number of responses given regardless of originality or flexibility). In convergent thinking, however, only one response is possible, for instance, answering multiple-choice test items in a scholastic aptitude test.

Thorndike and Hagen (1977, p. 390) emphasize that if creativity tests are to be useful, they must meet three criteria:

1. They must be relatively uncorrelated with the tests of convergent thinking that make up conventional aptitude batteries.

2. They must show some coherence in the sense that different tests of "creativity" should correlate with each other.

3. They must have some significant correlates in the world of practical events.

They conclude that the tests have had only modest success in meeting any of these criteria, and therefore they should be considered research tools rather than instruments of proven utility.

Differential Aptitude Test Battery

The *Differential Aptitude Tests* are popular instruments for use in differential testing. They form a battery of eight tests: *Verbal Reasoning, Numerical Ability, Abstract Reasoning, Clerical Speed and Accuracy, Mechanical Reasoning, Space Relations, Spelling, and Language Usage*. These abilities are defined as follows:

Verbal reasoning: To understand, think, and reason with words.

Numerical ability: To reason with numbers and solve mathematical problems.

Abstract reasoning: To think logically without words or numbers; to see and manipulate mentally the relationships among things, objects, patterns, diagrams, or designs.

Clerical speed and accuracy: To compare and mark simple letter and number symbols quickly and accurately.

Mechanical reasoning: To understand mechanical principles and devices and apply laws of everyday physics—to understand how appliances work and how tools are used.

Space relations: To "think in three dimensions" or mentally picture the shape, size, and position of objects.

Spelling: To recognize correct and incorrect spellings of common English words.

Language usage: To be sensitive to language structure, to recognize correct and incorrect word usage, grammar, and punctuation.

Content overlapping is minimized in the various tests, and the level of difficulty is related to the particular age group. Except for *Clerical Speed and Accuracy*, which is actually a speed test, the tests are essentially power tests. In addition to the norms for each subtest, there are norms for a composite of the *Verbal Reasoning* and *Numerical Ability* scores. The composit score is considered a good indicator of general scholastic aptitude.

Students' patterns of aptitude scores can be integrated with their responses to a career planning questionnaire, yielding a computer-produced career planning report. The appropriateness of their occupational choices might be confirmed or, if not, suggestions made for further exploration.

Profile Chart. Two types of profile charts are available, with a basic design identical for each. Only the orientation varies. For computer printing the profile is horizontal. The hand-plotted profile illustrated in Figure 12.3 is vertical. Through statistical formulas the authors arrived at a convenient method for approximating the significance of the differences between test scores (see "How Big a Difference is Important" in Figure 12.3).

It is important that the individual tests in a battery have high reliability; it is also essential, however, that tests not correlate highly with each other if important differences among the abilities of an individual are to be determined. The *DAT* subtests are highly reliable but interrelated.

Validity. The *Differential Aptitude Tests* are models of carefully prepared test construction and interpretation. Every detail of their development is so well explained in the test manual that by studying these discussions, you can readily develop an understanding of the important considerations of test construction in general. However, despite this commendation, one must be aware that many of the reported validation coefficients are low and differential predictions of performance must be made carefully.

PROBLEM

9. Study Jane's *DAT* profile as displayed in Figure 12.3. Is she a potential college student? What additional major features might a counselor point out to Jane and her parents?

Use of Aptitude Tests in Schools

Scholastic Aptitude Tests

The commonly used tests of scholastic aptitude differ greatly. Choosing the right test for a given purpose requires careful consideration. Test specialists are not in agreement on their utility. Some believe that tests of general mental ability are of limited value. They argue that most of the uses to which they have been put can be better served by using properly constructed achievement tests of more specialized abilities. Nevertheless, it is useful to have an estimate of a student's academic potential and the scholastic aptitude test is helpful for this purpose.

Aptitude tests can be used for instructional, guidance, and administrative purposes (Mehrens and Lehmann, 1978). Test scores should help a teacher make better decisions about what level and kinds of class materials would best suit the aptitude level of the group. Aptitude has a bearing on instructional strategies; brighter students can assume more personal responsibility for learning, for example. Knowledge of a student's ability is helpful to a teacher in understanding behavior. A bright child may be bored; a slow learner may be frustrated. In the evaluation of learning, aptitude scores provide a base for determining progress.

Guidance personnel are concerned with helping students better understand themselves and therefore improve their decision-making processes. Students should certainly have positive self-concepts, but they should also be able to make realistic evaluations of themselves. Along with other information, aptitude test scores can be useful in this respect.

There are many decisions that administrators must make, such as early admission to school, assignment of students to special groups, and a host of public

DIFFERENTIAL APTITUDE TESTS

G. K. Bennett, H. G. Seashore, and A. G. Wesman

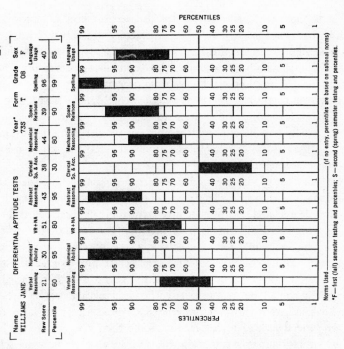

PROFILING YOUR DAT SCORES

The numbers that tell how you did on each test are in the row marked "Percentile." Your percentile tells where you rank on a test in comparison with boys or girls in your grade in numerous schools across the country. If your percentile is 50, you are just in the middle — that is, one-half of the students in the national group did better than you and one-half did less well.

If your percentile on one test is 80, you are at the top of 80 percent of the group — only 20 percent made higher scores than yours. If you scored in the 25th percentile, this means about 75 percent of the group did better than you on the test. These percentiles indicate your relative standing among students of your sex and grade. They do NOT tell you how many questions (or what percent of them) you answered correctly.

Using the information printed in the "Percentile" row, you can now draw your aptitude profile on the chart provided. There are nine columns to be marked; in each of these make a *heavy short line* across the column at the level corresponding to your percentile on that test. (In some cases, the line you draw will coincide with a dotted or solid line already printed on the chart.) Then blacken each column for a distance of one-half inch above and one-half inch below the short line you have drawn, so that you end up with a solid black bar in each column. (For extremely high or low percentiles, you will not be able to blacken one-half inch in both directions without running off the chart.)

HOW BIG A DIFFERENCE IS IMPORTANT?

Since tests cannot be perfectly accurate, you should not overestimate the importance of small differences between two percentiles in comparing your aptitudes. The bars on your profile help by indicating the more important differences.

Look at the bars for any *two* tests and notice whether or not the ends of the bars overlap. If they do not, chances are that you really are better in the kind of ability represented by the bar that is *higher* on the profile chart. If the bars overlap, but not by more than half their length, consider whether other things you know about yourself agree with this indication; the difference may or may not be important. If they overlap by more than half their length, the difference may be disregarded; so small a difference is probably not meaningful. This method of looking at the overlap of bars works for any two abilities you want to compare, whether they are listed next to each other or several columns apart on the chart.

FIGURE 12.3. Sample Profile from the Differential Aptitude Tests

Reproduced by permission. Copyright © 1973 by the Psychological Corporation, New York, N.Y. All rights reserved.

relations problems. Obviously, their knowledge of the children's scholastic ability is a base from which they can move to more satisfactory decision making.

In all of these suggested uses, great care must be exercised that scores are not used rigidly or without additional information. Aptitude test scores provide one more tool to help the educator improve the learning process.

Group, rather than individual, tests of verbal mental ability have the greater utility and can provide helpful information in any school testing program. Because of their economy and practicality, they do not require a trained examiner; yet they generally tend to be as reliable as individual tests. For school use their degree of validity is satisfactory.

It must be emphasized, however, that students do not always perform as well as they might, and this invalidates the scores. If the scores seem to deviate widely from other data available, a teacher may want some children retested on an individual basis with an instrument such as the *Stanford-Binet* or the *WISC-R*. In administering the individual test, the examiner can observe the student and better evaluate the validity of the test. If personnel trained for administering individual tests are unavailable, another form of the group test already used or a different group test should be administered. The nonlanguage test is a helpful supplementary instrument for discovering students whose scores are affected by poor reading or general lack of verbal facility. Some tests give a language and a nonlanguage IQ in addition to a composite IQ, and are popular in some schools. However, in interpreting these scores, one must realize that differences may be due to measurement error.

Special Aptitude Tests for Children

A recurring criticism of scholastic aptitude tests is that they do not provide enough helpful information to the teacher for instructional purposes. Some believe that there does not seem to be a significant relationship to student performance in certain situations in which a significant relationship might be expected (Weiner, 1976, p. 16). Also, the usefulness of the typical scholastic aptitude test for inner-city schools is often questioned because of possible test bias. In fact, they have been discontinued in certain parts of the country.

Let's Look at Children.   In some large cities commonly-used aptitude tests have been discontinued and other programs have been initiated. One of these is entitled *Let's Look at Children,* which uses common sets of material for both instruction and assessment. In this program, children are taught and given an opportunity to practice those tasks on which they are to be later evaluated, thus increasing the opportunity for equality of exposure. The primary objective of the project is to help teachers better understand and assess the intellectual development of each entering school child so that they can teach more effectively.

In order to accomplish this goal, three steps were taken. First, a guide for teachers, entitled *Let's Look at First Graders,* was written. It illustrates logical concrete behavior in six different areas: *basic language skills, concepts of space and time, beginning logical concepts, beginning mathematical concepts,* the *growth of reasoning skills,* and *general signs of development.* The second step was the development of tasks for eliciting intellectual behavior. The tasks not only allow children to demonstrate their understanding and the teacher to observe it, but they also have instructional value. They are game-like situations for the child to discover new concepts and develop new skills in thinking. The final step is the development of a series of written exercises designed to determine the child's understanding and developed ability in the areas of *shapes and forms, spatial relations, time concepts, mathematics, communication skills,* and *logical reasoning.* They provide practice for the child before any record is made of the measurement.

The unique aspect of the entire program is the attempt to make instructional materials and "test" materials one and the same thing. This is quite unlike other readiness tests or scholastic aptitude tests. Furthermore, the developmental progress of the child is presented only through qualitative descriptions rather than norms.

Circus. In response to the desire of educators to diagnose the instructional needs of children in the preprimary and primary grades, *CIRCUS* was developed. It is designed to determine each child's level of maturation and provides suggestions for capitalizing on this information. *CIRCUS* tries to inform teachers about a child's strengths and weaknesses, avoiding global descriptions such as those typical of "readiness" and "mental ability" tests.

Four levels are available covering the period from nursery school through the beginning of third grade:

Levels	Grade Levels
A	Nursery school to beginning kindergarten
B	End of kindergarten to first grade
C	End of first grade to beginning of second grade
D	Beginning of second grade to beginning of third grade

The various levels of *CIRCUS* measure both achievement and interests. There are seventeen tests at *Level A* divided into seven areas: language and reading, perception, mathematics, information processing and experience, divergent production, and attitudes and interests. *Level B* has fourteen tests in the above areas. Both *Levels C* and *D* include measures of reading, writing skills, mathematics, and listening, as well as problem solving, productive language, phonics, and school interests and preferences. The results of a student's performance on each test are reported as raw scores, percentile norms, and unique sentence reports. All levels are criterion- as well as norm-referenced.

The instruments can be administered individually or to small groups, and are intended to be effective with children for a wide variety of backgrounds. Furthermore, the series is integrated with *STEP III* (see page 299), thereby providing continuous achievement measures from kindergarten through twelfth grade.

Grouping

We have suggested that test scores may be administratively helpful in class grouping and occasionally for problems of promotion. Furthermore, it should be emphasized that no group determined by one criterion is homogeneous. A typical scholastic ability test contains both verbal and quantitative problems. Students making the same total score may vary considerably in their abilities. Students with identical scores also may have quite different motivations and interests. As one psychologist concluded, "The only way it is possible to have a homogeneous group is to have one student—and that student even continues to change." Grouping alone is not the answer to effective learning.

Teachers must plan in terms of materials and method to meet the needs and potential of each group. Furthermore, they must make special provisions for the unusual child within a group, whether this individual is very bright or very dull or has problems of an affective nature. Most schools are unable to organize special classes for these individuals.

It is perhaps easier to group for academic achievement in high school than in the elementary school. In the latter, many subjects are taught in one class. In high school, subjects are typically separated and an achievement test can be used along with an aptitude test for grouping. A word of caution is in order, however. The courts have not looked too kindly on the manner in which many schools select students in tracking procedures (see page 338).

Differential Testing

At the secondary school level, differential aptitude testing may provide some information for educational as well as vocational counseling; yet testing alone should not be used as the only criterion for determining the aptitude of boys and girls. The alert teacher is aware of their interests, their performance in and out of the classroom, the kinds of questions they ask, and so forth. Complete evaluation is necessary for valid interpretation.

An increasing number of secondary schools are realizing the importance of obtaining information about other student aptitudes. With the advent of differential testing, such instruments as the *Differential Aptitude Tests* have provided a means to identify the aptitude patterns in areas other than those most generally measured by the typical scholastic aptitude test. This added information provides many more data for the school to help all students plan their studies.

To be specific, a few special problems more readily identified by differential testing are listed below:

1. A boy may be failing verbally oriented courses, but has excellent mechanical ability.
2. A girl from a bilingual home with few cultural opportunities makes high scores on the *Numerical Ability, Mechanical Reasoning,* and *Space Relations* tests but is failing in school.

3. A boy's tested abilities are mostly below average but he does well in the *Clerical Speed and Accuracy* test.

4. A girl aspires to be a physicist, but her *Numerical Ability* score is low.

The school must have adequate information about its superior students if it is to help them achieve. Gifted students are too often overlooked or are unmotivated to continue their education. School authorities should identify such students and exercise every effort to appreciate and develop their talents.

It is also important to accurately identify the aptitude patterns of those who appear less able. The common practice is to direct them into vocational courses without regard for any other criterion except that they are doing poorly in their academic classes. Yet the chances of students' succeeding in a commercial course are not good if their scores on the *Clerical Speed and Accuracy* test are valid and low. In addition, those less mechanically inclined are not served best in a shop course. It is necessary to assign courses that correspond with the interests and abilities of all students.

Overachievement and Underachievement

Teachers want to know if their students are achieving as much as they should. In the past, teachers have attempted to label students as underachievers when they haven't measured up to the average achievement of all students. Using the average as the standard is grossly unfair to slow students who, though they try hard, do not reach the average level of achievement. Similarly, bright but lazy students are not seen as the underachievers they are because they can still achieve above average.

For these reasons, educators most often define underachievement and over-achievement as the discrepancy between the students' achivement level and the achievement predicted for those of their academic ability. Underachievers are so labeled because their achievements, in comparison with others of like academic ability, do not measure up to expectations. Overachievers are not achieving more than is possible, but more than is expected, based on the past achievement of students with similar academic ability.

The causes and characteristics of underachievement are suggested by a wealth of labels such as "free-floating" anxiety, negative self-value, hostility toward authority, high dependence-independence conflict, and negative interpersonal relations. However, there are many technical, measurement-related reasons why a student's actual and expected achievement may differ.

First, the tests of academic ability used to predict achievement only measure a narrow range of abilities, frequently verbal and mathematical ability. Achievement depends on other abilities. Students labeled as overachievers or as under-achievers may actually be achieving as they should, given their status on the specialized abilities most related to the achievement being considered.

Second, the difference between actual and expected achievement may be due solely to errors of measurement. As indicated on pages 295–296, the reliability of difference scores is notoriously unreliable. A student labeled an overachiever based on scores from one form of the tests could be labeled an underachiever had a different form of the tests been administered.

Third, if the scores on the achievement and academic ability tests were not referenced to the same norm group, the differences in performance on the achievement and academic ability measures could be bogus. This is due entirely to the noncomparability of the publishers' standardization groups. Fortunately, some test companies publish achievement test batteries and academic ability tests that are normed on the same population, as in the case of the *Metropolitan Achievement Tests* and the *Otis-Lennon School Ability Test* (see page 316). Such companies often provide test score reports that indicate expected achievement levels for each student based on his or her academic ability score.

Fourth, students scoring very high on academic ability tests are more likely to be labeled underachievers than overachievers. This is because students who are tops on one measure, relative to a given group, have no place to go but down on the other measures. Similarly, low ability students are most often labeled overachievers, for chances are that students who score toward the bottom on the ability measure will not perform quite so poorly on the achievement measure. Students who score very high or very low on one measure are not expected to score that extremely on a second measure, even if they were working up to capacity. Unless statistical prediction formulas called *regression equations* are used, differences between achievement and academic ability measures can be due to these bogus effects called regression effects.

For the reasons given above, many test experts suggest that the concepts of overachievement and underachievement be stricken from the teacher's vocabulary. At the least, the teacher must be very careful not to assume too quickly that any discrepancy between a student's achievement and academic ability levels is due merely to laziness or exceptional hard work. (For additional study of some of the problems encountered in determining whether students are working up to their potentials, see Spache, 1976; for a more technical discussion, read Thorndike, 1963.)

PROBLEM

10. In advising students about curriculum choices, what relative weights would you assign to aptitude scores as compared with final grades? Why?

Legal Issues in the Use of Aptitude Tests

There have been a number of court cases in recent years challenging the grouping of students for instructional purposes. In some instances, mental ability tests were used heavily to place students in a tracking system in which, for example, the school was organized into honor, average, and low groups. In one known instance, certain students were assigned to educable mentally retarded classes. Subsequently, the parents and guardians of some children argued that placement decisions based on mental ability scores were unfair to many children since a higher proportion of certain racial groups and lower socioeconomic students were classified as having low learning potentials.

Grouping Students.   In *Hobson v. Hansen* (1967) the major issue was the heavy use of mental ability tests to place students in a tracking system in which, for example, the school was organized into honor, college preparatory, general, and basic groups. The basic track was designed for students who were variously described as "slow learners," "retarded," "academically retarded," or "retarded slow learners." The educational program of this track was designed to provide a useful education for students who could not successfully compete in the normal curriculum because of their limited abilities. This track also provided remedial instruction in the basic subjects, particularly reading and arithmetic, for students who might eventually be upgraded to the general curriculum.

The plaintiffs argued that a disproportionate number of blacks were placed in this lower group, indicating racial discrimination. Furthermore, they argued that the assignment tended to be both permanent and complete as far as classroom contacts were concerned. They also maintained that the achievement and scholastic aptitude tests used were inappropriate for making predictions about the academic potential of these children. They maintained that, because of the disadvantaged students' impoverished circumstances, it was not possible to determine whether test scores reflect lack of ability or lack of opportunity.

The court found substantial evidence that adequate techniques and facilities for determining innate learning abilities of the majority of children in this district were not available. Also, since this was true, the placement and retention of children in the lower tracks, based on the premise that they could perform no better given the opportunity to do so, could not be justified.

In discussing the defendants' position, the court frowned on claims that selection procedures provided for flexibility so that students would be reclassified as their development permitted. Evidence presented indicated that 90 percent of the students tended to be rigidly classified. Furthermore, most testing programs had three-year periods between test administrations, thereby allowing only infrequent opportunities for reclassification of the students. Also, they were discouraged from seeking admission to higher levels of instruction because it was believed that they could not be successful at those levels.

In the testimony presented on behalf of the children, aptitude tests were described as being highly verbal and as penalizing low socioeconomic groups because these children had limited exposure to standard English. Noise levels of their environment were high, making it difficult for them to discriminate among various sounds. Also, there was less exposure to books and other serious reading material.

Furthermore, stress was placed on the emotional and psychological factors that precluded good test performance. Often there was a lack of motivation prompted by low self esteem; the students could not perceive that performing well on these tests made any difference in their lives. At other times worry or fear could increase anxiety past an optimum point of effective performance.

Tracking itself was not rejected by the court. However, when there was a disproportionate number of minorities in the lower track, the court stipulated that there had to be a justification for the classification pattern. Justification, it concluded, is also necessary when a disproportion of whites populate the upper track.

Assigning Students to Special Classes.   In *Larry P. v. Riles*, the plaintiffs asked the court to issue a preliminary injunction restraining the San Francisco Unified School District from administering IQ tests for purposes of determining whether to place black students in classes for the educable mentally retarded (EMR). The plaintiffs were San Francisco black elementary school children who had been placed in educable mentally retarded classes because they had IQs of 75 or less on mental ability tests. The plaintiffs argued that they were not mentally retarded. They held that their 14th Amendment rights were violated by this action because the tests were biased against the culture and experience of black children as a class.

The injunction was granted, and in its final decision the court stated that "IQ tests discriminate against black children and those who used them should have known better" (*Larry P. v. Riles*, 1979). The court also noted that intelligence tests "are racially and culturally biased, have a discriminatory impact on black children, and have not been validated for the purpose of [consigning] black children into educationally dead-end, isolated and stigmatizing classes." In short, the court held that placing black children in special classes with the use of IQ tests violated the 14th Amendment guarantee of equal protection, and it ordered the California schools to reevaluate all black children in EMR classes by other measures.

The State of California defended the use of mental ability tests in labeling large numbers of black children as retarded by raising the "poverty" argument— that these tests discriminate against all those who live in a culture of poverty. Furthermore, they maintained that poverty causes a high incidence of disease and malnutrition—that is, brain damaging factors. The court found that the most reliable scientific studies did not support the "damaged brain" theory.

Since this theory was rejected and because the genetic inferiority theory was ruled out, the court turned to the possibility of cultural bias in the tests. The court traced test bias to the origins of the testing movement in this country. Its opinion states that "we must recognize at the outset that the history of the IQ test, and of special education classes built on IQ testing, is not the history of neutral scientific discoveries translated into educational reform. It is, at least in the early years, a history of racial prejudice, of Social Darwinism, and of the use of the scientific 'mystique' to legitimate such prejudices." The court concluded that current mental ability tests are no different even though they have been updated.

Evaluating.   The *Hobson v. Hansen* court decision has been questioned by knowledgeable educators since the decision was based on the premise that the aptitude tests are designed to measure "innate ability." To this Goodman (1972, pp. 434–435) responds:

Few educators are so naive as to suppose that an IQ or scholastic aptitude test reveals a child's inborn potential. Most realize that the attribute measured by such tests is the joint product of endowment and experience, that the verbal and conceptual skills demanded are acquired skills, and that children of minority and lower-class background are at a disadvantage in obtaining them. But it by no means follows that such tests are an arbitrary or inappropriate basis upon which to classify students for purposes of educational groupings. Whatever may have been true in the District of Columbia, the declared purpose of homogeneous grouping in most school systems is not to pigeonhole the student on the basis of genetic potential, but to provide him an education better adapted to his present level of proficiency and better designed to meet his immediate learning problems than the standard fare he would receive in a heterogeneous classroom. So long as the aptitude or intelligence test accurately identifies those students who are not likely to do well in a heterogeneous classroom (and therefore stand to gain from a more specialized treatment), it accomplishes that purpose.

Psychologists and educators differ on the effect of the *Larry P. v. Riles* decision. There are those who believe that black children will be hurt the most because of it. Others feel that it will help to spur educational and testing psychologists to change. They believe it will lead to positive results and educational reform.

It is mandatory that users of tests understand their limitations and strengths in order to prevent serious injustices by misclassification. It is possible to obtain a test score and, along with other supporting data, to provide a valid estimate of a child's present optimal instructional level. However, we may still do that child an injustice if our main concern in the special group is only to adjust a program to that child's present capabilities. Our goal must be to change those children's capabilities so that they will have the opportunity for reclassification and a higher level of educational experiences. There is a difference. In the first instance we are concerned only with making the child successful at his or her present performance level. In the second instance our goal is to change and develop that ability.

Scholastic Aptitude Tests for College Admission

Test scores are among the various criteria used by colleges for the selection of members of their freshman classes. To provide these scores, several independent testing agencies develop tests, arrange for their administration, score the answer sheets, and report information to the students and the colleges to which they seek admission.

CEEB Scholastic Aptitude Test

The College Entrance Examination Board *Scholastic Aptitude Test* (*SAT*) is probably the oldest test still in use for this purpose. New forms are constructed for each administration. Generally, students take these tests during their senior year in high school. However, because there is need to have test scores before the last high-school year, the *Preliminary Scholastic Aptitude Test* is made available to juniors in secondary schools. This test also serves as the qualifying test for the National Merit Scholarship Program.

The *Scholastic Aptitude Test* has three parts, the *Verbal, Mathematical* (these are both seventy-five minutes in length), and a thirty-minute multiple-choice section to measure mastery of English grammar and sentence structure. The last test is called the *Test of Standard Written English* (*TSWE*) and is the newest of the three. It is designed to place individuals in appropriate English composition courses and to identify those who would benefit from remedial courses.

Candidates who have read widely, and who have well-developed vocabularies and skills, have a definite advantage in the verbal section. Performance on this test depends on developed skills rather than knowledge of specific information. The quantitative part of the test measures the ability to deal with concepts rather than mathematical achievement. Although a knowledge of basic mathematics is necessary, emphasis is on the student's application of basic knowledge in the solution of problems. The ceiling of this test is high enough to discriminate among able students, even though their training in formal mathematics may be limited.

American College Testing Program

Another program for testing college-bound students is the *American College Testing Program* (*ACT*). It is a battery of tests of educational development, having one test in each of four major fields: English, mathematics, social studies, and natural sciences.

Unlike *SAT* items, which tend to be more homogeneous and focus on abstract reasoning, the *ACT* requires students to perform tasks similar to those they will face in college. These tend to require complex reasoning in concrete situations in the social studies and the natural sciences. Other responses demand mathematical reasoning and the interpretation of literary passages.

Preparation for the Tests

Teachers wonder if they can prepare students for these tests by tutoring them. The effect of coaching for the College Entrance Examination Board's *Scholastic Aptitude Test* has been studied extensively. Results show that special short-term coaching does not increase test scores substantially in the case of the verbal test, with the possible exception of slight gains for "underachievers" (Fields, 1979). Test-taking skills may be improved but this does not affect scores significantly. In the case of the mathematical test, however, a review of basic mathematics through elementary algebra and geometry is helpful to individuals who have not had courses in mathematics in the recent past.

These findings are not unexpected. Scholastic aptitude tests require both innate ability and achievement. To demonstrate this fact, solve the problem below:

If 5 postcards cost y cents, how many cents will 15 postcards cost? (A) 3y
(B) 15y   (C) 5y   (D) 75y   (E) 16y.

The answer is $3y$. However, the purpose of the problem is not to determine whether students can multiply 3 by y, which is one computation that might be used in determining the answer, but to determine if they know how to attack the solution of the problem—finding the cost of one postcard and then 15. Nevertheless, it is obvious that if they cannot divide 15 by 5 correctly and then state the product of 3 and y, the answer will be wrong. Therefore, achievement in mathematics is basic to success in this test item. It follows that scores will tend to rise somewhat when students prepare for tests like the *SAT* by using well-developed materials embedded in the school curriculum (Slack and Porter, 1980, p. 164). Such preparation is more effective if it covers an appropriate period of time.

The following analogy is similar to those found in the *Verbal* section of the *SAT:*

Trigger: Bullet::	(A) handle: drawer	(B) holster: gun
	(C) bulb: light	(D) switch: current
	(E) pulley: rope	

The purpose of the item is to determine the examinees' ability to see the relationship among these words rather than to measure understanding of each. However, the examinee has to know the meanings of trigger, bullet, switch, and current to select response D as the correct answer.

Teachers can do nothing to increase the innate intellectual capacity of their students, but can do much to improve their effective intelligence. Verbal and mathematical facility are based on good intellectual ability, but poor achievement in language and mathematics precludes the use of this ability. If it were possible to select two students of equal capacity, the one who had read more widely, had a broader vocabulary, and had developed more critical skills in reading and thinking than the other would be at an advantage in taking the various scholastic aptitude tests. Students pay a penalty for a meager educational environment, since with their deficiencies they may not do so well in further school work, and are rightfully steered to other paths.

The "Truth-in-Testing" Movement

Through the years, organizations that develop college admission tests such as the *SAT* have distributed sample test forms, background information on preparing for the test, and information on the manner in which the test will be scored and used. In spite of this, concern has been expressed that the public does not have direct knowledge of the content of the items included in these tests, and that the corrected answer sheets are not returned to those to whom the tests are administered. This feeling has led to a "truth-in-testing" movement designed to force disclosure of test content and scored answer sheets. In turn, the issue has caught the attention of state legislatures and the U.S. Congress. One state, for example, has enacted rather sweeping disclosure standards for college admissions tests. These require, in effect, that the tests be released to the public after they are administered (Smith, 1979).

Reasonable as it is to argue that, in general, anyone who takes a test should be provided as much information as possible about the outcome, the release of college admissions tests creates a number of practical problems regarding the quality of the tests. Building test items for them is time consuming and expensive; and, over time, test quality will drop if items cannot be reused when review of them justifies this decision. Using test items more than once helps maintain high levels of reliability and validity and makes it possible to equate scores over several years and across different parts of the country. In short, responding to public concern while at the same time developing sound measuring instruments is difficult.

Decline in College Scholastic Test Scores

Reports about the lowering trend of *ACT* and *SAT* test scores have been widely publicized. The decline has been about two to three percent of a standard deviation per year in the late 1960s and in most of the 1970s for both the *ACT* and *SAT*. Studies on the *ACT* indicate that social studies scores have declined most, with little change in the natural sciences. English and mathematics scores have become somewhat lower. While the percentage of *ACT* high-scoring examinees has remained the same over the last five years, the percentage of low-scoring ones has increased. Scores of women have declined more than those of men, with more women being tested. Munday (1976) gives two possible explanations for the declining ACT scores. First, a more heterogeneous group is taking the test, and second, they tend not to be as well prepared academically.

The College Entrance Examination Board has made a serious attempt to identify the reasons for the *SAT* test score decline (Wirtz, 1977). Four general causes were investigated:

1. The psychometric qualities of the test.
2. The nature of the population administered the test.
3. The changes taking place in secondary education.
4. The factors bearing generally on the conditions of society.

The first cause proved to be unimportant; the others did not. In the case of the second, between two-thirds and three-fourths of the decline between 1963 and 1970 was attributed to changes in the composition of the population tested. During this period increased numbers of college-bound youths from low-income families were tested, and they scored lower on the tests. On the other hand, only about 20 to 30 percent of test score declines beyond 1970 appeared to be attributable to changes in the composition of the group tested.

Other factors blamed for the decline were diminished emphasis on the mastery of verbal and mathematical skills in precollege schooling; increased television viewing; less competition in entering higher education; and various social problems, such as broken homes and national disillusionment and unrest among youth. In other words, there is no single reason for the *SAT* score decline, and the evidence regarding those cited is largely circumstantial.

SUMMARY

In this chapter, a number of significant points have been developed:

1. Scholastic aptitude tests are often verbal and mathematical in nature and closely related to school work. They measure not only aspects of innate ability, but also the effects of learning.

2. Measuring aptitude can be useful in planning programs to help children attain their growth potential. However, care must be exercised in predicting achievement from aptitude test scores because many factors determine achievement.

3. Individual mental ability tests provide a wealth of information about the student but are only occasionally used in schools because of administration and cost considerations.

4. Aptitude tests may be classified as verbal, performance, or nonlanguage tests. To perform successfully on verbal tests, the subject must understand oral and often written language. Performance tests are individual tests and emphasize the manipulation of objects rather than verbal skill. Nonlanguage tests are constructed as paper-and-pencil tests and, unlike performance tests, are designed for group administration. Although some oral instructions in the administration of a nonlanguage test may be required, in general no written or spoken language is necessary to obtain correct responses.

5. For all practical purposes, the ratio IQ has been replaced by the deviation IQ for translating scores of children's mental ages.

6. A rough classification of a child's IQ generally holds throughout life; that is, dull, normal, or bright children tend to become dull, normal, or bright adults.

7. Differential aptitude tests are helpful for measuring specific aptitudes such as mechanical, spatial, and clerical abilities. A series of such tests are standardized on the same population so that meaningful profiles can be constructed to interpret a student's strengths and weaknesses.

8. The courts have generally opposed the use of aptitude tests for grouping students.

9. Culture-fair tests have been constructed to reduce the influence of the examinee's environment when measuring aptitude. Because of environmental factors we must look for different meanings in many of the aptitude scores of disadvantaged children. Great care must be exercised to avoid test bias due to improper use of tests and faulty interpretation of scores.

10. Dissatisfaction with the conventional scholastic aptitude tests used with young children has led to the termination of such use in some regions of the country. This, in turn, has led to the development of alternative instruments that provide helpful instructional information.

11. Evidence has been found that the decline in scholastic aptitude scores for college-bound youth in the 1960s and 1970s is associated with the heterogeneity of the population tested, a declining emphasis on the mastery of verbal and mathematical skills in the classroom, and certain social conditions. It is not associated with the psychometric qualities of the tests used.

SUGGESTED READINGS

ANASTASI, A. *Common fallacies about heredity, environment, and human behavior.* (ACT Research Report No. 58). Iowa City, Iowa: The American College Testing Program, 1973.
A discussion of the controversy of the environment-heredity issue and the place of test scores for developing human potential.

ANASTASI, A. *Psychological Testing* (4th ed.). New York: Macmillan, 1976.
Chapter 12 includes an excellent discussion of the important psychological issues of intelligence testing.

BERSOFF, D. N. Silk purses into sows' ears: The decline of psychological testing and a suggestion for its redemption. *American Psychologist*, 1973, 28, 892–899.
After reviewing some of the problems associated with psychological tests, the author suggests remedies, emphasizing naturalistic observation of behavior.

BLOCK, N. J., & DWORKIN, G. (Eds.). *The IQ controversy: Critical readings.* New York: Pantheon Books, 1976.
The volume is divided into four parts: a historical review, genetic issues, social and educational topics, and a summary.

EDUCATIONAL TESTING SERVICE. *Test use and validity.* Princeton, N.J.: Author, 1980.
This is a response to the Needes/Nairn Report on ETS. (Nairn, A., and Associates. The reign of ETS: The corporation that makes up minds. *Washington, D.C., 1980) Interesting concepts concerning validity are explored, particularly as they relate to the* Scholastic Aptitude Test.

FLAUGHER, R. I. The many definitions of test bias. *American Psychologist*, 1978, 33, 671–679.
The many ways that test bias can be defined are described, with emphasis on those associated with test content and the interpretation of test results.

JAEGER, R. M. (Ed.). On bias in selection. *Journal of Educational Measurement*, 1976, 13, 1–99.
A thorough discussion of test bias in selection for admission to educational programs and for employment.

SATTLER, J. M. *Assessment of children's intelligence.* Philadelphia: W. B. Saunders, 1974.
An excellent source of all phases of individual intelligence testing.

SPACHE, G. D. *Investigating the issues of reading disabilities.* Boston: Allyn and Bacon, 1976.
In chapter 6, the author discusses the problems in using "intelligence tests" for estimating student potential; he does not advise eliminating their use.

THORNDIKE, R. L. Mr. Binet's test 70 years later. *Educational Researcher*, 1975, 4, 3–6.
The author provides a discussion of the historical development of the various revisions of this classic instrument, with some hypotheses as to why there has been a rise in IQ level.

WILSON, B. J., & SCHMITS, D. W. What's new in ability grouping? *Phi Delta Kappan*, 1978, 59, 535–536.
Research has not supported the idea that homogeneous grouping improves achievement.

REFERENCES CITED

ANASTASI, A. *Common fallacies about heredity, environment, and human behavior.* Iowa City, Iowa: The American College Testing Program, 1973.

CLEARY, T. A., HUMPHREYS, L. G., KENDRICK, S. A., & WESMAN, A. Educational uses of tests with disadvantaged students. *American Psychologist*, 1975, *30*, 15–41.

CRONBACH, L. J. *Essentials of psychological testing* (3rd ed.). New York: Harper & Row, 1970.

CRONBACH, L. J. The BITCH test (Black Intelligence Test of Cultural Homogeneity). In O. K. Buros (Ed.). *The eighth mental measurements yearbook*. Lincoln, Nebr.: University of Nebraska Press, 1978.

DE AVILA, E. A., & PULOS, S. Developmental assessment by pictorially presented Piagetian material: The cartoon conservation scale. In *Proceedings of the Conference on Piagetian Theory and the Helping Professions*. Los Angeles: University of Southern California, 1978.

FIELDS, C. M. "Coaching" courses may help some students increase SAT scores, study concludes. *The Chronicle of Higher Education*, 1979, *18* (15), 3–4.

FLAUGHER, R. L. The many definitions of test bias. *American Psychologist*, 1978, *33*, 671–679.

GARBER, H., & HEBER, R. The efficacy of early intervention with family rehabilitation. In *Proceedings of the Conference on Prevention of Retarded Development in Psychosocially Disadvantaged Children*. Madison, Wis.: Center on Mental Retardation and Human Development, University of Wisconsin, 1978.

GERRY, M. H. Cultural myopia: The need for a corrective lens. *Journal of School Psychology*, 1973, *11*, 307–315.

GLASER, R., & NITKO, A. J. Measurement in learning and instruction. In R. L. Thorndike (Ed.), *Educational measurement* (2nd ed.). Washington, D.C.: American Council on Education, 1971.

GOODMAN, F. I. Defacto school segregation: A constitutional and empirical analysis. *California Law Review*, 1972, *60*, 275–437.

GUILFORD, J. P. Three faces of intellect. *American Psychologist*, 1959, *14*, 409–479.

HARRIS, A. J., & SIPAY, E. R. *How to increase reading ability* (6th ed.). New York: David McKay, 1975.

HEARNSHAW, L. S. *Cyril Burt, psychologist*. Ithaca, N.Y.: Cornell University Press, 1979.

HOBSON v. HANSEN, 269 F. Supp. 401 (D.D.C. 1967), affirmed sub nom. *Smuck v. Hobson*, 408 F.2d 175 (D.C. Cir. 1969).

HOPKINS, K. D., & BRACHT, G. H. Ten-year stability of verbal and nonverbal IQ scores. *American Educational Research Journal*, 1975, *12*, 469–477.

JAEGER, R. M. (Ed.). On bias in selection. *Journal of Educational Measurement*, 1976, *13*, 1–99.

JENSEN, A. R. *Bias in mental testing*. New York: Free Press, 1980.

JENSEN, A. R. How much can we boost IQ and scholastic achievement? *Harvard Educational Review*, 1969a, *39*, 1–123.

JENSEN, A. R. Reducing the heredity-environment uncertainty: A reply. *Harvard Educational Review*, 1969b, *39*, 449–483.

LARRY P. v. RILES, No. C—71-2270 RFP (N.D. Cal. Oct. 16, 1979).

LAOSA, L. M. Cross-cultural and subcultural research in psychology and education. *Interamerican Journal of Psychology* (Revista Interamericana de Psicologia) 1973, *7*, 241–248.

LAOSA, L. M. Nonbiased assessment of children's abilities: Historical antecedents and current issues. In T. Oakland (Ed.), *Psychological and educational assessment of minority children*. New York: Bruner/Mazel, Publishers, 1977.

LAZAR, I., & DARLINGTON, R. B. *Summary: Lasting effects after preschool.* (Final report on HEW Grant 90C-1311). Urbana, Ill.: ERIC/ECE, University of Illinois, 1978.

MCCALL, R. B., APPELBAUM, M. I., & HOGARTY, P. Developmental changes in mental performance. *Monographs of the Society for Research in Child Development*, 1973, *38.*

MEHRENS, W. A., & LEHMANN, I. J. *Measurement and evaluation in education and psychology* (2nd ed.). New York: Holt, Rinehart and Winston, 1978.

MERCER, J. R., & YSSELDYKE, J. Designing diagnostic-intervention programs. In T. Oakland (Ed.), *Psychological and educational assessment of minority children.* New York: Bruner/Mazel, Publishers, 1977.

MUNDAY, L. A. *Declining admissions test scores: ACT Research Report 71.* Iowa City: American College Testing Program, 1976.

NUTTALL, E. V. Test review of the System of Multi-Pluralistic Assessment (SOMPA). *Journal of Educational Measurement*, 1979, *16*, 285–290.

PINNEAU, S. R. *Changes in intelligence quotient, infancy to maturity.* Boston: Houghton Mifflin, 1961.

SANDAY, P. R. An alternative interpretation of the relationship between heredity, race, environment, and IQ. *Phi Delta Kappan*, 1972, *54*, 250–254.

SHOCKLEY, W. Dysgenics, geneticity, raceology: A challenge to the intellectual responsibility of educators. *Phi Delta Kappan*, 1972, *53*, 297–307.

SLACK, W. V., & PORTER, D. The scholastic aptitude test: A critical appraisal. *Harvard Educational Review*, 1980, *50*, 154–175.

SMITH, R. J. "Truth-in-Testing" attracts diverse support. *Science,* September 14, 1979, *205*, pp. 1110–1111; 1113–1114.

SPACHE, G. D. *Investigating the issues of reading disabilities.* Boston: Allyn and Bacon, 1976.

STROUD, J. B. The intelligence test in school use: Some persistent issues. *Journal of Educational Psychology*, 1957, *48*, 77–85.

TERMAN, L. M., & MERRILL, M. A. *The Stanford-Binet Intelligence Scale: 1972 norms edition.* Boston: Houghton Mifflin, 1973a.

TERMAN, L. M., & MERRILL, M. A. *The Stanford-Binet Intelligence Scale: Manual.* Boston: Houghton Mifflin, 1973b.

THORNDIKE, R. L., & HAGEN, E. P. *Measurement and evaluation in psychology and education* (4th ed.). New York: John Wiley & Sons, 1977.

THORNDIKE, R. L. *The concepts of over- and under-achievement.* New York: Bureau of Publications, Teachers College, Columbia University, 1963.

WEINER, I. B. *Clinical methods in psychology.* New York: John Wiley & Sons, 1976.

WIRTZ, W. *On further examination: Report of the advisory panel on the scholastic aptitude test score decline.* New York: College Entrance Examination Board, 1977.

13

Evaluating Affective Behavior

The discussion in this chapter will make it possible for you to

1. Describe the various methods of measuring affective behavior and list their strengths and weaknesses for specific purposes

2. Delineate some of the problems in obtaining objective data when measuring affective behavior

3. Enumerate criteria for effective observation

4. List positive and negative aspects of anecdotal records

5. Explain how the reliability and validity of rating scales and check lists can be increased

6. Outline the important aspects of interview procedures

7. State your position with respect to the ethical considerations involved in collecting data on affective behavior

8. Differentiate among sociograms, social distance scales, and "guess who" questionnaires in terms of their construction and use

9. Explain how self-reporting instruments measure interest and attitudes, personality traits, and personal-social adjustment

10. Differentiate between the stylistic and thematic types of projective techniques

The Greek myth of Daedalus and his son Icarus tells how Icarus met his death because he could not adjust to a new situation. When Daedalus, who had been held captive, made his escape from prison, he found no other way to flee the heavily guarded island but by air. Rarest of craftsmen, he set to work making great feathered wings for himself and for his son, binding the large feathers with thread, the small with wax. When all was ready for flight, he gravely cautioned the boy Icarus always to fly close to him in a moderate course between sky and sea. He warned his son that if he flew too low the weight of sea spray in the feathers would drag him down, and if too high, the heat of the sun would melt the wax that bound them.

All went well until Icarus, lacking his father's realistic caution and giddy with the joy of flight, soared away into the heavens. The blazing sun melted the wax bonds and, as the wings and feathers fell away, nothing was left to hold the boy in the air but his flailing arms. Suddenly missing his beloved son, Daedalus cried out to him but was answered only by the terrible sight of scattering feathers swirling in the sea beneath. Icarus' behavior seems to defy explanation. What foolhardiness had caused him to behave this way?

People have always been concerned with human behavior; its study offers the ultimate challenge. It was once believed that patterns of adjustment were entirely inherited, and personality traits were passed on to children in the same way as blue eyes and red hair. Even today we hear people say of nonconforming children: "Well, he comes by it honestly"; or, "she's a chip off the old block." They are assuming, however unconsciously, that there is a hereditary basis for atypical behavior.

But as is true of the cognitive and psychomotor domains, proficiency in the affective domain is also predicated on learning. To effectively teach affective concepts and skills, objectives must be formulated and learning experiences provided for children, just as they are in the development of cognitive behaviors. Following the development of a taxonomy for objectives in the cognitive domain, a comparative taxonomy in the affective domain appeared and gained acceptance. It established a hierarchy with five major categories (see pages 40–41). Teachers need to be aware of this hierarchy and the objectives associated with it in order to instruct and evaluate students effectively in this area.

Furthermore, teachers must be aware of the interrelationship of the domains. Interest in a subject often develops when a student becomes knowledgeable in that subject. Skill in coping with the emotions associated with a subject is achieved by understanding the influence of all three domains and their interactions.

Modern psychology has also shown that affective behavior depends on the interplay of many factors—not only on learned patterns of adjustment, but on such elements as the chemical function and physical structure of the body and the general level of intelligence. The small boy may become aggressive to compensate for his size, or he may withdraw from physical contact and compensate through intellectual prowess or fantasy. The dull girl with high standards may resort to atypical actions in an attempt to adjust to an impossible situation, but her reaction is learned, not inherited.

Maladjusted individuals are no longer assumed to be immoral or "suffering for their sins." Neither are they accused of deliberate nonconformist behavior. The clinician accepts individuals and approaches their problems with sympathy, but looks at the situation objectively and tries to determine possible reasons for it. Instead of focusing on symptoms, causes are sought.

Yet some parents and teachers still subject "different" children to sarcasm, and believe that if these children would only "try," they would improve. The shy child is urged to show more spunk; daydreamers are asked to wake up. Too often this approach convinces children that they are right in their poor estimation of themselves; too often, they accept the situation as hopeless. Thus, their behavior may actually be reinforced by exhortations to reform. Admonishing or ridiculing are not effective ways to initiate a positive change in behavior.

The process of adjustment is the attempt of individuals to create a more congruous relationship between themselves and their environment. The process may consist of an effort to change either the environment or their behavior, or to modify both. Teachers should play a very important role in helping the child manage the adjustment. Certainly, they cannot assume that the burden to adjust rests entirely on the individual. Yet, if they are careless of their responsibility, teachers may establish a social climate in which it is impossible for their students to meet even their basic personality needs. A teacher who stipulates equal requirements for all is frustrating many students by denying them any opportunity for success. Equally, when able children are forced to repeat much that they have already experienced and learned, the teacher is denying them the challenge that comes through new experience and that stimulates new learning and growth. Authoritarian taskmasters who expect everyone in their classrooms to conform are stifling not only creativity but also the satisfaction that comes through self-expression.

Evaluation of Affective Behavior

We all know that individuals must adjust to their psychological needs; they eat when they are hungry, they seek warmth if they are cold. But much broader dimensions of adjustment must be taken into account when evaluating affective behavior. We must consider the relationship of students to their social environments, as well as their behavior with respect to their own psychological needs. These environments can support or hinder them as they strive to satisfy vital psychological needs such as the need for achievement, love, and self-esteem.

Responses to psychological needs are typically more significant than responses to those that are physiological. It is highly important that society—particularly its schools—recognize this fact and respond to it. For the educational enterprise this means affording affective objectives their proper place and evaluating student behavior in terms of them.

Numerous instruments for evaluating affective behavior are available to the teacher. Some of these are based on formal observations, some are paper-and-pencil inventories to be administered to a group of students, others are individual instruments designed primarily for use by clinicians. The following outline is indicative of the variety of useful instruments and techniques in this area of evaluation.

Evaluation Methods Based on Observation

Anecdotal records
Rating scales
Check lists
Interviews

Sociometric and Related Techniques

Sociograms
Social-distance scales
"Guess who" questionnaires

Self-Report Inventories

Biographical data banks
Personal inventories
Interest inventories
Attitude scales and questionnaires

Projective Techniques

Inkblot and picture presentations
Presentations of verbal stimuli
Sentence completions

Neither the standardized instruments nor less formal ones for evaluating affective behavior are as reliable or valid as the better achievement and scholastic aptitude tests. As there are extremists who are indefensibly enthusiastic about measurement instruments in the affective domain, there are many prophets of gloom who totally mistrust these instruments and advocate a "hands-off" policy. It seems reasonable to adopt a middle-of-the-road position. The following discussion emphasizes the limitations of various methods and techniques included in the foregoing outline, but goes on to suggest some practical approaches to this area of evaluation.

Evaluation Methods Based on Observation

What teachers can learn from student observation in natural situations is generally useful to them, and is, for many reasons, a valuable addition to the study of affective behavior. First, the results of such observation supplement information gathered elsewhere. A student may do well on a mechancial aptitude test, but be awkward and uninterested in the shop. Another may give the desired answers on an adjustment inventory, but be unable to work cooperatively with peers.

Second, daily student observation provides teachers with information unobtainable in other ways. They have a chance to notice numerous incidents that reveal significant interests and attitudes. This opportunity may not exist in artificial situations. Even if teenagers answer "yes" to the question, "Is it fun to do nice things for other boys and girls?" their behavior may not be indicative of personal adjustment within the peer group. The teacher may observe that these teenagers are really self-centered.

Third, observation affords an opportunity to sample a student's actual behavior. Under informal observation, students are not asked to conform to what they might feel in an artificial situation, as in answering a questionnaire, and are not required to report on their own behavior. Direct observation will, therefore, be more valid in certain instances.

Finally, the results of such observation benefit the observer. It is important that teachers develop proper relationships with their students. When they observe students objectively, bias can be lessened and understandings deepened. Too often teachers judge students in terms of their own feelings and prejudices and therefore find it impossible to help them. It should be said, however, that the teacher may need help in developing the skill of accurate reporting. A serious limitation of observation may lie within the observers themselves, for what people see or hear depends in part on what they are predisposed to see or hear.

Teacher Observations

What should the teacher observe in the behavior of children in the classroom? Do the students volunteer or offer to share experiences, or do they withdraw and fail to participate? What kind of questions do they ask? Does the nature of their questioning indicate that they have a genuine interest in learning, or are they more interested in their grades? What do they like to talk about? Do they ever mention their interests, problems, or families? How does the group react to contributions by individual members? The teacher will find that the group will support certain individuals, contradict some, and ignore others.

The teacher should also observe the interactions within a group. Which students are aggressive, withdrawn, or hostile? Which students lead and which follow? Does group behavior within the freedom of the playground differ from that in the classroom? The student who appears listless and uninterested in the classroom may come alive in a ball game. Are some students more aggressive when freed from the teacher's control? Do they exhibit leadership characteristics in the rough-and-tumble of sports while they are withdrawn in the classroom?

Finally, a great deal is revealed about students' affective development through observation of their creative activities. These activities enable students to translate feelings into action. Do they prefer working with abstract symbols or concrete objects? Do they enjoy participating in dramatics and role playing? Are they overly anxious when they appear before others? What emotions do they tend to express in their drawings and paintings?

Danger of Bias.   Bias in observation is common. Take, for example, the commonly accepted fallacy that the "only child" is spoiled. Teachers often interpret negative behavior in students without siblings as a direct result of having their own way at home. This may or may not be the cause underlying the behavior. Simply knowing that a student is an "only child," without further examining the student's actual relationship with his or her parents, is not grounds for assuming that the "onlyness" will result in a social handicap.

Bias may also result when observers do not admit their own feelings and weaknesses to themselves. If they fail to do so, they may attribute their inadequacies to others, and certain student behaviors will be interpreted accordingly. This same projective type of reporting may also be reflected in a "Pollyanna" attitude toward all students. While it is commendable to look for strengths in children, total behavior must be evaluated objectively, and that is not easy. Many people well-versed in factual knowledge of human behavior have never learned to apply this information to themselves or to others. As an astute observer you must be able to analyze your feelings toward others as they relate to your own behavior, and attempt to discover causes through an objective approach. Why do you dislike certain students and champion others? What makes you unhappy with the behavior of some students? Observation alone cannot yield valid answers. Lack of objectivity makes it impossible to report behavior truthfully.

Objectivity in reporting may be improved by separating description from judgment. "Johnny is undependable," and "Mary will assume no responsibility" are judgments that do not specify what happened and how Johnny handled it, nor do they specify what responsibilities Mary failed to assume. As they stand, there is no way to check their validity; possibly they express only the teacher's dislike for a child. The following illustrates a more useful description of behavior.

I said, "Eddie, you haven't done the work assigned you this period. Don't you understand it?" Eddie answered by saying, "I don't know." When I checked to see if he understood, he knew the answers to all of my questions relating to the assignment. Eddie seldom completes more than one assignment per week during the allotted time.

On the playground I overheard Susie say, "Don't choose Eddie, because he won't try hard if he doesn't like the game." Janie said, "But someone has to choose him."

Note that this is a report; it injects no judgment. This is what the teacher said, how Eddie answered, and what was done as a result. In the same manner, the playground incident consists simply of the children's conversation.

Sampling.   Adequate sampling is also important for valid observation. Teachers who concern themselves only with classroom behavior may have a very biased picture of students' total affective behavior. The boy who is hostile and aggressive in English class may be a cooperative and respected leader in the chemistry club or have a helpful attitude toward his mathematics classmates.

To improve sampling, one must make observations in varied situations. However, care should also be given to timing. A girl under observation may have a toothache on the day you have chosen to make mental notes about her actions, or perhaps difficulties have arisen at home; what you see or hear may not be the child's typical behavior at all. Naturally, the more you observe children in a variety of situations, the more likely you are to synthesize an accurate picture of their problems, and the more reliable your observations will become.

Teachers must plan for reliability and economy of effort in observing students. It is not practical to use the technique, valuable in certain research, of planning a schedule of short observations in advance where, by randomizing the schedule, numerous students are seen in more or less comparable situations. Nevertheless, the teacher can schedule observation to a reasonable degree, and, through a conscious effort, somewhat avoid the bias resulting from a nonrepresentative or improperly timed situation.

PROBLEM

1. Elementary school teachers who remain with the same children all day have ample opportunity to obtain a wide variety of behavior samples. In what specific ways might junior and senior high school teachers meet the problem of less opportunity to sample behavior?

Purposeful Observation. Teachers always seek information that will help them promote learning; this is, however, a very general objective. It is more helpful to look for something specific. Why does one student seem to have difficulty in getting along with other boys? Why does another refuse to make reports or enter class discussion? An intelligent search for the answers will be guided by what we already know. It may be necessary to arrange some special occasions in which there is an opportunity to test guesses and hypotheses about the source of difficulty. Some simple structuring can elicit reactions to social stimuli that are encountered in the normal course of events—perhaps assigning certain students specific responsibilities, formulating key questions, or organizing games that present some individual and social problems.

Anecdotal Records

Observation techniques function most effectively when the information is written. One way of recording such information is in anecdotal records. These are systematic and significant records of student behavior that generally form part of the permanent record passed on from grade to grade. In studying a behavior problem,

ANECDOTAL RECORD FORM

Date: 1/24/80   *Student's Name:* Sue Collings

Observer: Dorothy Larson

Description of incident:
   Sue had won our first essay contest. When she was offered a prize for her second success, she gave it to Marlene, who was runner-up. Marlene accepted it without any expression of appreciation.

Comments:
   Sue seems to be a very well-adjusted child and quite sensitive to the needs of the other children. It was a particularly noble gesture for her to give Marlene the prize since Marlene is very selfish and uncooperative with her peers.

FIGURE 13.1.   Sample Anecdotal Record

it is important to look for signs of its development, because change can be evaluated only through knowledge of previous events.

A sample anecdotal record is shown in Figure 13.1. Notice that the description of the incident is separated from the teacher's comments about it. In both instances, more details can be added if necessary. Incidentally, a copy of this anecdote could be placed in the files of both girls mentioned.

Students may periodically exhibit deviant behavior. Sometimes, taxing school events, like issuing report cards, coincides with this behavior. The amount of security that home life affords a child varies as it does in school. Therefore, adequate sampling is necessary for a valid interpretation of behavior. Extended observation also provides an opportunity to detect improvement or lack of it in an individual's behavior.

Note that there is federal legislation (see page 471) permitting parents access to their children's school records; school personnel therefore should be forwarned. Carelessly written reports could have serious implications.

PROBLEM

2. An important use of the anecdotal record is to serve as a reference, along with other data, when the teacher is making inferences and formulating hypotheses about behavior. What other important uses can you see for this technique?

Rating Scales

Rating scales are useful in the making and recording of observations. These instruments are popular in many schools because they emphasize important aspects of adjustment and provide data that can be treated statistically. They also make it possible for several judges to rate the same student, a procedure that usually increases the reliability of the rating.

Most of the rating instruments used in the elementary and secondary schools are graphic scales, constructed so that the rater can mark any point along a continuum. For example:

Is he/she moody?

never   seldom   usually   always

The foregoing scale can be improved by substituting brief behavioral statements for the more general terms like "seldom" or "usually." For example:

Is he/she even-tempered or moody?

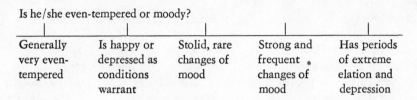

Generally very even-tempered	Is happy or depressed as conditions warrant	Stolid, rare changes of mood	Strong and frequent changes of mood	Has periods of extreme elation and depression

If some of these expressions, such as "even-tempered," were defined more specifically, they would provide a more common basis on which to evaluate students. Specific examples of behavior will do much to offset the disparity of judgment that arises because different raters employ different criteria in judging students according to general descriptive terms.

There are several types of error affecting the reliability and validity of ratings. They are

1. Rating all students too high or too low (the "personal bias" or "personal equation")
2. Rating everyone near the central point of the scale (the error of central tendency)
3. Rating inaccurately because of ambiguity in the scale or misunderstanding on the part of the raters
4. Rating largely in terms of one's general impression of a student (the "halo effect")

The fourth type of error occurs when the rater is favorably impressed by a student and so tends to give a higher evaluation than deserved on many items. Lower ratings may result for a student of whom the rater is not particularly fond.

The reliability of ratings can be improved by increasing the number of judges. This poses a practical problem in many elementary schools where a child may have only one teacher. In secondary school, the large student-teacher ratio prevents teachers from knowing all their students well, but because each student has contact with a number of teachers, there is a better opportunity to get reactions from several observers. It should be emphasized that rating students without sufficient evidence to make a highly reliable and valid opinion is a waste of time.

An interesting variation of the common rating scale is that involving the forced-choice technique. This, in its simplest form, requires the rater to choose between two descriptive statements, deciding which is more characteristic of the person rated. In one instance, both paired choices may represent desirable behavior; in another instance, undesirable behavior. In either case, the members of the pair appear to be equally acceptable in terms of desirability, but actually they represent different kinds of behavior. Instruments have been developed using groups of three, four, and even five statements.

Below is a pair of statements concerning one aspect of a student's social relationships:

A. Shares interests with the group.
B. Listens attentively while others relate their experiences.

Since raters must choose between what appear to be equally complimentary statements, the "halo effect" is countered, and the judges are prevented from giving only cursory attention to the items. Actually, as determined by validity studies, the choices do not represent equal degrees of personal-social development. Choice A might reflect more maturity than Choice B.

The forced-choice technique may prove to be helpful in developing more adequate instruments for evaluating personal-social adjustment in our schools. This technique is also be used in self-report inventories, such as the *Gordon Personal Profile*. In completing these items, the students determine which statements best describe their behavior.

PROBLEM

3. The United States Armed Forces have made use of the "man-to-man" type of rating scale in evaluating officers. The individual doing the rating is first asked to think of the best, the poorest, the average, etc., officer in his experience. Each man to be rated is then compared with these models. Could this procedure be successfully adapted to the classroom situation?

Check Lists

Check lists make it possible to record aspects of behavior rapidly. They are simply lists of personality descriptions or traits that the recorder notes as present or absent in individual students. Some schools construct their own, and a particularly valuable device is developed when the whole staff cooperates under a leader who is well-informed about child growth and development. The experience of constructing a check list may then prove to be effective in in-service training.

Standardized check lists have been published, such as the *Vineland Social Maturity Scale*. The items are arranged in the order of their increasing average difficulty and represent progressive maturation in self-help, self-direction, locomotion, occupation, communication, and social relations. Below are some excerpts from the scale, ranging from those designed for very young children to those for an adult:

"Crows"; laughs

Follows simple instructions

Relates experiences

Goes to school unattended

Makes telephone calls

Performs responsible routine chores

Buys own clothing

Looks after own bath

Assumes responsibilities beyond own needs

Shares community responsibility

This scale has many possible uses. It can serve as: (1) a standard schedule of normal development to be used repeatedly for the measurement of growth or change; (2) a measure of individual differences and, consequently, of extreme deviation that may be significant in such problems as mental deficiency, juvenile delinquency, and child placement or adoption; (3) a qualitative index of development variation in abnormal subjects such as the maladjusted, the unstable, the psychopathic, the epileptic; (4) a measure of improvement following special treatment, therapy, and training; and (5) a schedule for reviewing developmental histories in the clinical study of retardation, deterioration, and rates of growth and decline.

Interviews

Interviews with students often supplement and verify other information about their behavior. Since teachers are able to observe children in only a limited variety of situations, a face-to-face encounter with no peers present provides an opportunity to observe reactions closely and with greater attention than is possible in the classroom. Since the interview is less objective and reliable than paper-and-pencil inventories, it should not supplant them. Furthermore, its lack of economy precludes its use with all students. At times it is most helpful with those students having special problems.

Several schools of thought exist concerning the interview approach. Part of the disagreement concerns the degree to which the student is allowed to dominate the interviews—in other words, the degree of permissiveness the teacher exercises. Despite differences of opinion on this point, a number of suggestions will serve as guides for effective interviewing.

1. Be certain that you have a desirable purpose for the interview. With a purpose in mind, you can prepare for the interview by checking relative available data and formulating what you hope to accomplish.

2. Establish rapport. Certainly, teachers cannot expect to get helpful information if they call in a student after a misdemeanor and use this as the basis for a conference. A good relationship between the student and the teacher can hardly be expected if the discussion revolves around an inter-

personal difficulty. What teachers say in establishing rapport is not nearly so important as how they say it and whether they are encouraging positive feelings between the students and themselves. Try to help the students see that you are sincerely interested in them and their problems.

3. Guide the discussion so students have an opportunity to express their feelings. If you ask questions that can be answered with a simple "yes" or "no," they may respond that way. Avoid a climate that prompts a student to give an answer he or she thinks the interviewer wants.

4. Avoid communicating a note of finality at the end of the interview. Suggest that there will be opportunities for other conferences if they seem desirable. Students should feel that the interviews have been helpful and satisfying to them. If it appears that they have not been successful, set times for other meetings.

5. After students leave, make short written summaries of the salient points of the interviews to place in their cumulative records. Do not trust your memory.

Interviews with parents can also yield useful information for evaluating a student's affective behavior. As in interviewing the student, it is important to have a purpose in mind. Know what gaps of information you need to fill; parents can be an excellent source of missing information about behavior problems.

There are advantages in having the parents come to the school for the interview, as well as in visiting them at home. As a home visit gives the teacher a picture of a student's home life, a school visit lets the parents see how their children spend the day. Some parents may feel more secure in their homes because many of them recall painful childhood experiences that are, unfortunately, associated with school. Among the disadvantages of visiting the home are the shame some parents may feel about their home's physical appearance and the possibility of other family members interrupting the interview.

In getting to know the father and mother, a teacher may come away with a better understanding of the student in the light of parental reactions. One teacher wrote of a home visit:

> The time could have been spent to no better advantage. I developed an insight into Ann's problems that I've never had before. It will be much easier for me to be sympathetic with her at school now. I'm certain that I shall conserve considerable emotional energy. Frankly, I wonder how Ann has been able to adjust so well to our classroom environment. Coming from a middle-class home, I'm afraid I didn't realize how some people live.

PROBLEM

4. What behavioral symptoms of the student might indicate the need for a home visit? What factors should teachers keep uppermost in their minds when interviewing parents? How might you proceed with the hostile or withdrawn parent?

Sociometric and Related Techniques

One of the most valuable sources of information about the affective behavior of students is their peers. Instruments that ask students to rate their classmates in various ways are known as sociometric techniques. Teachers will find it helpful to use these means to verify their judgments of students for a number of reasons. First, the teacher has an opportunity to observe boys and girls in a limited number of situations only. Second, the relationship between teachers and students is different from that between students and their peers; teachers represent authority and children respond to authority in different ways. Third, teachers may lack objectivity in their observations.

Teachers may look on sociometric techniques as a lot of unnecessary bother, feeling that very little additional information can be obtained through their use, since, on the whole, good teachers have been quite successful in determining a student's relationship to the group. There continue to be some very bad misjudgments, however. As an example, students who carefully cultivate the friendship of their teachers may be highly rated by the teachers but not so highly rated by their peers.

Teachers who use sociometric techniques are quick to admit that they have at times misjudged the relationship among students. Social interaction is so complex a process that many feelings are expressed in such a way that even the keenest observer cannot detect them. Students may admire certain traits in each other that completely overshadow behavior the teacher considers undesirable. It is also possible that observers may, because of their own backgrounds, emphasize undesirable characteristics disproportionately.

Sociograms

The sociometric test is a device for determining preferences among peers to determine the social structure of a group. One method of administering the test is to ask students to list, in order of preference, the three persons in the class with whom they would most like to work on a project. A sociogram is constructed by drawing a map showing, by means of names and lines, the choices of each student. This depicts the social structure of the group for a particular moment in a particular situation that prompted the members' choices. To obtain a complete picture of the social interaction in the group, it is necessary to give several tests involving varied situations. Students do not always choose the same persons for work on different assignments. The choices expressed by students represent what they would like. They do not necessarily indicate what the situation is. For example, several students may indicate by their choices that they would like to be a part of the group populated by two or three leaders. If we were to observe these students in the classroom, however, we might find no interaction between them and the students of their choice. This explains why the sociometric tests can provide information that may not be available to an observer.

A natural circumstance should be selected to initiate the test, such as reseating a group, forming committees, or a similar activity. Teachers should emphasize that they will keep the students' preferences confidential. Students must understand that they may choose anyone; in some schools, where separation of boys and girls is encouraged, children may think that they must select only from their own sex. Finally, sufficient time should be given for all students to make their choices.

The following is an effective way of wording the sociometric question (adapted from Jennings, 1973):

> Our next unit is on the western movement in the United States. You have decided that you would like to take certain projects and work on them in committees. Each of you knows with whom you would like to work. Now I am going to pass out some cards. Print your name in the upper right-hand corner and then number from "1" to "3" on the left-hand side of the card like this. (Illustrate on the blackboard.) Beside the "1" write the complete name of the person with whom you would like most to work in a committee. After "2" indicate your second choice and after "3" your third choice. You may choose either a boy or a girl, but of course the person must be in this class. I will arrange the committee members so that you will be with at least one of those whom you have chosen.

It is also possible to ask the children to list at the bottom of the card the name of anyone with whom they would prefer not to work. This procedure has serious limitations, however, since it is in contradiction to the social philosophy the teacher should wish to develop in the class. When a group of eleventh graders was asked to list classmates whom they preferred not to have on their committees, a number of parents said that the students were disturbed by the request. Even though there were a number of cliques that operated among them, the students were unhappy about having to "blackball" others.

The primary-grades teacher may let the children give their choices orally if they cannot write. One second-grade boy reported that he had chosen Tom because he couldn't write Marjorie, the name of his best friend. A problem also arises when children do not know each other's names. Students must be well acquainted before the sociometric test can be used effectively.

Figure 13.2 is an illustration of a sociogram of a fourth-grade class of twenty-five students. Only first and second choices are shown; the solid lines indicate first choices and the broken lines, second choices. The boys' names are enclosed by boxes, the girls' by circles.

Notice the sex division in this class. Only one student, Joe, has chosen another of the opposite sex. Sue, Ann, and Jean form a clique. There are a number of mutual choices. Prominent among these are Mike and Dan, Rick and Loran, Sharon and Shirley, and Milton and Robert. There are also several isolates—students whom no one has chosen: Donna, Wesley, Philip, and Jack. Complete directions for constructing a sociogram such as this are given by Jennings (1973).

After the sociogram is constructed, it should be evaluated. The individual student should be considered first: Who are his or her preferences? Who has chosen him or her? The students should be considered as a group: Who was chosen most often, very seldom, or not at all? Are there any small groups who have chosen each other and seem to stand apart from the class as a whole? Does the group tend

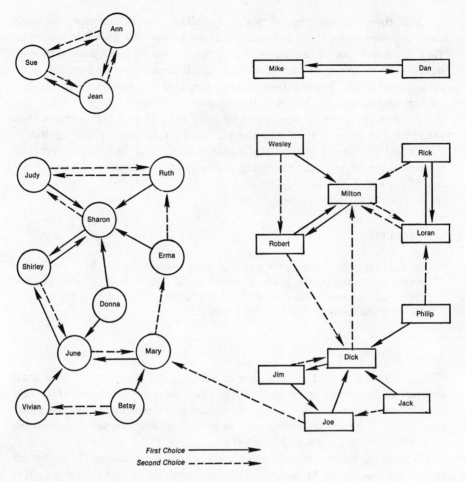

FIGURE 13.2.   Sociogram of a Fourth-Grade Class

toward sex divisions, boys choosing boys and girls choosing girls? Do urban children fail to choose rural children and vice versa? The answers to these questions may prove surprising when teachers compare them with their own reactions.

The sociometric interview, a by-product of the sociometric test, is used to obtain information and explanations from children. For example, John, a high-school junior, said he chose Bill because he wasn't as cocky as Tom. Actually, the sociogram indicated that Tom was well liked and had shown his effectiveness as a leader many times. John and Tom were rivals for high marks as well as for social position in the school, and this struggle had had its effect on John's feeling toward his rival. Tom, on the other hand, had given John his first choice for committee work. When queried about his reasons for this choice, he said simply, "John has good ideas."

Care must be taken in the interview not to place the students on the defensive because of their choices. The teacher should not say, "Why did you choose Bill?" but "How did you decide to choose Bill?"

If teachers find that their duties do not allow time to interview the whole class, they may select those few students about whom they are most concerned. They might also get written statements of the reasons for their choices from all students. Of course they must assure children of their intent to keep the information confidential. Written statements of this kind are seldom effective unless teachers have excellent rapport with their classes.

Jennings gives specific suggestions for using the sociogram. However, teachers would be wise not to use set formulae for dealing with group problems. Rather, they should use the information as a basis for formulating hypotheses concerning procedures for helping isolates, coping with cliques, and improving the cohesiveness of a group.

PROBLEM

5. In a junior high school, sociograms of each seventh- and eight-grade section were constructed by the guidance counselor on the basis of choices made in group guidance sessions during the fall semester. These data were then released to the teachers. Evaluate this procedure.

Social-Distance Scales

The sociogram is limited in the degree to which it can show the complete social structure of the group. Since students typically have only three choices, we have no information on why they failed to choose other classmates. As one fourth grader said, "I didn't have enough choices to choose Sally." However, she did not choose Billy because "He is such a tattletale."

The social-distance scale overcomes this particular weakness. It is possible to use this instrument to determine the degree to which individuals accept or reject the group as well as the degree to which the group accepts or rejects them. Table 13.1 shows how thirty-two elementary school students reacted to two classmates in terms of certain social situations. The number of checks for each item on the scale received by the most accepted child and the least accepted child are listed. Interestingly enough, every student is usually accepted by at least one classmate, and even the most popular are not approved by everyone.

The questions used in this technique have certain limitations. For example, if our objective is to promote peer acceptance, we may wonder about the effect of an item like "Wish he/she were not in our room." Some teachers prefer not to use social-distance scales because items of this kind are in opposition to their goals.

"Guess Who" Questionnaires

Another method of obtaining reports from students is to have them match their peers with a list of behavioral characteristics. The teacher makes a list of characteristics ranging from complimentary to unfavorable. The students then indicate those classmates who, in their opinion, fit each description. Since students

TABLE 13.1. Social Acceptance of Two Pupils

Item on scale	Checks for pupil 1 (most accepted)	Checks for pupil 2 (least accepted)
1. Would like to have him as one of my best friends.	20	2
2. Would like to have him in my group but not as a close friend.	7	15
3. Would like to be with him once in a while but not too often or for a long time.	3	4
4. Do not mind his being in our room but do not want to have anything to do with him.	1	3
5. Wish he were not in our room.	1	8

From Cunningham and others, 1951, p. 172; reproduced by permission of the Bureau of Publications, Teachers College, Columbia University.

often know each other better than the teacher does, it is possible to get a great deal of information about many aspects of their adjustment. The following examples illustrate the kind of item that has proved helpful.

Here is someone who likes to talk a lot, usually has something to say ———.

Here is someone who waits for somebody else to think of something to do and usually likes to follow the suggestions which others make ———.

Here is someone who is very friendly, who has lots of friends, who is nice to everybody ———.*

Children may list themselves or as many students as fit the description. It is also possible that some students will feel that certain items apply to no one in the class. When teachers tabulate the number of times each student is mentioned for each description and find some individuals referred to by a large number of the class, it is significant information. No doubt they should disregard mention by only one or two, although possibly some children are not well-known and are mentioned infrequently for this reason.

There is some disagreement about the listing of negative statements. Some educators believe that it is unwise to ask students to make judgments about their peers in anything other than a positive way. They feel that emphasizing the negative might be harmful both to the individual and to the group. On the other hand, others believe that determining negative characteristics of individuals and then working to remove them outweighs any possible damage.

* From Cunningham and others, 1951, pp. 419, 420, and 422; reproduced by permission of the Bureau of Publications, Teachers College, Columbia University.

Self-Report Inventories

Since individuals themselves have the most knowledge and awareness about their own behavior, self-report inventories can elicit important information. They attempt to tap the wealth of information that persons have about their background, feelings, interests, and attitudes. If a number of standardized questions are chosen that can be relied upon to show differences among individuals, one has the basis for the so-called paper-and-pencil "personality," interest, and attitude inventories. It is obvious that the reliability and validity of these instruments depend to a great degree on how adequately the individual can or will report the facts. It is possible that some students with severe emotional problems cannot satisfactorily interpret their feelings and behavior to make a valid report.

Biographical Data Blanks

Factual information about an individual's past history has been found helpful in predicting future success on the job or in higher learning. Hobbies, special activities in and out of school, skills, success with past education, and so on, can be used by an evaluator to make a clinical judgment about an individual. In some cases, items have been analyzed to determine the relationship of responses to future behavior of the individual. For example, it may be that in a question such as

> How many things have you built out of wood?
>   (a)   none
>   (b)   several
>   (c)   many

the student answering *many* probably is more successful in shop class than one answering *none* or *several*. On the other hand the question may have no predictive value for success in general mathematics.

Serious efforts have been made to use biographical data to predict student achievement. For instance, data yielded by a biographic blank (Schaefer & Anastasi, 1968) were used to predict creativity in adolescents. A 165-item inventory was grouped into five sections: physical characteristics, family history, educational history, leisure-time activities, and miscellaneous. *Project Talent* also employed numerous questions of the biographical-data-blank type in the nationwide inventory of human talent. Typical of the questions used are the following:

> How many times have you been president of a class, a club, or other organization (other than athletic) in the last 3 years?
>   (a)   none
>   (b)   once
>   (c)   twice
>   (d)   three times
>   (e)   four times
>   (f)   five or more times

How many books are in your home?
- (a)   none, or very few (0–10)
- (b)   a few books (11–25)
- (c)   one bookcase full (26–100)
- (d)   two bookcases full (101–250)
- (e)   three or four bookcases full (251–500)
- (f)   a room full—a library (501 or more)

Instruments of this type probably have some degree of predictive value because they reflect interests, personality traits, and certain abilities related to performance.

Personality Inventories

One of the typical personality inventories designed for school use is the *California Test of Personality*. This instrument was developed in five series so that it can be administered to students from kindergarten to adulthood. According to the authors, the primary purpose of the inventory is to reveal the extent to which students are adjusting to the conditions facing them and to indicate whether they are developing normal, happy, and socially effective personalities.

Each series is divided into two sections. The first part indicates the students' feelings about themselves (personal adjustment), and the second reflects social adjustment. Each division is further subdivided into six headings having an equal number of questions: eight in the primary series; twelve in the elementary series; and fifteen in the intermediate, secondary, and adult series. Such questions as these are asked of children in the primary grades: "Do the children think you can do things well?" "Are you asked to play in other people's yards?" Older students are queried as follows: "Do you visit with several young men and women in your neighborhood?" A "yes" or "no" response is made to each question. The authors suggest that a profile be made for each student so that serious deviations may be determined and dealt with. This is a questionable recommendation.

The foregoing inventory is designed to be a measure of traits or components of adjustment. Another approach to the evaluation of personal-social adjustment is through the determination of problem areas. The *Mooney Problem Check List*, which can be used with junior and senior high school students, is a self-report instrument designed to help individuals express their personal problems. Students read through the check list and underline the problems that concern them. After completing the first step, they are asked to go back over the items they have underlined and circle the numbers of those of greater concern to them. The high school form lists 330 problems commonly faced by adolescents. These were collected from student reports and some of the items are listed below:

Getting sick too often

Awkward in meeting people

Not being attractive to the opposite sex

Being different

Too little freedom in class

Worrying about grades

Afraid of the future

The items are set up in problem areas to facilitate counseling. For the high school form there are eleven areas: health and physical development; finances; living conditions and employment; social and recreational activities; social-psychological relations; courtship, sex, and marriage; home and family; morals and religion; adjustment to school work; the future; vocations and education; and curriculum and teaching procedures.

It would appear offhand that the student who has checked the most problems is in serious need of counseling. However, individuals may check an item even though it bothers them very little. Since the number of problems checked depends on the willingness of students to express themselves, some individuals may not check their most serious problems. It is also possible that one problem may seem more difficult for one student than a series of problems for another. It should be noted that what may not seem to be a problem to an adult, or may seem one of little importance, may be a very real source of concern to the student.

Reliability and Validity. Extensive investigations of the reliability and validity of the adjustment inventories, particularly of the type represented by the *California Test of Personality,* have been made. Evidence exists that, in many instances, these inventories are not measuring the student traits that they claim to measure. Also, results from one inventory regularly do not agree closely with results from others even though the descriptions of the scales would lead one to believe that they should. Whether these weaknesses are due to the fact that responses are easily faked is not clear. No doubt this is a contributing factor.

When these instruments are used in a school setting, the data yielded by them must be interpreted with extreme care. Unless teachers are well trained in personality measurement, the use of these inventories should be restricted to counselors. Note that subtest scores are quite unreliable, although total scores might be used for screening to select some individuals for further study. Answers to specific questions on these inventories occasionally may furnish tiny hints with respect to further diagnosing a child's problems. However, under no circumstances should scores from these inventories be the basis for educational or vocational decisions without further corroborating evidence.

Ethical Considerations. Questions have been raised about the ethics of requiring individuals to answer very personal questions that are included in some personality tests and personal-social adjustment inventories. These have caused some to inquire as to whether such questions constitute an invasion of privacy. Particular attention has been focused on requiring individuals who are not thought to be emotionally ill to answer questions about private feelings in such areas as religion, family relationships, patriotism, and so forth.

Psychologists defending the use of personal-social adjustment inventories stress their present basic limitations, but emphasize their usefulness when the results yielded by them are considered along with other data. Self-regulation by the psychological profession is helpful, but a basic conflict exists. While psychologists believe firmly in the dignity and worth of the individual, they are also committed to increasing man's understanding of himself and others. Hence, is the use of personal-social adjustment inventories in a given instance an invasion of privacy or a legitimate investigation of man's behavior?

Concern has been expressed about the collection, maintenance, and dissemination of student records, particularly data from personal-social adjustment inventories. Guidelines have been prepared that protect the privacy of students and their families without seriously inhibiting the school's efforts to help children (Goslin, 1970). In the case of research involving questionnaires, inventories, and tests, the procedures to be used are routinely and carefully screened in accordance with established ethical principles in order to protect the rights of human subjects (American Psychological Association, 1973).

PROBLEM

6. Three major issues associated with the invasion of privacy questions are (1) respecting the dignity of those tested; (2) the permissibility of deception in the procedures; and (3) the limits on freedom of scientific inquiry (Cronbach, 1970, pp. 509–515). Evaluate each. In view of your evaluations, should schools routinely gather personal-social adjustment data about students?

Interest Inventories

Experienced teachers know that interest plays an important part in the affective behavior of children. The girl who likes sciences and has books available to her in this area will be motivated to read, thereby developing basic reading skills and a sense of adequacy at the same time. Teachers who involve their students in projects that interest them will find that the students' facility in social situations will develop much more readily than if they are forced to do uninteresting or irrelevant work.

Informal methods (for example, interviews) of obtaining information about student interests are commonly used. In addition, standardized interest inventories are comparatively popular. Two of these are the *Strong-Campbell Interest Inventory (SCII)* and the *Kuder Preference Record—Vocational (Form C)*. The *SCII* and *Kuder* inventories are used repeatedly for vocational guidance in the secondary schools, and are described in the following sections.

Strong-Campbell Interest Inventory. For many years the *Strong Vocational Interest Blank (SVIB)* was widely used to determine the pattern of interests of adolescents and adults. Separate booklets, each containing about 400 items, were used for men and women. Examinees were asked to express their like or dislike for a wide variety of activities such as various occupations, school subjects, and amusements. These responses were empirically keyed for different occupations. In other words, persons in a specific occupation (such as nursing) are found to have reasonably common interests that differentiate them from those in other occupations. Hence, a comparison can be made between an examinee's pattern of interests and those of individuals successfully employed in various occupations. Knowledge of similarities and dissimilarities is useful information for the examinee, teacher, and counselor.

Major changes were made in the *SVIB* in 1974, and it was then published as the *Strong-Campbell Interest Inventory (SCII)*. The changes include the combining of the man's and women's test booklets into a single form, and the use of a new theoretical approach for profile interpretation. Items with sexual bias were eliminated, and those with reference to gender were changed (police*man* to police *officer*). Also, changes in traditional male-female vocational roles are reflected in new empirical scales (female college professors, male nurses).

The *SCII* materials include an inventory booklet, an answer sheet, and a profile form. Some scoring agencies also offer an explanatory profile to aid in score interpretation. The inventory contains 325 items divided into seven sections. For the first five sections, responses are scored by marking "like," "indifferent," or "dislike." The five sections are

I. *Occupations* (names of occupations, e.g., banker, artist, fireman)

II. *School Subjects* (lists of subjects, e.g., botany, speech, mathematics)

III. *Activities* (diverse activities, e.g., studying, arguing, cooking)

IV. *Amusements* (leisure-time activities, e.g., hobbies, games, entertainments)

V. *Types of People* (a broad assortment, e.g., babies, thrifty people, people who live dangerously)

Section VI, *Preference Between Two Activities,* requires choices to be made between two activities (dog trainer/juvenile parole officer). One of three possible responses must be selected: "prefer," "like the same," or "can't decide." Section VII, *Your Characteristics,* asks respondents to mark "yes" if the statement describes them, "no" if the statement does not describe them, and "?" if they cannot decide.

The *SCII* yields a great deal of information. Reports for examinees include information regarding 6 general occupational theme scales, 23 basic interest scales, 124 occupational scales, an introversion-extroversion scale, an academic orientation scale, and several administrative indices to detect carelessness and test-taking response habits. The general occupational themes are

Realistic
Investigative
Artistic
Social
Enterprising
Conventional

These represent a type of person as well as the type of working environment that such a person would probably find comfortable. Classified under the six themes are twenty-three basic interest scales. Within the realistic theme, for example, are basic interest scales entitled agriculture, nature, adventure, military activities, and mechanical activities.

In many ways the occupational scales are the heart of the *SCII.* They show the degree of similarity between the examinee's responses and those of the criterion group for each of the 124 occupations included in the inventory. Standard scores are used in this report, and profiles are plotted in terms of degree of similarity of interests.

Extensive research has been done with the *SVIB* and now with its successor, the *SCII.* It has been found that interests change very little from age twenty-five to fifty-five, that there is a little change from twenty to twenty-five years of age, but that the shifts are considerable between the ages of fifteen and twenty. Therefore it would be wise not to use the test with students under the age of seventeen unless they are unusually mature; in any event, an allowance should be made for their youth. Interest scores may be helpful to high school juniors and seniors if the emphasis is on the general direction of a career rather than in a specific vocation.

The Kuder Preference Record—Vocational. This instrument illustrates another method of constructing interest inventories. As in the *SCII* a large number of items were collected describing everyday life. However, instead of emphasizing the interests of those in the various occupations and then attempting to determine if a person's interests were similar, Kuder sought to describe the interesting aspects of a subject through a logical grouping of items. If students showed an interest in a certain group of items, it could be said that they had an interest in activities related to that group. There are ten areas of interest and a verification scale to identify those who answer the items carelessly or without understanding.

The *Kuder Preference Record—Vocational* has 168 items organized in groups of 3. Students decide which one of the three they like most and which one they like least. They are forced to choose even though they may like or dislike them all equally. In the first example shown in Figure 13.3, the examinee has punched a hole in the left-hand circle in front of the letter *R.* In this way, she has indicated that of the three activities, *P, Q,* and *R,* she would most like to visit a museum. By punching the hole in the right-hand circle beside letter *Q,* she indicates that of the three activities she would like least to browse in a library. Similarly, in the second example, she would like most to collect autographs and would least like to collect butterflies.

A sample *Kuder* profile is shown in Figure 13.4. This profile of Jim Spencer, a high school junior, shows that he has very little interest in the computational and scientific areas. Jim's father is an engineer and holds an important executive position in his firm. Both parents are anxious that their son choose engineering as a vocation. Jim's record throughout elementary school has been satisfactory. His SAI on the *Otis-Lennon School Ability Test* administered at the end of the eighth grade was 130. His scores on the *Iowa Tests of Basic Skills* showed no difficulty in the basic subjects.

A number of activities are listed in groups of three. Read over the activities in each group. Decide which of the three activities you like *most*. There are two circles on the same line as this activity. Punch a hole with the pin through the left-hand circle following this activity. Then decide which you like *least* and punch a hole through the right-hand circle.

P	Visit an art gallery	O	P	O
Q	Browse in a library	O	Q	◉
R	Visit a museum	◉	R	O
S	Collect autographs	◉	S	O
T	Collect coins	O	T	O
U	Collect butterflies	O	U	◉

FIGURE 13.3.   Instructional Examples of the Kuder Preference Record—Vocational, Form CP

From Kuder, 1976; reproduced by permission of Science Research Associates. © 1948, G. F. Kuder.

However, in high school his final marks in algebra, plane geometry, and general science were below average. He had to repeat biology during the summer session. During his junior year he was having serious difficulty with mathematics and science courses, though he had completed one of the best projects in social studies. He had also become a behavior problem and was absent from school quite often. Because he refused to cooperate at band practice, he was suspended from that organization.

Although the preceding data do not represent a complete case history, it seems apparent that Jim's interests are more closely related to other vocational fields than to engineering. His superior academic ability will probably be wasted if he is forced to continue his present course of study. Quite possibly a career in social science would be appropriate for him.

Scoring and Interpreting Results. The *Kuder* and the *SCII* differ in terms of their scoring procedures. Scoring the *SCII* is complex and time-consuming, although it can be scored commercially for a nominal fee. On the other hand, students can score their own *Kuder* records in a few minutes and the results are available immediately. It is not surprising, therefore, to find the *Kuder* used in the secondary school much more extensively than the *SCII*.

Faking is an important consideration in the test validity of interest inventories, just as it is in the personal-adjustment inventories. An examinee suitably motivated can successfully fake the *Kuder Preference Record*. Because the intent of the items is not so obvious in the *SCII*, it is less easily faked. When tests are given for

NAME **Spencer Jim R.** AGE **16** SEX **M** GROUP **Grade 11** DATE OF TEST **1–8**
Print   Last   First   Initial   M or F

PROFILE SECTION

MEN and WOMEN

DIRECTIONS FOR PROFILING

1. Copy the V-Score from the back page of the answer section in the box at the right.

If your V-Score is 37 or less, there is some reason for doubting the value of your answers and your other scores may not be very accurate. *If your V-Score is 45 or more,* you may not have understood the directions, since 44 is the highest possible score. *If your score is not between 38 and 44, inclusive,* you should see your adviser. He or she will probably recommend that you read the directions again and that you then fill out the blank a second time, being careful to follow the directions exactly and give sincere replies.

If your V-Score is between 38 and 44, inclusive, go ahead with the following directions.

2. Copy the scores 0 through 9 in the spaces at the top of the profile chart. Under "outdoor" find the number that is the same as the score at the top. Find this number in both the column headed M (for male) and the column headed F (for female). You may want to plot your scores on both male and female norms, using a different color for each or a solid line for one and a dashed line for the other. Keep in mind, though, that it is the profile based on your own sex group that counts.

Draw a line through the number from one side to the other of each half column under "outdoor." If your score is not shown, draw a line *between* the scores above and below your own. Do the same thing for the scores you wrote at the top of each of the other columns. If a score is larger than any number in the column, draw a line across the top of the column; if it is smaller, draw a line across the bottom.

3. With your pencil blacken the entire space between the lines you have drawn and the bottom of the chart. The result is your profile for the *Kuder Preference Record—Vocational.*

An interpretation of the scores will be found on page 35.

This page is to be kept by your counselor.

SCIENCE RESEARCH ASSOCIATES, INC.
155 North Wacker Drive, Chicago, Illinois 60606
A Subsidiary of IBM

7-296-FORM-22

FIGURE 13.4. Kuder Preference Record Profile Sheet

Profile Section (Men and Women) from the *Kuder Preference Record, Vocational, Form CP.* © 1976, 1951, G. Frederic Kuder. Reprinted by permission of the publisher, Science Research Associates, Inc.

employment purposes, apparent motives could promote untruthful answers, but when used with secondary school students, it would seem that little is gained from faking.

The stability of the interest patterns of adolescents has been questioned repeatedly. For instance, shifts of high school students' low and high interest scores have been found when there is a difference of several years between two administrations of the *Kuder Preference Record—Vocational*. Nevertheless, this instrument is of some help to the counselor and teacher, since it focuses attention on general fields of interest rather than on the interests of successful people in various occupations, as in the case with the *SCII*. However, the teacher or counselor needs to exercise caution against over-interpretation. Effective evaluation must include the use of other data gathered from varied sources as an adjunct to the interest inventory scores.

Other Kuder Inventories.   A number of *Kuder* inventories are available besides the *Kuder Preference Record—Vocational (Form C)*. The *Kuder General Interest Survey (Form E)* is a revision and downward extension of *Form C*. It is designed for grades six through twelve. The *Kuder Preference Record-Personal (Form A)* reflects an individual's personal and social preferences rather than those related to vocations. It is therefore more like an adjustment inventory than the other *Kuder* forms. Its five scales reflect the following personal and social preferences: (1) preference for being in active groups; (2) preference for familiar and stable situations; (3) preference for working with ideas; (4) preference for avoiding conflict; and (5) preference for directing or influencing others.

The *Kuder Occupational Interest Survey (KOIS)* is designed to replace the *Kuder Preference Record—Vocational*. It is an empirically keyed inventory, but it uses the same type of items as its predecessor. Individuals indicate the activity in each triad that they like best and the one they like least. Scores are designed to reflect the relationship of an individual's preferences to those in various occupations and fields of study. A person whose responses are the same as those made frequently by physical therapists receives a high coefficient for physical therapist. If, however, the person's responses are unlike those of a physical therapist, the person's coefficient would be low or perhaps negative. For the occupational and college major scales, generally the ten highest scores are reported separately by sex. No general reference group was used in developing the scales.

The *KOIS* has more occupational scales than its forerunner. There has also been an addition of scales for college majors. New scales have been normed for women for 37 occupations and for 19 college majors. Additional scores on 20 occupational scales and 8 college major scales are awarded women.

The major limitation of the *KOIS* to date is a lack of studies on reliability and validity. At present, the test cannot be confidently used in counseling individuals because of insufficient evidence about its degree of validity in various testing situations.

PROBLEM

7. Interest inventories are often administered during the ninth grade as an aid in the selection of high school courses and for prevocational planning for the student. Although counselors know that interests may shift, they find the inventory useful. Why?

Attitude Scales and Questionnaires

Attitudes are the result of individuals' previous experiences, and they are reflected in the way individuals act toward and think about the people, objects, and situations they encounter. The school is committed to the development of certain basic social attitudes in its students. Among the attitudes that can be learned are those toward race prejudice, bigotry, consideration, religion, democracy, and the quality of man. Evaluation of attitude formation and change becomes just as important, then, as achievement in the basic skills.

The formal instruments for attitude measurement fall into two categories: opinion polling and attitude scales. Neither is very useful to the classroom teacher. Their value often lies in their utility as research tools. The Gallup poll is a typical opinion survey. Individuals are generally approached with a single question that they are usually asked to answer with "yes," "no," or "undecided." The results are typically reported in terms of the percentage of answers given in each of those categories.

Attitude scales are generally of the Thurstone or Likert types. Both are designed so that an attitude can be measured by degrees, from very unfavorable to highly favorable. In a Thurstone scale, a number of statements representing levels of agreement or disagreement about a subject (for example, law) give the respondents an opportunity to express their feelings. Scale values for each statement are determined empirically. The composite attitude score is the numerical average of the scale values given to the statements with which each respondent agrees.

With the Likert method, statements are never neutral toward the object in question but are favorable or unfavorable in varying degrees. Examinees react to each statement usually on a five-point scale, indicating that they either strongly agree, agree, are uncertain, disagree, or strongly disagree. Their scores are computed simply by weighting the responses from five to one for a favorable statement beginning with strong agreement. Values are assigned in reverse order for unfavorable statements.

The Likert method is illustrated by the following two items taken from a scale designed to measure a student's attitude toward science courses.

Encircle one of the symbols preceding each of the following statements: A stands for "Agree," SA for "Strongly Agree," D for "Disagree," SD for "Strongly Disagree," and "?" for "Uncertain."

SA (A) ? D SD   Science books are very interesting to study.
SA (A) ? D SD   Laboratory work in science classes is drudgery.

Note that both items have the *A* circled, which means that the subject agreed with both statements. However, since the first item is favorable to science education, the "Agree" has a value of four. The second item is essentially unfavorable, and so the reverse order of scoring gives it a value of two. The total score on the scale is the sum of the values of all items. The maximum possible score is five times the total number of items.

Criterion-Referenced Inventories.   When evaluating achievement using criterion-referenced methods, it is easier for the busy teachers to select from objectives already developed with illustrative test items rather than to design their own. Instructional Objectives Exchange (IOX) provides compilations for many subject and topic areas including both the cognitive and affective domains. In certain instances, short tests have been constructed to measure achievement in terms of a small group of related objectives. Such is the case with *Attitudes Related to Tolerance,* an attitude inventory for ninth through twelfth graders. It is a criterion-referenced test designed to be used to assess in part the effectiveness of educational programs. Consequently, it was not planned that the responses of individual students be used in a clinical setting.

In this test students respond to a variety of statements of opinion by selecting one of the following: *Strongly agree; Agree; Disagree; Strongly Disagree;* or in some instances, *I would not mind; I would mind—but would accept it;* and *I would mind and would do something to try and change the situation or remove myself from the situation.* There are several scales, five of which are the following:

Scale	Purpose
Personal Perspective Scale I	Indicates attitudes toward certain groups of people.
	Example: "People who help others have an ax to grind."
Personal Perspective Scale II	Assesses attitudes toward diverse experiences.
	Example: "I like to associate with students whose families are different from mine."
Policy scale	Reflects attitudes toward policies which are tolerant or intolerant of others
	Example: "Boys with long hair should be required to have it cut."
Group Description Scale	Determines attitudes toward ethnic groups.
	Example: "There is one ethnic group whose chief value is money."

Scale	Purpose
Interaction Attitude Index	Assesses reaction to a situation with various social groups. *Example:* "My new club leader is a person of another race."

In addition to these scales, sociometric techniques can be used to determine whether there have been changes in the choices of companions made by students. Unobtrusive observations are also helpful such as allowing students to do an alternate assignment on interracial relations and noting their reactions. Another approach is to determine the checkout rate of value-laden books from the school library. If these optional choices increase, there is evidence of an increase in tolerance.

Validating Attitude Inventories. Determining the relative validity of attitude scales has been a difficult problem, chiefly because of a lack of adequate criteria by which to judge test scores. The question arises as to whether verbalized opinions actually represent attitudes. Although behavior can be checked, of course, individuals behave in different ways for different reasons. Students may say that they like school and show outward signs of full cooperation. They may nonetheless dislike teachers and classwork intensely, but find it expedient to foster good will so that they can stay on the basketball team. As is true of other self-report techniques, attitude evaluation is likely to be most valid when the student has no reason for falsification.

Unfortunately, standardized instruments for attitude measurements have not developed to the point where they can be practically useful to classroom teachers, who must in large part depend on other evidences of attitude formation and change. Through observation and sociometric data, teachers are able to evaluate these changes if they direct their attention toward them and systematize their approaches.

To obtain objective data, a teacher must look for attitudes in student behavior. Students may say that honesty is the best policy, but do they cheat, lie, or steal? Do they accept other students despite their social status? Are they responsive to the needs of others? Do they have a scientific attitude? Do they get all the facts? Do they draw logical conclusions? Teachers who have stated their educational objectives in terms of changes in student behavior will be able to infer attitude development and change from the modified actions of their students. If they then record such developments as anecdotal records, if they file their notes regarding all pertinent observations, and if they summarize these data for the group, they are then making important progress toward effective evaluation of attitudes.

PROBLEM

8. There is common agreement that the degree of validity of attitude scales is generally low at best. Nevertheless, describe possible uses of these instruments in a classroom or in a group guidance session.

Projective Techniques

The general idea of projective techniques is to present students with some unstructured and ambiguous situation and then to note their reaction to it. Since the individuals have no clues from the examiner, they will tend to react to the situation in terms of their own personalities. Whatever they do or say in such a situation will be influenced by their experiences and how they feel at the moment.

Two very common projective tests used by highly trained specialists in clinical diagnosis are the *Rorschach Inkblot Test* and the *Thematic Apperception Test*, commonly called the *TAT*. The *Children's Apperception Test* (*CAT*) is similar in type to the *TAT* and is designed for children of ages three through ten.

The *Rorschach* is composed of ten inkblots that serve as unstructured and ambiguous stimuli prompting individuals to give expression to the patterns of their personalities. The inkblots are presented in a given order, and the subjects tell what they "see" in each one.

The *TAT* consists of a series of pictures that may be interpreted in many ways. The subject is asked to tell a story about each picture, emphasizing how the scene was initiated, what is happening, how the characters feel, and what will probably result. The test is based upon the well-recognized fact that when people interpret an ambiguous social situation, they are likely to expose their own personalities as much as the scene under scrutiny. Absorbed in their attempts to explain the objective occurrence, the subjects become naively unconscious of themselves and of the observation of others and are, therefore, less vigilant and/or defensive. To a trained ear, they are disclosing certain inner tendencies, wishes, fears, and traces of past experience.

Cronbach (1970, p. 651) emphasizes the difference between the two kinds of tests. He classifies the *Rorschach* as a stylistic-type test and the *TAT* as a thematic type. In other words, the stylistic type indicates the style with which students handle problems, while the thematic type emphasizes the content of their thoughts and fantasies. He indicates, however, that the specific strengths are not mutually exclusive and that of the two, the thematic test more nearly examines "the whole person," yielding possible information about emotions, attitudes, and cognitive processes.

Numerous other projective procedures are less well-known than the above instruments. Several of these are quite similar to the *TAT*. Some present pictures, as does the *TAT*, while others require the examinee to draw their own pictures and interpret them. Varied approaches employ the use of finger painting, clay modeling, and doll play in unstructured situations with an opportunity for the students to project themselves through the materials.

Verbal materials can also be used in projective testing. For example, in word association, a list of stimulus words is read and the subjects respond with another word. When they produce unusual words or state them with hesitation, it may be indicative of problem areas.

An additional example of the use of verbal materials is the sentence completion test. Partial sentences are presented and the subjects choose the word or words that would complete the sentences and best express their feelings. For example:

My greatest difficulty is ———.

In working with other people I ———.

The completed sentences may be scored for content, as in the case of the *TAT*, or the responses may be coded in terms of healthfulness of adjustment.

Rarely is the classroom teacher trained to use these instruments and procedures. Their administration and interpretation require the knowledge and experience of trained clinicians; they will be familiar with the instruments' limitations of validity and reliability and the bases for their use and interpretation. Schools fortunate enough to have psychologists on their staffs may find that they will employ projective testing for certain difficult behavioral problems. In skilled hands, these procedures may provide helpful information with a comparatively small outlay of time and effort. Reports from these clinicians can be most helpful to classroom teachers and counselors concerned with serious behavioral problems.

SUMMARY

The main ideas in this chapter can be condensed as follows:

1. Fostering achievement in the affective domain is a very important responsibility for our schools.

2. Teachers must be able to differentiate between adequate and atypical affective behavior. Furthermore, they should be able to determine causes and facilitate solutions to behavioral problems.

3. The methods for evaluating affective behavior may be grouped as follows: observation of students, sociometric and related techniques, self-report inventories, and projective techniques.

4. Anecdotal records are helpful in providing a means for recording observational data in evaluating the affective behavior of children. To prevent bias, it is well to separate reports of behavior from interpretations of it.

5. Rating scales and checklists direct and objectify observation. They can also provide quantitative data as a basis for pooling the evaluations of several observers.

6. Teacher-parent and teacher-student interviews are useful means of gathering data about students' personal-social development. A high degree of rapport is desirable for maximum effect.

7. Still another source of information comes from children themselves. The use of such devices as the sociogram, social-distance scale, and "guess who" questionnaire can indicate how well students are accepted by their peers and can reveal specific strengths and weaknesses in their personalities. Follow-up interviews for interpretation are recommended.

8. Further information from children can be garnered by the use of self-report tests, such as personal inventories, interest inventories, attitude scales, and biographical data banks. Care should be exercised in the interpretation of data; faking can occur.

9. There is genuine concern about the need to protect the privacy of students and their families. Some school systems have adopted carefully formulated procedures to avoid abuses, particularly with respect to information about a student's personal-social adjustment.

10. Standardized projective instruments to evaluate affective characteristics of children are designed chiefly for specialists such as clinical psychologists. The teacher's role is to be informed of the utility of these instruments and to be alert to refer students when a need arises.

11. Because affective behavior is so complex, its evaluation demands extensive and varied approaches. There is a fine line, however, between the idea that a teacher should collect as much information about a student from as many sources as possible and the ethical problems in doing so.

SUGGESTED READINGS

ANASTASI, A. *Psychological testing* (4th ed.). New York: Macmillan, 1976.
Of particular interest are the discussions of self-report inventories (Chapter 17) and measures of interests and attitudes (Chapter 18). Chapter 19 is devoted to projective techniques; miscellaneous topics such as situational tests and self-concept assessment are included in chapter 20.

BLOOM, B. S., HASTINGS, J. T., & MADAUS, G. F. *Handbook on formative and summative evaluation of student learning.* New York: McGraw Hill, 1971.
In chapter 10, the authors discuss the Taxonomy of Educational Objectives, Handbook 2, Affective Domain *by Krathwohl, Bloom, and Masia and various modifications and additions. They also describe methods of evaluating affective objectives.*

CARTWRIGHT, C. A., & CARTWRIGHT, G. P. *Developing observation skills.* New York: McGraw-Hill, 1974.
The authors emphasize the need for observation and then delineate the principles, procedures, and problems that can be applied to all observational situations. Finally, they deal with specific types of records used for observation: behavior tallying and charting, check lists, rating scales and participation charts, and anecdotal records.

DYER, H. S. *The interview as a measuring device in education.* Princeton, N.J.: ERIC Clearinghouse on Tests, Measurement, and Evaluation; Educational Testing Service, 1976.
Interviews are classified as standardized or "open," with the former further subdivided into diagnostic and survey types. Interviews conducted in various educational settings are examined.

MISCHEL, W. On the future of personality measurement. *American Psychologist,* 1977, 32, 246–254.
In this article the issues that are troublesome in the assessment of personality are reviewed. Particularly interesting is the discussion of the interface of personality and cognition.

PAYNE, D. A. *The assessment of learning: Cognitive and affective.* Lexington, Mass.: D. C. Heath, 1974.
In Chapter 15 illustrative standardized measures in the affective domain are described and cautions for their use are listed. Observational methods used in the affective and cognitive domains are discussed in Chapter 16.

SEVERY, L. J. *Procedures and issues in the measurement of attitudes.* Princeton, N.J.: ERIC Clearinghouse on Tests, Measurement, and Evaluation; Educational Testing Service, 1974.
Traditional approaches to attitude scale construction are reviewed, followed by a good description of the guidelines for developing Likert scales.

TYLER, R. W. Assessing educational achievement in the affective domain. *NCME Measurement in Education*, 1973, 4, 1–8.
Affective behavior is described, and attention is given to selecting objectives and appropriate evaluation techniques in this important domain.

REFERENCES CITED

AMERICAN PSYCHOLOGICAL ASSOCIATION. *Ethical principles in the conduct of research with human participants.* Washington, D.C.: Author, 1973.

CRONBACH, L. J. *Essentials of psychological testing* (3rd ed.). New York: Harper & Row, 1970.

CUNNINGHAM, R., AND ASSOCIATES (ELZI, A., HALL, T. A., FARRELL, M., & ROBERTS, M.). *Understanding group behavior of boys and girls.* New York: Bureau of Publications, Teachers College, Columbia University, 1951.

GOSLIN, D. A. *Guidelines for the collection, maintenance, and dissemination of pupil records.* New York: Russell Sage Foundation, 1970.

JENNINGS, H. H. *Sociometry in group relations.* Washington, D.C.: American Council on Education, 1959. (Reprinted in 1973 by Greenwood Press.)

KUDER, G. F. *Kuder Preference Record—Vocational, Form C.* Chicago: Science Research Associates, 1951.

SCHAFFER, C. E., & ANASTASI, A. A. Biographical inventory for identifying creativity in adolescent boys. *Journal of Applied Psychology*, 1968, 52, 42–48.

PART FIVE

Using Evaluation to Improve Learning

Part Five will help you apply your understanding of measurement and evaluation in the classroom. Chapter 14, "Diagnosis and Remediation of Problems," is devoted to outlining procedures and suggesting materials and tests to aid in diagnosing and prescribing remediation for severe learning difficulties. There are practical examples that provide information about the selection of tests and interpretation of test data. Specific difficulties in such subjects as reading and mathematics are addressed. The philosophy of diagnostic teaching as effective teaching directs the discussion throughout.

Chapter 15, "Grading and Reporting," focuses attention on student progress and how we can best use the results of measurement to aid educators and parents in helping students achieve their potential. In this context, the purposes of final marks (grades) for informing students, parents, and school personnel are discussed. Also discussed is the principle that specific evidence of student progress should be based on the school's educational objectives, and that the evidence should include data from test performance, procedure and product evaluation, class participation, and projects and reports. Various methods of marking and reporting these data are given, such as the letter-number systems, checklists, written correspondence, teacher-parent conferences, and criterion-referenced methods. Finally, suggestions for improving grading and reporting are outlined. The chapter concludes with a discussion of promotion as it relates to final marks.

The last chapter is Chapter 16, "A Schoolwide Program of Evaluation." It stresses the importance of organizing a program of evaluation rather than one of testing alone. It also emphasizes that we must be concerned with the inputs and operations of the educational program rather than the outputs alone. The program should be developed democratically rather than imposed on the teachers by administrative officers.

14

Diagnosis and Remediation of Problems

After reading this chapter you will be able to

1. Differentiate between diagnostic and other kinds of evaluation and describe the purposes of each type

2. Explain the major causes of unsatisfactory achievement

3. Identify procedures for determining specific causes of learning difficulties

4. Identify and explain the importance of specific principles for the facilitation of remediation

5. Explain the use of various evaluation techniques for surveying class achievement

6. Identify an achievement problem for a student and explain possible diagnostic and remedial procedures

7. Explain when you would use individual and group diagnostic procedures and why

There is more to gardening than having a "green thumb." When expert gardeners' plants do not grow well, they know there is a reason, and they try to determine the source of the trouble. Is an insect, a fungus, or an improper soil condition causing the damage? They search for evidence that will help solve their problems. When they have identified the parasite or disease they determine the treatment, which may consist of spraying fungicides or insecticides on the affected plants. Every gardener knows, however, that all insecticides are not lethal to all insects, that a certain fungicide will not destroy all fungi, and that plants differ in their tolerance of various kinds of chemicals.

The gardener's approach is like that of teachers who realize that all members of the group they are teaching do not have the same abilities. Some of them are not growing well scholastically, and the causes must be found and remedies applied. They know that the textbook for the class will be too difficult for some students, too easy for others. Some children are not able to do long-division exercises because they lack skill in multiplication, addition, and subtraction. Others are proficient in long division and can be challenged only by more advanced work in mathematics. Teachers try to avoid the mistake of frustrating the slower students or boring the more able. With a range of ability and achievement from three to nine grade levels in most classes, they know that good teaching must begin with information about the ability and achievement of each student.

Diagnostic Evaluation

Diagnostic evaluation is closely associated with formative and summative evaluation. Recall that formative evaluation is useful at the intermediate stages of curriculum development, teaching, and learning. In curriculum development, it is helpful in the tryout process to determine where students find difficulty. For the learner, formative evaluation also provides feedback about strengths and weaknesses. It tells the student whether important learning has occurred and whether the prerequisites for further educational tasks have been mastered. This information is also important for teachers who plan for instruction. Summative evaluation, on the other hand, is applied at the end of a learning sequence for grading, evaluating progress, or determining the effectiveness of an educational program.

Diagnostic evaluation, although closely related to formative and summative evaluation, has two specific purposes: proper placement of students at the beginning of instruction and the determination of the causes of students' learning difficulties. Diagnostic evaluation attempts to carefully analyze causes of learning problems so that proper remediation can be applied. The goal is to determine the best possible instructional situation for students in terms of their present learning status.

Meaning of Diagnosis and Remediation

If a school is to reach its educational objectives, each teacher must recognize and understand the complex aspects of behavioral changes. Since a student's development tends to be sequential, schools must provide the most effective sequence of experiences, that is, those that will bring about behavior consonant with the abilities of the individual. Because growth patterns differ among individuals, causing various degrees of maturity at the same age, and because a developmental sequence in behavior is necessary, the teacher must determine where students stand in this sequence and how they may best achieve their full potential.

The teacher sees each individual within the group as having different problems. In practice, of course, students in a class have many common difficulties and can be grouped for instruction. For example, in a class where a few advanced students know how to multiply common fractions, those who do not can be taught as a group. And certainly, as a gardener waters the whole garden, there are many opportunities to bring the entire class together for instruction, like listening to a poem or story, watching a demonstration, or discussing initiation of a project.

In helping students, the teacher must determine the stages of their development and their peculiar learning difficulties. This is educational diagnosis. Some years ago, educational diagnosis was confined for the most part to academic knowledge and skills, but its scope has kept pace with the modern concept of education, which emphasizes all aspects of development. Thus the development of the nonintellectual aspects of students' personalities is as much the legitimate concern of teachers as is academic knowledge and skills. Indeed, affective learning cannot be divorced from learning knowledges and skills.

Remediation is possible only when teachers understand the bases of student difficulties; seeing specific needs, they teach to meet them. Good teaching implies several things: first, that we meet children at their own levels of achievement and start from there; second, that we know something of the experiences and problems they have had in reaching those levels; and third, that we are aware of how present learning relates to future school experiences. Children who have suffered the agonies of frustration and humiliation in arithmetic classes will present a more complex problem of remediation than those who simply do not understand long division.

Diagnosis

Educational diagnosis centers on three questions. Which students have learning difficulties? What are the strengths and weaknesses in their achievement? What factors have caused their unsatisfactory achievement?

Identifying Students Having Difficulty

There are a number of ways to locate students with learning difficulties. One of the most effective is the survey approach. Survey achievement tests included in a school testing program are specifically designed to find students who need remediation. When a serious lack of achievement shows up, the teacher will need information about the students' scholastic aptitude to make the achievement score more meaningful. Perhaps the children are achieving as well as can be expected in terms of their potential; students may not be less able simply because their scores are lower than the class average. Some may have average or above average achievement but are still below their potential. Others, particularly at the secondary level, may need to change their educational and vocational goals. It is these brighter students who generally benefit most from remediation because there is a wider gap between their achievement and their ability.

Teachers will often discover from test data that entire classes have a specific weakness. One fifth-grade teacher found that all students were below the grade norm in rate of reading, although they were above average in scholastic ability. Another teacher uncovered a weakness in study skills; another, difficulties with fractions; and a fourth, problems in spelling.

Many sources of information are helpful in locating the student who needs help. One may contact a child's former teacher, because past achievement must be evaluated. Attendance records and data on personal-social adjustment may provide clues. Information in a student's cumulative record, such as an anecdotal record, may prove helpful. For example, some of the highest academic achievers are in serious need of guidance in their social relations. Case histories show that some students, having no friends, strive for high scholastic achievement as a means of compensating for lack of affective development.

PROBLEMS

1. Describe the characteristics of academic "slowness." Illustrate with specific examples.

2. A high school biology teacher who meets with 150 students per day, and who is also responsible for a tenth-grade homeroom, maintains that under these circumstances individual student diagnosis is an impossible task. What arguments would you use to refute this position?

Determining Strengths and Weaknesses

Student improvement is the goal of all diagnosis and remediation, and to achieve it, good teachers help students correct their weaknesses by building on their strengths. For example, if reading disabilities exist, it is just as important to know that students are good in their word attack skills as it is to know that they are poor in their use of context clues. One of the basic principles in effective remediation is that students must experience success, and building on their strengths makes this possible.

Competencies in Diagnosis. Determining the strengths and weaknesses of students requires essential diagnostic skills that teachers must develop even though they are not trained clinicians. They should first understand the principles of learning and their application. Second, they should be able to recognize behavioral symptoms that suggest the causes of specific difficulties. Third, they should be able to apply diagnostic and remedial techniques.

Before teachers can be successful diagnosticians, they must be familiar with the psychology of learning in general and with specific subject areas. They can formulate useful hypotheses about the nature of children's difficulties far more readily if they understand how learning normally develops in a subject area and if they are aware of the difficulties most frequently encountered. Take, for example, the problem of transfer of learning. If we learn how to shift gears in one automobile with a three-forward-speed transmission, we can then shift gears in another with a similar transmission. Learning from the original task has been transferred to the new. But if we are then asked to drive an automobile with a four-forward-speed transmission, our previous learning tends to interfere with the new task. This is known as the negative transfer effect.

Research in transfer of learning indicates that although considerable transfer occurs from some learning tasks to others, there are cases in which there is little transfer unless we teach for it. In one such instance, a teacher discussed word endings and rhyming with a class. Prescribed procedures were carefully followed; *Jane* rhymes with *rain, cane, train.* A little girl went home and announced, "We learned about rhyming today. Try me. You say *Jane.*" When the parent dutifully obeyed, the child responded with a triumphant *"rain, cane, train."* Asked whether other words rhymed with *Jane,* the child said no, only the three she had just given them. Clearly her concept of rhyming was the relationship among four specific words and no useful learning transfer was gained.

We can further illustrate the importance of understanding in learning as it applies to concept formation. Teachers cannot give students concepts; concepts can only be formed by individuals out of their own experiences. Research shows, for instance, that difficulties in arithmetic processes can be traced to a failure to understand basic number concepts. Too often understanding is evaluated on the basis of the products of learning without considering the learning processes. When students' answers are correct, do they understand the problem? They may not. It is possible that they got the correct answer by coincidence or, having dutifully learned a method, followed it blindly down a corridor of computation to the proper reply. Can you explain why you invert and then multiply when you divide by a fraction? If you cannot, you were probably taught how to perform the operation without understanding the process. Understanding number concepts comes through many experiences in which the student is required to think through the reasons for performing an operation. Therefore, diagnosis in mathematics should begin by studying how basic number concepts relate to specific difficulties.

A second competency in diagnosis is the ability to recognize symptoms related to the physical and psychological aspects of growth. Sometimes the underlying causes of students' difficulties are so complex that teachers will need to rely on the services of a specialist for diagnosis. Still, they should be familiar with symptoms of poor vision, inadequate hearing, and lack of energy. Further, the informed teacher understands the common mental mechanisms used by poorly adjusted children to reduce their tension. Students with severe anxieties are not ready for learning. Remediation is, after all, exceedingly demanding of the student, requiring both concentration and a high degree of motivation.

The psychological bases of a problem may be hard to reach. For instance, one girl of above average intelligence was having great difficulty with arithmetic. Her achievement in subjects demanding verbal facility was high, relationships with her peers appeared satisfactory, and rapport with her teacher was excellent. The teacher tried many approaches to help the student, but made little progress. Finally, in a case history, a discovery was made. The child's mother had always done poorly in arithmetic and persisted in talking about it. The youngster had identified with her mother, building up a self-concept of inability that completely negated all efforts to succeed.

The third competence is the ability to use the various diagnostic and remedial techniques, devices, and materials available with understanding. Among these devices are standardized and classroom tests and practice exercises. Detailed discussions of specific difficulties, particularly in arithmetic and reading, can be found elsewhere, and suggested remedial procedures are outlined in detail. The teacher can do much diagnosis and remediation without a clinical specialist. Printed materials are available for classroom help, and experience expands the teacher's skills.

Determining the Causes of Unsatisfactory Achievement

Teachers who know the more common causes of unsatisfactory achievement have some basis for making intelligent hypotheses about the difficulties of their students. Lack of achievement may be attributed to personal and/or environmental factors reflected in scholastic aptitude and physical development and health, with special emphasis on visual and auditory abilities, and personal-social adjustment.

Scholastic Aptitude. When children have low scholastic aptitude, lack of achievement cannot necessarily be interpreted as the result of faulty teaching or lack of application. They may be doing as well as they can. Many students who are poor in reading and mathematics have low scholastic aptitude scores, but a low score does not necessarily mean that a student has low innate mental ability. The score on most group tests of scholastic aptitude can be seriously affected by poor reading ability, lack of motivation, or distractions from poor test administration. Therefore, a principal diagnostic problem is to get as accurate an estimate of the student's potential as possible. Teachers should not conclude that students have a low scholastic aptitude unless they have carefully considered various data.

If at all possible, an individual intelligence test should be administered to those students who have low achievement and low group scholastic aptitude scores. It is often surprising to learn that some of these students have higher mental ability than some of the high achievers. Too often teachers equate ability to pass tests, conformity, good grooming, and verbosity with high intelligence. Many shy, withdrawn, poorly groomed, or nonconformist students excel intellectually.

There have been many suggested procedures for comparing students' aptitude and achievement test scores to determine whether they are working up to their capacities. However, there are precautions one must take in seeking this kind of information (Hills, 1976, pp. 284–288). As an example, the norms for both types of tests must be determined on the same standardization group, at the same time, and in the same norming operation. Another consideration is the degree of content similarity in the instrument's items.

Health. Because learning is hard work, the health of students influences their ability to achieve. Many things cause inadequate stamina; examples are malnutrition, glandular difficulty, or improper rest. In one fourth-grade class a teacher discovered that forty percent of the students were consistently watching television until after ten o'clock on school nights. It is understandable that this group was difficult to teach. Poor health may also cause excessive absences, which can be especially detrimental to achievement in arithmetic and reading—subjects that require cumulative skill learning.

There is no unequivocal evidence that visual anomalies are a primary cause of educational disability. While some students with good vision are poor readers, others who fail to pass vision tests read well, but the latter perform with considerable discomfort. Many cannot attend to print and can only read for short periods of time. If students are nearsighted, and if their teachers use a visual approach, the students may miss basic instruction.

Poor hearing is a distinct disadvantage. Students may successfully camouflage hearing anomalies with apparent attention and go unnoticed by the teacher. Even students who pass common hearing tests may have serious auditory deficiencies. If there is a high tonal frequency loss, it is difficult to differentiate among consonant sounds, so that an oral approach to beginning reading distinctly handicaps such a student.

An alert teacher can often detect symptoms of poor hearing. Students so handicapped may speak without expression and with the voice pitched unnaturally. Because they cannot differentiate among sounds, they are often poor spellers, and their speech and pronunciation lack clarity and precision. When they cannot understand what is being said, their attention often wanes; they may stare out the window or disturb their classmates. Others may frequently request that statements or questions be repeated. Whether speech defects result from loss of hearing or some other cause, they seriously impair a student's achievement.

There are also organic symptoms of poor hearing, such as earache, sinus condition, and ear discharge. Because such disorders can be corrected, teachers can prevent permanent disabilities by referring these students for medical attention.

Motor coordination is another physical factor to which the elementary teacher in particular should be attentive, since it can have a detrimental effect on handwriting. Because handwriting is important in developing other skills, a disability may have far-reaching effects. If students write slowly, they may understand test items but find it impossible to complete them within the time limit. Their scores imply low achievement but the real deficiency lies in the handwriting.

Federal Law (PL 94–142).   Federal legislation in 1975 entitled the "Education for All Handicapped Children Act" (PL 94–142) mandated early identification of children who need special services and special education. The Bureau of Education for the Handicapped has determined that approximately ten percent of school age children are handicapped. These include the mentally retarded, hard of hearing, deaf, speech impaired, visually handicapped, emotionally disturbed, physically handicapped, learning disabled, and other children who require special educational assistance and other services.

A complete educational assessment program for handicapped children requires the assistance of classroom teachers, educational diagnosticians, and school psychologists. Both standardized and informal methods are required so that multidimensional analyses can be made for each child. Furthermore, additional specialized procedures need to be employed for each area of exceptionality.

Personal-Social Adjustment.   Emotionally disturbed students dissipate their energy before they can apply it. It is difficult to determine whether emotional difficultie s are causing learning difficulties or vice versa. Learning problems can at times be cause or effect. Indeed, a student may become an outstanding achiever to compensate for some emotional problem. But too often children with emotional disturbances find themselves caught in a vicious circle, anxious over lack of achievement, and performing poorly because of the emotional disturbance.

Harris and Sipay (1975, pp. 301–304) list ten kinds of emotional problems that contribute to reading disabilities, but which can also be applied to other subjects.

1. Conscious refusal to learn.

2. Overt hostility. Because some children have built up intense feelings of resentment, they find it difficult to exercise control of their emotions. Student-teacher relationships are not conducive to learning.

3. Negative conditioning to reading. Reading has been associated with something the child dislikes intensely like a teacher or punishment. Therefore, he or she learns to dislike reading.

4. Displacement of hostility. Suppose a child dislikes or fears a parent or a teacher. The child realizes that this person enjoys reading. Since it may arouse feelings of anxiety and guilt to direct hostility toward this individual, the child expresses these hostile feelings toward reading.

5. Resistance to pressure. When an overambitious parent pressures a child to achieve, the reaction of the child may be a disinterest in reading.

6. Clinging to dependency. To avoid growing up a child may cling to a symbol of early childhood—inability to read.

7. Quick discouragement. Because some children lack a feeling of security, they become quickly discouraged. They have little confidence and respect.

8. Success is dangerous. Success may symbolize entering adult society and competing as a rival with a parent. There is an implication for the child that this competition will result in extreme retaliation.

9. Extreme distractability or restlessness. When a child has a high degree of tension, he or she finds it difficult to control his physical activity. This results in inattention and inability to learn.

10. Absorption in a private world. Daydreams, through which some children fulfill their wishes, result in lack of concentration and inability to learn.

Teachers should be continually aware of significant symptoms. If students cannot solve their problems in the classroom, they may need to be referred for clinical treatment. Symptoms of aggression, withdrawal, and general problem behavior are often indicative of personal-social adjustment problems. Sometimes antisocial behavior results from a particular incident and passes quickly. Serious and deep-seated problems, however, can be identified by persistence of symptoms.

Environmental Causes.   Although it is not easy to identify environmental causes of a student's learning problems, the difficulties associated with them are likely to surface quickly. Feelings of rejection traced to a poor home environment, for example, may cause school adjustment problems in the child in short order.

Some students are handicapped by the failure of their parents to serve successfully as surrogate teachers. Moreover, there may be an absence of intellectual stimulation in the home. Few if any books or magazines are available. Lack of travel and other cultural opportunities make it difficult, if not impossible, for the child to develop the concepts so readily attainable by those with broader experiences.

Poor teaching may be the cause of serious learning problems. Students may have learning difficulties that become cumulative. They may be underequipped to learn and may be emotionally disturbed. Suffice it to say that, in diagnosing learning difficulties, one must investigate a student's environment to find if the principal cause lies there.

Specific Subject Difficulties.   Learning difficulties often stem from the subject itself. The complex skills demanded by mathematics, language, spelling, and reading present learning problems. Considerable research on learning difficulties has indicated typical specific errors and has resulted in the design of many diagnostic instruments to help locate them. But the teacher need not always administer a standardized instrument in diagnosis, because informal techniques are effective when used competently. Criterion-referenced test items are particularly helpful when trying to identify specific learning difficulties.

A variety of common errors can be observed in the work of children as they solve problems in basic arithmetic skills. For example, they make mistakes in carrying, counting, and subtracting because of inability to cope with zeroes. The interrelationships among the fundamental processes must be taken into account in any diagnosis. If children are struggling with long division because they cannot subtract or multiply, for example, giving them more division problems to work without analyzing their difficulties is an inefficient way of helping them. Learning to subtract will make them competent in long division.

Oral language provides its share of common errors, such as misplaced accents, confusion with silent letters, and incorrect vowel and consonant quality. Also, failure to write legibly often requires attention. Illegibility of handwriting can often be traced to a few improperly formed letters repeated many times. The lower case *e* is written with a closed loop resembling an *i*, or the *i* is written with a loop to resemble an *e*. Often letters like *o*, *s*, *a*, and *b* are not closed, thereby making them illegible. If legibility is to be improved, the teacher must concentrate on letters causing the most difficulty. It is a waste of valuable time to have students drilling on every letter of the alphabet.

Spelling errors may be related to mispronunciation, speech disability, or inability to use phonic skills. A classification of typical spelling errors can reveal this relationship and give the teacher a basis for helping the student. For instance, average spellers add fewer letters to words than poor spellers, which may be due to greater use of phonics among the average spellers.

Students having difficulty with spelling often have problems with reading and vice versa; the skills are closely related. Another, and subtler, cause of reading disability is lack of background, a difficulty in all grades and areas. A first-grade student may not have had the visual and auditory experiences to acquire a sight vocabulary. A student in secondary school may lack the vocabulary to comprehend assignments in social studies and physical science. One gifted student thought that a cow was about the size of a large dog. The child had never seen a cow, though verbalization about one was easy. Field trips provide experiences that help make classroom learning meaningful. A lesson in conservation will be much more effective if students have actually seen the results of erosion. A discussion of city government will be aided by a visit to the municipal buildings. Words have no intrinsic meaning; they trigger associations from the experiences of individuals. When students have no experiences to associate with the symbols, they can only memorize.

Another cause of poor reading is lack of the systematic development of the basic skills in reading, such as a sight vocabulary, techniques of word recognition, comprehension, and the work-study skills. For example, if children have not developed an adequate sight vocabulary, they may become overanalytical in their reading and break words apart without learning how to blend the syllables, use meaningful phrases, or find the context to help them understand. In other cases, structural analysis, syllabication, phonics, and so on, have been too little emphasized, and the students find themselves handicapped in attacking new words. Independent reading demands a system of word-attack skills.

Failure to transfer reading skills to other assignments is another difficulty. Teaching reading without applying it to assignments in, for example, biology, too often results in the student's inability to do everyday reading tasks. Teachers of science or other subjects need to discuss the main ideas of paragraphs with their students. They should show how skimming, thorough reading, and rapid reading can be applied to assignments. They should help their students initiate vocabulary development programs for themselves, because skills must be applied, not allowed to remain in isolation.

PROBLEMS

3. A sixth-grade teacher reports that students can do arithmetic computations fairly well but that they are experiencing frustration in the areas of arithmetic reasoning and problem solving. Apply the principles of diagnosis to this situation by outlining specific steps for this teacher to follow to gain a thorough understanding of the learning problems involved.

4. Common learning difficulties in the basic skill subjects have been presented. How might teachers in the following curriculum areas approach similar analyses?
    a. Middle school physical education
    b. Elementary art
    c. Tenth-grade biology
    d. French I

Remediation

In addition to recognizing what children need to learn, teachers must also determine how they can best learn (Rutherford, 1972). Remediation would be much simpler if we could apply a trusted formula to each learning disability—a notion as sadly impossible as every other cure-all. Students differ, and it may be said that learning disabilities are rooted in different soils. The source of one student's difficulty may be emotional while another suffers from faulty teaching. One student's handwriting is illegible because of inadequate motor development while his or her neighbor is simply careless.

Despite the different techniques and methods for remediation, certain guiding principles apply to all subjects and provide an operational framework:

1. Remediation should be accompanied by a strong motivational program.
2. Remediation should be individualized in terms of the psychology of learning.
3. A continuous evaluation that informs a student of results is vital.

Providing Motivation

No remedial technique will be successful unless students can see the relationship between the purposes of the technique and their own needs. Many failing students have acute feelings of inadequacy and feel they are unable to succeed, that they are different. Some of them withdraw and refuse to try; others rationalize by thinking that success is unimportant and that whatever they might learn will never be useful.

The teacher is the catalyst for changing these attitudes. Such students long to be understood. Many of them have been lectured, threatened, and rejected until often the first task is to help them rebuild self-confidence. Good teachers let students know that they are liked and appreciated; above all, teachers are optimistic and stay that way during the students' "downs" as well as their "ups." By accepting students, teachers help them to build a sense of security that is vital for effective learning.

Since students develop confidence when they experience success, it is important that teachers know their strengths as well as their weaknesses. The teacher must build on those strengths, starting at the child's level of achievement. It helps if the student's first success is dramatized. Presenting progress concretely is effective, particularly for younger children. Charts, graphs, and pictures can all be used successfully, though the device must be attuned to the maturity of the students. A device that lets them see their improvement works well. When they compete with themselves they can improve their past records and this proves highly motivating.

To sustain motivation, the teacher should stimulate interest in the remedial program and monotony should be avoided at all costs. Different approaches prevent mental fatigue, and so do materials with high motivational value. If students can help plan their programs by selecting materials and procedures, their involvement will often generate a permanent interest basic to the development of their independence.

Students' interests may wane if they are forced into remedial activity. Some students honestly feel that their skills are adequate in spite of painful indications to the contrary. Sometimes allowing them to take a standardized test and helping them analyze the results produces the desired effect. Ingenious teachers use many methods to help a student want to improve, and social recognition is not the least of them. Most students find it rewarding to demonstrate progress to their peers and parents. Above all, remedial activities should not be scheduled when they conflict with other things the student would like to do. To be required to work a sheaf of arithmetic exercises while a "big game" is going on is hardly motivating.

Evaluating the Program

No remedial program can be based on initial diagnosis without consistent follow-through. In the first place, students' needs will change as they overcome their learning difficulties. Just as their problems have been cumulative in nature, remedial instruction will be cumulative in impact. The new is learned in terms of the old.

Second, the teacher will want to judge the success of a program. Methods and materials may have to be shifted to help the student learn; all students do not respond equally to the same treatment. Only a continual evaluation can determine progress and future procedure.

Third, evaluation is important because it lets students know how they are progressing. Motivation to learn is increased when students know the results of their efforts. The less mature the child, the more it is necessary to depict results graphically.

Using Clinical Personnel

Although most teachers are responsible for remedial work, special teachers are occasionally employed to help them with their problems and often to work with students who have severe learning difficulties. Because reading problems are the source of many educational problems, a number of schools employ reading specialists. Although they are most often found in the elementary schools, some secondary schools are also providing their services. In other schools, a subject specialist handles problems in all basic skill or curriculum areas.

School psychologists can also substantially contribute to a child's improvement. Although a great share of their work will be corrective in nature, much of it will also be preventive. Their task is to sensitize school personnel to students' needs, to diagnose individual problems, and to make the proper referrals when necessary. In this role, they serve as coordinators for all the special services in the school as well as the community. Through them, the varying contributions of remedial programs, mental health clinics, social agencies, and the home can be effectively utilized.

PROBLEMS

5. Imagine that you are a foreign language teacher. Three of your students are having difficulties. Robert works hard but stumbles desperately in dictations and oral work. Al has a natural ear for the language but seemingly cannot understand the grammar. Donna is a rote learner who memorizes long vocabulary lists with ease, but cannot grasp the essential meaning when translating. Describe how you would provide individualized remediation for these pupils.

6. Some teachers do not report standardized test scores to their students as they fear that poor results may be discouraging. Do you agree?

Examination of Class Achievement

A good way to identify students with learning difficulties is to administer a survey achievement test battery and a scholastic aptitude test. Students who appear to be underachieving may then undergo thorough diagnosis and remediation. The discussion that follows is based on the results of seven basic skills subtests from an achievement test battery and on a group-administered scholastic aptitude test that primarily measures verbal aptitude. The tests were administered in October to twenty-three students of a fifth-grade class. These students attended a public elementary school in a small city, and their families varied in socioeconomic status. Data analysis provides a description of the use of the class record and the class analysis chart in identifying group as well as individual strengths and weaknesses. Suggestions for individual diagnosis and remediation are presented through a discussion of one student's difficulties.

Class Record

A class record was prepared on the basis of the test scores from all tests and is shown in Table 14.1. The students' names are listed in the order of their overall achievement, as represented by a composite value for all subtests in the battery. The sex of each student is recorded in the first column following the name. Age is listed in the next two columns, the scholastic aptitude score in the fourth column, and the grade equivalent and stanines for the seven subtests of the battery in the following columns.

Class Analysis Chart

The numbers preceding the students' names serve as identification numbers when preparing a class analysis chart, such as that shown in Figure 14.1. A column is available for each subtest score. Note that these scores are in terms of stanines. The distribution of stanines for each column is found by writing the identification

TABLE 14.1.   Class Record of Achievement Test Scores for a Fifth-Grade Class

Student's name	Sex	Age (yr–mo)	Scholastic aptitude	Vocabulary	Reading comp.	Math concepts	Math comp.	Math applic.	Spelling	Language
1. Mary Jones	G	10–2	132	8.8–9[a]	9.3–8	8.4–9	7.8–9	9.5–9	7.0–7	8.5–8
2. William Seeber	B	10–1	128	8.8–9	9.3–8	8.4–9	6.5–7	8.6–8	8.1–8	9.0–8
3. Mary Hillhouse	G	9–8	125	8.8–9	7.9–8	5.2–5	5.2–5	5.4–5	8.1–8	9.5–9
4. Ann Chitwood	G	9–10	130	8.3–8	9.3–8	7.5–8	5.9–6	7.4–8	6.0–6	8.7–8
5. Celia Graham	G	10–4	120	7.3–7	6.7–7	5.2–5	5.6–6	5.6–6	7.3–8	9.5–9
6. Carol Smith	G	10–5	125	6.8–7	6.2–6	6.5–7	6.9–8	7.4–8	6.3–6	6.4–6
7. Gloria Behrens	G	10–7	122	6.1–6	6.4–6	5.8–6	5.6–6	7.4–8	8.1–8	7.4–7
8. Sandra Black	G	10–4	123	6.8–7	7.3–7	5.2–5	4.6–5	5.6–6	6.3–6	9.5–9
9. June Nelson	G	9–10	128	6.8–7	5.1–5	6.0–6	4.1–4	7.4–8	6.3–6	6.4–6
10. Trudy Lincoln	G	10–4	115	7.0–7	6.2–6	5.6–6	5.1–5	5.4–5	6.3–6	7.4–7
11. Joe Sills	B	10–3	110	6.3–7	5.9–6	5.2–5	4.6–5	5.6–6	6.4–7	7.4–7
12. Albert Uken	B	9–11	115	5.7–6	6.2–6	5.6–6	4.6–5	5.1–5	6.3–6	7.8–7
13. John Sevaar	B	10–2	110	6.3–7	5.3–5	4.9–5	3.0–2	5.1–5	5.3–5	6.2–6
14. Cindy Bockwitz	G	10–5	104	4.4–4	2.7–2	4.7–5	5.1–5	5.4–5	7.3–8	4.8–5
15. Florence Weber	G	10–6	98	5.7–6	4.6–5	3.7–3	3.9–3	4.0–4	4.8–5	4.5–4
16. Meg Adams	G	10–8	102	4.4–4	5.1–5	4.0–4	4.1–4	4.4–4	4.3–4	2.8–3
17. Stanley Seward	B	10–4	98	4.1–4	4.4–4	3.7–3	3.5–3	4.4–4	3.2–3	4.9–5
18. Beverly Hill	G	10–8	122	3.8–3	3.6–3	6.2–6	4.6–5	6.2–6	3.6–3	3.5–4
19. Carol Jones	G	10–6	94	3.8–3	3.3–3	3.2–3	3.0–2	4.0–4	4.5–4	3.5–4
20. Peter White	B	9–10	98	3.8–3	3.6–3	3.2–3	3.0–2	4.0–4	3.2–3	3.5–4
21. Floyd Echart	B	9–9	90	3.8–3	2.7–2	3.7–3	3.0–2	3.5–3	3.2–3	2.3–3
22. Oscar Biggs	B	10–1	88	2.7–2	2.5–2	2.0–1	3.0–2	2.9–3	2.7–2	2.3–3
23. Helen Brown	G	10–7	85	2.4–2	2.5–2	2.0–1	2.7–2	2.9–3	2.7–2	2.6–3

[a] The first score is the grade equivalent; the second score is the stanine based on the standardization group.

number of each student in the box on the same line as the stanine score. For example, Meg Adams (#16) has a stanine score of three for the *Language* test. Therefore, a "16" is written in the language column in the box opposite the stanine score of three. The remaining twenty-two numbers are similarly recorded in this column.

For each column, the median stanine score was determined by locating the twelfth score from the top or bottom and plotted by placing a rectangle at the appropriate stanine in each column. As you can see, the class analysis chart is a summary of the test results for the entire class. At a glance, the teacher can identify the areas in which the best and poorest work is being done. There is considerable variability in all areas of achievement. Few students have scores at the very top or bottom of the class in all subtests.

Notice that the low point in achievement for this class is in mathematics computation. Obviously, certain computational skills are not being mastered. The class does somewhat better in mathematics application because only low-level computation skills are needed in this subtest.

Finally, the highest points of achievement are in vocabulary, language, and spelling. Vocabulary is related to good scholastic ability. In this connection, note that the median of the scholastic aptitude score for the class is 115, which is above average. The comparatively high degree of success in spelling can be attributed to the special emphasis given this subject.

Stanine	Vocabulary	Reading Comp.	Math Concepts	Math Comp.	Math Applic.	Spelling	Language
9	1,2, 3		1,2	1	1		3,5, 8
8	4	1,2, 3,4	4	6	2,4,6, 7,9	2,3,5, 7,14	1,2, 4
7	5,6,8,9, 10,11,13	5,8	6	2		1,11	7,10, 11,12
6	7,12, 15	6,7,10, 11,12	7,9,10, 12,18	4,5, 7	5,8, 11,18	4,6,8, 9,10,12	6,9, 13
5		9,13, 15,16	3,5,8, 11,13,14	3,10,11, 14,18	3,10,12, 13,14	13,15	14,17
4	14,16, 17	17	16	8,9, 12,16	15,16,17, 19,20	16,19	15,18, 19,20
3	18,19, 20,21	18,19, 20	15,17,19, 20,21	15,17	21,22, 23	17,18, 20,21	16,21, 22,23
2	22,23	14,21, 22,23		13,19,20, 21,22,23		22,23	
1			22,23				

FIGURE 14.1.   Class Analysis Chart for a Fifth-Grade Class

Study of the class analysis chart reveals a good deal of useful information about individual students. For instance, Cindy Bockwitz (#14) has a much higher score in spelling than in other parts of the achievement test. Is this an indication that Cindy could improve in other areas? Does it mean that her parents have been drilling her in spelling and find that she excels in this skill? Spelling is not as high level a verbal skill as is reading for comprehension.

The teacher cannot assume that two students with about the same average (or composite) are alike in terms of their patterns of achievement. This is true of Meg Adams (#16) and Stanley Seward (#17). Even though their average achievement differs little, Meg is at the third stanine in language usage, while Stanley is at the fifth. There are also differences in spelling and reading comprehension, but in the opposite direction (see Table 14.1).

Item Analysis

Another useful aid is an item-analysis chart constructed from the right and wrong answers to each item in a subtest. Table 14.2 lists the responses of the fifth-grade class on the mathematics computation subtest.

This diagnostic device gives the teacher a more detailed picture of the areas of lowest achievement. For example, the content represented by items like 1, 4, and 6 has been fairly well learned by the class as a whole, while several items missed by a large percentage of the group represent areas of low achievement.

Items 24, 25, 29, and 37 require knowledge about how to cope with zeros in the minuend when subtracting. The results indicate that only a few of the students have mastered these skills. Poor performance on some of the other items reveals that many students had trouble with mathematical computations involving fractions.

In a multiple-choice test, it is possible to determine the number of students choosing each of the distracters as well as the number answering correctly. When items are machine-scored, the test-scoring machine can easily run the analysis. Because a good test item included plausible distracters, a study of students' choices will often give the teacher insight into their difficulties. This information provides a better basis for diagnosis and, as a result, enables prescription of more effective remediation.

Table 14.2 provides information about how well the class as a whole performs specific tasks. In a sense, we are now using data from a norm-referenced test in a criterion-referenced way (Fremer, 1972). Certainly a well-constructed criterion-referenced test would provide better information in these instances. Yet an item analysis as shown in Table 14.2 has much value.

It should be further noted that, in working with the learning disabled where instruction must be individualized, norm-referenced measurement devices are of use in determining how deviant from the "normal" certain children are. However, after student problems are evaluated, these devices provide less flexibility for making the frequent measurements of educational progress needed for this type of child (Proger & Mann, 1973).

TABLE 14.2.   Item Analysis of the Mathematics Computation Subtest

Test item	Right No.	%	Wrong No.	%	Test item	Right No.	%	Wrong No.	%
1	19	83	4	17	21	13	56	10	44
2	17	74	6	26	22	10	44	13	56
3	16	70	7	30	23	17	74	6	26
4	19	83	4	17	24	4	17	19	83
5	16	70	7	30	25	7	30	16	70
6	18	78	5	22	26	3	13	20	87
7	16	70	7	30	27	5	22	18	78
8	16	70	7	30	28	9	39	14	61
9	14	61	9	39	29	7	30	16	70
10	14	61	9	39	30	4	17	19	83
11	11	48	12	52	31	4	17	19	83
12	5	22	18	78	32	12	52	11	48
13	8	35	15	65	33	7	30	16	70
14	3	13	20	87	34	6	26	17	74
15	5	22	18	78	35	9	39	14	61
16	12	52	11	48	36	8	35	15	65
17	11	48	12	52	37	3	13	20	87
18	10	44	13	56	38	8	35	15	65
19	11	48	12	52	39	8	35	15	65
20	16	70	7	30	40	9	39	14	61

PROBLEMS

7. Can you find specific instances of a serious lack of achievement in the fifth-grade class in question? Are any of the students overachievers? In your opinion, what is the chief problem confronting the teacher of this class? What additional information about the students would be highly useful?

8. What advantages would criterion-referenced tests have over norm-referenced instruments in working with severely disabled learners?

Individual Diagnosis and Remediation

At this point it is clear that group strengths, weaknesses, and range of ability can be determined from the class record and the class analysis chart. Some individual problems also become apparent. Consider the case of Beverly Hill (#18), who is significantly below the average achievement in language skills of a normal fifth-grade child in the second month of the school year. Beverly has ability that surpasses the average child. Her scholastic aptitude score is 122 (see Table 14.1). Despite her superior scholastic aptitude, she is definitely below the point a student with average mentality should be, except in mathematics. Even her mathematics scores represent some retardation considering her scholastic aptitude.

Inability to Read

Because there was evidence that inability to read might be the cause of Beverly's difficulties, the teacher wanted to explore several related elements, but needed more information about her specific reading difficulties. Many teachers like to use an informal oral reading test for this purpose. Beverly's teacher selected several interesting narrative passages, each about 200 words long, from material that Beverly had not read. The reading level of the first passage was of first- or second-grade difficulty, the others of increasing difficulty.

This procedure threw considerable light on Beverly's reading problems. Typical questions asked in an informal reading test are: Does she know the sounds of the vowels and consonants? Can she break a new word into syllables? Can she blend individual sounds together so that she can recognize the word? Does she read with expression, indicating that she is using the context to help identify new words? Does she rely too much on context and fail to recognize certain words, substituting those that make sense but distorting the meaning?

In addition to the informal reading test, the teacher administered the *Gates-McKillop Reading Diagnostic Tests*, a standardized instrument to analyze reading difficulties. Table 14.3 contains some of Beverly's grade scores on these tests. Her oral score is 3.8, approximately the same as her silent reading score. The other scores indicate her serious weakness in reading fundamentals.

Beverly had developed no systematic method for attacking words. She tended to concentrate on words themselves, rather than on the relationship among them, and thereby lost the train of thought. Even her word-by-word reading was marked at times with considerable confusion. Not only did she make a considerable number of reversal errors, but she had difficulty in blending word parts. A number of letter sounds were confused, particularly *a* and *e*. Recognition of syllables and phonograms was weak and because of her undue attention to word parts and units, she made very little use of context to aid her in pronunciation or comprehension.

Survey vs. Diagnostic Test Data.   What are the differences between a diagnostic and a survey test? A survey test provides a general appraisal of overall achievement in some subject area such as reading. It is not designed to give a detailed picture of deficiencies; that is the province of the diagnostic test. Nor is it constructed

TABLE 14.3.   Scores on the Gates-McKillop Reading Diagnostic Tests, First Administration

Subtests	Beverly's grade score	Highest possible grade score
Oral reading	3.8	7.5
Reversals	Poor score	
Recognizing and blending common word parts	Very low score	
Syllabication	Low score	

to indicate possible causes of inadequate achievement. A good diagnostic test should provide cues for the formulation of hypotheses concerning lack of growth and possible remedial procedures.

The survey test showed Beverly Hill to be very low in achievement of language skills, but it required a diagnostic test to emphasize weakness in syllabication, recognizing and blending common word parts, and so forth, which are the bases of low performance in the language arts.

Determination of the Cause

The teacher found from Beverly's cumulative record,* Figures 14.2 and 14.3, that she had a long history of underachievement. She had complained of headaches during her first year of school and, in the second grade, was required to wear glasses for close work. Also, during that year her father had been killed in an accident and her mother had been compelled to work. Beverly had symptoms of anxiety and insecurity, and her early school experience probably accounts for the reading difficulty. She was severely handicapped because learning basic skills is a cumulative process and she lacked a foundation on which to build. Beverly's mother remarried, and both parents expressed concern about the child's achievement. They asked for a conference, so the teacher had an opportunity to enlist their help.

The teacher realized the importance of involving the parents in learning and giving them a positive role in the process. There was an understanding that parental nagging, forcing children to forego normal social activities, or a lack of genuine parental interest in the child can prevent a remedial program from being a success. The parents were also given specific instructions so they could help. They were never told that "there was nothing they could do," or that "everything would work out all right."

Of course it is sometimes difficult if not impossible to elicit parental co-operation. Some parents' own lack of personal-social adjustment prevents them from being close to their children. Some are so absorbed in their own interests and professional lives that they find it impossible to become involved in their children's problems.

During the conference with Beverly's parents, the teacher explained that their child was bright and that her difficulty stemmed from immature word-recognition skills and lack of concentration on the meaning and the relationship among the words. It was decided that Beverly should have individual remedial reading instruction each day. Her parents were helped to realize the need for supporting the child emotionally and were asked to praise her liberally for any improvement. They were advised against exerting pressure either overtly or through expression of concern about her progress.

The teacher was also able to discuss television and its relation to Beverly's reading problem. Her parents were helped to see that if their own chief interest was television, not reading, it would be impossible to convince the child of the

* For additional information about cumulative records, see page 477.

CALIFORNIA CUMULATIVE RECORD
ELEMENTARY FORM
Confidential Information for use by Professional Personnel

FILE No. (Pencil)

1. IDENTIFICATION DATA

PHOTOGRAPHS

LAST NAME	FIRST NAME	MIDDLE NAME	NICKNAME (Pencil)	CHECK SEX
Hill	Beverly	Jane		M F X

BIRTH DATE	BIRTH DATE VERIFICATION	CITY (OR COUNTY)	PLACE OF BIRTH STATE (OR NATION)
2/20/69	Birth Certificate	Surburban	New York

HOME	NAME	ADDRESS	TELEPHONE
	Mary L. Hill	101 Olds Ave.	748-3218

COMMENTS

IN CASE OF EMERGENCY NOTIFY

	NAME	ADDRESS	TELEPHONE
(Pencil) (OR)	Joe S. Brown	1805 Lotus St.	748-4532

COMMENTS

DATES PHOTOGRAPHED (Pencil) _____ SCHOOL DISTRICT _____

	NAME	ADDRESS	TELEPHONE
(Pencil) (OR)	Dr. Ralph Ogden	16 Main Street	744-8072

COMMENTS

2. GROUP SCHOLASTIC CAPACITY TESTS
(LABEL OTHER SUB SCORES USED, e.g. PERFORMANCE, PERCEPTION, ETC. DOUBLE SPACES PROVIDED.)

DATE TEST GIVEN	GRADE	NAME OF TEST	FORM	LEVEL	C.A.	M.A.	5 Total	6 Verbal	7 Non-Verb.	8	9	10	11	12	13	COMMENTS	EXAMINER
10/75	1	Basic Skills		Prim			124										
10/79	5	Basic Skills		Inter			122										

3. INDIVIDUAL TESTS

DATE TEST GIVEN	GRADE	NAME OF TEST	C.A.	RESULTS AND REMARKS	EXAMINER
11/79	5	Mental Abilities		130 I.Q. Had trouble with tests demanding reading skill.	A. J. Smith

4. GROUP ACHIEVEMENT TESTS (Including Reading Readiness) (LABEL VARIOUS SUB SCORES, e.g. VOCABULARY)

DATE TEST GIVEN	GRADE	NAME OF TEST	FORM	LEVEL	3 READING	4	5	6	7 ARITHMETIC	8	9	10	11 LANGUAGE	12	13	14	15	COMMENTS	EXAMINER
11/76	2	Basic Skills		Prim	Par M Word M	1.1 1.5			Reas Comp	3.1 1.8			Spell	1.5					
10/77	3	Basic Skills		Prim	Par M Word M	1.8 2.3			Comp Conc	2.9 2.9			Spell	2.5					
10/78	4	Basic Skills		Inter	Par M Word M	2.4 2.8			Appl Comp Conc	5.1 3.8 5.0			Spell Lang	3.6 3.6					
10/79	5	Basic Skills		Inter	Read Voc	3.6 3.8			Appl Comp Conc	6.2 4.6 6.2			Spell Lang	3.6 3.5					

5. PERSONALITY AND INTEREST INVENTORIES, APTITUDE TESTS, AND OTHER TESTS (LABEL VARIOUS SUB SCORES, e.g. EMOTIONAL, SOCIAL)

DATE TEST GIVEN	GRADE	NAME OF TEST	FORM	LEVEL	1	2	3	4	5	6	7	8	9	10	11	12	13	14	15	COMMENTS	EXAMINER

6. INFORMATION CONCERNING INDIVIDUAL ADJUSTMENT

YEAR AND GRADE	INTERESTS, ACTIVITIES, LEADERSHIP	FAMILIES AND HOME RELATIONSHIPS OUT OF SCHOOL RESPONSIBILITIES	ATTITUDES AND FEELINGS ABOUT: SELF; PEERS; SCHOOL	REFERRALS TO SCHOOL SERVICES AND/OR COMMUNITY AGENCIES
YEAR 1974-1975 KINDERGARTEN	Quiet child. Very cooperative.	Shares family experiences. Close family ties.	Has adjusted well to school and to her peers.	
YEAR 1975-1976 GRADE 1	Likes to do activities with hands. Doesn't choose books in free time.	Family watches television a great deal.	Sometimes appears to be daydreaming.	
YEAR 1976-1977 GRADE 2	Seems withdrawn since death of father.	Mother is now working. Does not spend as much time with Beverly.	Retarded in reading. Seems un-interested.	
YEAR 1977-1978 GRADE 3	Evidences of some leadership. Has several close friends.	Seems to be a close relationship with the Mother.	Has shown considerable interest in arithmetic.	
YEAR 1978-1979 GRADE 4	Continues to be liked and accepted by her peers.	Has done some baby sitting with neighbor children during the day hours.	Has applied herself to her school work.	
YEAR 1979-1980 GRADE 5				
YEAR 19 -19 GRADE				
YEAR 19 -19 GRADE				
YEAR 19 -19 GRADE				

FIGURE 14.2.   Inside Half of an Elementary School Cumulative Record

Reproduced by permission of the California State Department of Education.

7. GROWTH AND DEVELOPMENT THROUGH SCHOOL EXPERIENCES   FORM LM.—A. Carlisle & Co., S.F., 1955

INDICATE MAJOR CURRICULUM UNIT, DESCRIPTION OF EXPERIENCE, AND DURATION. INITIAL EACH ENTRY. THIS SPACE MAY ALSO BE USED FOR INDICATING DEGREE OF SUCCESS IN SCHOOL EXPERIENCES AND READERS USED

YEAR 1975-1976 KINDERGARTEN	YEAR 1976-1977 GRADE 1	YEAR 1977-1978 GRADE 2	YEAR 1978-1979 GRADE 3	YEAR 1979-1980 GRADE 4

Works well with group and plays independently. Neat; follows directions. Sings in tune; knows many nursery rhymes.
 	
Knows the letters of the alphabet, names of the colors.
Can write her name.
 	
Cooperative
 	
Seems ready for first grade work
	Reading: S-F series.
	Readiness bks.
	3 pre-primers,
	jr. primer and
	primer completed.
	Also 3 pre-primers of
	supp (H-M) rdrs.
	
	Did not start first reader, but should be ready for it in Sept.
	Did all bks.
	
	Math: Knows combinations and understands meaning of concepts
		Readers: S-F series.
		
		1^1 reader ...11/20
		1^2 " (H-M)..2/2
		          4/15
		L-C phonics bks, A & B
		Cowboy Sam, 1 & 2
		
		(started 2^1 reader in May, but finds it difficult. Cannot concentrate. Wears glasses, but forgets them)
		
		Math: Understands add. & sub., knows basic facts. S-B bk.
			Readers: S-F series.
			
			2^1 of S-F and of H-M; workbooks
			Eye & Ear Fun,1, 2, 3
			L-C phonics, bk C
			
			Completed S-F 2^2 and began 3^1,but finds it difficult. Dislikes reading.
			
			Social Studies: Local history, Indians
			
			Math: Average in class S-B bk 3; knows all combinations and 4 processes; accurate and neat.
				Readers: In lowest group. S-F 3^1 & 3^2
				Workbooks: S-F &
				   Readers Digest Skill
				   Builders, 2, 3, 4
				Merrill Skilltexts:
				   Nibs, Nicky, Uncle
				   Funny Bunny
				
				Math: S-B bk 4. Neat, accurate. Understands problems but has trouble reading them.
				
				Social Studies — Foll. Regional studies. Can't read text. Does not participate in disc.
				
				Science: enjoys experiments, can't read text.

YEAR 1980-1981 GRADE 5	YEAR 19 -19 GRADE	YEAR 19 -19 GRADE	YEAR 19 -19 GRADE	YEAR 19 -19 GRADE

Requirements of U. S. Constitution, American History, State and Local Government satisfactorily completed.

Date Certified   INITIAL

8. SCHOOL HISTORY

DATE ENTERED	HOME ADDRESS & TELEPHONE	CITY OR COUNTY	SCHOOL & SCHOOL DISTRICT	GRADE	TEACHER	ATTENDANCE	TRANSFERRED TO:	DATE LEFT
9/75	101 Olds 748-3218	Suburban	Suburban Central	K	Shapiro	Perfect		
9/76	"	"	"	1	Wilson	1st week — trip		
9/77	"	"	"	2	Eddy	1 week — death of F.		
9/78	"	"	"	3	Wood	Periodic absences		
9/79	"	"	"	4	Bannar	No absences		
9/80	"	"	"	5	Green			

9. PARENTS' EDUCATIONAL AND/OR VOCATIONAL PLANS FOR PUPIL: (Pencil)

COMPLETED GRADE 6 OR 8 OR ( ) ON   CIRCLE   Month   Day   Year

	HOME ADDRESS (Pencil)	SPECIFIC OCCUPATION (Pencil)	BUSINESS ADDRESS AND TELEPHONE (Pencil)
10. FATHER'S NAME Deceased			
11. MOTHER'S NAME Mary L. Hill	101 Olds Ave.	Teacher	Elmwood School
12. OR GUARDIAN'S NAME			

CIRCLE (Pencil)

Pupil Living With	Living?
Yes (No)	Yes (No)
Pupil Living With	Living?
(Yes) No	(Yes) No
Pupil Living With	Living?
Yes No	Yes No

13. CHILDREN OF FAMILY

NAMES	Year of Birth	RELATIONSHIP TO PUPIL	Living at Home
Beverly Hill	1969		

14. ADULTS OTHER THAN PARENTS LIVING CONTINUOUSLY IN PUPIL'S HOME (Pencil)

NAME	RELATIONSHIP TO PUPIL
DATE	

15. SIGNIFICANT HEALTH FACTORS

DATE	RECOMMENDATIONS OF HEALTH ADVISER	ADVISER'S NAME
9/76	Classes prescribed	Jones
	Audiometer reading normal	Jones

DATE	TEACHER'S COMMENTS ON PUPIL'S HEALTH CONDITIONS	TEACHER
11/76	Symptoms of extreme anxiety	

FIGURE 14.3.   Outside Half of an Elementary School Cumulative Record
Reproduced by permission of the California State Department of Education.

importance of improving her reading. In other words, their habits would have a marked effect on Beverly's. They were advised to discuss both television programs and their reading, and to draw Beverly into the conversation, thereby signifying the importance of both in acquiring and formulating ideas.

Remedial Instruction

Removing the cause of a learning difficulty is only the first step. Now Beverly had to be taught to read. In her case, stress was placed on recognition of sounds, syllables, and blending. She was given the opportunity to practice a systematic attack on unfamiliar words and helped to use context for determining meanings. Her left to right orientation was developed.

Attention was also given to improving her reading rate. Beverly was encouraged to time herself on short easy exercises and to keep a record of her progress. To keep her abreast of class work, the teacher made available easy materials on topics under study.

A student who has had difficulty in such a basic skill as reading is probably short on confidence. Beverly was given an opportunity to read an easy passage to the class occasionally, but first her teacher made sure that she was well-prepared. Recognition of this kind provided a high degree of motivation.

At the end of the year, several tests from the second form of the *Gates-McKillop Reading Diagnostic Tests* were administered to Beverly. The scores are listed in Table 14.4. Notice the vast improvement. The total score in oral reading increased from 3.8 to 7.2. All other scores are now satisfactory. Moreover, her scores on the *Gates-MacGinitie Reading Tests* are as shown in Table 14.5.

Beverly kept a record of the books she read during the year, and at the last count, she had over forty to her credit. Although some were very short and easy, she also had read a number of considerable substance.

All remedial teaching does not have to be done on an individual basis. Elementary school teachers can group students in various ways so that special help can be given for special difficulties. More secondary school teachers need to utilize these grouping procedures. The teacher might begin with two groups. Four or five students who excel in the course may be grouped for special projects while the

TABLE 14.4.   Scores on the Gates-McKillop Reading Diagnostic Tests, Second Administration

Subtests	Beverly's grade score
Oral reading	7.2
Reversals	Normal progress
Recognizing and blending common word parts	Normal progress
Syllabication	Normal progress

TABLE 14.5.   Scores on the Gates-MacGinitie Reading Tests

Test	Grade level
Vocabulary	6.8
Speed and accuracy	6.3
Comprehension	6.5

teacher works with the majority of the class. Gradually, as teachers develop skill and confidence, they can increase the number of groups.

PROBLEM

9. An analysis of Beverly's reading scores has been presented. Does the interpretation given indicate a need for a certain degree of sophistication on the part of the teacher to make maximum use of these tests? How would you explain the meaning of the *Gates* subtest scores to a parent?

Criterion-Referenced Diagnostic and Remedial Programs

Another approach to individual diagnosis and remediation is the use of criterion-referenced instruments based on a hierarchy of objectives developed for a subject-matter area. The *Diagnostic Mathematics Inventory (DMI)* is an example. It measures student mastery of 325 behaviorally stated objectives and is divided into seven levels covering grades 1.5 through 7.5 and beyond. To identify strengths and weaknesses of individual students, two report forms are used: the premastery analysis and the individual diagnostic report.

Figure 14.4 is a sample premastery analysis of the arithmetic skills of a class in which John Ames was a student. It provides diagnostic information that allows teachers to detect and correct the errors students are making. For example, in the category *Subtracting Whole Numbers,* John did not borrow from zero when solving these problems. Many of his classmates had the same trouble. In general, the group needs instruction in subtraction and multiplication more than addition.

The individual diagnostic report in Figure 14.5 identifies those objectives that John mastered and those yet to be mastered. A plus sign (+) is recorded for the objectives mastered, and a minus sign (−) for those not mastered. An *R* appears opposite omitted items. As you can see, John mastered most objectives in addition (e.g., addition of 3-, 4-, and 5-digit whole numbers with regrouping), but still needs help in subtraction (e.g., subtraction of one 2-digit whole number for another to obtain a 2-digit answer.)

Learning materials keyed to John's specific mathematics needs are easily available to his teacher. A *Learning Activities Guide* contains suggested instructional activities for each of the objectives included in the test. Also, a *Mastery Reference Guide* lists all objectives and cites pages from common textbooks in which those

TEACHER COMDON J
SCHOOL SAN ANDREAS
CITY REEF CITY
STATE CA
GRADE 5.1
BATCH 5001-004
DATE OF TESTING 10/75
RUN DATE 10/30/75

TEST DIAGNOSTIC MATHEMATICS INVENTORY
LEVEL D/ORANGE

NUMBER OF CASES - 32	N
ADDING WHOLE NUMBERS	
AW1 MISADDED	12
AW2 DID NOT CARRY	8
AW3 CARRIED WRONG DIGIT	3
AW4 MULTIPLIED INSTEAD	1
AW5 ADDED LEFT TO RIGHT	3
AW6 SUBTRACTED INSTEAD	2
SUBTRACTING WHOLE NUMBERS	
SW1 MINUEND FROM SUBTRAHEND	2
SW2 BORROWED COLUMN NOT REDUCED	20
SW3 DID NOT BORROW FROM ZERO	18
SW4 SUBTRAHEND > MINUEND ZERO	13
SW5 ADDED INSTEAD	4
SW6 CARRIED INSTEAD OF BORROWING	11
SW7 MISSUBTRACTED	19
MULTIPLYING WHOLE NUMBERS	
MW1 MULTIPLIED WITHIN COLUMN ONLY	14
MW2 DID NOT ADD CARRIED DIGIT	10
MW3 MISALIGNED PARTIAL PRODUCTS	8
MW4 ADDED INSTEAD	7
MW5 SUBTRACTED INSTEAD	19
MW6 MISMULTIPLIED	12
MW7 MISMULTIPLIED (REPEAT ADD)	12
MW8 MISMULTIPLIED (MATRIX)	10
MW9 RECORDED UNRELATED PRODUCT	3

CTB®/McGRAW-HILL

Published by CTB/McGraw-Hill, Del Monte Research Park, Monterey, California 93940. Copyright © 1975 by CTB/McGraw-Hill, Inc. All Rights Reserved. Printed in the U.S.A.

FIGURE 14.4. A Sample Pre-Mastery Analysis in Mathematics

CTB®/McGRAW-HILL

ADDITION OF WHOLE NUMBERS NO REGROUPING
003 NUMBER LINE (POINT)	+
012 NUMBER LINE (ADDITION)	+
019 ADDITION 5-DIGIT	+

ADDITION OF WHOLE NUMBERS, REGROUPING
021 ADDITION 2-DIGIT (RG)	−
022 ADDITION 3-DIGIT (RG)	+
023 ADDITION 4-DIGIT (RG)	+
024 ADDITION 5-DIGIT (RG)	+
025 ADDITION COLUMN	−

SUBTRACTION OF WHOLE NUMBERS NO REGROUPING
026 NUMBER LINE (SUBTRACTION)	+
032 SUBTRACTION 1D − 1D = 1D	+

SUBTRACTION OF WHOLE NUMBERS, REGROUPING
034 SUBTRACTION 2D − 2D = 2D (RG)	−
036 SUBTRACTION 3D − 3D = 3D (RG)	+
037 SUBTRACTION 4D − 4D = 4D (RG)	−
038 SUBTRACTION 5D − 5D = 5D (RG)	−

MULTIPLICATION OF WHOLE NUMBERS NO REGROUPING
039 NUMBER LINE (MULTIPLICATION)	+
040 MULTIPLICATION: REPEATED ADDITION	+
041 MULTIPLICATION: ROWS/COLUMNS	+
045 MULTIPLICATION: BASIC FACTS	−
054 MULTIPLICATION: POWERS OF TEN	+

MULTIPLICATION WHOLE NUMBERS REGROUPING
046 MULTIPLICATION 1D X 2D	+
047 MULTIPLICATION 1D X 3D	+
049 MULTIPLICATION 1D X 4D	+
050 MULTIPLICATION 2D X 2D	+

DIVISION OF WHOLE NUMBERS
056 NUMBER LINE (DIVISION)	+
058 DIVISION, BASIC FACTS, NO REMAINDER	+
059 DIVISION 3D ÷ 1D, NO REMAINDER	−
060 DIVISION 2D ÷ 1D, WITH REMAINDER	−
067 DIVISION, POWERS OF TEN	+

ADDITION OF DECIMAL NUMBERS NO REGROUPING
101 DECIMAL FRACTIONS ONE PLACE	−
102 DECIMAL FRACTIONS TWO PLACES	+
103 DECIMAL FRACTIONS THREE PLACES	+

ADDITION OF DECIMAL NUMBERS REGROUPING
104 DECIMAL FRACTIONS ONE PLACE RG	+
105 DECIMAL FRACTIONS TWO PLACES RG	+
106 DECIMAL FRACTIONS THREE PLACES RG	−

SUBTRACTION DECIMAL NUMBERS NO REGROUPING
107 DECIMAL FRACTIONS ONE-DIGIT	+
108 DECIMAL FRACTIONS TWO-DIGIT	+

SUBTRACTION OF DECIMAL NUMBERS REGROUPING
109 DECIMAL FRACTIONS ONE-DIGIT RG	−
110 DECIMAL NUMBER TWO PLACES	+
111 DECIMAL FRACTION THREE-DIGIT RG	−

COMMUTATIVE, ASSOCIATIVE, DISTRIBUTIVE PROPERTIES
137 MISSING ADDEND, COMMUTATIVITY	+
139 MISSING FACTOR, COMMUTATIVITY	−
141 MISSING ADDEND, ASSOCIATIVITY	+
143 MISSING FACTOR, ASSOCIATIVITY	−
145 MISSING NUMBER, DISTRIBUTIVE	+

IDENTIFY ELEMENT, INVERSE RELATIONSHIPS
148 MISSING ADDEND OR SUM, IDENTITY	−
150 MISSING FACTOR, IDENTITY	+
153 MISSING ADDEND, ADD/SUBT.	−

NUMBER SEQUENCES
164 LETTERS	+
165 ADDITION − WHOLE NUMBERS	+
166 SUBTRACTION − WHOLE NUMBERS	+

INEQUALITIES, ODDS, MULTIPLES
185 WHOLE NUMBERS	+
187 EVEN AND ODD NUMBERS	+
188 MULTIPLES	+

METRIC GEOMETRY
200 AREA (WHOLE NUMBERS)	−
201 VOLUME (WHOLE NUMBERS)	−
204 GRAPHS	+

LINEAR MEASURE
209 LINEAR (NON-STANDARD UNITS)	−
210 LINEAR (M., CM., MM.)	−

MONEY
217 MONEY (CONCEPT)	+
218 MONEY (ADDITION)	−
219 MONEY (SUBTRACTION)	−
220 MONEY (MULTIPLICATION)	+

WEIGHT AND LIQUID MEASURE
223 WEIGHT (LBS. OZS.)	−
226 LIQUID MEASURES (CONCEPT)	+
227 LIQUID MEASURES (ADD)	+
228 LIQUID MEASURES (SUBT.)	−

TEMPERATURE AND TIME
230 TEMPERATURE	+
232 CLOCK (CONCEPT)	+
233 CALENDAR (DATES)	+

SEGMENTS, LINES, RAYS
239 LINE SEGMENTS	+
240 PARALLEL LINES	+
241 PERPENDICULAR LINES	+
243 RAY	−

PLACE VALUE
279 0-999	+
282 1,000 − 99,999	−

EXPANDED NOTATION
280 EXPANDED NOTATION (3-DIGIT)	+
281 EXPANDED NOTATION (ADDITION)	+

FIGURE 14.5.   A Sample Individual Diagnostic Report in Mathematics

objectives are discussed. Lastly, there is a *Guide to Ancillary Materials* that shows over seventy different sets of nontext materials (such as manipulative aids, task cards, etc.) that are available to aid learning.

In short, the analysis of the criterion-referenced test results leads directly to aids for individualized remedial action. This can be expanded to group diagnosis and remediation as well. An analysis of results from diagnostic tests can assist greatly in grouping students initially for instructional purposes. Their needs are identified by means of the patterns of scores from these tests. Students with similar profiles can be grouped for remedial work.

SUMMARY

The highlights of this chapter can be summarized as follows:

1. Diagnostic evaluation is closely related to formative and summative evaluation but has somewhat different purposes.

2. Good teaching implies that all students should achieve in terms of their interests, needs, and potential. "Lockstep" teaching forces some children to repeat what they already know and confronts others with tasks too difficult for them. It precludes effective learning.

3. The first step in diagnoses of learning difficulties is to ascertain the strengths and weaknesses of the student. Underlying causes of the difficulty should be largely or totally eliminated before remedial instruction begins.

4. Although teachers are not expected to develop clinical skills, they must have several competencies in diagnosing and providing for remediation:
   a. An understanding of the psychology of learning as it applies to specific subject areas
   b. An ability to recognize those physical and psychological aspects of human development related to learning
   c. An understanding of the important diagnostic techniques and the remedial methods and materials in various subject areas

5. A number of factors affect student achievement. These include scholastic aptitude, health, vision, hearing, motor coordination, personal-social development, and environment.

6. Difficulties peculiar to a specific subject may be responsible for learning problems, and such elements have been identified in arithmetic, language, handwriting, spelling, and reading.

7. The following considerations should be emphasized in remediation:
   a. Motivating the learner
   b. Individualizing learning
   c. Evaluating continuously

8. A school testing program is an excellent way to initiate a sound program of diagnosis and remediation. Both norm-referenced and criterion-referenced instruments are useful.

9. Survey testing of the student body provides information that lends itself to the remediation of groups of students and/or further diagnosis of groups and individuals.

10. Analysis of test scores and use of cumulative records are the basis on which to build a remedial program.

SUGGESTED READINGS

DAVIS, J. A. Use of measurement in student planning and guidance. In R. L. Thorndike (Ed.), *Educational measurement* (2nd ed.). Washington, D.C.: American Council on Education, 1971.
In chapter 18, the selection of measures for student evaluation and the interpretation of the information they provide are principal topics.

HAMMELL, D. D. Evaluating children for instructional purposes. *Academic Therapy,* 1971, 6, 341–353.
This article focuses on children with learning disabilities. The author provides a helpful bibliography to aid the teacher in coping with these problems, and describes methods for translating diagnostic information into remediation procedures.

HARRIS, A. J. & SIPAY, E. R. *How to increase reading ability* (6th ed.). New York: David McKay, 1975.
This is one of the best and most widely-used references in the field of diagnosis and remediation in reading. The authors base their discussion on research and practical information. The book is a thorough and practical source of information.

OTTO, W., SMITH, R. J., & MCMENEMY, R. A. *Corrective and remedial teaching* (2nd ed.). Boston: Houghton Mifflin, 1973.
The focus of this book is on student underachievement in the basic skills. In addition, the author examines what can be done to solve underachievement problems in the schools. Primary emphasis is given to reading (5 chapters), with additional chapters devoted to spelling, arithmetic, listening, handwriting, and oral and written expression. Examples of test score interpretations are given.

WILSON, R. M. *Diagnostic and remedial reading for classroom and clinic* (2nd ed.). Columbus, Ohio: Charles E. Merrill, 1972.
This is a diagnostic teaching-oriented volume with practical suggestions for the teacher.

REFERENCES CITED

FREMER, J. *Criterion-referenced interpretations of survey achievement tests* (Test Development Memorandum). Princeton, N.J.: Educational Testing Service, 1972.

HARRIS, A. J. & SIPAY, E. R. *How to increase reading ability* (6th ed.). New York: David McKay, 1975.

HILLS, J. R. *Measurement and evaluation in the classroom.* Columbus, Ohio: Charles E. Merrill, 1976.

PROGER, B. B. & MANN, L. Criterion-referenced measurement: The world of gray vs. black and white. *Journal of Learning Disabilities,* 1973, 6, 72–84.

RUTHERFORD, W. L. From diagnosis to treatment of reading disabilities. *Academic Therapy,* 1972, 8, 51–55.

15

Grading and Reporting

After reading this chapter, you should be able to

1. Explain how marking (or grading) and reporting are used for various purposes

2. Illustrate how educational objectives can become a basis for grading and reporting

3. Differentiate between the concepts of student growth and final achievement, and explain the problems in using growth as a focus for reporting

4. Contrast norms and standards of performance

5. Understand the differences among the various marking systems and illustrate their strengths and weaknesses

6. Explain the theory and concepts involved in weighting the components used to grade a class

7. List and explain the factors that are important in designing an effective report card

8. Indicate the strengths and weaknesses of correspondence to parents and teacher-parent conferences, delineating the steps needed to prepare for each

9. Explain the problems encountered in using criterion-referenced marking, mastery learning, and self-evaluation procedures

10. Suggest how marking and reporting in the open classroom are likely to differ from that in the conventional classroom

11. Specify how the by-products of marking and reporting might interfere with learning

12. Outline methods for improving marking and reporting

13. Take a position on the issues surrounding student promotion policies

Suppose you have asked your physician to give you a thorough physical examination. After you run through a complex series of clinical and laboratory examinations and your physician has evaluated them, you receive the report: "Well, I guess you're worth about a *B+*." You leave cheerfully enough—a *B+* always sounds good when you are told achievement test results—but a bit puzzled. Perhaps it means that there are not many people as physically able as you. But these seem to be the only conclusive judgments you can come to. You do not know how to improve your health, because you do not know what deficiencies kept you from getting an *A*.

Clearly a letter grading system is inadequate for summarizing the results of a physical examination. Often physicians must interpret extensively before patients understand the meaning of the evaluations, because many bits of information are related and balanced. Furthermore, physicians relate their diagnoses to remediation, and are likely to modify patient activities or diets.

Similarly, evaluating students' competence requires careful reflection on many aspects of their personalities and abilities. Much more is examined than their knowledge of subject matter; teachers are concerned with their affective, cognitive, and often psychomotor behavior. Moreover, not all evidence is completely objective. Every source of data available for assessing both psychological and physical characteristics must be tapped. It is impossible to summarize the evaluation with a single symbol.

Teachers agree that giving and reporting marks (or grades) is one of their most uncomfortable responsibilities. Some lack confidence in the marks they assign; others believe their marks are fair, but find them difficult to defend. Behind these negative attitudes lies the fact that the basis for assigning marks is often unclear. Should the intelligent student who loafs be given a low mark? Should the students who work very hard but whose mental capacities are limited be upgraded in spite of their below-average performance on tests and assignments? Should the students who adjust well to their peers but receive failing marks be promoted? What would be the effect on these children's future development if they were held back? Should a teacher give inflated grades just because everyone else is doing so? Should marks be eliminated entirely? There are very strong reasons for doing so. With so many factors to consider, it is small wonder that teachers regard giving final marks as a chore and wish that they could be relieved of the responsibility.

In many modern schools, there is a definite trend toward revising methods of marking and reporting. Child psychology and a redefinition of the objectives of the school have had their influence. Attention has been centered on the entire child, emphasizing achievement in relation to potential for development. The complexity of this kind of evaluation is reflected in changed methods of reporting leading to such devices as checklists, personal letters, teacher-parent conferences, pass/fail or credit/no credit grading, criterion-referenced marking, and contracting for grades.

Marks can make a positive contribution to learning. They can perform an evaluative function that cannot be served or served as well by other forms of evaluation (Feldmesser, 1972). Unfortunately, marks have not always represented valid measures of achievement, because the meaning of marks and the evidence for determining them have not been carefully determined. The elimination of marks will not guarantee the elimination of undesirable competition in the classroom, nor will this act alone foster the elimination of conformity and the development of creativity. There seems to be agreement on all sides that evaluation of learning is important. Disagreement focuses on how it should be reported.

There is no method of reporting that will prevent all of the problems inherent in the evaluation of students. However, certain flagrant violations can be eliminated by a knowledge of acceptable procedures. Furthermore, newer methods of marking and reporting, such as criterion-referenced marking, can be used in association with traditional methods. They may eventually be more widely used as teachers become more knowledgeable about them.

Purposes of Reporting

The purposes of marking and reporting can best be defined in terms of those who use them—students, parents, teachers, school administrators, and employers. In the final analysis, reports should serve the paramount purpose of facilitating the educational development of each student in relation to ability, and their effectiveness should be judged by this criterion. Reports succeed insofar as they help all students realize their potentials.

Informing the Student

Originally, one of the purposes of reports was to exhort students to greater effort in school. Fear of failure, it was argued, would produce greater achievement; if students knew they would be passed automatically from grade to grade, they wouldn't work as hard.

It has been found that certain students will be challenged to work for higher marks. Although they may have little interest in the subject matter at first, interest may develop through feelings of accomplishment and success. Yet there are dangers in working for marks. Students who conform rigidly to a teacher's set standards for an A may sacrifice creativity and imagination in the process. Others, those who lack the mental ability to meet the standards set by their teachers, may not be motivated to learn when they know they cannot succeed despite their best efforts. If marks represent improvement rather than status alone, however, these students may have an incentive to strive for higher marks.

Final marks must be interpreted in terms of the quality of instruction and the general ability of the students in the class. In some schools where there may be a lack of talent among the students, it is possible for high marks to give a distorted picture of a student's achievement. The lower marks of some students in our better schools may depict more achievement than an A in schools inadequately staffed and equipped. A final mark of C in an honors class may represent greater achievement than an A in an average class.

The interpretation of marks, then, is very important. The value of the report increases as the student is helped to understand what it means. This implies that the teacher is prepared to defend its accuracy and show its significance. There are teachers who make it a practice to explain the meaning of marks and other data to students before the reports go home. This procedure also provides an opportunity to review the school's objectives with the students.

Informing Parents, School Personnel, and Employers

Parents must understand the school's objectives to advance cooperation between home and school; otherwise, there is likely to be conflict. When parents accept the educational objectives of the school, they are in a position to support and supplement the educational program for their children. A truly informative system of reporting is formulated in terms of the school's objectives and the children's growth and progress toward them. It provides a basis for intelligent cooperation of the parent with both teacher and child.

A composite evaluation of students' achievement and growth should be available for their future teachers and the administration. The cumulative record is most helpful. Periodic reports should be filed therein, since they represent summative evaluations of much of the data. Whether or not students remain in the same school system, their teachers will have information about their progress in previous grades.

The school administrator or guidance officer often must evaluate the competence and potentiality of the school's graduates. For instance, many colleges and universities exercise stringent selection, and well-organized evaluations of college-bound students should be available for them.

Students who do not go to college generally seek employment. Because the tendency to practice social promotion has changed the meaning of a high school diploma, their prospective employers often request information about them. While competence in secretarial or machine-shop skills are important for certain types of jobs, employers may also want people who can get along with others, who can assume responsibility, and who have leadership potential and a general attitude of cooperation. Periodic reports over the years provide an indication of the future pattern of behavior that an employer might expect of an individual.

PROBLEMS

1. If we accept the premise that report cards and final marks exist to help students develop according to their abilities, how then can we justify the use of rigid standards of passing and failing?

2. If standardized test scores yield information comparable to secondary school marks, could we then abolish report cards and concentrate on thorough interpretation of the achievement test results in individual conferences with the parents and child? Explain your answer.

Objectives of the School

If evaluation is to be made in terms of all of the school's objectives, general and specific, then marking and reporting become very complex. In the first place, evaluation of some aspects of student behavior cannot be as adequate as we would like, yet even so may be more valuable than a paper-and-pencil test indicating only what the students can do. If one of our objectives is to develop effective citizenship, for example, statements such as "Individuals vote in all elections for which they are eligible," and "Students assume responsibility in group work," give some direction and basis for evaluation. Second, it is impractical to sample enough behavior of every student to obtain an adequate evaluation. This is especially true for the secondary school, where a teacher meets many students every day. Third, to report on each one of a great number of behavioral patterns would give the false impression that valid judgments can be made in every instance. A fourth problem would arise in presenting such a report to parents, since it would be too long and complex to be interpreted easily; certainly the evaluation could not be given in a single number or letter.

So teachers face something of a dilemma. On the one hand, they want to base their marking and reporting on all pertinent educational objectives, general and specific. On the other, the list of these objectives is so long, and sometimes the evidence concerning them so difficult to obtain, that they face an almost impossible task. To make their reporting task more manageable, they compromise, however reluctantly. Rather than try to report student progress in terms of all educational objectives each time a report is to be made, they may select a group of objectives, perhaps reporting on a different group on the next occasion. Or they may report on each student, on each reporting occasion, in terms of a group of basic objectives of special importance to the student and the school. Each of these may really be a combination of related specific objectives. Typically, however, grading is done more simply. Marks are awarded on what can be easily measured, namely, subject content. Too often the subject content is factual information, and skills such as problem solving, critical thinking, application, and so forth, are not emphasized in the report. Unfortunately even these marks reflect a teacher's bias in such factors as amount of work completed, neatness, and correctness of expression.

Growth and Achievement

A mark may depict growth or achievement, or both. These are distinct concepts. Growth means change or gain. To interpret it adequately, we must consider the individual in terms of ability, background experience, present environmental stimulation, and so on. Achievement means the students' present status—what they know or can do now. Achievement is generally judged against norms or a teacher's standards, and all too often it is evaluated without respect to ability and prior experiences.

Differences between the two concepts can be described by use of diagrams. Figure 15.1 is a record of John's and Bill's growth and achievement in reading

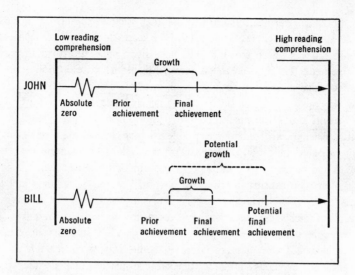

FIGURE 15.1.   Diagram of Growth and Achievement in Reading
Comprehension of Two Fifth-Grade Students

comprehension. The top line is a description of John's progress, the bottom line describes Bill's. Clearly there was a point in the life of each boy when his achievement in this basic skill was zero; this is represented on the far left of the two lines by the position labeled absolute zero. Proceeding to the right represents an increase in achievement. Let us assume that John and Bill have just entered the fifth grade. Each boy's achievement in reading comprehension at this particular time is represented by a point called prior achievement. Bill's prior achievement in reading comprehension exceeds John's considerably.

If we examine the boys' achievement at the end of the academic year (final achievement), we find that Bill still surpasses John. Their growth in reading comprehension is represented by the difference between prior and final achievement. Both boys have grown in this skill, but John has made a tremendous spurt. Several interpretations are possible, depending on the other information we have about these students. Suppose that they have equal potential in reading. We might then conclude that Bill is an overachiever who could not be expected to make tremendous growth strides whereas John may be achieving according to his ability. It is more likely that John achieved less in the earlier grades and, through good teaching, was able to make great strides in the fifth grade. Bill, on the other hand, may or may not have shown adequate growth during the year. But suppose that Bill is a brighter boy than John. His actual growth is then inadequate; his potential growth may then be as great as that shown in Figure 15.1. Although his final achievement may be the highest in the class, it is still unsatisfactory in terms of what he could do.

We see from the above illustration that both growth and final achievement guide the teacher in evaluating student progress. However, it is questionable whether to assign marks on the basis of achievement gains rather than present status. First, gains are very unreliable because they include the errors of both the initial and final achievements. Second, if initial scores are obtained from instruments that are too easy, able students will have little opportunity to improve on the final assessment. Third, it is much more difficult to raise a high score even higher than to raise a low score. A gain of one-half standard deviation from a score below the mean may not be of the same substance as a gain of one-half standard deviation above the mean. The regression effect is operating.

Typically, teachers are much better able to give grades that represent final achievement rather than growth. Growth, or the lack of it, can be reported by supplementary comments or by means of an accompanying check list.

One problem confronting teachers is how to prevent students who receive only low marks from getting discouraged. One way, of course, is to have them compete against themselves and to evaluate them on the basis of their own gains. If this is not defensible, however, then we can give all students opportunities within the school and the class to excel in some way even though it is not through overall achievement status in the subject matter. Life dictates that all students must eventually learn that present status, rather than growth, is what counts for the most part. Standards of the working world demand that grades reflect achievement. Standards exist as much to protect society as to select qualified applicants.

Standards and Ability to Learn

Whether to evaluate students in terms of standards or achievement in relation to learning ability is a part of the growth-versus-achievement question. Standards of achievement are typically teacher estimates of the level of achievement that students must reach before they have done acceptable work. The use of such standards is sometimes defended in the following manner:

> When I pass a student in this course I am certifying to his next instructor that he has covered the material of the course, and that if he works reasonably hard he is capable of continuing with the next course in this field at least approximately at the level indicated by his letter grade. In the first place, I will not give a fraudulent certification. In the second place, it would be no kindness to your child to let him get into college or into a job only to find out that he is not prepared to do good work. Moreover, if I lower the standards, the result is a disservice to your children and your community, handicapping all future students by making colleges and universities reluctant to accept them or give them scholarships, and prospective employers mistrustful of them. (Green, 1956, p. 72)

This issue may be, for all practical purposes, a "straw man." In many instances, teacher standards are derived from the observed performance of the students themselves, which means that they are relative and not absolute measures of subject matter achievement.

But there are other clear-cut issues that at best are difficult to resolve. If the teacher does in fact employ norm-referenced grading (for example, grading "on the curve"), are certain students doomed always to receive low marks? Furthermore, if grading is done on a relative basis, are standards compromised? One answer to the first question is the use of more flexible marking systems. For example, these can be designed so that high achieving students with low ability receive appropriately high grades, and furthermore, that high achieving students with high ability also receive high grades even though they are in an honors class. This is not a flawless solution to our first question, but it does a better job of solving the problem than does marking on what are called "standards;" this inevitably results in the maneuvering of marks in order to produce some kind of acceptable grade distribution. Those who would eliminate grades mention this as one of their major criticisms. They often advocate other kinds of reporting systems such as criterion-referenced marking (see p. 433).

The second question is more easily answered, in that there is no evidence that the quality of learning need suffer with relative marking. The concern should be focused instead on improved instruction and providing experiences for all students with varied individual differences. This may require regrouping into more homogeneous classes and, of course, differential instruction within the classroom.

Specific Evidence of Student Progress

The specific evidence needed for accurate assessment and reporting of a student's progress must come from the many measuring instruments and techniques discussed in detail in other chapters. Certainly, data from both teacher-constructed and standardized paper-and-pencil tests, ranking and rating scales, and check lists must be used. Data from observation of class participation and student success in projects and reports are helpful as well.

The key to success is the use of a wide variety of evidence. In some ways paper-and-pencil achievement tests, particularly standardized ones, provide the most impressive looking data about student achievement. But these have a verbal or mathematical emphasis only. In contrast, sample products like student essays are more difficult to interpret, yet serve well as a means of explaining to them and their parents the degree of their achievement. Furthermore, reports of class participation often reflect student attitudes and even interpersonal relationships. Use of all of the foregoing will strengthen the marking and reporting effort.

PROBLEM

3. If there are to be multiple standards of achievement in the interests of healthful psychological development on the part of the student, is there a need to revise the high school diploma system as it now exists in many schools? Why?

Methods of Marking and Reporting

Typical procedures for marking and reporting are letter-number systems, check lists, correspondence with parents, teacher-parent conferences, and criterion-referenced marking. It is important that these methods be critically evaluated in terms of purposes, bases, and the sources of information available for reporting. Whatever system is used must be established as the best possible under existing circumstances.

Letter-Number Systems

The letter-number system has been and remains a popular method of reporting student progress. In essence, it is an effort to summarize a variety of information about such characteristics of students as their growth, final achievement, effort, ability, and general deportment. Each report period, the summary is given in the form of a letter, usually *A* through *E* or *F*, or a number, usually *100* through *0*, reported for each subject matter area.

There are two reasons why these marks are difficult to assign. First, the teacher cannot be certain whether appropriate credit is being given to growth and to final achievement for each educational objective considered. Second, since the mark represents student progress in terms of a combination of objectives, the teacher is uncertain whether each objective within the combination is being appropriately weighted.

Multiple Marking Systems.   An interesting variation of the traditional letter-number system is the use of two or more marks for each subject matter area. One may represent the student's final achievement in relation to the teacher's standards. Another is often an evaluation of effort put forth by the student; in some school systems it represents student growth in the area of achievement listed. A three-point letter system is sometimes used for recording the student's effort: *H* if students exceed what is expected of them, *S* if their levels of work correspond approximately to their levels of ability, and *U* if they are capable of better work. Students evaluated according to this system might receive marks such as *A/S* or *91/S,* each indicating high final achievement and normal effort. Marks such as *C/H* or *83/H* mean that the students are average in terms of final achievement and that their efforts are superior.

Clearly the success of multiple marking systems depends on a teacher's ability to evaluate final achievement and effort by a letter or number. Some teachers find evaluation of effort particularly troublesome since satisfactory judgment requires more accurate evaluation techniques than are available. If a second mark represents growth rather than effort, an extensive pretesting program must be set up to establish achievement levels before instruction begins, and then careful consideration must be given to the problems of interpreting gains.

In actual practice, a halo effect may exist when assigning good marks to bright students on their relative achievement and on subjective factors such as effort. Teachers often tend to equate effort with achievement, disregarding individual differences of intelligence.

These are central issues. In theory, multiple marking systems should be expected to give a clearer picture of a student's progress than a single mark. However, multiple reporting often presents an oversimplified picture of the teacher's evaluation. Each subject matter area encompasses many educational objectives. It is difficult, at best, to obtain enough evidence to give one valid mark. When the number of marks is increased, the problem is compounded.

Relative vs. Absolute Standards for Marking.   Because there is no absolute zero for achievement test scores, it is impossible to assign marks on an absolute scale or standard. If students respond correctly to all items on a test, it does not necessarily mean that they know one hundred percent of what is to be learned in the subject, and a mark of fifty percent does not mean that they have learned half of the subject matter. Test items are a sampling of what is learned in the subject. Furthermore, whether a student receives credit for having mastered a particular concept depends on how it is measured by a particular test item. Even a question about a difficult concept may be answered correctly by almost all students if the question requires only superficial understanding. In other words, the difficulty of an item often depends as much on how a concept is measured as what is measured.

Actually, teachers who convert raw scores or percentages directly into final marks usually adjust them near the end of the year by giving bonus points; they construct an easy or difficult test as the situation may warrant, or use some such procedure, until the raw scores or percentages will convert to a distribution of final marks that was largely predetermined. This distribution involves an arbitrary decision. It may be determined by school policy, the ability and vocational plans of the students, gaps in the distribution of composite scores, and so forth. In a high ability class, for example, a teacher might give thirty percent *A*'s, forty percent *B*'s, twenty percent *C*'s, and ten percent *D*'s. Rarely are there as many *F*'s as there are *A*'s; the median final mark in many classes is often *B* rather than *C*.

Regardless of the marking system adopted, it is important that the marks present a clear message to students, parents, employers, and college admission officers. The meaning of marks is much clearer when school personnel agree on the criteria for choosing the percentage of students in a given class who will be assigned a particular mark.

To illustrate how final marks may be assigned unfairly, imagine three English classes taught by different teachers. Classes 1 and 2 are made up of college-bound students of comparable ability; Class 3, of students of lesser ability. The teacher of Class 1 assigns sixty percent *A*'s and *B*'s. The teacher of Class 2, who is less liberal, gives only forty percent *A*'s and *B*'s. Consequently a girl whose English achievement is typical of college-bound students would probably receive a *B* if she were in Class 1, a *C* if in Class 2, and an *A* if she were a member of Class 3, in which she would probably be one of the best students.

One way of rectifying this situation is to obtain some common and relevant measure by which the three English classes could be compared. Scores from a scholastic aptitude test or from standardized or teacher-constructed English achievement tests with acceptable degrees of content validity might be used. Suppose it is decided that fifteen percent of the students will receive A's. Then the cutoff score, above which only fifteen percent of the students score on the common measure, would be determined. The number of students in a particular class who surpass this cutoff score provides the approximate number of A's to be given in that class. The same is true of the percentages of B's, C's, and so on. Note that the final marks students receive depend on their total performance in their classes, not on their scholastic aptitude scores. The scholastic aptitude tests serve here to determine percentages of letter grades assigned, not the students to whom they will be assigned. Some students will receive higher final achievement marks than their fellows who scored higher on the scholastic aptitude test. (For a more sophisticated method of assigning final marks in classes having different levels of academic ability, see Ebel, 1979, pp. 247–248.)

Weighting Data.   One of the problems teachers encounter in giving final marks is weighting the data gathered from such various sources as informal quizzes, final examinations, and reports to obtain valid composite scores for ranking students. There is no consensus on the emphasis each of these types of data should receive in the total evaluation. Some teachers maintain that a final examination should count far more than the quizzes and other tests given during the course. They point out that since the final examination measures long-term retention, and the ability to organize and deal with large units of subject matter, this score should logically be weighted more heavily than others. Other teachers are quick to retort that it is unfair to students to determine such a large proportion of their final evaluations from their performance at a specified time within an interval of several hours at most. They also object to the limitations of most final examinations that preclude measurement in terms of many important educational objectives.

The last point is vital. The weighting of various data must be determined in terms of the educational objectives of the specific grade level or class. Those data that reflect student progress in terms of the most important objectives must be given greater weight when computing a composite mark than those relating to less important objectives. This is equally true whether the data come from a final examination or from any other measuring instrument.

There is a precaution that must be taken in determining a composite mark no matter what weightings are chosen. Suppose we wish to base one-fifth of the final mark for a course on class reports, one-fifth on daily assignments, one-fifth on quizzes and unit tests, and two-fifths on the final examination. Inspection of the ranges and standard deviations of these measures in the following table reveals a definite lack of uniformity. If we hope to maintain the weighting scheme originally chosen, we must take into consideration these differences in variability. A failure to do this will result in inequities.

To illustrate this point, let us suppose that Mary made a total of 55 points for class reports, the highest number of points for this category. However, on quizzes and unit tests her score was the lowest, 30 points. For daily assignments and the final examination she earned 61 and 91, respectively. Frank, on the other

TABLE 15.1. Variability of Scores on Tests and Assignments

Source of points	Nominal weight	Range	Standard deviation
Class reports	1	26	5.1
Daily assignments	1	46	8.6
Quizzes and unit tests	1	110	20.8
Final examination	2	90	16.4

hand, did the poorest of anyone in the group on class reports; his score was 29. On the quizzes and unit tests he had a high score of 140. It happens that he also made the same scores as Mary on daily assignments and the final exam, namely 61 and 91. (See Table 15.1.)

If we weight Mary's and Frank's scores for each source and add them to obtain a composite, we have Table 15.2. Note that although class reports, quizzes, and unit tests are to have the same weight, Mary is penalized because of the lesser variability of scores of class reports when compared with that of quizzes and unit tests. In other words, class-report scores with a relatively low standard deviation ($\sigma = 5.1$) have less influence than scores of quizzes and unit tests ($\sigma = 20.8$) in determining the class rankings on the composite score.

A procedure for avoiding errors like the one above would be to convert the raw scores into standard scores so that the variability of the scores for each category would be the same. When the scores for each category are converted into stanines the following formula to compute the composite is appropriate:

$$C = \frac{\Sigma WS}{\Sigma W}$$

where

C = composite average
Σ = the sum
W = weight for a particular category
S = standard score for that category for each student

TABLE 15.2. Weighting of Students' Scores without Consideration of Score Variability

	Mary	Frank
Reports	$55 \times 1 = 55$	$29 \times 1 = 29$
Assignments	$61 \times 1 = 61$	$61 \times 1 = 61$
Quizzes	$30 \times 1 = 30$	$140 \times 1 = 140$
Final exam.	$91 \times 2 = 182$	$91 \times 2 = 182$
Total points	328	412

To illustrate the use of the formula let us assume that Mary received stanine scores of 9, 5, 1, and 7 for class reports, daily assignments, quizzes, and unit tests, and the final examination respectively. Frank's stanine scores were 1, 5, 9, and 7. The composite averages would be

Mary

$$C = \frac{(1 \times 9) + (1 \times 5) + (1 \times 1) + (2 \times 7)}{1 + 1 + 1 + 2} = \frac{29}{5} = 5.8$$

Frank

$$C = \frac{(1 \times 1) + (1 \times 5) + (1 \times 9) + (2 \times 7)}{1 + 1 + 1 + 2} = \frac{29}{5} = 5.8$$

Although these composite averages are not stanines, they do provide means for a ranking of students that reflects the desired weightings of the scores for the several categories. On the basis of this distribution, the teacher may assign final marks.

Grade Contracts.   Contracts are agreements between teachers and students, detailed in writing, as to what is to be achieved over a period of time for a particular grade. Everyone does the work required to earn a *D* for the course. A *C* grade demands additional accomplishments. To earn a *B* the student must first complete the requirements for the *D* and *C* marks, and then do further work. An *A* can be earned by doing *D*, *C*, and *B* contracts and then completing the additional *A* requirements.

The contract idea has some of the characteristics of criterion-referenced marking (see page 433) in that there is at least an attempt to specify achievement, albeit in a rather global fashion. Instead of representing relative standing, the marks of *A*, *B*, *C*, and *D* represent specified achievement. There should be no failures since pupils continue to work until they at least have done satisfactory *D* work.

Reliability and Validity.   The reliability of scores from paper-and-pencil tests is sometimes not as great as we wish it to be. Reliability of data from a teachers' observations of students' procedures and their affective behavior is usually even lower. Yet both are used to determine final marks. Consequently, the reliability of final marks is often less than desired.

Such evidence as is available suggests that the usual reliability coefficients of semester marks may be as high as 0.70 to 0.90. This means that in many, if not all, cases it is difficult to defend the practice of interpreting such differences as those between an *83* and an *84* or a *91* and a *92*. For that matter, the difference between a *C+* and a *B−* may be due purely to chance. This evidence raises the question of the number of divisions that should be used in a marking system. The more categories one makes, such as *90, 91,* and *92,* the more likely errors in student placement. The fewer the categories, such as *Pass/Fail*, the smaller the number of students who will be given an incorrect mark, but the more serious the error. These facts must be balanced with concern for the amount of information a mark reveals; *S* and *U* reveal less than *90, 91,* and *92*.

Evidence of the validity of final marks is also limited. They seem to be quite valid as a measure of mastery of subject matter by the student, with the correlation coefficient estimated to be 0.70 or possibly higher. This estimate was arrived at by summarizing the results of a number of studies concerning the correlation between the final marks in question and (1) other marks in the same subject matter area, (2) test scores from appropriate standardized tests, and (3) the students' estimates of the marks they deserved.

The validity of final marks has been investigated with respect to a number of different criteria, such as college entrance examination scores, college marks, economic success, and success on the job. The correlation coefficients vary a great deal. The most widely investigated use of secondary school final marks is that of predicting academic success in college. The correlation coefficients are often as high as 0.50 and seldom higher than 0.70. It has been repeatedly shown that final marks in secondary school are one of the best means of predicting college success, whether used alone or as part of a prediction battery.

Interpretation. The typical letter or number system of marking is based primarily on final achievement. Confusion results when a teacher also attempts to include an evaluation of effort and other personality traits in this single mark. Interpretation becomes almost impossible. There is no way to determine whether a low mark is the result of lack of achievement or effort. Even when a single letter mark is used to report final achievement alone, it is very difficult to make a valid interpretation. What does a *B* in general science mean? Does it show that the student did *A* work in quizzes, *C* work in laboratory, *B* work in class participation? Or more important still, does it mean that the student achieved at an *A* level with respect to one educational objective, a *B* level with respect to another, and a *C* level with a third? We have no way of knowing. Therefore when letter or numerical marks are used, there must be additional data in the report that provide diagnostic information.

The mark is also influenced by other factors, one of which is the nature of the student population. Too often students who have been graduated magna cum laude from their high schools find to their dismay when they face competition in a university that they do not have exceptional ability. Another factor is the peculiarity of the individual teacher who does the marking. Some teachers give consistently high marks, while others pride themselves in never being so easy as to give an *A* or a *95*. Students may find it very difficult to identify a criterion by which they can judge the value of their marks.

Marks as they are now generally assigned are far from being as meaningful as people think. They are being overinterpreted; they reveal far less about the student than is commonly supposed, and their meaning is often ambiguous. Hence it is imperative that standardized test scores be used to supplement final marks whenever possible. It is particularly important for secondary school students to have this objective basis for comparing their own capacity and achievements with a broader sample of students, giving them a better opportunity to interpret their potential for future academic work.

Pass/Fail or Credit/No Credit Marking

The surge of reaction against grading with letter or numerical marks on a scale of five or more points prompted a number of colleges and universities to provide the option of *Pass/Fail* or *Credit/No Credit* marking for some of the courses in the curriculum. In various modified forms, this two-point procedure has also been used in secondary schools. The most common justification for the *P/F* and *C/NC* plans is the provision it offers for students to take courses that they might have omitted from their schedules for fear of failure. Other reasons supporting the plan are that it reduces student anxiety, provides for their own control of study time, and places emphasis on learning rather than "grade getting."

Studies of the *P/F* and *C/NC* plans reveal that students report that they feel less anxious and they reduce study time in those courses in order to concentrate on others. There is also reason to believe that they do not perform as well in *P/F* and *C/NC* courses as in other courses.

The weakness of *P/F* and *C/NC* marking is that it does not promote learning and it does not provide students with an adequate record of their achievement. It is questionable whether motivation to learn would be equalized in a system where all courses were graded on a *P/F* or *C/NC* basis; learning in all courses might deteriorate. This question can only be answered if and when *P/F* or *C/NC* marking is used more extensively.

Grade Inflation

The large increase in students' grade averages and the greater number of students admitted to honors groups have been of concern to educators and the general public. Although the focus has been on marking in higher education, attention has also been given to the problem in elementary and secondary schools.

The chief functions of grades are to serve as reinforcement/motivation and selective agents. These functions may have been severely impaired as a result of high marks that do not present a realistic evaluation of students' competence.

Although substantive empirical evidence is lacking, there appear to be several hypotheses explaining this explosion of high grades. Faculty permissiveness has often been cited as one reason. During the unpopular Vietnam War students could escape the draft if their grades were satisfactory. Many faculty found it most distasteful to send their students into the conflict because of a low grade. In other situations, an instructor's popularity may have hinged on high marks.

A second explanation offered is the changing student population. Paradoxically, the explanation for higher marks has been attributed to both a higher quality student population and to a lower quality student population. Obviously, if students were more able and well motivated, higher marks would be in order.

But it is also argued that, because of declining enrollment, a lower quality of student must be selected. This results in a poorer performance expectation.

The third hypothesis revolves around rule changes in our colleges and universities. Course withdrawal times have been lengthened. This provides an opportunity for students to drop courses where they are doing poorly. Poor or failing course grades have been dropped from transcripts if the course was repeated successfully. Provision for *Pass/Fail* grading has provided an opportunity to eliminate what might turn out to be poor grades. Students often wish to register for courses outside their majors or minors. Their preparation may be meager compared to majors in the field with whom they will be competing. In other instances, difficult offerings are often required of students.

Indications now lead us to believe that grade inflation has run its course and that more conservative marking is appearing (Bromley et al., 1978). A more realistic evaluation of student competencies is required in this period of greater teacher accountability.

Types of Report Cards

The report cards used to record the assigned marks can take many different forms. Commonly they provide for the recording of marks for all marking periods during the school year. Parents or guardians are requested to sign the card before it is returned at the end of each marking period.

Reports of academic achievement are often accompanied by a checklist of personality traits and attitudes. The teacher may generally place a check in any one of several categories, such as "unsatisfactory," "satisfactory," or "improving." If these checklists are carefully worded, the instrument can save the teacher time and effort.

Reporting must not become a stereotyping procedure. In the past, many students have been checked "satisfactory" in every characteristic from kindergarten through the sixth grade. The "halo effect" seems to keep some teachers from making a realistic evaluation of the student. This can be eliminated if teachers base their reports on adequate data, carefully compiled and critically interpreted. Space left on the checklist form for comments on students' problems will help individualize the method.

At the secondary level, checklists are usually used to supplement numerical or letter marks, both providing information not discernible from the mark alone and helping to clarify the mark itself. In elementary school, checklists are often the only report given. The example shown in Figure 15.2 represents the type that can be used for this purpose. Observe that all main aspects of the academic program are included, and also health, music, art, and personal development. The common three-point letter system is used to represent the teacher's judgment of the student's success. In this case, the letters are *O* for outstanding, *S* for satisfactory, and *N* for not satisfactory. Such a checklist can give a great deal of information about the student's school life.

A number of schools, wishing to conserve time, are employing computers for reporting marks and organizing and analyzing data about them. In one school system (Crisler & Wogaman, 1963) each school's master class schedule and individual student programs are converted into punched cards. There is a deck of cards for each class with one mark-sense card for each student (see Figure 15.3). All the decks are arranged alphabetically by teacher name and each teacher's decks by period sequences.

At the time of reporting, teachers receive a deck of mark-sense cards for each of their classes. They mark these in the space representing the final mark earned by each student. One to four comments, such as "excellent," "satisfactory," and so on, from a list of nine on each card are also marked.

The cards are then returned to the processing center where the teachers' marks are printed on the report card (see Figure 15.4). Four copies of this report are available. The original is given to the student to take home and the other three copies are for office use. The reports are cumulative during a semester; that is, the students' previous marks also appear on successive reports. Parents do not sign these cards and students do not return them.

This system of reporting provides readily available data about marks to the school staff. The number of times students received each letter mark and each

---

REPORT CARD FORM

What the letters mean:

O—Outstanding for your child; commendation for special effort and achievement.
S—Satisfactory for your child; achievement consistent with ability.
N—Not Satisfactory for your child; improvement needed.
Note: Any further information in regard to the standing of your child may be secured in personal conference.

Growth in Skills	1st Report	2nd Report	3rd Report
Reading			
Understands what he reads _____	_____	_____	_____
Works to develop independent reading habits _____	_____	_____	_____
Writing			
Expresses himself well_____	_____	_____	_____
Uses basic writing skills _____	_____	_____	_____
Writes legibly _____	_____	_____	_____
Spells correctly _____	_____	_____	_____
Uses good sentence structure _____	_____	_____	_____
Learns to use new words _____	_____	_____	_____
Arithmetic			
Knows arithmetic facts _____	_____	_____	_____
Understands arithmetic processes (addition, subtraction, multiplication, division)____	_____	_____	_____
Applies skill in solving problems _____	_____	_____	_____
Social studies			
History, geography, civics, government, development of American ideals_____	_____	_____	_____
Works to develop a knowledge and understanding of home, community, state, country, world _____	_____	_____	_____
Works to develop skill in the use of materials (newspapers, maps, encyclopedias, etc.)	_____	_____	_____

Science
Works to develop keen observation _____   _____   _____   _____
Is growing in scientific knowledge _____   _____   _____   _____

Listening
Understands what he hears and responds
    wisely _____   _____   _____   _____

Health
Works to develop good health habits _____   _____   _____   _____
Helps to maintain safety _____   _____   _____   _____
Plays and enjoys games _____   _____   _____   _____
Works to develop skill in physical education   _____   _____   _____

Music
Takes part in group singing _____   _____   _____   _____
Responds to rhythm _____   _____   _____   _____
Works to develop basic music skills_____   _____   _____   _____

Art
Expresses ideas creatively _____   _____   _____   _____
Works to develop a variety of skills _____   _____   _____   _____

Personal development
Is developing a variety of interests _____   _____   _____   _____
Is courteous and considerate _____   _____   _____   _____
Respects the rights and property of others   _____   _____   _____
Shares outside experience, skills and mate-
    rials with others _____   _____   _____   _____
Accepts responsibility _____   _____   _____   _____
Works to the best of his ability _____   _____   _____   _____

FIGURE 15.2.   Modified Form of Checklist

From Heffernan and Marshall, 1955, pp. 75–76; reproduced by permission of the
California State Department of Education.

comment is totaled along with their average marks. Data on teachers include the
number of times they made a comment such as "excellent," or "inattentive." The
average mark of each teacher's class and the average for all their classes are tabulated. Marks are also available for each class grouped by subject matter area, as
are the comments marked, the percentage of each mark given, and the average
mark for the class.

With information showing how teachers mark, this school has the basis to
set up guidelines for assigning marks; it also gives the teachers feedback on their
own marks and also those of their colleagues. There is an excellent opportunity
to make marks more meaningful to students and their parents.

Criterion-Referenced Marking

Typical marking systems are norm-referenced, that is, they tend to rank an individual in relation to other students such as those in his class, his school, or some
other specified norm group. Two major trends in education, namely, individualized

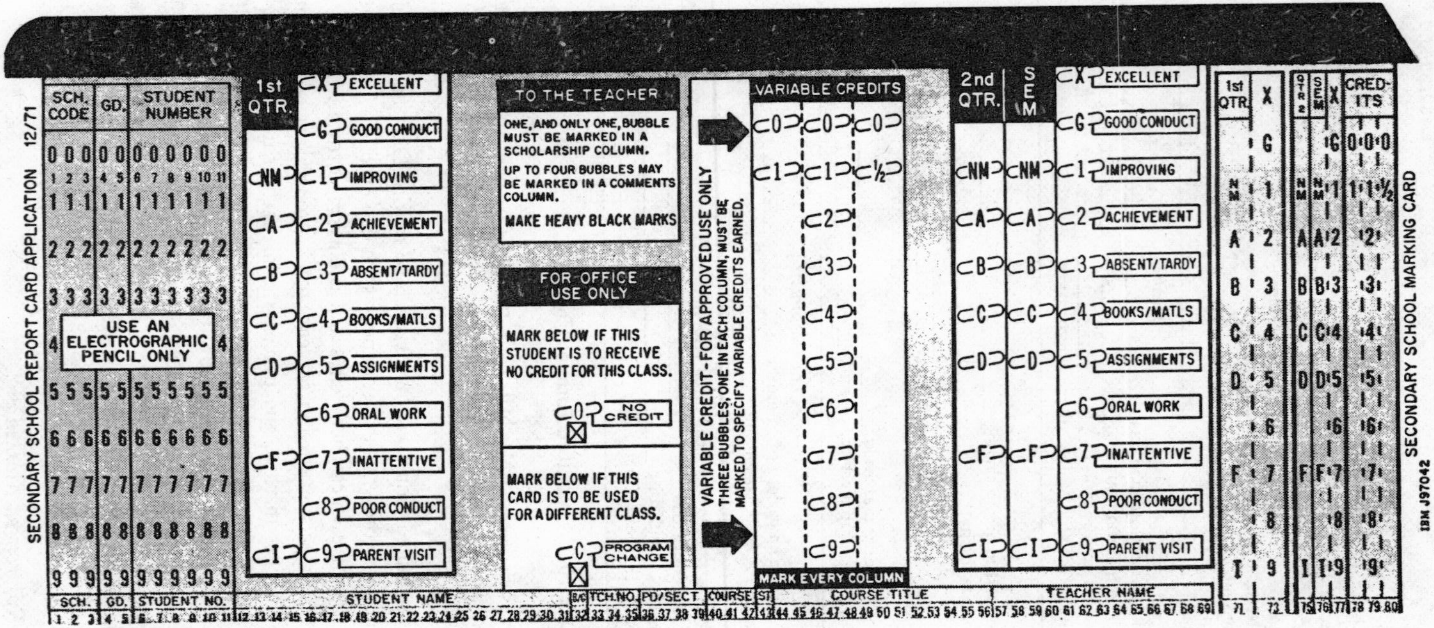

FIGURE 15.3. Student's Mark-Sense Card

Reproduced by permission of the Richmond (California) Schools.

RICHMOND UNIFIED SCHOOL DISTRICT

REPORT CARD

School Name	School Term	Counselor	Gd.	Adv.	Student Name

EXPLANATION OF MARKS

A — Outstanding achievement
B — Good achievement
C — Satisfactory achievement
D — Minimum achievement
F — Failure due to unsatisfactory achievement
I — Incomplete due to justifiable absence

EXPLANATION OF COMMENTS

X — Excellent progress
G — Good attitude/conduct
1 — Showing some improvement
2 — Achievement is not up to apparent ability
3 — Absences/tardiness affecting school work
4 — Books/materials are not brought to class
5 — Assignments are incomplete or unsatisfactory
6 — Oral participation needed
7 — Inattentive/wastes time/does not follow directions
8 — Conduct in class is not satisfactory
9 — Please contact teacher through counselor

Per./Sect.	COURSE	MARKS		Comments	TEACHER	Credits
		1	2 Sem.			

Normal credits for a semester are 30.   You may keep this card for your records.

FIGURE 15.4.   Report Card

Reproduced by permission of the Richmond (California) Schools.

instruction and the emphasis on criterion-referenced instruments, invite a different format for reporting school progress known as criterion-referenced marking. If the key task of schools is to maximize the amount of each learning area that a student has mastered, then one must know whether the student can perform in ways specified by the objectives.

The essential features of a criterion-referenced report are a list of objectives (or an abbreviated description of tasks), spaces for indicating whether proficiency has been demonstrated, and a system to identify objectives achieved since the previous report (Millman, 1970). Figure 15.5 is an example of such a report card.

Of course, one of the important tasks in the marking system is the formulation of objectives and the construction of test items to measure the criterion perform-

---

MATHEMATICS
Grade Two

Skill	Date
Concepts	
Understands commutative property of addition (e.g., $4 + 3 = 3 + 4$)	9/27
Understands place value (e.g., $27 = 2$ tens $+ 7$ ones)	10/3
Addition	
Supplies missing addend under 10 (e.g., $3 + ? = 5$)	10/8
Adds three single-digit numbers	
Knows combinations 10 through 19	
*Adds two 2-digit numbers without carrying	
*Adds two 2-digit numbers with carrying	
Subtraction	
Knows combinations through 9	10/4
*Supplies missing subtrahend — under 10 (e.g., $6 - ? = 1$)	
*Supplies missing minuend — under 10 (e.g., $? - 3 = 4$)	
*Knows combinations 10 through 19	
*Subtracts two 2-digit numbers without borrowing	
Measurement	
Reads and draws clocks (up to quarter hour)	
Understands dollar value of money (coins up to $1.00 total)	
Geometry	
Understands symmetry	
Recognizes congruent plans figures — that is, figures which are identical except for orientation	
Graph Reading	
*Knows how to construct simple graphs	
*Knows how to read simple graphs	

*In Jefferson Elementary School, these skills are usually learned toward the end of grade two. Some children who need more than average time to learn mathematics may not show proficiency on tests of these skills until they are in grade three.

FIGURE 15.5.   Report Card Based on a System of Criterion-Referenced Measurement

ance. This has already been done commercially for a number of curricula to aid school personnel in this arduous undertaking.

Criterion-referenced testing (which is the basis for criterion-referenced marking), is clearly not a panacea for all the grading and sorting problems that exist in education. More thoughtful reflection and research is required before all the difficulties associated with criterion-based measurement are resolved. However, the criterion-referenced approach serves two very valuable functions within the instructional context. First, it directs attention to the performances and behaviors that are the main purpose of instruction. Secondly, it rewards students on the basis of their attainment relative to these criterion performances rather than to their peers. Under this system, it is conceivable that intrinsic student motivation will dominate over the extrinsic, which has been the result of common marking and reporting practices (Van Hoven, 1972).

Computerized Alternative to Grading.   A computerized alternative to grading has also been developed. In the case of one school district, locally developed criterion-referenced tests are used to determine attainment of twenty instructional objectives for each elementary student in mathematics and in communication skills. Objectives are not based on grade level expectations, but are selected according to each student's "functional level" or ability level. Individualization is the key.

Results of fall pretesting are shared with parents in the form of computerized narrative reports (see Figure 15.6) that list the specific objectives assigned to each student. Thus, parents are apprised of the instructional goals established by the school for their children. During conferences throughout the year, they are given progress reports. These conferences also provide an opportunity to discuss the total educational experiences of each child. During the spring, students are posttested to determine how well they have met their objectives for the year; it is decided which ones have been mastered, and which need further work. This individually tailored evaluation program provides both feedback and direction in a positive manner.

There are a number of advantages to this effective use of computerization as an alternative to grading. First, the clear language of each report is especially helpful; teachers do not fall into the trap of using general clichés and educational jargon in explaining the progress of the student. Second, the system is flexible. Individual narratives can be added or deleted at any time. Third, the method is more realistic than grading in that the focus is on the mastery of some skill, concept, or attitude. Fourth, the role of the teacher is more carefully delineated; while keeping track of student progress, teachers are encouraged to look more closely at each child's development. And finally, the computerized narrative approach focuses on individual progress and experiences and does not compare students with each other (Burba, 1976, pp. 67–69).

PROBLEM

4. Argue for and against criterion-referenced marking in comparison to a letter-number system.

STUDENT PROFILE OF READING/MATH OBJECTIVES

Student _____ Grade _____ Teacher _____ Programs _____

Reading Objectives

( ) 067 Matches cause with effect
( ) 068 Arranges words in alphabetical order
( ) 071 Uses table of contents
( ) 072 Relates pronoun to subject
( ) 073 Places events in sequential order
( ) 075 Spells words with ending diagraphs
( ) 076 Punctuates given sentences
( ) 077 Spells words with ending consonant cluster
( ) 078 Writes sentences with correct punctuation
( ) 080 Arranges data
( ) 081 Writes city and state of birth
( ) 082 Alphabetizes words
( ) 084 Categorizes words
( ) 085 Watches phrases of same meaning
( ) 086 Defines figurative language
( ) 088 Identifies mood of characters
( ) 089 Draws conclusions (short story)
( ) 090 Uses prefixes correctly
( ) 091 Makes use of context
( ) 092 Matches appropriate action to quotation

Mathematics Objectives

( ) 577 Order of the days of the week
( ) 579 Solve subtraction word problems (1–18)
( ) 580 Multiply any number by 1
( ) 582 Subtraction facts vertical/horizontal (1–18)
( ) 583 Multiply two numbers (0–5) in head
( ) 584 Identify pictures for 1/2, 1/3, 1/4
( ) 587 Write in missing multipliers
( ) 590 Multiply any number by 0
( ) 591 Identify pictures for 2/3 or 3/4
( ) 593 Subtraction, 2-digit — 1-digit, borrowing
( ) 595 Draw a set with twice as many objects
( ) 598 Money equivalents (to $1.00)
( ) 599 Make change (to $1.00)
( ) 600 Interpret a chart with 4 or 6 entries
( ) 601 Multiply two numbers (0–6) in head
( ) 602 Multiplication, 1-digit × 2-digit, no carrying
( ) 603 Multiplication, 1-digit × multiple of 100
( ) 604 Write multipliers for answer
( ) 605 Multiplication, 1-digit × 2-digit, carrying
( ) 606 Solve number sentences with 1 or 0

FIGURE 15.6.   Student Profile of Reading/Mathematics Objectives
Reproduced by permission of the Beecher School District, Flint, Michigan.

Mastery Learning

Mastery learning is closely related to criterion marking. Usually we distribute our grades according to the normal curves on the assumption that students will achieve to varying degrees because of different levels of aptitude. However, Bloom, Hastings, and Madaus (1971, pp. 43–57) believe that most students can master what we have to teach them, as long as they receive the kind and quality of teaching needed to meet their needs and have adequate time to learn. Aptitude and achievement should then have a relationship approaching zero.

Typically in mastery learning a course is broken into small learning units, involving a week or two of learning activity. Monitoring of a diagnostic nature provides continuous feedback for student and teacher while learning occurs; it also paces and motivates the student. Furthermore, it is designed to reduce the negative effect associated with evaluation by reducing judgmental aspects. Grades or quality points should not be assigned. Formative tests should be marked to show *mastery* and *nonmastery* with respect to specified instructional goals.

For students who lack mastery of a particular unit, the formative tests should reveal the particular points of difficulty—the specific ideas, skills, and processes they still need to work on. It is most helpful when the feedback shows the elements in a learning hierarchy that the student still needs to learn. Students respond best to the diagnostic results when they are referred to particular instructional materials or processes intended to help them correct their difficulties. The diagnosis should be accompanied by a very specific prescription if they are to do anything about it.

As in any instructional methodology, it is important in mastery learning that objectives of instruction be carefully specified in terms of the products and processes the student is expected to learn. These must be used in summative evaluation for the purpose of judging and grading the student's achievement. Summative evaluation is a summing up of the student's achievement that has been attained throughout an entire course or some substantial part of it.

One of the most difficult tasks is to set the standards for mastery. Some suggest that at least eighty to eighty-five percent of the skills be mastered in each learning unit. Numerical procedures for setting passing scores for domain-referenced tests have been devised, and all require the use of judgment at some stage of their execution (Millman, 1973, p. 214).

If grades are to be given, we must go one step further than the criterion-referenced marking previously described. This can be done by using standards from nonmastery teaching of the subject. For example, Block (1971) suggests using scores earned by students receiving *A*'s and *B*'s with this type of instruction as the grading standard. The procedure will result in many more students receiving *A*'s and *B*'s with mastery learning. Under the latter type of instruction, students have an opportunity to take parallel tests if they do not attain mastery under a particular test administration.

Mastery learning presents several issues. Its proponents claim that it improves the self-concept and mental health of the student. This is not always true. Considerable frustration and hostility can be developed among students when they must continue to work on tasks that were easily accomplished by their classmates.

Another issue that is not resolved even in the minds of mastery-learning proponents is whether mastery learning is effective for all subjects. Some believe that the strategy is most effective for learning areas whose content is stable (closed) and where the emphasis is on convergent rather than divergent thinking. For this reason, among others, the concept of mastery is criticized as being too limiting (Cronbach, 1971, p. 52).

Use of Report Cards

The two most widely used methods for reporting student progress to parents are teacher-parent conferences and a classified scale of letters, that is, *A, B, C,* and so on (National Education Association, 1971). More elementary teachers use the conference, while the letter classification is employed to a greater extent in the secondary school. The majority of the teachers feel that the conference is more effective in the elementary school. Opinion seems to be divided among secondary school teachers among a classified scale of letters, teacher-parent conference, and a *Pass/Fail* system. A number of teachers use more than one method of reporting to parents. For example, sometimes reports are accompanied by a check list.

PROBLEM

5. What difficulties might parents face in interpreting information from a check list? How can these be minimized?

Correspondence with Parents

Communications sent to parents may range from a little notation on a report card to a long letter discussing many aspects of their child's school experiences and growth. It is possible to emphasize both student development and subject matter achievement. With an adequate cumulative record, teachers have evidence to interpret patterns of development. They may discuss problems and emphasize factors pertinent to individual students. If some phases of their work would profit from help at home, this can be explained to the parents. Parental comments should be requested, to provide for two-way communication. The interchange of information may lead to some fruitful conferences between teachers and parents.

One of the serious weaknesses of letters to parents is that they tend to be generalized and stereotyped, all too often appearing to have been run off an assembly line, with little variation in wording to relate to a particular student. For instance, the following letter is far less helpful to the parent than it might have been:

> Mary is an exceptionally likeable child. In general her progress has been quite satisfactory in all phases of her school work. She seems to be interested in all activities and is purposeful in the tasks she undertakes. Her personal-social adjustment is proceeding at a very normal rate.

What has the parent learned? Do Mary's peers accept her, or is she just liked by the teacher? Perhaps the teacher likes her because she is retiring and does not bother anyone. Certainly there must be some strength or weakness in her academic progress that could be emphasized. Does she question what she reads or is she inclined to accept it without critical evaluation? Do her reports show imagination or does she tend to string together some of the words she has read in the encyclopedia? What does the teacher mean by "purposeful?" What is "normal" personal-social adjustment?

Often the reason for inadequate reporting can be traced to vaguely stated objectives. Objectives like the following do not ensure that the teachers understand the criterion behavior. There is no suggestion of how they are to determine whether an objective has been achieved (see Chapter 2).

To develop good citizenship.

To improve health habits.

To understand the scientific method.

Even with sharpened objectives, communicating with parents by letter is not easy. In one community, parents received among other comments the statement "Your child is nervous." They reacted at once with concern about the youngster's mental health, a notion the startled teacher had not meant to convey at all. Letters may annoy the parent or fail to express what the teacher means. The following note concerning a fifth-grade student is not helpful in cementing effective relations between home and school:

Dear Mr. and Mrs. Knowles:

John has been a real problem in our class this year. Unlike most of the children in the group, he doesn't enjoy working with others. He is really a lone wolf. Instead of cooperating, he seems to find satisfaction in disturbing others, and he. . . .

This could be changed to a much more effective report for securing parental cooperation. For example:

Dear Mr. and Mrs. Knowles:

We find that it is difficult to summarize in a single mark the things we would like to share with you about John's development this year. In addition to achievement in academic skills, there are many other aspects of growth that we feel are important.

John can be depended upon to see a task through to completion. In preparation for a recent play, he volunteered to get a number of props and he had them for us on time. When he offered to interview several city officials about our town's history, he brought back information that was exceptionally well organized and interesting. Even in activities that require considerable effort, John will finish the task. I recall a particularly long assignment in fractions with which he had some difficulty. He worked longer than he usually has to, but the paper he handed in was well done.

John seems to have no serious trouble in mastering the basic skills. He reads with understanding and he has learned how to make effective use of source materials for research reports. He is a good speller and has missed no words on our weekly spelling tests. In class discussions, he expresses himself well and reflects a background of reading and travel.

We have been trying to help John this year in associations with his classmates. He tends to prefer working by himself rather than with others. At times he is quite aggressive in a group and finds it difficult to cooperate with his classmates on a project. We feel, however, that he has made considerable progress in this respect. Of late he has commented favorably on the good ideas of his group members. He was also chosen as chairman of the entertainment committee for the last day of school.

John tells us that most of the children in his neighborhood are younger than he. It might be helpful if John had some opportunities this summer to play with children of his own age. This would enable him to enter into the "give-and-take" that is so important for his continued development.

I have enjoyed working with John this year. We anticipate that he will have a good relationship with his sixth-grade teacher and class group.

Sincerely,

Because poorly written letters may cause serious troubles, many principals supervise this type of reporting closely. Some schools have provided such suggestions as the following:

Suggestions for Writing Letters to Parents*

I.   Begin the letter with encouraging news.

II. Close with an attitude of optimism.

III. Solicit the parents' cooperation in solving the problems, if any exist.

IV. Speak of the child's growth—social, physical, and academic.
   A. Social (Citizenship traits)
      1. Desirable traits: attention, attitude toward school, care of property, cooperation, honesty, effort, fair play, neatness, truthfulness, obedience, promptness, reliability, self-control, self-reliance, concentration, courtesy and consideration, thrift, patience, appreciation, kindness, sympathy, orderliness, interests in associates, decision-making, politeness, respect for the rights of others.
      2. Undesirable traits: selfishness, wastefulness, untruthfulness, dishonesty, spitefulness, slow to respond, impudence, carelessness, untidiness, rudeness, noisiness, insolence, cheating, inattention, lack of self-reliance, discourtesy, tattling, snobbishness, conceit, impatience, stealing.
   B. Physical (Health conditions): posture, weight, vitality, physical handicaps, cleanliness (personal), muscular coordination, nervousness, emotional traits.
   C. Academic
      1. Interests: (a) in school activities, (b) in extra-school activities.

* Reproduced by permission of the Santa Monica Unified School District.

2. Methods of work: (a) methods of attack, (b) purposing, (c) planning, (d) executing, (e) judging, (f) consistency in finishing work.
3. Achievements: (a) growth in knowledge, appreciation, techniques; (b) subjects in which the child is making progress and those in which he is not making progress; (c) relationship of his accepted standards to his capacities.

V. Compare the child's efforts with his/her own previous efforts and not with those of others.

VI. Speak of achievements in terms of his/her ability to do school work.

VII. Remember it is our professional duty to know the reason why if the child is not making normal progress. (Some possible reasons for lack of progress—late entry; absence; lack of application; health defects, such as hearing, sight, undernourishment.)

VIII. Teacher's advice to parents in matters pertaining to health in which the home is a vital factor; such as diet, rest, clothing, exercise, etc.

IX. Please remember that every letter is a professional diagnosis, and as such is as sacred as any diagnosis ever made by any physician.

Obviously it requires a great deal of time to compose a thoughtful and helpful letter and teachers are faced with an enormous taks if they must report on thirty or forty students. Some elementary schools have abandoned reporting by letter for just this reason. It is impractical in most secondary school situations.

The problem can be eased if reports are sent out in staggered lots rather than on all students at once. The number of letters for each student can be limited. It is better to have one good letter than three poor ones, and to use other methods for other reporting periods. Perhaps some students will benefit more than others by frequent letter reports, and the load can thereby be reduced.

Time spent on reporting is never lost and often produces rich dividends in parental cooperation. If the report concerns a problem child, the energy saving from better relations may be very rewarding. Too often teachers become so involved in unimportant details that they overlook more fruitful approaches.

PROBLEM

6. What is the most serious limitation in reporting both positive and negative student behavior by means of a letter? If a school system requires this type of evaluative procedure, what steps can be taken to avoid poor public relations?

Teacher-Parent Conferences

The conference method of reporting is most generally used in the elementary school, although for special situations it should be more widely employed at the secondary level. It has potential for providing more information and better understanding between home and school; misunderstanding can be eliminated far more readily when either conferee is able to raise questions than when communication is by letter. Certainly there are optimum conditions for conferences. They should not be called only when a special problem arises—rapport can hardly be at its best if this is the only basis for meeting. They should be planned periodically to serve as a regular report on the child's progress.

Sufficient time must be allowed—a minimum of thirty minutes. Attempting to rush through one interview to be prompt for the next is unfair to parent and teacher. Conferences are just as much a part of a good instructional program as teaching the multiplication table, and teachers should be given time to prepare and hold them during their working schedules. Some schools dismiss classes for half-day periods; others provide substitutes to relieve teachers of classroom responsibilities. Because conferences involve a great deal of time, some schools arrange only one per student during the school year, using other methods for the remaining report periods.

Conference Preparation.   Preparation is basic to an effective conference. Some school systems orient their teachers in the conference technique by distributing bulletins describing the conference purpose, policy, records to be kept, time and preparation. These typically contain numerous illustrations suggesting ideas for preparation. The following are examples:*

> Bobby Bates, in second grade, an only child, is 7 years, 6 months. He is sturdy, well-developed physically, energetic, and active. He seems to have superior mental ability, reads very well, and possesses distinct creative language ability. He loves music and the arts, expressing himself creatively and freely. He is doing very satisfactory number work. Bobby has never been able to get along in a group—he exhibits a quarrelsome and domineering attitude and a tendency to be very aggressive with his peers. He also evidences a negative and often openly resistant attitude toward adults. His parents need to give him more experience in children's groups and gradually add responsibility for certain home tasks. They have a "perfectionist" attitude and want him to excel.

Show Mrs. Bates puppet stage (point out Bobby's ideas)
Refer to room-mothers' meeting
Growth in skills
    Reading (books, reading records)
    Language arts (sample stories—dictionary—broad writing vocabulary)
    Doing two-column addition, gaining mastery of facts
    Attendance records
    Help in broadening interests
Group adjustments
    Home interests and attitudes
    Seems resistant to suggestion (examples)
    Sometimes domineering—aggressive (examples), makes group acceptance
        difficult—good ideas
    Plans for helping Bobby—home—school (boys' groups? hobbies? help
        to share his ability)

* Reproduced by permission of the Schenectady (New York) Public Schools.

Individual work habits
    Perfectionist
    Sharing and helping others is difficult (examples—games, books, Monday play)
    How can we help him accept and profit by occasional failures?
    Parents' support and encouragement (suggestions)

James, age 12–8, entering junior high school, has reached sixth grade with normal physical and social growth and development. His academic achievement ranges from a year to a year and one-half beyond normal sixth grade as per the fall testing scores.

    Safety Patrol work—fine job
    Review academic progress Kgn through 6
    Indicate seventh-grade adjustment problems
    Emphasize adequate social growth for age
    Successful six years of growth
    Meeting of sixth-grade parents and junior high school guidance teachers on May 20.

Some schools have organized worshops and various kinds of training sessions for their teachers. Role playing, in which the teachers assume the roles of both parent and teacher, is helpful. Writing a script of a hypothetical conference and inviting criticism from colleagues develops insight into conference skill. Bulletins may be issued outlining suggestions, including "dos and don'ts." They often include helpful materials such as a summary sheet for each child, to be completed before the conference, and a report form to record what took place at the conference. One copy of the latter is placed in the student's cumulative record, and another copy may be given to the parents.

One reason why teachers do not get as much information as needed from parents is that they do not ask good questions. Typical questions like the following lack the sharpness so necessary to get at specific behaviors that would be helpful for teachers to know about.

Is Barbara generally good-natured?

Does Nancy like mathematics?

Does Jack seem to be in good health?

Parents can and will provide, under adequate stimulation, information that will help the teacher determine how effective teaching has been in transferring to students' behavior outside of school. Note the questions below:

Is Nancy interested in graphs printed in the local newspaper?

Does she ask questions when cost-of-living data are broadcast?

Does Jack accept food that he has disliked or ask for a substitute to maintain a healthful diet?

Parents can also provide information to aid in remediation. Too often, in answer to queries about their child's difficulties, they have been told that everything is all right. They are advised not to concern themselves with instructional problems. Nothing is more frustrating to the interested and intelligent parent than this approach. It is important for teachers to accept parents and look objectively at any problems that might relate to the child's welfare. Resenting parents for their treatment of children is more likely to reinforce parental attitudes than to change them.

Limitations. Conferences have several important limitations, one of which is the time factor. Yet, as in the case of letters to parents, this time can be very important in developing an improved learning environment for the child. Educating the parents may be as important as working with the child in the classroom. Teachers also find that the information gathered and the thinking they must do in preparing for the conference may be very useful in class instruction. Often they are forced by a conference to collect information they should already have.

Another limitation sometimes mentioned is that parents will not come to conferences. A great deal of the blame for this can be attributed to school administrators who fail to involve the community in the affairs of the school and to teachers who are not well trained in the conference method. The inadequately trained teacher can do more harm than good, for the parent is often antagonized and refuses to cooperate readily in the future. In such a case, the usefulness of conference-type reporting is greatly reduced.

A third limitation is that the conference technique is difficult to use in the secondary school. It is true that most experimentation with conferences has been in the elementary school. Moreover, there is reason to believe that secondary school students do not want their parents to participate in formal teacher-parent conferences. On the other hand, as the educational level of parents increases over the years, parental concern about student growth in the secondary school will undoubtedly be as great as for the elementary grades now. Such a trend appears to be developing. Nonetheless, a very practical problem must be solved before there can be extensive conferences at the secondary school level, namely, the large student-teacher ratio. In many instances, the guidance staff is able to alleviate the teacher's load by conferring with some of the parents.

PROBLEM

7. The teacher-parent conference is often more helpful to the teacher than to the parents in terms of understanding the child. If you were allowed only one conference each year, during what month would you prefer to schedule these meetings? Support your answer.

Marking and Reporting in the Open Classroom

In a number of instances, alternate methods of organizing schools based on certain British ideas of education have been adopted in this country. Designated by such terms as "open" education, the "informal" classroom, the "Leicestershire plan," and the "integrated day," these methods produce classrooms quite different from the typical American model. The British system is child- rather than teacher-centered. The learners are responsible for directing their activities. Many and varied kinds of materials in the classroom provide the student with a laboratory to explore and opportunities to create and learn.

Permeating the "open" classroom philosophy is the belief that children learn from their errors and that these errors may be only a temporary condition. Proponents do not believe that the teacher needs to find and correct all mistakes that children make. They maintain that teachers must learn to accept the idea that when consequences of children's mistakes become known to the children themselves, their behavior will change. The teacher must learn to accept children's expressions of mathematics and reading like they accept artwork, namely, as only temporary manifestations of a student's thinking.

Obviously this type of classroom organization presents special challenges for evaluating students' work that are different from those in the classroom in which the teacher directs the entire class or a very few groups in a sequence of activities. First, in the "open" classroom, students are completing many and varied tasks so there are few comparable products to evaluate. Secondly, "open" classrooms place greater emphasis on such qualities as initiative, independence, social skill, curiosity, and creativity, in addition to the basic skills. Development of these personal characteristics is much more difficult to measure.

Evidence of learning is typically assessed by direct observation, or perhaps by criterion-referenced test items. Even norm-referenced tests are sometimes appropriate as well. No matter which techniques are used, it is particularly important that teachers in "open" classrooms keep detailed records that chronicle the student's work. These records, as opposed to commonly used report cards, will provide information to children and their parents and give organized feedback to teachers. Records that are kept carefully day by day might be similar to the following:

Alice Blue: Week of May 1

Worked on fractions. Measured various storage boxes to determine the amount of decorative paper necessary to cover them.

Read several plays. Began writing one of her own.

Assigned her Task Card #1 on electricity. Worked one hour with the materials and read from several references to find the answers to a number of questions raised.

Observations: Needs more practice in subtracting fractions. Has difficulty in word syllabification. Shows signs of developing a greater sense of personal worth. Is able to easily accept praise and criticism.

In addition to teacher records, children maintain logs of their activities. These often include pictures, essays, graphs, charts, and the like. With these data, one of two methods or a combination of the two are sometimes used in more formal reporting. One method is the use of a criterion-referenced-type report card. School learning is analyzed and the desired outcomes indicated. Personal characteristics such as dependability, leadership, and persistence are listed as well as cognitive and psychomotor skills. Another method is to report to parents by using anecdotal records. The skills necessary for writing such reports are basically the same as those for preparing correspondence with parents.

PROBLEM

8. Outline a specific program in your subject matter area for implementing self-evaluation procedures. What are your underlying objectives for following this program?

By-Products of Marking and Reporting

Emotional Problems

Invariably, a cartoonist playing on some aspect of reporting will emphasize the defensive behavior of the student or the fear of adult disapproval. The judgment always seems to be punitive, with the implication that life would be wonderful if report cards could somehow vanish. Certainly in many instances parents do withhold privileges or administer corporal punishment when their child brings home a bad report. Some offer prizes and rewards for an *A*; then the child's problems may be overlooked and the mark becomes all important. Other parents identify with their children and may blame the school for bad grades, and the necessary cooperation between the home and school diminishes. In some cases, students develop feelings of inferiority which keep them from trying to solve their difficulties. It is not uncommon for gifted children with specific difficulties in arithmetic or reading to be convinced of their general lack of intellectual prowess.

Marking and reporting need not cause these reactions. In many school systems, children are eager for reporting time. The spirit is one of helpful cooperation, with the child likely to gain. Prevailing attitudes promote helpfulness rather than criticism.

How Marking Affects Teaching

Some teachers assign marks as rewards or prizes, an approach that is not successful with all students. When marks are used for motivation, they can too often become an end in themselves. They should be a tool for the improvement of learning, not a crutch for ineffective teaching. The process of determining them should result in feedback of a diagnostic nature for the teacher as well as the student.

Too often, the only bases for giving grades are typical class assignments that incorporate equal requirements for all, regardless of individual differences in learning ability. The simpler aspects of student achievement are emphasized while more complex aspects are ignored. It's much easier to teach and measure in terms of the lower levels of the taxonomy of the cognitive domain (i.e., knowledge and comprehension), than at the upper levels (i.e., application, analysis, synthesis, and evaluation). Measuring achievement in the affective domain is often disregarded. It is also a simple process to evaluate only in terms of test averages, grades for papers, and class participation, rather than by trying to understand students and evaluate their growth in terms of their own inherent characteristics and environmental problems.

Grade-Seeking

Pressures to earn high marks may result in cheating, or at best, in conforming to a teacher's wishes to obtain good grades. Students generally do what teachers want them to do in order to improve their grade-point averages. If students are only graded on how well they memorize, this is all they are likely to do; creativity, problem-solving, and critical thinking rarely become part of the learning process. If the teacher expects specific and routine answers during recitation, the student who wants high marks will probably not challenge the teacher or present new ideas and hypotheses.

Unfortunately, grade-seeking often pits the student against both teacher and peer. This happens particularly when competition rather than cooperation is emphasized. Some teachers stress their roles as evaluators and judges at the expense of their responsibilities as guides and helpers. But teachers can make evaluation a part of the learning process with positive results. All of us learn through our mistakes when we have feedback about the source of our errors.

PROBLEM

9. A high-school teacher felt that Johnny was lazy and was concerned about his sloppy work in algebra. The teacher reasoned that this boy needed a good jolt. Knowing that Johnny's father held rigid, high standards for his son, the teacher assigned Johnny a low mark. Evaluate this decision by the teacher.

Improvement of Marking and Reporting Systems

Why is there such a violent controversy concerning the marking of student achievement? The most important reason is that it is such a difficult and complex problem. There are so many factors related to marking and reporting, ranging from the emotional impact on students to their opportunities in selected vocations or professions, that we shall probably never discover a procedure that will be satisfactory for everyone. We can, however, improve on the effectiveness with which marking systems are used.

The following are suggestions for improvement advanced by schools that have studied their marking and reporting systems seriously and initiated programs of effective improvement (Strang, 1955, pp. 15–17):

Have teachers, parents, and students study the problem cooperatively. Involving representatives of all groups who will be concerned with marks and re- ports is the best way to ensure understanding and cooperative effort for continued critical analysis and improvement of the system. This means calling on teachers from a range of grade levels and subjects and also a variety of specialists among school personnel, such as administrators and guidance staff. There should be representatives from the parent-teacher association and other interested organizations. It is important to provide a hearing for a cross section of the students and for parents from several socioeconomic backgrounds, as their goals for their children will differ.

Begin by studying the present reporting system. The experience of all representatives with the existing marking practices of the school will generate interest, should produce profitable discussion, and do much to involve all members of the representative group. They should determine the effectiveness of communication under the current reporting system and the usefulness of the information that reports give to students and parents. Certainly the group will be concerned with how well the marking and reporting evaluate in terms of the educational objectives of the school. This provides an excellent opportunity to interpret the school program to parents and students.

Determine what marking and reporting should accomplish. The answer to this problem will evolve from the previous discussion. The group must decide what it believes important to know about the student, and whether it is feasible to report it. Furthermore, they should decide on suitable measurement tools and procedures. There must be exploration of such issues as the use of universal standards in marking and marking achievement in terms of the student's ability. The breadth of achievement and growth must be determined. If only final achievement is to be assessed, the group's problem is comparatively simple; if there is a desire for some of the reporting to be based on student growth, then serious consideration must be given to the problems involved.

Explore the marking and reporting systems of other schools. The group can often glean helpful ideas from the experiences and reports of other schools. Though no two school systems have identical problems, there is enough similarity to make it helpful to examine effective methods, difficulties that have been met, and suggestions made for improvement elsewhere.

Prepare a tentative form. The starting point for a reporting system is always the objectives of the school. The group must select those objectives on which they wish reports made and examine the feasibility of various methods of reporting in terms of those objectives. It is important to consider such factors as the time available to the teacher. Possibly there should be time released from teaching to prepare and make the reports. If a printed form of some kind is to be used, specific suggestions should be made for its construction.

Present the tentative form to students, teachers, and the general public. A considerable amount of study may be necessary if a basic change in reporting is involved. Questions that may not have been considered in the representatives' group will surely be raised on general presentation. Another meeting of the group may be necessary to resolve some of them. Possibly teachers will find it helpful to meet in special session to study means of administering the system effectively. Understanding and agreement should be reached. If there is a change to teacher-parent conferences or the writing of letters, in-service training conferences will undoubtedly be needed. Possibly some basic curriculum changes will be recommended if educational objectives are reformulated. A new look at school and community relationships may be in order, and some aspects of the school program may have to be revised, such as promotional policies, guidance services, and curriculum offerings.

Give the tentative form a trial. When the basic groundwork has been completed, the new system is ready for its trial run. Plan on several semesters to appraise its strengths and weaknesses. Set up machinery to collect all general public. Emphasize the growth of the students as the criterion for possible suggestions and criticisms from students, parents, teachers, and the judgment. Has the student's attitude toward learning been improved? Has his or her personal-social adjustment matured? Is there a better relationship among students, teachers, parents?

We should not stop here. The new system must always be subject to revision. Parents and students should be continuously involved in a study of the educational program of the schools. This includes evaluation of the extent to which the program achieves the educational objectives. It also means that evaluation must keep pace when objectives are changed.

Schools and communities that follow the seven steps above to the best of their ability will not necessarily arrive at the same system of marking and reporting, for there is no single system that is best for schools of all types or for all grade levels within these schools. Because of differences, however slight, in educational objectives, pupil talent, and points of view about the function of reports, the reporting systems selected vary from place to place and time to time. Furthermore, it is common to find variations within a school system. Different combinations of several of the reporting techniques may be used.

Regardless of which reporting system or combination of systems is chosen, it is most important that the result should receive widespread approval and that its purposes should be clearly understood by all concerned. If understanding and approval exist, cooperation among teachers, students, parents, and school administrators will come more easily, and the likelihood of misinterpretation (usually in the form of overinterpretations) of the reports themselves will be greatly lessened.

PROBLEM

10. A suggested program of improving marks and reporting has been outlined. Choose one of the seven steps, and assume that you are to head a committee that is to carry out this phase of the program. Describe in detail the procedures you and your committee would follow.

Promotion and Final Marks

Problems and Principles

If the philosophy of the school is concerned with the most effective development of the whole student, policies for promotion must be consistent with the criterion of "what is best for the student." Widely different practices are currently in effect in an effort to meet this criterion. Students in some schools must meet or exceed a "passing level" of achievement before they are promoted. Other schools have the policy of "social promotion," or one hundred percent promotion. Both approaches have serious limitations.

Requiring all students, without respect to their talents and goals, to reach a "passing level" before promotion creates a threat of failure that can in some cases do great harm to the student. To students of modest ability, this perpetual threat of failure can undermine their self-confidence, creating feelings of inadequacy and insecurity that can do irreparable damage to their personalities. Moreover, failing them not only leaves the cause of their difficulties unchanged but aggravates the situation by increasing their feelings of inadequacy.

The very nature of today's school population greatly complicates the mental health problem. The schools are committed to accept all children with few exceptions and to give them twelve or thirteen years of free education. State laws force the children to stay in school for most of these years. Great heterogeneity results. Unfortunately, the curriculum of many schools has not been expanded to meet the different needs of their students. Consequently, those placed in classes in which they may have no interest and for which they are ill-prepared are faced with failure. The result may be boredom, apathy, anxiety, belligerence, or hostility. The teacher is confronted with a complex teaching situation.

Thus the use of a "passing level" is not the source of the problem. A much more basic cause is the limited nature of the curriculum in many schools. Until they are placed in classes better suited to their needs and talents, some students will experience a series of failures. To assume that every student should receive the same dosage of subject matter in a particular grade level is to ignore the fact that, at any grade level, there are students at all levels of achievement with a wide range of learning capacities. There must be appropriate levels of instruction with appropriate standards.

Yet "social promotion" is not the answer. In the first place, there are some students who profit by repeating a course or grade level. A student who is generally immature might find considerable satisfaction in being with a younger group of children and a teacher who instructs accordingly. A second and more important factor is that students do not become a homogeneous group by some magic after they are promoted. The fact that they are all now fourth graders or sophomores in high school does not suddenly create homogeneity. Students must still be taught on the basis of their experiences, backgrounds, and learning capacities. Data show that there are from three to nine grades of achievement levels in any one grade level. Indeed, effective teaching tends to make a group more heterogeneous relative to achievement. Therefore, if we are to promote students regardless of achievement, considerable attention must be given to the problems of each.

Failure to promote students can be very costly from both an economic and a social point of view. Educators who favor retention in a grade feel that such action provides an opportunity for remediation and allows immature students the time required for their social development. After reviewing the available studies, however, Jackson (1975, p. 627) concludes that there is no reliable body of evidence to indicate that grade retention is more beneficial than grade promotion for students with serious academic or adjustment difficulties. This is not to be interpreted to mean that promotion is better than retention. It is clear that further research is needed before the relative benefits of the two options can be validly determined. In the meantime, judgment must be exercised in evaluating the effect either option is likely to have on a particular student.

Improving Promotion Policies.   Trying to establish the best promotion policy is about as difficult as trying to find the best marking and reporting system. In fact, there are many problems common to the two issues. In both cases, differences among schools in terms of educational objectives, student populations, and the opinions of all parties concerned can be reasons for differences in policies.

Six basic principles that can be used as the basis for a policy for promotion are the following:

1. Promotion should be decided on the basis of the individual student.
2. Promotion should be on the basis of many factors. The final decision as to whether a particular student should be promoted should rest not merely on academic accomplishment, but on what will result in the greatest good to the all-around development of the individual.
3. In order that promotion procedures may be more or less uniform throughout a particular school system, a definite set of factors should be agreed upon. Each teacher will take these into consideration in forming a judgment as to whether a particular student should be promoted.
4. Criteria for promotion must take into consideration the curriculum offerings of the next higher grade or unit and the flexibility of its organization, its courses of study, and its methods.
5. It is the duty of the next higher grade or unit to accept students who are properly promoted to it from the lower grade or unit and to adapt its work to fit the needs of these students.
6. Promotion procedures demand continuous analysis and study of cumulative case history records in order that refinement of procedures may result and that guesswork and conjecture may be reduced to a minimum.

The foregoing principles were stated many years ago by the National Education Association, and then only as a basis for discussion. They are, however, still sound and applicable in today's classroom. Notice that they stress the individual child as the central factor. In many instances, uniform promotion is the answer, yet to make a blanket policy would work against the needs and interest of some students. There can be no substitute for the careful study of individuals. Decisions must be made on the basis of what is best for each person.

PROBLEM

11. Paul has failed four seventh-grade subjects. He is of average mental ability and has a stable home background. He is physically immature, has low

vitality, and has progressed very little academically and socially in the past few years. This year he has been absent a great deal due to illness. The seventh-grade teachers have made the decision that he should repeat the seventh grade. What other information would you need before you could evaluate their action?

SUMMARY

The following are the key points presented in this chapter:

1. No other teacher activity has greater potential for interpreting the school program, for securing cooperation between home and school, and for promoting student development than determining and reporting student progress.

2. Reporting exists to inform students, parents, school personnel, and employers about the degree to which teachers judge the student to be achieving certain educational objectives.

3. The chief sources of information used for evaluating the student are classroom and standardized tests, procedure and product evaluation, class participation, and projects and reports.

4. Common methods of marking and reporting are the letter and number system, checklists, *Pass/Fail* or *Credit/No Credit* marking, correspondence to parents, and teacher-parent conferences. Criterion-referenced marking is gaining attention, and mastery learning is also being emphasized.

5. There can be negative by-products of marking and reporting that must be dealt with in a positive manner. Some of these are student emotional problems, cheating, and overemphasis on grades.

6. The best plan of reporting is a combination of different methods tailored to meet the needs of the students, school, and community.

7. Parents should be active participants in the evaluation process. They have opportunities to observe many phases of their children's development that the teacher does not see and are in a position to provide helpful information.

8. Promotion policies should be based on what is best for the student. Although there are tendencies toward social promotion, promoting all students does not solve all the problems of organizing effective learning experiences.

SUGGESTED READINGS

CURETON, L. W. The history of grading practice. *NCME Measurement in Education*, 1971, *2* (4).
This well-documented history of marking and reporting student achievement concludes with a list of five major problems that still perplex us.

EBEL, R. L. Shall we get rid of grades? *NCME Measurement in Education*, 1974, *5* (4).
Twenty-two reasons for eliminating grades are listed and responses to the major ones are summarized. The author concludes that, on balance, grades make a positive contribution to the educational process.

FELDMESSER, R. A. The positive function of grades. *Educational Record*, 1972, *53*, 66–72.
The author believes that grades serve an evaluative function that cannot be served or served as well by some other form of evaluation.

HUNTLEY, J. F. Academic evaluation and grading: An analysis and some proposals. *Harvard Educational Review*, 1976, *46*, 612–631.
A new model for grading based on intrinsic *rather than* extrinsic *evaluation is proposed. The author contends that this system will eliminate many of the evils of current grading practices, such as grade inflation.*

LOSEN, S. *Parent conferences in the schools: Procedures for developing effective partnership.* Boston: Allyn & Bacon, 1978.
This guidebook is designed to help teachers and parents have effective conferences.

MARSHALL, M. S. Why grades are argued. *School and Society*, 1971, *99*, 350–353.
This article discusses the relative merits of using grades, emphasizing their limitations.

THORNDIKE, R. L. Marks and marking systems. In R. L. Ebel (Ed.), *Encyclopedia of Educational Research* (4th ed.). New York: Macmillan, 1969.
This chapter contains a thorough review of marking and reporting. Such topics as objections to marks, substitutes for marks, what a mark should represent, and proportions to be awarded each symbol are included.

REFERENCES CITED

BLOCK, J. H. (Ed.). *Mastery learning: Theory and practice.* New York: Holt, Rinehart and Winston, 1971.

BLOOM, B. S., HASTINGS, J. T., & MADAUS, G. F. *Handbook on formative and summative evaluation of student learning.* New York: McGraw-Hill, 1971.

BROMLEY, D. G., CROW, M. L., & GIBSON, M. S. Grade inflation: Trends, causes, and implications. *Phi Delta Kappan*, 1978, *59*, 694–697.

BURBA, K. V. A computerized alternative to grading. In S. B. Simon & J. A. Bellanca (Eds.), *Degrading the grading myths: A primer of alternatives of grades and marks.* Washington, D.C.: Association for Supervision and Curriculum Development, 1976.

CRISLER, R. D., & WOGAMAN, T. D. Educational data processing at Richmond. *Journal of Secondary Education*, 1963, *38*, 71–76.

CRONBACH, L. J. Comments on mastery learning and its implications for curriculum development. In E. W. Eisner (Ed.), *Confronting curriculum reform.* Boston: Little, Brown, 1971.

EBEL, R. L. *Essentials of educational measurement* (3rd ed.). Englewood Cliffs, N.J.: Prentice-Hall, 1979.

FELDMESSER, R. A. The positive function of grades. *Educational Record*, 1972, *53*, 66–72.

GREEN, C. D. What shall we do with the dullards? *Atlantic Monthly*, 1956, *197*, 72–74.

HEFFERNAN, H., & MARSHALL, L. E. Reporting pupil progress in California cities. *California Journal of Elementary Education*, 1955, *24*, 67–77.

JACKSON, G. B. The research evidence on the effects of grade retention. *Review of Educational Research*, 1975, *45*, 613–635.

MILLMAN, J. Reporting student progress: A case for a criterion-referenced marking system. *Phi Delta Kappan*, 1970, *52*, 226–230.

MILLMAN, J. Passing scores and test lengths for domain-referenced measures. *Review of Educational Research*, 1973, *43*, 205–216.

NATIONAL EDUCATION ASSOCIATION. Reporting pupil progress to parents. *National Education Association Research Bulletin*, 1971, *49*, 81–82.

STRANG, R. *How to report pupil progress.* Chicago: Science Research Associates, 1955.

VAN HOVEN, J. B. Reporting progress: A broad rationale for new practices. *Phi Delta Kappan*, 1972, *53*, 365–366.

16

A Schoolwide Program of Evaluation

After reading this chapter you will be able to

1. State the purposes of a school evaluation program
2. Outline the steps to initiate a schoolwide program of evaluation
3. Describe various testing programs for different grade levels
4. State acceptable guidelines for testing the educationally disadvantaged
5. List guiding principles for test selection
6. Explain the factors involved in effective test administration and scoring
7. Appreciate the need to keep test scores confidential
8. State and defend your position with regard to the criticisms of standardized tests
9. List guidelines for the use of the cumulative record by teachers, counselors, and administrators

All football coaches probably have one overall objective—to win as many games as possible. To have a successful season, they must accomplish numerous other objectives centering around individual performance and team play. Blocking, running, tackling, and passing should be developed in terms of each player's ability. Then these skills have to be orchestrated to form a smooth-functioning team.

The coaches will measure progress in various ways. This is important. They want to note continuous improvement. Evaluation of the success of their programs is based on data collected in various ways at various times. Speed can be timed. Effects of blocking can be visually judged. Distance and accuracy of passing can be measured. But data are not so easily obtained for other important performance objectives. On what basis do the coaches measure motivation and eagerness? How can they judge player morale? How will they estimate sensitivity to, and ability to profit from, suggestion? How may they determine a team's confidence in the quarterback? They rely on reports, observations, a sensitivity to certain cues, and comparative mental images of past performance. From this information they evaluate progress. These evaluations continue throughout the season and into the following year.

To evaluate the school's total educational program is even more complex than the task of the coach. We sometimes lose sight of the broad range of our goals and how difficult it is to measure change in such areas as attitudes, interests, and personal-social adjustment. To collect data for evaluation, many types of instruments and procedures, in addition to tests, must be used. But we must not lose sight of the fact that these are all selected on the basis of measuring the degree of attainment of the school's objectives. One does not ask the question "What is the best achievement test?" Rather, one asks "What is the best test for obtaining data about my school program under the conditions that it must operate?"

Purposes of an Evaluation Program

Evaluation is the discovery of the nature and worth of something. We can evaluate students, teachers, curricula, administrative systems, teaching materials, and much more. Evaluation contributes to understanding substance, function, and worth.

The ultimate goal of a student evaluation program is to inform various persons and groups who are strongly interested in the school how to assist students in the development of their abilities. We must be able to translate measurement data into teaching prescriptions (Fleming, 1971). To accomplish this, we must know the students' interests and achievement. Furthermore, we must have instructional objectives that lend themselves to the evaluation process. Stated objectives like "to develop good citizenship" are of limited value if good citizenship is not defined and delineated so that the degree of the students' development can be determined. It is much less bewildering to assess progress toward the following objective, representing one facet of good citizenship: "The students do not destroy, or mutilate in any way, property that does not belong to them."

A schoolwide program of student evaluation is based on the complete set of educational objectives held by that school. The task is exceedingly complex. Too often testing is confused with evaluation, and the school initiates a testing program per se. Though an important part of the evaluation program, testing is still only one part. Many kinds of evidence are needed, and from various sources. Because we do not have effective tests to measure all aspects of behavior, many other approaches including observation, rating scales, questionnaires, and interviews must be used. Evaluation that considers a variety of data can also focus on the process of learning rather than on the product alone. Data collected can then be the basis for evaluating individuals in terms of their abilities and needs.

But there should be more to a schoolwide program of evaluation than student evaluation. It can be vastly strengthened by the presence of program and product evaluation (see pages 27–29). Now we can take steps to evaluate the inputs and processes as well as the outputs of the instructional program. What programs are effective for learning? What procedures can be used to overcome specific weaknesses? We need information to aid in selecting among various competing instructional approaches.

Unfortunately, we are more able to predict from test scores the possible success or failure of a student than we are able to suggest instructional procedures to prevent failure and ensure success. We are much more sophisticated in using measurement techniques that determine students' ranks in a particular norm group than we are in describing what they can and cannot do, as in the case of a criterion-referenced testing. Happily, a number of instruments employing methodologies attuned to identifying barriers to learning and related to specific instructional techniques have been developed. These include programs with stated objectives arranged in hierarchical order for sequential learning, criterion-referenced diagnostic tests to determine students' strengths and weaknesses, and keyed instructional materials to enable boys and girls to focus on their deficiencies. These programs fit nicely into schoolwide programs of evaluation.

Initiation of the Program

Since a program of evaluation cannot be separated from the total educational program, school personnel in administration, guidance, and instruction must participate in its inception, organization, and promotion. It should be a truly cooperative venture. The authoritarian principal who dictates a program may compel the staff to comply mechanically. They may administer, score, and record the results of tests, but it is doubtful that they will be motivated to understand student behavior and motivation. Such understanding only comes through in-service education and democratic participation of a staff; it is the basis of a good evaluation program.

In a small school, the general staff meeting should involve all teachers and specialists; everyone should have a chance to ask questions and discuss procedures. The administrator should probably assume leadership to stimulate interest, perhaps by posing such a problem as "Why do our students always do better on the mathematical parts of standardized achievement test batteries than on the verbal parts?"

Perhaps community criticism of achievement may prompt the staff to evaluate its educational program. It is also possible to interest the staff by showing them the results of the administration of a standardized achievement test, like a reading survey test; from this they can determine the students' strengths and weaknesses. When properly directed, this approach will stimulate thinking about the total evaluation problem in the school.

In the large city system it is impractical, if not impossible, to involve the entire staff in the initial evaluation discussions, so a representative committee should work out preliminary details. In smaller schools, however, one person should be responsible for coordinating the program. This individual should be adept in working with people and sophisticated in measurement and statistics. It is important that time be allotted for the coordinator to do the assignment effectively. Nevertheless, before any final action is taken in test selection or evaluation procedures, the entire staff should discuss and evaluate the proposals. This is a necessity in the evaluation is to be integrated with the total educational program.

In the initial discussions, teachers should understand that evaluation is a comprehensive process requiring continuous administrative and guidance functions in addition to the more obvious instructional ones. Suggestions as to the kinds of evidence needed for evaluating, in terms of a group of related objectives, and where that evidence can be sought can be meaningful if presented in chart form (see Table 16.1). This will help prevent the limited approach of paper-and-pencil alone.

TABLE 16.1. Educational Objectives in Communication for the Primary Period and Means of Evaluation

Educational objective	Means of evaluation
Knowledge and Understanding	
Can define common words that are used orally	Standardized word meaning tests
	Observation (The teacher listens to student's use of words.)
	Classroom tests (The student writes definitions of words.)
Can read orally in a meaningful way	Standardized oral reading tests
	Classroom tests
	Checklists (Smooth reading, good phrasing, correct interpretation of punctuation marks are some items included.)
Understands that many words "pair off" as opposites, e.g., *yes-no, little-big*	Classroom and standardized tests
	Workbook exercises
	Informal questioning during group instruction
Can distinguish between the names of persons and things and action words	Classroom tests
	Observation (The student is able to follow directions and to make up directions for others to follow.)
	Classification lists

Educational objective	Means of evaluation
Skill and Competence	
Can recall the sequence of a story or the facts read in a story	Standardized reading tests Classroom reading tests (The student recalls and writes facts.) Observation (The student answers well-phrased questions during group discussion, illustrates the sequence in pictures, and acts out the sequence.)
Reads third-grade material with a comprehension of 80 percent	Standardized reading tests Classroom tests
Can read seven out of ten paragraphs of third-grade material and recognize many of the main ideas	Standardized reading tests Classroom tests Informal questioning during individual instruction
Can read from 95 to 120 words silently each minute	Standardized reading tests (timed) Classroom tests (timed)
Attitude and Interest	
Enjoys reading for recreation or information	Observation (The student talks or writes about what was read, brings objects related to it to school, and is anxious to read new material.)
Likes to recite poems and retell favorite stories	Observation (The student displays interests by what he/she says and does.)
Is interested in the sounds of words in word-families, in rhymes, and in secret languages and codes	Observation (Questions asked by the student indicate this interest; the student knows how to determine word-families.)

Paraphrased from Part II, "Recommended Goals for the Elementary School Years: Communication," in ELEMENTARY SCHOOL OBJECTIVES, by Nolan C. Kearney, © 1953 by the Russell Sage Foundation, New York.

Illustrative objectives concerning communication are shown in Table 16.1. Although it is desirable to refine the wording of some of the objectives in this table, by following the chapter 2 suggested guidelines for stating specific objectives, note that these are not loosely phrased. Rather than a vague statement, such as "to develop comprehension," the objective listed is "he/she reads third-grade material with a comprehension of 80 percent." Rather than "to read rapidly," the objective is stated "he/she can read from 95 to 120 words silently each minute." The last objective could be improved by adding "and is able to answer correctly 80 percent of the comprehension questions sampling the passage." The criterion of acceptable performance is now definite. A few other objectives could be more crisply stated in behavioral terms.

In Table 16.1, the statement of objectives is followed by a suggested means for gathering information to be used as a basis for evaluation. Note that the use of both these teacher-constructed and standardized tests is advised. Although tests are often very helpful, there are some areas of achievement where they are not applicable. For example, no test can determine whether students do their assigned reading independently. Certainly, improved skill will be reflected in test results, but the teacher can only observe them in the classroom for effective evaluation of this achievement. Incidentally, not all students will be limited to the specific objectives stated in Table 16.1, which are only general guides for primary teachers. A number of students should be able to read more difficult material than those at third grade level, just as some will read faster than 120 words per minute.

Packaged Programs

There are a number of programs, such as the *Skills Monitoring System (SMS)*, that have stated objectives for a given subject area. Table 16.2 includes a few of the third-grade objectives in word identification. You will note that the objectives are skill statements, following our suggestions for well-formulated goals. Criterion-referenced tests based on these skill statements are available for determining student strengths and weaknesses and for evaluating progress. Furthermore, there is a *Coded Instructional Resource Index* for choosing materials keyed to teaching specific skills.

Programs similar to the *SMS* are the *Diagnostic Mathematics Inventory* (see page 411), and the *Prescriptive Reading Inventory* (see page 301). It is obvious

TABLE 16.2.   Illustrative Skill Statements for Word Identification, Third Grade Level

Morphemic Elements (Meaning)	
Rootwords: No change	Identify the root word contained in a printed affixed word when no spelling change is involved
Rootwords: Change	Identify the root word contained in a printed affixed word when a spelling change is involved
Compound words	Discriminate between printed compound and non-compound words
Plurals	Identify the one noun printed in plural form when only a plural noun is appropriate for the printed context
Time indicators	Identify the printed verb tense that is appropriate to answer the printed time-frame question
Comparatives	Identify simple, comparative or superlative form of a printed word appropriate for the printed context
Contractions	Identify the two printed words that make up the printed contraction
Possessives	Identify the printed word in possessive form when only the possessive word is appropriate to answer the printed question
Prefixes	Identify the correctly affixed root word when the printed definition requires the appropriate prefix (*dis-, im-, mis-, over-, re-, un-, under-*)
Suffixes	Identify the correctly affixed root word when the printed definition requires the appropriate suffix (*-able, -er, -ful, -ing, -less, -ness, -or, -ship, -some, -tion*)

From *Skills Monitoring System*; reproduced by permission of Harcourt Brace Jovanovich, Inc. Copyright © 1975 by Harcourt Brace Jovanovich, Inc.

that such programs are of invaluable help to busy teachers because they provide for individualized instruction and progress determination and contribute to overall evaluation.

PROBLEMS

1. The board of education of a small community hired a team of educational specialists from a nearby university to evaluate the testing program of the school system and to make specific recommendations for improvement. The team prepared a comprehensive report, which was then presented to the faculty. Although this report was complimentary for the most part, there was a general feeling of dissatisfaction among both faculty and administration. Criticize the procedure followed by the board of education. Suggest a better approach.

2. Prepare a list of general educational objectives for a secondary school program in a slum area in a large city, and another list for a secondary school program in a small rural community. In what respects are your lists similar? Are the differences sufficiently large to cause the schoolwide evaluation program at one school to be greatly different from that of the other school?

3. Choose one or more of the educational objectives that you have stated for your subject matter and devise reasonably reliable and valid methods to systematically and objectively evaluate each student in a class.

Use of Standardized Tests

Although standardized tests represent only one means of obtaining data for evaluation, they are very important tools in measurement. Therefore their selection, administration, scoring, and interpretation are significant aspects of educational evaluation. Selection of the wrong test, its improper administration or scoring, or inadequate interpretation of the results can waste time and money and harm students.

Scope of the Program

Infant and Preschool Tests.   There has been a resurgence of interests in infant and preschool tests largely because of concern for retarded children and the establishment of compensatory school programs for culturally disadvantaged boys and girls. These tests are either performance or oral tests and must be individually administered. Generally, infant tests are designed for children up to eighteen months of age, and preschool tests are considered applicable to the eighteen-to-sixty month period

Some of these instruments are rating scales rather than tests to aid in the observation of children. Others are downward extensions of the *Binet* scales such as the *Cattell Infant Intelligence Scale.* At the lower end of these scales, the required responses are largely perceptual, such as following a moving object or focusing on sounds. There may be some motor tasks requiring movement of parts of the body or changing an object from one hand to another. Of course, as one proceeds up the scale the tasks become more complex. Some verbal responses are required and manipulative tasks require added skill.

Regarding the use of infant and preschool tests, we must conclude that infant tests have no validity in predicting future intelligence test performance. Beginning with the age of twelve months, however, there is a constant increase in predictive power so that the preschool tests have a moderate correlation with subsequent intelligence test scores. One may conclude that the value of infant tests is to aid in the diagnosis of children who may later be judged mentally defective.

Elementary and Junior High School.   A minimum testing program for the elementary and junior high school consists of periodic measurement of scholastic aptitude and yearly achievement testing. Although authorities differ about the best grade level for administering scholastic aptitude tests, they generally agree that four or five administrations should occur between the time children enter school and the completion of high school. A suggested sequence is at the beginning of the first, fourth, seventh, and tenth grades. Some schools add two more administrations in the second and eighth or ninth years. These are transitional points in the student's educational life, representing the beginning of formal study and of the intermediate, junior high, and senior high periods. In addition to the administrations suggested above, the student should be tested again whenever results are at variance with the teacher's judgment.

Another argument for frequent administrations of scholastic aptitude tests is the variation in the test results that typically occurs. IQs commonly vary as much as ten or more points when two or more tests are given. A student may therefore be penalized unless previous test results are continually checked. Fluctuations tend to be greater in the primary grades.

The courts have expressed concern that when students are grouped in terms of their abilities, too often they are frozen in status for periods as long as three years. Evaluation should be continuous, and additional tests should be administered whenever needed to confirm judgment concerning change of status.

Achievement batteries should be administered yearly. The minimal program should emphasize tests of basic skills. The basic responsibilities of the school at this level are proficiency of work-study, language arts, and arithmetic skills. These are of greater importance than content areas.

An optimum program for the elementary and junior high school would include access to all available tests that would help the student. In addition to survey tests of achievement, criterion-referenced diagnostic tests would be administered whenever necessary. Special reading tests, such as readiness tests, could be added to the first-grade battery. An optimum program might also include interest inventories administered late in the junior high school program.

A number of programs, particularly in the basic skills, are built around criterion-referenced tests. They tend to be diagnostic and keyed to instructional procedures and materials. They can be coordinated within the overall testing program.

Senior High School. The minimum program in the senior high school should include a test of scholastic aptitude or a differential aptitude test and measures of achievement in various subjects. It is particularly important that college-bound students know their adequacy in such areas as mathematics; the social, biological, and physical sciences; and the language arts. Every program should also include a recheck of the basic skills. It is especially important to administer a reading test. Whether or not a student is college-bound, reading is important.

The optimum program for the secondary school might employ personal-social adjustment inventories, problem check lists, and interest inventories. These can be used for screening purposes or educational and vocational guidance. In this regard, the limitations of adjustment inventories should be carefully considered.

Guidelines for Testing the Disadvantaged.   Attention has been given to the problem of obtaining valid scores in aptitude testing for disadvantaged students (see p. 320). In addition, test scores from achievement and personal-social adjustment instruments may need special interpretation for the disadvantaged. Fishman et al. (1964) cite three critical issues in testing the disadvantaged: (1) unreliable differentiation within their range of scores, (2) the possible difference in predictive validity between disadvantaged groups and standardization groups, and (3) the importance of understanding the group's social and cultural background. They believe that it is important to compare disadvantaged children's test performances with their previous test results. Progress can best be judged by using the children themselves as controls and employing the norms as "benchmarks."

To improve the quality of aptitude test administration for disadvantaged pupils, the following guidelines should be observed (Gronlund, 1976, pp. 341–342):

1. Provide adequate orientation to the test to be administered.

2. Arrange preliminary practice in test taking.

3. Administer the test under normal conditions—in the classroom, for example.

4. Observe carefully the students' behavior during testing. Watch for problems such as lack of motivation or understanding.

5. Retest low-scoring students with a lower form of the test.

6. Obtain both verbal and nonverbal measures of ability whenever possible.

7. Interpret the test scores as measures of present performance only; avoid inferences concerning inherited ability.

8. Verify the test results by comparing them with other information, for example, observation, achievement test scores, and grades.

It should be emphasized that informed test users must be sensitive to the various characteristics of a given test, the student, and the interpretation of test scores. If they are knowledgeable about general test use, they are not likely to make gross errors with any specific individual or group, including disadvantaged students.

Mainstreaming. For many years parents of handicapped children were concerned that their offspring were set apart in special educational programs and considered to be inferior. As a result, court decisions, state legislation and finally federal legislation (PL 94-142, passed in 1975) have mandated that schools must provide education in the "least restrictive environment" for all handicapped children. In many instances, schools must now provide for the integration of handicapped children into the regular classroom. This is commonly called mainstreaming.

Mainstreaming places special demands upon school testing programs. First of all, there are test administration problems. Children with a wide variety of handicapping conditions very often cannot be tested with the group tests ordinarily used, and special care must be taken when using individual tests. Furthermore, standardized tests often fail to consider the value of nonconventional responses. Finally, norm tables are hard to apply since relatively few standardized tests include handicapped students in the standardization sample. In short, the tests often included in a typical school testing program have serious shortcomings when administered to many handicapped students. Special accommodations are needed in that a greater variety of individual tests will be required, and school counselors and psychologists must be actively involved.

Illustrative Tests for School Testing Programs.   School testing programs often vary considerably in terms of the tests used. Table 16.3 lists the various types of tests

TABLE 16.3.   An Illustrative Outline of a School Testing Program[a]

Testing area	Age or grade level of the instruments[b]	Suitable grade level for administering
Achievement		
Reading Achievement		I through VI: IX
Gates-MacGinitie Reading Tests	I–XI	
Iowa Silent Reading Tests	VI–XII	
Basic Skills Achievement		II through VI
California Achievement Tests	K–XII	
Iowa Tests of Basic Skills	III–IX	
Content Achievement		VI and IX
Sequential Tests of Educational Progress	III–XII	
Stanford Achievement Test	I–IX	
Tests of Achievement and Proficiency	IX–XII	
Diagnostic Tests		As needed
Diagnostic Mathematics Inventory	I–VII	
Gates-McKillop Reading Diagnostic Test	II–VI	
Prescriptive Reading Inventory	K–VI	

Testing area	Age or grade level of the instruments[b]	Suitable grade level for administering
Aptitude[c]		
Group Mental Ability Tests		I, IV, VII, and X
Cognitive Abilities Test	K–XII	
Otis-Lennon School Ability Test	K–XII	
School and College Ability Test	IV–XIV	
Short Form Test of Academic Aptitude	I–XII	
Differential Aptitude Tests		VIII
Differential Aptitude Tests	VIII–XII	
General Aptitude Test Battey	IX–XII	
College Admissions Tests		XII
CEEB Scholastic Aptitude Test	XI–XII	
American College Testing Program	XI–XII	
Individual Intelligence Tests		As needed
Stanford-Binet Intelligence Scale	3–18	
Wechsler Preschool and Primary Scale of Intelligence	4–6½	
Wechsler Intelligence Scale for Children (R)	6–16	
Affective Behavior		
Interest		IX
Kuder Preference Record-Vocational	IX–Adult	
Minnesota Vocational Interest Survey	IX–Adult	
Strong-Campbell Interest Inventory	17 and over	
General		As needed
California Test of Personality	K–Adult	
Mooney Problem Check List	VII–Adult	

[a] One of the tests from each group is normally used, not all of them. The courts have criticized the inflexibility of grouping when several years pass between administrations of aptitude tests. In addition to the overall testing program, attention to each student must be continuous and further tests administered when judgment dictates.
[b] Age levels are given in Arabic numbers, grade levels in Roman numbers.
[c] Also available are alternative instruments such as *CIRCUS* and *Let's Look at Children.*

included in most well-developed programs. For each type, some commonly used tests are listed. These lists are by no means complete.

Note that many of these tests are only used for special purposes with a few students. For instance, individual intelligence tests would be given only when group mental ability tests produce questionable results. Diagnostic tests would be administered when there is a need to study the basic learning problems experienced by certain students.

Also, some tests are designed for special groups only. Examples are the *General Aptitude Test Battery* and the *Minnesota Vocational Interest Survey*, which are designed for non-college bound youth.

Overtesting should be avoided at all costs. Any nonfunctional tests should be eliminated. The staff should be satisfied that each part of the testing program is contributing new and useful information each time it is used.

PROBLEM

4. A middle school teacher complains because the *Iowa Tests of Basic Skills* are the only standardized achievement tests administered to her classes. She feels that they do not measure all that she teachers her students. What steps do you recommend that she take to broaden her testing program?

Test Selection

Tests should be selected on the basis of their contribution to evaluation in terms of the school's educational objectives. Therefore, a test must be studied carefully to determine both its content and its relationship to other tests and information available. The best way to do this is to take the test yourself. This indicates the processes required for correct responses, makes clear the obvious content, and enables you to anticipate difficulties in administration.

In selecting tests, the teacher should consult Buros' *Mental Measurements Yearbooks.* These references are revised continually and provide quantities of information about all types of tests. At least one specialist discusses the strengths and weaknesses of most of the popular tests. Often individual items are criticized, and sometimes problems in administration and scoring are discussed. As well as being helpful in selection, these volumes provide a great deal of general information about tests. Studying tests by referring to these critiques is an excellent way to become more sophisticated about tests in general.

It is important to keep the continuity of a testing program in mind for all the grades from kindergarten through high school. The cumulative record (see page 477) is more meaningful if related tests are used at the different grade levels. If the *Stanford Achievement Tests* are selected, for example, the norms from level to level would be based on similar populations, and the relative emphasis on various types of content in the tests would tend to be similar, thereby making it easier to assess achievement. Likewise, the scores from a given scholastic aptitude test would be more comparable from level to level than comparisons made between tests having different authors.

After tests have been selected, administered, and proved functional for a school, they should not be replaced unless it appears that other instruments will be more effective, since it is necessary to compare results from year to year if the cumulative record is to be meaningful. A more recent copyright date on another test does not necessarily guarantee a better test. At times, because of the development of new instruments, it is wise to make a change. Then, study of the results of groups of students will be helpful in making comparisons with previous test data.

In selecting the test, special attention must be given to its degree of validity and reliability, the adequacy of its norms, its ease of administration and scoring, and its cost in time and money. Furthermore, tests with equivalent forms are necessary for testing different classes at different times or for multiple testing of one class. Aids for test interpretation, such as class charts and profile blanks, ease and clarify recording and interpreting test results.

Criterion-Referenced Tests.   Many publishing companies have published criterion-referenced tests for only a few years, and sufficient theory coupled with practical guidelines for developing such tests was initially lacking. Therefore, extreme care must be taken when selecting these instruments. Although many of the guidelines used in selecting norm-referenced tests are relevant for criterion-referenced tests, there are additional considerations (Popham, 1978, pp. 175–186). Primary among these are

1. *The test must possess an unambiguous descriptive scheme.* In other words, we need to know what the test results for a student means. What is it that the examinee can or can't do?

2. *There should be an adequate number of test items per measured behavior.* A criterion-referenced test attempting to measure behavior with as few as one, two, or three items typically fails to adequately measure the behavior. The optimum number of items is at least five, and probably lies between ten and twenty.

3. *The focus of the test should be limited.* The question before us is whether we should measure a few things very well or many things with poor accuracy. Typically we do neither; instead we try to find a middle position. Probably about five to ten measured behaviors per subject per year is reasonable.

4. *The test must be highly reliable.* In other words, does the test measure student behavior consistently?

5. *The test must be highly valid.* The three types of validity to be considered are descriptive, functional, and domain-selection validity, the first of which is the most important. At a minimum, evidence is needed to support the claim of adequate descriptive validity.

6. *A wide range of comparative data indicating how other students performed on the test should be made available.* To be highly useful in many settings, each test must have field trial data that help us answer the question "How *good* is the performance of our students?" In addition to knowing what students can and cannot do, we need help when judging adequacy of performance. Comparative data by geographic region, sex, and so on, provide useful benchmarks.

Because of the increasing importance of criterion-referenced achievement and their rapid state of development, it is most necessary that we select them with care. This requires rigorous scrutiny of all of their major facets, which no doubt will prove to be time-consuming. This is a small sacrifice when one considers the massive investment made in achievement testing at all levels.

PROBLEM

5. A middle school is using a new battery of achievement tests this year. A faculty committee has been appointed to evaluate the usefulness of the new tests and to recommend either retaining or discontinuing them. Outline a procedure for the committee to follow.

Test Administration

If results are to be successfully interpreted, tests must be carefully administered according to the specific instructions. Results from various classes cannot be compared unless administration is standardized, nor can norms be of any value. This applies not only to reading printed instructions carefully, but to motivating the students to do their best on a test. Time limits must be followed rigidly. Proper administration requires very careful planning from ordering tests on time to their distribution to the classrooms.

Test Administrators.   Who should administer the tests? Some individual tests will be given by the school psychologist. In large school systems, a testing specialist may be employed to administer group tests. In most instances, however, teachers give the tests. This method informs teachers about the testing program, since they must familiarize themselves with the instruments. In addition, because they know their students, teachers can motivate them more effectively, interpret their reactions, and establish the necessary rapport.

Those who criticize administration of tests by teachers usually focus their arguments on inaccurate timing or improper instructions. Teachers should be given instruction in the administration of the tests. The first step is to familiarize them with standardized test construction, for they must understand the importance of standardized procedure. Group instruction is advised when provision can be made for a question period. Instruction had best be given by a specialist in testing, whether from the local school or from a college or university.

If the instructions are particularly complex, teachers should be encouraged to give the test to each other. Many a test has been spoiled because instructions were not completely understood.

Special emphasis should be given to proper timing. Instructions generally appear quite simple; but when an ordinary watch, rather than a stopwatch, is used as the timing instrument, it is easy to make mistakes. When possible, teachers should use stopwatches that they have operated with checks on readings before they administer the test. When a regular watch is used, the starting time should be recorded in minutes and seconds. Then the testing time should be added to record the exact moment to stop the test. Memory should never be trusted in timing any more than in memorizing instructions. Record the time and read the instructions.

Test Administration.   Scheduling is one of the biggest problems in a testing program. On the surface it may appear simple, but when test booklets are being reused for economy, when separate answer sheets are used on which all the answers for several sittings are recorded, or when test length does not coincide with the length of the class periods, some complicated situations can arise. For example, since the test booklets must be checked for marks after each administration, the same booklets cannot be used in consecutive periods. Getting students started at the right place when their answer sheets are collected at the close of one sitting is another problem. When testing time is longer than class periods or a combination of them, it is probably wise to set up a testing timetable.

Proper physical conditions for testing will allow students to work with freedom without crowding, poor lighting, or interruptions. A sign should be placed on the door to indicate that a test is in progress. All testing equipment must be in the room and readily available, along with extra pencils and erasers and carefully spaced functional chairs. Cheating should not be tolerated, but it should dealt with firmly without emotional outbursts that disturb other students.

An additional factor requiring planning is the allowance of the proper amount of time for passing out test booklets, answer sheets, and pencils, which must also be collected. Too often the time requirement for these procedures is underestimated.

Even when directions are carefully followed, timing is accurately completed, and interruptions are eliminated, test results may not be highly valid if students are not motivated to do their best. Students must be confident that testing is for their own welfare and not for determining promotion or for assigning final marks. They must understand the purpose of the test and the demands it will make on them. Unless testing is of value to them, they may not do their best work.

On the other hand, overstimulation produces anxiety, and this interferes with good performance. It is particularly apparent among those students who have the greatest need to earn high marks. Test administrators provide the best testing atmosphere for dealing with anxiety when they establish a relaxed, businesslike atmosphere with a touch of humor. They encourage students to do their best, but do not threaten.

Furthermore, students need to have a certain amount of sophistication or test-wiseness to give evidence of their best performance. Teachers should exhort students to listen carefully to instructions, mark their papers neatly and accurately, plan wise use of their time, leave enough time to recheck their answers, and understand when to omit or answer a question.

Time of Year for Test Administration. An important decision in any evaluation program is the time for test administration. Should standardized tests be administered in the spring or fall? Fall administration has a number of advantages:

1. With today's itinerant population, fall administration assures the teacher a record for each student. Transfer students may not bring adequate records with them from other schools. If tests are administered in the spring, teachers are more likely to have inadequate data for some students throughout the year—a deficit which prevents them from focusing their attention on student needs rather than on what is supposed to be taught in a certain class. If students have specific weaknesses and teachers know about them, remedial work can be planned. If students rank high in achievement,

teachers won't make the serious mistake of having them repeat what they already know just because it appears in the syllabus. The information enables teachers to meet the needs of individuals through grouping or through any other practical approach.

2. Fall testing provides a more realistic measure of students' achievement. During the summer vacation, certain skills may improve; others may deteriorate. If the children know a great deal of arithmetic, they may not be as proficient in September as they were in June. On the other hand, they may have done considerable reading during the summer, thereby improving their skills in this area.

3. Testing can be helpful to students in self-evaluation. If the results are used wisely, they can provide aid in formulating goals. The objective data from standardized tests can give the pupil direction and purpose for the new school year.

4. Too often it appears that tests are administered to determine the effectiveness of the teacher rather than the status of the students. This may result in coaching the students for tests or in invalid administration, such as lengthening the time limits. Fall testing lessens this possibility.

5. Testing in the spring is generally done under pressure of time. As the school year draws to a close, teachers are busy filling out reports and completing final details. Testing may tend to be more of a chore than an aid to good teaching.

Although fall testing is generally recommended, certain conditions may require spring testing. This is particularly true when ability grouping requires that data be available for determining programs for the following year.

PROBLEMS

6. Imagine that you are in charge of a schoolwide achievement testing program in which classroom teachers will administer the results. What steps would you take to ensure standard testing procedures? What difficulties would have to be anticipated?

7. Some school systems do not tell students in advance when standardized tests are to be administered. They hope that undue anxiety and absenteeism will thereby be avoided. Evaluate this practice.

Test Scoring

Although essay and objective tests of the supply type are generally scored by hand, many standardized and classroom objective tests can be machine-scored. Central agencies providing this scoring service at a nominal fee offer some definite advantages:

1. Accuracy is greater; machine-scoring results in fewer errors.

2. It saves time for busy teachers, who can spend their time more profitably than by doing clerical work. For some tests a pressure-sensitive label,

containing each student's scores, is available to attach to the cumulative record. Scores are easily recorded without retyping.

3. Item-analysis data can be quickly prepared when needed.

Hand-scoring by the teacher also results in certain benefits:

1. Results are generally more quickly available.
2. It is possible that by scoring tests the teacher will gain better insight into a student's strengths and weaknesses. However, this is not as likely to occur in the case of the objective test as it is in the case of the essay test.

The advantages and disadvantages of hand-scoring notwithstanding, the fact remains that many test papers are scored in this manner—so the scorer must avoid injustice due to inaccuracy. This is so important a matter that school officials must exert considerable effort and care in training teachers and checking scoring accuracy.

Two types of errors are frequently made: compensating and biased. In the first category are those errors made by carelessness in checking, adding, or using formulas; teachers score too high in one instance and too low in another. The other type of error is a misinterpretation of a scoring formula, which slants scores all in one direction, high or low. There is no opportunity for them to be cancelled out.

How should these errors be prevented? Teachers must be taught how to score, and carry out the scoring instructions to show they have understood them. A discussion of procedures is not enough. The papers first scored should be rescored. When high accuracy is maintained, only a sampling of papers need be checked. One out of five or ten papers may be selected for this purpose. Because biased errors prove to be so serious, the second scoring should be done by a different person. In some schools all papers are scored twice with different colored pencils. One helpful idea is to have one or more teachers responsible for each subtest. They can then become thoroughly proficient in their task; scoring becomes much more efficient and accurate.

Another check is to see if any extreme scores show up in a student's profile. It is possible that they are valid, but if such scores occur, these subtests should be scored again. Also, if scores seem unrealistic in terms of a student's past achievement, the corresponding parts or the entire test should be rescored.

PROBLEM

8. Some argue that if teachers score the tests of those students they meet every day, test results become more meaningful; in the process of scoring, the teacher will become conscious of specific areas of subject matter difficulty. Evaluate this point of view.

Interpretation and Use of Test Results

Test Data. Regardless of the care with which the tests have been selected, administered, and scored, they will prove of little value unless the results are used in the evaluation program. This means that they must be available to teachers, counselors, school administrators, school boards, communities, and others. In Chapter 14, summarization and interpretation of group and individual test scores provide information for improving diagnostic and remedial programs. In Chapter 15, suggestions are given for the use of test scores in reporting to students and their parents.

It is advantageous to use test scores in interpreting the school program for the public or special community groups; presenting information comparing student achievement with national norms of those having comparable ability is one procedure. It may focus attention on a school's educational objectives to portray achievement in various subjects, and at different grade levels. Such a summary may, on the other hand, reveal specific weaknesses that should be remedied through increased financial support by the community.

Test data should be presented in the most meaningful ways. The use of numerical or graphic charts is clearer than a narrative. Figure 16.1 shows the distribution of mental ability scores of a senior high school class compared with national norms. Information about achievement in various subject areas would be helpful. Insight could also be gained from comparing achievement in various subject areas for specific groups through several grades. Groups could vary in terms of racial and socioeconomic characteristics. It is possible that comparisons

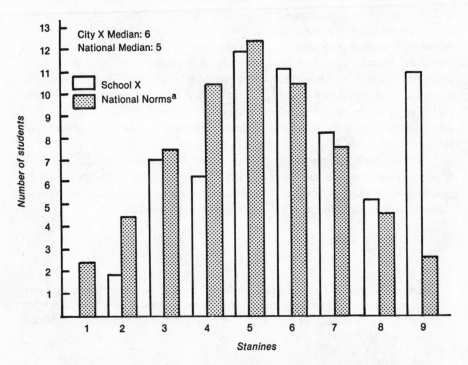

aExpected frequencies of a representative sample; the same number of students were selected from the standardization group.

FIGURE 16.1.   Distribution of the School and College Ability Test, Total Score, for a Twelfth-Grade Class

of groups exposed to different curricula would also be timely. In Figure 16.1 it would also have been possible to graph the achievement of the group to provide a comparison with their ability. Note that stanines are employed.

The group of students from School X tends to be above the national norms. No students have a stanine score of 1, and fewer have stanine scores of 2, 3, 4, and 5 than is true of those from the national norm group; there is a larger proportion of students from School X having stanine scores of 6, 7, 8, and 9.

Confidentiality of Test Scores.   *The Family Educational Rights and Privacy Act* of 1974 (commonly called the "Buckley Amendment"), has had a significant impact on the manner in which schools handle test scores of individual students. Schools may be denied federal funds if they do not permit parents to inspect their children's school records. Furthermore, schools may not allow other persons or agencies access to these records without the written consent of the parent. A special problem facing the schools is how to present a student's records to parents. Great care must be exercised so that lay people understand the meaning of scores, as well as the weaknesses and strengths of particular tests.

Accountability Measures for Schools

Accountability is a very important concern of schools, as uneasy parents may demand evidence about school effectiveness. In fairness to teachers, we must realize that the input from students is a big factor in the end product. Teachers have little control over their "raw material." Therefore, accountability must be tempered in terms of those outcomes that can be affected by teachers' and administrators' actions and decisions (Barro, 1970). Sound program evaluation recognizes this point.

Furthermore, the purpose of accountability should not be punitive, but to improve instruction and learning (Campbell, 1971). In order to do this, the school must have its goals clearly in mind. It makes a great difference how resources are allocated. For instance, should the major responsibility of the school be to try (1) to bring all students up to some basic minimum level of achievement or (2) to help all children develop their full potentials?

The latter is the better choice, even though, with our present state of knowledge and restricted resources, our efforts are limited. It is very difficult for schools to guarantee a specific level of student performance. Educators must keep informed of student needs, then try to meet those needs within the limits of what they know about the teaching-learning process.

One outcome of the accountability movement in education is the requirement in some state and local education agencies that students attain at least a minimum competency level in the basic skills before leaving high school. Typically, paper-and-pencil tests are administered to all students one or more times during their secondary school years. Those who fail to reach a predetermined minimum level of achievement are provided remedial work and must be retested.

In some districts minimal competency testing programs are an important part of the school testing program. Either specially designed tests are developed or commercial tests are administered. These normally cover reading, mathematics, and composition skills. By using these tests, school systems feel that they are demonstrating their accountability for student learning of important basic skills. Furthermore, graduating seniors can demonstrate actual mastery of these skills rather than just present a transcript of grades and a diploma as evidence of academic achievement.

There have been legal challenges to the use of minimum competency testing when it is required that students must pass these tests in order to receive a standard high school diploma (Tractenberg, 1977). The issue becomes particularly complicated when a disproportionately large number of students from minority groups fail to meet the minimum standards established. Such legal challenges raise the question of the degree of validity and reliability of the tests as well as the reasonableness of interpreting the results in terms of absolute standards (Glass, 1978).

Criticisms of Standardized Tests

At the same time that the accountability movement in education is gaining strength, criticisms of standardized tests and testing in general are frequent. Prominent among these criticisms are the following:

1. Achievement tests are largely invalid because they measure mostly superficial or trivial knowledge.
2. Aptitude tests lead to labeling some student as talented or not talented, which may distort their expectations and change their level of effort.
3. Test content often has a middle-class bias, and hence test scores misrepresent the level of achievement and potential of disadvantaged students.
4. Testing places students under stress and is harmful to their emotional health, especially when their scores are compared to others, as in the case of norm-referenced testing.
5. External testing programs impose external controls on the school curriculum and often cause teachers to "teach to the test" (Ebel, 1976, p. 4).

Other criticisms include accusations that (1) test scores represent test-taking skills rather than achievement, (2) a small number of scores cannot adequately represent the complex achievement of each student, and (3) tests generate harmful competition. Examples of each of the foregoing can be found if one wishes to search for them. Obviously, abuses have occurred from time to time. But do these justify eliminating all tests?

Those who defend the use of standardized test scores believe that no better way of measuring academic progress within the acceptable limits of the resources available has been developed to replace them. Safeguards against the kind of problems mentioned do exist, they say. In the case of impact of test-taking skills on test scores, for example, most tests have practice exercises and clear instructions to be augmented by an examiner before actual testing begins. Also, even though there may be flaws in some test items, these are rare indeed among the questions in modern standardized tests.

As for the question of one or two scores on a test representing total achievement of a student, no proponent of testing would argue that this is true or even possible. There is a much broader curriculum in our schools than that sampled by the typical batteries of standardized tests. They test primarily for proficiency of knowledge in terms of the educational objectives on which they are based, and secondarily for application of that knowledge. Test results should be used as a supplement to other information.

The suggestion sometimes made that competition is caused largely by tests seems to be a very weak one indeed. Life becomes a series of instances in which we are compared with others; eliminating tests will not eliminate competition. Rather, the chief function of tests is to improve learning and instruction.

Achievement and aptitude tests provide an immense quantity of useful information that cannot be conveniently obtained by any other known means. In short, tests as we know them should not be eliminated unless more suitable methods of gathering data about students are developed. Since this is unlikely for the immediate future at least, we need to contribute to use standardized tests, being ever vigilant for the possible misuses and misinterpretations associated with them.

The Cumulative Record

The cumulative record is a device for recording and filing all pertinent data that will lead to a better understanding of the student for educational and vocational guidance purposes. Various kinds of data from many sources are more helpful than data obtained from a single source. A systematic, long-range accumulation of data clearly produces more intelligent interpretation than data collected at one time.

Cumulative records take various forms, the most common of which are the card and the folder, or a combination of the two. The folder is printed for recording data, and any pertinent materials such as anecdotal records may be placed inside. A typical cumulative record of the folder type for the elementary grades is shown in Chapter 14 (pages 406–408). Notice the information required, the recording method, and the insert for recording additional health data. A surprisingly large amount of information can be permanently recorded on such a form.

If possible, the school staff should plan the record form cooperatively. The following are guiding principles for its construction (Traxler, 1971, pp. 74–75):

1. It should agree with the educational objectives of the local school.
2. It should be the result of the group thinking of the faculty members.
3. It should either provide for a continuous record of the development of the student from the first grade to the end of the junior college or be one of a series of forms which make provision for such a record.
4. It should be organized by time sequence; that is, it should be set up by yearly divisions which run throughout the form.
5. It should contain ample and carefully planned space for a record of the results of all types of tests and for an explanation of the norms in terms of which the results were interpreted.
6. It should provide for the annual recording of personality ratings of behavior descriptions, which represent the consensus of the student's counselors and teachers.

7. While it should be as comprehensive as possible it must be simple enough to avoid overwhelming the clerical resources of the school.

8. It should be accessible to the teachers as well as to the counselors and principal. Highly confidential information that the counselor may possess should be filed elsewhere.

9. The record form should be reevaluated periodically and revised as needed to take account of educational change and progress.

Information Needed

One of the best ways to select data to include in the cumulative record is to determine the usefulness of each type in understanding the student. In general, the following information is thought helpful.

1. *Identifying data.* These include items such as name, address, age, and date of birth.

2. *Scholastic achievement and mental development.* This would include not only information about the student's achievement in various areas but data concerning general and special aptitudes. Some of this information can be recorded in anecdotal form. Other data can be tabulated as the results of classroom and standardized tests and as school marks.

3. *School attendance record.* Many factors, such as the suitability of the curriculum, home conditions, and the student's health, are related to a poor attendance record. These should be reported as well as the source of this information.

4. *Home and family background.* The educational and cultural backgrounds of the parents should be noted. It is also important to know the father's occupation, whether parents are living together, and any other information about home conditions that may be reflected in the student's behavior.

5. *Personal-social development.* Such factors as self-confidence, emotional stability, predominant moods, relationship to peers and authority figures, and general mental health should be recorded.

6. *Health.* Under this category, items such as a history of medical and dental care, disabilities, and special information on vision and hearing are included. If students have disabilities, it is also wise to record their attitudes toward them.

7. *Special activities and interests.* Discovering how students use their free time in and outside school often provides answers to important questions about their behavior. Any skills in athletics, music, or art, other special talents, and any work experiences should be reported.

8. *Educational and vocational plans.* For students in secondary school, future plans are a prime factor in the selection of subjects and other related decisions. As students' plans develop they should be noted.

It should be noted that because parents now have access to data in their children's files, great care must be exercised in the selection of information to be included. Data requiring professional interpretation may be misinterpreted by the lay person. The situation now presents a dilemma in many instances. Some material that should be included for the good of the student may cause, if misinterpreted, legal action involving school personnel.

Interpretation and Use of the Cumulative Record

The cumulative record will be useful to all school personnel concerned with educational and vocational guidance. The three key persons involved are the teacher, the counselor, and the school administrator.

The Teacher. Teachers facilitate learning through improved instruction. The discussion of the class record and the class analysis chart in chapter 14 show how an orderly presentation of data enables teachers to analyze the needs of their classes and know the strengths and weaknesses of a group as a whole. For example, a large percentage of a class may be having trouble with decimals, finding the main idea in a paragraph, or problem solving in science. Knowing this, the teacher can use group instruction effectively. Those students who do not need help can explore new material.

But teachers must go further than to release students from areas they have already mastered. They must help them select projects and materials. The general direction for these students should be detected in the cumulative record from achievement and aptitude scores, samples of their work, and indications of their interests.

The cumulative record can also aid in finding students' weaknesses. For example, children often appear to succeed, but this is only in comparison with their lackluster classmates. A mediocre performance often looks good if the competition is weak. Because the students seem to be doing all right, teachers attend to those whose difficulties are more obvious and who are generally less able. But when teachers match achievement with ability, and notice from the record of the able students that they do poorly in certain areas, instructional problems are seen that would otherwise have been overlooked.

After teachers locate learning difficulties they must prescribe remediation and try to prevent such difficulties in the future. Chapter 14 includes a discussion of the process of identifying group and individual difficulties and suggesting remedial help. Again, in attacking remedial problems, the importance of data from the cumulative record is emphasized.

The cumulative record may be expanded for records of individualized instruction programs. Evaluation is central to the effective functioning of these plans. Pretests, posttests, and the continuous monitoring of each student become integral parts of the systems. In some instances, computers are used to collect and systematize the data for feedback.

To be sure, the cumulative record can play an important role in teacher-parent conferences. To make these conferences helpful, the teacher must have such data as objective test scores, illustrative work samples, and reports of critical behavioral incidents.

The Counselor. Seven significant measurements needed in the counseling process are (Darley and Anderson, 1951, pp. 75–76)

1. General scholastic ability
2. Differential measures of achievement
3. Evidence of special aptitudes or disabilities
4. Interests
5. Attitudes and beliefs
6. Socioeconomic status
7. Health and physical attributes

Darley and Anderson also list four types of questions with regard to counseling students that may be answered in part by data obtained from the above measurements:

1. Questions regarding vocational planning
2. Questions regarding underachievement
3. Questions regarding personal development and adjustment
4. Questions regarding motivation and interest

The choice of a vocation should depend on the student's ability, often with emphasis on scholastic aptitude. In certain cases, vocational choice must be made on the basis of past achievement, health, physical attributes, or the ability to adjust to people. Jobs are classified into families; if students are interested in a particular area, they may select a vocation appropriate to their talents. The low-IQ student who is interested in medicine can, after all, be a hospital orderly.

Although students may have excellent academic potential, and be well adjusted individuals, their lack of interest can result in underachievement. For a determination of the causes, it is helpful to turn to interest inventory scores, notations of hobbies, leisure-time activities, and anecdotal records. Possibly parents may be insisting on a particular course of study because they think it is prestigious; or, thwarted in their own lives, perhaps they are trying to live through their children. Parents may exhort their children so vigorously to greater effort that the child refuses to try at all.

To be most effective, counselors and teachers must cooperate. Evaluation is improved as additional data are added to the record available to both. Teachers, through observation of student behavior, can give important information to the counselor, just as the counselor can share interpretations of test scores and other information found in the student's cumulative record.

An important objective for the counselor is to develop in the student a capacity for self-evaluation. Society is competitive and students must have an understanding of their behavior to cope effectively with it. It is encouraging that more and more information and tools are becoming available so that counselors can advise all students, no matter what their level of occupational interest. Students should see test scores and other discreetly selected portions of information in the cumulative record to help them understand their strengths and weaknesses; decisions must be based on adequate data.

The School Administrator. Data from cumulative records prove helpful to the school administrator in organizing class groups and in providing information to colleges, prospective employers, and schools to which students may transfer. Some of the data can be used in a public information program, particularly such elements as recorded group results of standardized achievement and aptitude tests.

As our population increases, even small schools have more than one class at each grade level. Combination grades, such as a fifth and sixth, may be formed. At other times, particularly at the secondary level, students may be grouped because of such factors as lack of basic skills in English.

Applications for higher education need to be reviewed, and college officials must have data on which to base selection. One source is a systematic record of standardized test scores. Because final marks given in small schools are often not comparable to those assigned in larger ones, and because the quality of instruction varies from school to school, standardized test data provide a basis for comparison of candidates across the country. Though many colleges use college entrance examinations, the data from a school testing program represent a child far more completely than the single test administration.

Many students work after high school. As recently as fifty years ago, graduation from secondary school was a measure of achievement. Today, when most children receive high school diplomas and as variability of achievement becomes the rule, the wise employer will contact the high school administration about a prospective employee. As inquiries of this kind are increasing, the administrator must have a well-kept cumulative record.

But this is not the whole of the administrators' informational obligation. They must also interpret the school program for the general public, a task that may involve the publishing of brochures, speech making, and instigating public discussion. The better the data on which these are based, the more profitable the public information effort is likely to be.

PROBLEM

9. The cumulative record folder accompanies students as they move from elementary to junior high school and also when they enter senior high school. At the transfer points, many counselors go through the folders and discard materials that, in their opinion, are no longer useful or that might jeopardize children in a new setting. What kinds of material might they prefer to discard? Is this a wise practice?

SUMMARY

The principal ideas in this chapter can be summarized as follows:

1. A sound evaluation program should be based on measureable objectives of the school. The data gathered should reflect the educational program and include information about the personal characteristics of students and their environment.

2. All school personnel—teachers, counselors, and school administrators—should be involved in the evaluation program from its initiation throughout its integration with other activities of the school. Staff members should receive training to prepare them for their roles in the program.

3. A minimal testing program includes tests of scholastic aptitude and achievement. The optimum program adds other aptitude tests as well as interest and personality inventories. Alternative scholastic aptitude tests, as well as programs built around criterion-referenced tests, can be helpful.

4. Standardized achievement tests are most useful when administered yearly. Scholastic aptitude tests often are scheduled at the beginning of the first, fourth, seventh, and tenth grades.

5. In selecting a test, the first consideration should be its usefulness to the evaluation program as a whole. Attention should be given to its degree of validity and reliability, the adequacy of its norms, and the complexity of its administration and scoring. Consideration should also focus on ease of interpretation by selecting one test series for all grade levels, if this is possible. Buros' *Mental Measurements Yearbooks* prove helpful guides in test selection.

6. Valid test results depend on effective administration and scoring. This includes proper training of personnel and good judgment when selecting the time and place of test administration.

7. Test data should be presented in the most meaningful way possible. Test and inventory scores transformed into charts and diagrams are helpful in a public information program, but they are only one source of data. Rating scales aid in observation, and are an effective technique for collecting certain kinds of information.

8. Teachers and administrators should be aware that parents have the right to see their children's records, and that parental permission is required before the school can release information to a third party.

9. The use of cumulative records is recommended for making data available for diagnostic teaching and guidance.

10. School administrators not only need data for interpreting the school program to the public, to satisfy its concern for accountability, but also for supplying information to colleges, prospective employers, and schools to which students transfer.

SUGGESTED READINGS

BRACEY, G. W. Some reservations about minimum competency testing. *Phi Delta Kappan*, 1978, 59, 549–552.
Concern is expressed that minimum competency testing will do little to improve teaching and learning in our schools.

EBEL, R. L. The case for minimum competency testing. *Phi Delta Kappan*, 1978, 59, 546–549.
The author believes that the minimum competency movement helps restore

our concern for cognitive development as the first mission of the school. Reasons for supporting minimum competency testing programs are given.

MEHRENS, W. A. Evaluators, educators, and the public: A detente? *NCME Measurement in Education,* 1974, *5,* (3).
This issue is devoted to the major problems raised by test critics—accountability, privacy, and the role of evaluators. A bibliography is included.

OAKLAND, T. (Ed.). *Psychological and educational assessment of minority children.* New York: Brunner/Mazel Publishers, 1977.
Major topics in this volume are nondiscriminatory assessment and diagnostic-intervention programs.

SAJON-SHEVIN, M. Another look at mainstreaming: Exceptionality, normality, and the nature of difference. *Phi Delta Kappan,* 1978, *60,* 119–121.
The author feels that mainstreaming requires a consideration of conceptual and ethical changes in all areas of education. Attention to administrative details is not enough.

SEWELL, W. H., HAUSER, R. H., & FEATHERMAN, D. L. (Eds.). *Schooling and achievement in American society.* New York: Academic Press, 1975.
This text provides information about the effects of schooling on educational and socioeconomic achievement in American society. It is a helpful volume for the school administrator.

SMITH, F. M. (Ed.). Improving the use of test results. *NCME Measurement News,* 1974, *17,* 3–9.
Suggestions are given for answering the test critics and for developing effective communication of test results.

Testing program. *Childhood Education,* 1973, *49,* 338–372.
A symposium on testing and accountability is summarized. Included are such topics as the assessment of young children, the use of norms, and decision-making based on accountability data.

WARD, A. W., et al. *Guide for school testing programs.* East Lansing, Mich.: National Council on Measurement in Education, 1977.
This monograph contains useful information for a system-wide test director who must organize and operate a testing program. In addition, it is helpful to teachers who need to know how the testing program relates to the rest of the school program.

REFERENCES CITED

BARRO, S. M. An approach to developing accountability measures for the public schools. *Phi Delta Kappan,* 1970, *52,* 196–205.

CAMPBELL, R. E. Accountability and stone soup. *Phi Delta Kappan,* 1971, *53,* 176–178.

DARLEY, J. G., & ANDERSON, G. W. The functions of measurement in counseling. In E. F. Lindquist (Ed.), *Educational Measurement.* Washington, D.C.: American Council on Education, 1951.

EBEL, R. L. The paradox of educational testing. *NCME Measurement in Education,* 1976, *7* (4).

FISHMAN, J. A., DEUTSCH, M., KOGAN, L., NORTH, R., & WHITEMAN, M. Guidelines for testing minority group children. *Journal of Social Issues* (Supplement), 1964, *20,* 129–145.

FLEMING, M. Standardized tests revisited. *The School Counselor,* 1971, *19,* 71–72.

GLASS, G. V. Standards and criteria. *Journal of Educational Measurement*, 1978, *15*, 237–261.

GRONLUND, N. E. *Measurement and evaluation in teaching* (3rd ed.). New York: MacMillan, 1976.

KEARNEY, N. C. *Elementary school objectives.* New York: Russell Sage Foundation, 1953.

POPHAM, W. J. *Criterion-referenced measurement.* Englewood Cliffs, N.J.: Prentice-Hall, 1978.

TRACTENBERG, P. L. The legal implications of statewide pupil performance standards. (Paper prepared for the Education Commission of the States National Institute of Education Workshops on Minimal Competency Testing, 1977.)

TRAXLER, A. E., JACOBS, R., SELOVER, M., & TOWNSEND, A. *Introduction to testing and the use of test results in the public schools.* Westport, Conn.: Greenwood Press, 1971.

Appendices

Appendix A: Statistical Methods*

Part One

Measure of central tendency: the arithmetic mean. The arithmetic mean is a measure of central tendency or central location. In other words, it is a value that attempts to represent the clustering that is so commonly found in test-score distributions. In the cases in which the test scores are for all practical purposes normally distributed, the arithmetic mean corresponds closely to two other measures of central tendency, the mode, (the most common score) and the median (the point below which fifty percent of the test scores fall).

The arithmetic mean is the sum of all test scores in a distribution divided by the number of test scores. Many people call is "the average." This definition can be translated into the following equation:

$$M = \frac{N}{\Sigma X}$$

where

M = arithmetic mean
Σ = the sum
X = any test score
N = number of test scores

This formula can be applied to any of ungrouped data to determine the arithmetic mean, for example, the following mental ability scores of twenty fifth-grade students.

107	123	112	97	100
93	88	83	109	91
101	96	98	114	106
115	105	85	118	111

* For those who wish to engage in independent study of statistical concepts useful in tests and measurements, many textbooks are available. Furthermore, it is recommended that hand-held calculators or computers be used to complete the arithmetic steps required. In this case, formulas based on ungrouped data are of primary concern.

The sum of the twenty values (ΣX) is 2052. The arithmetic mean is 2052 divided by 20, or 102.6. The substitution in the formula is as follows:

$$M = \frac{2052}{20} = 102.6$$

Test scores are not always available in the ungrouped fashion illustrated in the foregoing table. Occasionally they are grouped in a frequency distribution, as in the case of the 360 vocabulary scores shown in Table 8.1 (see p. 213). In a frequency distribution, the exact test score for any particular student is unknown, and the formula for the arithmetic mean as presented above cannot be applied.

One method of computing the arithmetic mean of test scores included in a frequency distribution is to guess the arithmetic mean and then correct the guess. The only requirement for a guessed mean is that it be the midpoint of one of the intervals of the frequency distribution. The guessed mean is corrected by a simple coding operation.

The first steps of the computation of the arithmetic mean of the 360 vocabulary scores included in the frequency distribution cited are shown in Table A.1. The guessed mean is 57, the midpoint of the 55–59 interval. The values in the deviation column are found by counting, in terms of the number of intervals, how far each interval deviates from the interval containing the guessed mean. Thus, the d value of the 60–64 intervals is $+1$ because it is one interval above the 55–59 interval; the d value of the 50–54 interval is -1 because it is one interval below the 55–59

TABLE A.1. Frequency Distribution of 360 Vocabulary Test Scores

Raw-score interval	Frequency (f)	Deviation (d)	fd
90–94	4	7	28
85–89	6	6	36
80–84	12	5	60
75–79	20	4	80
70–74	28	3	84
65–69	36	2	72
60–64	40	1	40
55–59	46	0	0
50–54	43	−1	−43
45–49	39	−2	−78
40–44	32	−3	−96
35–39	24	−4	−96
30–34	13	−5	−65
25–29	9	−6	−54
20–24	5	−7	−35
15–19	3	−8	−24
Total	360		−91

interval. The *fd* values are determined by multiplying each frequency by the corresponding *d* value.

The complete formula for finding the arithmetic mean of a frequency distribution is as follows

$$M \ = \ G.M. \ + \ (h) \ \left[\frac{\Sigma fd}{N} \right]$$

where

M = arithmetic mean
$G.M.$ = guessed mean
h = size of the intervals of the frequency distribution
Σfd = algebraic sum of the entries in the *fd* column
N = number of test scores

The expression following the plus sign corrects the guessed mean by increasing it if it is too small or reducing it if it is too large.

The appropriate values can be readily taken from the table and substituted in the equation as follows:

$$M \ = \ 57 \ + \ (5) \ \left[\frac{-91}{360} \right] \ = 55.7$$

The fact that the guessed mean is slightly higher than the actual arithmetic mean causes the sign of the Σfd to be negative.

The formula for computing the arithmetic mean of test scores arranged in a frequency distribution is nothing more than a convenient substitute for the definition formula for the arithmetic mean that is applied to ungrouped data. The frequency distribution formula is none too satisfactory at times. It often yields inaccurate answers when the number of cases in the frequency distribution is small.

The formula for computing the median of test scores included in a frequency distribution is shown in Part Four of Appendix A. For the frequency distribution of 360 vocabulary test scores, the median is 55.8. Since the distribution of test scores is approximately normal, it is very close to the arithmetic mean.

Part Two

Measure of variability: the standard deviation. The standard deviation, like the range, is a measure of variability or dispersion, as it is sometimes called. It is a distance expressed in test-score units rather than a point such as the arithmetic mean. If the test scores of a distribution are widely scattered above and below the arithmetic mean of the scores, the standard deviation is large; the distribution has considerable variability. If the test scores of a distribution cluster closely around the arithmetic mean, the standard deviation is small; the distribution has little variability.

Like the arithmetic mean, the standard deviation can be computed for un-grouped data or test scores arranged in a frequency distribution. The formula for computing the standard deviation of ungrouped data can serve as a definition of the standard deviation. The formula for computing the standard deviation of test scores arranged in a frequency distribution is a somewhat imperfect substitute for the first formula.

To compute the standard deviation of ungrouped test scores, the following formula is used:

$$\sigma = \sqrt{\frac{\Sigma X^2 - [(\Sigma X)^2/N]}{N}}$$

where

σ = standard deviation
Σ = the sum
X = any test score
N = number of test scores

This formula was used to determine the standard deviation of the 200 American history achievement test scores cited in Chapter 9. In Table A.2 are a few of the 200 test scores, and opposite each is its square.

Summing the two columns yields the two values needed for the numerator of the standard deviation equation. Substitution of all values gives the following equation:

$$\sigma = \sqrt{\frac{585,979 - [(10,620)^2/200]}{200}} = 10.5$$

Finding the standard deviation of test scores arranged in a frequency distri-bution is a simple extension of the process used to compute the arithmetic mean of

TABLE A.2.   Array of American History Achievement Test Scores

Pupil	Test score X	X^2
1	80	6,400
2	21	441
3	62	3,844
4	76	5,776
5	32	1,024
6	47	2,209
.	.	.
.	.	.
.	.	.
200	75	5,625
Total	10,620	585,979

TABLE A.3.   Computation of the Standard Deviation of a Frequency Distribution

Raw-score interval	Frequency (f)	Deviation (d)	fd	fd²
90–94	4	7	28	196
85–89	6	6	36	216
80–84	12	5	60	300
75–79	20	4	80	320
70–74	28	3	84	252
65–69	36	2	72	144
60–64	40	1	40	40
55–59	46	0	0	0
50–54	43	−1	−43	43
45–49	39	−2	−78	156
40–44	32	−3	−96	288
35–39	24	−4	−96	384
30–34	13	−5	−65	325
25–29	9	−6	−54	324
20–24	5	−7	−35	245
15–19	3	−8	−24	192
Total	360		−91	3,425

those test scores. A convenient interval is selected, the deviations of the remaining intervals from the selected interval are identified, and a systematic series of multiplications follow.

The frequency distribution of vocabulary test scores shown in Table 8.1 (see p. 213) is reproduced in Table A.3. Again, the 55–59 interval is chosen as the starting point and all other intervals are identified in the deviation column according to the number of intervals they happen to be above or below the selected interval. The entries in the fd column are found by multiplying each frequency by the corresponding d value. The entries in the fd^2 column are determined by multiplying each fd value by the corresponding d value.

The sums of the fd column and fd^2 columns are needed if the standard deviation is to be found. The complete formula for the standard deviation is as follows:

$$\sigma = (h) \sqrt{\frac{\Sigma fd^2}{N} - \left(\frac{\Sigma fd}{N}\right)^2}$$

where

σ = standard deviation
h = size of the intervals of the frequency distribution
Σfd^2 = sum of the entries in the fd^2 column
Σfd = algebraic sum of the entries in the fd column
N = number of test scores

Substitution of the values computed in the table yields the following:

$$\sigma = \sqrt{\frac{3425}{360} - \left(\frac{-91}{360}\right)^2} = 15.3$$

A simpler method of determining the size of a standard deviation is available provided that the distribution of the test scores is approximately normal. All that is necessary is to (a) sum the scores for the top sixth of the group of students, (b) sum the scores for the bottom sixth, (c) find the difference between these two values, and (d) divide the difference by half of the number of students in the total group. The formula is as follows:

$$\sigma = \frac{\Sigma X_t - \Sigma X_b}{N/2}$$

where

σ = standard deviation
ΣX_t = sum of scores for top sixth
ΣX_b = sum of scores for bottom sixth
$N/2$ = half of the number of students in the total group

Values yielded by this formula are often quite satisfactory for the needs of a classroom teacher.

Part Three

Measure of relationships: the product-moment coefficient of correlation. The Pearson product-moment coefficient of correlation represents the degree of straight-line relationship between two sets of measurements, such as those of two characteristics of a group of students. The correlation coefficient reflects the tendency of these students to have, in some systematic manner, similar relative positions or dissimilar relative positions in the two distributions. If students who are high in one distribution tend to be high in the second, and if those who are low in one distribution tend to be low in the other, the correlation coefficient is positive: a direct relationship exists between the two characteristics. If students who are high in one distribution tend to be low in the other, and if those who are low in one distribution tend to be high in the other, the correlation coefficient is negative: an inverse relationship exists between the two characteristics.

The amount of straight-line relationship between two characteristics is indicated by the size of the correlation coefficient. If the correlation coefficient is +1.00 or −1.00, the straight-line relationship is perfect, that is, plotting one measurement against the other will yield a series of points that can be joined by a single straight line. If the correlation coefficient were 0.00, there would be absolutely no straight-line relationship between the two characteristics. Thus, correlation coefficients can vary in size from +1.00 to −1.00, the sign reflecting the direction of the relationship and the size reflecting the amount of the relationship. The fact that two characteristics are correlated does not necessarily mean that one is the immediate cause of the other.

A correlation coefficient is useful in situations such as that described in Chapter 10 in connection with the discussion of criterion-related validity. Table 10.2 (see p. 266) shows the test scores of the scholastic aptitude and social studies achievement of each of twenty pupils.

The following formula is used to compute the coefficient of correlation:

$$r = \frac{\Sigma XY - [(\Sigma X)(\Sigma Y)/N]}{\sqrt{\left[\Sigma X^2 - \frac{(\Sigma X)^2}{N}\right]\left[\Sigma Y^2 - \frac{(\Sigma Y)^2}{N}\right]}}$$

where

r = product-moment coefficient of correlation
Σ = the sum
X = any test score of one characteristic (i.e., any scholastic aptitude test score)
Y = any test score of the other characteristic (i.e., any social studies test score)
N = number of students

Solution of the formula can be simplified by preparing a worksheet. Table A.4, based upon Table 10.2, is such a worksheet.

TABLE A.4.   Computation of a Coefficient of Correlation for Ungrouped Data

Student	Scholastic aptitude test X	Social studies test Y	XY	X²	Y²
Leo	135	66	8,910	18,225	4,356
Margaret	130	90	11,700	16,900	8,100
Brian	120	68	8,160	14,400	4,624
Carrie	117	85	9,945	13,689	7,225
Brett	116	81	9,396	13,456	6,561
Louise	114	47	5,358	12,996	2,209
Ralph	113	69	7,797	12,769	4,761
Joyce	112	77	8,624	12,544	5,929
Quinton	111	65	7,215	12,321	4,225
Sandra	109	56	6,104	11,881	3,136
Larry	107	89	9,523	11,449	7,921
Norma	106	49	5,194	11,236	2,401
Frank	101	57	5,757	10,201	3,249
Milton	100	58	5,800	10,000	3,364
Dave	97	71	6,887	9,409	5,041
Joe	95	60	5,700	9,025	3,600
Bill	94	38	3,572	8,836	1,444
Sally	90	31	2,790	8,100	961
Mary	88	40	3,520	7,744	1,600
Sue	87	59	5,133	7,569	3,481
Total	2,142	1,256	137,085	232,750	84,188

The new entries in the worksheet are products, either the square of a test score or the cross-product of two test scores. The sums of these products as they are listed in the last row of the table are the values necessary to solve the r formula. The following needed values can be taken from the table:

$$\Sigma X \ = \ 2{,}142 \qquad\qquad \Sigma Y \ = \ 1{,}256$$
$$\Sigma X^2 \ = \ 232{,}750 \qquad\qquad \Sigma Y^2 \ = \ 84{,}188$$
$$\Sigma XY \ = \ 137{,}085 \qquad\qquad N \ = \ 20$$

Substitution of these values into the formula for the correlation coefficient yields the following:

$$r = \frac{137{,}085 \ - \ [(2142)\ (1256)/20]}{\sqrt{\left[232{,}750 \ - \ \dfrac{(2142)^2}{20}\right]\left[84{,}188 \ - \ \dfrac{(1256)^2}{20}\right]}} = 0.61$$

As in the case of arithmetic means and standard deviations, coefficients of correlations can also be computed by use of measurements arranged in frequency distributions. The formula must be altered somewhat to do this. A complete description of the computation of a correlation coefficient from a two-way frequency distribution can be found in most introductory textbooks of statistical methodology.

A simple means of obtaining a somewhat accurate estimate of the size of the product-moment coefficient of correlation is to compute a Spearman rank-difference coefficient of correlation, known as rho (ρ). It represents the tendency of the students to have similar or dissimilar ranks in terms of two variables. Rho values are computed by means of the following formula:

$$\rho = 1 - \frac{6\Sigma D^2}{N(N^2 - 1)}$$

where

ρ = rank-difference coefficient of correlation
Σ = the sum
D = difference between a pair of ranks
N = number of students

In Table 10.2 are shown the ranks of each of the twenty students for both a scholastic aptitude test and a social studies achievement test. When the differences between these pairs of ranks are squared and added, a sum of 526 is found. Hence,

$$\rho = \frac{(6)\ (526)}{20\ (400 - 1)} = 0.60$$

Another quick way of obtaining an estimate of the degree of relationship that exists between two variables is to compute a tetrachoric correlation coefficient. Such coefficients can be determined by finding the percentage of students who are in the top half of the class in terms of both sets of test scores being correlated, and then looking up the correlation coefficient corresponding to this percentage in a table (see Table A.5) published by the Educational Testing Service.

TABLE A.5.   Simplified Method for Estimating the Size of Tetrachoric Correlation
Coefficients

%	ρ	%	ρ	%	ρ	%	ρ	%	ρ
45	.95	37	.69	29	.25	21	−.25	13	−.69
44	.93	36	.65	28	.19	20	−.31	12	−.73
43	.91	35	.60	27	.13	19	−.37	11	−.77
42	.88	34	.55	26	.07	18	−.43	10	−.81
41	.85	33	.49	25	.00	17	−.49	9	−.85
40	.81	32	.43	24	−.07	16	−.55	8	−.88
39	.77	31	.37	23	−.13	15	−.60	7	−.91
38	.73	30	.31	22	−.19	14	−.65	6	−.93

Unfortunately, the tetrachoric correlations yielded by this table are not precise. At best they can be thought of as a rough approximation of the size of the product-moment coefficient of correlation for the data in question.

Part Four

Measure of relative performance: the quartile, decile, and percentile. Quartiles, deciles, and percentiles are points in a distribution of test scores. The first quartile, often identified as Q_1, is the point in the distribution below which twenty-five percent of the test scores fall; the first decile (D_1) is the point below which ten percent of the test scores fall; the first percentile (P_1) is the point below which one percent of the test scores fall. Other quartiles, deciles, and percentiles are similarly defined and symbolically identified.

Quartiles divide the test-score distribution into four equal parts in terms of the number of test scores. Deciles divide such a distribution into ten equal parts, and percentiles divide it into one-hundred equal parts.

A computation of any quartile, decile, or percentile can be based on a frequency distribution of test scores such as that shown in Table 8.1 (see p. 213). This frequency distribution contains vocabulary test scores obtained by testing 360 students. It is reproduced in Table A.6.

The formula for determining any quartile, decile, or percentile is as follows:

$$Q, D, \text{ or } P = l + (h) \left[\frac{(F)\ (N) - f_c}{f_w} \right]$$

where

l = theoretical lower limit of the interval containing the quartile, decile, or percentile desired
h = size of the intervals in the frequency distribution
F = a fraction that varies according to which quartile, decile, or percentile is desired
N = number of test scores
f_c = cumulative frequency below the interval containing the quartile, decile, or percentile desired
f_w = number of test scores within the interval containing the quartile, decile, or percentile desired

TABLE A.6.   Computation of Quartiles, Deciles, and Percentiles Based on a Frequency
Distribution

Raw-score intervals	Frequency (f_w)	Cumulative frequency (f_c)
90–94	4	360
85–89	6	356
80–84	12	350
75–79	20	338
70–74	28	318
65–69	36	290
60–64	40	254
55–59	46	214
50–54	43	168
45–49	39	125
40–44	32	86
35–39	24	54
30–34	13	30
25–29	9	17
20–24	5	8
15–19	3	3
Total	360	

Two of the values used in the formula, l and F, deserve further explanation.
That l is a theoretical lower limit of an interval and not a reported lower limit
simply recognizes the fact that all measurements are limited in accuracy. Although
test scores are reported to the nearest whole number, theoretically each score
represents the interval that extends from 0.5 below the test score in question to
0.5 above it. A reported score of 50 represents an interval from 49.5 to 50.5 in a
test-score distribution. Whenever test scores are reported to the nearest whole
number, the value of l is 0.5 less than the reported value of the lower limit of the
frequency distribution interval containing the quartile, decile, or percentile to be
computed.

The value of F is defined as the size of a fraction associated with the quartile,
decile, or percentile. For the median, the point below which fifty percent of the
scores fall, the fraction is 50/100 or $\frac{1}{2}$. For the third decile (D_3), the point
below which thirty percent of the scores fall, the fraction is 30/100 or 3/10. For
the sixty-third percentile (P_{63}), the fraction is 63/100. All other fractions can be
found in a similar manner.

Suppose that P_{32} is to be computed. The first step is to find the interval
containing P_{32}. The most rapid way of doing this is to determine F, which is
32/100, and multiply it by N, which is 360. The answer, 115.2, is entered in the
cumulative frequency column of the table. Observe that 86 students have test scores
of 44 or less, whereas 125 have test scores of 49 or less. Therefore, P_{32}, which
corresponds to 115.2, falls somewhere within the 45–49 interval.

Now that the interval is identified, three of the required values can be quickly found. The number of test scores within the interval (f_w) is 39; the cumulative frequency below the interval (f_c) is 86; the theoretical lower limit of the interval (l) is 44.5. Substitution of these and other needed values yields the following equation:

$$P_{32} = 44.5 + 5 \left[\frac{32/100(360) - 86}{39} \right] = 48.2$$

The determination of a decile or quartile is equally simple. The steps needed to compute D_6 are as follows:

1. $F = 60/100$, or $6/10$
2. $(F)(N) = 6/10 (360) = 216$
3. Therefore, interval containing D_6 is 60–64 interval
4. $f_w = 40$
5. $f_c = 214$
6. $l = 59.5$

Therefore

$$D_6 = 59.5 + 5 \left[\frac{6/10 (360) - 214}{40} \right] = 59.8$$

A quartile, such as Q_3, is computed as follows:

1. $F = 75/100$, or $3/4$
2. $(F)(N) = (3/4)(360) = 270$
3. Therefore, interval containing Q_3 is 65–69 interval
4. $f_w = 36$
5. $f_c = 254$
6. $l = 64.5$

Therefore

$$Q_3 = 64.5 + 5 \left[\frac{3/4 (360) - 254}{36} \right] = 66.7$$

Quartile, decile, and percentile ranks can be determined by inspecting the appropriate quartiles, deciles, and percentiles; inspecting an appropriate ogive curve; or computing from ungrouped test scores arranged according to size from low to high. These techniques are described in many introductory textbooks of statistical methodology.

Appendix B: Free and Inexpensive Materials on Measurement and Evaluation

I. Test Bulletins Published at Irregular Intervals

Test Data Reports, Harcourt Brace Jovanovich, Inc.
Test Service Bulletins, The Psychological Corporation
Test Service Notebook, Harcourt Brace Jovanovich, Inc.
Testing Today, Houghton Mifflin Company

II. Newsletters Concerning Measurement

ACTivity, American College Testing Program
College Board News, College Entrance Examination Board
ETS Developments, Educational Testing Service
Evaluation Comment, UCLA Center for the Study of Evaluation
Evaluation News, Phi Delta Kappa Evaluation Network
How to Evaluate Educational Programs, Capitol Publications
Measurement in Education, National Council on Measurement in Education
Measurement News, National Council on Measurement in Education
NAEP Newsletter, National Assessment of Educational Progress

III. Educational and Psychological Journals

Applied Psychological Measurement
American Educational Research Journal
Behavioral Assessment
CEDR Quarterly
Contemporary Educational Psychology
Educational and Psychological Measurement
Educational Evaluation and Policy Analysis
Educational Researcher
Evaluation and Program Planning
Evaluation in Education
Evaluation Quarterly
Journal of Educational Measurement
Measurement and Evaluation in Guidance
Review of Educational Research
Studies in Educational Evaluation

IV. Annual Reports and Proceedings

Annual Reports, College Entrance Examination Board
Annual Reports, Educational Testing Service
Proceedings, Annual Invitational Conference on Testing Problems, Educational Testing Service

V. Miscellaneous Paperback Books and Bulletins

A Directory of Information on Tests. TM Report 62, prepared by T. E. Backer.

Guide for School Testing Programs, National Council on Measurement in Education

Tests and Measurement Kit. Educational Testing Service, 1973.
  Making the Classroom Test: A Guide for Teachers
  Multiple-Choice Questions: A Close Look
  Selecting an Achievement Test: Principles and Procedures
  Short-Cut Statistics for Teacher-Made Tests

Guidance Monograph Series, Set III: Testing. Houghton Mifflin Company, 1968.
  Modern Mental Measurement: A Historical Perspective
  Basic Concepts in Testing
  Types of Test Scores
  School Testing Programs
  Intelligence, Aptitude, and Achievement Testing
  Interest and Personality Inventories
  Tests on Trial
  Automated Data Processing in Testing
  Controversial Issues in Testing

TM Reports. ERIC Clearinghouse on Tests, Measurement, and Evaluation; Educational Testing Service.

New Directions for Program Evaluation

New Directions for Testing and Measurement

Indexes

Author Index

Subject Index

A

Absolute zero, 209–211
Academic Promise Tests, 329
Accountability for schools, 457–476
Achievement:
  academic, 31, 36–37, 53–54
  aptitudes and, 131, 284–285
  changes in level over time, 29–30
  complex, 113–115, 181–182
  differential, 248, 251
  evaluation of, 6–10
  final, 420–422
  over- and underachievement, 317,
    337–338
Achievement tests (*see* Criterion-referenced
  tests, Essay tests, Norm-referenced
  tests, Objective tests, Standardized
  achievement tests)
Affective behavior evaluation:
  anecdotal records, 355–356
  attitude scales and questionnaires,
    375–377
  biographical data blank, 366–367
  check lists, 358–359
  ethical considerations, 368–369
  "guess who" questionnaires, 364–365
  interest inventories, 369–374
  interviewing, 359–360
  methods of, 351–352
  observation, 352–361
  personal inventories, 367–369
  projective techniques, 378–379
  rating scales, 356–358
  self-report inventories, 24, 366–377
  social-distance scales, 364
  sociograms, 361–364
  sociometry and related techniques,
    361–365
Age equivalents, 228
American College Testing Program, 342, 467
Anecdotal records, 186, 191, 355–356
Answer sheets, 102–103
Aptitude tests (*see* Standardized aptitude
  tests)
Aptitudes:
  achievement and, 131, 284–285
  changes in level over time, 344
  defined, 284–285, 308–309
  genetic differences, 323–324
  measurement of (*see* Standardized
    aptitude tests)
Arithmetic mean (*see* Mean)

Assessments of achievement, large-scale, 7,
  29–31
Attitude scales and questionnaires, 375–377
Ayres Measuring Scale for Handwriting, 186

B

Bias in evaluation, 320–323, 338–341,
  354–355
Biographical data blanks, 366–367
Blueprint for test (*see* Table of
  specifications)

C

California Achievement Test, 297, 317, 466
California Test of Personality, 367–368, 467
Chance errors, 238–239
Check lists:
  in evaluating affective behavior, 358–359
  in procedure and product evaluation,
    185–186, 188–190
  as report cards, 431–433
CIRCUS, 300, 335, 467
Class analysis chart, 168–169, 400–401
Class record sheet, 400
Classroom achievement tests, 14 (*see also*
    Objective tests, Essay tests, Criterion-
    referenced tests, Norm-referenced
    tests)
"Coaching" for tests, 342–343
Coefficient of correlation:
  computation of, 490–493
  defined, 242, 267–268, 490
  interpretation, 242, 267–268, 490
  rank order, 268, 492
  tetrachoric coefficient, 493
Coefficient of reliability (*see* Reliability
    coefficients)
Coefficient of validity, 273–274
Cognitive Abilities Test, 316–317, 467
College admission tests, 341–344, 467
Completion test items, 73, 75–78
Computer-assisted test construction, 60
Conferences (*see* Teacher-parent conferences)
Confidentiality of test scores, 475
Construct validity (*see* Validity, construct)
Content validity (*see* Validity, content)
Correcting for guessing, 105–107
Correlation coefficient (*see* Coefficient of
    correlation)
Correspondence with parents, 400–443
Creativity, 329–330
Criterion-referenced marking, 423, 433–437
Criterion-referenced tests:
  attitude inventories, 376–377